GAIL E. TOMPKINS
California State University, Fresno

LEA M. McGEE
Boston College

TEACHING READING WITH LITERATURE

Case Studies to Action Plans

Merrill, an imprint of
Macmillan Publishing Company
New York

Maxwell Macmillan Canada
Toronto

Maxwell Macmillan International
New York   Oxford   Singapore   Sydney

Cover art: Clare Wood
Editor: Linda James Scharp
Production Editor: Jonathan Lawrence
Art Coordinator: Lorraine Woost
Photo Editor: Anne Vega
Text Designer: Angela Foote
Cover Designer: Cathleen Norz
Production Buyer: Patricia A. Tonneman
Illustrations: Academy ArtWorks, Inc.

This book was set in Korinna by Compset, Inc., and was printed and bound by R. R. Donnelly & Sons Company. The cover was printed by Phoenix Color Corp.

Copyright © 1993 by Macmillan Publishing Company, a division of Macmillan, Inc. Merrill is an imprint of Macmillan Publishing Company.

Printed in the United States of America

Macmillan Publishing Company
866 Third Avenue
New York, NY 10022

Macmillan Publishing Company is part of the
Maxwell Communication Group of Companies.

Maxwell Macmillan Canada, Inc.
1200 Eglinton Avenue East, Suite 200
Don Mills, Ontario M3C 3N1

Library of Congress Cataloging-in-Publication Data
Tompkins, Gail E.
    Teaching reading with literature : case studies to action plans /
Gail E. Tompkins, Lea M. McGee.
        p. cm.
    Includes bibliographical references and index.
    ISBN 0-675-21303-7
    1. Reading (Elementary) 2. Children—Books and reading—Case
studies. 3. Children's literature—Study and teaching—Case
studies. 4. Curriculum planning. I. McGee, Lea M. II. Title.
LB1575.T63   1993
372.4′1—dc20   92-22203
                                                          CIP

Printing: 1   2   3   4   5   6   7   8   9   Year: 3   4   5   6   7

PREFACE

Today teachers are experimenting with new ways to use literature in reading instruction. In *Teaching Reading with Literature: Case Studies to Action Plans* we describe literature-based reading, present the theory and research findings that support this reform movement, and share anecdotes from teachers we have worked with who use literature in their kindergarten through eighth grade classrooms. Our purpose is to guide teachers as they make a transition to this approach or as they refine their current literature-based programs. We focus on the decisions that teachers must make as they plan, organize, implement, and assess literature-based reading programs, and we present action plans that describe how teachers have revolutionized literacy learning in their classrooms.

The book is divided into two sections. Part I includes nine chapters that explain how to implement a literature-based reading program. In Chapter 1, "Using Literature in the Reading Program," we discuss the advantages of using literature to teach reading and describe the characteristics of these programs. In Chapter 2, "Choosing Literature for Children," we discuss the three major categories of literature—stories, informational books, and poems—and offer guidelines for selecting books for children. In Chapter 3, "Learning About Authors and Illustrators," we provide background information about authors, illustrators, and illustration styles. This information is useful for teachers who are planning author and illustrator units, and teachers can use the information on illustration styles and techniques as they talk about picture books with students.

The next four chapters focus on the reading process. In Chapter 4, "Identifying Perspectives on Reading Instruction," we discuss the reading process and delineate three perspectives—reader response, critical, and interactive—that teachers often use in teaching reading with literature. The first perspective is explored more thoroughly in Chapter 5, "Teaching from a Reader Response Perspective," the second in Chapter 6, "Teaching from a Critical Perspective," and the third in Chapter 7, "Teaching from an Interactive Perspective."

The last two chapters focus on planning, organizing, and assessing instruction. In Chapter 8, "Putting It All Together," we describe the steps in developing a literature-based reading program, and we talk about ways to keep records and evaluate students' reading in Chapter 9, "Assessing Students' Learning."

In Part II we present eight action plans that show how teachers in kindergarten through eighth grade use literature-based reading in their classrooms. In each action plan we discuss the teacher's perspective in reading instruction, the teacher's daily schedule, components of the teacher's literacy program, a lesson plan showing how the teacher "puts it all together," and the teacher's recordkeeping and assessment procedures.

Special Features

We have incorporated a number of special features into *Teaching Reading with Literature: Case Studies to Action Plans* to increase its usability:

Case Studies.   Each chapter begins with one, two, or three brief case studies that provide glimpses into literature-based reading classrooms. The teachers and students we describe demonstrate key concepts that will be presented and teaching techniques that will be explained later in the chapter. Each "Case in Point" will provide a realistic point of reference for readers.

Core Literature and Reading Workshop Approaches.   The two major approaches to literature-based reading instruction—core literature and reading workshop—are an integral part of the book. We explain these approaches and, in the Action Plans, share descriptions of how elementary teachers use components of the core literature and reading workshop approaches in their own classrooms.

Making Decisions.   We believe that teachers who use literature as the basis of their reading programs are decision makers. They need to make decisions about philosophy, daily schedules, approaches, books for focus units and theme cycles, reading and response activities, and assessment procedures. At the beginning of each chapter we present a list of decision points related to that chapter. We hope that these decision points will spur readers to read more reflectively and to consider how they will develop their own literature-based reading programs. The last section in each chapter ("Making Decisions about . . .") summarizes the information presented in the chapter in light of the decision points.

Acknowledgments

We want to thank the teachers who welcomed us into their classrooms and shared their innovative ideas for teaching literature-based reading with us. In addition to the teachers named in the case studies and action plans, we thank Agnes Dauphinais, Boyden Elementary School; Annmarie Hunter, Old Post Elementary School; Sharon Schmidt, Idyllwild School; Shirley Carson, Wayne School; and Thayer McCaffree, Laurel Tompkins, and all the teachers at Western Hills School. The students in these classrooms have shared their interpretations of literature and response projects with us. In particular, we express appreciation to the students whose writing and art samples appear in this book: Vicki Garcia, Davide Bernard, Adrienne Alvarez, Devann Knox, Shanna, Jeffrey, Lawrie Donovan, Jennifer Goguen, and Kristen Lomax.

Our thanks, too, to the teachers and students who appear in the photos: Kathy Morehouse, Mia White, Davide Bernard, Arron Lopez, Darlene Torres, Andy Florentino, Steven Kyhn, Timmy Rosenberger, Jacob Mariano, Derrick Olzack, and Jenny Gonzales, Shaffer School; Cheryl Landrum, Marcus McCowan, Wayne Drumm, Kristy Wiggins, Shaun Bates, Edward Tart, Darrell Brewer, Pat Blackburn, Judy Reeves, and Thayer McCaffree, Western Hills School; and Judy Cochran, Wilson Elementary School.

We want to acknowledge the support we received from our colleagues and students at Boston College and California State University–Fresno. Special thanks to Elizabeth Gonsalves, Fran Loftus, and Susan Cookson, who spent many hours tracking down books of children's literature and journal articles, collecting students' writing and art samples, and attending to other details for us. Our gratitude goes to the reviewers who carefully read the manuscript in its many stages and offered insight and suggestions for shaping the book: Martha Combs, University of Nevada; Bonnie Ericson, California State University–Northridge; Pose Lamb, Purdue University; Beverly Otto, Northeast Illinois University; and Dixie M. Turner, Olivet Nazarene College.

The people at Merrill/Macmillan are very special to us. We want to express our appreciation to Jeff Johnston, who gave us the green light to begin this project, and to our editor, Linda Scharp, who guided our struggle toward coherence and style. We also want to thank our production editor, Jonathan Lawrence, who competently dealt with the myriad of responsibilities related to transforming our manuscript into a book, and our copyeditor, Cindy Peck, who polished our words and sentences.

Gail E. Tompkins
Lea M. McGee

BRIEF CONTENTS

CONTENTS

PART I

Literature-Based Reading Instruction

CHAPTER 1

USING LITERATURE IN THE READING PROGRAM

> **In this chapter you will learn to make decisions about:**
> * **Using literature as the focus of your literacy program**
> * **Integrating the four language arts**
> * **Making your classroom literature-rich**
> * **Using the core literature and reading workshop approaches**

THE CASE STUDY at the beginning of this chapter features Mrs. Blackburn, a fourth grade teacher who uses literature in her reading program. She and her students are involved in a focus unit on Chris Van Allsburg, and they are reading his fantasy picture books and exploring and extending their understandings of the stories using all four of the language arts—listening, talking, reading, and writing.

A CASE IN POINT

Mrs. Blackburn Uses Literature in Her Reading Program

Mrs. Blackburn prepares to read aloud a copy of Chris Van Allsburg's newest book *The Wretched Stone* (1991) to her fourth graders. *The Wretched Stone* is an old captain's log of an ocean voyage and the bizarre things that happened after the crew picked up a strange glowing stone when they stopped at an island to take on drinking water. Many of her students are already familiar with one or two of Van Allsburg's other books and they anticipate that this new book will also be a gripping fantasy. Brian says, "All of Chris Van Allsburg's books are g-r-e-a-t! *Jumanji. The Polar Express.* They're so good I just can't get enough of them." Mrs. Blackburn points out, "This story is a little different; Mr. Van Allsburg wrote it as a ship captain's log." Her students nod in agreement; they, too, have written simulated journals, stepping into the role of a book character or a historical personality.

Mrs. Blackburn reads *The Wretched Stone* aloud, stopping several times to invite her students to make predictions about what they expect will happen next. When she finishes reading, her students get into a circle to talk about the book. Mrs. Blackburn begins the grand conversation by saying, "Let's talk about Mr. Van Allsburg's newest book," and Luther begins the discussion:

LUTHER: That one's really weird.

SEAN: I thought it was good even though it was weird. I liked when the crew turned into monkeys.

AARON: Me, too.

ELIZABETH: Why did they change into monkeys?

SEAN: Well, whatever it was, they changed back.

SASHA: Could that really happen?

ADRIANNA: It's just pretend like in *The Polar Express* when the little boy went to see Santa Claus.

TONY: It's more like *The Garden of Abdul Gasazi* when the magician changed the dog into a duck and then back to a dog.

KRISTEN: I didn't see the dog anywhere, and there's always a white dog in his books. (Mrs. Blackburn hands the book to Kristen and she looks for the picture of the dog and finally finds the dog's white tail hidden in an illustration.)

The conversation continues and after a few minutes, Kelly, who has been sitting quietly, says, "It's a television. That's what the glowing rock is. You stop reading and you stop talking when you watch too much TV." Everyone is taken aback by her thoughtful analogy. Then Brian comments:

BRIAN: Yeah, couch potatoes are monkeys.

KARI: People didn't have TVs back then.

KELLY: I know they didn't, but I still think that's his message.

BRIAN: I think Kelly's right. It is confusing because they didn't have TVs then, but what else could the glowing stone be?

Mrs. Blackburn asks if her students would like to continue reading Chris Van Allsburg's books as a focus unit for the next several weeks. The students are unanimous in their agreement. They take a few minutes to plan the unit. Together Mrs. Blackburn and her students decide to spend two weeks reading and responding to Chris Van Allsburg's books. (Of course, Mrs. Blackburn had already done some planning for the focus unit, but she involves her students in the planning so that they are more interested in what they are learning and more responsible as well.) Students brainstorm a list of the activities they want to do:

- Read four of his books.
- Write about each book in a lit log.
- Make a chart to tell where the dog is in each book.
- Write to Chris Van Allsburg.

- Do a response project about one book.
- Share the project with the class.

Mrs. Blackburn adds these items to the class list:

- Use the writing process.
- Learn about Chris Van Allsburg.
- Learn about fantasies because most of Van Allsburg's books are fantasies.

Mrs. Blackburn has a class set of *Jumanji* (1981), a Caldecott Award book about two children who play an adventure game that comes to life, and several copies of each of his other books. She has borrowed copies from other teachers, and students lend a few of their own copies. Together they collect 42 copies of Van Allsburg's books in addition to the class set of *Jumanji* and place them on a special shelf in the class library.

During their two-week study, Mrs. Blackburn's students spend one hour each day reading and writing in response to Van Allsburg's books. During the first week, students spend most of the time reading and during the second week, they continue to read but spend more time writing and working on response projects. At the end of the second week, students also share their completed response projects with the class.

Over the two-week focus unit, Mrs. Blackburn teaches brief 10 to 15 minute minilessons every other day or so to share information about the author and about fantasies. She also teaches minilessons on alliteration (repetition of initial sounds in words) using Van Allsburg's *The Z Was Zapped* (1987) and on point of view using *Two Bad Ants* (Van Allsburg, 1988).

Many students read independently and others form small groups to read and discuss his books. Mrs. Blackburn circulates around the classroom, conferencing briefly with students about their reading and reading their lit log entries. One day the class reads *Jumanji* together. Before reading, they talk about games and quickwrite, or write informally to reflect on their ideas for five or ten minutes, about their favorite games. Then students read the book independently or with partners. After reading, they write an entry in their lit logs and talk about the book in a grand conversation, or discus-

FIGURE 1.1 Response Projects for Chris Van Allsburg's Books

Jumanji
- Write a sequel.
- Make a gameboard of the game.
- Research a favorite game and make a poster to share what you learn.

The Stranger
- Make a chart about the four seasons.
- Make a cluster and write a descriptive paragraph about fall.

The Polar Express
- Write about a Christmas memory.
- Write about another holiday.
- Research Christmas customs and share what you learn in an oral report.

Two Bad Ants
- Retell a favorite story from a different point of view.
- Make ant puppets and use them to retell the story.

The Z Was Zapped
- Make an ABC book on Chris Van Allsburg.
- Write an ABC book on any topic and remember to use alliteration.
- Collect five ABC books and read and compare them.

The Garden of Abdul Gasazi
- Make a wordless picture book to retell the story.

The Mysteries of Harris Burdick
- Write a story about one of the pictures.

Ben's Dream
- Research one of the great monuments and share the information with the class.
- Construct one of the monuments.
- Trace Ben's trip on a world map.

The Wretched Stone
- Write a simulated journal from a crew member's point of view.
- Make a wretched stone.

Just a Dream
- Read a book to learn how to clean up the environment.
- Make a poster to put in the hallway to tell kids not to pollute.

Other
- Write to Chris Van Allsburg.
- Make a poster about Mr. Van Allsburg for the library center.
- Make a quilt with your favorite quotations from each book.
- Dramatize your favorite story.
- Do an art project about your favorite story.

FIGURE 1.2   Mrs. Blackburn's Assessment Checklist

Chris Van Allsburg Focus Unit Checklist

Name: _____   Week of: _____

1. Read four CVA books.   _____
2. Write in lit log about the four books.   _____
3. Take notes about minilessons in lit log.   _____
4. Do a response project.   _____
5. Share with the class.   _____
6. Use the writing process.   _____
7. Use good work habits.   _____

---

sion, sharing ideas and feelings as they did about *The Wretched Stone.* After students make their comments, Mrs. Blackburn asks if they would like to play Jumanji, and the grand conversation continues as students talk about whether or not they would want to play the game. Some students are so excited about the book that they decide to write a sequel as their response project.

At the end of the first week, the class talks about response projects and compiles a list of ways they might extend their reading. In these projects, students choose to respond to one of the books they have read through talk, drama, writing, research, art, or additional reading. These response projects that Mrs. Blackburn's students suggest are listed in Figure 1.1. Each student works on one or more response projects during the second week and shares the finished project with the class.

During the second week the students also use the writing process as they draft, revise, and edit a composition related to the focus unit. Some students write letters to Van Allsburg, some write se-

quels to *Jumanji,* some write about Christmas memories after reading *The Polar Express* (1985), and others write stories about an illustration from *The Mysteries of Harris Burdick* (1984).

On the last few days of the second week, students share their compositions and the response projects with the class. On the last day of the focus unit, one group of students makes a chart about where the white dog is hidden in each book, and another group graphs the frequency of the class's favorite Van Allsburg books.

Mrs. Blackburn uses checklists to track and assess students' work. She makes a checklist of the activities students will be involved in after the class plans the unit. Then she distributes a copy to each student. Students keep the checklist in their language arts folders with their lit logs and other papers related to the unit and check off each item as they complete it. At the end of the focus unit, Mrs. Blackburn collects the language arts folders and reviews all the materials in them. A copy of Mrs. Blackburn's assessment checklist for this focus unit is presented in Figure 1.2.

INTRODUCTION

Mrs. Blackburn uses a literature-based reading program because she believes that her students learn to read by reading literature and by using the four language arts— listening, talking, reading, and writing—as they respond to literature. She has a large collection of literature in her classroom library including multiple copies of some of Chris Van Allsburg's books. These books form the core of Mrs. Blackburn's reading program, and students read real books independently, in small groups, and together as a class.

In this chapter we describe the new movement toward literature-based reading and the benefits of using literature to teach reading and language. We discuss the power of literature to enhance children's talk, reading, and writing development as well as their cognitive and social development. Next, we examine the four language arts—listening, talking, reading, and writing, and the connections among the four of them. In the third part of the chapter, we describe materials that are found in literature-rich classrooms and we discuss characteristics of literature-based reading programs. In the final section of this chapter (and each of the chapters that follow), we consider the decisions that teachers must make about teaching literature-based reading.

THE MOVEMENT TOWARD LITERATURE-BASED READING

Today more teachers than ever are interested in learning how to use literature in their reading programs. While teaching reading with literature is not a new idea in American education, this resurgence is the result of both teachers' disenchantment with traditional reading practices and the abundant selection of quality literature being published for children today. Even though teachers worry about how students will perform on state-mandated achievement tests, they recognize that new approaches to literacy instruction are needed. In addition to these concerns, teachers are faced with adapting their programs to meet the needs of culturally and linguistically diverse students and other at-risk students.

Teachers' Disenchantment with Traditional Reading Practices

Many teachers believe that literature-based reading programs can solve two growing problems in American society: illiteracy and aliteracy. *Illiteracy* is not being able to read and write, whereas *aliteracy* is being able to read but choosing not to. Research has shown that only a small percentage of children will become lifelong readers and one in four will not learn to read well enough to function in the workplace. These statistics are grim; less than 1 percent of children spend their free time reading and 40 percent of adult Americans who can read books choose not to (Anderson et al., 1985; Honig, 1988). These frightening statistics may be the result of too much attention to reading skills and not enough concern for fostering a love of reading.

The literature-based reading movement is changing what teachers believe about how children learn to read and about how they teach reading. Teachers are making decisions about reading instruction for their own classrooms; these decisions are to reallocate time, reorganize their classroom schedule and space, expand reading options, and integrate the language arts (Henke, 1988). Teachers who want to implement literature-based reading programs must become risk-takers and accept that change might make them anxious and uncomfortable at times, but the result— changing students' attitudes about reading—is worth it.

The Abundant Selection of Literature for Children

A second reason for the growing popularity of literature-based reading programs is literature itself. Literature is the core of the literacy program because of its universal appeal: "Literature asks universal questions about the meaning of life and human relationships with nature and other people" (Huck, Hepler, & Hickman, 1987, p. 10). It enriches children's personal lives and contributes to their educational development. Reading is enjoyable, and as they read, students meet characters they can relate to and heroes who grapple with all of life's tragedies, joys, and triumphs. Students learn about the world around them as they read and are vicariously transported to other lands or back or forward in time to experience lives very different from their own. Literature can also help them understand how they are affected by the institutions of society and the forces of nature. Through reading, students learn about the power of language to narrate a story or persuade our thinking. Literature is our cultural heritage and our curriculum.

As teachers experiment with literature in their classrooms, they are becoming convinced that exposing children to the best in literature and helping them make choices about their literacy experiences will ensure that children not only become expert readers but also become lifelong readers. Bernice Cullinan, a past president of the International Reading Association says, "There is a sense of determination among teachers who believe that this educational movement must succeed" (1989, p. 113).

The Issue of Accountability

Many teachers would like to use literature in their reading programs, but they are often concerned about how this program might affect students' achievement test scores. Accountability is a major issue for many teachers, and one of the first questions teachers ask when they consider implementing a literature-based reading program is, "Won't my students' achievement test scores go down?" Our answer is "no." The teachers we work with tell us that literature-based reading programs are effective, and research supports this conclusion (McWhirter, 1990; Reutzel & Cooter, 1990; Tunnell & Jacobs, 1989).

Teachers are documenting their success with literature-based reading programs in articles that they write for professional journals. For instance, Cora Lee Five, a fifth grade teacher in Scarsdale, New York, reported that her students' standardized achievement test scores were "gratifying": [their] test results remained constant or showed gains of from two to six years in reading comprehension (1988, p. 104). Other teachers and researchers have reported that all students including at-risk students, bilingual students, and emotionally disturbed students benefit from literature-based reading instruction (Allen, Michalove, Shockley, & West, 1991; D'Alessandro, 1990; Roser, Hoffman, & Farest, 1990).

The California Reading Initiative (Honig, 1988) and the California *English-Language Arts Framework* (1987) recommend literature-based reading programs that allow children to discover that reading is enjoyable. The *Framework* calls these changes "a revolution":

> We are in the midst of a revolution—a quiet, intellectual revolution spinning out dramatic insights into how the brain works, how we acquire language, and how we construct meaning in our lives. (p. 1)

Teachers in California studied the research about learning, language, and literacy, and based on their review, they have identified these themes for their statewide literature-based reading program:

- Reading is enjoyable as well as educational.
- Learning to read is a means toward the goal of becoming a lifelong reader.
- Teachers should inspire students as well as teach them.
- Parents are teachers, too. When they read aloud, listen to children read, and encourage reading, they enhance the learning process.
- Literature should be the core of the language arts curriculum. (Honig, 1988, p. 237)

Interest in the California Reading Initiative has spread nationwide to create the National Reading Initiative (Cullinan, 1989), and teachers, curriculum directors, administrators, state departments of education, and parents in communities sprinkled across the United States are questioning traditional practices that do not reflect current theories and research about learning and that have not successfully taught all children how to read, shared the pleasures of reading, or made them lifelong readers. The result of this reform movement is that literature-based reading is being implemented by individual teachers at the classroom level and groups of teachers and administrators at the school, school district, or state level.

VALUES OF LITERATURE IN THE READING PROGRAM

Children read literature first and foremost for entertainment, as an aesthetic experience that illuminates the human condition. In the case study at the beginning of this chapter, Mrs. Blackburn's students eagerly read Chris Van Allsburg's fantasies because they were enjoyable. Some of the other benefits from reading literature include enhanced aesthetic, oral language, reading, writing, and social-cognitive development.

Aesthetic Development

Louise Rosenblatt (1985) described aesthetic reading as the kind of reading that occurs when we focus attention on what we are "seeing and feeling and thinking, on what is aroused within [us] by the very sounds of the words, and by what they point to in the human world" (p. 70). As we read, we create an imaginary place, and the construction of this imaginary place and all of the feelings and thoughts that we experience as a part of that world is an aesthetic experience. It is like creating a work of art—we make something real from the stuff of our imaginations. Reading literature develops children's aesthetic sensibilities by encouraging them to use their imaginations and savor aesthetic experiences they create. Reading picture books that have vivid and creative illustrations begins this process, and the process is refined by reading increasingly more sophisticated chapter books.

Researchers have learned that not all students enjoy literature aesthetically. Some students, especially poor readers, seem to have a difficult time constructing and stepping into imaginary worlds of literature as a natural part of reading (Purcell-Gates, 1991). Teachers need to support students' aesthetic development by encouraging them to imagine and picture characters and events and to describe their feelings and thoughts as they read various portions of books and poems. These and other personal responses to literature form an important foundation in students' aesthetic development.

Literature-based reading programs provide important support for children's aesthetic development. Children respond to books personally as they write their thoughts in response journals and talk about books in discussions that are not dominated by teachers' questions. Children are allowed to choose the kinds of activities they want to engage in to extend their responses to stories. In the case study at the beginning of this chapter, the students in Mrs. Blackburn's class recorded their personal responses in quickwrites and lit logs, participated in grand conversations, and selected their own response activities. All of these activities provided children the opportunity to grow aesthetically.

Oral Language Development

Literature is a powerful force in children's oral language development, and a high correlation exists between the amount of experience children have with literature and the sophistication of their linguistic development (Chomsky, 1972). As students listen to literature read aloud, they learn about the rhythm and flow of language. The language of stories, informational books, and poems provides a rich source of vocabulary and sentence patterns that students incorporate into their talk (Galda, 1990).

As they read and listen to literature read aloud, students learn about literary language and gain an appreciation for literary styles (Geller, 1985; Norton, 1991). Researchers have found that children's oral retellings of stories reflected the richness of the language and patterns of the stories that they were retelling (Hade, 1988).

Literature-based reading programs support children's oral language development by surrounding them with books and poems that use language of the highest quality. Children are encouraged to enjoy the language of literature as they talk about books they are reading, share personal experiences that books bring to mind, compare versions of a story, perform puppet shows and skits, and give reports about information they have learned from reading. Children are allowed to ask questions and share observations about authors and illustrators and their craft, and they present projects they have pursued to extend their reading.

Reading Development

Literature exerts a strong influence on children's reading development. Clark (1976) found that young children whose parents began reading literature to them at an early age often learned to read before entering school, and Butler (1980) described the crucial role that literature played in the reading development of a child who has multiple handicaps. Reading good literature aloud has long-term effects; Sostarich (1974), for example, found that among upper elementary students who are good readers, those who had been read to from the time they were 3 years old valued reading more and expected they would be lifelong readers. Other studies (Cohen, 1968; Cullinan, Jaggar, & Strickland, 1974) found that reading aloud to children who had not previously been exposed to literature helped them learn to read.

Experiences with literature develop many abilities that contribute to effective reading. Young children learn the kinds of language patterns and literary words that are found in literature by listening to stories read aloud (Purcell-Gates, l988). Experiences with literature develop children's concept of story—knowing the literary elements of a story such as characters and complications and being able to anticipate and construct the meaning of a story. For example, children quickly learn that events often occur in threes in folktales so that even kindergartners and first graders predict that after Goldilocks has eaten the porridge and broken the chair, she will do something else (Huck, Hepler, & Hickman, 1987).

Repeated readings of literature are another important avenue for reading development. Researchers have found that through rereading students gain control over the parts of a story and are better able to synthesize the story parts into a whole (Yaden, l988). The quality of children's responses to stories improves with repeated experiences with those stories (Beaver, 1982), and children become more independent users of the classroom library center when they are able to select favorite books to read again and again (Martinez & Teale, 1988).

The most significant value of literature for reading development is that students read more when they read literature, and wide reading is essential to the development of fluent readers. Children in literature-based reading classrooms often read between 50 and 100 books in a school year, whereas in traditional programs, students read an average of only seven minutes during the reading class and typically read only the one or two reading textbooks during the school year (Anderson et al., 1985). Hepler (1982) found that the fifth and sixth graders in her study each read between 25 and 122 books for an average of 45 books in a school year.

Writing Development

Exposure to good literature also supports students' writing development. Dressell (1990) found that the quality of the stories students read affected the quality of the stories they wrote. Students who read quality literature with well-defined literary elements wrote better quality stories. Similarly, Eckhoff (1983) found that primary grade students' writing reflected the style of their reading texts. She compared children who read the typical simplified basal reader texts with those who read children's literature. Children in the literature group wrote more complex sentences, whereas children in the the basal reader group copied the style and format of their readers—simple sentence structures written with one sentence per line.

In a similar study, DeFord (1981) examined primary grade students' writing in classrooms where teachers used different instructional methods and found that both the method and reading materials influenced students' writing. Students in the literature-based reading classroom wrote using a wider variety of literary forms and were more competent at retelling stories. The content of their stories also reflected the literature they read and listened to read aloud.

It is not surprising that students who read quality literature write better quality compositions than students who are not given these opportunities. We know that there is an important connection between the processes involved in reading and writing. Frank Smith (1983) argued that this connection involves the way that readers who are writers read:

> To read like a writer we engage with the author in what the author is writing. We can anticipate what the author will say, so that the author is in effect writing on our behalf, not showing how something is done but doing it with us. . . . Bit by bit, one thing at a time, but enormous numbers of things over the passage of time, the learner learns through reading like a writer to write like a reader. (pp. 563–564)

Literature-based reading programs offer students many opportunities to read like writers and to write like readers. They use writing to respond to what they read by writing quickwrites, sequels to stories, reports of information gathered from several sources, and poems about characters they have read. Reading and writing are intimately connected so that students write what they are reading about and read to find out more for their writing.

Cognitive and Social Development

Literature is a vehicle for students' cognitive and social development, and the response activities that students engage in support them as they move from egocentric to abstract thinking and learn how to interact socially with classmates. The elementary years are a particularly important period in children's cognitive development. Literature encourages children's cognitive development as they view problems from different viewpoints and grapple with abstract concepts, issues, and motivations. Reading and talking about literature often engage students in a higher level of thinking than might usually be expected. For example, kindergartners who are involved in listening to stories read aloud and responding to them are able to abstract generalized themes from literature (Lehr, 1991). Many activities in literature-based reading programs support and encourage children's cognitive growth, such as taking on the perspective of different characters when they retell a story from a character's perspective or assuming a character's role in a dramatization.

In literature-based reading programs, students are exposed to literature that illustrates human relations in its richest variety. Through discussions and response activities, they make connections between the events and characters in literature and their own lives. One outcome of reading and responding to literature is that students develop a stronger sense of self and learn how to get along with others.

Students learn about the interesting diversity of both human relations and cultures as they read books set in different cultural groups within the United States, in locations around the world, and in other times. Developing positive attitudes toward our own culture and other cultures is an important part of social development, and literature-based reading programs foster these positive feelings.

During the elementary grades, students develop social-cognitive competence, the ability to make connections between literature and life. Being able to make these connections depends on students' interactions and relationships in home and school communities and their experiences with literature. Developing students' social-cognitive competence is important because it is related to the likelihood that students will become lifelong readers (Dyson, 1984; Harste, Woodward, & Burke, 1984; Heath, 1985; Hepler & Hickman, 1982).

Experienced readers think about characters and their relationships with others to understand what they are reading and to generalize to the larger world. However, not all students are able to capitalize on literature experiences because they may not make connections between literature and life (Hynds, 1989). When teachers model literature as a way of learning about life, participate as learners rather than experts, and offer students choices in how they respond to literature, students are more likely to make strong connections between literature and life.

INTEGRATING LITERATURE ACROSS THE LANGUAGE ARTS

Literature is not read in isolation; instead, literature study is integrated with the other language arts. Students use oral language to talk about literature, to listen to stories read aloud, and to dramatize stories. Students use informal writing such as quick-writes to expand their understanding of stories and informational books, and they apply their knowledge of literary structures and language through more formal process writing projects such as writing sequels to stories or poems and writing reports. Although our focus in this book is on reading, we cannot talk about reading literature without integrating reading with listening, talking, and writing.

The Four Language Arts

Traditionally, language arts has been defined as the four modes of language: listening, talking, reading, and writing. Children use these four language modes interrelatedly in literature-based reading programs as they get ready to read a book and go beyond the book after reading as the case study about Mrs. Blackburn's class illustrates.

Listening. Students use listening for genuine and meaningful communication purposes in literature-based reading classrooms. They listen to the teacher read aloud books and poems, listen to monitor their understanding in book discussions, listen to the information teachers provide in minilessons, and listen to classmates talk about books in book talks and share response projects. In these activities, students are listening for appreciative, comprehensive, and critical purposes (Tompkins & Hoskisson, 1991).

Appreciative listening is at the heart of literature-based reading. Students use appreciative listening as they listen for enjoyment and engage in an aesthetic experience. Students listen for appreciative purposes when they listen to teachers read aloud a book or to other students as they perform a puppet show or a readers' theater presentation of a story.

Comprehensive listening is listening to remember; students determine their purpose for listening, and they may use strategies such as noting the speaker's organization or keeping track of main points as an aid to recall. Students are listening for comprehension purposes when they listen to an informational book being read aloud to note specific details to use in a project they are working on or listen to a story read aloud a second time to check their sequencing of story events.

When students use *critical listening,* they are listening to understand and then evaluate the information. Students listen for critical purposes when they participate in discussions about books they have read and in writing groups as they critique each other's writing. They also use critical listening when they listen to classmates compare different versions of a folktale, identify which of an author's books they like best, or talk about whether they prefer the book or film version of the book. These three purposes for listening are summarized in Figure 1.3.

Talking.   Talk is a cornerstone of literacy experiences and is an essential part of life and learning in elementary classrooms (Heath, 1983; Hepler, 1982). Too often, quiet classrooms are considered the most conducive to learning even though research shows that talk is a necessary ingredient for learning. In literature-based reading classrooms, teachers create a classroom atmosphere that encourages students to talk to each other and students to take a more active role in their own learning (Staab, 1991). Children use talk in many ways as they respond to literature—to make predictions about stories they are reading, discuss stories they have read, reflect on experiences, ask questions, retell and dramatize stories, and give book talks to share books they have read—to name only a few of the ways. Researchers are examining the types of talk that students use as they respond to literature and Figure 1.4 presents a list of these types and sample activities.

The teacher's role shifts in literature-based reading programs. Teachers encourage talk because they understand its value and importance in learning. Teachers become one source of information, but not the only one in the classroom. It is not a matter of control or losing control; instead, the teacher and students share both con-

FIGURE 1.3   Purposes for Listening

Appreciative Listening	Comprehensive Listening	Critical Listening
Listening to the text for enjoyment	*Listening to understand the text*	*Listening to understand and evaluate the text*
Enjoy a story, informational book, or poem.	Follow the plot of a story.	Compare versions of a folktale.
Select a favorite sentence for a "Notable Language" poster.	Identify the facts in an informational book.	Determine the structure of an informational book.
	Gain knowledge related to a theme cycle.	Compare book and film versions.

FIGURE 1.4   Types of Talk Students Use to Respond to Literature

Type	Description	Examples
Conversing	Talk informally with class-mates or the teacher.	• Share a personal experience. • Have a conference with the teacher about a book or response project. • Express opinion about an illustrator's style.
Collaborating	Talk as students work to-gether to read and respond to a book.	• Read a book with a buddy. • Plan a puppet show. • Do a response project with classmates.
Negotiating	Talk about roles and respon-sibilities in reading and re-sponding to literature.	• Decide how many chapters to read before the next lit group meeting. • Select a response project. • Determine roles for a readers' theater presen-tation.
Directing	Lead classroom routines and other procedures.	• Lead a literature discussion group. • Serve on class editorial boards. • Oversee production of a theatrical production.
Presenting	Give a planned talk to an audience.	• Retell a favorite story. • Give a book talk. • Give an oral report.
Informing	Ask questions and make statements of factual information.	• Ask about the meaning of an unfamiliar word. • Give information in response to a classmate's question. • Suggest a book that a classmate might want to read.
Hypothesizing	Make guesses and other ex-ploratory comments.	• Predict what will happen next in a story. • Make tentative comments in discussions. • Wonder what might happen to favorite char-acters in a sequel.
Interpreting	Put information together in new ways; reflect; draw con-clusions.	• Link literature to life in literature discussion groups. • Discuss a character's motivations. • Infer themes in literature.
Inventing	Experiment with language and play with words.	• Create a story or poem. • Coin new words and sayings. • Invent dialogue for a favorite book character.
Reflecting	Talk to self-evaluate and value reading and response activities.	• Critique a book for a classmate. • Judge work habits in a conference with the teacher. • Compare versions of a folktale.

Camp & Tompkins, 1992.

trol and responsibility for learning. Reardon (1988) describes her role in literature discussion group meetings in her classroom:

> Reading groups meet around a table. The children have notes they have made in response to the discussion questions and their "reading books" are filled with paper slips to mark important passages. The discussion begins. It is a conversation. Children do not raise their hands but respond to what the previous speaker has said. I sit in for part of the meeting, but the children control the discussion. I rarely give my ideas. I listen, question, and help make connections. It is an exciting and thoughtful time as the children explain their ideas. They read passages to substantiate points, laugh and argue with each other, with the author, and with characters. They make discoveries. (p. 59)

Drama is a special type of talk activity; it plays a central role in language learning because students use drama as a tool for learning (Kardash & Wright, 1987; Wagner, 1988). In literature-based reading classrooms, students participate in dramatic activities to explore what they are reading and to respond to that reading. These activities can be classified as informal drama, interpretive drama, and dramatic productions. These three types of drama activities are summarized in Figure 1.5 (and are more thoroughly described in Chapters 5, 6, and 7).

In informal drama, students participate in spontaneous and unrehearsed dramatic activities, such as role-playing. They assume roles in a story and act out the events to better understand the plot and the characters. Interpretive drama is slightly more formal; students use voice, facial expressions, and gestures to dramatize a story or an event from an informational book. Some rehearsal is needed and there is usu-

FIGURE 1.5   Types of Dramatic Activities

Type	Description	Examples
Informal Drama	Students' spontaneous and unrehearsed dramatic activities *Characteristics:* • few props • little rehearsal • usually no audience	• Role-play a story or episode from a chapter book. • Pantomime as a poem is read aloud.
Interpretive Drama	Students use voice, facial features, and gestures to dramatize a story *Characteristics:* • few props • some rehearsal • usually no audience	• Retell a favorite story with puppets or storyboards. • "Read" a wordless picture book. • Present a readers' theater. • Present a choral reading.
Dramatic Productions	Students stage theatrical productions *Characteristics:* • use props and scenery • rehearsal • dialogue to learn • an audience	• Present a play. • Present a puppet show. • Videotape a commercial. • Dramatize scripts that students have written.

ally an audience—often a small group of children. In dramatic productions students interpret stories through storytelling, readers' theatre, puppet shows, and plays. Dramatic productions are the most formal type of drama and involve rehearsal, collecting props, and more elaborate planning and rehearsal. Sometimes students write their own scripts for stories or sequels of stories. These productions are not always live, and sometimes the dramatic production is videotaped.

Reading.   Four ways that students read literature in literature-based reading classrooms are reading aloud, shared reading, guided reading, and independent reading. The type of reading that students use depends on the teacher's purpose, the availability of reading materials, and students' reading proficiencies. In some classrooms all four types of reading take place daily; in others, teachers and students use two or three types. Over a school year, however, all four types are used in most classrooms. These four types of reading are summarized in Figure 1.6.

   Reading aloud.   In literature-based reading classrooms, reading aloud to students is a valuable way of sharing literature with students, not an "extra" or a reward for good behavior. It is used at all grade levels, kindergarten through eighth grade, not just with primary grade students who do not read independently yet. Teachers (or other fluent readers) read aloud at least once daily (and usually more often than that) to the class to nurture a love of literature, model what good readers do, introduce students to authors and genres, and share books that students cannot read by themselves. Teachers read a variety of literature aloud including stories, biographies, informational books, and poems.

FIGURE 1.6   Four Types of Reading Activities

Type	Description	Examples
Reading Aloud	Teacher or another fluent reader reads the text aloud while students listen.	• Read stories or poems aloud to the class. • Readers' theater presents a script.
Shared Reading	Teacher or another fluent reader reads the text aloud while one or more students follow along in individual copies or an enlarged text.	• A small group reads a big book. • Teacher and class read a chapter book together. • Do a choral reading of a poem. • Reread a book with a buddy. • Read a book at the listening center.
Guided Reading	Students and the teacher read, think, and discuss a book as a class or in a small group.	• Read a core literature book. • Participate in a literature study group.
Independent Reading	Students read self-selected books on their own without teacher direction.	• Have a reading workshop. • Students participate in DEAR time. • Students read books in connection with a unit or author study.

Reading aloud is an informal and pleasurable activity in which students build a shared understanding and interpretation of the piece of literature that was read. Reading aloud helps students gain the confidence about reading and literature that they need to be successful independent readers. After listening to a book read aloud, some students may want to revisit it by listening to it read aloud again at the listening center or by choosing to reread it independently.

Teachers use reading aloud for a variety of instructional purposes. They read aloud to share literature with students when the book is too difficult for them to read on their own but it is appropriate for their interests or when there is only one copy of the story, poem, or book available. Teachers usually read an entire picture book or short story aloud in one sitting, but for longer chapter books they read one or two chapters aloud each day until the book is finished. Even when they have class sets of books available, teachers might read part or all of it aloud as an introductory activity before distributing individual copies to students. Teachers also reread favorite books that students ask to have read again.

Shared reading.   In shared reading, the teacher or another fluent reader reads the literature aloud while students follow along in the text and often join in the reading (Holdaway, 1979). It is similar to reading aloud in that the teacher or another expert reader does the reading, but unlike reading aloud, students can see the text as it is being read in shared reading. Students might follow along by looking at an enlarged or *big book* version of a story, at a chart of a song, rhyme, chant, or poem that the teacher has made, or in individual copies of books. As in reading aloud, the reading experience is relaxed and social, and the teacher accepts and encourages all efforts and approximations that students make as they join in the reading.

Shared reading is a good way to immerse students in literature without worrying about the reading level of the story, book, or poem. Young emerging readers, linguistically and culturally different readers, and reluctant readers feel more success through shared reading than when they struggle to read the text by themselves (Trachtenburg & Ferruggia, 1989; Wicklund, 1989).

Shared reading can also be used with upper grade students when reading a chapter book. The teacher or another fluent reader reads aloud while students follow in their individual copies of the book. Some proficient readers may read ahead independently, but most students read along with the person reading aloud. This allows access to literature that might be beyond some students' reading level but not outside their range of interests. Other ways to use shared reading include choral reading in which students read lines of a poem in unison and buddy reading in which two students read a text together, with one student reading and the other following along.

A listening center is another way to use shared reading to give access to all students. At the listening center a small group of students follows along in individual copies of a book as they listen to a commercially prepared tape of the book or a tape prepared by the teacher. Students can follow along in individual copies of a book for a first reading or as they listen a second time to a favorite story.

Guided reading.   In guided reading, students and the teacher read, think, and talk their way through the reading of a text. This approach is "guided" in that the teacher supports students and directs their attention during reading to focus on events, vocabulary, the author's craft, a genre, or an author's style. Guided reading can also be used when teachers read aloud to students or when students are reading individual copies of a book. This approach can be used with the whole class or with small heterogeneous groups called "literature discussion groups."

During guided reading students and the teacher ask questions, make predictions, and talk about their reading. Most of the time is spent in appreciating and enjoying the language of the book and in sharing personal insights through discussion. Often there is oral reading, such as when students read a passage aloud to make a point or share a description of a character. Several vocabulary words might also be discussed within the context of the story, poem, or book.

In the case study at the beginning of the chapter, Mrs. Blackburn guided students as they read *Jumanji* by talking and writing about games before they read the book, quickwriting about the story after reading, and having students discuss the book in a grand conversation. Through these activities, students explored and elaborated their interpretations of the book.

Independent reading.   In independent reading, students are in charge of their own reading (Hornsby, Sukarna, & Parry, 1988). They choose books to read from the class or school library or they bring a book from home. Sometimes, teachers ask students to read particular types of books—biographies or books written by Beverly Cleary, for example—but students choose which books they will read.

Students read by themselves and at their own pace. Young children often tell a story by looking at the pictures or from memory rather than by reading the text conventionally. However young children approach reading, it is important that they spend time looking at books and thinking about literature regardless of whether they can read every word in the book. At the primary grade level, students may read independently for only 10 to 20 minutes each day while older students read independently up to 45 minutes daily.

The students in Mrs. Blackburn's class selected books for independent reading from a special collection of Van Allsburg's books. Mrs. Blackburn believes that self-selection is a crucial part of her reading program because students learn how to select literature and they read books that they are interested in reading. She confers with individual students about the books they are reading and uses these brief conferences to keep track of students' learning.

Writing.   In literature-based reading classrooms, students write informally to explore what they are learning and use the writing process to share what they have learned (Tompkins, 1990). A list of informal and writing process activities is presented in Figure 1.7. (See Chapters 5, 6, and 7 for more explanation of these activities.)

Students use informal writing when they use quickwrites and clusters to clarify their interpretations about a book. The students in Mrs. Blackburn's class, for example, used quickwrites and lit log entries to explore their understanding of the books they read. Another way students make personal connections with books is by writing in response journals. These journals go by many names, including reading logs, literature journals, and reading notebooks. No matter what they are called, students at all grade levels use them to focus and sharpen their understandings about what they read (Atwell, 1987; Barone, 1990; Dekker, 1991, Five, 1986; Graves, 1989).

FIGURE 1.7   Informal and Formal Writing Activities

Informal Writing Activities (Exploratory)	Formal Writing Activities (The Writing Process)
Quickwrites • Quickwrite on a topic related to the book. • Quickwrite a response to the book. • Quickwrite a prediction before reading. *Response Journals* • Write a response to reading. • Write predictions before reading. • Pretend to be a character from the book and write simulated journal entries. *Clusters, Maps, and Charts* • Cluster the beginning-middle-end of story. • Cluster a character. • Use a Venn diagram to compare two versions of a book. • Cluster a topic related to book.	*Stories* • Write a retelling of a story. • Rewrite a story from a different point of view. • Write a prequel or sequel to a story. • Use the pattern of a story to write an original story. *Letters* • Write a letter to a favorite author or illustrator. • Pretend to be a character from the book and write a letter to another character. • Write a letter to request information related to a theme cycle. *Poems* • Write an acrostic poem using the title of the book or a character's name. • Write a found poem using words and phrases from the book. • Write a poem using the format of a favorite poem. • Write a formula or free-form poem related to a book. *Essays* • Write to compare versions of a familiar story. • Write to compare a book and film version of a book. • Write about the theme of a story. *Reports* • Research and write a report on a topic related to a book. • Write an ABC book on a topic related to a book.

At other times, students' writing is more polished, written to share learning, such as when they are

- writing a *prequel* (story to precede) or a *sequel* (story to follow) to a favorite story
- writing a report as part of a theme cycle
- writing an essay to compare a book and the film version of the book
- writing a letter to an author or illustrator
- writing a poem to describe a favorite character

For these more polished writings, students use a process approach to writing. Students view spelling and handwriting as tools that writers use to communicate effectively with their readers. When students are making final copies of their compositions, they take care to use conventional spelling and write legibly as a courtesy to classmates (and others) who will read their compositions.

In recent years, the emphasis in writing instruction has shifted from the finished product that students have written to the process they use as they gather and organize ideas, draft their ideas, refine, and polish their compositions. The teacher's role has shifted from merely assigning and grading the finished product to working with students throughout the writing process. The writing process includes five stages: prewriting, drafting, revising, editing, and publishing. The key features of each stage are shown in Figure 1.8. The labeling and numbering of the stages should not be construed to suggest that the writing process always proceeds in the same order; instead writers work in recurring cycles. The labeling is only an aid to discussing the activities that represent each stage. In the classroom, the stages merge and repeat, and students personalize the process to meet their needs and vary the process according to the writing assignment.

FIGURE 1.8 Key Features of the Writing Process

Stage 1: Prewriting

Students write on topics based on their own experiences.
Students engage in rehearsal activities before writing.
Students identify the audience to whom they will write.
Students identify the purpose of the writing activity.
Students choose an appropriate form for their compositions based on audience and purpose.

Stage 2: Drafting

Students write a rough draft.
Students emphasize content rather than mechanics.

Stage 3: Revising

Students share their writing in writing groups.
Students participate constructively in discussions about classmates' writing.
Students make changes in their compositions to reflect the reactions and comments of both teacher and classmates.
Between the first and final drafts, students make substantive rather than only minor changes.

Stage 4: Editing

Students proofread their own compositions.
Students help proofread classmates' compositions.
Students increasingly identify and correct their own mechanical errors.

Stage 5: Publishing

Students publish their writing in an appropriate form.
Students share their finished writing with an appropriate audience.

Stage 1: Prewriting.   Prewriting is the getting-ready-to-write stage. Writers do not have a topic completely thought-out and ready to flow onto the page; instead, they begin tentatively—talking, reading, drawing, writing—to see what they know and what direction they want their writing to go. Three of the activities that writers are involved in during the prewriting stage are

1. *Choose a topic.* Traditionally, teachers supplied topics by suggesting gimmicky story starters to relieve students of the "burden" of topic selection. Often these topics stymied students, who were forced to write on topics they knew little about or were not interested in. Instead students who use the writing process take responsibility for choosing their own writing topics. Sometimes students write about completely self-selected topics; at other times, they choose a specific topic related to a more general theme. For example, after reading *The True Story of the Three Little Pigs* (Scieszka, 1989), students might rewrite a familiar folktale from one character's viewpoint; after *Jumanji* (Van Allsburg, 1981), they might write a sequel; after *Number the Stars* (Lowry, 1989), they might write a poem about bravery; and after Burningham's *Would You Rather . . .* (1978), they might write their own books of outrageous choices.

2. *Consider the purpose, form, and audience.* As students prepare to write, they need to think about their purpose for writing. Are they writing to entertain? To inform? To persuade? Understanding the function of a piece of writing is important because purpose influences other decisions students make.

Students write for an audience, and the quality of their writing is influenced by their sense of audience. When writing for others, students adapt what and how they write to fit their audience. Possible audiences include classmates, younger children, parents, foster grandparents, children's authors, and pen pals.

Another important consideration is the form the writing will take: a poem? a letter? a newspaper article? A writing project could be handled in any one of these ways; too often students' writing is limited to stories, poems, and reports. Instead, they need to experiment with a variety of writing forms and explore the purposes and formats of language used to communicate to authentic audiences (Hidi & Hildyard, 1983; Langer, 1985).

3. *Gather and organize information.* Students need to collect ideas that they will write about and experiment with different ways to organize those ideas. One way students gather and organize information is by constructing clusters. A cluster is a graphic display of key words, phrases, and pictures that are arrayed into main ideas and details. A cluster that a first grader made to get ready to write a retelling of *The Day Jimmy's Boa Ate the Wash* (Noble, 1980) is presented in Figure 1.9.

Stage 2: Drafting.   In the process approach to writing, students write and refine their compositions through a series of drafts. During the drafting stage, students focus on getting their ideas down on paper. Because writers do not begin writing with their compositions already composed in their minds, students begin with tentative ideas developed through prewriting activities. The drafting stage is the time to generate ideas, with little concern about spelling, punctuation, and other mechanical errors.

FIGURE 1.9 A First Grader's Cluster for *The Day Jimmy's Boa Ate the Wash* (Noble, 1980)

Students should skip every other line when they write their rough drafts so that they will have space to make revisions later. They write on only one side of a sheet of paper so they can cut it apart and rearrange it later when they revise. As word processors become more accessible in classrooms, revising text will become much easier, but for the time being wide spacing is crucial. (Students can make small *x*'s on every other line of their papers as a reminder to skip lines when they draft their compositions.)

Students label their drafts by writing "rough draft" at the top of the paper or by stamping it with a ROUGH DRAFT stamp. This label indicates to the writer, other students, parents, and administrators that the composition is a draft, in which the emphasis is on content, not mechanics, and explains why the teacher has not marked mechanical errors.

When drafting their compositions, students may need to modify earlier decisions about function, audience, and especially, form; for example, a composition that began as a story may be transformed into a report, letter, or a poem because the new format allows the student to communicate more effectively. The process of modifying earlier decisions continues into the revising stage.

Stage 3: Revising.   During this stage, writers refine ideas in their compositions. Students often break the writing process cycle as soon as they complete a rough draft, believing that once they have jotted down their ideas, the writing task is complete. Experienced writers, however, know they must turn to others for reactions and revise on the basis of these comments. Revision is not just polishing; it is meeting the needs of readers by adding, substituting, deleting, and rearranging material. Revision means seeing again, and in this stage writers see their compositions again with the help of classmates and teacher. Activities in the revising stage are:

1. *Rereading the rough draft.* After finishing the rough draft, writers need to distance themselves from the draft for a day or two, and then reread the draft from a fresh perspective, as a reader might. Writers must be able to see what they have actually written, rather than what they intended to write. As students reread, they make changes—adding, substituting, deleting, and moving—and place question marks by sections they need help with so they remember to bring them up in their writing group.

2. *Sharing the rough draft.* Students meet in writing groups to share their compositions with small groups of classmates (Calkins, 1986; Mohr, 1984). Writing groups can form spontaneously when several students have completed drafts and are ready for feedback, or they can be established groups with identified leaders. The writing group begins with one writer reading his or her composition aloud. Everyone listens politely, thinking of compliments and suggestions to make. Next, listeners offer compliments, stating what they liked about the writing. These positive comments should be specific and focus on strengths. General remarks such as "I like it" or "It was good" are not effective feedback. Teachers should model appropriate responses so students will know how to offer specific and meaningful comments about organization, word choice, sequence, dialogue, character development, and point of view. After compliments, the writer asks for assistance with trouble spots, and members of the writing group ask questions about things that were unclear and make suggestions for revising the composition. Students make suggestions about adding more details, sequencing events, expanding an underdeveloped section, eliminating redundant text, substituting better words for *it* or *said,* combining sentences, or adding a lead sentence to grab the reader. This process is repeated for each student's composition.

3. *Revising the rough draft.* Students revise their compositions based on the feedback they received in writing groups. They add words, substitute sentences, delete paragraphs, and move phrases (Faigley & Witte, 1981). They cross out, draw arrows, and write in the space left between the doublespaced lines of their rough drafts. Messiness is inevitable, but despite the scribbles, students are usually able to decipher what they have written.

Stage 4: Editing.   Editing is putting the piece of writing into its final form. Until this stage, the focus has been on content; now the focus changes to mechanics, and students polish their writing by correcting spelling and other mechanical errors. The goal here is to make the writing "optimally readable" (Smith, 1982).

Mechanics are the commonly accepted conventions of written Standard English. They include capitalization, punctuation, spelling, sentence structure, usage, and formatting considerations specific to poems, scripts, letters, and other writing forms. The use of these commonly accepted conventions is a courtesy to those who will read the composition.

Students move through three activities in the editing stage:

1. *Getting distance.* Students are more efficient editors if they set the writing aside for a few days before beginning to edit. After working so closely with the piece of writing, they are too familiar with it to locate many mechanical errors.

2. *Proofreading to locate errors.* Students proofread their compositions to locate and mark possible errors. Proofreading is a unique type of reading in which students read slowly, word by word, hunting for errors rather than reading for meaning (King, 1985). After proofreading their own papers, students often trade papers with a classmate and proofread each other's papers.

3. *Correcting errors.* Students correct errors they have located on their own or with their editor's assistance. Editing can end there or students can then meet with the teacher for a final editing. When mechanical correctness is crucial, this conference is important. Teachers proofread the composition with the students and identify and correct the remaining errors together. After all the errors are corrected, students make the final copy of their compositions.

Teachers can use the editing stage to assess students' mechanical and spelling skills informally and to give minilessons on a skill that one student or several students are having trouble with.

Stage 5: Publishing. In the final stage of the writing process, students bring the composition to life by publishing their writing or sharing it orally with an appropriate audience. This stage is crucial because when students share their writing with a real audience of classmates, other students, parents, or the community, students come to think of themselves as authors.

The writing process is an important component of literature-based reading classes. It is a time-consuming process, but it is how real writers work. If students, for example, rewrote a familiar folktale from a character's point of view after reading *The True Story of the Three Little Pigs* (Scieszka, 1989), wrote a single draft paper, and placed it on the teacher's desk to be graded, they would learn little about point of view, folktales, or written language. Instead, students need to learn how to craft a folktale, make decisions about what information to include in the retelling according to the perspective of the character telling the story, and choose words and sentence structures to make their version as compelling as Jon Scieszka's. Juggling all these considerations requires that students use the revising and editing stages of the writing process, and in the end students publish a book—not just a piece of paper.

Connections Among the Language Arts

All four language modes are used in literature-based reading programs for an important reason: developing fluency and strength in one language art supports the growth of fluency and strength in the others. More competent readers are more competent talkers, listeners, and writers. Over a 13-year period, researcher Walter Loban

(1976) documented the language growth of a group of 338 students from kindergarten through 12th grade (ages 5–18). He examined differences between students who used language effectively and those who did not. Three of Loban's conclusions are especially noteworthy to our discussion of the relationship among the language modes. First, Loban reported positive correlations among the four language modes. Second, he found that students with less effective oral language (listening and talking) competencies tended to have less effective written language (reading and writing) competencies. And, third, he found a strong relationship between students' oral language ability and their overall academic ability. Loban's seminal study demonstrates clear relationships among the language modes.

Research shows that students learn to read and write better when the two processes are connected. Shanahan (1988) identified seven instructional principles for relating reading and writing:

1. Teachers should provide daily opportunities for students to read literature and write in response to literature.
2. Teachers should introduce reading and writing in kindergarten and provide opportunities for these students to read and write for genuine purposes.
3. Teachers should understand that students' reading and writing reflects the developmental nature of the reading-writing relationship.
4. Teachers should make the reading-writing connection explicit to students by providing opportunities for them to share their writing with classmates, publish their own books, and learn about authors.
5. Teachers should emphasize the process and product relationships in reading and writing as students reread and talk about literature to clarify interpretations and revise writing to communicate more effectively.
6. Teachers should emphasize the communicative functions of reading and writing and involve students in reading and writing for genuine communication purposes.
7. Teachers should teach reading and writing in meaningful contexts with literature.

The grouping of language arts into listening, talking, reading, and writing activities, while convenient for discussion, is both arbitrary and artificial. This arrangement wrongly suggests that the modes develop separately or that children use different mental processes for listening, talking, reading, and writing (Smith, 1979). It has generally been assumed that children learn to use the language modes in sequence from listening to talking before they come to school, to reading in the elementary grades, and then to writing in the middle school and high school. Although listening is the first language mode to develop, with talking beginning soon after, parents and preschool teachers have recently documented children's early interest in both reading and writing (Baghban, 1984; Bissex, 1980). Carol Chomsky (1971) and other researchers have observed young children experimenting with writing earlier than with reading. On the basis of reports from parents, teachers, and researchers, we can no longer assume that there is a definite sequence in learning and using the four language modes.

LITERATURE-RICH CLASSROOMS

Literature-rich classrooms are social settings in which students read, talk, and write about literature. These classrooms have certain characteristics, specific materials and classroom arrangements, and instructional methodologies that are conducive to learning and support students' interactions with literature.

Characteristics of Literature-Rich Classrooms

Literature-rich classrooms are special places where teachers establish a community of readers and writers. Susan Hepler (1991) explains that "The real challenge to teachers . . . is to set up the kind of classroom community where children pick their own ways to literacy and continue to learn to read" (p. 179). Students read literature and make choices about books they will read and the activities they will engage in, and from these experiences they become responsible, independent learners (Calkins, 1986; Hansen, 1987).

Through her observations of successful literature-based reading classrooms, O'Brien (1991) recommends these practices:

1. Students discuss the words in the context of the story and the author's effect in using particular words after reading rather than looking up definitions of vocabulary words before reading.
2. Students discuss their feelings and interpretations with classmates to negotiate a personal meaning and return to the story to learn more about the author's craft. They do not complete fill-in-the-blank or question-and-answer worksheets to demonstrate that they understood the story they have read.
3. Students read whole books rather than excerpts and avoid breaking chapter books up into a chapter-by-chapter reading format. Students read shorter chapter books in their entirety before discussing them, and decisions about how to divide longer books are made logically, after thinking about plot development and theme.
4. Students in the class read a story together using a class set of books. At other times they may choose which books they want to read and read in small literature study groups or independently.
5. Teachers use a broad definition of grade level when they consider which books to use with students. Books are not written for any particular grade level; instead, they can be read and reread at different grade levels and each time students read a book, their responses to it will deepen.
6. Students are encouraged to develop individual interpretations of books and responses to them even though they may reach a general consensus about the literary elements or the author's craft.
7. Students discuss literary elements such as plot, characters, and theme in books they read so that they can understand how these elements work together to create a work of literature.
8. Students lead the discussions about books they have read and the

teacher serves mainly as the facilitator so that the discussion is based on students' response.

9. Students study themes, authors, and genre by reading and discussing several related books, called *text sets.*
10. Students focus on what the author reveals about the characters and about life as they read and discuss a book; they do not focus on short vowel sounds, sequence of events in the book, or other skills.
11. Students make connections between what they read and their own lives.
12. Students read literature from various cultures and ethnic groups.

New Zealand educator Brian Cambourne has identified seven conditions of learning (Butler & Turbill, 1984) that can be found in literature-rich classrooms. These conditions suggest that students are immersed in reading literature in a supportive classroom environment that encourages students to learn by trial and error and to become more responsible by making choices. The teacher provides a model of a reader and writer, expects students to learn to read, and manages the classroom environment in a way that actively engages students in literacy activities. Cambourne's conditions for learning are summarized in Figure l.10.

Materials and Centers in Literature-Rich Classrooms

Literature-rich classroooms have a variety of materials including literature, audiovisual materials, drama materials, and writing and art materials that students use as they read and respond to literature. These materials are collected in centers and other locations, and literature-rich classrooms have large, comfortable, and visually appealing library centers, listening centers, and other locations to house drama, writing, and art materials.

Literature.   Literature-based reading classrooms are filled with books because real communities of readers need their own collections of books to read. While school

FIGURE 1.10   Seven Conditions of Learning in Literature-Based Reading Classrooms

1. *Immersion.* Students need to be immersed in a wide variety of literature that they find interesting and use these books for reading and writing instruction.
2. *Demonstration.* Students learn from demonstrations—explanations and models—that show them that texts are written and read.
3. *Expectation.* Students are supported or thwarted by the expectations of parents, teachers, and classmates.
4. *Responsibility.* Students who make choices about what they read and the activities they are involved in become more self-reliant.
5. *Employment.* Students must have time to read literature, extend their reading, share their reading with genuine audiences, and participate in other authentic literacy-related activities.
6. *Approximation.* Students read and write more confidently when they understand that teachers do not expect correctness but improvement by trial and error.
7. *Engagement.* Students are actively involved in reading and are willing to take chances when the classroom environment is inviting and supportive as these conditions suggest.

libraries and public libraries are good sources of books, they are not enough. Robert Frost suggested that we "surround youngsters with so many books they stumble on them" (quoted in Henke, 1988, p. 43). Many of the teachers we work with have 500 or more books in their classrooms that they have collected over the years. Some books in classroom libraries have been bought using school funds and others are on loan from the teacher next door, the school library, and the public library, but most teachers purchase a great number of the books themselves from local children's book stores, yard sales, and through paperback book clubs.

Whether teachers purchase or borrow the books, they collect the best of children's literature. The classroom library should include books representing a wide variety of genres—stories, informational books, biographies, and poetry. Most importantly the collection should include multicultural books—books written for and by various racial and ethnic cultures in America.

Literature-rich classrooms have *literature sets* of books (also called *lit sets*) with multiple copies of the same book. Classrooms typically have four to six sets of books with sufficient copies so that the whole class can read the book together. These books must be carefully chosen to launch author studies or to illustrate a genre, and often they lend themselves to the study of a literary element or the author's craft (for more information, see Chapters 2 and 3).

Literature-rich classrooms also have many other literature sets of six to eight copies of a book that small groups of students can read and discuss together. Even when only two or three copies of a book are available, students can buddy-read together and discuss the book.

Library Center.   In literature-rich classrooms teachers create a library center to display the books of children's literature in their classrooms. The library center is an attractive area large enough for several children to browse through books and read together. It includes posters and projects about books and authors that students have made and displays of special books related to a theme, written by the same author, or versions of the same story. The books should be organized in some way, usually by genre or author with special sections for sets of books related to units of study or topics of special interest. Most teachers devise a system for checking out and returning books and involve students as librarians to keep the library center neat. A file with information about favorite authors and illustrators might also be included. After studying library centers in classrooms, Leslie Morrow (1989) compiled 10 recommendations for library centers which are presented in Figure 1.11.

Audiovisual Materials.   In literature-rich classrooms, teachers have a variety of audiovisual materials to support and extend students' reading. Some of these audiovisual materials are

- filmstrips, videotapes, and films of children's literature
- filmstrips and videotapes featuring interviews with children's authors and illustrators
- kits for students to use in making filmstrips to retell favorite stories
- videotape camera to use in filming children's skits and other dramatic productions
- the equipment to produce and view audiovisual materials

FIGURE 1.11   Recommendations for Library Centers

- The library center should be inviting and afford privacy.
- The library center should have a physical definition with shelves, carpets, benches, sofas, or other partitions.
- Five or six students should fit comfortably in the center at one time.
- Two kinds of bookshelves are needed. Most of the collection should be shelved with the spines facing outward, but some books should be placed so that the front covers are displayed.
- Books should be shelved by category and color-coded by type.
- Books written by one author or related to the theme being studied should be displayed prominently, and the displays should be changed regularly.
- The floor should be covered with a rug and the area furnished with pillows, beanbag chairs, or comfortable furniture.
- The center should be stocked with at least four times as many books as students in the classroom.
- A variety of types of reading materials, including books, newspapers, magazines, posters, and charts, should be included in the center.
- Attractive posters that encourage reading, especially if they relate to books in the library center, should be added.

These materials are available for students to use in literature-based reading classrooms, and the teacher spends time early in the school year to introduce the materials to students and demonstrate how to operate the equipment.

Listening Centers. A listening center is an essential part of a literature-based reading classroom. Too often teachers think of them only for primary grade students, and do not realize their potential usefulness with older students. Many commercially prepared tape recordings of children's literature are available so that students can listen to them for any of these purposes:

- as an introduction before reading
- as another presentation mode
- to learn about techniques of oral or dramatic reading
- to learn how to use background music and other sound effects that they can use in their own storytelling, choral reading, and readers' theater productions
- for rereading favorite books
- to compare versions of folktales and other stories

Teachers also tape-record when they read aloud chapter books so that when students are absent, they can catch up by listening to the taped version of the book when they return.

Dramatic Materials. Students in literature-rich classrooms use a variety of dramatic materials in retelling and dramatizing stories they have read and producing stories they have written. Examples of materials that support dramatic activities include

- commercially prepared finger puppets to use in retelling a familiar folktale
- stick puppets that students make using scrap art materials to retell a favorite story
- a puppet stage that students use in retelling stories they have read and new stories students have written
- story boards that students sequence and use in retelling a story or pattern book (These may be made by cutting apart two copies of a picture book and glueing the pages to sheets of tag board.)
- props such as hats, magic wands, mustaches, and other small objects that students use in dramatizing a story or an episode from a chapter book

These materials are kept in a corner of the classroom where students have free access to them as they are working on projects and other activities related to books they are reading.

Writing and Art Materials. Literature-rich classrooms are well stocked with a variety of writing and art materials for students to use as they respond to the books they are reading. Some materials are

- a variety of pens, pencils, crayons, markers, and other writing materials to use in writing and illustrating books, posters, and other displays

- lined and unlined paper of varied sizes and colors that children use in writing books, making posters, murals, and other displays
- materials for making and binding books including cloth scraps, contact paper, and cardboard for covers; gift wrap and other decorated papers for end papers; a saddleback stapler, brads, and rings for binding books; and paper cut in various shapes for shape books
- one or more computers with word processing systems and printers that children can use to write books and posters
- a camera and film to use in taking photos for illustrations and photos of children for "All about the author" pages
- a variety of scrap art materials for collages, dioramas, and mobiles
- paint, markers, crayons, chalk, and other art materials to use in art projects and for illustrating children's books

These materials are stored in a writing or art center for students to use as they write and illustrate response projects.

Instructional Approaches in Literature-Rich Classrooms

Teachers put literature at the center of their instructional programs and use components of two approaches for their literature-based reading programs: core literature and reading workshop. In the case study at the beginning of this chapter, Mrs. Blackburn used a combination of the core literature and reading workshop approaches. The core literature approach involves all the students in the class or small heterogeneous groups of students reading and responding to the same core book, such as *Jumanji* (Van Allsburg, 1981). In the other approach, reading workshop, students select and read whatever books they wish to read or select books from a special collection of related books, such as books written by Chris Van Allsburg.

Core Literature.   In the core literature approach, students read and respond to a single book as a class or in small groups. When students read a book as a class, the teacher plans a variety of activities to introduce students to the core literature selection, support students as they listen to the book read aloud or read the book using shared reading or guided reading, explore the ideas and language of the book through writing and talk, and extend the book through activities after reading.

Reading Workshop.   Reading workshop is quite different from the core literature approach. In the reading workshop approach, students select books to read and spend from 15 to 45 minutes reading independently. After reading, students complete response activities they have selected, such as writing a sequel to a story, writing a poem about a character, or writing a report about an animal in a poem. Teachers hold meetings with the whole class and read aloud to students. They also present brief minilessons on reading strategies or demonstrations such as how to write in response journals or keep records of books and poems. The final activity in reading workshop is sharing; all the students gather together and a few students talk about books they have read or present their finished response activities.

FIGURE 1.12   Summary Chart for Decision Tree

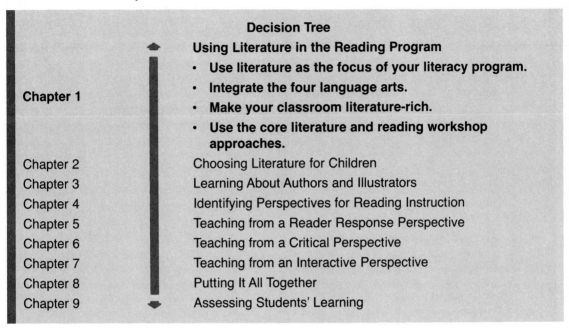

	Decision Tree
	Using Literature in the Reading Program
	• **Use literature as the focus of your literacy program.**
	• **Integrate the four language arts.**
Chapter 1	• **Make your classroom literature-rich.**
	• **Use the core literature and reading workshop approaches.**
Chapter 2	Choosing Literature for Children
Chapter 3	Learning About Authors and Illustrators
Chapter 4	Identifying Perspectives for Reading Instruction
Chapter 5	Teaching from a Reader Response Perspective
Chapter 6	Teaching from a Critical Perspective
Chapter 7	Teaching from an Interactive Perspective
Chapter 8	Putting It All Together
Chapter 9	Assessing Students' Learning

MAKING DECISIONS ABOUT TEACHING LITERATURE-BASED READING

In contrast to basal reading programs, which provide guidelines for teachers to follow, literature-based reading programs call on teachers to become independent decision-makers if they are to teach reading successfully. Teachers must be informed, committed, and courageous to create literature-based reading programs in their classrooms. They must become knowledgeable about children's literature, reading, and language arts in order to plan, teach, and assess children's learning. They must be prepared to devote time to reading children's literature, think about the kinds of activities and instruction that children indicate they need, and reflect on their beliefs about literacy learning.

Recent reform efforts in education have attempted to control rather than support teachers because they have been dominated by attempts to "teacher-proof" the curriculum (Burchby, 1988). These efforts have limited teacher autonomy rather than empowered teachers to become decision-makers. Literature-based reading is a different kind of movement.

Some teachers feel torn between their personal beliefs about teaching reading and writing and their concern that students do well on state-mandated achievement tests (Zancanella, 1991). Over the past three or four years, teachers and researchers have reported that literature-based reading programs are successful and students' scores on achievement tests improve or at least remain constant. We urge teachers to take up the challenge and surround their students with the best that children's literature has to offer.

Teachers should consider the following points as they make decisions about using children's literature in the reading program:

- Use literature as the focus of your literacy program.
- Integrate the four language arts.
- Make your classroom literature-rich.
- Use the core literature and reading workshop approaches.

The decisions are presented in a chart in Figure 1.12.

REFERENCES

Allen, J., Michalove, B., Shockley, B., & West, M. (1991). "I'm really worried about Joseph": Reducing the risks of literacy learning. *The Reading Teacher, 44,* 458–472.

Anderson, R. C., Heibert, E., Scott, J., & Wilkinson, I. (1985). *Becoming a nation of readers: The report of the commission on reading.* Washington, DC: National Institute of Education.

Atwell, N. (1987). *In the middle: Writing, reading, and learning with adolescents.* Portsmouth, NH: Heinemann.

Baghban, M. (1984). *Our daughter learns to read and write: A case study from birth to three.* Newark, DE: International Reading Association.

Barone, D. (1990). The written response of young children: Beyond comprehension. *The New Advocate, 3,* 49–56.

Beaver, J. M. (1982). *Say it!* over and over. *Language Arts, 59,* 143–149.

Bissex, G. L. (1980). *Gnys at wrk: A child learns to write and read.* Cambridge, MA: Harvard University Press.

Burchby, M. (1988). Literature and whole language. *The New Advocate, 1,* 114–123.

Butler, A., & Turbill, J. (1984). *Towards a reading-writing classroom.* Portsmouth, NH: Heinemann.

Butler, D. (1980). *Cushla and her books.* Boston: Horn Book.

Calkins, L. M. (1986). *The art of teaching writing.* Portsmouth, NH: Heinemann.

Camp, D. J., & Tompkins, G. E. (1992). *Categorizing students' talk about literature.* Unpublished manuscript.

Chomsky, C. (1971). Write now, read later. *Childhood Education, 47,* 296–299.

Chomsky, C. (1972). Stages in language development and reading exposure. *Harvard Educational Review, 42,* 1–33.

Clark, M. (1976). *Young fluent readers.* London: Heinemann.

Cohen, D. (1968). The effect of literature on vocabulary and reading achievement. *Elementary English, 45,* 209–213, 217.

Cullinan, B. E. (1989). The National Reading Initiative: Outgrowth of the California Reading Initiative. *The New Advocate, 2,* 105–113.

Cullinan, B. E., Jaggar, A., & Strickland, D. (1974). Language expansion for black children in the primary grades: A research report. *Young Children, 29,* 98–112.

D'Alessandro, M. (1990). Accommodating emotionally handicapped children through a literature-based reading program. *The Reading Teacher, 44,* 288–293.

DeFord, D. (1981). Literacy: Reading, writing, and other essentials. *Language Arts, 58,* 652–658.

Dekker, M. M. (1991). Books, reading, and response: A teacher-researcher tells a story. *The New Advocate, 4,* 37–46.

Dressel, J. H. (1990). The effects of listening to and discussing different qualities of children's literature on the narrative writing of fifth graders. *Research in the Teaching of English, 24,* 397–414.

Dyson, A. H. (1984). Learning to write/learning to do school: Emergent writers' interpretations of school literacy tasks. *Research in the Teaching of English, 18,* 233–264.

Eckhoff, B. (1983). How reading affects children's writing. *Language Arts, 60,* 607–616.

English-language arts framework. (1987). Sacramento: California State Department of Education.

Faigley, L., & Witte, S. (1981). Analyzing revision. *College Composition and Communication, 32,* 400–410.

Five, C. (1986). Fifth graders respond to a changed reading program. *Harvard Educational Review, 56,* 395–405.

Five, C. (1988). From workbook to workshop: Increasing children's involvement in the reading process. *The New Advocate, 1,* 103–113.

Fox, C. (1985). The book that talks. *Language Arts, 62,* 374–384.

Galda, L. (1990). Children's literature as a language experience. *The New Advocate, 3,* 247–259.

Geller, L. G. (1985). *Word play and language learning for children.* Urbana, IL: National Council of Teachers of English.

Graves, D. (1989). When children respond to fiction. *Language Arts, 66,* 777–783.

Hade, D. D. (1988). Children, stories, and narrative transformations. *Research in the Teaching of English, 22,* 310–325.

Hansen, J. (1987). *When writers read.* Portsmouth, NH: Heinemann.

Harste, J. C., Woodward, V. A., & Burke, C. L. (1984). Examining our assumptions: A transactional view of literacy and learning. *Research in the Teaching of English, 18,* 84–108.

Heath, S. B. (1983). Research currents: A lot of talk about nothing. *Language Arts, 60,* 999–1007.

Heath, S. B. (1985). Being literate in America: A socio-historical perspective. In J. Niles & R. Lalik (Eds.), *Issues in literacy: A research perspective.* Rochester, NY: National Reading Conference.

Henke, L. (1988). Beyond basal reading: A district's commitment to change. *The New Advocate, 1,* 42–51.

Hepler, S. (1982). *Patterns of response to literature: A one-year study of a fifth and sixth grade classroom.* Unpublished doctoral dissertation, The Ohio State University.

Hepler, S. (1991). Talking our way to literacy in the classroom community. *The New Advocate, 4,* 179–191.

Hepler, S. I., & Hickman, J. (1982). The book was okay. I love you—social aspects of response to literature. *Theory Into Practice, 21,* 278–283.

Hidi, S., & Hildyard, A. (1983). The comparison of oral and written productions in two discourse modes. *Discourse Processes, 6,* 91–105.

Holdaway, D. (1979). *The foundations of literacy.* New York: Ashton Scholastic.

Honig, B. (1988). The California reading initiative. *The New Advocate, 1,* 235–240.

Hornsby, D., Sukarna, D., & Parry, J. (1988). *Read on: A conference approach to reading.* Portsmouth, NH: Heinemann.

Huck, C. S., Hepler, S., & Hickman, J. (1987). *Children's literature in the elementary school* (4th ed.). NY: Holt, Rinehart & Winston.

Hynds, S. (1989). Bringing life to literature and literature to life: Social constructs and contexts of four adolescent readers. *Research in the Teaching of English, 23,* 30–61.

Kardash, C. A. M., & Wright, L. (1987, Winter). Does creative drama benefit elementary school students: A meta-analysis. *Youth Theater Journal,* 11–18.

King, M. (1985). Proofreading is not reading. *Teaching English in the Two-year College, 12,* 108–112.

Langer, J. A. (1985). Children's sense of genre. *Written Communication, 2,* 157–187.

Lehr, S. S. (1991). *The child's developing sense of theme: Responses to literature.* New York: Teachers College Press.

Loban, W. (1976). *Language development: Kindergarten through grade twelve* (Research Report No. 18). Urbana, IL: National Council of Teachers of English.

Lukens, R. J. (1986). *A critical handbook of children's literature* (3rd ed.). Glenview, IL: Scott Foresman.

Martinez, M., & Teale, W. H. (1988). Reading in a kindergarten classroom library. *The Reading Teacher, 41,* 568–572.

McWhirter, A. M. (1990). Whole language in the middle school. *The Reading Teacher, 43,* 562–565.

Mohr, M. M. (1984). *Revision: The rhythm of meaning.* Upper Montclair, NJ: Boynton/Cook.

Morrow, L. M. (1989). Designing the classroom to promote literacy development. In D. S. Strickland & L. M. Morrow (Eds.), *Emerging literacy: Young children learn to read and write* (pp. 121–134). Newark, DE: International Reading Association.

Norton, D. E. (1991). *Through the eyes of a child: An introduction to children's literature* (3rd ed.). New York: Merrill/ Macmillan.

O'Brien, K. L. (1991). A look at one successful literature program. *The New Advocate, 4,* 113–123.

Purcell-Gates, V. (1988). Lexical and syntactic knowledge of written narrative held by well-read-to kindergartners and second graders. *Research in the Teaching of English, 22,* 128–160.

Purcell-Gates, V. (1991). On the outside looking in: A study of remedial readers' meaning-making while reading literature. *Journal of Reading Behavior, 23,* 235–253.

Reardon, S. J. (1988). The development of critical readers: A look into the classroom. *The New Advocate, 1,* 52–61.

Reutzel, D. R., & Cooter, R. B. (1990). Whole language: Comparative effects on first-grade reading achievement. *Journal of Educational Research, 83,* 252–257.

Rosenblatt, L. (1985). Viewpoints: Transaction versus interaction—A terminological rescue operation. *Research in the Teaching of English, 19,* 98–107.

Roser, N. L., Hoffman, J. V., & Farest, C.(1990). Language, literature, and at-risk children. *The Reading Teacher, 43,* 554–559.

Shanahan, T. (1988). The reading-writing relationship: Seven instructional principles. *The Reading Teacher, 41,* 636–647.

Smith, F. (1979). The language arts and the learner's mind. *Language Arts, 56,* 118–125.

Smith, F. (1982). *Writing and the writer.* New York: Holt, Rinehart & Winston.

Smith, F. (1983). Reading like a writer. *Language Arts, 60,* 553–564.

Sostarich, J. (1974). *A study of the reading behavior of sixth graders: Comparisons of active and other readers.* Unpublished doctoral dissertation, The Ohio State University.

Staab, C. (1991). Talk in whole-language classrooms. In V. Froese (Ed.), *Whole-language: Practice and theory* (pp. 17–49). Needham Heights, MA: Allyn and Bacon.

Tompkins, G. E. (1990). *Teaching writing: Balancing process and product.* New York: Merrill/ Macmillan.

Tompkins, G. E., & Hoskisson, K. (1991). *Language arts: Content and teaching strategies* (2nd ed.). New York: Merrill/Macmillan.

Trachtenburg, P., & Ferruggia, A. (1989). Big books from little voices: Reaching high risk beginning readers. *The Reading Teacher, 42,* 284–289.

Tunnell, M. O., & Jacobs, J. S.. (1989). Using 'real' books: Research findings on literature-based reading instruction. *The Reading Teacher, 42,* 470–477.

Wagner, B. J. (1988). Research currents: Does classroom drama affect the arts of language? *Language Arts, 65,* 46–55.

Wicklund, L. (1989). Shared poetry: A whole language experience adapted for remedial readers. *The Reading Teacher, 42,* 478–481.

Yaden, D. (1988). Understanding stories through repeated read-alouds: How much do it take? *The Reading Teacher, 41,* 556–560.

Zancanella, D. (1991). Teachers reading/readers teaching: Five teachers' personal approaches to literature and their teaching of literature. *Research in the Teaching of English, 25,* 5–32.

CHILDREN'S LITERATURE REFERENCES

Burningham, J. (1978). *Would you rather . . .* New York: Crowell.

Lowry, L. (1989). *Number the stars.* Boston: Houghton Mifflin.

Noble, T. H. (1980). *The day Jimmy's boa ate the wash.* New York: Dial.

Scieszka, J. (1989). *The true story of the three little pigs.* New York: Viking.

Van Allsburg, C. (1979). *The garden of Abdul Gasazi.* Boston: Houghton Mifflin.

Van Allsburg, C. (1981). *Jumanji.* Boston: Houghton Mifflin.

Van Allsburg, C. (1982). *Ben's dream.* Boston: Houghton Mifflin.

Van Allsburg, C. (1983). *The wreck of the zephyr.* Boston: Houghton Mifflin.

Van Allsburg, C. (1984). *The mysteries of Harris Burdick*. Boston: Houghton Mifflin.

Van Allsburg, C. (1985). *The polar express*. Boston: Houghton Mifflin.

Van Allsburg, C. (1986). *The stranger.* Boston: Houghton Mifflin.

Van Allsburg, C. (1987). *The Z was zapped.* Boston: Houghton Mifflin.

Van Allsburg, C. (1988). *Two bad ants.* Boston: Houghton Mifflin.

Van Allsburg, C. (1990). *Just a dream.* Boston: Houghton Mifflin.

Van Allsburg, C. (1991). *The wretched stone.* Boston: Houghton Mifflin.

CHAPTER 2

CHOOSING LITERATURE FOR CHILDREN

> **In this chapter you will learn to make decisions about:**
> - **Reading a wide variety of stories, informational books, and poems**
> - **Using the guidelines presented in this chapter for choosing stories, informational books, and poems**
> - **Consulting reviews of children's books published in professional magazines and journals**
> - **Sharing literature with children and noting their responses and preferences**

K NOWING ABOUT CHILDREN'S literature and making informed decisions when selecting books for students to read is essential for a literature-based reading program, as the following three case studies show.

A CASE IN POINT

Mr. Penton's Author Study

Mr. Penton's kindergarten class is studying Bill Martin, Jr., one of their favorite authors. During this two-week author study, Mr. Penton reads aloud many of Martin's books, but he focuses on two related books, *Brown Bear, Brown Bear, What Do You See?* (1983), a book about animals and colors that is written in a predictable verse, and *Polar Bear, Polar Bear, What Do You Hear?* (1991). This second book has a similar predictable verse but focuses on sounds rather than sights. "I use these two books," Mr. Penton explains, "because my 5- and 6-year-olds can be successful reading them. The text is so predictable that every child in my class can read these two books." In the library center of the classroom, Mr. Penton sets out a display of Bill Martin, Jr.'s books and hangs a poster about the author on the "Author in the Spotlight" bulletin board. He also collects concept books on colors and sounds and places them in a special bucket in the library area. These books include: *Growing Colors* (McMillan, 1988), *Rat-a-*

Tat, Pitter Pat (Benjamin, 1987), *Wobble Pop* (Burningham, 1984), *Is It Red? Is It Yellow? Is It Blue?* (Hoban, 1978), and *Color Zoo* (Ehlert, 1989). Mr. Penton shares these books with the kindergartners and uses them in center activities during the author study to further extend their understanding of colors and sounds.

Mr. Penton begins the author study by introducing the collection of Bill Martin, Jr. books in the class library, sharing information about the author, and rereading *Brown Bear, Brown Bear, What Do You See?* After talking about the book, Mr. Penton brings out a puppet of a brown bear and the children take turns holding the puppet and answering the question, "Brown bear, brown bear, what do you see?" The children to try to include a color word in their answers, and by the time the puppet has been passed to each child in the class, more than 20 colors have been mentioned.

The next day Mr. Penton reads *Polar Bear, Polar Bear, What Do You Hear?* After reading the book once, he introduces a big book version that he has constructed using large sheets of poster board and bound together with yarn. Mr. Penton has cut out tissue paper animals for the illustrations, using the same techniques that illustrator Eric Carle used. Mr. Penton uses shared reading techniques to read the big book, and soon the kindergartners join in reciting the verses. After Mr. Penton finishes reading the big book, students talk about book, telling what parts they liked best, recalling the sound words in the book, and spontaneously creating additional verses.

During the author study, the kindergartners are involved in a variety of response activities. Mr. Penton demonstrates how to draw and cut out tissue paper animals and the children make a mural with tissue paper animals. Later Mr. Penton helps them add sound words in "talking balloons." They also make their own copies of one of the two books. Some children create new verses following Martin's pattern while others use the familiar verses in Martin's book. They begin by drawing large pictures on each page, and some children write their own text using "kid spelling" that they invent while others ask Mr. Penton to write as they dictate. After the books are completed, the children share their books with their third grade reading buddies.

Mr. Penton also reads aloud other Bill Martin, Jr. books from the display in the library center, including *Barn Dance* (1986), and *Chicka Chicka Boom Boom* (1989). He reads each book at least once and rereads them when children show interest. Mr. Penton also tape records his reading so that the kindergartners can listen to the books again at the listening center. At the end of the two week unit, the children make a graph to determine which Bill Martin, Jr. book they like best and they write a class letter and mail it to the author.

A CASE IN POINT

Mrs. Levi's Theme Cycle

Students in Mrs. Levi's seventh grade humanities class are studying medieval life. Mrs. Levi uses an integrated approach to teach Language Arts and Social Studies in a 100-minute block. For this month-long theme cycle, she has collected more than 50 stories, poems, and informational books on the medieval period for the class library. These books include *A Medieval Feast* (Aliki, 1983) in which the author describes the preparations and activities of a feast, *Merry Ever After* (Lasker, 1976) which compares the prenuptial and wedding festivities of a peasant couple and a wealthy couple, and *Illuminations* (Hunt, 1989), a medieval alphabet book.

The students spend the first week of the theme cycle reading two or more of these books independently, taking notes in learning logs, and sharing what they have learned in class discussions. "I begin most theme cycles with a week of 'wide reading' as I call it," Mrs. Levi explains. "My students need a chance to develop background knowledge and vocabulary about our themes, and reading books in our class library during this first week gives them that opportunity." Mrs. Levi uses the last 15 or 20 minutes of each period to bring the students together to discuss what they have learned through their "wide reading."

Students spend the second week reading David Macaulay's Caldecott Honor Book *Castle* (1977), which describes how a castle is planned, built, and furnished. There is a class set of copies of this book, and they read the book in literature study groups with seven or eight students in each group. As they read, students talk about what they are reading with classmates and make notes and drawings in their learning logs. The students work together to construct a table-top model of a castle in the classroom as a response project and use the terminology introduced in *Castle* to label the architectural components and rooms.

During the third week, students read Charles Keeping's picture book version of the classic hero tale *Beowulf* (1982) together as a class. Mrs. Levi begins by introducing the characters and their names. A class set of copies of this book is available for students to use, but because Beowulf is a difficult tale, students do not read it independently. Instead, Mrs. Levi spends several days reading the book aloud as students follow along in their copies. Each day students use the last 15 minutes to discuss the story. They get into a large circle and share their reactions to the story and make predictions about what will happen next. Then students spend a day or two rereading the book at their own pace and locating their favorite passages for a read-around and a class quilt. The next day, students take turns reading aloud their favor-ite passages and writing them on strips of paper for the bulletin board class quilt.

As they finish reading *Beowulf,* students choose response projects to work on individually or in small groups to extend their learning about medieval life. Some students write stories set in the middle ages, some pursue art, music, or drama activities, and others research topics of special interest and share what they have learned in oral or written reports. "I think this theme cycle is my students' favorite one. We end the theme cycle with a culminating activity—a medieval feast; otherwise my students would continue the theme for months," Mrs. Levi explains. The students share their response projects at the feast as the after dinner entertainment.

A CASE IN POINT

Ms. Missakian's Reading Workshop

Ms. Missakian's second graders spend an hour and a half each morning in reading workshop. "I begin each reading workshop by reading a picture book aloud," Ms. Missakian explains, "because I want to share good literature with my students and to model what fluent readers do." This week Ms. Missakian is focusing on characters, and today she reads aloud Gloria Houston's *My Great-aunt Arizona* (1992), a story about Houston's great aunt who grew up in the Blue Ridge Mountains and was a teacher. After she finishes reading, students talk about the book and interesting people in their own families and neighborhoods. Ms. Missakian asks if any student is reading a book about an interesting person. Caleb shares his book, *Keep the Lights Burning, Abbie* (Roop & Roop, 1985), a true story about a girl in Maine who had to keep the lighthouse lamps burning during a storm in 1856, and Sherilyn shares *The Josefina Story Quilt* (Coerr, 1986) about the adventures of a girl and her family who are going to California in a covered wagon.

Then students begin reading books they have selected from the class library. They read independently for 20 minutes, and as they read, Ms. Missakian walks around the classroom, stopping to chat briefly with each child during the week. Her students are reading and rereading a wide range of books. Lionel is rereading a favorite book—Dr. Seuss' *Green Eggs and Ham* (1988)—and Missy is reading *Mama, Do You Love Me?* (Joosse, 1991), a repetitive book about an Eskimo mother's unconditional love that Ms. Missakian read aloud two weeks earlier. Other students are reading *If the Dinosaurs Came Back* (Most, 1978), *If You Give a Mouse a Cookie* (Numeroff, 1985), *The Very Busy Spider* (Carle, 1984), and *The Jolly Postman or Other People's Letters* (Ahlberg & Ahlberg, 1986). Students are successful in their reading. Occasionally one student might stop to ask a classmate or Ms. Missakian about a word or to share a favorite passage, but they are familiar with a wide variety of books and know how to choose books for independent reading.

After independent reading time, Ms. Missakian's second graders write in reading logs and work on response projects. In their reading logs, students write the titles and authors of the books they are reading and they draw and/or write at least three comments. Ms Missakian wants her students to make comments that connect the book to their own personal experiences and opinions. Each week students choose one book they have read and written about in their reading logs for a response project. Students draw, write, dramatize, read, or research about the book. For instance, Kristen has read *If You Give a Mouse a Cookie,* and she collects props in a shoebox to use in retelling the story for the class. David writes a book about dinosaurs after reading *If the Dinosaurs Came Back.*

Students also meet with Ms. Missakian for minilessons on reading skills and strategies. This week the focus is on characters and how authors develop characters in stories. She asks students to identify main and supporting characters in the stories they are reading and to think about how the author developed the characters. She asks, "Do you know what your main character looks like? What that character says? What that character does? What that character thinks?" The students discuss character development, and Kristen talks about the mouse in *If You Give a Mouse a Cookie*: "The mouse is cute and neat and he wears little overalls. He can give himself a haircut and he always wants to sweep and clean up. But more than all these nice things, he is very, very clever. I mean, he is almost tricky. In the book you don't know what he is thinking, but you almost do. Well, he gets another cookie and more milk, doesn't he?" The other students agree that the mouse is well behaved, clever, and a little bit tricky.

The class ends each reading workshop by sitting in a circle and sharing some of the books they have finished reading and their completed response projects with classmates. Through these activities, students are responding to the literature they have read and learning more about reading and literature.

INTRODUCTION

A wide variety of literature is available today for children, and these books can be used effectively for reading instruction as well as to connect reading and literature across the curriculum. To plan effective literature-based reading programs, teachers must be familiar with children's literature. Mr. Penton, Mrs. Levi, and Ms. Missakian are familiar with books currently available for elementary students and choose books of high quality literature for their literature-based reading programs. Moreover, they select books for specific educational purposes. Mr. Penton selected stories written by Bill Martin, Jr. for an author study and supplemented these books with color and sound concept books. Mrs. Levi connected literature and history through the books she selected for the theme cycle on medieval life, and she planned how she would use the books to their best advantage. Ms. Missakian has a vast collection of books at her second graders' reading levels in her classroom library and she selects books to read aloud that exemplify concepts, such as characterization, that she is teaching.

In this chapter, we provide an overview of the wide variety of trade books written for children in kindergarten through eighth grade. These books are classified in three broad categories: (a) stories, (b) informational books, and (c) poetry. Within each category, we introduce you to some of our favorite books, describe the characteristics of various types of literature and the literary elements of books in that category. We also present guidelines to assist teachers as they choose stories, informational books, and poetry to use with their students.

STORIES

We read stories for entertainment. Shorter stories are often presented in picture book format such as *Where the Wild Things Are* (Sendak, 1963). In these books, the story is told as much through the large pictures as through the line or two of text on each page. Many of these books are designed for young children, but other stories such as *Beauty and the Beast* (Mayer, 1978) have more text on each page and deal with more mature themes, making them more appropriate for older students. Other short stories have been collected and published in one book, such as Lobel's *Frog and Toad Together* (1972), Kipling's *Just So Stories* (1987), and *The Tales of Uncle Remus* (Lester, 1987).

Some stories that are longer may be presented as chapter books or novels. Examples of chapter books include *Sarah, Plain and Tall* (MacLachlan, 1985) and *Charlotte's Web* (White, 1952). Most chapter books are more appropriate for middle and upper grade students, but second and third graders can enjoy some of these stories, especially when the teacher reads them aloud.

Types of Stories

Stories can be categorized in several different ways, one of which is according to *genre,* or types of literature within a broad category. Three broad categories are (a) folk literature, (b) fantasies, and (c) realistic fiction. We will examine the characteristics of each of these genre and identify stories for elementary students that represent each one.

Folk Literature. Stories that began hundreds and hundreds of years ago and were passed from generation to generation by storytellers before being written down are classified as *folk* or *traditional literature* (Bosma, 1987). Three distinct types are (a) fables, (b) folk and fairy tales, and (c) myths and legends. A list of stories representing each of the three types of folk literature is presented in Figure 2.1. Many are spectacular picture book versions with award-winning illustrations. These three types of folk literature are an important part of our cultural heritage.

Fables. Fables are brief narratives designed to teach a moral. They employ a story format to make the lesson easier to understand, and the moral is usually stated at the end. The characteristics of fables include the following:

1. They are short, often less than a page long.
2. The characters are usually animals.
3. The characters are one-dimensional, strong or weak, wise or foolish.
4. The backdrop setting is barely sketched.
5. Fables involve only one event.
6. The conflict is between the characters.
7. The theme is usually stated as a moral at the end of the story.

Our best-known fables, including "The Hare and the Tortoise" and "The Ant and the Grasshopper," were written by a Greek slave named Aesop in the sixth century B.C. Collections of Aesop's fables for elementary students include Eric Carle's *Twelve Tales from Aesop* (1980), *Aesop's Fables* selected by Michael Hague (1985),

FIGURE 2.1   Traditional or Folk Literature Stories

Fables

Castle, C. (1985). *The hare and the tortoise.* New York: Dial. (P–M)

Cauley, L. B. (1984). *The town mouse and the country mouse.* New York: Putnam. (P–M)

Hague, M. (1985). *Aesop's fables.* New York: Holt, Rinehart & Winston. (M)

Lionni, L. (1985). *Frederick's fables.* New York: Pantheon. (P–M)

Lobel, A. (1980). *Fables.* New York: Harper & Row. (M)

Paxton, T. (1988). *Aesop's fables.* New York: Morrow. (M–U)

Wildsmith, B. (1963). *The lion and the rat.* Oxford, England: Oxford University Press. (P)

Wildsmith, B. (1966). *The hare and the tortoise.* Oxford, England: Oxford University Press. (P)

Wildsmith, B. (1969). *The miller, the boy, and the donkey.* Oxford, England: Oxford University Press.
   (P–M)

Folktales

Aardema, V. (1975). *Why mosquitoes buzz in people's ears.* New York: Dial. (M)

Carrick, C. (1989). *Aladdin and the wonderful lamp.* New York: Scholastic.

Cauley, L. B. (1979). *The ugly duckling.* San Diego: Harcourt Brace Jovanovich. (P–M)

Cauley, L. B. (1981). *Goldilocks and the three bears.* New York: Putnam. (P)

Cauley, L. B. (1983). *Jack and the beanstalk.* New York: Putnam. (P–M)

Cauley, L. B. (1988). *The pancake boy.* New York: Putnam. (P)

Climo, S. (1989). *The Egyptian Cinderella.* New York: Crowell. (U)

Ehrlich, A. (1985). *Cinderella.* New York: Dial. (P–M)

Galdone, P. (1968). *Henny Penny.* New York: Seabury. (P)

Galdone, P. (1972). *The three bears.* Boston: Houghton Mifflin. (P)

Galdone, P. (1973). *The little red hen.* New York: Seabury. (P)

Galdone, P. (1973). *The three billy goats Gruff.* Boston: Houghton Mifflin. (P)

Galdone, P. (1975). *The gingerbread boy.* New York: Seabury. (P)

Hague, K., & Hague, H. (1980). *East of the sun and west of the moon.* New York: Harcourt Brace
   Jovanovich. (M–U)

Heins, P. (1974). *Snow White.* Boston: Little, Brown. (M)

Howe, J. (1989). *Jack and the beanstalk.* Boston: Little, Brown. (M)

Huck, C. (1989). *Princess Furball.* New York: Greenwillow. (M–U)

Hyman, T. S. (1977). *The sleeping beauty.* Boston: Little, Brown. (M)

Hyman, T. S. (1983). *Little red riding hood.* New York: Holiday House. (P–M)

Jacobs, J. (n.d.). *Johnny cake.* New York: Putnam. (P–M)

Louie, A. (1982). *Yeh-Shen: A Cinderella story from China.* New York: Philomel Books. (M–U)

Mahy, M. (1990). *The seven Chinese brothers.* New York: Scholastic. (P–M)

Mayer, M. (1978). *Beauty and the beast.* New York: Four Winds Press. (U)

Perrault, C. (1990). *Puss in boots.* New York: Farrar, Straus & Giroux. (P–M)

Stevens, J. (1987). *The three billy goats Gruff.* San Diego: Harcourt Brace Jovanovich. (P–M)

Yolen, J. (1986). *The sleeping beauty.* New York: Knopf. (U)

Zemach, H. (1973). *Duffy and the devil.* New York: Farrar, Straus & Giroux. (M)

Zemach, M. (1976). *It could always be worse.* New York: Farrar, Straus & Giroux. (P–M)

P = Primary grades (K–2); M = middle grades (3–5); U = upper grades (6–8)

Myths and Legends

Colum, P. (1948). *The children of Odin: The book of northern myths.* New York: Macmillan. (U)

Colum, P. (1949). *The golden fleece and the heroes who lived before Achilles.* New York: Macmillan. (U)

Crossley-Holland, K. (1982). *Beowulf.* Oxford, England: Oxford University Press. (U)

D'Aulaire, I., & D'Aulaire, E. P. (1962). *D'Aulaires' book of Greek myths.* Garden City, NY: Doubleday. (M–U)

D'Aulaire, I., & D'Aulaire, E. P. (1967). *D'Aulaires' Norse gods and giants.* Garden City, NY: Doubleday. (M–U)

de Paola, T. (1983). *The legend of the bluebonnet.* New York: Putnam. (M)

de Paola, T. (1988). *The legend of the Indian paintbrush.* New York: Putnam. (M)

Felton, H. W. (1968). *True tall tales of Stormalong: Sailor of the seven seas.* Englewood Cliffs, NJ: Prentice-Hall. (M) (See other tall tales written by this author.)

Fritz, J. (1982). *The good giants and the bad pukwudgies.* New York: Putnam. (M–U)

Goble, P. (1988). *Iktomi and the boulder.* New York: Orchard Books. (M)

Haddithi, M., & Kennaway, A. (1986). *Hot hippo.* Boston: Little, Brown. (P–M) (See other tales by the same authors.)

Haviland, V. (Ed.). (1979). *North American legends.* New York: Collins. (U)

Heyer, C. (1991). *Excalibur.* Nashville, TN: Ideals. (M–U)

Highwater, J. (1977). *Anpao: An American Indian odyssey.* Phildelphia: Lippincott. (U)

Hodges, M. (1984). *Saint George and the dragon.* Boston: Little, Brown. (M–U)

Houston, J. (1973). *Kiviok's magic journey: An Eskimo legend.* New York: Atheneum. (M)

Howe, J. (1988). *Rip Van Winkle.* Boston: Little, Brown. (M–U)

Keats, E. J. (1965). *John Henry: An American legend.* New York: Knopf. (M)

Kellogg, S. (1984). *Paul Bunyan.* New York: Morrow. (M)

Kellogg, S. (1988). *Johnny Appleseed.* New York: Morrow. (M)

Kipling, R. (1984). *How the camel got his hump.* New York: Peter Bedrick Books. (M) (See other tales in the same series of "Just so stories.")

Kipling, R. (1985). *The beginning of the armadillos.* San Diego: Harcourt Brace Jovanovich. (M)

McGovern, A. (1968). *Robin Hood of Sherwood Forest.* New York: Scholastic. (M–U)

Steptoe, J. (1984). *The story of jumping mouse.* New York: Mulberry Books. (M–U)

Stoutenburg, A. (1966). *American tall tales.* New York: Puffin. (M–U)

Sutcliff, R. (1977). *The chronicles of Robin Hood.* New York: Oxford University Press. (M)

Eve Rice's *Once Upon a Wood: Ten Tales from Aesop* (1979), and *Doctor Coyote: A Native American's Aesop's Fables* (Bierhorst, 1987). Also Arnold Lobel has written *Fables* (1980), a collection of 20 original fables in Aesop's style with short narratives and clearly stated morals.

Other well-known fables include *Once a Mouse,* an Indian fable retold by Marcia Brown (1961), and Chaucer's *Chanticleer and the Fox* (Cooney, 1958). These fables are longer than Aesop's and the moral is implied rather than clearly stated in the text.

Folktales. Folktales are relatively short stories that originated as part of the oral tradition. Characteristics of these tales include the following:

1. The story is often introduced with the words "Once upon a time."
2. The setting is usually generalized and could be located anywhere.
3. The plot structure is simple and straightforward.
4. The problem usually revolves around a journey from home to perform some tasks, a journey that involves a confrontation with a monster, the miraculous change from a harsh home to a secure home, or a confrontation between a wise beast and a foolish beast.
5. Characters are portrayed in one dimension, either good or bad, stupid or clever, industrious or lazy.
6. The end is happy, and everyone "lives happily ever after."

Folktales include four distinct types of stories. One type is *cumulative tales,* such as *Henny Penny* (Galdone, 1968) and *The Gingerbread Boy* (Galdone, 1975). These stories are built around the repetition of words and events. Another kind of folktales is the *talking beast tales.* In these stories, animals act and talk like humans. Favorite talking beast tales include *The Three Little Pigs* (Zemach, 1988) and *Puss in Boots* (Perrault, 1990). *Noodlehead stories* are a third kind of folktales. These stories are humorous tales of absurdity. *The Three Wishes* (Galdone, 1961) shows what happens when a farmer makes a foolish wish. *Wonder tales* or *fairy tales* are the fourth type. Well-known examples are *Snow White* (Heins, 1974), *The Sleeping Beauty* (Yolen, 1986), and *Jack and the Beanstalk* (Howe, 1989). These tales include fantastic characters, including witches, giants, and fairy godmothers.

Storytellers often added their own variations to these stories, which is why some differences exist among the various versions of folk and fairy tales. Well-known tales with different versions include "The Three Little Pigs," "The Gingerbread Boy," "Cinderella," and "Jack and the Beanstalk." For example, in one version of "The Gingerbread Boy" titled *The Runaway Pancake* (Asbjornsen & Moe, 1980), the main character is a pancake and it is eventually eaten by a pig, not a fox!

Folktales have *motifs* or small, recurring elements, such as three wishes, a magical ring, or a character who is a trickster. Every folktale has at least a few of these motifs. Six of the most common motifs, according to Huck et al. (1987) are the following:

• *A long sleep or enchantment. The Sleeping Beauty* (Yolen, 1986) is an example of a story with the long sleep motif.

- *Magical powers.* Characters in folktales often have magical powers, such as the fool's companions in *The Fool of the World and the Flying Ship* (Ransome, 1968).
- *Magical transformations.* In stories such as *Beauty and the Beast* (Mayer, 1978) and *The Princess and the Frog* (Isadora, 1989), characters are magically transformed from one form to another.
- *Magical objects.* In some folktales, magic objects play an important role in the story. One example is *Aladdin* (Lang, 1981).
- *Wishes.* Characters are granted wishes but they use them unwisely in folktales, such as *The Stonecutter* (Newton, 1990).
- *Trickery.* Animals and people trick other characters in many folktales. The wolf tricks the little girl in *Little Red Riding Hood* (Hyman, 1983), and Brer Rabbit is a trickster in *Jump! The Adventures of Brer Rabbit* (Harris, 1986).

There are other motifs as well. Teachers and their students may want to make a list of these and other motifs that they encounter in stories they read.

African and Afro-American folktales are becoming increasingly available for elementary students. Storytelling in Africa is a highly prized talent. African folktales feature tricksters such as Anansi the spider, Zomo the rabbit, and Ijapa the tortoise. Ashley Bryan's *The Ox of the Wonderful Horns and Other African Folktales* (1971) contains many examples of these delightful tales. Newbery Medal-winning author Virginia Hamilton has gathered a collection of black folklore in *The People Could Fly: Black American Folktales* (1985). These stories include familiar trickster tales about Buh Fox, Doc Rabbit, and the Tar Baby with layers of meaning about the relations between slaves and owners.

Myths and legends. People around the world have created myths to explain natural phenomena. Some *myths* explain the origin of the world and how human beings were brought into existence; some were created to explain the seasons, the sun and moon, and the constellations; and others explain the mountains and other physical features of the earth. Ancient peoples used myths to explain many things that have more recently been explained by scientific theories and investigations. Characteristics of myths include the following:

1. Myths explain creations.
2. Characters are often heroes with supernatural powers.
3. The setting is barely sketched.
4. Magical powers are required.

Collections of myths from many cultures have been compiled for children. Hodges' retelling of the Greek myth *Persephone and the Springtime* (1973) tells how spring originated, and Native American myths such as *The Fire Bringer* (Hodges, 1972) and *The Legend of the Bluebonnet* (de Paola, 1983) tell how natural phenomena came to be. Myths that explain physical features of animals are very appealing to elementary students, and Rudyard Kipling's *Just So Stories* (1987) tell how the camel got its hump, the leopard acquired its spots, and how other animals developed their unique features.

Legends are stories that have been passed from generation to generation that are thought to have some basis in history but are not verifiable. They exemplify many of same elements as myths; the hero does something important enough to be remembered in story. Three well-known legends are *Johnny Appleseed* (Kellogg, 1988), *The Pied Piper of Hamelin* (Mayer, 1987), and *The Chronicles of Robin Hood* (Sutcliff, 1977). The tall tales of Paul Bunyan, Mike Fink, John Henry, Casey Jones, and Pecos Bill are legends created as the American West was settled.

Fantasies.   *Fantasies* are stories that could not really take place. Authors create new worlds for their characters, but these worlds must be based in reality so that readers will believe they exist. There are many types of fantasies, ranging from *Charlotte's Web* (White, 1952) to *Mary Poppins* (Travers, 1934), *The Hobbit* (Tolkien, 1938), and *Watership Down* (Adams, 1974). Four genre of fantasies that we will discuss are (a) modern literary tales, (b) fantastic stories, (c) science fiction, and (d) high fantasy. A list of stories exemplifying each of the four genre is presented in Figure 2.2.

Modern literary tales.   *Modern literary tales* are related to folktales and fairy tales because they often include many characteristics and conventions of traditional literature, but they have been written more recently and have identifiable authors. The best-known author of modern literary tales is Hans Christian Andersen, a Danish writer of the last century who wrote *The Emperor's New Clothes* (Westcott, 1984), *The Nightingale* (Le Gallienne, 1965), *The Snow Queen* (Ehrlich, 1982), *The Ugly Duckling* (Cauley, 1979), and other favorites. Other examples of modern literary tales include *The Paper Bag Princess* (Munsch, 1980) and *The Five Chinese Brothers* (Bishop, 1938). According to Russell (1991), an interesting variation of modern literary tales is a spoof or satire of the genre, such as James Thurber's *Many Moons* (1943).

Fantastic stories.   *Fantastic stories* are realistic in most details, but some events require readers to suspend disbelief. According to Norton (1991), "the impossible becomes convincingly possible" (p. 294). The characteristics of fantasies are the following:

1. The events in the story are extraordinary; things that could not happen in today's world.
2. The setting is realistic.
3. Main characters are people or personified animals.
4. Themes often deal with the conflict between good and evil.

Through character and theme, readers are drawn to suspend their disbelief (Lukens, 1990). In Chris Van Allsburg's *Jumanji* (1981), for example, Judy and Peter, the two children who find themselves playing the fantastic adventure game called Jumanji, are believable because they find they are able to cope with the jungle dangers that threaten them, despite their fear. The theme—to bravely finish what you start—also seems reasonable.

Fantastic stories are often subdivided into four categories. The first category is *animal fantasies,* such as *Watership Down* (Adams, 1974), *The Wind in the*

FIGURE 2.2   Fantasies

Modern Literary Tales

Babbitt, N. (1969). *The search for delicious.* New York: Farrar, Straus & Giroux. (M)
Calmenson, S. (1989). *The principal's new clothes.* New York: Scholastic. (P)
Cauley, L. B. (1979). *The ugly duckling.* New York: Harcourt Brace Jovanovich. (P–M)
Ehrlich, A. (1982). *The snow queen.* New York: Dial. (P–M)
Grahame, K. (1923). *The reluctant dragon.* New York: Holiday House. (M)
Kasza, K. (1987). *The wolf's chicken stew.* New York: Putnam. (P)
Le Gallienne, E. (1965). *The nightingale.* New York: Harper & Row. (M–U)
Lionni, L. (1969). *Alexander and the wind-up mouse.* New York: Knopf. (P–M)
Thurber, J. (1943). *Many moons.* New York: Harcourt Brace Jovanovich. (P–M)
Yolen, J. (1972). *The girl who cried flowers.* New York: Crowell. (M)

Fantastic Stories

Babbitt, N. (1975). *Tuck everlasting.* New York: Farrar, Straus & Giroux. (U)
Banks, L. R. (1980). *The Indian in the cupboard.* New York: Doubleday. (U)
Barrett, J. (1978). *Cloudy with a chance of meatballs.* New York: Macmillan. (P–M)
Brittain, B. (1983). *The wish giver.* New York: Harper & Row. (M–U)
Carroll, L. (1985). *Alice's adventures in Wonderland.* New York: Holt, Rinehart & Winston. (M–U)
Dahl, R. (1964). *Charlie and the chocolate factory.* New York: Knopf. (M–U)
Erickson, R. E. (1974). *A toad for Tuesday.* New York: Lothrop, Lee & Shepard. (M)
Grahame, K. (1961). *The wind in the willows.* New York: Scribners. (M–U)
Howe, D., & Howe, J. (1979). *Bunnicula: A rabbit-tale of mystery.* New York: Atheneum. (M–U)
Juster, N. (1961). *The phantom tollbooth.* New York: Random House. (U)
King-Smith, D. (1988). *Martin's mice.* New York: Crown. (M–U)
Lawson, R. (1972). *Rabbit hill.* New York: Viking. (M–U)
Norton, M. (1980). *The borrowers.* San Diego: Harcourt Brace Jovanovich. (M–U)
Selden, G. (1960). *The cricket in Times Square.* New York: Farrar, Straus & Giroux. (M–U)
Sendak, M. (1983). *Where the wild things are.* New York: Harper & Row. (P)
Van Allsburg, C. (1981). *Jumanji.* Boston: Houghton Mifflin. (M)
Van Allsburg, C. (1985). *The polar express.* Boston: Houghton Mifflin. (M)
Wahl, J. (1987). *Humphrey's bear.* New York: Henry Holt. (P)
White, E. B. (1952). *Charlotte's web.* New York: Harper & Row. (M)

Science Fiction

L'Engle, M. (1980). *A ring of endless light.* New York: Farrar, Straus & Giroux. (U)
O'Brien, R. C. (1971). *Mrs. Frisby and the rats of NIMH.* New York: Atheneum. (U)
Marzollo, J., & Marzollo, C. (1987). *Jed and the space bandits.* New York: Dial. (P)
Sleator, W. (1984). *Interstellar pig.* New York: Dutton. (U)
Yolen, J. (1990). *The devil's arithmetic.* New York: Viking. (U)

High Fantasy

Cooper, S. (1973). *The dark is rising.* New York: Atheneum. (U)
L'Engle, M. (1962). *A wrinkle in time.* New York: Farrar, Straus & Giroux. (U)
Lewis, C. S. (1950). *The lion, the witch, and the wardrobe.* New York: Macmillan. (M–U) (See other
   books in the Narnia series.)
Tolkien, J. R. R. (1974). *The lord of the rings.* Boston: Houghton Mifflin. (U)

Willows (Grahame, 1961) and *Mrs. Frisby and the Rats of NIMH* (O'Brien, 1971). In these stories, the main characters are animals that are endowed with human traits. Middle and upper grade students often realize that the animals symbolize human beings and that these stories explore human relationships. Other fantasies are toy fantasies, such as *Winnie-the-Pooh* (Milne, 1961), *Alexander and the Wind-up Mouse* (Lionni, 1969), and *Miss Hickory* (Bailey, 1968). *Toy fantasies* are similar to animal fantasies except that the main characters are talking toys, usually stuffed animals or dolls. A third category includes *fantasies about eccentric characters and extraordinary beings.* The main characters in these fantasies possess magical or extraordinary powers. Examples are *Mr. Popper's Penguins* (Atwater & Atwater, 1966), *Mary Poppins* (Travers, 1934), and *The Adventures of Dr. Dolittle* (Lofting, 1920). The fourth category is *enchanted journey fantasies,* in which characters (usually children) go from the real world into another world where all sorts of wondrous things can happen. The journey must have a purpose, but it is usually overshadowed by the thrill and delight of the fantastic world. Examples are *Peter Pan* (Barrie, 1950), *Alice's Adventures in Wonderland* (Carroll, 1984), and *Charlie and the Chocolate Factory* (Dahl, 1964).

Science fiction.   In *science fiction stories,* authors create a world in which science interacts with every area of society (Norton, 1991). Many stories involve traveling through space to distant galaxies or meeting alien societies. Authors hypothesize scientific advancements and imagine technology of the future to create the plot. Characteristics of science fiction include the following:

1. The story is set in the future.
2. Conflict is usually between the characters and natural or mechanical forces, such as robots.
3. The characters believe in the advanced technology.
4. There is detailed description of scientific facts.

Most science fiction stories are written for upper grade students, and Madeleine L'Engle and Lloyd Alexander are two well-known authors of this genre.

High fantasy.   *High fantasy* is a genre of modern fantasy in which heroes and heroines confront evil for the good of humanity. The primary characteristic of the genre is the focus on the conflict between good and evil, as in C. S. Lewis' Narnia series (e.g., *The Lion, the Witch, and the Wardrobe,* 1950) and *The Lord of the Rings* (Tolkien, 1974). Other characteristics are the following:

1. Main characters are fully developed heroes.
2. The setting is integral and in some stories it is a fully created world.
3. The point of view encourages us to believe the story.
4. Time is flexible and may expand and constrict so that the story moves back and forth in time.
5. Theme involves a broad concern for humanity, usually focusing on good versus evil.

High fantasy is related to folk literature in that it is characterized by certain motifs and themes. Most stories of high fantasy include magical kingdoms, quests, tests of courage, magical powers, and fantastic characters, and their themes touch on the struggle between goodness and evil as do many folktales and fairy tales. In *The Dark Is Rising* (Cooper, 1973), for example, the author shows Will Stanton as the last of the Old Ones who must find the six signs of life in order to defeat the rising of the dark. Similarly, a young village lay-about is transformed into a king in *The First Two Lives of Lukas-Kasha* (Alexander, 1978). He must rescue his kingdom from the grasp of an evil wizard.

High fantasies also embody some of the characteristics of myths. Myths are filled with tales of young gods or heroes who partake in successful adventures and endure great dangers but eventually emerge safely. The hero's quest involves a philosophical reflection on life. They include elements of paradise and hell, dreams and nightmares, romance and tragedy. One of the archetypes associated with myths is the cyclical journey in which the hero or heroine returns home after a quest is completed. This cycle is used in *The Hobbit* (Tolkien, 1938), a well-known and popular story of high fantasy. Bilbo goes on a quest and meets adventure. He is tested but finally returns home safely.

Another archetype is the cyclical pattern of the seasons used to reveal life's cycles. Spring and summer are associated with youth, hope, and vigor. In contrast, autumn and winter are associated with old age, despair, and death. The land of Narnia is caught in forever-winter in *The Lion, the Witch, and the Wardrobe* (Lewis, 1950). Monsters of all kinds as well as evil witches and wizards, symbolizing the forces of evil, abound in the story. Similarly, Ged in *The Wizard of Earthsea* (Le Guin, 1968) must fight the shadow.

Realistic Fiction. These stories are lifelike and believable, without magic or supernatural powers. The outcome is reasonable and the story is a representation of action that seems truthful. Realistic fiction can help children discover that their problems and desires are not unique and that they are not alone in experiencing certain feelings and situations. Realistic fiction also broadens children's horizons and allows them to experience new adventures. A list of stories representing each type of realistic fiction is presented in Figure 2.3.

Contemporary fiction. As children read contemporary fiction, they identify with characters their own age who have similar interests and problems, such as in *Ramona Quimby, Age 8* (Cleary, 1981), a story about Ramona and her typical family tensions, and *The Incredible Journey* (Burnford, 1961), a realistic story of three animals who walk several thousands of miles to rejoin their human family who moved away without them. Characteristics of contemporary fiction include the following:

1. Characters act like real people or like real animals.
2. The setting is in the world as we know it today.
3. Stories deal with everyday occurrences or "relevant subjects."

Some contemporary fiction stories deal with controversial issues of violence, drugs, sexuality, and profanity.

Historical fiction. *Historical fiction* stories are placed in the past, and in this genre, authors combine history and imagination. Details about the food, clothing, and transportation must be typical of the era in which the story is set because the

FIGURE 2.3   Realistic Fiction

Contemporary Fiction

Bauer, M. D. (1986). *On my honor.* Boston: Houghton Mifflin. (M)

Blume, J. (1972). *Tales of a fourth grade nothing.* New York: Dutton. (M)

Bunting, E. (1988). *How many days to America: A Thanksgiving story.* New York: Clarion. (M–U)

Bunting, E. (1991). *Fly away home.* New York: Clarion. (M)

Burch, R. (1966). *Queenie Peavy.* New York: Viking. (U)

Burnford, S. (1961). *The incredible journey.* Boston: Little, Brown. (U)

Byars, B. (1977). *The pinballs.* New York: Harper & Row. (M–U)

Cleary, B. (1981). *Ramona Quimby, age 8.* New York: Morrow. (M)

Fox, M. (1988). *Wilfrid Gordon McDonald Partridge.* Brooklyn, NY: Kane/Miller. (P–M–U)

George, J. C. (1959). *My side of the mountain.* New York: Dutton. (M–U)

Giff, P. R. (1984). *Fish face.* New York: Bantam. (P)

Gilson, J. (1983). *Thirteen ways to sink a sub.* New York: Lothrop. (M–U)

Greenfield, E. (1974). *Sister.* New York: Harper & Row. (M)

Jukes, M. (1984). *Like Jake and me.* New York: Knopf. (P–M)

Paterson, K. (1977). *Bridge to Terabithia.* New York: Crowell. (M–U)

Rockwell, T. (1973). *How to eat fried worms.* New York: Franklin Watts. (M)

Spinelli, J. (1990). *Maniac Magee.* Boston: Little, Brown. (U)

Steptoe, J. (1980). *Daddy is a monster . . . sometimes.* New York: Harper & Row. (P)

Viorst, J. (1972). *Alexander and the terrible, horrible, no good, very bad day.* New York: Atheneum. (P–M)

Waber, B. (1972). *Ira sleeps over.* Boston: Houghton Mifflin. (P)

Historical Fiction

Avi. (1990). *The true confessions of Charlotte Doyle.* New York: Orchard Books. (U)

Coerr, E. (1986). *The Josefina story quilt.* New York: Harper & Row. (P)

Cohen, B. (1983). *Molly's pilgrim.* New York: Lothrop. (M)

Collier, J. L., & Collier, C. (1983). *War comes to Willy Freeman.* New York: Delacorte Press. (M–U) (See other books in the series.)

Dalgliesh, A. (1982). *The courage of Sarah Noble.* New York: Scribner. (P–M)

Fleischman, S. (1963). *By the great horn spoon!* Boston: Little, Brown. (M–U)

Fleischman, S. (1986). *The whipping boy.* New York: Greenwillow. (M)

Forbes, E. (1970). *Johnny Tremain.* Boston: Houghton Mifflin. (M–U)

Fox, P. (1973). *The slave dancer.* New York: Bradbury Press. (U)

Fritz, J. (1958). *The cabin faced west.* New York: Coward-McCann. (P–M)

Greene, B. (1973). *Summer of my German soldier.* New York: Dutton. (U)

Hunt, I. (1966). *Across five Aprils.* Chicago: Follett. (U)

Lowry, L. (1989). *Number the stars.* Boston: Houghton Mifflin. (U)

Nixon, J. L. (1987). *A family apart.* New York: Bantam. (U) (See other books in the series.)

O'Dell, S. (1970). *Sing down the moon.* Boston: Houghton Mifflin. (U)

Speare, E. G. (1957). *Calico captive.* Boston: Houghton Mifflin. (M–U)

Speare, E. G. (1958). *The witch of Blackbird Pond.* Boston: Houghton Mifflin. (M–U)

Speare, E. G. (1983). *The sign of the beaver.* Boston: Houghton Mifflin. (M)

Wilder, L. I. (1953). *Little house in the big woods.* New York: Harper & Row. (M)

Uchida, Y. (1971). *Journey to Topaz.* Berkeley, CA: Creative Arts. (U) setting influences the plot. Examples of historical fiction include *Sarah, Plain and Tall* (MacLachlan, 1985), a pioneer story, and *Summer of My German Soldier* (Greene, 1973) which is set during World War II. Characteristics of historical fiction include the following:

1. The setting is integral and must be historically accurate.
2. Conflict is often between the character and society or between characters.
3. Characters are described within the time and place in which they live.
4. Language is appropriate to the setting.
5. Themes are universal, both within the historical period of the book and for today.

Through historical fiction, children are immersed in historical events, appreciate the contributions of people who have lived before them, and understand human relationships.

Literary Elements

Another way to examine stories is according to their literary elements. Whether stories are short and written to appeal to 5- and 6-year-olds or written for adolescents, they have the same basic structure. Five basic literary elements are (a) characters, (b) plot, (c) setting, (d) point of view, and (e) theme.

Characters.   *Characters* are the people or personified animals who are involved in the story. Often characters are the most important literary element because the reading experience is centered around a character or group of characters. Usually, one or two fully rounded and several supporting characters are introduced and developed in a story. Fully developed or round main characters have many character traits, both good and bad. That is to say, they have all the characteristics of real people. Knowing and inferring a character's traits is an important part of reading. Through character traits we get to know a character well and the character seems to come alive. Several stories that have fully developed characters are listed in Figure 2.4.

The supporting characters may be individualized, but they will be portrayed much less vividly than the main character. The extent to which the supporting characters are developed depends on the author's purpose and the needs of the story. In *Sarah, Plain and Tall* (MacLachlan, 1985), for instance, Sarah is the main character and we get to know her as a real, multi-dimensional person. In contrast, what we know best about Caleb and Anna in this story is how much they want Sarah to become a part of their lives.

We learn about characters and their traits in four ways: their (a) appearance, (b) actions, (c) talk, and (d) thinking.

Appearance.   Readers learn about characters through physical description. Authors tell readers about a character's facial features, body shapes, habits of dress, mannerisms, and gestures. In the title of the book, MacLachlan describes Sarah as "plain" and "tall." As we read, we learn that she has a yellow bonnet, wears her brown hair in a bun, is large, has rough hands, and sometimes wears overalls. This appearance suggests that Sarah will not be meek and mild. She is strong and hardworking,

FIGURE 2.4   Stories with Fully Developed Main Characters

Blume, J. (1972). *Tales of a fourth grade nothing.* New York: Dutton. (M)
Burch, R. (1966). *Queenie Peavy.* New York: Viking. (U)
Cleary, B. (1981). *Ramona Quimby, age 8.* New York: Morrow. (P–M)
Cohen, B. (1983). *Molly's pilgrim.* New York: Lothrop. (M)
Fox, M. (1988). *Wilfred Gordon McDonald Partridge.* Brooklyn, NY: Kane/Miller. (M–U)
Galdone, P. (1978). *Cinderella.* New York: McGraw-Hill. (P–M)
Jukes, M. (1984). *Like Jake and me.* New York: Knopf. (P–M)
MacLachlan, P. (1985). *Sarah, plain and tall.* New York: Harper & Row. (M)
Speare, E. (1983). *The sign of the beaver.* Boston: Houghton Mifflin. (M–U)
Steig, W. (1982). *Doctor De Soto.* New York: Scholastic. (P–M)
Steig, W. (1986). *Brave Irene.* New York: Farrar, Straus & Giroux. (M)
Taylor, M. (1976). *Roll of thunder, hear my cry.* New York: Dial. (U)
Uchida, Y. (1971). *Journey to Topaz.* Berkeley, CA: Creative Arts Book Company. (M–U)
Waber, B. (1972). *Ira sleeps over.* Boston: Houghton Mifflin. (P)
Zelinsky, P. O. (1986). *Rumpelstiltskin.* New York: Dutton. (M)

---

and she may be independent. Undoubtedly, she is unconventional for a woman of her time.

Actions. A second way readers learn about characters is through their actions. In *Sarah, Plain and Tall,* the author demonstrates that Sarah is hardworking through her actions: She can braid hair, make stew, bake bread, build bookshelves, paint, keep a fire going all night, sing, dry flowers for winter, cut hair, draw pictures, write letters, plow fields, swim, and fix the roof. MacLachlan also shows us that Sarah can be playful when she slides down haystack dunes and goes swimming in a cow pond.

Talk. Readers also learn about characters through their talk. What characters say is important, and so is the way they speak. Some characters might speak informally; others may speak quite formally. Sometimes characters are given dialectical speech patterns that reflect the geographic location of the story or the socioeconomic status of the characters. Sarah's speech is characteristically New England, and she speaks with a Maine accent, saying "Ayuh" for "yes." We can infer that Sarah also acts like a New Englander, and from our knowledge of cultures, we might conclude that Sarah is hardworking, frugal, and direct.

Thinking. A fourth way to learn about characters is through their thoughts. Sometimes readers gain glimpses into characters through the characters' thoughts; however, in other stories characters' thoughts are not revealed. In *Sarah, Plain and Tall,* we do not know what Sarah is thinking; instead, we must infer her thoughts from what she says and does. After Sarah's return from town and in response to Anna's worry that Sarah would leave, Sarah says that while she will always miss Maine, she would miss her new family on the plains more. Then we know she will stay.

Plot. Plot is the sequence of events involving characters in conflict situations in the beginning, middle, and end of a story. It is based on the goals of one or more characters and the processes involved in attaining these goals (Lukens, 1990). The main character or characters want to achieve a goal, and other characters are introduced to oppose or prevent the main characters from being successful. The story events are put in motion by characters as they attempt to overcome conflict, reach their goals, and solve their problems.

Beginning-Middle-End.   The most basic aspect of plot is the division of the main events of a story into three parts: the *beginning, middle,* and *end.* (Upper grade students may substitute the terms *introduction, development* or *complication,* and *resolution.*) In Chris Van Allsburg's *Jumanji* (1981), for example, the three story parts can be picked out easily. As the story begins, two bored children find a box with a game inside and take it home to play. In the middle, the children play the fantasy game, with bizarre results. Finally, the children finish the game and with relief they return it to the park where they found it. As the story ends, the children notice two boys pick up the game and head out of the park with it.

Specific types of information are included in each of the three story parts. In the beginning, the author introduces the characters, describes the setting, and presents a problem. The author uses the characters, the setting, and events to develop the plot and sustain the theme through the story. In the middle, the author adds events to prepare readers for what will follow. Conflict heightens as the characters face roadblocks that prevent them from solving their problems. How the characters tackle these problems adds suspense to keep readers interested. In the end, all that has happened in the story is reconciled, and readers learn whether or not the characters' struggles are successful.

Almost any story can be divided into these three parts. Stories that have easily identifiable beginnings, middles, and ends are listed in Figure 2.5.

FIGURE 2.5   Stories with Identifiable Beginnings, Middles, and Ends

Aardema, V. (1975). *Why mosquitoes buzz in people's ears.* New York: Dial. (P–M)
Bunting, E. (1988). *How many days to America?* New York: Clarion. (M)
Cauley, L. B. (1979). *The ugly duckling.* San Diego: Harcourt Brace Jovanovich. (P–M)
Fleischman, S. (1986). *The whipping boy.* New York: Greenwillow. (M)
Freeman, D. (1968). *Corduroy.* New York: Viking. (P)
Gallo, D. R. (Ed.). (1984). *Sixteen short stories by outstanding writers for young adults.* New York: Dell. (U)
Heins, P. (1974). *Snow White.* Boston: Atlantic Monthly. (M)
Keeping, C. (1982). *Beowulf.* Oxford, England: Oxford University Press. (U)
Kellogg, S. (1979). *Pinkerton, behave!* New York: Dial. (P)
Kellogg, S. (1985). *Chicken Little.* New York: Mulberry. (P)
Locker, T. (1987). *The boy who held back the sea.* New York: Dial. (M)
Locker, T. (1988). *Washington Irving's Rip Van Winkle.* New York: Dial. (U)
MacLachlan, P. (1985). *Sarah, plain and tall.* New York: Harper & Row. (M)
Mayer, M. (1978). *Beauty and the beast.* New York: Macmillan. (M–U)
Noble, T. H. (1980). *The day Jimmy's boa ate the wash.* New York: Dial. (P)

Conflict.   *Conflict* is the tension or opposition between forces in the plot, and it is introduced to interest readers enough to continue reading the story. Conflict usually occurs

1. between a character and nature
2. between a character and society
3. between characters
4. within a character (Lukens, 1990)

Conflict between a character and nature is represented in stories in which severe weather plays an important role, as in Jean Craighead George's *Julie of the Wolves* (1972), a story of about an Eskimo girl who is lost in the Alaskan wilderness, and in stories set in isolated geographic locations, such as Scott O'Dell's *Island of the Blue Dolphins* (1960) in which the Indian girl Karana struggles to survive alone on a Pacific island.

In some stories, a character's activities and beliefs are different from those held by other members of society, and these differences cause conflict between that character and the local society. One example is Elizabeth Speare's *The Witch of Blackbird Pond* (1958) in which Kit Tyler is accused of being a witch because her actions, which were acceptable in the Caribbean community where she grew up, are not acceptable in a New England Puritan community.

Conflict between characters is commonly used in children's literature. In Judy Blume's *Tales of a Fourth Grade Nothing* (1972), for instance, the never-ending conflict between Peter and his little brother Fudge is what makes the story interesting.

The fourth type of conflict occurs within a character, and stories such as Bernard Waber's *Ira Sleeps Over* (1972) and Betsy Byars's *The Summer of the Swans* (1970) are examples. In *Ira Sleeps Over,* 6-year-old Ira must decide whether to take his teddy bear with him when he goes next door to spend the night with a friend, and in *The Summer of the Swans,* Sara feels guilty when her mentally retarded brother wanders off and is lost. A list of stories illustrating the four conflict situations is presented in Figure 2.6.

Plot development.   *Plot* is developed through the introduction, development, and resolution of the conflict in the beginning, middle, and end of the story. Plot development involves four components:

1. A problem that introduces conflict is presented in the beginning of a story.
2. Characters face roadblocks as they attempt to solve the problem in the middle of the story.
3. The high point in the action occurs when the problem is about to be solved. This high point separates the middle and end of the story.
4. The problem is solved and the roadblocks are overcome at the end of the story.

The problem is introduced at the beginning of the story, and the main character is faced with trying to solve it. This problem determines the conflict. In *Jumanji,* the problem is that the children must continue playing the game despite the wild animals, natural disasters, and havoc around them until they finish it. This conflict might be

FIGURE 2.6   Stories Illustrating the Four Conflict Situations

---

Conflict Between a Character and Nature

George, J. C. (1972). *Julie of the wolves.* New York: Harper & Row. (M–U)
Locker, T. (1987). *The boy who held back the sea.* New York: Dial. (M)
Peet, B. (1976). *Abel's island.* Boston: Houghton Mifflin. (M–U)
Steig, W. (1971). *Amos and Boris.* New York: Farrar, Straus & Giroux. (P)

Conflict Between a Character and Society

Kellogg, S. (1973). *The island of the skog.* New York: Dial. (P–M)
Nixon, J. L. (1987). *A family apart.* New York: Bantam. (M–U)
Speare, E. G. (1958). *The witch of Blackbird Pond.* Boston: Houghton Mifflin. (M–U)
Uchida, Y. (1971). *Journey to Topaz.* Berkeley, CA: Creative Arts Book Company. (M–U)

Conflict Between Characters

Blume, J. (1972). *Tales of a fourth grade nothing.* New York: Dutton. (M)
Howe, D., & Howe, J. (1979). *Bunnicula: A rabbit-tale of mystery.* New York: Atheneum. (M)
Lewis, C. S. (1950). *The lion, the witch, and the wardrobe.* New York: Macmillan. (U)
Zelinsky, P. O. (1986). *Rumpelstiltskin.* New York: Dutton. (P–M)

Conflict Within a Character

Bunting, E. (1987). *Ghost's hour, spook's hour.* New York: Clarion. (P)
Byars, B. (1970). *The summer of the swans.* New York: Viking. (M–U)
Lowry, L. (1979). *Anastasia Krupnik.* Boston: Houghton Mifflin. (M–U)
Waber, B. (1972). *Ira sleeps over.* Boston: Houghton Mifflin. (P)

---

characterized as conflict within a character, the last of the four types of conflict described in the previous section.

Once the problem has been introduced, authors use conflict to throw roadblocks in the way of an easy solution. As one roadblock is removed, another is devised to thwart the characters as they strive to reach their goals. Postponing the solution by introducing roadblocks is the core of plot development in the middle of the story. Stories may contain any number of roadblocks, but many children's stories contain three, four, or five roadblocks.

In *Jumanji,* author Chris Van Allsburg introduces the first conflict as the children begin playing the game and the lion appears on top of the piano. Next, monkeys ransack the kitchen, rhinos charge, a lost guide appears in the living room, a boa constrictor begins to slither off the mantle, and so on. There are eight roadblocks in all.

The high point of the action occurs when the solution of the problem hangs in the balance. It is the dividing point between the middle and end of the story. Tension is high, and readers continue reading to learn whether or not the main characters will solve the problem. In *Jumanji,* the high point occurs when one child rolls two sixes so she can win the game. Tension is high because readers aren't sure if winning the game will solve the problem of the wild animals and natural disasters that have wreaked havoc on the house and put the children into danger.

At the end of the story, the problem is solved and the goal is achieved. The house has resumed its normal appearance and the children are safe. They quickly put the gameboard and pieces back in the box and return the game to the park where they found it. However, *Jumanji* has an unusual ending: the two children notice two other boys—boys who are known not to complete what they start—pick up the game and head home with it. The theme of the book is reinforced with this ending.

Setting.   In some stories the setting is barely sketched, and these settings are called *backdrop settings.* In other stories, however, the setting is elaborated and integral to the story's effectiveness. These settings are called *integral settings* (Lukens, 1990). The setting in these stories must be specific and authors take care to ensure the authenticity of the historical period or geographic location in which the story is set. There are four dimensions of setting: (a) location, (b) weather, (c) time period, and (d) time.

Location.   Location is a very important dimension of setting in many stories. The Boston Commons in *Make Way for Ducklings* (McCloskey, 1969), the Alaskan North Slope in *Julie of the Wolves* (George, 1972), and New York City's Metropolitan Museum of Art in *From the Mixed-up Files of Mrs. Basil E. Frankweiler* (Konigsburg, 1983) are integral to these stories' effectiveness. In other stories, location is not important, and readers take little notice of the setting.

Weather.   The second dimension of setting is weather, and, like location, it is crucial in some stories. For example, a rainstorm is essential to the plot in *Bridge to Terabithia* (Paterson, 1977) and a snowstorm to *Brave Irene* (Steig, 1986). At other times, weather is not even mentioned because it does not affect the outcome of the story. For example, readers may not even think about the setting as they read stories that take place on warm, sunny days.

Time period.   The third dimension of setting is the time period in which a story is set. The time period is important in stories that are set in the past or in the future. If *Sarah, Plain and Tall* (MacLachlan, 1985) was set in a different era, for example, it would lose much of its impact. Today, few men advertise for a wife in a newspaper or find it surprising that a woman wears overalls. Other stories, such as *A Wrinkle in Time* (L'Engle, 1962), take place in the future where things are possible that are not possible today.

Time.   The fourth dimension of setting, time, includes both time of day and the passage of time within a story. The time of day is ignored in most stories, except for scary stories, which typically take place after dark. For example, in Bill Martin, Jr., and John Archambault's *The Ghost-eye Tree* (1985), a story of two children who must walk past a scary tree at night to get a pail of milk, time is a more important dimension than in stories that take place during the day because night makes things more scary.

Many short stories span a brief period of time, often less than a day, and sometimes less than an hour. In Chris Van Allsburg's *The Polar Express* (1985), for instance, the little boy's trip to the North Pole lasts only an hour or two. Other stories, such as *Charlotte's Web* (White, 1952) and *The Ugly Duckling* (Mayer, 1987), span a year or more. A list of stories in which setting plays an integral role is presented in Figure 2.7.

Point of View. Stories are written from a particular viewpoint, and this focus determines to a great extent readers' understanding of the characters and the events of the story. One way to demonstrate point of view is to contrast *The Three Little Pigs* (Galdone, 1970), which is told from an objective, third person viewpoint, with *The True Story of the Three Little Pigs* (Scieszka, 1989), which is told by Mr. A. Wolf from his first person viewpoint. In this unusual and satirical retelling, the wolf tries to explain away his bad image. Four common points of view are (a) first person, (b) omniscient, (c) limited omniscient, and (d) objective (Lukens, 1990). A list of stories written from each point of view is presented in Figure 2.8.

First person point of view. The first person viewpoint is used to tell a story through the eyes of one character using the first person pronoun *I*. This point of view is used so the reader can experience the story as the narrator tells it. The narrator, usually the main character, speaks as an eyewitness and a participant in the events. For example, in *The Slave Dancer* (Fox, 1973), Jessie tells the story of his kidnapping and frightful voyage on a slave ship, and in *Alexander and the Terrible, Horrible, No*

FIGURE 2.7 Stories with Integral Settings

Location

George, J. C. (1972). *Julie of the wolves.* New York: Harper & Row. (M–U)
Konigsburg, E. L. (1983). *From the mixed-up files of Mrs. Basil E. Frankweiler.* New York: Atheneum. (M)
McCloskey, R. (1969). *Make way for ducklings.* New York: Viking. (P)
Polacco, P. (1988). *Rechenka's eggs.* New York: Philomel. (P–M)

Weather

Locker, T. (1987). *The boy who held back the sea.* New York: Dial. (M)
Ness, E. (1966). *Sam, Bangs, and moonshine.* New York: Holt. (P)
Paterson, K. (1977). *Bridge to Terabithia.* New York: Crowell. (M–U)
Steig, W. (1986). *Brave Irene.* New York: Farrar, Straus & Giroux. (M)

Time

Bunting, E. (1984). *The man who could call down owls.* New York: Macmillan. (M)
Martin, Jr., B., & Archambault, J. (1985). *The ghost-eye tree.* New York: Henry Holt. (P)
Mayer, M. (1987). *The ugly duckling.* New York: Macmillan. (P–M)
White, E. B. (1952). *Charlotte's web.* New York: Harper & Row. (M)

Time Period

L'Engle, M. (1962). *A wrinkle in time.* New York: Farrar, Straus & Giroux. (U)
Lowry, L. (1989). *Number the stars.* Boston: Houghton Mifflin. (M–U)
Mayer, M. (1987). *The pied piper of Hamelin.* New York: Macmillan. (P–M)
Nixon, J. L. (1987). *A family apart.* New York: Bantam Books. (U)

FIGURE 2.8   Stories Illustrating the Four Points of View

First Person Viewpoint

Greene, B. (1974). *Philip Hall likes me. I reckon maybe.* New York: Dial. (M–U)

Howe, D., & Howe, J. (1979). *Bunnicula.* New York: Atheneum. (M)

MacLachlan, P. (1985). *Sarah, plain and tall.* New York: Harper & Row. (M)

Viorst, J. (1977). *Alexander and the terrible, horrible, no good, very bad day.* New York: Atheneum. (P)

Omniscient Viewpoint

Babbitt, N. (1975). *Tuck everlasting.* New York: Farrar, Straus & Giroux. (M–U)

Grahame, K. (1961). *The wind in the willows.* New York: Scribner. (M)

Lewis, C. S. (1981). *The lion, the witch, and the wardrobe.* New York: Macmillan. (M–U)

Steig, W. (1982). *Doctor De Soto.* New York: Farrar, Straus & Giroux. (P)

Limited Omniscient Viewpoint

Burch, R. (1966). *Queenie Peavy.* New York: Dell. (U)

Cleary, B. (1981). *Ramona Quimby, age 8.* New York: Random House. (M)

Lionni, L. (1969). *Alexander and the wind-up mouse.* New York: Pantheon. (P)

Lowry, L. (1979). *Anastasia Krupnik.* Boston: Houghton Mifflin. (M)

Objective Viewpoint

Brown, M. (1954). *Cinderella.* New York: Scribner. (P)

Lobel, A. (1972). *Frog and toad together.* New York: Harper & Row. (P)

Wells, R. (1973). *Benjamin and Tulip.* New York: Dial. (P)

Zemach, M. (1983). *The little red hen.* New York: Farrar, Straus & Giroux. (P)

Good, Very Bad Day (Viorst, 1977), Alexander tells about a day when everything seemed to go wrong for him. One limitation to this viewpoint is that the narrator must remain an eyewitness.

Omniscient point of view.   In the omniscient viewpoint, the author is god-like, seeing all and knowing all. The author tells the readers about the thought processes of each character without worrying about how the information is obtained. William Steig's *Doctor De Soto* (1982), a story about a mouse dentist who outwits a fox with a toothache, is an example of a story written from the omniscient viewpoint. Steig lets readers know that the fox is thinking about eating the dentist as soon as his toothache is cured and that the mouse dentist is aware of the fox's thoughts and plans a clever trick to protect himself.

Limited omniscient point of view.   The limited omniscient viewpoint is used so that readers can know the thoughts of one important character. The story is told in third person and the author concentrates on the thoughts, feelings, and significant past experiences of the important character. Robert Burch used the limited omniscient viewpoint in *Queenie Peavy* (1966), the story of a misfit girl in the 1930s whose father is in jail. Burch concentrates on the character Queenie, showing why she has a chip on her shoulder and how she overcomes it.

Objective point of view. In the objective viewpoint, readers are eyewitnesses to the story and are confined to the immediate scene. It is as though we were viewing a film of the story and learn only what is visible and audible and what others say about the characters and situations. Fairy tales are usually told from the objective viewpoint. In these stories, the focus is on recounting the events of the story rather than on developing the personalities of the characters.

Theme. *Theme* is the underlying meaning of a story and embodies general truths about society or human nature. According to Lehr (1991), the theme "steps back from the literal interpretation" to state the more general truths (p. 2). It usually deals with the characters' emotions and values.

Themes can be stated explicitly or implicitly. Explicit themes are stated openly and clearly in the story, while implicit themes are implied through the characters' actions, dialogue, and monologue as they strive to resolve their problems. Friendship, responsibility, courage, and kindness to others are common topics around which authors build themes in children's literature.

The theme in *Sylvester and the Magic Pebble* (Steig, 1969), for instance, revolves around the importance of family and the futility of wishing for trivial things. After a first reading, we are likely to say that the theme of the story is to be happy with what you have. Through repeated readings, careful observation of the illustrations, and thoughtful, reflective discussions, we notice the importance of family, especially in the final illustration when the reunited Duncan family sits entwined in each others' arms. Thus, the theme is expanded to show that families often take their special worth for granted.

A secondary theme focuses on Sylvester and his misuse of the magic pebble. He was tested when the lion appeared, and he failed when he turned himself into a rock rather than wishing the lion away or turning the lion into a rock. We recognize that Sylvester was not mature enough to control the magic and that families are needed to help, support, and guide children until they mature.

Guidelines for Choosing Stories

The best way to evaluate a picture book or a chapter book is to share it with a child and observe his or her reaction and the depth of that response. However, this method is not very practical when many books must be evaluated. There are methods, though, that teachers can use to identify well-written books to use in their classrooms. The criteria used to evaluate books are based primarily on the literary elements discussed in this chapter. Understanding the characteristics of the various genre is also important because the literary elements vary from one genre to another. For example, setting is very important in historical fiction, but it is unimportant in fables.

A list of guidelines that teachers can use as they choose well-written books for literature-based reading is presented in Figure 2.9. Not all of the qualities need to be present in each book, but many excellent picture books and chapter books embody all or almost all of the qualities. Some criteria that relate to specific genre are also included in the figure.

FIGURE 2.9   Guidelines for Choosing Stories

1. Is the book a good story?
2. Is there action?
3. Is the plot original and believable?
4. Are the characters real and believable?
5. Do the characters grow and change in the story?
6. Does the author avoid stereotyping?
7. How does the setting affect the action, characters, or theme?
8. Does the story move beyond the setting and have universal implications?
9. Is the theme worthwhile?
10. Is the style of writing and use of language appropriate?
11. Does the book exemplify the characteristics of a genre?
12. How does the book compare with other books on the same subject or in the same genre?

Adapted from Sutherland & Arbuthnot, 1986; Huck, Hepler, & Hickman, 1987; Norton, 1991.

INFORMATIONAL BOOKS

Informational books provide information, concepts, and facts on topics ranging from sea otters to the solar system and careers in journalism to Christopher Columbus's voyages to the New World. These books are very useful in literature-based reading classrooms; there are many benefits for students who read informational books. First and foremost is the fascinating information these books provide. Informational books enrich content area study and theme cycles in a way that textbooks cannot. Norton (1991) and Vardell (1991) have identified these other qualities. Information books

- stretch imaginations
- stimulate thinking
- develop critical reading abilities
- promote discussion
- expand vocabularies, especially understanding of technical terms
- generate enthusiasm
- encourage independence

Informational books have become an exciting and popular genre. The information presented in these books is relevant, well researched, clearly organized and written in an interesting style (Vardell, 1991). Several recently published informational books exhibit many of these qualities and have received critical acclaim as Caldecott or Newbery Award winners or honor books. Some of these include *Lincoln: A Photobiography* (Freedman, 1987), *Volcano: The Eruption and Healing of Mount St. Helen's* (Lauber, 1986), *Alphabatics* (MacDonald, 1986), and *Truck* (Crews, 1980).

These books not only provide information about a variety of topics, but they are enjoyable reading. Too often teachers ignore the pleasure—experiences, personal associations, and feelings—that come from reading informational books and assume that students read informational books to learn facts or abstract generalizations. Rosenblatt (1991) distinguishes between reading to take away information, which she calls *efferent reading,* and reading to experience, think, and feel, which she calls *aesthetic reading.* Whether readers assume an aesthetic or efferent stance depends on the purpose for reading. To complicate matters, readers often move back and forth along a continuum between aesthetic and efferent reading as they read. Rosenblatt cautions that teachers should not ask students to read informational books efferently but should encourage reading primarily as an aesthetic experience in which students savor a book's images and the associations and feelings that come from their reading.

Characteristics of quality informational books include the following:

1. Information is presented objectively without anthropomorphism (ascribing human characteristics to animals, plants, and inanimate things) or over-simplification.
2. Both sides of controversial issues are presented and significant facts are not omitted.
3. Photographs, diagrams, and drawings are used to illustrate and clarify the text.
4. The organization is clear and logical.
5. Organizational aids, such as headings and subheadings, a table of contents, index, and a glossary, make the book easier to read and more usable.
6. The book stimulates curiosity and a sense of wonder.
7. The author has the scientific or educational qualifications to write the book or the book has been reviewed by a qualified person.

Types of Informational Books

Students who are curious about the world and want to learn about animals, machines, earthquakes, sports stars, the Civil War, and other nonfiction topics read informational books. Informational books have been written for elementary students on topics related to the biological sciences (plants, animals, and human beings), physical sciences (chemistry, physics, astronomy, geography, and geology), social sciences (economics, history, and culture), and the arts (art, music, drama, dance, architecture, and crafts and hobbies). Examples of informational books include *Weather Forecasting* (Gibbons, 1987), *The Buck Stops Here: The Presidents of the United States* (Provensen, 1990), and *Sugaring Time* (Lasky, 1983). Other examples of informational books on a variety of topics are listed in Figure 2.10.

Three other types of informational books are concept books, alphabet books, and biographies, and they are discussed in the following sections.

Concept Books. *Concept books* present information about basic concepts, such as colors, shapes, numbers, sounds, and the alphabet, and they are young children's introduction to informational books. These books are valuable because they help children to see relationships between objects, stimulate talk, and expand their awareness of the world around them.

Concept books present familiar concepts such as machines (Rockwell & Rockwell, 1972), a school bus (Crews, 1984), and the airport (Barton, 1982). (Even

FIGURE 2.10   Informational Books

Biological Sciences

Aliki. (1985). *Dinosaurs are different.* New York: Harper & Row. (P–M)

Arnold, C. (1985). *Saving the peregrine falcon.* Minneapolis: Carolrhoda. (M)

Cole, J. (1989). *The magic school bus inside the human body.* New York: Scholastic. (M)

Cole, J. (1991). *My puppy is born.* New York: Morrow. (P)

Heller, R. (1984). *Plants that never bloom.* New York: Grosset & Dunlap. (M)

Miller, J. (1983). *The human body.* New York: Viking. (M–U) (moveable book)

Smith, R. (1990). *Sea otter rescue.* New York: Cobblehill Books. (M–U)

Squire, A. (1991). *Understanding man's best friend: Why dogs look and act the way they do.* New York: Macmillan. (M–U)

Physical Sciences

Gibbons, G. (1987). *Weather forecasting.* New York: Four Winds Press. (P–M)

Hartman, G. (1991). *As the crow flies: A first book of maps.* New York: Bradbury Press. (P–M)

Krementz, J. (1987). *A visit to Washington, DC.* New York: Scholastic. (P–M)

Lauber, P. (1990). *Seeing earth from space.* New York: Orchard. (P–M)

Lowry, L. (1991). *Earth day.* Minneapolis: Carolrhoda. (P)

Pollard, M. (1978). *How things work.* New York: Larousse. (M–U)

Simon, S. (1979). *Danger from below: Earthquakes—past, present, and future.* New York: Four Winds Press. (M–U)

Social Sciences

Fritz, J. (1987). *Shh! We're writing the Constitution.* New York: Putnam. (P–M)

Goor, R., & Goor, N. (1986). *Pompeii: Exploring a Roman ghost town.* New York: Harper & Row. (M–U)

Hamanaka, S. (1990). *The journey: Japanese Americans, racism, and renewal.* New York: Orchard Books. (M–U)

Horwitz, J. (1984). *Night markets: Bringing food to a city.* New York: Harper & Row. (M)

Macaulay, D. (1975). *Pyramid.* Boston: Houghton Mifflin. (U)

Provensen, A. (1990). *The buck stops here: The presidents of the United States.* New York: Harper & Row. (M–U)

Pryor, B. (1987). *The house on Maple Street.* New York: Morrow. (P–M)

Ziefert, H. (1986). *A new coat for Anna.* New York: Knopf. (P)

The Arts

Arnosky, J. (1982). *Drawing from nature.* New York: Lothrop, Lee & Shepard. (M–U)

Bjork, C. (1991). *Elliot's extraordinary cookbook.* New York: Farrar, Straus & Giroux. (P–M–U)

Brown, L. K., & Brown, M. (1986). *Visiting the art museum.* New York: Dutton. (P–M)

Gibbons, G. (1985). *Lights! Camera! Action! How a movie is made.* New York: Crowell. (P–M)

Gibbons, G. (1987). *The pottery place.* San Diego: Harcourt Brace Jovanovich. (P–M)

Haldane, S. (1988). *Painting faces.* New York: Dutton. (M)

Krementz, J. (1976). *A very young dancer.* New York: Dell. (P–M)

Macaulay, D. (1973). *Cathedral: The story of its construction.* Boston: Houghton Mifflin. (M–U) though alphabet books are concept books, they will be discussed separately in the next section.) Many books have little or no text and use photographs or clearly drawn illustrations instead to describe concepts.

Most concept books are written for young children, but others focus on language concepts—opposites, homographs, nouns, prepositions—and are more appropriate for middle and upper grade students. Figure 2.11 presents a list of concept books.

Alphabet Books. *Alphabet* or *ABC books* are commonly used to introduce preschool children and kindergartners to common objects, letters of the alphabet, and letter-sound correspondences. In these ABC books, the objects in the illustrations should be familiar and easy for children to identify, such as in Cleaver's *ABC* (1985). Other alphabet books have been designed for older children. The books are more complex and have detailed illustrations. Many of these books are puzzles, tell a story, or introduce vocabulary related to a topic such as flowers or medieval life.

Puzzle and game alphabet books are appropriate for first and second graders. For example, *I Unpacked My Grandmother's Trunk* (Hoguet, 1983) is a popular alphabet word game in which children remember and recite objects for each letter of the alphabet which are packed in a suitcase, and *On Market Street* (Lobel, 1981) has richly detailed illustrations with several objects for each letter that students must study carefully to identify.

Other alphabet books are more sophisticated and appeal to middle and upper grade students. One of the best known of these alphabet books for older children is Graeme Base's *Animalia* (1987), an animal ABC book with lush, detailed illustrations and alliterative sentences for each letter. Some of these complex alphabet books deal with language and literature, and others are useful in social studies and science thematic units. *Aster Aardvark's Alphabet Adventures* (Kellogg, 1987) is a wordplay book, and two alphabet books that are illustrated with poems are *Halloween ABC* (Merriam, 1987) and *If There Were Dreams to Sell* (Lalicki, 1984). Flowers are the topic of *Alison's Zinnia* (Lobel, 1990). *Ashanti to Zulu: African Traditions* (Musgrove, 1976) focuses on customs of 26 African tribes, and *Illuminations* (Hunt, 1989), a book about the Middle Ages, introduces words such as *falconry* and *troubadour.* Not only are these books informative and interesting to read, but students can also use this format in writing their own alphabet books about concepts they are learning in social studies and science. A list of ABC books is presented in Figure 2.12.

Biographies and Autobiographies. *Biographies* and *autobiographies* are life-stories. Biographies focus on the life of well-known personalities and people who have overcome great odds, and autobiographies are life-stories written by the person himself or herself. Life-stories have been written about a wide range of people, including artists, sports figures, explorers, and authors—not just American historical personalities.

The two most important characteristics of biographies and autobiographies are accuracy and authenticity. Readers turn to these books for information, and authors are increasingly documenting the sources they used in researching their books, either

FIGURE 2.11   Concept Books

Aliki. (1990). *My feet.* New York: Harper & Row. (P)
Aliki. (1990). *My hands.* New York: Harper & Row. (P)
Allen, M. N., & Rotner, S. (1991). *Changes.* New York: Macmillan. (P)
Anno, M. (1977). *Anno's counting book.* New York: Crowell. (P)
Bang, M. (1983). *Ten, nine, eight.* New York: Greenwillow. (P)
Barton, B. (1981). *Building a house.* New York: Puffin. (P)
Barton, B. (1982). *Airport.* New York: Harper & Row. (P)
Barton, B. (1987). *Machines at work.* New York: Crowell. (P)
Burningham, J. (1985). *John Burningham's 1, 2, 3's.* New York: Crown. (P)
Burningham, J. (1986). *Cluck baa, jangle twang, slam bang, skip trip, sniff shout, wobble pop.* New York: Viking. (P)
Carle, E. (1968). *1, 2, 3 to the zoo.* Cleveland: World. (P)
Carle, E. (1971). *The grouchy ladybug.* New York: Crowell. (P)
Carle, E. (1974). *My very first book of colors.* New York: Crowell. (P)
Carle, E. (1974). *My very first book of shapes.* New York: Crowell. (P)
Crews, D. (1978). *Freight train.* New York: Greenwillow. (P)
Crews, D. (1980). *Truck.* New York: Greenwillow. (P)
Crews, D. (1982). *Carousel.* New York: Greenwillow. (P)
Crews, D. (1982). *Harbor.* New York: Greenwillow. (P)
Crews, D. (1984). *School bus.* New York: Puffin. (P)
Emberely, R. (1989). *City sounds.* Boston: Little, Brown. (P–M)
Emberely, R. (1980). *Jungle sounds.* Boston: Little, Brown. (P–M)
Feelings, M. (1971). *Moja means one: A Swahili counting book.* New York: Dutton. (P–M)
Gibbons, G. (1987). *Trains.* New York: Holiday House. (P)
Gibbons, G. (1990). *Up goes the skyscraper!* New York: Aladdin Books. (P–M)
Goor, R., & Goor, N. (1983). *Signs.* New York: Crowell. (P)

in endnotes or bibliographies at the back of the book. Often photos are used as illustrations because they are accurate and reflect the culture and time period. Even so, life-stories are more than a collection of facts; authors seem to bring the person to life through their writing style. Authors are no longer merely glorifying heroes that they write about; instead, they try to present a more balanced picture of the person. Sometimes authors fictionalize parts of biographies by inventing dialogue for their characters or filling in events. When little is known about the person, some fictionalizing is necessary, but fictionalized life-stories can easily merge into historical fiction. The line between them is not clear.

Life-stories can be classified in several ways. Some are picture book biographies, such as David Adler's *A Picture Book of Martin Luther King, Jr.* (1989) and Jeanette Winter's book about the Mexican painter *Diego* (1991) in which the brief text is extended through illustrations. Others such as *Stonewall* (Fritz, 1979) are written in a chapter book format with only a few illustrations. Some life-stories focus on one part of the person's life, such as Jean Fritz's *Will You Sign Here, John Hancock?* (1976) and her other American Revolution period biographies. Still others are complete life-stories that trace the person's entire life, such as Russell Freedman's Newbery Medal book *Lincoln: A Photobiography* (1987).

Hoban, T. (1972). *Count and see.* New York: Macmillan. (P)
Hoban, T. (1972). *Push-pull, empty-full: A book of opposites.* New York: Macmillan. (P–M)
Hoban, T. (1973). *Over, under, through and other spatial concepts.* New York: Macmillan. (P)
Hoban, T. (1974). *Circles, triangles, and squares.* New York: Macmillan. (P)
Hoban, T. (1975). *Dig, drill, dump, fill.* New York: Greenwillow. (P)
Hoban, T. (1976). *Big ones, little ones.* New York: Greenwillow. (P)
Hoban, T. (1983). *Round & round & round.* New York: Greenwillow. (P)
Hoban, T. (1986). *Shapes, shapes, shapes.* New York: Greenwillow. (P)
Kohn, B. (1971). *How high is up?* New York: Putnam. (P–M)
Maestro, B., & Maestro, G. (1981). *Traffic: A book of opposites.* New York: Crown. (P–M)
McMillan, B. (1983). *Here a chick, there a chick.* New York: Lothrop, Lee & Shepard. (P)
McMillan, B. (1988). *Fire engine shapes.* New York: Lothrop, Lee & Shepard. (P)
McMillan, B. (1991). *One, two, one pair!* New York: Scholastic. (P)
Provensen, A., & Provensen, M. (1978). *The year at Maple Hill Farm.* New York: Aladdin Books. (P–M)
Rockwell, H. (1975). *My dentist.* New York: Greenwillow. (P)
Rockwell, H. (1985). *My doctor.* New York: Harper & Row. (P)
Rockwell, H. & Rockwell, H. (1972). *Machines.* New York: Harper & Row. (P)
Rockwell, H., & Rockwell, H. (1979). *The supermarket.* New York: Macmillan. (P)
Samton, S. W. (1991). *Moon to sun: An adding book.* Honesdale, PA: Boyds Mills Press. (P)
Schwartz, D. M. (1989). *If you made a million.* New York: Lothrop, Lee & Shepard. (M)
Tafuri, N. (1983). *Early morning in the barn.* New York: Greenwillow. (P)
Wildsmith, B. (1965). *Brian Wildsmith's 1 2 3's.* New York: Franklin Watts. (P)
Yabuuchi, M. (1985). *Whose baby?* New York: Philomel. (P)
Yabuuchi, M. (1985). *Whose footprints?* New York: Philomel. (P)

While many kinds of biographies are available today, only a few autobiographies have been written for children. Several autobiographies are especially interesting, such as *The Land I Lost: Adventures of a Boy in Vietnam* (Huynh, 1982), Jane Goodall's *My Life with the Chimpanzees* (1988), and Roald Dahl's *Boy* (1984) in which the popular author recounts his childhood. Other biographies and autobiographies recommended for elementary students are included in Figure 2.13.

Structure of Informational Books

One way that informational books can be examined is by their organization. Biographies, for example, are often organized in a time sequence. The organizational patterns of informational books are called *expository text structures*. The five most common expository text structures are (a) description, (b) sequence, (c) comparison, (d) cause and effect, and (e) problem and solution (Niles, 1974; Meyer & Freedle, 1984).

Description. *Descriptions* are lists of characteristics, features, and examples related to a topic. Phrases such as *for example* and *characteristics are* are often used in

FIGURE 2.12   ABC Books

Anno, M. (1975). *Anno's alphabet: An adventure in imagination.* New York: Crowell. (P–M)
Base, G. (1987). *Animalia.* New York: Abrams. (M–U)
Bayer, J. (1984). *A my name is Alice.* New York: Dial. (P)
Belling, J. (1984). *A-B-Cing: An action alphabet.* New York: Crown. (M)
Bourke, L. (1991). *Eye spy: A mysterious alphabet.* San Francisco: Chronicle Books. (M–U)
Brown, M. (1974). *All butterflies: An ABC.* New York: Scribner. (P)
Downie, J. (1988). *Alphabet puzzle.* New York: Lothrop. (P)
Duke, K. (1983). *Guinea pig ABC.* New York: Dutton. (P)
Ehlert, L. (1989). *Eating the alphabet: Fruits and vegetables from A to Z.* San Diego: Harcourt Brace Jovanovich. (P)
Feelings, M. (1974). *Jambo means hello: Swahili alphabet book.* New York: Dial. (P–M)
Fisher, L. E. (1991). *An ABC exhibit.* New York: Macmillan. (M)
Gag, W. (1933). *The ABC bunny.* New York: Coward, McCann. (P)
Hague, K. (1984). *Alphabears: An ABC book.* New York: Holt, Rinehart & Winston. (P)
Hoban, T. (1982). *A, B, see!* New York: Greenwillow. (P)
Hoguet, S. R. (1983). *I unpacked my grandmother's trunk.* New York: Dutton. (P)
Hunt, J. (1989). *Illuminations.* New York: Bradbury Press. (M–U)
Kellogg, S. (1987). *Aster aardvark's alphabet adventures.* New York: Morrow. (M)
Lalicki, B. (1984). *If there were dreams to sell.* New York: Lothrop, Lee & Shepard. (M–U)
Lobel, A. (1981). *On market street.* New York: Greenwillow. (P)
MacDonald, S. (1986). *Alphabatics.* New York: Bradbury. (P)
Martin, Jr., B., & Archambault, J. (1989). *Chicka chicka boom boom.* New York: Simon & Schuster. (P)
Mayers, F. C. (1986). *ABC: Museum of Fine Arts, Boston.* New York: Abrams. (M–U)
Mayers, F. C. (1986). *The National Air and Space Museum ABC.* New York: Abrams. (M–U)
McPhail, D. (1988). *David McPhail's animals A to Z.* New York: Scholastic. (P)
Mendoza, G. (1975). *Norman Rockwell's Americana ABC.* New York: Dell. (P–M–U)
Merriam, E. (1987). *Halloween ABC.* New York: Macmillan. (M–U)
Musgrove, M. (1976). *Ashanti to Zulu: African traditions.* New York: Dial. (M–U)
Pallotta, J. (1989). *The yucky reptile alphabet book.* Watertown, MA: Charlesbridge Publishing Co. (M–U)
Paul, A. W. (1991). *Eight hands round: A patchwork alphabet.* New York: HarperCollins. (P–M–U)
Provensen, A., & Provensen, M. (1978). *A peaceable kingdom: The Shaker abecedarius.* New York: Viking. (M)
Van Allsburg, C. (1987). *The Z was zapped.* Boston: Houghton Mifflin. (M–U)
Wildsmith, B. (1962). *Brian Wildsmith's ABC.* New York: Franklin Watts. (P–M)

descriptions, and topics, such as the Mississippi River or eagles, are often described using this structure.

Sequence.   In the *sequence* structure, items or events are listed in numerical or chronological order. Words that often signal this organizational structure include *first, second, third, next, then,* and *finally.* Steps in building a road or the events in the life cycle of an animal are often written using the sequence pattern.

Comparison.   *Comparison* structures consist of descriptions of how two or more topics are similar and different. *Different, in contrast, alike, same as,* and *on the other hand* are words that are often used to signal this stucture. When reptiles and

FIGURE 2.13   Life-stories

Biographies

Adler, D. A. (1989). *A picture book of Martin Luther King, Jr.* New York: Holiday House. (P–M) (See other biographies by the same author.)

Aliki. (1988). *The many lives of Benjamin Franklin.* New York: Simon & Schuster. (M)

Bulla, C. R. (1954). *Squanto: Friend of the pilgrims.* New York: Crowell. (M)

Collins, D. R. (1989). *The country artist: A story about Beatrix Potter.* Minneapolis: Carolrhoda. (M)

Dobrin, A. (1975). *I am a stranger on earth: The story of Vincent Van Gogh.* New York: Warne. (M–U)

Felton, H. W. (1976). *Deborah Sampson: Soldier of the revolution.* New York: Dodd, Mead. (M)

Ferris, J. (1988). *Walking the road to freedom: A story about Sojourner Truth.* Minneapolis: Carolrhoda. (M)

Freedman, R. (1987). *Lincoln: A photobiography.* New York: Clarion. (M–U)

Freedman, R. (1991). *The Wright brothers: How they invented the airplane.* New York: Holiday House. (M)

Fritz, J. (1979). *Stonewall.* New York: Putnam. (M–U)

Fritz, J. (1983). *The double life of Pocahontas.* New York: Putnam. (M)

Giff, P. R. (1987). *Laura Ingalls Wilder.* New York: Viking. (M)

Golenbock, P. (1990). *Teammates.* San Diego: Harcourt Brace Jovanovich. (M)

Hamilton, V. (1974). *Paul Robeson: The life and times of a free black man.* New York: Harper & Row. (U)

Jakes, J. (1986). *Susanna of the Alamo: A true story.* San Diego: Harcourt Brace Jovanovich. (M)

Lauber, P. (1988). *Lost star: The story of Amelia Earhart.* New York: Scholastic. (M–U)

Provensen, A., & Provensen, M. (1983). *The glorious flight across the channel with Louis Bleriot.* New York: Viking. (P–M)

Quackenbush, R. (1989). *Pass the quill, I'll write a draft: A story of Thomas Jefferson.* New York: Pippin Press. (M–U)

Say, A. (1990). *El Chino.* Boston: Houghton Mifflin. (M–U)

Stanley, D. (1986). *Peter the great.* New York: Four Winds Press. (P–M)

Autobiographies

Bean, A. (1988). *My life as an astronaut.* New York: Minstrel Books. (M)

Dahl, R. (1984). *Boy.* New York: Farrar, Straus & Giroux. (M–U)

de Paola, T. (1989). *The art lesson.* New York: Putnam. (P–M)

Fritz, J. (1982). *Homesick: My own story.* New York: Putnam. (M–U)

Gish, L. (1988). *An actor's life for me.* New York: Viking. (U)

Goodall, J. (1988). *My life with the chimpanzees.* New York: Simon & Schuster. (M)

Keller, H. (1980). *The story of my life.* New York: Watermill Press. (M–U)

Nuynh, Q. N. (1982). *The land I lost: Adventures of a boy in Vietnam.* New York: Harper & Row. (M–U)

O'Kelley, M. L. (1983). *From the hills of Georgia: An autobiography in paintings.* Boston: Atlantic Monthly/Little, Brown. (P–M–U)

Peet, B. (1989). *Bill Peet: An autobiography.* Boston: Houghton Mifflin. (P–M)

Schulz, C. M. (with R. S. Kiliper). (1980). *Charlie Brown, Snoopy and me: And all the other Peanuts characters.* New York: Doubleday. (M–U) amphibians are compared or life in ancient Greece and modern Greece are contrasted, this organizational pattern is being used.

Cause and Effect. In the *cause and effect* pattern, one or more causes and the resulting effect or effects are presented. *Reasons why, if . . . then, as a result, therefore,* and *because* are words and phrases that cue the use of this structure. Explanations of why the dinosaurs died, the effects of pollution on the environment, or the causes of the Civil War might use the cause and effect pattern.

Problem and Solution. In the *problem and solution* structure, a problem is stated and one or more solutions are suggested. A variation is the question and answer format in which a question is posed and then answered, as in the book . . . *If You Traveled West in a Covered Wagon* (Levine, 1986). Cue words and phrases include *the problem is, the puzzle is, solve,* and *question . . . answer.* Books about using immunizations to protect people from disease, explanations of why locks were invented, or question-and-answer books about dinosaurs often use this structure.

These patterns are reviewed in Figure 2.14. For each pattern, a sample passage, cue words that signal the pattern, and sample books illustrating the pattern are listed.

Not all informational books fit neatly into one of the five expository text structures. Many books use a combination of two or more structures. In *Digging Up Dinosaurs* (1981), for instance, Aliki uses the problem and solution structure as the overarching one to explain how scientists discover dinosaur bones, dig them up, preserve and study them, and finally reconstruct them into skeletons so that people can see and learn about them in museums. In addition, within the book Aliki uses sequence to explain how dinosaurs become fossils, description to introduce the experts who work together to dig up dinosaurs, and sequence again to outline the steps involved in excavating the fossils. There are also some books that don't appear to use any structure at all, and research suggests that these books may be more difficult for students to comprehend (Thorndyke, 1977).

Guidelines for Choosing Informational Books

Many informational books are available today and teachers should select the very best nonfiction books to use in their classrooms. Too often teachers select stories for primary grade students to read, assuming that they are more appropriate for young readers or that these students prefer stories. These assumptions may not be true, and children need many opportunites to read informational books that feature different organizations and styles of nonfiction (Newkirk, 1989; Pappas, 1991). Four general criteria for selecting informational books are accuracy, organization, design, and style. A list of guidelines based on these criteria for selecting well-written informational books is presented in Figure 2.15.

POETRY

Children grow rather naturally into poetry. The Opies (1959) have verified what we know from observing children: children have a natural affinity to verse, songs, riddles, jokes, and chants. Young children are introduced to poetry through Mother Goose rhymes, *The House at Pooh Corner* (Milne, 1956) and Dr. Seuss stories. During the elementary grades, students chant and clap favorite poems, dramatize and dance as poems are read aloud, play with words, visit with poets, and read and write many kinds of poetry. Educator Nancy Larrick (1991) believes that children become enthralled with poetry because of the way teachers share poems—through active involvement with the music and language of poetry.

Poetry that is being written for children today is fun. No longer is it confined to rhyming verse about daffodils, clouds, and love. For example, Jack Prelutsky wrote about dinosaurs in *Tyrannosaurus Was a Beast* (1988), Arnold Adoff about his love of chocolate in *Eats Poems* (1979), and Paul Fleischman about insects in *Joyful Noise: Poems for Two Voices* (1988).

Forms of Poetry

Poems for children assume many different forms. The most common form of poetry is *rhymed verse* in which sounds, usually at the ends of lines, match or rhyme. An example is John Ciardi's "Mummy Slept Late and Daddy Fixed Breakfast" (Prelutsky, 1983), a humorous description of what happened when daddy tried to fix waffles for breakfast. Poems that tell a story are called *narrative poems.* Longfellow's "Paul Revere's Ride" (1990) and "A Visit from St. Nicholas" by Clement Moore (1980) are well-known examples. A Japanese form, haiku, is popular in anthologies of poetry for children. *Haiku* is a three-line form of nature poetry containing just 17 syllables. Because of its brevity, teachers often assume that it is an appropriate form for children, but researchers report that children prefer to read other forms of poetry.

Free verse has lines that do not rhyme, and rhythm is less important than in other types of poetry. Instead, images take on greater importance in free verse, and the arrangement of lines on the page may be unusual. In his collection of *Eats Poems* (1979), for example, Arnold Adoff uses free verse to create vivid images about loving chocolate, always being hungry, and end-of-the-summer apple pies. In these poems, all the letters are printed in lower case, the letters in words are spread across the page, and sometimes they drop into the next line.

Another poetic form is *limericks,* which are short five-line rhymed verse poems popularized by Edward Lear. Arnold Lobel wrote a book of limericks about pigs, which he called "pigericks" (1983) that are very popular with children.

Three types of poetry books are published for children. A number of picture book versions of single poems in which each line or stanza is illustrated on a page are available, such as *Lewis Carroll's Jabberwocky* (1977) and *Paul Revere's Ride* (Longfellow, 1990). Other books are specialized collections of poems, either written by a single poet or related to a single theme, such as dinosaurs, Christmas, or foods. Examples are Jack Prelutsky's popular collection of his poems *The New Kid on the Block* (1984) and Eric Carle's beautifully illustrated collection of animal poems, *Animals, Animals* (1989). The third type of poetry books for children is the comprehensive anthology, which features 50 to 500 poems or more arranged by category. *The Random House Book of Poetry for Children* (Prelutsky, 1983) is an example. A list of poetry books representative of each of the three categories is presented in Figure 2.16 (pp. 78–79).

FIGURE 2.14   The Five Expository Structures

Pattern	Description	Cue Words	Graphic Organizer	Sample Passage
Description	The author describes a topic by listing characteristics, features, and examples.	*for example* *characteristics are*		The Olympic symbol consists of five interlocking rings. The rings represent the five continents—Africa, Asia, Europe, North America, and South America—from which athletes come to compete in the games. The rings are colored black, blue, green, red, and yellow. At least one of these colors is found in the flag of every country sending athletes to compete in the Olympic games.
Sequence	The author lists items or events in numerical or chronological order.	*first, second, third* *next* *then* *finally*	1. 2. 3. 4. 5.	The Olympic games began as athletic festivals to honor the Greek gods. The most important festival was held in the valley of Olympia to honor Zeus, the king of the gods. It was this festival that became the Olympic games in 776 B.C. These games were ended in A.D. 394 by the Roman Emperor who ruled Greece. No Olympic games were held for more than 1,500 years. Then the modern Olympics began in 1896. Almost 300 male athletes competed in the first modern Olympics. In the games held in 1900, female athletes were allowed to compete. The games have continued every four years since 1896 except during World War II, and they will most likely continue for many years to come.
Comparison	The author explains how two or more things are alike and/or how they are different.	*different* *in contrast* *alike* *same as* *on the other hand*		The modern Olympics is very unlike the ancient Olympic games. Individual events are different. While there were no swimming races in the ancient games, for example, there were chariot races. There were no female contestants and all athletes competed in the nude. Of course, the ancient and modern Olympics are also alike in many ways. Some events, such as the javelin and discus throws, are the same. Some people say that cheating, professionalism, and nationalism in the modern games are a disgrace to the Olympic tradition. But according to the ancient Greek writers, there were many cases of cheating, nationalism, and professionalism in their Olympics, too.

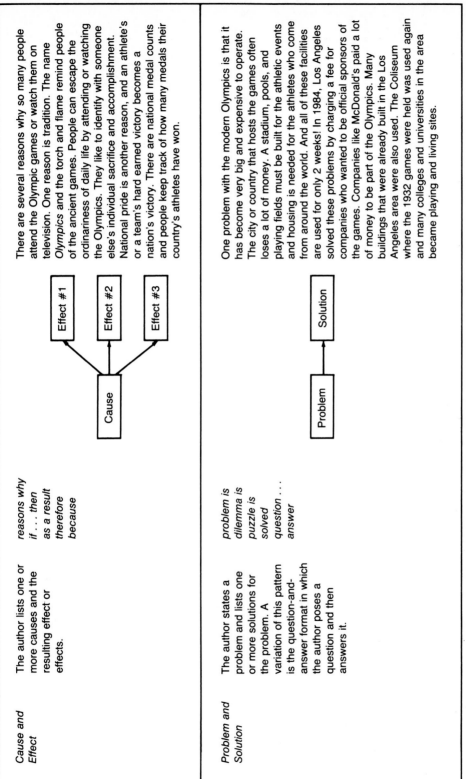

Cause and Effect

The author lists one or more causes and the resulting effect or effects.

reasons why
if . . . then
as a result
therefore
because

Effect #1

Effect #2

Effect #3

Cause

There are several reasons why so many people attend the Olympic games or watch them on television. One reason is tradition. The name *Olympics* and the torch and flame remind people of the ancient games. People can escape the ordinariness of daily life by attending or watching the Olympics. They like to identify with someone else's individual sacrifice and accomplishment. National pride is another reason, and an athlete's or a team's hard earned victory becomes a nation's victory. There are national medal counts and people keep track of how many medals their country's athletes have won.

Problem and Solution

The author states a problem and lists one or more solutions for the problem. A variation of this pattern is the question-and-answer format in which the author poses a question and then answers it.

problem is
dilemma is
puzzle is
solved
question . . .
answer

Problem

Solution

One problem with the modern Olympics is that it has become very big and expensive to operate. The city or country that hosts the games often loses a lot of money. A stadium, pools, and playing fields must be built for the athletic events and housing is needed for the athletes who come from around the world. And all of these facilities are used for only 2 weeks! In 1984, Los Angeles solved these problems by charging a fee for companies who wanted to be official sponsors of the games. Companies like McDonald's paid a lot of money to be part of the Olympics. Many buildings that were already built in the Los Angeles area were also used. The Coliseum where the 1932 games were held was used again and many colleges and universities in the area became playing and living sites.

Adapted from McGee & Richgels, 1985; Smith & Tompkins, 1988.

FIGURE 2.15   Guidelines for Choosing Informational Books

1. Does the author stimulate children's curiosity and wonder?
2. Is the author qualified to write a book on this subject?
3. Is the information accurate, complete, and up-to-date?
4. Is there a balance between facts and theories?
5. Does the author use facts to support generalizations?
6. Is the information presented without anthropomorphism (assigning human characteristics and feelings to animals, plants, or objects)?
7. Are there any racial, cultural, or sexual stereotypes?
8. Is the scientific method or analytical thinking demonstrated?
9. Is the organization clear and logical?
10. Is vocabulary related to the subject introduced in the text?
11. Do illustrations (including photographs and charts) complement and clarify the text?
12. Does the author use a lively and stimulating writing style?
13. Are reference aids, such as a table of contents, a glossary, and an index, included?
14. Does the design of the book enhance the clarity, organization, and readability of the book?
15. For what age child is this book appropriate?

Adapted from Sutherland & Arbuthnot, 1986; Huck, Hepler & Hickman, 1987; Norton, 1991; and Vardell, 1991.

Elements of Poetry

Poetry has very compact language in which carefully chosen words create images, play with rhyme and rhythm, repeat sounds within a word or stanza, and imitate sounds. The arrangement of words, lines, and stanzas of the poem on the page is also important. Usually poems are arranged in lines, but sometimes poems are arranged in shapes on the page. For example, in *Seeing Things: A Book of Poems* (1974), Robert Froman arranged the words of his poems as waves, telephone poles, and light bulbs to create the images in shape as well as in words.

Rhythm and Rhyme.   *Rhythm* is the pattern of accented and unaccented syllables in lines of poetry, and *rhyme* is matched ending sounds of words, usually at the end of lines of poetry. Together rhythm and rhyme create the musical qualities of a poem, and children respond to this word play, often preferring poems with strong rhythm and rhyme. One reason young children enjoy Mother Goose rhymes is their delight in the rhyme and rhythm. Similarly, school-age children amuse themselves with jump rope rhymes, street chants, and other verses. Many poems written for children have rhythm and rhyme, such as Jack Prelutsky's nighttime poems in *My Parents Think I'm Sleeping* (1985) and Mary O'Neill's collection of color poems *Hailstones and Halibut Bones* (1961).

Alliteration.   *Alliteration* is the repetition of initial sounds in consecutive words or in words in close proximity to one another. Repeating the same initial sound makes poetry and tongue twisters fun to read, and children enjoy reading and reciting alliterative verses in wordplay books such as *A My Name Is Alice* (Bayer, 1984) and *Alison's Zinnia* (Lobel, 1990).

Onomatopoeia.   Another aspect of sound is onomatopoeia. Often poets add sound words, such as *crack* or *hiss* to their poems to represent actions. One example of onomatopoeia is David McCord's "The Pickety Fence" (1980) in which he uses words to imitate the sound of hitting a picket fence with a stick. Students enjoy reading poems because it is so much fun to add the sound effects and play with words. Sometimes students work together, and while one student reads the poem aloud, the other student does an accompaniment of sound words.

Repetition.   Sometimes certain words or phrases are repeated in a poem for specific emphasis or to develop a theme. In Langston Hughes' poem "Dreams" (Prelutsky, 1983), the same line begins each stanza, and the word *because* is repeated in almost every line of Mary Ann Hoberman's poem "Giraffes" (Carle, 1989). Children enjoy reading poems with repetition, and the repeated words and lines make the poem easier for beginning readers to manage. When students are doing choral reading, they often choose poems with repetition and read the repetitions together as a chorus.

Imagery.   Poets paint pictures or images with the words they carefully choose and arrange in their poems. To create these mental images, they use descriptions, comparisons, and sensory words. For example, in Tennyson's "The Eagle" (Prelutsky, 1983), his vivid descriptions of the bird make you feel as though you can actually see the eagle in your mind, and in Carl Sandburg's quiet poem "Fog" (Prelutsky, 1983), his comparison of fog to a cat makes you see fog in a new and fresh way. Students are impressed with imagery and often name poems with strong images as the most memorable, if not the most fun to read and share.

Children's Favorite Poems

Children have definite preferences about which poems they like best, just as adults do. Fisher and Natarella (1982) surveyed the poetry preferences of first, second, and third graders; Terry (1974) investigated fourth, fifth, and sixth graders' preferences; and Kutiper (1985) researched seventh, eighth, and ninth graders' preferences. The results of these three studies are important for teachers to consider when they select poems to share with children. The most popular forms of poetry were limericks and narrative poems; least popular were haiku and free verse. In addition, children preferred humorous poems, poems about animals, and poems about familiar experiences. The most important elements were rhyme, rhythm, and sound. Primary grade children preferred traditional poetry, middle graders preferred modern poetry, and upper grade students preferred rhyming verse. The 10 best-liked poems for each grade group are ranked in Figure 2.17. The researchers found that children in all three studies liked poetry, enjoyed listening to poetry read aloud, and could give reasons they liked or disliked particular poems.

Guidelines for Choosing Poems

The research suggests that children like poetry with rhythm and rhyme, humorous poems, and poems that tell a story. Beyond these basic qualities, it is probably wise to have a wide selection of poetry books in the classroom and have students choose

FIGURE 2.16   Books of Poetry

Picture Book Versions of Single Poems

Brown, R. (1988). *Ladybug, ladybug.* New York: Dutton. (P–M)

Carroll, L. (1977). (Ill. by J. B. Zalben). *Lewis Carroll's Jabberwocky.* New York: Warne. (M–U)

Degen, B. (1983). *Jamberry.* New York: Harper & Row. (P)

Field, E. (1982). (Ill. by S. Jeffers). *Wynken, Blynken, and Nod.* New York: Dutton. (P)

Frost, R. (1988). (Ill. by E. Young). *Birches.* New York: Henry Holt. (U)

Lear, E. (1986). (Ill. by L. B. Cauley). *The owl and the pussycat.* New York: Putnam. (P–M)

Longfellow, H. W. (1990). (Ill. by T. Rand). *Paul Revere's ride.* New York: Dutton. (M–U)

Mahy, M. (1987). *17 kings and 42 elephants.* New York: Dial. (M)

Moore, C. (1980). *The night before Christmas.* New York: Holiday House. (P–M)

Noyes, A. (1981). (Ill. by C. Keeping). *The highwayman.* Oxford, England: Oxford University Press. (U)

Stevenson, R. L. (1984). (Ill. by D. Saldutti). *The moon.* New York: Harper & Row. (M)

Thayer, E. L. (1988). (Ill. by P. Polacco). *Casey at the bat: A ballad of the republic, sung in the year 1888.* New York: Putnam. (M–U)

Westcott, N. B. (1988). *The lady with the alligator purse.* Boston: Little, Brown. (P–M)

Specialized Collections

Carle, E. (1989). *Animals, animals.* New York: Philomel. (P–M)

Dickinson, E. (1978). *I'm nobody! Who are you? Poems of Emily Dickinson for children.* Owing Mills, MD: Stemmer House. (M–U)

Fleischman, P. (1985). *I am phoenix: Poems for two voices.* New York: Harper & Row. (M–U)

Fleischman, P. (1988). *Joyful noise: Poems for two voices.* New York: Harper & Row. (M–U)

Frost, R. (1982). *A swinger of birches: Poems of Robert Frost for young people.* Owing Mills, MD: Stemmer House. (U)

Greenfield, E. (1988). *Under the Sunday tree.* New York: Harper & Row. (M)

Hopkins, L. B. (1984). *Surprises* (An I can read book). New York: Harper & Row. (P)

---

their own favorite poems. Children's choice of poems may be very different from the teacher's. With this caution in mind, a list of guidelines for choosing poems and books of poetry is presented in Figure 2.18.

MAKING DECISIONS ABOUT CHOOSING LITERATURE FOR CHILDREN

In the case studies at the beginning of this chapter, Mr. Penton, Mrs. Levi, and Ms. Missakian were familiar with the wide range of books available for children today. Because they knew about literature, they were able to make wise choices and connect language arts and literature with social studies and science. Teachers who want to use literature as the basis for their reading programs must be knowledgeable about children's literature.

The first step in becoming knowledgeable about children's literature is to read a great many of the stories, informational books, and poems available for children today. Children's librarians and the salespeople in children's bookstores are very help-

Hopkins, L. B. (1987). *Click, rumble, roar: Poems about machines.* New York: Crowell. (M)

Lewis, R. (1965). *In a spring garden.* New York: Dial. (haiku) (M–U)

Livingston, M. C. (1985). *Celebrations.* New York: Holiday House. (M)

Lobel, A. (1983). *The book of pigericks.* New York: Harper and Row. (limericks) (P–M)

Livingston, M. C. (1986). *Earth songs.* New York: Holiday House. (See also *Sea songs* and *Space songs.*) (M–U)

Pomerantz, C. (1982). *If I had a paka: Poems in 11 languages.* New York: Greenwillow. (M–U)

Prelutsky, J. (1981). *It's Christmas.* New York: Scholastic. (Collections for other holidays, too.) (P–M)

Prelutsky, J. (1984). *The new kid on the block.* New York: Greenwillow. (P–M)

Prelutsky, J. (1989). *Poems of A. Nonny Mouse.* New York: Knopf. (P–M)

Prelutsky, J. (1990). *Something big has been here.* New York: Greenwillow. (P–M)

Silverstein, S. (1974). *Where the sidewalk ends.* New York: Harper & Row. (P–M–U)

Yolen, J. (1990). *Bird watch: A book of poetry.* New York: Philomel. (M–U)

Comprehensive Anthologies

de Paola, T. (compiler). (1988). *Tomie de Paola's book of poems.* New York: Putnam. (P–M)

de Regniers, B. S., Moore, E., White, M. M., & Carr, J. (compilers). (1988). *Sing a song of popcorn: Every child's book of poems.* New York: Scholastic. (P–M–U)

Dunning, S., Leuders, E., & Smith, H. (compilers). (1967). *Reflections on a gift of watermelon pickle, and other modern verse.* New York: Lothrop, Lee & Shepard. (U)

Kennedy, X. J. (compiler). (1985). *The forgetful wishing well: Poems for young people.* New York: McElderry Books. (U)

Kennedy, X. J., & Kennedy, D. M. (compilers). (1982). *Knock at a star: A child's introduction to poetry.* Boston: Little, Brown. (P–M–U)

Prelutsky, J. (compiler). (1983). *The Random House book of poetry for children.* New York: Random House. (P–M–U)

ful and willing to suggest books for teachers. As teachers read, they should keep in mind the guidelines for selecting stories (Figure 2.9), informational books (Figure 2.15), and poems (Figure 2.18) and think about which of the books they would want to share with students.

Each year a number of books written for children are recognized for excellence and receive awards. The two best-known awards are the Caldecott Medal for excellence in illustration and the Newbery Medal for excellence in writing. Another prestigious award is the Coretta Scott King Award, which is given to black authors and illustrators for their outstanding contributions to children's literature. Lists of the previous winners of the Caldecott and Newbery Medal, honor books, and books that have received the Coretta Scott King Award are presented in Appendix A. Teachers should be familiar with many of these outstanding books.

Many professional magazines and journals provide reviews of newly published children's books and other information about choosing books for children. In these reviews, bibliographical information is provided, the book is summarized, appropriate grade levels are suggested, and a critical review of the book is offered. A list of professional magazines and journals is presented in Figure 2.19. Most of these resources

FIGURE 2.17   Children's Favorite Poems

First, Second, and Third Graders' Favorite Poems

Rank	Title	Author
1	"The Young Lady of Lynn"	Unknown
2	"The Little Turtle"	Vachel Lindsay
3	"Bad Boy"	Lois Lenski
4	"Little Miss Muffet"	Paul Dehn
5	"Cat"	Eleanor Farjeon
6	"Adventures of Isabel"	Ogden Nash
7	"Mummy Slept Late and Daddy Fixed Breakfast"	John Ciardi
8	"The Lurpp Is on the Loose"	Jack Prelutsky
9	"A Bookworm of Curious Breed"	Ann Hoberman
10	"The Owl and the Pussy-cat"	Edward Lear

Fourth, Fifth, and Sixth Graders' Favorite Poems

Rank	Title	Author
1	"Mummy Slept Late and Daddy Fixed Breakfast"	John Ciardi
2	"Fire! Fire!"	Unknown
3	"There was an old man of Blackheath"	Unknown
4	"Little Miss Muffet"	Paul Dehn
5	"There once was an old kangaroo"	Edward S. Mullins
6	"There was a young lady of Niger"	Unknown
7	"Hughbert and the Glue"	Karla Kuskin
8	"Betty Barter"	Unknown
9	"Lone Dog"	Irene Rutherford McLeod
10	"Eletelephony"	Laura E. Richards

Seventh, Eighth, and Ninth Graders' Favorite Poems

Rank	Title	Author
1	"Sick"	Shel Silverstein
2	"Oh, Teddy Bear"	Jack Prelutsky
3	"Mother Doesn't Want a Dog"	Judith Viorst
4	"Mummy Slept Late and Daddy Fixed Breakfast"	John Ciardi
5	"The Unicorn"	Shel Silverstein
6	"Why Nobody Pets the Lion at the Zoo"	John Ciardi
7	"Homework"	Jane Yolen
8	"Dreams"	Langston Hughes
9	"Questions"	Marci Ridlon
10	"Willie Ate a Worm Today"	Jack Prelutsky

Fisher & Natarella, 1982, p. 344; Terry, 1974, p. 15; Kutiper, 1985, p. 51.

FIGURE 2.18   Guidelines for Choosing Poems

Poems

1. Is the poem lively, with exciting meters and rhythms?
2. Is the poem humorous?
3. Does the poem emphasize the sounds of language and encourage wordplay?
4. Does the poem encourage children to see or hear the world in a new way?
5. Does the poem tell a well-paced story?
6. Does the poem allow children to feel emotions?
7. Does the poem create an image that appeals to a child's imagination?
8. Does the poem encourage children to make comparisons?
9. Is the poem good enough for children to want to hear it again and again?

Books of Poetry

1. Is the cover of the book appealing to children?
2. Do poems in the book meet the criteria listed above?
3. Are the poems arranged on the page so as to not overwhelm children?
4. Do the illustrations clarify and extend the image the poem creates, or do they merely distract the reader?
5. Are there reference aids such as a table of contents or indexes?

Adapted from Norton, 1991.

FIGURE 2.19   Professional Magazines and Journals that Review Children's Books

Book Links
American Library Association
50 E. Huron Street
Chicago, IL 60611

Horn Book
14 Beacon Street
Boston, MA 02108

Language Arts
National Council of Teachers of English
1111 Kenyon Road
Urbana, IL 60801

The New Advocate
Christopher-Gordon Publishers
480 Washington Street
Norwood, MA 02062

The Reading Teacher
International Reading Association
800 Barksdale Road
Newark, DE 19711

School Library Journal
249 West 17th Street
New York, NY 10011

FIGURE 2.20   Summary Chart for Decision Tree

Decision Tree

Chapter 1	Using Literature in the Reading Program
	Choosing Literature for Children
	• **Read a wide variety of stories, informational books and poems.**
	• **Use the guidelines presented in this chapter for choosing stories, informational books, and poems.**
Chapter 2	• **Consult reviews of children's books published in professional magazines and journals.**
	• **Share literature with children and note their responses and preferences.**
Chapter 3	Learning About Authors and Illustrators
Chapter 4	Identifying Perspectives on Reading Instruction
Chapter 5	Teaching from a Reader Response Perspective
Chapter 6	Teaching from a Critical Perspective
Chapter 7	Teaching from an Interactive Perspective
Chapter 8	Putting It All Together
Chapter 9	Assessing Students' Learning

are available in school libraries and local public libraries. Teachers may also want to subscribe to one or two of them.

We further recommend that teachers share stories, informational books, and poems with children and ask them for their opinions and preferences. So often teachers use their own adult preferences and recommendations made by other adults in deciding which books to use with children. Sometimes the child's point of view is different than ours. Each year the International Reading Association publishes a list of "Children's Choices" in the October issue of *The Reading Teacher,* which is another good resource for teachers who want to keep up-to-date about books for children.

In summary, as teachers become familiar with children's literature, they should consider the following points:

- Read a wide variety of stories, informational books and poems.
- Use the guidelines presented in this chapter for choosing stories, informational books, and poems.
- Consult reviews of children's books published in professional magazines and journals.
- Share literature with children and note their responses and preferences.

This information is added to the decision-making diagram shown in Figure 2.20 that was begun in the first chapter and will be added to throughout this book.

REFERENCES

Bosma, B. (1987). *Fairy tales, fables, legends, and myths.* New York: Teachers College Press.

Fisher, C. J., & Natarella, M. A. (1982). Young children's preferences in poetry: A national survey of first, second, and third graders. *Research in the Teaching of English, 16,* 339–354.

Huck, C. S., Hepler, S., & Hickman, J. (1987). *Children's literature in the elementary school* (4th ed.). New York: Holt, Rinehart & Winston.

Kutiper, K. (1985). *A survey of the poetry preferences of seventh, eighth, and ninth graders.* Unpublished doctoral dissertation, University of Houston.

Larrick, N. (1991). *Let's do a poem: Introducing poetry to children.* New York: Delacorte.

Lehr, S. S. (1991). *The child's developing sense of theme: Responses to literature.* New York: Teachers College Press.

Lukens, R. (1990). *A critical handbook of children's literature* (4th ed.). New York: HarperCollins.

McGee, L. M., & Richgels, D. J. (1985). Teaching expository text structure to elementary students. *The Reading Teacher, 38,* 739–748.

Meyer, B. J., & Freedle, R. O. (1984). Effects of discourse type on recall. *American Educational Research Journal, 21,* 121–143.

Newkirk, T. (1989). *More than stories: The range of children's writing.* Portsmouth, NH: Heinemann.

Niles, O. S. (1974). Organization perceived. In H. L. Herber (Ed.), *Perspectives in reading: Developing study skills in secondary schools.* Newark, DE: International Reading Association.

Norton, D. E. (1991). *Through the eyes of a child: An introduction to children's literature* (3rd ed.). New York: Merrill/Macmillan.

Opie, I., & Opie, P. (1959). *The lore and language of school children.* Oxford, England: Oxford University Press.

Pappas, C. C. (1991). Fostering full access to literacy by including information books. *Language Arts, 68,* 449–462.

Rosenblatt, L. M. (1991). Literature-S.O.S! *Language Arts, 68,* 444–448.

Russell, D. L. (1991). *Literature for children: A short introduction.* New York: Longman.

Smith, P. L., & Tompkins, G. E. (1988). Structured note-taking: A new strategy for content area readers. *Journal of Reading, 32,* 46–53.

Sutherland, Z., & Arbuthnot, M. H. (1986). *Children and books* (7th ed.). Glenview, IL: Scott Foresman.

Terry, A. (1974). *Children's poetry preferences: A national survey of upper elementary grades* (NCTE Research Report No. 16). Urbana, IL: National Council of Teachers of English.

Thorndyke, P. (1977). Cognitive structures in comprehension and memory of narrative discourse. *Cognitive Psychology, 9,* 77–110.

Vardell, S. (1991). A new 'picture of the world': The NCTE Orbis Pictus Award for outstanding nonfiction for children. *Language Arts, 68,* 474–479.

CHILDREN'S LITERATURE REFERENCES

Adams, R. (1974). *Watership down.* New York: Macmillan.

Adler, D. A. (1989). *A picture book of Martin Luther King, Jr.* New York: Holiday House.

Adoff, A. (1979). *Eats Poems.* New York: Lothrop.

Ahlberg, J., & Ahlberg, A. (1986). *The jolly postman or other people's letters.* Boston: Little, Brown.

Alexander, L. (1978). *The first two lives of Lukas-Kasha.* New York: Dutton.

Aliki. (1981). *Digging up dinosaurs.* New York: Harper & Row.

Aliki. (1983). *A medieval feast.* New York: Crowell.

Asbjornsen, P. C., & Moe, J. (1980). *The runaway pancake.* New York: Larousse.

Atwater, R., & Atwater, F. (1966). *Mr. Popper's penguins.* Boston: Little, Brown.

Bailey, C. S. (1968). *Miss Hickory.* New York: Viking.

Barrie, J. (1950). *Peter Pan.* New York: Scribner.

Barton, B. (1982). *Airport.* New York: Harper & Row.

Base, G. (1987). *Animalia.* New York: Abrams.

Bayer, J. (1984). *A my name is Alice.* New York: Dial.

Benjamin, A. (1987). *Rat-a-tat, pitter pat.* New York: Crowell.

Bierhorst, J. (1987). *Doctor coyote: A native American Aesop's fables.* (Trans.). New York: Macmillan.

Bishop, C. (1938). *The five Chinese brothers.* New York: Coward, McCann & Geoghegan.

Blume, J. (1972). *Tales of a fourth grade nothing.* New York: Dutton.

Brown, M. (1961). *Once a mouse.* New York: Aladdin Books.

Bryan, A. (1971). *The ox of the wonderful horns and other African folktales.* New York: Atheneum.

Burch, R. (1966). *Queenie Peavy.* New York: Viking.

Burnford, S. (1961). *The incredible journey.* New York: Little, Brown.

Burningham, J. (1984). *Wobble pop.* New York: Viking.

Byars, B. (1970). *The summer of the swans.* New York: Viking.

Carle, E. (1980). *Twelve tales from Aesop.* New York: Philomel.

Carle, E. (1984). *The very busy spider.* New York: Philomel.

Carle, E. (1989). *Animals, animals.* New York: Philomel.

Carroll, L. (1977). (Ill. by J. B. Zalben). *Lewis Carroll's Jabberwocky.* New York: Warne.

Carroll, L. (1984). *Alice's adventures in wonderland.* New York: Macmillan.

Cauley, L. B. (1979). *The ugly duckling.* New York: Harcourt Brace Jovanovich.

Cleary, B. (1981). *Ramona Quimby, age 8.* New York: Morrow.

Cleaver, E. (1985). *ABC.* New York: Atheneum.

Coerr, E. (1986). *The Josefina story quilt.* New York: Harper & Row.

Cooney, B. (1958). *Chanticleer and the fox.* New York: Crowell.

Cooper, S. (1973). *The dark is rising.* New York: Atheneum.

Crews, D. (1980). *Truck.* New York: Greenwillow.

Crews, D. (1984). *School bus.* New York: Puffin.

Dahl, R. (1964). *Charlie and the chocolate factory.* New York: Knopf.

Dahl, R. (1984). *Boy.* New York: Farrar, Straus & Giroux.

de Paola, T. (1983). The legend of the bluebonnet. New York: Putnam.

Ehlert, L. (1989). *Color zoo.* New York: Lippincott.

Ehrlich, A. (1982). *The snow queen.* New York: Dial.

Fleischman, P. (1988). *Joyful noise: Poems for two voices.* New York: Harper & Row.

Fox, P. (1973). *The slave dancer.* New York: Bradbury Press.

Freedman, R. (1987). *Lincoln: A photobiography.* New York: Clarion.

Fritz, J. (1976). *Will you sign here, John Hancock?* New York: Coward-McCann.

Fritz, J. (1979). *Stonewall.* New York: Putnam.

Froman, R. (1974). *Seeing things: A book of poems.* New York: Crowell.

Galdone, P. (1961). *The three wishes.* New York: McGraw-Hill.

Galdone, P. (1968). *Henny Penny.* New York: Clarion.

Galdone, P. (1970). *The three little pigs.* New York: Seabury.

Galdone, P. (1975). *The gingerbread boy.* New York: Seabury.

George, J. C. (1972). *Julie of the wolves.* New York: Harper & Row.

Gibbons, G. (1987). *Weather forecasting.* New York: Four Winds Press.

Goodall, J. (1988). *My life with the chimpanzees.* New York: Minstrel Books.

Grahame, K. (1961). *The wind in the willows.* New York: Scribner.

Greene, B. (1973). *Summer of my German soldier.* New York: Dutton.

Hague, M. (1985). *Aesop's fables.* New York: Holt, Rinehart & Winston.

Hamilton, V. (1985). *The people could fly: Black American folktales.* New York: Knopf.

Harris, J. C. (1986). *Jump! The adventures of Brer Rabbit.* San Diego: Harcourt Brace Jovanovich.

Heins, P. (1974). *Snow white.* Boston: Atlantic/Little, Brown.

Hoban, T. (1978). *Is it red? Is it yellow? Is it blue?* New York: Greenwillow.

Hodges, M. (1972). *The fire bringer: A Paiute Indian legend.* Boston: Little, Brown.

Hodges, M. (1973). *Persephone and the springtime.* Boston: Little, Brown.

Hoguet, S. R. (1983). *I unpacked my grandmother's trunk.* New York: Dutton.

Houston, G. (1992). *My great-aunt Arizona.* New York: HarperCollins.

Howe, J. (1989). *Jack and the beanstalk.* Boston: Little, Brown.

Hunt, J. (1989). *Illuminations.* New York: Bradbury Press.

Huynh, Q. N. (1982). *The land I lost: Adventures of a boy in Vietnam.* New York: Harper & Row.

Hyman, T. S. (1983). *Little red riding hood.* New York: Holiday House.

Isadora, R. (1989). *The princess and the frog.* New York: Greenwillow.

Joosse, B. M. (1991). *Mama, do you love me?* San Francisco: Chronicle Books.

Keeping, C. (1982). *Beowulf.* Oxford, England: Oxford University Press.

Kellogg, S. (1987). *Aster aardvark's alphabet adventures.* New York: Morrow.

Kellogg, S. (1988). *Johnny Appleseed.* New York: Morrow.

Kipling, R. (1987). *Just so stories.* (Illustrated by M. Foreman). New York: Viking.

Konigsburg, E. L. (1983). *From the mixed-up files of Mrs. Basil E. Frankweiler.* New York: Atheneum.

Lalicki, B. (1984). *If there were dreams to sell.* New York: Lothrop, Lee & Shepard.

Lang, A. (1981). *Aladdin.* New York: Viking.

Lasker, J. (1976). *Merry ever after.* New York: Viking.

Lasky, K. (1983). *Sugaring time.* New York: Macmillan.

Lauber, P. (1986). *Volcano: The eruption and healing of Mount St. Helen's.* New York: Bradbury.

Le Gallienne, E. (1965). *The nightingale.* New York: Harper & Row.

Le Guin, U. (1968). *The wizard of earthsea.* New York: Parnassus.

L'Engle, M. (1962). *A wrinkle in time.* New York: Farrar, Straus & Giroux.

Lester, J. (1987). *The tales of Uncle Remus.* New York: Dial.

Levine, E. (1986). *. . . If you traveled west in a covered wagon.* New York: Scholastic.

Lewis, C. S. (1950). *The lion, the witch, and the wardrobe.* New York: Macmillan.

Lionni, L. (1969). *Alexander and the wind-up mouse.* New York: Pantheon.

Lobel, A. (1972). *Frog and toad together.* New York: Harper & Row.

Lobel, A. (1980). *Fables.* New York: Harper & Row.

Lobel, A. (1981). *On market street.* New York: Greenwillow.

Lobel, A. (1983). *The book of pigericks.* New York: Harper & Row.

Lobel, A. (1990). *Alison's zinnia.* New York: Greenwillow.

Lofting, H. (1920). *The adventures of Dr. Dolittle.* Philadelphia: Lippincott.

Longfellow, H. W. (1990). *Paul Revere's ride.* New York: Dutton.

Macaulay, D. (1977). *Castle.* Boston: Houghton Mifflin.

MacDonald, S. (1986). *Alphabatics.* New York: Bradbury.

MacLachlan, P. (1985). *Sarah, plain and tall.* New York: Harper & Row.

Martin, B., Jr. (1983). *Brown bear, brown bear, what do you see?* New York: Holt, Rinehart & Winston.

Martin, B., Jr. (1991). *Polar bear, polar bear, what do you hear?* New York: Holt, Rinehart & Winston.

Martin, B., Jr., & Archambault, J. (1985). *The ghost-eye tree.* New York: Holt, Rinehart & Winston.

Martin, B., Jr., & Archambault, J. (1986). *Barn dance.* New York: Henry Holt.

Martin, B., Jr., & Archambault, J. (1989). *Chicka chicka boom boom.* New York: Henry Holt.

Mayer, M. (1978). *Beauty and the beast.* New York: Macmillan.

Mayer, M. (1987). *The pied piper of Hamelin.* New York: Macmillan.

Mayer, M. (1987). *The ugly duckling.* New York: Macmillan.

McCloskey, R. (1969). *Make way for ducklings.* Boston: Houghton Mifflin.

McCord, D. (1980). *One at a time: His collected poems for the young.* Boston: Little, Brown.

McMillan, B. (1988). *Growing colors.* New York: Lothrop.

Merriam, E. (1987). *Halloween ABC.* New York: Macmillan.

Milne, A. A. (1956). *The house at pooh corner.* New York: Dutton.

Milne, A. A. (1961). *Winnie-the-pooh.* New York: Dutton.

Moore, C. (1980). *The night before Christmas.* New York: Holiday House.

Most, B. (1978). *If the dinosaurs came back.* New York: Harcourt Brace Jovanovich.

Munsch, R. N. (1980). *The paper bag princess.* Toronto: Annick Press.

Musgrove, M. (1976). *Ashanti to Zulu: African traditions.* New York: Dial.

Newton, P. (1990). *The stonecutter.* New York: Putnam.

Numeroff, L. J. (1985). *If you give a mouse a cookie.* New York: Harper & Row.

O'Brien, R. (1971). *Mrs. Frisby and the rats of NIMH.* New York: Atheneum.

O'Dell, S. (1960). *Island of the blue dolphins.* Boston: Houghton Mifflin.

O'Neill, M. (1961). *Hailstones and halibut bones.* Garden City, NY: Doubleday.

Paterson, K. (1977). *Bridge to Terabithia.* New York: Crowell.

Perrault, C. (1990). *Puss in boots.* New York: Farrar, Straus & Giroux.

Prelutsky, J. (1983). *The Random House book of poetry for children.* New York: Random House.

Prelutsky, J. (1984). *The new kid on the block.* New York: Greenwillow.

Prelutsky, J. (1985). *My parents think I'm sleeping.* New York: Greenwillow.

Prelutsky, J. (1988). *Tyrannosaurus was a beast.* New York: Greenwillow.

Provensen, A. (1990). *The buck stops here.* New York: HarperCollins.

Ransome, A. (1968). *The fool of the world and the flying ship.* New York: Farrar, Straus & Giroux.

Rice, E. (1979). *Once upon a wood: Ten tales from Aesop.* New York: Greenwillow.

Rockwell, A., & Rockwell, H. (1972). *Machines.* New York: Harper & Row.

Roop, P., & Roop, C. (1985). *Keep the lights burning, Abbie.* Minneapolis: Carolrhoda Books.

Scieszka, J. (1989). *The true story of the three little pigs.* New York: Viking.

Sendak, M. (1963). *Where the wild things are.* New York: Harper & Row.

Seuss, Dr. (1988). *Green eggs and ham.* New York: Random House.

Speare, E. G. (1958). *The witch of Blackbird Pond.* Boston: Houghton Mifflin.

Steig, W. (1969). *Sylvester and the magic pebble.* New York: Windmill Books.

Steig, W. (1982). *Doctor De Soto.* New York: Farrar, Straus & Giroux.

Steig, W. (1986). *Brave Irene.* New York: Farrar, Straus & Giroux.

Sutcliff, R. (1977). *The chronicles of Robin Hood.* New York: Oxford University Press.

Thurber, J. (1943). *Many moons.* New York: Harcourt Brace Jovanovich.

Tolkien, J. R. R. (1938). *The hobbit.* Boston: Houghton Mifflin.

Tolkien, J. R. R. (1974). *The lord of the rings.* Boston: Houghton Mifflin.

Travers, P. L. (1934). *Mary Poppins.* New York: Harcourt Brace Jovanovich.

Van Allsburg, C. (1981). *Jumanji.* Boston: Houghton Mifflin.

Van Allsburg, C. (1985). *The polar express.* Boston: Houghton Mifflin.

Viorst, J. (1977). *Alexander and the terrible, horrible, no good, very bad day.* New York: Atheneum.

Waber, B. (1972). *Ira sleeps over.* Boston: Houghton Mifflin.

Westcott, N. B. (1984). *The emperor's new clothes.* Boston: Atlantic.

White, E. B. (1952). *Charlotte's web.* New York: Harper & Row.

Winter, J. (1991). *Diego.* New York: Knopf.

Yolen, J. (1986). *The sleeping beauty.* New York: Knopf.

Zemach, M. (1988). *The three little pigs.* New York: Farrar, Straus & Giroux.

CHAPTER 3

LEARNING ABOUT AUTHORS AND ILLUSTRATORS

In this chapter you will learn to make decisions about:

- **Becoming informed about children's favorite authors and illustrators**
- **Learning about artistic elements, media, styles, and how they are used in children's literature**
- **Supporting students as they develop a concept of author and a concept of illustrator**
- **Focusing students' attention on illustrations and helping them develop visual literacy**
- **Teaching minilessons about authors, illustrators, and illustration**
- **Planning and teaching a focus unit on an author, illustrator, or type of illustration**

THESE CASE STUDIES DEMONSTRATE two ways that elementary students learn about authors and illustrators.

A CASE IN POINT

Mrs. Smiley's Class Learns About Ezra Jack Keats

Mrs. Smiley's first grade class is studying Ezra Jack Keats. In the library center, Mrs. Smiley has a display of Keats' books and a picture of the author/illustrator on the wall over the display. Mrs. Smiley begins the author study on a snowy day by reading aloud his Caldecott-winning book *The Snowy Day* (1962), a story about Peter's experiences playing in the snow. After reading, the children talk about their snow experiences and draw and write their own snowy day books.

The next day, Mrs. Smiley reads two more stories about Peter. She reads *Peter's Chair* (1967) about a time Peter was so upset that his baby furniture is being repainted for his baby sister that he wanted to run away from home. The chil-

dren talk about the story and their own feelings about their brothers and sisters. She also reads *Whistle for Willie* (1964), about a time Peter tries to learn to whistle so that he can whistle to call his dog Willie. The children demonstrate their whistling talents and talk about the story.

Mrs. Smiley explains that the first graders will get to know a number of children who are characters in Ezra Jack Keats' books. She suggests that they make a chart of the characters. She has photocopied pictures of Peter from each of the books she has read, and students cut out the pictures and glue them on a chart that they decide to call "The Characters in Ezra Jack Keats' Books." The class also adds a picture of Willie and will continue to add pictures of Archie, Louie, and other characters in Keats' urban neighborhood. As Mrs. Smiley reads each book, she tape-records her reading and then places the tape and a copy of the book at the listening center so that students can "reread" it.

One day the first graders watch the Weston Woods filmstrip about author/illustrator Ezra Jack Keats in which he demonstrates how he uses paint and collage to illustrate his books. Mrs. Smiley collects a variety of art materials for the first graders to experiment with. After some practice making collages, they decide to create a paint and collage mural about the urban neighborhood and the characters in Keats' books.

Today Mrs. Smiley reads *Hi, Cat!* (1970), and students talk about their pets. Then Mrs. Smiley asks, "How do you know that *Hi, Cat!* is one of Ezra Jack Keats' books?" Students mention the familiar characters, the real-life events in the story, and the paint and collage illustrations. After their discussion, students paint faces on large brown grocery bags as the characters did in the story and assume roles of the characters in the book to act it out.

During the three weeks that Mrs. Smiley's class spends on this author/illustrator study, the students will listen to 10 of Keats' stories read aloud and reread them many times at the listening center and during independent reading time. They will talk about the characters and relate the experiences described in the stories to their own lives. They will explore the artistic media that Keats used and create their own art. Each child will also create a "box" project about a favorite book. They will draw a banner, make an object, write a booklet, or construct something related to one of Keats' books and place the completed project in a shoe box. On the last day of the author/illustrator study, students will share their projects with their classmates.

A CASE IN POINT

Mr. Jurey's Students Learn About Expressionism

In Mr. Jurey's art class, seventh grade students are studying expressionism, a style in which artists use brilliant colors and somewhat abstract or simple shapes. Mr. Jurey begins the unit by sharing prints of expressionistic art, such as Van Gogh's "The Starry Night," and reading *Meet Matisse* (Munthe, 1983). As they talk and read about expressionism, the class adds these words to their word wall: *simplicity, vibrate, space, color, sensations, impressions, forms, cut-outs, cold and hot colors, brillant, swirling lines, geometric shapes, texture, strong feelings, melody, rhythm, bold patterns, abstract, negative and positive shapes, dark background, images, balance, personalized vision, light and dark colors, colors play with each other, colors vary,* and *dappled texture.* Students also experiment with cut-outs. They cut shapes from paper they have painted and texturized and play with colored backgrounds, much like Matisse did.

Next students look for picture books in the school library in which illustrators have used brilliant colors and simple shapes in an expressionistic style. They work in small groups to read the books and closely examine the illustrations. Today they share the books with the class and explain why the illustrations are expressionistic:

- Chris shares Lois Ehlert's *Feathers for Lunch* (1990), a rhyming story about an escaped housecat who tries to catch 12 birds but ends up only eating feathers for lunch. He explains, "Lois Ehlert's illustrations are expressionistic. You can see that they are brightly colored and grab your eye. These pictures of the cat, the birds, and the plants are built from basic shapes like circles and squares. Lois Ehlert used cut-outs. It looks like she built the pictures using white pieces of paper that she had brushed with watercolor paint. She also cut pieces of tissue paper and colored paper to vary the texture. You see the birds and the cat up close and get a very strong impression of prey and predator."

• Anna shares Vera B. Williams's Caldecott Honor Book *A Chair for My Mother* (1982), a story of a little girl, her mother, and grandmother who save their money to buy a comfortable armchair after all their furniture is lost in a fire. She explains, "These colors are really vivid, and that's why Vera B. Williams's illustrations are expressionistic. She uses lots of bright reds and blues in the pictures. Even though the colors are bright, they are soft and the feeling is warm and homey. You know the people in this family love each other. You can see that every bit of the page is colored—even behind the words—and the colorful border around each page adds to the intensity of the illustrations. These illustrations are painted; there are no cut-outs. Mr. Jurey said that Vera B. Williams probably used opaque watercolors."

• Jason shares Gerald McDermott's Caldecott Honor Book *Anansi the Spider* (1972), an African myth about how the moon came to be in the sky. He explains, "Gerald McDermott used bold African designs in this book. The spiders are simple geometric patterns—lines, circles, angles, squares, and triangles. The spiders in the foreground seem to vibrate and the designs in the background are softer and give the texture. Mr. McDermott also used very bright, intense colors. The colors and designs make me think of Africa and the hot climate there. It says in the back of the book that he only used four colors in the book—the primary

colors and black. Orange and green are in some of the illustrations but they were made by mixing the primary colors and, of course, there is white. This book is interesting because the words are left white, and like in Anna's book, the illustrations cover the whole page."

• Michelle shares *Celebrations,* a collection of 16 holiday poems written by Myra Cohn Livingston and illustrated by Leonard Everett Fisher (1985). She explains, "These illustrations were painted with acyrlic paint, and they have a lot of texture because they were painted on textured paper. I think the texture makes the illustrations softer, kind of like a memory. The colors are bright and what you expect for each holiday. You know, the St. Patrick's Day illustration is green and the Valentine's Day illustration is red. Usually Mr. Fisher painted one or two things to symbolize each holiday. For the Fourth of July, there are fireworks in the night sky. They remind me of the stars in Vincent Van Gogh's 'The Starry Night.' The illustrations cover the entire page and the poems are printed on top of the illustrations. I think these illustrations are expressionistic because the colors are intense and soft and the images are simple."

• Will shares Eric Carle's *The Mixed-up Chameleon* (1984), a pattern book about a chameleon who wishes he could be like other animals, and with each wish, the chameleon's appearance changes to incorporate a feature of that animal. At the end, the chameleon decides it is best to be himself. He explains, "I loved this book when I was a child and that's why I chose it. Eric Carle is the neatest illustrator, and I think his illustrations are expressionistic because they are cut-outs and they are brightly colored. The background is light and the cut-outs really stand out. On this page you can see the body, legs and head of the chameleon turned white because he wanted to be a polar bear. And he has pink wings and webbed feet to be like a flamingo. He has a red, bushy fox's tail, and orange goldfish fins. On this page he wants to run like a deer so Eric Carle added antlers. I think Eric Carle used fingerpaint and a pointed stick or something like that to make the texture interesting. The illustrations are simple and I think Eric Carle was smart to do that because the message of the book is so deep."

• Kevin shares *Chicka Chicka Boom Boom* (Martin & Archambault, 1989), an alphabet rhyme about what happens when the letters climb a coconut tree, and illustrated by Lois Ehlert. Kevin explains, "I'm sure this is an expressionistic book. These illustrations are really simple—just cut-outs of the upper and lower case letters and a coconut tree on a white background. The colors are more than bright; they are brilliant. You can see there is a hot-pink and orange polka-dotted border around three sides of each page. I think these illustrations look a lot like Matisse's—especially the palm leaves. There is no texture at all, but balance is important in these illustrations because, when too many letters climb the coconut tree, the trunk bends and the letters fall down. Lois Ehlert placed the shapes on the page very carefully."

Later students will apply what they have learned about expressionism as they write stories or poems and illustrate them in the expressionistic style.

INTRODUCTION

When students read and compare books written by an author, experiment with art media, and locate picture books representative of an artistic style, they are involved in genuine literature study. Literature-based reading as we discuss it in this book is much more than just reading the words on a page. The goal of these literature explorations is to help students acquire personal literary preferences and develop an appreciation for the crafts of writing and illustration.

In this chapter, we focus on authors, illustrators, and illustration. The first section provides information about the people who write and illustrate books, including lists of authors and illustrators recommended for study in the elementary grades. These people have written or illustrated more than one or two books, are known well enough that information about them is available, and many have received awards or other recognition for their work. Then we examine the components of illustration: the visual elements of art, art media used in children's literature, and artistic styles. In the third section, we discuss ways to teach students about authors and illustrators. We conclude this chapter with a section on making decisions about how to incorporate the information about authors and illustrators in literature-based reading classrooms.

PEOPLE WHO WRITE AND ILLUSTRATE BOOKS FOR CHILDREN

Very talented people are writing and illustrating children's books today. Not only do these people share their genius through their books, but they also share something of themselves through letters they write back to children who have written to them, their autobiographical books for children, their visits to schools, and audiovisual productions about their lives which are used in schools. Children are fascinated by favorite authors and illustrators, just as adults are. Adults watch television talk shows to catch a glimpse of a favorite author or stand in line at bookstores to have a favorite author autograph a book; similarly, children want to learn about authors and illustrators of books they have read and enjoyed. Children often decide what book they will read next based on books they have already read by a particular author. They build on this practice when they know some personal facts about authors.

Beyond this fascination, there are other reasons for connecting students with authors and illustrators. Children learn about the crafts of writing and art from authors and illustrators. For example, in a Random House filmstrip (1981), award-winning author and illustrator Arnold Lobel explained how he writes by "unwriting," or deleting excess text. Children want to experiment with this technique after watching the filmstrip. Similarly, after examining how illustrators such as George Ancona and Tana Hoban use photography, students may choose to take photographs to illustrate a class book they are making. As they learn about authors, illustrators, and their crafts, children come to see themselves as writers and illustrators, rather than as students who are completing school assignments when they read and write.

Almost all children who have been given the opportunity to read literature have favorite authors and are familiar with a number of authors and illustrators such as Eric Carle, Beverly Cleary, Jean Fritz, and Chris Van Allsburg. Teachers can build on children's interests by planning units that focus on specific authors and illustrators. Through these units, students are introduced to authors and illustrators they might otherwise miss and become familiar with a wider range of literary and artistic styles.

Authors

Many authors are writing for children today, and more information is available about them than ever before. Although we feature only four authors in this section, we list others who are recommended for study in Figure 3.1. Through these thumbnail sketches, we hope to demonstrate that these people are not only talented writers, but interesting people as well.

Bernard Waber, Author of Picture Books for Children.   Bernard Waber is the author of the popular series of books about Lyle the Crocodile (*The House on East 88th Street,* 1962; *Lyle, Lyle Crocodile,* 1965; *Lyle and the Birthday Party,* 1966; *Lovable Lyle,* 1969; *Lyle Finds His Mother,* 1974; *Funny, Funny Lyle,* 1987). Waber's stories are about Lyle, a crocodile who shares Mr. and Mrs. Primm's home on East 88th Street in New York City. Lyle is a friendly crocodile who can perform many tricks. In the series of books, Lyle moves from one adventure to another. Since Lyle's debut, Waber has collected crocodile bric-a-brac which he uses to decorate his home. Children and friends who enjoyed the Lyle books have given him many stuffed crocodile toys, mobiles, drawings, and dishware.

Perhaps Waber's most popular book may be *Ira Sleeps Over* (1972), the story about a young child who wants to spend the night next door with his best friend Reggie but can't decide whether to take along his teddy bear—the one he always sleeps with. A sequel is *Ira Says Goodbye* (1988) in which his friend Reggie moves away.

FIGURE 3.1   Authors for Focus Units

Verna Aardema (M)	Lillian Hoban (P–M)
David A. Adler (P–M)	Tana Hoban (P)
Arnold Adoff (P–M)	Lee Bennett Hopkins (M)
Lloyd Alexander (U)	Trina Schart Hyman (M)
Aliki (Brandenburg) (P–M)	Ezra Jack Keats (P)
Frank Asch (P–M)	Steven Kellogg (P–M)
Avi (U)	Fernando Krahn (P–M)
Marion Dane Bauer (M–U)	Steven Kroll (P–M)
Byrd Baylor (P–M)	Madeleine L'Engle (U)
Jan Brett (P–M)	Leo Lionni (P–M)
Norman Bridwell (P)	Myra Cohn Livingston (M–U)
Raymond Briggs (P)	Arnold Lobel (P–M)
Bill Brittain (U)	Lois Lowry (M–U)
Marc Brown (P–M)	David Macauley (M–U)
Eve Bunting (M)	James Marshall (P–M)
Robert Burch (U)	Bill Martin, Jr. (P)
John Burningham (M)	Mercer Mayer (M–U)
Betsy Byars (M)	Gerald McDermott (M)
Eric Carle (P)	David McPhail (M)
Lorinda Bryan Cauley (M)	Scott O'Dell (U)
Beverly Cleary (M)	Katherine Paterson (M–U)
Lucille Clifton (P–M)	Bill Peet (M)
Christopher Collier (U)	Patricia Polacco (M)
Barbara Cooney (M)	Beatrix Potter (P–M)
Susan Cooper (U)	Jack Prelutsky (M–U)
Roald Dahl (M–U)	Robert Quackenbush (M)
Tomie de Paola (P–M)	Cynthia Rylant (M)
Lois Ehlert (P)	Maurice Sendak (P–M)
Sid Fleischman (M–U)	Elizabeth George Speare (M–U)
Paula Fox (M–U)	Peter Spier (M)
Russell Freedman (M–U)	William Steig (M)
Don Freeman (P)	John Steptoe (P–M)
Jean Fritz (M–U)	Judith Viorst (M)
Dick Gackenbach (P–M)	Bernard Waber (P)
Paul Galdone (P–M)	Laura Ingalls Wilder (M–U)
Jean Craighead George (M–U)	Brian Wildsmith (P–M)
Gail Gibbons (M)	Nancy Willard (M–U)
Patricia Reilly Giff (M–U)	Vera B. Williams (P–M)
Jamie Gilson (M–U)	Don and Audrey Wood (M)
John Goodall (M–U)	Jane Yolen (M)
Eloise Greenfield (M–U)	Ed Young (M–U)
Gail E. Haley (M)	Margot Zemach (M)
Virginia Hamilton (M–U)	Charlotte Zolotow (P)
Ruth Heller (M)	

P = Primary grades (K–2); M = Middle grades (3–5); U = Upper grades (6–8)

Another popular book that teachers like to share with primary grade students in February is *Just Like Abraham Lincoln* (1964). This story is told by a young boy about his neighbor Mr. Potts who looks just like Abraham Lincoln and enjoys sharing stories about our sixteenth president. At the end of the story, Mr. Potts who is a lawyer (like Lincoln) is moving away and the new neighbor, Mr. Pettigrew, moves in. He looks just like—can you guess?—George Washington!

Jean Craighead George, Novelist with an Ecological Message.   Newbery Medal author Jean Craighead George, is a naturalist whose writing combines an understanding of early adolescence with a profound reverence for nature. She has studied wolves in Alaska and traveled in the Florida Everglades, and she has used these settings in some of her books. At her home in Chappaqua, New York, she has kept nearly 200 pets, not including dogs and cats! Many of these animals have become characters in the more than 40 books she has written for children. In her award-winning book *Julie of the Wolves* (1972), George created a poignant adventure of a 13-year-old Eskimo girl who is protected by a wolf pack after she becomes lost on the tundra. She runs away from an intolerable home situation, and while living with the wolves, she begins to appreciate her heritage and its oneness with nature that modern civilization is destroying. Other books by Jean Craighead George are briefly described in Figure 3.2. Through her books, George has given us a glimpse of animal worlds and how we can better respect and appreciate the world around us.

Jack Prelutsky, Poet for Children of All Ages.   Jack Prelutsky, one of the most popular contemporary poets, writes from the "child" within himself in rhymed, rhythmic verse. "My Parents Think I'm Sleeping" (1985) and "Tyrannosaurus Was a Beast" (1988), title poems in books of the same names, illustrate his special talents and unique understanding of children and childhood. He visits schools often to read and recite poems and these experiences help him to know children's preferences.

Prelutsky is best known for the collections of his own poems, including *The New Kid on the Block* (1984) and *Something BIG Has Been Here* (1990), as well as *The Random House Book of Poetry for Children* (1983), a collection of 572 poems selected by Prelutsky and illustrated by Arnold Lobel, which has become the standard poetry resource in classrooms across the United States. Another interesting collection is *Poems of A. Nonny Mouse* (1989). In the introduction Prelutsky tells readers that the 70 traditional rhymes and silly poems in this collection have been incorrectly labeled as anonymous due to a typographical error when in fact they were penned by Ms. A. Nonny Mouse. Some of his other books of poetry are

> *Toucans Two and Other Poems* (1970)
> *Circus* (1974)
> *Nightmares: Poems to Trouble Your Sleep* (1976)
> *The Snopp on the Sidewalk and Other Poems* (1977)
> *It's Halloween* (1977)
> *The Headless Horseman Rides Tonight: More Poems to Trouble Your Sleep* (1980)
> *It's Christmas* (1981)
> *It's Valentine's Day* (1983)
> *It's Snowing! It's Snowing!* (1984)
> *Ride a Purple Pelican* (1986)

FIGURE 3.2   Books by Jean Craighead George

1959	*My side of the mountain.* New York: Dutton. A first person account of a boy who goes to live in the wilderness. (1960 Newbery Honor Book) (M–U)
1971	*Who really killed Cock Robin?* New York: Dutton. An ecological mystery that focuses on the cause of Cock Robin's death. (U)
1971	*All upon a stone.* New York: Crowell. A mole cricket's search for other crickets that reveals the microcosm on a large weathered stone. (P–M)
1972	*Julie of the wolves.* New York: Harper & Row. A 13-year-old Eskimo girl is protected by a wolf pack after she becomes lost on the tundra. (Winner of the 1973 Newbery Medal) (U)
1978	*The wounded wolf.* New York: Harper & Row. A true story of a wounded wolf who is saved by the food brought to him by the leader of the wolf pack. (P)
1980	*The cry of the crow.* New York: Harper & Row. A touching story of a young girl in the Florida Everglades who keeps a crow for a pet even though her father thinks of the birds as pests. (M–U)
1982	*The grizzly bear with golden ears.* New York: Harper & Row. The story of an Alaskan bear who feeds herself and her cub by bluffing other bears and fishermen out of their food. (P)
1982	*The wild, wild cookbook: A guide for young wild-food foragers.* New York: Crowell. An informational book with more than 60 recipes for dishes prepared from wild foods readily found on roadsides, fields, waterways, and vacant city lots. Also, a guide for identifying edible wild foods is included. (M–U)
1983	*The talking earth.* New York: Harper & Row. In this contemporary adventure, Billie Wind is a Seminole Indian in the Florida Everglades. (M–U)
1984	*One day in the alpine tundra.* New York: Crowell. An account of the actions of wild creatures during a day on the tundra. (M–U)
1986	*One day in the prairie.* New York: Crowell. An account of prairie ecology including a description of a tornado forming and its effect on the buffalo herd, the prairie dogs, and other animals. (M–U)
1987	*Water sky.* New York: Harper & Row. A gripping adventure story about whaling set in Alaska. (M–U)
1988	*One day in the woods.* New York: Crowell. An account of an expedition to the Teatown Woods in New York. (M–U)

Jack Prelutsky lives in Seattle, Washington, and continues to write poetry. He has expressed concern that while young children delight in poetry and wordplay, "something happens to this early love affair with poetry," and during the elementary grades, students "lose their interest and enthusiasm for poetry and their easygoing pleasure in its sounds and images" (1983, p. 18). Through his poems, Prelutsky is reawakening older children's interest in poetry.

Ruth Heller, Author and Illustrator of Informational Books.   Ruth Heller writes and illustrates nonfiction picture books. Her first book was *Chickens Aren't the Only Ones* (1981), an unusual concept book about egg-laying animals that appeals to both primary and middle grade students. This book is also available as a big book for classroom use and as a filmstrip. Heller's other science concept books about plants and animals are

Animals Born Alive and Well (1982)
The Reason for a Flower (1983)
Plants That Never Ever Bloom (1984)

In each of these books, Heller writes in rhyme and supplements the minimal text with brightly colored double-page illustrations. She has also written a series of six small "how to hide" books (c.f., *How to Hide a Whip-poor-will and Other Birds*, 1986) which explain how animals and insects use camouflage as protection.

Ruth Heller is currently writing a series of five books about the parts of speech. In each book, one part of speech, such as adjectives, is explained and rules are reviewed along with examples. Four of the five concept books have been published thus far:

A Cache of Jewels and Other Collective Nouns (1987)
Kites Sail High: A Book About Verbs (1988)
Many Luscious Lollipops: A Book About Adjectives (1989)
Merry-go-round: A Book About Nouns (1990)

These books, too, are written in rhyme, as this excerpt from *Many Luscious Lollipops: A Book About Adjectives* shows:

An adjective's terrific
even when it's not specific . . .
SOME jellybeans
a FEW gumdrops
and
MANY luscious lollipops. (1989, n.p.)

Each adjective in the book is typed in upper case letters to reinforce the concept. These books are gaily illustrated with brightly colored line drawings that fill each page. Heller's books make grammar instruction much more interesting for elementary students than was possible with traditional language arts textbooks.

Illustrators

Illustrators have made an enormous contribution to children's literature through their art. Their illustrations enhance and extend the text of children's books. Many illustrators draw and paint their illustrations. Paul O. Zelinsky's dazzling oil paintings in his retelling of *Rumpelstiltskin* (1986) bring the medieval setting of the tale vividly to life, and David Macaulay's painstakingly detailed line drawings in *Castle* (1977) clarify the information presented in the text. Some illustrators use photographs, such as Christopher G. Knight's photo illustrations in *Sugaring Time* (Lasky, 1983) and Russell Freedman's collection of period photos and prints in *Lincoln: A Photobiography* (1987). Other illustrators use watercolor and acrylic paints, cut paper, woodcuts, collage, paper sculpture, and other media.

Too often people think incorrectly that illustrations are appendages or at best, visual extensions of the text. However, illustrations actually serve several functions: to clarify the text, to add information that is not in the text, to enlarge and interpret the authors' meaning, to evoke an appropriate mood, to establish the setting, and to portray the characters as well as to be decorative (Rudman, 1989). By learning more about illustrators, their perspectives, and techniques, readers begin to appreciate the thought and intent that these artists bring to literature. In fact, sometimes it is the

FIGURE 3.3   Illustrators for Focus Units

Mitsumasa Anno (M–U)	James Marshall (P–M)
Jose Aruego (P–M)	Mercer and Marianna Mayer (M–U)
Marcia Brown (P–M)	Robert McCloskey (P)
Eric Carle (P)	Gerald McDermott (M)
Lorinda Bryan Cauley (M)	Charles Mikolaycak (M–U)
Barbara Cooney (P–M)	Peter Parnall (M)
Donald Crews (P)	Alice and Martin Provensen (M–U)
Tomie de Paola (P)	Ted Rand (M)
Leo and Diane Dillon (M–U)	John Schoenherr (M)
Paul Goble (P–M)	Maurice Sendak (P)
Tana Hoban (P–M)	Lane Smith (M)
Trina Schart Hyman (M)	Peter Spier (P–M)
Susan Jeffers (M)	Chris Van Allsburg (M–U)
Ezra Jack Keats (P)	Brian Wildsmith (P–M)
Leo Lionni (P–M)	Audrey and Don Wood (P–M)
Anita and Arnold Lobel (P)	Ed Young (M–U)
David Macauley (M–U)	Margot Zemach (M)

illustrations that you remember about a book. We highlight three illustrators in this section and list others who are recommended for in-depth study in Figure 3.3.

Tomie de Paola, Author and Illustrator of Books for Young Children. Tomie de Paola has written and illustrated more than 150 picture books for children, and he is well known for his unique folk style of art. De Paola often decorates his line drawings with hearts and little white birds. He began his career as an aritist and thinks of himself first and foremost as an artist. De Paola's major influences on his artistic style have been Fra Angelico, Giotto, Georges Rouault, and Ben Shahn. For his illustrations, de Paola has received a Caldecott Honor for *Strega Nona* (1975), an old Italian tale about a magic pasta pot that is misused by one of the villagers, and he has received many other awards for his work. Several of his books have been recognized as "Children's Choices" by the International Reading Association.

Tomie de Paola has written retellings of many folktales and legends, illustrated collections of Mother Goose rhymes, Bible stories, and poems, written Christmas and other religious stories, several wordless picture books, and several informational books. Some of his best known books are

> *The Legend of the Bluebonnet* (1985), a retelling of an Indian legend about how a little girl's sacrifice brought the bluebonnet flower to Texas.
> *The Legend of the Indian Paintbrush* (1988), a retelling of an Indian legend about how the colors of the sunset are brought down to earth.
> *Tony's Bread* (1989), a retelling of an Italian folktale about a baker who loses a daughter but gains a bakery.
> *Tomie de Paola's Mother Goose* (1985), an illustrated collection of more than 200 nursery rhymes.

An Early American Christmas (1987), an explanation of traditional American Christmas customs.

Pancakes for Breakfast (1978), a wordless picture book that recounts an old lady's attempts to cook pancakes for breakfast.

The Cloud Book (1984), an informational book about clouds.

The Popcorn Book (1978), an informational book about popcorn.

Charlie Needs a Cloak (1982), an explanation of how wool is grown and woven into cloth.

Tomie de Paola was born in 1934 and grew up in Connecticut. He made up his mind to be an artist by the time he was four, and took tap dancing lessons while in elementary school. De Paola has written four semi-autobiographical books about his childhood. In *The Art Lesson* (1989), he tells about wanting to draw with crayons, and in *Oliver Button Is a Sissy* (1979), he writes about a boy like himself who takes tap-dancing lessons. He has also written two stories about his grandparents. *Now One Foot, Now the Other* (1981) is about a boy's relationship with a grandfather who has had a stroke, and *Nana Upstairs and Nana Downstairs* (1973) is a story about de Paola's own grandmother and great-grandmother, one who lives upstairs and one downstairs. He received art training at the Pratt Institute in Brooklyn, New York and at the California College of Arts and Crafts.

De Paola has been a professional artist and designed greeting cards as well as a teacher and professor of art. He has painted murals for Catholic churches in New England and worked with children's theater groups. In 1965 de Paola published his first book, and since then he has been writing and illustrating books for children full time. Now he lives in a 100-year-old farmhouse in New Hampshire called Whitebird, and he plans to continue writing and illustrating books for children for many years to come.

Leo and Diane Dillon, Husband and Wife Team of Illustrators.   Leo and Diane Dillon are the first and so far the only artists who have won the Caldecott Medal in two consecutive years—1976 and 1977. In 1976 they received the Caldecott Medal for their illustrations in *Why Mosquitoes Buzz in People's Ears,* a retelling of a West African folktale by Verna Aardema (1975). This folktale is a repetitive story that explains why mosquitoes behave as they do and buzz in our ears. This is the first book that the Dillons illustrated for young children, and they decided it was the illustrator's job to go beyond the text to illustrate what was between the lines, not just to repeat the words. They concentrated on the interaction between the animals and added a little red bird that does not appear in the text at all to many of the pages. This bird witnesses events in the story, and they added her to many other pages. When the story ends, she flies away. They compare the little bird to the storyteller who passes a story from one generation to the next.

The bright, double-page illustrations in this book are stunning. The style the Dillons' used was inspired by African batik. The illustrations are stylized and colors are separated by narrow white borders. They use a technique called *frisket,* which is like a stencil. Rubber cement is used to separate areas of paint, and after the paint dries, the rubber cement is removed to create the white borders. To get a light, airy look, they use both watercolors and pastels. The watercolor paint is applied with an airbrush, and the pastels are scraped with a knife to make dust. The dust is rubbed on by hand with cotton.

In 1977, the Dillons won their second Caldecott Medal for their illustrations in Margaret Musgrove's *Ashanti to Zulu: African Traditions* (1976), an alphabet book describing the customs of 26 African tribes. In each magnificently composed picture, the Dillons included a man, and woman, and child, their home, an artifact, and a local animal even though these elements might not be seen together ordinarily. The illustrations were done with pastels, watercolors, acrylics, and black ink. The Dillons chose warm earth tones—yellow, red, green, and brown—to reflect the African landscape and climate in their illustrations. They used pen and ink to add authentic details about African grooming and costumes. This book features more attention to detail than does *Why Mosquitoes Buzz in People's Ears* because of the artistic techniques and media that they used. On each page, the illustration is placed above the text, and a border with Nigerian Kano Knots in the four corners frame the page.

The Dillons met in art school 30 years ago and are married. They live in Brooklyn, New York and have one son, Lee. The husband and wife team have worked together for their entire career developing their unique style of illustration, and all of their pictures are created jointly. In fact, they say that their talents are so melded that their art is done by a third artist, the combination of the two of them. Many of the Dillons' illustrations deal with African subjects, but they have not been to Africa. They research their illustrations at their local public library. The Dillons have experimented with a variety of media, including embroidery and stained glass but are best known for their innovative frisket technique.

The Dillons have illustrated other books, including the following:

1. *The Hundred Penny Box* (Mathis, 1975) is the story of Michael's 100-year-old Great-great-aunt Dew, who lives mostly in the memories of her past. The 100 pennies that she keeps in a wooden box represent these memories. Michael's mother struggles to convince Aunt Dew to live in the present, not the past. This book is a Newbery Honor Book. Through their illustrations, the Dillons wanted to give readers the feeling they were looking at pictures in an old family photo album. They used the frisket technique to protect the outside edge and began the illustrations with a brown watercolor background. Then they used bleach to etch out the lighter tones in the pictures.

2. *Who's in Rabbit's House?* (Aardema, 1977) is a dramatization of an African folktale about a rabbit who can't go into his house because he's afraid a dangerous animal is in the house. The Dillons used pastels for the background and tempera paint for the foreground. The illustrations are similar in style to *Ashanti to Zulu,* and the same care was taken to authentically depict the grooming and costumes of the Masai people, their housing and landscape.

3. *Honey, I Love, and Other Love Poems* (Greenfield, 1978) is a collection of poetry about the black experience. The Dillons' soft, subdued illustrations are similar to those in *The Hundred Penny Box.*

4. *The Tale of the Mandarin Ducks* (Paterson, 1990) is a popular Japanese folktale about a pair of Mandarin ducks who are separated by a cruel lord who wants the magnificently plumed drake as a pet and the reward a compassionate

couple receives who risk their lives to reunite the ducks. The Dillons' illustrations are brilliant, double-page watercolor and pastel paintings in the style of eighteenth-century woodcuts called *ukiyo-e*.

5. *Aida* (Price, 1990) is a retelling of Verdi's opera about an Ethiopian princess who is forced into slavery by the Egyptians. She then falls in love with an Egyptian soldier and has to choose between her love and her country. In their most recent work, the Dillons have created vibrant illustrations using acrylics on acetate and marblized paper. The illustrations are single-page paintings, placed opposite pages of text. The husband and wife team use the royal colors purple and gold in many of the paintings, and Egyptian motifs are featured in the paintings and in the designs at the top of the text pages. Around the bottom and sides of each page are double frames of African flowers that were designed in metal by Lee Dillon, the couple's son.

TYPES OF ILLUSTRATIONS

Illustrations in picture books add immeasurably to children's enjoyment and understanding of the text. Advanced technology in the printing industry makes possible the wide variety of media and unique graphics used in today's books. In *The Polar Express* (Van Allsburg, 1985), for instance, both the striking illustrations and the magical mood they create help to make the story memorable; the hole-cuts in *The Very Hungry Caterpillar* (Carle, 1975) and *Fish Eyes* (Ehlert, 1990) add a playful quality to these books; and the creative paper sculpture and movable pictures in *Leonardo da Vinci* (Provensen & Provensen, 1984) and other movable books invite active participation in reading.

In some books, called wordless picture books, the story is told entirely through pictures, and few words other than the title appear in the book. Well-known illustrators, including Mitsumasa Anno, Tomie de Paola, Fernando Krahn, Mercer Mayer, and John Goodall have created a number of these marvelous books. In some books, the author tells a complete story through the illustrations. For example, *Frog Goes to Dinner* (Mayer, 1974) is a hilarious story about a frog's misadventures in a fancy restaurant, and Goodall's *Above and Below Stairs* (1983) compares the lifestyle of English lords and peasants during the middle ages. Other wordless books, such as *Anno's USA* (Anno, 1983), contain hidden pictures that readers must examine closely to notice. These books are fun to read and are useful for nonreaders and limited English-speaking students. A list of wordless picture books is presented in Figure 3.4.

Three dimensions of illustrations in literature are (a) visual elements, (b) art media, and (c) artistic styles. Information about these art qualities is provided in the following sections, and books of children's literature are listed as examples. A list of guidelines to use in evaluating illustrations is presented in Figure 3.5. It must be stressed, however, that this information is intended to help teachers and students examine how illustrators create meaning and expand and extend the text of the book, not to provide terms and definitions for students' use in workbook exercises or to memorize for tests.

Visual Elements

Artists make decisions about line, space, color, shape, texture, and perspective as they compose illustrations. These components are called visual elements.

Line. The most basic element of art is *line*. Artists use lines to suggest shape, direction, and movement. Lines may be straight or curved, wide or thin, light or heavy, jerky or smooth, and feathery or bold. They are drawn in horizontal, vertical, or diagonal directions. The overall effect of the lines contributes to the mood that the illustration evokes. The lines are big, broad, and bold in McDermott's African folktale, *Anansi the Spider* (1972), whereas Ronald Himler's soft, shaded lines in *Nettie's Trip South* (Turner, 1987), a letter about a Northern girl's trip to Richmond, Virginia, in the pre-Civil War days, suggests blurred images of a memory. The curved lines in *Follow the Drinking Gourd* (Winter, 1988) project the surrealistic, haunting mood of this book about the underground railroad.

Space. *Space* is another visual element. Depending on where artists place illustrations on the page, they can give us an up-close-and-personal or a more detached view of the story. In *Miss Rumphius* (1982), for example, Barbara Cooney uses wide panoramic illustrations to review her aunt's life and accomplishments. When the pages are crammed with details, a frantic pace is suggested and when they are more spacious, a calmer environment is implied. In *Now One Foot, Now the Other* (1981), author/illustrator Tomie de Paola shows the grandfather and grandson's love by placing them together in scenes at the beginning and end of the book. After the grandfather has a stroke and is hospitalized, de Paola draws the boy alone in each picture, making the boy's loneliness much more clear than the text could alone.

Illustrators use space creatively for special effects. Trina Schart Hyman, for example, in *Saint George and the Dragon* (Hodges, 1984) extended her romantic illustrations of the legend into the borders. Jan Brett used side panels in *The Mitten* (1989) to present before and after scenes. Eric Carle enlarged the space for his illustrations in *Papa, Please Get the Moon for Me* (1986); he created four illustrations on double-sized pages which are folded into the book. Another way artists can create space is through three-dimensional paper sculpture in moveable books. The illustrations of the organs in *The Human Body* (Miller, 1983) seem more realistic because they are three-dimensional.

Color. *Color* is another important visual element. Some illustrators use black and white, such as Wanda Gag in *Millions of Cats* (1956) or shades of gray as in Chris Van Allsburg's *Jumanji* (1981). In contrast, other artists use color in their illustrations, choosing their colors carefully depending on the mood they wish to create in the book. Different colors suggest different emotions. Yellow and red are warm while blue and purple are cool colors. Green suggests life, and orange and black suggest autumn. Peter Parnall used bright yellows, oranges, and reds in *I'm in Charge of Celebrations* (Baylor, 1986), a book about special days in the American southwest, whereas Ted Rand used darker night colors in *The Ghost-eye Tree* (Martin & Archambault, 1985) to create a spooky mood.

How Many Days to America? A Thanksgiving Story (Bunting, 1988) is the story of refugees from a Caribbean island and their dangerous boat trip to freedom

FIGURE 3.4   Wordless Picture Books

Alexander, M. (1968). *Out! Out! Out!* New York: Dial. (P)
Alexander, M. (1970). *Bobo's dream.* New York: Dial. (P)
Anno, M. (1978). *Anno's Italy.* New York: Collins. (M–U)
Anno, M. (1978). *Anno's journey.* New York: Philomel. (M–U)
Anno, M. (1982). *Anno's Britain.* New York: Philomel. (M–U)
Anno, M. (1983). *Anno's USA.* New York: Philomel. (M–U)
Aruego, J. (1971). *Look what I can do.* New York: Scribner. (P)
Bang, M. (1980). *The grey lady and the strawberry snatcher.* New York: Four Winds. (M–U)
Briggs, R. (1980). *The snowman.* New York: Random House. (P)
Carle, E. (1971). *Do you want to be my friend?* New York: Crowell. (P)
Carroll, R. (1965). *What whiskers did.* New York: Walck. (P)
Day, A. (1985). *Good dog, Carl.* New York: Green Tiger Press. (M)
de Groat, D. (1977). *Alligator's toothache.* New York: Crown. (P–M)
de Paola, T. (1978). *Pancakes for breakfast.* New York: Harcourt Brace Jovanovich. (P)
de Paola, T. (1979). *Flicks.* New York: Harcourt Brace Jovanovich. (P)
de Paola, T. (1981). *The hunter and the animals: A wordless picture book.* New York: Holiday House.
   (P–M)
de Paola, T. (1983). *Sing, Pierrot, sing.* New York: Harcourt Brace Jovanovich. (M)
Dupasquier, P. (1988). *The great escape.* Boston: Houghton Mifflin. (M–U)
Goodall, J. S. (1975). *Creepy castle.* New York: Macmillan. (M)
Goodall, J. S. (1979). *The story of an English village.* New York: Atheneum. (M–U)
Goodall, J. S. (1980). *Paddy's new hat.* New York: Atheneum. (M)
Goodall, J. S. (1983). *Above and below stairs.* New York: Atheneum. (U)
Goodall, J. S. (1987). *The story of a high street.* London: Andre Deutsch. (M–U)
Goodall, J. S. (1988). *Little red riding hood.* New York: McElderry Books. (P–M)
Henstra, F. (1983). *Mighty mizzling mouse.* New York: Lippincott. (P–M)
Hoban, T. (1971). *Look again.* New York: Macmillan. (P)

in America. Only the first page of the book before the soldiers come and force the family to flee from their home and the last pages when the family arrives safely in America are "happy" pages. On the pages in-between the family faces danger, cold, hunger, and fear. Illustrator Beth Peck's choice of colors reflects these feelings. She chose a golden background on the first and last pages of the story, but the background colors on the other pages are somber, ranging from blue to purple to gray.

Shape.   Some illustrators use natural, realistic *shapes* whereas others use more abstract cartoon or geometric shapes. Donald Carrick uses natural shapes in *The Wednesday Surprise* (Bunting, 1989), a story about how a girl teaches her grandmother to read. The natural shapes in the pictures add authenticity to the story. In contrast, Leo and Diane Dillon used geometric shapes in their illustrations for *Why Mosquitoes Buzz in People's Ears* (Aardema, 1975), an African pourquoi tale. This stylized art is more fitting for an African folktale than it would have been for a more realistic story.

   The placement of the shapes in the illustrations makes them symmetrical or asymmetrical. Symmetrical pictures are more comfortable and secure than asymmetrical pictures, which often seem unbalanced, more dynamic. The symmetrical,

Hoban, T. (1988). *Look! Look! Look!* New York: Greenwillow. (P)

Hutchins, P. (1971). *Changes, changes.* New York: Macmillan. (P)

Keats, E. J. (1973). *Psst! Doggie.* New York: Franklin Watts. (P)

Krahn, F. (1970). *A flying saucer full of spaghetti.* New York: Dutton. (P–M)

Krahn, F. (1977). *The mystery of the giant footprints.* New York: Dutton. (P–M)

Krahn, F. (1978). *The great ape.* New York: Penguin. (P–M–U)

Mayer, M. (1967). *A boy, a dog, and a frog.* New York: Dial. (P–M)

Mayer, M. (1973). *Bubble, bubble.* New York: Parents. (P–M)

Mayer, M. (1974). *Frog goes to dinner.* New York: Dial. (P–M)

Mayer, M. (1976). *Ah-choo.* New York: Dial. (P–M)

Mayer, M. (1977). *Oops.* New York: Dial. (P–M)

McCully, E. A. (1984). *Picnic.* New York: Harper & Row. (P)

McCully, E. A. (1985). *First snow.* New York: Harper & Row. (P)

McCully, E. A. (1987). *School.* New York: Harper & Row. (P)

McCully, E. A. (1988). *New baby.* New York: Harper & Row. (P)

Monro, R. (1987). *The inside-outside book of Washington, D.C.* New York: Dutton. (M–U)

Prater, J. (1987). *The gift.* New York: Viking. (P–M)

Spier, P. (1977). *Noah's ark.* New York: Doubleday. (P–M–U)

Spier, P. (1982). *Rain.* New York: Doubleday. (P–M–U)

Tafuri, N. (1985). *Rabbit's morning.* New York: Greenwillow. (P)

Tafuri, N. (1986). *Have you seen my duckling?* New York: Viking. (P)

Turkle, B. (1976). *Deep in the forest.* New York: Dutton. (P–M)

Ward, L. (1973). *The silver pony.* Boston: Houghton Mifflin. (P–M)

Wiesner, D. (1988). *Free fall.* New York: Lothrop, Lee & Shepard. (M–U)

Winters, P. (1976). *The bear and the fly.* New York: Crown. (P–M–U)

Winters, P. (1980). *Sir Andrew.* New York: Crown. (P–M)

Young, E. (1984). *The other bone.* New York: Harper & Row. (P–M)

cartoon shapes in James Marshall's *Red Riding Hood* (1987) are much less threatening than the impressionistic, asymmetrical illustrations in Ed Young's version, *Lon Po Po: A Red-riding Hood Story from China* (1989).

Texture.   Illustrators use *texture* to make their pictures look more lifelike and real to readers; the texture helps to create the illusion that readers can almost touch the objects and people. Illustrators create texture using lines and shades of color. Two picture books with particularly realistic illustrations are *The Story of Jumping Mouse* (Steptoe, 1984), an American Indian myth about a little mouse whose sacrifices and compassion for others bring him great rewards, and *Owl Moon* (Yolen, 1987), the description of a father and child who go owling (or looking for owls) one winter night.

Perspective.   *Perspective* is the point of view the illustrator takes. The illustrations in many books are rendered to make the page appear to be a window or a door through which we can peer into the world of the book. We often don't think about perspective as we are reading and examining the illustrations. Sometimes, though, one or more pictures in a book catch our attention because of a change of perspective, for example as we follow the school bus through the organs of the body in *The*

FIGURE 3.5   Guidelines for Evaluating Illustrations

1. Does the illustrator's use of line, space, color, shape, texture, and perspective extend the development of plot, characterization, setting, and theme?
2. Does the illustrator's use of art media extend the development of plot, characterization, setting, and theme?
3. Does the artistic style enhance the author's style?
4. Are the illustrations an integral part of the book?
5. Do the illustrations reflect the mood of the book?
6. Are the illustrations accurate in historical, cultural, and geographic details?
7. Do the illustrations extend the text or help readers to anticipate upcoming events?
8. Do the illustrations conflict with the text in any way?

Adapted from Sutherland & Arbuthnot (1986), Huck, Hepler, & Hickman (1987), and Norton (1991).

Magic School Bus Inside the Human Body (Cole, 1989). Other books, such as Chris Van Allsburg's *Two Bad Ants* (1988), are illustrated completely from an unusual perspective. In this book, the illustrations are from the ants' viewpoint.

Art Media

Illustrators use a variety of media in creating pictures for trade books. These media include pens and pencils, paints, collage, photographs, woodcuts and other prints, and paper sculpture. Each type of media is described in the following sections, and Figure 3.6 lists books illustrated with each art medium. Some illustrators use other art media. One of the most unusual is batik, which artist Patricia MacCarthy used in *17 Kings and 42 Elephants* (Mahy, 1987).

Pens and Pencils.   Artists use pencils, pens, crayons, and colored pencils for line drawings and coloring illustrations. The art for Wanda Gag's classic *Millions of Cats* (1956) was rendered in bold black ink line drawings, and Chris Van Allsburg used finer black ink line drawings for greater detail in *Ben's Dream* (1982). David Macaulay's thin line drawings in *Pyramid* (1975) are similar to Van Allsburg's but have a softer quality. Many picture books are illustrated with colored pencils, including Lionni's *Swimmy* (1963) and Bill Peet's *Huge Harold* (1961).

Paints.   Illustrators use a variety of paints, including watercolors, acrylics, pastels, and oils, to evoke the mood in a book, from festive holiday moods to cold moonlight nights. Leonard Everett Fisher used acrylic paints to create the brightly colored holiday backgrounds for the poems in *Celebrations* (Livingston, 1985), whereas Barbara Cooney's illustrations—also done with acrylics—in *Miss Rumphius* (1982) are much softer and more controlled. Ted Rand's intense watercolor illustrations for *Paul Revere's Ride* (Longfellow, 1990) heighten the tension of the famous midnight ride, and Chris Van Allsburg's oil pastel pictures in *The Polar Express* (1985) create a peaceful, white Christmas eve scene. Paul O. Zelinsky's oil paintings in *Rumpelstiltskin* (1986) and Fred Marcellino's in *Puss in Boots* (Perrault, 1990) depict rich medieval settings for the familiar folktales.

Collage.   Several well-known artists use collage to create unique illustrations. To make a *collage,* artists cut or tear paper into shapes and paste the paper onto a background sheet. The paper they use may be plain or painted, printed, or textured. Sometimes marblized paper (paper that has been streaked with paint to look like the surface of a marble) is also used. Eric Carle used collage in *The Very Hungry Caterpillar* (1975) and other well-known favorites, and Ezra Jack Keats used marblized paper in the collages he made for *The Snowy Day* (1962).

Photographs.   Photographs are often used to illustrate informational books because of the authenticity they add to the book. Dr. Ronald H. Cohn's color photographs enriched the text of *Koko's Kitten* (Patterson, 1985), and Russell Freedman collected old black-and-white photographs to illustrate his Newbery Medal winning *Lincoln: A Photobiography* (1987). Tana Hoban used photos to illustrate her concept books for preschool and primary grade students. One of her newest books is *Shadows and Reflections* (1990), illustrated with black-and-white photographs.

Woodcuts and Other Prints.   To prepare woodcuts, artists carve designs in blocks of wood and use other materials to make print illustrations. Then they ink the wood blocks or other materials and stamp the designs on paper. Marcia Brown used woodcuts to illustrate the Indian fable, *Once a Mouse* (1961), and Gail Haley used linoleum block prints in *Jack Jouett's Ride* (1973).

Three-dimensional Paper Sculpture.   A few illustrators create three-dimensional paper sculpture that unfolds or opens as the book is opened or the pages are turned. Tomie de Paola created three-dimensional illustrations of a Renaissance town that unfold as pages are opened in *Giorgio's Village* (1982), and David Pelham designed multilayer, working illustrations of the organs and systems for *The Human Body* (Miller, 1983).

Mixed Media.   Many books of children's literature are illustrated with combinations of two or more media. For example, John Goodall combined watercolor paints and line drawings (drawn with black ink) in *The Story of a Castle* (1986), and Ed Young combined watercolor and pastels in *Lon Po Po: A Red-riding Hood Story from China* (1989), which won the Caldecott Medal.

Sometimes readers can identify the art medium used in a trade book because it is obvious or because a note on the copyright page (which follows the title page) or at the back of the book explains it. In many other books it is not possible to identify the medium or combination of media. Watercolor paintings sometimes look like pastels, and woodcuts can look like line drawings. In fact, some publishers deliberately do not identify the medium because in the printing process colors are separated and reproduced in such a way that the medium becomes less obvious. They argue that it is preferable to provide no information in order not to confuse readers.

Artistic Styles

Style encompasses both the distinctive features and the elusive quality of the artist's work, and it is based on how the illustrator combines the visual elements and artistic media. Artists have a unique personal style that readers recognize from book to book.

FIGURE 3.6   Art Media

Acrylics

Brown, R. (1981). *A dark, dark tale.* New York: Dial. (P)
Cooney, B. (1982). *Miss Rumphius.* New York: Viking. (M)
Livingston, M. C. (1985). (Ill. by L. E. Fisher). *Celebrations.* New York: Holiday House. (M)
Price, L. (1990). (Ill. by L. & D. Dillon). *Aida.* San Diego: Harcourt Brace Jovanovich. (U)

Collage

Brown, M. (1982). *Shadow.* New York: Scribner. (P–M)
Keats, E. J. (1962). *Snowy day.* New York: Viking. (P)
Lewis, R. (1965). (Ill. by E. J. Keats). *In a spring garden.* New York: Dial. (M–U)
Lionni, L. (1969). *Alexander and the wind-up mouse.* Natick, MA: Picture Book Studio. (P)
Martin, B., Jr. (1991). (Ill. by E. Carle). *Polar bear, polar bear, what do you hear?* New York: Henry Holt. (P)

Crayons and Colored Pencils

Brown, M. (1972). *The bun: A tale from Russia.* New York: Harcourt Brace Jovanovich. (P–M)
Lionni, L. (1970). *Fish is fish.* New York: Knopf. (P)
Peet, B. (1961). *Huge Harold.* Boston: Houghton Mifflin. (M)
Van Allsburg, C. (1986). *The stranger.* Boston: Houghton Mifflin. (M–U)

Oil Paints

Johnston, T. (1988). (Ill. by L. Bloom). *Yonder.* New York: Dial. (M)
Locker, T. (1984). *Where the river begins.* New York: Dial. (M–U)
Locker, T. (1987). *The boy who held back the sea.* New York: Dial. (M–U)
Perrault, C. (1990). (Ill. by F. Marcellino). *Puss in boots.* New York: Farrar, Straus & Giroux. (M)
Wood, A. (1984). *The napping house.* San Diego: Harcourt Brace Jovanovich. (P)
Zelinsky, P. O. (1986). *Rumpelstiltskin.* New York: Dutton. (M–U)

Pastels

Howe, J. (1987). (Ill. by E. Young). *I wish I were a butterfly.* San Diego, CA: Harcourt Brace Jovanovich. (P–M)
Jukes, M. (1984). (Ill. by L. Bloom). *Like Jake and me.* New York: Knopf. (M)
Van Allsburg, C. (1985). *The polar express.* Boston: Houghton Mifflin. (M–U)

Pens and Pencils

Gag, W. (1956). *Millions of cats.* New York: Coward, McCann & Geoghegan. (P)
Macaulay, D. (1977). *Castle.* Boston: Houghton Mifflin. (U)
Mayer, M. (1974). *Frog goes to dinner.* New York: Dial. (P–M–U)
Turner, A. (1987). (Ill. by Ronald Himler). *Nettie's trip south.* New York: Macmillan. (M–U)
Van Allsburg, C. (1981). *Jumanji.* Boston: Houghton Mifflin. (M–U)
Viorst, J. (1972). (Ill. by R. Cruz). *Alexander and the terrible, horrible, no good, very bad day.* New York: Atheneum. (P–M–U)

Photographs

Freedman, R. (1987). *Lincoln: A photobiography.* New York: Clarion. (U)

Hoban, T. (1990). *Shadows and reflections.* New York: Greenwillow. (P)

Lasky, K. (1983). (Ill. by C. S. Knight). *Sugaring time.* New York: Macmillan. (M)

Lauber, P. (1990). *Seeing earth from space.* New York: Orchard. (M–U)

Patterson, F. (1985). (Ill. by R. H. Cohn). *Koko's kitten.* New York: Scholastic. (P–M)

Three-dimension Paper Sculpture

Ahlberg, J., & Ahlberg, A. (1986). *The jolly postman or other people's letters.* Boston: Little, Brown. (P–M)

de Paola, T. (1982). *Giorgio's village.* New York: Putnam. (P–M)

Miller, J. (1983). *The human body.* New York: Viking. (M–U)

Prokofiev, S. (1985). (Ill. by B. Cooney). *Peter and the wolf.* New York: Viking. (P–M)

Provensen, A., & Provensen, M. (1984). *Leonardo da Vinci.* New York: Viking. (M–U)

Watercolor Paints

Bunting, E. (1990). (Ill. by R. Himler). *The wall.* New York: Clarion. (P–M)

Castle, C. (1985). (Ill. by P. Weevers). *The hare and the tortoise.* New York: Dial. (M)

Longfellow, H. W. (1990). (Ill. by T. Rand). *Paul Revere's ride.* New York: Dutton. (M–U)

Potter, B. (1902). *The tale of Peter Rabbit.* New York: Warne. (P)

Say, A. (1990). *El chino.* Boston: Houghton Mifflin. (U)

Williams, V. B. (1982). *A chair for my mother.* New York: Mulberry Books. (P)

Yolen, J. (1987). (Ill. by J. Schoenherr). *Owl moon.* New York: Philomel. (P–M)

Woodcuts and Other Prints

Brown, M. (1961). *Once a mouse.* New York: Aladdin Books. (P–M)

Emberley, E., & Emberely, B. (1967). *Drummer Hoff.* Englewood Cliffs, NJ: Prentice-Hall. (P)

Haley, G. E. (1970). *A story, a story.* New York: Atheneum. (P–M)

Haley, G. E. (1973). *Jack Jouett's ride.* New York: Viking. (M)

Lionni, L. (1963). *Swimmy.* New York: Random House. (P)

Tejima. (1987). *Owl lake.* New York: Philomel. (M)

Mixed Media

Burningham, J. (1989). *Hey! Get off our train.* New York: Crown. (M)

Crews, D. (1982). *Carousel.* New York: Greenwillow. (P)

Most, B. (1978). *If the dinosaurs came back.* New York: Harcourt Brace Jovanovich. (P–M)

Wildsmith, B. (1963). *The lion and the rat.* Oxford, England: Oxford University Press. (P–M)

Young, E. (1989). *Lon po po: A red-riding hood story from China.* New York: Philomel. (M)

For example, Chris Van Allsburg's illustrations are unmistakable. He often uses finely detailed line drawings, sometimes in a monotone gray color, and in each book he includes a picture of a white dog.

Artistic style is also associated with periods in art, such as realism or impressionism. Van Allsburg's illustrations, to continue the example, might be described as surrealistic because of their mix of realism and fantasy. Although designations of realism, impressionism, surrealism, and other artistic styles are not exact, six styles will be discussed and sample books identified. For a list of other books representing each style, see Figure 3.7.

Realism. In the *realistic style,* artists depict their subjects as they are seen in daily life. The pictures are not photographically exact images, but they are visually accurate. For example, Winslow Homer's paintings of the American scene are representative of this category. In the past, the illustrations in most children's books were realistic. It was assumed that realistic pictures were easier for children to understand and that they helped children learn new concepts. Two examples are Robert McCloskey's line drawings for *Make Way for Ducklings* (1969) that realistically depict Mallard ducklings and Anita Lobel's paintings that show post-war Europe in *A New Coat for Anna* (Ziefert, 1986). Many children's trade books will undoubtedly continue to be illustrated with realistic pictures; however, more recently illustrators have been using other styles as well.

Impressionism. As the name suggests, the *impressionistic style* concentrates on the general impression produced by a scene. Claude Monet, the best-known impressionist painter, focused on light and color and their impressions on natural subjects, such as water gardens, rather than realistic details. Ed Young's illustrations in *I Wish I Were a Butterfly* (Howe, 1987) have many of the same impressionistic characteristics as Monet's works.

Expressionism. The *expressionistic style* grew out of impressionism as artists such as Vincent Van Gogh used visual elements to express intense emotions. Matisse's abstract paintings with vivid colors are also representative of this category. Jeannette Winter's dramatic, swirling illustrations in *Follow the Drinking Gourd* (1988) are expressionistic. Her illustrations of slaves escaping to Canada on the underground railroad evoke the same intense emotions that some of Van Gogh's paintings do. We also classify as expressionistic Lois Ehlert's vivid abstract shapes, which are reminiscent of Matisse's art, in *Color Zoo* (1989) and *Chicka Chicka Boom Boom* (Martin & Archambault, 1989).

Surrealism. The *surrealistic style* is dreamlike, and Salvador Dali's painting "The Persistence of Memory" is a good example. This style of art "combines incongruous images in unnatural juxtapositions" (Huck, Hepler, & Hickman, 1987, p. 212). Lane Smith's surrealistic illustrations in *The True Story of the Three Little Pigs* (Scieszka, 1989) make us question Mr. Wolf's version of the story. Illustrators of fantasies often use surrealism. In *Come Away from the Water, Shirley* (1977), John Burningham juxtaposes the fantasy of Shirley's dreams with the reality of Shirley's parents' inane chatter during a trip to the beach. Burningham used the arrangement of illustrations on the page and different media to emphasize the dichotomy.

FIGURE 3.7 Artistic Styles

Realism

Holling, H. C. (1969). *Paddle-to-the-sea*. Boston: Houghton Mifflin. (M)
McCloskey, R. (1969). *Make way for ducklings*. New York: Viking. (P)
Turkle, B. (1976). *Deep in the forest*. New York: Dutton. (P)
Viorst, J. (1972). (Ill. by R. Cruz). *Alexander and the terrible, horrible, no good, very bad day*. New York: Atheneum. (P–M–U)
Ziefert, H. (1986). (Ill. by A. Lobel). *A new coat for Anna*. New York: Knopf. (P–M)

Impressionism

Baker, O. (1981). (Ill. by S. Gammell). *Where the buffaloes begin*. New York: Warne. (M)
Bjork, C. (1985). (Ill. by L. Anderson). *Linnea in Monet's garden*. Stockholm: R & S books. (M–U)
Howe, J. (1987). (Ill. by E. Young). *I wish I were a butterfly*. San Diego, CA: Harcourt Brace Jovanovich. (P–M)
Wildsmith, B. (1966). *The hare and the tortoise*. Oxford, England: Oxford University Press. (P–M)
Zolotow, C. (1962). (Ill. by M. Sendak). *Mr. Rabbit and the lovely present*. New York: Harper & Row. (P)

Expressionism

Carle, E. (1984). *The very busy spider*. New York: Philomel. (P)
Ehlert, L. (1989). *Color zoo*. New York: Lippincott. (P)
Livingston, M. C. (1985). (Ill. by L. E. Fisher). *A circle of seasons*. New York: Holiday House. (P–M–U)
Martin, B., Jr., & Archambault, J. (1989). (Ill. by L. Ehlert). *Chicka chicka boom boom*. New York: Simon & Schuster. (P)
Williams, V. B. (1982). *A chair for my mother*. New York: Mulberry. (P–M)

Surrealism

Bang, M. (1980). *The grey lady and the strawberry snatcher*. New York: Four Winds Press. (M–U)
Burningham, J. (1977). *Come away from the water, Shirley*. New York: Harper & Row. (M–U)
Scieszka, J. (1989). (Ill. by L. Smith). *The true story of the three little pigs*. New York: Viking. (P–M)
Van Allsburg, C. (1981). *Jumanji*. Boston: Houghton Mifflin. (M–U)
Winter, J. (1988). *Follow the drinking gourd*. New York: Knopf. (M)

Cartoon Style

Cole, J. (1989). (Ill. by B. Degen). *The magic school bus inside the human body*. New York: Scholastic. (M)
Schwartz, D. M. (1985). (Ill. by S. Kellogg). *How much is a million?* New York: Scholastic. (M)
Seuss, Dr. (1957). *Cat in the hat*. New York: Random House. (P)
Spier, P. (1980). *People*. New York: Doubleday. (M)
Westcott, N. B. (1984). *The emperor's new clothes*. Boston: Little, Brown. (P–M)

Folk Art

Aardema, V. (1975). (Ill. by L. Dillon & D. Dillon). *Why mosquitoes buzz in people's ears*. New York: Dial. (P–M)
Hall, D. (1979). (Ill. by B. Cooney). *The ox-cart man*. New York: Viking. (P–M)
Lindbergh, R. (1990). *Johnny Appleseed*. Boston: Little, Brown. (M–U)
O'Kelley, M. L. (1986). *Circus!* Boston: Little, Brown. (P–M)
Polacco, P. (1988). *Rechenka's eggs*. New York: Philomel. (M)
Provensen, A. (1990). *The buck stops here: The presidents of the United States*. New York: Harper & Row. (M–U)
Xiong, B. (1989). (Ill. by N. Hom). *Nine-in-one. Grr! Grr!* San Francisco: Children's Book Press. (M)

Cartoon Style.   *Cartoon art* is a familiar style in picture books. In cartoon art, illustrators use line drawings to detail characters, show movement, and create humor. Three of the best-known cartoon illustrators of children's books are Dr. Seuss, Steven Kellogg, and William Steig. Bruce Degan also used cartoons in his detailed illustrations for *The Magic School Bus Inside the Human Body* (Cole, 1989).

Folk Art.   *Folk art* is a primitive style of art, and the term is also used to describe the art of self-taught artists, such as Grandma Moses. Illustrators of children's books, such as Barbara Cooney in *The Ox-cart Man* (Hall, 1979), use this style as they imitate early American artists. Alice Provensen's delightful book about the presidents *The Buck Stops Here* (1990) is an example of folk art as are the Provensens' many other notable books.

We also categorize illustrations that are typical of particular cultures or regions as folk art (Cianciolo, 1976). Folk art is characterized by a simplification of line or use of abstracted forms as shown in the Dillons' striking illustrations for the African folktale *Why Mosquitoes Buzz in People's Ears* (Aardema, 1975). Two other examples are Patricia Polacco's Ukrainian decorations in *Rechenka's Eggs* (1988) and Nancy Hom's traditional story cloth illustrations for the Hmong folktale *Nine-in-one. Grr! Grr!* (Xiong, 1989).

HELPING CHILDREN TO LEARN ABOUT AUTHORS AND ILLUSTRATORS

Learning about authors, illustrators, and illustration techniques is an important part of literature-based reading. Teachers use minilessons as a part of literature studies or plan and teach focus units about an author, illustrator, or type of illustration.

Minilessons are brief lessons, often lasting about 15 minutes that may be taught to the whole class or small groups of students. In these lessons, the teacher draws on students' experiences, such as a book that they have previously read, and then teaches or reviews a concept or skill. Teachers can focus on events in an author's life, present information about letter writing prior to writing to favorite authors and illustrators, focus on a visual element such as color, discuss an art medium, or examine a style of art. After presenting the information, teachers provide opportunities for students to experiment with the materials or use the information in genuine reading or writing activities. For example:

- A teacher talks about the watercolor illustrations in a book read the previous day and asks students to locate two or three other books illustrated with watercolors in the class library. They discuss the effect of the illustrations on the reader and how the effect might be different if another art medium had been used. Then the teacher sets out a center with watercolor paints for students to experiment with. A week later students might meet a local watercolor artist or use watercolors to illustrate the next book they write.
- As a part of a theme cycle on the pioneers, the teacher might introduce folk art using a cross-stitched sampler, a print of a Grandma Moses painting, a pail painted in the Pennsylvania Dutch folk art style, and an old family quilt. Next, students would examine books illustrated with folk art, and later they might illustrate reports about pioneers that they wrote using folk art.

A list of general suggestions about teaching students about authors, illustrators, and illustration is presented in Figure 3.8. Many of these suggestions are elaborated on in the following sections.

Concept of Author and Illustrator

Students need to know about authors and illustrators as the people who write and illustrate the books they read, but they need to know much more than that. They need to develop a *concept of author and illustrator* so that students think of them as real people—real people who eat breakfast, ride bikes, and take out the garbage, just as they do. When students think of them as real people, they view reading and literature in a different, more personal way. This concept of author (and illustrator) also carries over to children's writing. As they learn about authors and illustrators, students realize that they too can write and illustrate books. They can learn about the writing process from these authors and about using illustrations to extend the meaning of the text from illustrators. They can hide their pets' initials in the illustrations for their books because Eric Carle hides his children's initials in the illustrations in his books. Students need to be familiar with authors and illustrators so that they can have favorites and compare them.

FIGURE 3.8   Guidelines for Learning About Authors and Illustrators

1. Research a favorite author or illustrator.
2. Collect materials about authors and illustrators and keep them in a file or scrapbook.
3. View filmstrips or videotapes about authors and illustrators.
4. Make posters, booklets, or brochures with information about a favorite author or illustrator.
5. Write letters to a favorite author or illustrator.
6. Collect and read all the books written by a favorite author or illustrated by a favorite illustrator.
7. Locate where authors/illustrators live on a United States (or world) map.
8. Read a biography or autobiography of an author or illustrator.
9. Teach minilessons about authors and illustrators.
10. Arrange a conference telephone call with a favorite author or illustrator.
11. Plan a young authors' conference with an author or illustrator.
12. Experiment with artistic media.
13. Develop students' visual literacy concepts.
14. Invite a local artist or illustrator to come to the classroom and demonstrate art media.
15. Study a well-known artist and then select trade books that are illustrated in the same style.
16. Read *If You Were a Writer* (Nixon, 1988) to get a glimpse of how a writer works.
17. Read Aliki's *How a Book Is Made* (1986) to learn how books are written, illustrated, and published.
18. Plan a focus unit on an author or illustrator.
19. Have students publish their writing in books.
20. Place an author's chair in your classroom for students to sit in as they share their writing.
21. Invite a local author to visit the classroom and talk about the writing process and share his/her books.
22. Have students add "All About the Author" and "All About the Illustrator" pages to the books they write and illustrate. (Duplicate copies of students' school photos for them to use on these pages.)
23. Visit a local publishing company or newspaper to see the publishing process in action.

One way that students learn about authors and illustrators is by reading about them. A number of biographies and autobiographies of well-known authors and illustrators, including Beatrix Potter (Aldis, 1969), Jean Fritz (1982), Bill Peet (1989), Roald Dahl (1984), and Tomie de Paola (1989), are appropriate for elementary students. A list of these books is presented in Figure 3.9 together with resource books that provide brief biographical sketches of many authors and illustrators.

Students can read newspaper, magazine, and journal articles to learn about favorite authors and illustrators. Many articles profiling these people have been published in *Language Arts, The New Advocate, Horn Book,* and other journals which teachers can clip and file. (A list of journal articles profiling authors and illustrators is presented in Appendix B.) Another source of information is the publicity brochures that teachers and students can request from publishers, usually free of charge. We suggest that teachers set up a file system and add information about students' favorite authors and illustrators as a part of literature study.

Filmstrips, videotapes, and other audiovisual materials about authors and illustrators are becoming increasingly available. Persons who have won the Caldecott or

FIGURE 3.9   Resources About Authors and Illustrators

Reference Books

(1962–1988). *Contemporary authors: A bio-bibliographical guide to current writers in fiction, general nonfiction, poetry, and journalism, drama, motion pictures, television, and other fields* (122 volumes). Detroit: Gale Research.

Commire, A. D. (Ed.). (1971–1988). *Something about the author: Facts and pictures about contemporary authors and illustrators of books for young people* (vols. 1–50). Detroit: Gale Research.

Estes, G. E. (Ed.). (1987). *Dictionary of literary biography. Volume 52: American writers for children since 1960: Fiction.* Detroit: Gale Research.

Estes, G. E. (Ed.). (1987). *Dictionary of literary biography. Volume 61: American writers for children since 1960: Poets, illustrators, and nonfiction authors.* Detroit: Gale Research.

Hopkins, L. B. (1987). *Pass the poetry, please.* New York: HarperCollins.

Loertscher, D. V., & Castle, L. (1991). *A state-by-state guide to children's and young adult authors and illustrators.* Englewood, CO: Libraries Unlimited.

McElmeel, S. L. (1988). *An author a month (for pennies).* Englewood, CO: Libraries Unlimited.

McElmeel, S. L. (1989). *Bookpeople: A first album.* Englewood, CO: Libraries Unlimited.

McElmeel, S. L. (1989). *Bookpeople: A second album.* Englewood, CO: Libraries Unlimited.

McElmeel, S. L. (1990). *An author a month (for nickels).* Englewood, CO: Libraries Unlimited.

Roginsky, J. (1985). *Behind the covers: Interviews with authors and illustrators of books for children and young adults.* Englewood, CO: Libraries Unlimited.

Roginsky, J. (1989). *Behind the covers: Interviews with authors and illustrators of books for children and young adults* (Vol. 2). Englewood, CO: Libraries Unlimited.

Sarkissian, A. (Ed.). (1986–1987). *Something about the author autobiography series* (vols. 1–4). Detroit: Gale Research.

Journals

Book Links, American Library Association, 50 E. Huron Street, Chicago, IL 60611

The Horn Book, 14 Beacon Street, Boston, MA 02108

Language Arts, National Council of Teachers of English, 1111 Kenyon Road, Urbana, IL 60801

The New Advocate, Christopher-Gordon Publishers, 480 Washington Street, Norwood, MA 02062

Newbery Medals, including Arnold Lobel, Katherine Paterson, and Russell Freedman, or who are very popular, like Dr. Seuss, are most often profiled. In these audiovisual profiles, authors and illustrators are shown in their homes or studios and they talk about themselves, their families, their work, and other interests. The profiles are very interesting for teachers as well as for children. Three companies that sell videotapes and filmstrips about authors and illustrators are

American School Publishers
PO Box 408
Hightstown, NJ 08520–9377

Houghton Mifflin Company
Wayside Road
Burlington, MA 01803

Weston Woods
Weston, CT 06883

A third way students learn about authors and illustrators is by writing letters to them. It is important to caution, however, that students should write only to authors and illustrators with whose work they are familiar. In their letters, students share their ideas and feelings about books they are reading, ask how a particular character was developed, or why the illustrator used a particular art medium or style. They can also describe the books they have written. Most authors and illustrators reply to children's letters; however, because they receive thousands of letters from children every year their replies might be a promotional brochure with answers to commonly asked questions.

Beverly Cleary's award-winning book, *Dear Mr. Henshaw* (1983) offers a worthwhile lesson about what children (and their teachers) can realistically expect from authors and illustrators. Sometimes children want to become pen pals with authors and illustrators, and as much as these people don't want to disappoint children, it simply is not possible. When students write letters, they should follow the correct letter format with a return address, and use the process approach to write, revise, and edit their letters. The final copy should be neat, and they should enclose a self-addressed, stamped envelope for a reply. If students do not know the author or illustrator's home or office address, they can mail letters to the author or illustrator's publisher (the address is usually found on the copyright page, which follows the title page in a book). If the complete mailing address is not available, check *Books in Print* or *Literary Market Place,* two reference books that are available in most public libraries.

Another way children can learn about authors is by meeting them in person. Authors and illustrators often make public appearances at libraries, bookstores, and schools. Students also meet authors at young authors' conferences, often held in schools as the culminating event for a year's work in writing, or in libraries to spotlight an author and his or her books. Students are usually selected to attend the special conference on the basis of their interest or expertise in writing and share their writing and listen to the guest author talk about his or her work. Special-interest sessions help students hone their writing skills or experiment with new techniques. The conferences give students recognition for their work and emphasize the importance of writing.

Visual Literacy

Literacy has traditionally been defined as the ability to read and write, but today the term *literacy* is also used to describe other competencies (e.g., computer literacy) needed for full participation in modern society. One of these is *visual literacy,* the ability to comprehend and evaluate illustrations and the visual elements, art media, and artistic style used by the artist (Camp & Tompkins, 1990). Children develop visual literacy not only by looking at art masterpieces, studying about great artists, and museum field trips but also by studying the illustrations in children's trade books.

According to Stewig (1989), children develop visual literacy as they describe, compare, and value illustrations in trade books. Children begin by focusing on an illustration and describing it clearly, concisely, and concretely. Next, they compare two illustrations using common terminology about visual elements, art media, and styles of art. Two good ways to do this are to compare illustrations in two or more versions of a folktale or to compare illustrations in different alphabet books. Figure 3.10 presents a list of folktales published in picture book versions. As children develop visual literacy, they come to value one of the books more than the others. They prefer the illustrations in one of the books and can explain their preference using convincing reasons.

Teachers teach visual literacy when they focus children's attention on the illustrations as a part of reading and sharing literature experiences. This teaching strategy includes Stewig's three components—describe, compare, and value—and can be used as a part of other reading and sharing literature experiences. (The teaching strategy is adapted from Camp and Tompkins, 1990.) The steps are

Step 1: Choose books.   Choose one picture book or a pair of picture books that are similar in some way to share with students. If you plan to focus on one book, be sure that other books by the same illustrator, illustrated in the same artistic style, or illustrated with the same art media are available in the classroom for the comparison step. A pair of books that might be used with first or second graders is *The Mitten,* a Ukrainian folktale about a child who loses a mitten on a snowy day and the series of animals who move into the mitten. Finally one animal too many tries to squeeze in and the animals lose their home. One version was written by Alvin Tresselt and illustrated by Yaroslava (1964), and the newer version was written and illustrated by Jan Brett (1989).

Step 2: Introduce one of the books.   The teacher introduces one of the books, often by asking a question or drawing on children's background knowledge. For *The Mitten,* the teacher might ask whether any students have ever lost a mitten or glove. After providing an opportunity for students to talk about their experiences, the teacher might ask students to speculate on what might have happened to the lost mitten or glove.

Step 3: Read the book.   The teacher reads the book aloud to students, the class reads the book together using shared reading, or students read the book independently. For *The Mitten,* the teacher might choose to share Tresselt's version of the story first, waiting to introduce Brett's version in the comparison step.

FIGURE 3.10   Picture Book Versions of Folktales and Related Books (pp. 115–117)

"Beauty and the Beast"

Brett, J. (1989). *Beauty and the beast.* New York: Clarion. (M–U)
Mayer, M. (1978). *Beauty and the beast.* (Ill. by M. Mayer). New York: Macmillan. (M–U)

"Cinderella"

Brown, M. (1954). *Cinderella.* New York: Scribner. (P–M)
Climo, S. (1989). (Ill. by R. Heller). *The Egyptian Cinderella.* New York: Crowell. (M–U)
Cole, B. (1987). *Prince Cinders.* New York: Putnam. (M)
Dahl, R. (1983). *Roald Dahl's revolting rhymes.* New York: Knopf. (M–U)
Ehrlich, A. (1985). (Ill. by J. Jeffers). *Cinderella.* New York: Dial. (P–M)
Galdone, P. (1978). *Cinderella.* New York: McGraw-Hill. (P–M)
Hogrogian, N. (1981). *Cinderella.* New York: Greenwillow. (P–M)
Hooks, W. H. (1987). *Moss gown.* New York: Clarion. (M–U)
Huck, C. (1989). (Ill. by A. Lobel). *Princess Furball.* New York: Greenwillow. (P–M)
Louie, A. L. (1982). (Ill. by E. Young). *Yeh-Shen: A Cinderella story from China.* New York: Philomel. (M–U)
Shorto, R. (1990). *Cinderella: The untold story.* New York: Birch Lane Press. (P–M–U)
Steptoe, J. (1987). *Mufaro's beautiful daughters: An African tale.* New York: Lothrop. (P–M–U)

"The Emperor's New Clothes"

Calmenson, S. (1989). *The principal's new clothes.* New York: Scholastic. (P–M)
Westcott, N. B. (1984). *The emperor's new clothes.* New York: Aladdin. (P–M)

"The Gingerbread Boy"

Asbjornsen, P. C., & Moe, J. (1980). *The runaway pancake.* New York: Larousse. (P)
Brown, M. (1972). *The bun: A tale from Russia.* New York: Harcourt Brace Jovanovich. (P)
Cauley, L. B. (1988). *The pancake boy: An old Norwegian folk tale.* New York: Putnam. (P)
Galdone, P. (1975). *The gingerbread boy.* New York: Seabury. (P)
Jacobs, J. (n.d.). *Johnny-cake.* New York: Putnam. (P)
Jarrell, R. (1964). (Ill. by G. Williams). *The gingerbread rabbit.* New York: Collier. (P–M)
Lobel, A. (1978). *The pancake.* New York: Greenwillow. (P)
Oppenheim, J. (1986). (Ill. by A. Shachat). *You can't catch me!* Boston: Houghton Mifflin. (P)
Sawyer, R. (1953). *Journey cake, ho!* New York: Viking. (P–M)

"Goldilocks and the Three Bears"

Brett, J. (1990). *Goldilocks and the three bears.* New York: Putnam. (P)
Cauley, L. B. (1981). *Goldilocks and the three bears.* New York: Putnam. (P)
Dahl, R. (1983). *Roald Dahl's revolting rhymes.* New York: Knopf. (M–U)
Galdone, P. (1972). *The three bears.* New York: Clarion. (P)
Marshall, J. (1988). *Goldilocks and the three bears.* New York: Dial. (P)
Tolhurst, M. (1990). (Ill. by S. Abel). *Somebody and the three Blairs.* New York: Orchard Books. (P)
Turkle, B. (1976). *Deep in the forest.* New York: Dutton. (P)

"The Hare and the Tortoise"

Castle, C. (1985). (Ill. by P. Weevers). *The hare and the tortoise.* New York: Dial. (M)
Galdone, P. (1962). *The hare and the tortoise.* New York: MacGraw-Hill. (P–M)
Stevens, J. (1984). *The tortoise and the hare.* New York: Holiday House. (M)
Wildsmith, B. (1966). *The hare and the tortoise.* Oxford, England: Oxford University Press. (P–M)

FIGURE 3.10, *continued*

"Jack and the Beanstalk"

Briggs, R. (1970). *Jim and the beanstalk.* New York: Coward, McCann & Geoghegan. (P–M)
Cauley, L. B. (1983). *Jack and the beanstalk.* New York: Putnam. (P–M)
Cole, B. (1986). *The giant's toe.* New York: Farrar, Straus & Giroux. (P–M)
Dahl, R. (1983). *Roald Dahl's revolting rhymes.* New York: Knopf. (M–U)
de Regniers, B. S. (1985). (Ill. by A. Wilsdorf). *Jack and the beanstalk.* New York: Macmillan. (P–M)
Galdone, P. (1974). *Jack and the beanstalk.* New York: Clarion. (P–M)
Haley, G. E. (1986). *Jack and the bean tree.* New York: Crown. (P–M)
Howe, J. (1989). *Jack and the beanstalk.* Boston: Little, Brown. (P–M)
Still, J. (1977). (Ill. by M. Tomes). *Jack and the wonder beans.* New York: Putnam. (P–M)

"Little Red Riding Hood"

Dahl, R. (1983). *Roald Dahl's revolting rhymes.* New York: Knopf. (M–U)
deRegniers, B. S. (1972). *Red riding hood.* New York: Atheneum. (M–U)
Emberley, M. (1990). *Ruby.* Boston: Little, Brown. (M–U)
Galdone, P. (1974). *Little red riding hood.* New York: McGraw-Hill. (P–M)
Goodall, J. S. (1988). *Little red riding hood.* New York: McElderry Books. (P–M–U)
Grimm, J. (1983). *Little red cap.* New York: Morrow. (M–U)
Hyman, T. S. (1983). *Little red riding hood.* New York: Holiday House. (P–M)
Marshall, J. (1987). *Red riding hood.* New York: Dial. (P–M)
Young, E. (1989). *Lon po po: A red-riding hood story from China.* New York: Philomel. (M–U)
Zwerger, L. (1983). *Little red cap.* New York: Morrow. (M)

"The Princess and the Frog"

Berenzy, A. (1989). *A frog prince.* New York: Henry Holt. (P–M–U)
Gwynne, F. (1990). *Pondlarker.* New York: Simon & Schuster. (M–U)
Isadora, R. (1989). *The princess and the frog.* New York: Greenwillow. (P–M–U)
Isele, E. (1984). *The frog princess.* (Ill. by M. Hague). New York: Crowell. (P–M–U)
Scieszka, J. (1991). *The frog prince continued.* New York: Viking. (M–U)
Tarcov, E. H. (1974). *The frog prince.* (Ill. by J. Marshall). New York: Scholastic. (P–M–U)

"Puss in Boots"

Brown, M. (1952). Puss in boots. New York: Scribner. (M)
Galdone, P. (1979). *Puss in boots.* New York: Clarion. (P–M)
Goodall, J. (1990). *Puss in boots.* New York: McElderry. (P–M)
Perrault, C. (1990). (Ill. by F. Marcellino). *Puss in boots.* New York: Farrar, Straus & Giroux. (M)

"Rumpelstiltskin"

Galdone, P. (1985). *Rumpelstiltskin.* New York: Clarion. (M)
Ness, E. (1965). *Tom tit tot.* New York: Scribner. (M)
Zelinsky, P. O. (1986). *Rumpelstiltskin.* New York: Dutton. (M)
Zemach, H., & Zemach, M. (1973). *Duffy and the devil.* New York: Farrar, Straus & Giroux. (M–U)

"Sleeping Beauty"

Hyman, T. S. (1977). *The sleeping beauty.* Boston: Little, Brown. (M)
Yolen, J. (1981). *Sleeping ugly.* (Ill. by D. Stanley). New York: Coward-McCann. (M)
Yolen, J. (1986). *The sleeping beauty.* New York: Knopf. (M)

FIGURE 3.10, *continued*

"Stone Soup"

Brown, M. (1975). *Stone soup.* New York: Aladdin Books. (P–M)
McGovern, A. (1968). *Stone soup.* New York: Scholastic. (P–M)
Ross, T. (1987). *Stone soup.* New York: Dial. (P–M)
Stewig, J. W. (1991). *Stone soup.* (Ill. by M. Tomes). New York: Holiday House. (P–M)
Van Rynbach, I. (1988). *The soup stone.* New York: Greenwillow. (P–M)

"The Three Little Pigs"

Dahl, R. (1983). *Roald Dahl's revolting rhymes.* New York: Knopf. (M–U)
Galdone, P. (1970). *The three little pigs.* New York: Seabury. (P)
Hooks, W. H. (1989). *The three little pigs and the fox.* New York: Macmillan. (P)
Scieszka, J. (1989). (Ill. by L. Smith). *The true story of the three little pigs.* New York: Viking. (P–M–U)
Zemach, M. (1988). *The three little pigs.* New York: Farrar, Straus & Giroux. (P)

Step 4: Discuss the book and describe the illustrations. Students and the teacher discuss the book, talking about both the text and the illustrations. Teachers ask students to focus on the illustrations and describe them in *The Mitten,* students talk about the events of the story and what happens to the mitten when the cricket tries to squeeze inside. (It bursts like a balloon into many little pieces.) They focus on the sequence of the animals moving inside the mitten and the irony that a tiny cricket is the animal that causes the mitten to burst apart. Then they discuss the illustrations. Yaroslava's illustrations are done in pen and ink and color is used for the child, the mitten, and the clothes each animal wears. This technique calls attention to the characters and events of the story. They notice that the pages alternate between white and aqua-colored backgrounds.

Step 5: Compare and contrast the book with another book. The teacher presents another book to compare and contrast with the first book, or students suggest a book to be compared. This book is then shared and discussed. Then students focus on the illustrations and make comparisons and contrasts between the books. They notice visual elements, media, and artistic styles. Now the teacher shares Jan Brett's version of *The Mitten.* Students notice the difference in illustrations immediately. In Brett's version, the illustrations are lavish, colorful, and full of details with side panels that review a previous event in the story on the left side of the page and suggest the next event on the right side of the page. Brett's retelling is similar to Tresselt's but different animals scramble into the mitten in each version. The ending is different, however. In Tresselt's version the mitten bursts apart when the cricket tries to squeeze in. In Brett's version a mouse climbs in and settles on the bear's nose, which causes the bear to sneeze and the mitten shoots into the air, leaving all the animals without their snug home. The boy finds his mitten but never knows why it is so stretched out of shape. While the illustrations are very different, students note that the ethnic flavor of the folktale is clear in both books. Students and the teacher work together to make a compare-contrast chart or Venn diagram on the chalkboard or on a large piece of paper as they discuss the two versions.

Step 6: Respond to the books.   Students respond to the books through different types of activities. For example, they might dramatize the story, write a retelling of it, make a mural or other art project, experiment with the art media used in one of the books, or read other books related to the books. Through these activities they explore their understanding of the book and develop an appreciation of it. After reading *The Mitten,* students might dramatize the story by crawling under a large sheet to pretend they are inside the mitten. Or, they might draw pictures of the events in the folktale and hang them on a story clothesline to sequence their retelling of *The Mitten.*

Step 7: Evaluate and value the books.   Students evaluate the books they have read or listened to by giving specific, meaningful explanations for their preferences and opinions. Sometimes, teachers have students write or dictate reasons for their preferences and list them on a chart or make a graph of them. Students' preferences for *The Mitten* are interesting. Many students prefer Brett's more colorful and detailed version, but other students prefer Tresselt's simpler retelling because they find that Brett's illustrations interrupt the story. They say that there is too much information in the illustrations.

When teachers ask students to focus on illustrations and how they enhance a story, students develop visual literacy. A list of other guidelines for developing visual literacy is presented in Figure 3.11.

MAKING DECISIONS ABOUT AUTHORS AND ILLUSTRATORS

In the case studies at the beginning of this chapter, students were reading and comparing books written by an author, experimenting with art media, and examining the art styles of illustrations in picture books. Mrs. Smiley and her kindergartners were reading books written and illustrated by Ezra Jack Keats and experimenting with collage, Keats' art medium. Mr. Jurey's focus was on illustration as his seventh grade art class studied expressionism and examined picture books to find examples of expressionistic art. The decisions these two teachers made about involving their students in activities to learn about authors, illustrators, and illustration were based on their goal of having students acquire personal literary preferences and develop an appreciation for the crafts of writing and illustration.

As a part of literature-based reading, teachers make decisions about authors, illustrators, and illustration, and these decisions must be based on knowledge. Through wide reading and some careful research, teachers learn about children's favorite authors and illustrators, and they use this information for minilessons and thematic units. Teachers also need to learn about artistic elements, media, and styles and how they are used in children's literature. Moreover, teachers should make it a point to be more observant of the illustrations as they read picture books; that is to say, that they should develop their own visual literacy.

With background knowledge about authors, illustrators, and illustration, teachers can support students as they develop a concept of author (and illustrator) and focus students' attention on illustrations as they develop visual literacy. Teachers should also plan and teach minilessons about and focus units on authors, illustrators,

FIGURE 3.11   Guidelines for Developing Visual Literacy

1. *Take time to talk about the illustrations in picture books.*
    When reading picture books, take time to talk about the illustrator's use of line, color, and other visual elements, media, artistic styles, the mood evoked by the illustration, and how the illustration enriches the text of the book.
2. *Teach the terminology used in discussing art.*
    As they talk about illustrations, teachers should use basic terms such as

    • line, space, color, shape, texture, and perspective to describe the visual elements of illustrations
    • media, such as watercolors, pen and ink, pastels, oils, woodcuts, collage used in illustrations
    • realistic, folk, impressionistic, and other art styles

3. *Compare the illustrations in different versions of a story.*
    Many folktales, such as "Stone Soup," "The Hare and the Tortoise," and "Little Red Riding Hood," have been published in different picture book versions. The text of each version is slightly different, and the illustrators use different media and artistic styles. Children compare these versions, noting differences in the texts and illustrations as well as the interrelationships between the text and illustrations.
4. *Experiment with various media.*
    Students experiment with various media used to illustrate children's literature. Through this experimentation and by using various media to illustrate their own writing, students will develop an appreciation for art.
5. *Plan focus units on illustrators.*
    Plan and teach focus units on the books illustrated by favorite illustrators, such as Eric Carle, Leo Lionni, Leo and Diane Dillon, Chris Van Allsburg, and the Provensens. In these units, provide opportunities for students to describe, compare, and value the illustrations as well as to experiment with the artistic media used by the illustrator.
6. *Encourage children to value favorite illustrations and illustrators.*
    Just as children have favorite books and authors, they should be so familiar with illustrators, artistic media and styles used in illustrations that they can develop preferences for illustrators and illustrations. Through experiences with literature and art, children learn to value illustrations and to make choices about the books they read based on these personal preferences.

and illustration. Literature-based reading, as it is discussed in this book, is much more than just reading the words on a page.

In summary, teachers should consider the following points as they make decisions about involving authors, illustrators, and types of illustration in literature-based reading:

• Become informed about children's favorite authors and illustrators.
• Learn about artistic elements, media, styles and how they are used in children's literature.
• Support students as they develop a concept of author and a concept of illustrator.
• Focus students' attention on illustrations and help them develop visual literacy.

FIGURE 3.12   Summary Chart for Decision Tree

Decision Tree

Chapter 1	Using Literature in the Reading Program
Chapter 2	Choosing Literature for Children

Learning About Authors and Illustrators

- **Become informed about children's favorite authors and illustrators.**
- **Learn about artistic elements, media, styles, and how they are used in children's literature.**
- **Support students as they develop a concept of author and a concept of illustrator.** (Chapter 3)
- **Focus students' attention on illustrations and help them develop visual literacy.**
- **Teach minilessons about authors, illustrators, and illustration.**
- **Plan and teach a focus unit on an author, illustrator, or type of illustration.**

Chapter 4	Identifying Perspectives for Reading Instruction
Chapter 5	Teaching from a Reader Response Perspective
Chapter 6	Teaching from a Critical Perspective
Chapter 7	Teaching from an Interactive Perspective
Chapter 8	Putting It All Together
Chapter 9	Assessing Students' Learning

- Teach minilessons about authors, illustrators, and illustration.
- Plan and teach a focus unit on an author, illustrator, or type of illustration.

This information is added to the decision-making diagram (in Figure 3.12) that was begun in the first chapter and will be added to throughout this book.

REFERENCES

Camp, D. J., & Tompkins, G. E. (1990). The abecedarius: Soldier of literacy. *Childhood Education, 66,* 298–302.

Cianciolo, P. (1976). *Illustrations in children's books* (2nd ed.). Dubuque, IA: William C. Brown.

Huck, C. S., Hepler, S., & Hickman, J. (1987). *Chil-* *dren's literature in the elementary classroom* (4th ed.). New York: Holt, Rinehart & Winston.

Norton, D. E. (1991). *Through the eyes of a child: An introduction to children's literature* (3rd ed.). New York: Merrill/Macmillan.

Rudman, M. K. (1989). People behind the books: Illustrators. In M. K. Rudman (Ed.), *Children's lit-*

erature: Resource for the classroom (pp. 19–36). Norwood, MA: Christopher-Gordon.

Stewig, J. W. (1989). Book illustration: Key to visual and oral literacy. In J. W. Stewig & S. L. Sebesta (Eds.), *Using literature in the elementary class-room* (rev. ed.) (pp. 55–74). Urbana, IL: National Council of Teachers of English.

Sutherland, Z., & Arbuthnot, M. H. (1986). *Children and books* (7th ed.). Glenview, IL: Scott, Foresman.

CHILDREN'S LITERATURE REFERENCES

Aardema, V. (1975). *Why mosquitoes buzz in people's ears.* New York: Dial.

Aardema, V. (1977). *Who's in rabbit's house?* New York: Dial.

Aldis, D. (1969). *Nothing is impossible: The story of Beatrix Potter.* New York: Atheneum.

Aliki. (1986). *How a book is made.* New York: Doubleday.

Anno, M. (1983). *Anno's USA.* New York: Philomel.

Arnold Lobel (Meet the Newbery Author Series). (1981). Westminster, MD: Random House.

Baylor, B. (1986). *I'm in charge of celebrations.* New York: Scribner.

Brett, J. (1989). *The mitten.* New York: Putnam.

Brown, M. (1961). *Once a mouse.* New York: Aladdin Books.

Bunting, E. (1988). *How many days to America: A Thanksgiving story.* New York: Clarion.

Bunting, E. (1989). *The Wednesday surprise.* New York: Clarion.

Burningham, J. (1977). *Come away from the water, Shirley.* New York: Crown.

Carle, E. (1975). *The very hungry caterpillar.* New York: Philomel.

Carle, E. (1984). *The mixed-up chameleon.* New York: Crowell.

Carle, E. (1986). *Papa, please get the moon for me.* Natick, MA: Picture Book Studio.

Cleary, B. (1983). *Dear Mr. Henshaw.* New York: Morrow.

Cole, J. (1989). *The magic school bus inside the human body.* New York: Scholastic.

Cooney, B. (1982). *Miss Rumphius.* New York: Viking.

Dahl, R. (1984). *Boy.* New York: Farrar, Straus & Giroux.

de Paola, T. (1973). *Nana upstairs and Nana downstairs.* New York: Putnam

de Paola, T. (1975). *Strega nona.* Englewood Cliffs, NJ: Prentice-Hall.

de Paola, T. (1978). *Pancakes for breakfast.* New York: Harcourt Brace Jovanovich.

de Paola, T. (1978). *The popcorn book.* New York: Holiday House.

de Paola, T. (1979). *Oliver Button is a sissy.* New York: Harcourt Brace Jovanovich.

de Paola, T. (1981). *Now one foot, now the other.* New York: Putnam.

de Paola, T. (1982). *Charlie needs a cloak.* Englewood Cliffs, NJ: Prentice-Hall.

de Paola, T. (1982). *Georgio's village.* New York: Putnam.

de Paola, T. (1984). *The cloud book.* New York: Holiday House.

de Paola, T. (1985). *The legend of the bluebonnet.* New York: Putnam.

de Paola, T. (1985). *Tomie de Paola's Mother Goose.* New York: Putnam.

de Paola, T. (1987). *An early American Christmas.* New York: Holiday House.

de Paola, T. (1988). *The legend of the Indian paintbrush.* New York: Putnam.

de Paola, T. (1989). *The art lesson.* New York: Putnam.

de Paola, T. (1989). *Tony's bread.* New York: Putnam.

Ehlert, L. (1989). *Color zoo.* New York: Lippincott.

Ehlert, L. (1990). *Feathers for lunch.* San Diego: Harcourt Brace Jovanovich.

Ehlert, L. (1990). *Fish eyes.* San Diego: Harcourt Brace Jovanovich.

Freedman, R. (1987). *Lincoln: A photobiography.* New York: Clarion.

Fritz, J. (1982). *Homesick: My own story.* New York: Putnam.

Gag, W. (1956). *Millions of cats.* New York: Scholastic.

George, J. C. (1972). *Julie of the wolves.* New York: Harper & Row.

Goodall, J. (1983). *Above and below stairs.* New York: Atheneum.

Goodall, J. S. (1986). *The story of a castle.* New York: Atheneum.

Greenfield, E. (1978). *Honey, I love and other love poems.* New York: Crowell.

Haley, G. E. (1973). *Jack Jouett's ride.* New York: Viking.

Hall, D. (1979). *The ox-cart man.* New York: Viking.

Heller, R. (1981). *Chickens aren't the only ones.* New York: Grosset & Dunlap.

Heller, R. (1982). *Animals born alive and well.* New York: Grosset & Dunlap.

Heller, R. (1983). *The reason for a flower.* New York: Grosset & Dunlap.

Heller, R. (1984). *Plants that never ever bloom.* New York: Grosset & Dunlap.

Heller, R. (1986). *How to hide a whip-poor-will and other birds.* New York: Grosset & Dunlap.

Heller, R. (1987). *A cache of jewels and other collective nouns.* New York: Grosset & Dunlap.

Heller, R. (1988). *Kites sail high: A book about verbs.* New York: Grosset & Dunlap.

Heller, R. (1989). *Many luscious lollipops: A book about adjectives.* New York: Grosset & Dunlap.

Heller, R. (1990). *Merry-go-round: A book about nouns.* New York: Grosset & Dunlap.

Hoban, T. (1990). *Shadows and reflections.* New York: Greenwillow.

Hodges, M. (1984). *Saint George and the dragon.* Boston: Little, Brown.

Howe, J. (1987). *I wish I were a butterfly.* San Diego: Harcourt Brace Jovanovich.

Keats, E. J. (1962). *The snowy day.* New York: Viking.

Keats, E. J. (1963). *Whistle for Willie.* New York: Viking.

Keats, E. J. (1967). *Peter's chair.* New York: Harper & Row.

Keats, E. J. (1970). *Hi, cat!* New York: Macmillan.

Lasky, K. (1983). *Sugaring time.* New York: Macmillan.

Lionni, L. (1963). *Swimmy.* New York: Knopf.

Livingston, M. C. (1985). *Celebrations.* New York: Holiday House.

Longfellow, H. W. (1990). *Paul Revere's ride.* New York: Dutton.

Macaulay, D. (1975). *Pyramid.* Boston: Houghton Mifflin.

Macaulay, D. (1977). *Castle.* Boston: Houghton Mifflin.

Mahy, M. (1987). *17 kings and 42 elephants.* New York: Dial.

Marshall, J. (1987). *Red riding hood.* New York: Dial.

Martin, B., Jr., & Archambault, J. (1985). *The ghost-eye tree.* New York: Holt, Rinehart & Winston.

Martin, B., Jr., & Archambault, J. (1989). *Chicka chicka boom boom.* New York: Simon & Schuster.

Mathis, S. B. (1975). *The hundred penny box.* New York: Viking.

Mayer, M. (1974). *Frog goes to dinner.* New York: Dial.

McCloskey, R. (1969). *Make way for ducklings.* Boston: Houghton Mifflin.

McDermott, G. (1972). *Anansi the spider: A tale from the Ashanti.* New York: Henry Holt.

Miller, J. (1983). *The human body.* New York: Viking.

Munthe, N. (1983). *Meet Matisse.* Boston: Little, Brown.

Musgrove, M. (1976). *Ashanti to Zulu: African traditions.* New York: Dial.

Nixon, J. L. (1988). *If you were a writer.* New York: Four Winds Press.

Paterson, K. (1990). *The tale of the Mandarin ducks.* New York: Dutton.

Patterson, F. (1985). *Koko's kitten.* New York: Scholastic.

Peet, B. (1961). *Huge Harold.* Boston: Houghton Mifflin.

Peet, B. (1989). *Bill Peet: An autobiography.* Boston: Houghton Mifflin.

Perrault, C. (1990). *Puss in boots.* New York: Farrar, Straus & Giroux.

Polacco, P. (1988). *Rechenka's eggs.* New York: Philomel.

Prelutsky, J. (1970). *Toucans two and other poems.* New York: Macmillan.

Prelutsky, J. (1974). *Circus.* New York: Macmillan.

Prelutsky, J. (1976) *Nightmares: Poems to trouble your sleep.* New York: Greenwillow.

Prelutsky, J. (1977). *It's Halloween.* New York: Scholastic.

Prelutsky, J. (1977). *The snopp on the sidewalk and other poems.* New York: Greenwillow.

Prelutsky, J. (1980). *The headless horseman rides tonight: More poems to trouble your sleep.* New York: Greenwillow.

Prelutsky, J. (1981). *It's Christmas.* New York: Scholastic.

Prelutsky, J. (1983). *It's Valentine's Day.* New York: Scholastic.

Prelutsky, J. (1983). *The Random House book of poetry for children.* New York: Random House.

Prelutsky, J. (1984). *It's snowing! It's snowing!* New York: Greenwillow.

Prelutsky, J. (1984). *The new kid on the block.* New York: Greenwillow.

Prelutsky, J. (1985). *My parents think I'm sleeping.* New York: Greenwillow.

Prelutsky, J. (1986). *Ride a purple pelican.* New York: Greenwillow.

Prelutsky, J. (1988). *Tyrannosaurus was a beast.* New York: Greenwillow.

Prelutsky, J. (1989). *Poems of A. Nonny Mouse.* New York: Knopf.

Prelutsky, J. (1990). *Something BIG has been here.* New York: Greenwillow.

Price, L. (1990). *Aida.* San Diego: Harcourt Brace Jovanovich.

Provensen, A. (1990). *The buck stops here.* New York: HarperCollins.

Provensen, A., & Provensen, M. (1984). *Leonardo da Vinci.* New York: Viking.

Sciesza, J. (1989). *The true story of the three little pigs.* New York: Viking.

Steptoe, J. (1984). *The story of jumping mouse.* New York: Mulberry Books.

Tresselt, A. (1964). *The mitten.* New York: Lothrop.

Turner, A. (1987). *Nettie's trip south.* New York: Macmillan.

Van Allsburg, C. (1981). *Jumanji.* Boston: Houghton Mifflin.

Van Allsburg, C. (1982). *Ben's dream.* Boston: Houghton Mifflin.

Van Allsburg, C. (1985). *The polar express.* Boston: Houghton Mifflin.

Van Allsburg, C. (1988). *Two bad ants.* Boston: Houghton Mifflin.

Waber, B. (1962). *The house on East 88th Street.* Boston: Houghton Mifflin.

Waber, B. (1964). *Just like Abraham Lincoln.* Boston: Houghton Mifflin.

Waber, B. (1965). *Lyle, Lyle crocodile.* Boston: Houghton Mifflin.

Waber, B. (1966). *Lyle and the birthday party.* Boston: Houghton Mifflin.

Waber, B. (1969). *Lovable Lyle.* Boston: Houghton Mifflin.

Waber, B. (1972). *Ira sleeps over.* Boston: Houghton Mifflin.

Waber, B. (1974). *Lyle finds his mother.* Boston: Houghton Mifflin.

Waber, B. (1987). *Funny, funny Lyle.* Boston: Houghton Mifflin.

Waber, B. (1988). *Ira says goodbye.* Boston: Houghton Mifflin.

Williams, V. B. (1982). *A chair for my mother.* New York: Mulberry.

Winter, J. (1988). *Follow the drinking gourd.* New York: Knopf.

Xiong, B. (1989). *Nine-in-one. Grr! Grr!* San Francisco: Children's Book Press.

Yolen, J. (1987). *Owl moon.* New York: Philomel.

Young, E. (1989). *Lon po po: A red-riding hood story from China.* New York: Philomel.

Zelinsky, P. O. (1986). *Rumpelstiltskin.* New York: Dutton.

Ziefert, H. (1986). *A new coat for Anna.* New York: Knopf.

CHAPTER 4

IDENTIFYING PERSPECTIVES ON READING INSTRUCTION

> **In this chapter you will learn to make decisions about:**
> - **Reflecting on your present beliefs about learning to read and teaching reading with literature**
> - **Becoming more knowledgeable about the reader response, critical, and interactive theoretical perspectives and their implications for instruction**
> - **Considering how all three theoretical perspectives can be woven into a literature program that helps children to prepare for reading, read, explore, and extend the text (story, poem, or informational book)**

IN THESE THREE CASE STUDIES, Mrs. Figlock, Ms. Chauvez, and Mr. Williams use literature to teach reading. These teachers have different beliefs about teaching reading with literature, and their beliefs reflect different theoretical perspectives. In this chapter we will identify and explore beliefs and theoretical perspectives that guide teachers as they teach literature-based reading.

A CASE IN POINT

Mrs. Figlock's Reading Workshop

Mrs. Figlock believes that one of the most important ways to help children become better readers is to listen to what they say about stories, poems, and informational books they are reading. She has found that children respond differently to the same story or poem and that they are able to share informally what they think that stories, poems, and informational books mean. To expand her students' ways of responding and articulating those responses, Mrs. Figlock demonstrates a variety of different ways that readers explore literature in minilessons.

Mrs. Figlock begins reading workshop by reading aloud the last chapter of *The Phantom Tollbooth* (Juster, 1961), a story about a lazy boy, Milo, who travels to a strange land to learn the importance of words and numbers, patience, and re-

sponsibility that she has been reading for nearly three weeks. Then she begins a minilesson by introducing the concept of character growth. She says, "One of the reasons I like this book is because Milo grows and changes during the story. At the end he is much more grown up; he wanted to go back through the tollbooth, but at the beginning he didn't. Milo reminds me of when I was 7 years old and I got some Lincoln Logs. I never wanted to play with them. Then my three cousins—all boys—came to visit for a week. They wanted to play with the Lincoln Logs all the time. I didn't want to, but pretty soon I was playing with the Lincoln Logs, too. When they left I really missed playing with them. Milo reminded me of myself and how I felt about playing with Lincoln Logs with my cousins. I didn't like the toy or my cousins very much, but after they left I missed playing with them." Several students tell about books they have read in which the characters grow and change. Marge recalls, "Leigh in *Dear Mr. Henshaw* (Cleary, 1983) learns to understand his dad and accept his parents' divorce," and Joe adds, "Al in *Hey, Al* (Yorinks, 1986) changes, too. He accepts and even finds joy in his life as a janitor."

During the next part of reading workshop students read their own self-selected books. Mrs. Figlock suggests that they might want to think about character growth or about how their book reminds them of their own lives as they read. The students read for 15 to 30 minutes and then begin writing in their response journals. Mrs. Figlock meets with a few students and they talk about what they are reading. Some students begin work on response activities to extend their reading, such as building a diorama (a table-top display of the setting of a story) or writing a readers' theatre script.

A CASE IN POINT

Ms. Chauvez's Circle Stories

Ms. Chauvez believes that good readers know a great deal about literature. They compare and contrast stories, poems, and informational books and discuss character, setting, plot, and theme. The students in her third grade class have recently read three stories: *Brave Irene* (Steig, 1986), *The Story about Ping* (Flack & Wiese, 1933), and *Hetty and Harriet* (Oakley, 1981). After students read each story they wrote responses in special literature journals and then talked together about the stories. Today they will examine what these stories have in common.

Ms. Chauvez has drawn a large circle on the chalkboard with the word *home* written at the top. She begins by saying, "*Brave Irene* is a circle story. The story begins with Irene at home with her mother who is a seamstress. She has just finished sewing a new ball gown for the duchess but is too sick to take it to her. So Irene decides to take the dress to the duchess herself even though it will be a long, difficult trip over the mountain during a snow storm. Irene packs the dress in a box and dresses warmly for the trip. Then Irene begins her trip. She faces danger as the winter storm gets worse. The temperature gets colder, the wind blows harder, and the snow piles deeper, but Irene keeps walking. A strong gust of wind blows open the dress box, and the new gown is blown away. Irene tries to get the dress back, but she can't. She continues walking to the palace to tell the duchess what happened. Then she sees the palace and uses the dress box as a sled. Outside the palace Irene finds the duchess's new dress caught on a tree. Finally, Irene arrives at the palace with the duchess's gown. Because the storm is so bad, she stays at the palace overnight and returns to her home the next day in a horse-drawn sleigh." As she talks, Ms. Chauvez writes these events around the circle she has drawn on the chalkboard, as shown in Figure 4.1.

Next, Ms. Chauvez asks the children to retell *The Story About Ping*. She says, "Before we begin retelling the events of this story, let's think about the story as a circle. Does it begin and end at home?" The children agree that the story has a circle structure and dictate the events in the story as Ms. Chauvez writes them around another circle drawn on the chalkboard. Next, the children divide into small groups to reread *Hetty and Harriet* and make a circle chart for it. Each group has a large sheet of paper on which they draw a circle and write the story events.

FIGURE 4.1   A Circle Chart for *Brave Irene* (Steig, 1986)

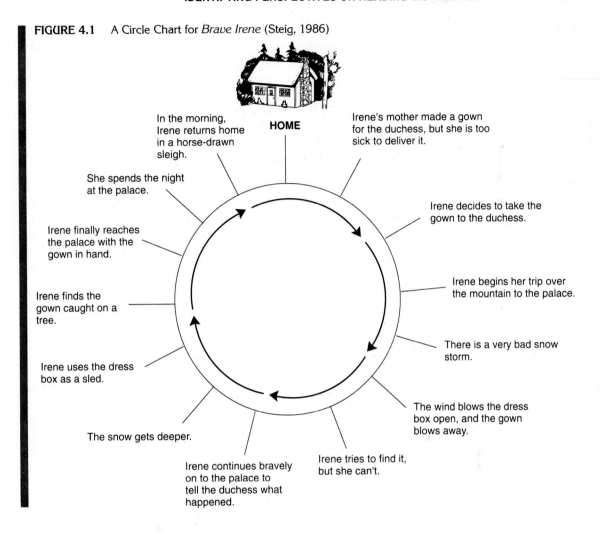

In the morning, Irene returns home in a horse-drawn sleigh.

HOME

Irene's mother made a gown for the duchess, but she is too sick to deliver it.

She spends the night at the palace.

Irene decides to take the gown to the duchess.

Irene finally reaches the palace with the gown in hand.

Irene begins her trip over the mountain to the palace.

Irene finds the gown caught on a tree.

There is a very bad snow storm.

Irene uses the dress box as a sled.

The wind blows the dress box open, and the gown blows away.

The snow gets deeper.

Irene tries to find it, but she can't.

Irene continues bravely on to the palace to tell the duchess what happened.

A CASE IN POINT

Mr. Williams' Science Lesson

Mr. Williams believes that good readers use their knowledge about a topic to understand what they read. He uses a variety of activities to help students think about what they know about a topic before reading and then to connect what they learned from reading to what they already knew. Mr. Williams and his first graders are studying about insects. They have read many stories, informational books, and poems about insects, and yesterday one child brought a caterpillar to school for the class insect collection. Today they will learn more about caterpillars. Mr. Williams will draw on what the children already know about caterpillars in teaching new concepts.

Mr. Williams has divided a large sheet of chart paper into three sections. The sections are labeled "Things We Know About Caterpillars," "Questions about Caterpillars," and "What We Learned about Caterpillars." Mr. Williams says, "Since so many of you were interested in the caterpillar that Derek brought yesterday, I found a book to read to you about caterpillars. Before we begin, let's talk about the things we already know about caterpillars." The children dictate things they know about caterpillars. Melissa says, "Caterpillars turn into butterflies," and Mr. Williams records this in the first section of the chart. After students dictate facts, they dictate their questions about caterpillars, which Mr. Williams records in the second section of the chart.

Next, Mr. Williams shares a big book, *The Caterpillar Diary* (Drew, 1987), an informational book about the life cycle of a butterfly, with the class. He reads the book pointing to the words as he reads and inviting children to predict and make comments. After sharing the book, the children talk about what they liked about the book, what interested them most, and what they learned. Then they dictate what they learned for Mr. Williams to write in the third column of the chart. Mr. Williams and the children reread the chart and compare what they knew before reading to what they learned through reading. The class adds other questions to the "Questions About Caterpillars" section of the chart for use later in their unit. Mr. Williams places the chart in the science center along with the big book and several other books on insects.

INTRODUCTION

In these case studies, Mrs. Figlock, Ms. Chauvez, and Mr. Williams used methods of instruction that reflected their beliefs about how children learn to read and how to teach reading with literature. Beliefs are our personal knowledge of how something works and why, and they are also, in part, a set of values that we have toward a certain activity or object. Beliefs influence the kinds of lessons that teachers teach and the kinds of things that children learn; therefore, important questions for teachers who are planning literature-based reading programs are, "What do I believe about how children learn to read?" and "How do I teach reading with literature?" The answers to these questions reveal your beliefs.

All teachers, even when they are unaware of it, have beliefs about how children learn to read and how to teach reading with literature. These beliefs unconsciously guide teachers' decisions about the kinds of instruction they plan, the manner in which they interact with children during reading, and the ways children extend and enrich their reading experiences.

We begin this chapter by asking you to examine your beliefs about how children learn to read and the role of children's literature in teaching them to read. Then we provide information about three theoretical perspectives that have implications for reading acquisition and teaching reading with literature. Unlike beliefs, which are based on personal values and understanding, theoretical perspectives come from research and theories. They are used to explain how something works based on the evidence gathered from observation or rational arguments. The three theoretical perspectives we present are the (a) reader response perspective, as demonstrated by Mrs. Figlock's instruction in the first case study, (b) critical perspective, as demonstrated by Ms. Chauvez's instruction in the second case study, and (c) interactive perspective, as demonstrated by Mr. Williams' instruction in the third case study.

This chapter is divided into six parts. In the first part of the chapter we offer activities designed to help teachers make their beliefs about learning to read and teaching reading with literature more explicit. In the next three sections we describe three theoretical perspectives that underlie many teachers' beliefs about learning to read and teaching reading with literature. We present information about each perspective and discuss the instructional implications. In the fifth section we describe an instructional framework for planning reading lessons and activities, and in the final section, we discuss making decisions about theoretical perspectives in literature-based reading.

EXAMINING PERSONAL BELIEFS

What is reading? How do children learn to read? How do teachers teach reading? Why is children's literature important for teaching reading? These questions are more difficult to answer than they may seem at first. In fact, there is no one right answer to any one of them. If there were, we would have no children with reading problems! Even reading specialists and researchers cannot agree on the answers. Instead, we have different answers to each question based on several theories that explain what reading is, how reading develops, and how teachers can best teach reading.

To help you to examine what you believe, read the following statements about reading, literature, and teaching which represent different beliefs and theories about learning to read and teaching reading, and select the five that you think are the most important.

1. Good readers will not always get the same meaning from a book.
2. What readers know about a topic before reading is the most important component for understanding what is read.
3. What readers know about literature is the most important component for understanding what is read.
4. The activities that readers engage in during reading is the most important component for understanding what is read.
5. Identifying with characters and reacting emotionally to ideas, events, or images in the book is the most important component for understanding what is read.
6. Good readers know characteristics of genre and use these to interpret stories, poems, and informational books.
7. Good readers analyze character, plot, setting, point of view, and theme.
8. Good readers relate the events, characters, or images in a book to personal experiences and understandings.
9. Comprehension must include emotions; readers identify with characters and react emotionally to stories and poems.
10. Comprehension must include learning; readers find out important information.
11. Studying authors and illustrators is an essential part of learning to read; children who do not know authors and illustrators are not truly readers.

12. Children learn the most about books by answering insightful questions.
13. Children learn the most about books when they talk about what interested them in a book.
14. To teach reading, it is more important to know a lot about children's literature than to know a lot about reading.
15. To teach reading, it is more important to know a lot about reading than to know a lot about children's literature.

We could have listed many more statements about reading, literature, and teaching than these 15; however, these statements should generate sufficient thought about what you believe the essential components in reading instruction are. Take a moment to look for similarities among the five statements that you selected, and as you read the remainder of the chapter, try to determine which theoretical perspective each of the statements you selected reflects. All five statements you selected may fit within one perspective or you may have selected statements that fit within two or three of the theoretical perspectives. Compare your thinking with the classification of the statements according to the three theoretical perspectives in Figure 4.15 at the end of this chapter.

Most teachers' beliefs about teaching reading with literature fit with within one or more of three theoretical perspectives: reader response, critical, or interactive. We describe each of these perspectives and explain the instructional implications that can be drawn from each. Although we describe them separately, many aspects of the three perspectives do overlap. So, many beliefs that teachers have about teaching reading and many activities that teachers plan may fit within more than one perspective.

READER RESPONSE PERSPECTIVE

The *reader response perspective* arises from reader response criticism, a collection of theories that describe how readers read literature (Tompkins, 1980). This perspective attempts to explain reading and interpretation of literature. According to reader response critics, literature is not an object that can be studied and does not have a single correct interpretation that can be found in the text. Rather, literature is the lived-through experience of reading.

Reading as Experience

Readers do many things as they read. They hypothesize, pause to reflect on what they have read, revise hypotheses, visualize, and make associations between ideas in the text and their own experiences. These activities create an experience. That is, literature is not a thing, but rather the meanings that are evoked during the experience of reading. Fish (1970) demonstrated what is meant by "meaning as an experience" by exploring the experience a reader has when reading this sentence from *Paradise Lost:* "Nor did they not perceive the evil plight" (Milton, *Book I,* Lines 335–336).

When you begin to read Milton's sentence, the first word *nor* leads you to expect that a negative assertion will follow. You do not know what this negative assertion will be; nevertheless, you expect that a subject and a verb will follow the word *nor* which will clarify the negative assertion set up by this word. Thus, you continue to read the next two words *did* and *they,* which confirm your earlier expectation that a subject (*they*) and a verb (*did* is an auxiliary verb and it suggests the main verb will follow) would come next in the sentence. However, reading the next word in the sentence, *not,* makes you pause because it is totally unexpected. You ask—did they or didn't they? To answer the question you might apply the double negatives rule: *not* cancels out *nor* to create a positive statement—they did. However, Fish insisted that having a question about the meaning in the first place—the experience of pausing in the middle of understanding the sentence—is part of the sentence's meaning. The sentence means more than "They perceived their evil plight." The act of reading this sentence is not the same as reading Milton's sentence; therefore, their meanings are different.

From the reader response perspective, everything a reader does or experiences during reading contributes to meaning. Rosenblatt (1978) has described a wide variety of activities that readers engage in while reading literature, and these activities are listed in Figure 4.2.

These activities evoke certain images, ideas, feelings, associations, and connections for readers which Rosenblatt (1978) calls *the poem.* Rosenblatt's poem does not refer to what we normally think of as a poem—a text perhaps with rhyme or rhythm or spatially arranged on paper. Instead, Rosenblatt's poem is that which is formed in the minds of readers as they read a piece of literature. It is an experience or event that happens at the time of reading; it is the lived-through experience of reading.

What readers do while reading is influenced by who the reader is, what the reader knows, and what the text is. Readers have characteristic ways of viewing the

FIGURE 4.2 Activities That Readers Engage in While Reading Literature

- Call to mind past experiences including events, objects, and images.
- Select from various alternative referents for words (e.g., when reading the word *bank,* readers select the meaning relevant to the context).
- Find contexts in which referents to many words or symbols can be related (e.g., consider situations in which the words *banks* and *bridges* can be related).
- Form initial expectations.
- Construct images (e.g., visualize a bank or a bridge).
- Pause to reflect on current meaning (e.g., consider the emerging meaning or the experience of creating those meanings).
- Think back to meanings constructed early during reading and compare to current meaning.
- Revise original expectations.
- Call to mind images, feelings, attitudes, associations, and ideas that the words and their referents evoke (e.g., the word *bank* calls to mind a grassy slope from which children can dangle their feet into a lazy, cool stream).
- Make metaphoric connections among qualities of feeling, images, and tone (e.g., readers feel the impartial image of a bridge and the warmth of the image of a child at a stream. This tension calls to mind a possible connection between the innocence of childhood and the harsh realities of adulthood.).

world and reacting to experiences. They have had certain experiences, read certain literary works, and have certain emotions and feelings. These experiences, assumptions, expectations, and senses guide the selection of ideas, images, associations, and feelings that are evoked by the text. The text guides the readers' activities as well. You might say that the text acts as a blueprint within which readers select, reject, and order meanings.

The reader and the text influence one another. When they read, readers bring certain orientations and past experiences to the text. Yet the text is also creating new experiences and new orientations for readers. The relationship between readers and text is a dynamic, ever-changing *transaction*. Readers influence texts by using their past experiences to select certain images, feelings, and referents, while at the same time texts influence readers by creating new past experiences and orientations.

Reading as Engagement

Many readers say, "I couldn't put the book down" or "I felt like I was right there in the story." They weep, laugh, and shake their heads as if saying, "That's just how I feel." Readers identify with characters; they see themselves in the way characters act or feel. Such feelings signal a reader's engagement with the experience of reading.

One way that readers become engaged is through images (Iser, 1978). The images that readers construct during reading are not fully conceptualized mental pictures of what objects look, smell, taste, or feel like. Rather these images are ideas about things. Many people create images of characters, yet these images are not like photographs or even films of what characters look like, say, or do. The image of Charlotte from *Charlotte's Web* (White, 1952), for instance, constantly changes as we read the chapter book. The image synthesizes all the various facets of meaning created during reading. Readers do not just see a spider, but imagine a caring, daring, and clever person. We are most aware of the kinds of images we create when something goes wrong—when the character acts "out of character" or contrary to the expectations we have built up in our image (Iser, 1978).

Images are one way that readers create what is called a *secondary world,* the world in which characters, act, think, and feel. Readers feel both as if they are hovering above the secondary world, or standing in it alongside the characters and as if they were standing back and reflecting on this world (Langer, 1990). While readers are in the secondary world, they must suspend thoughts about their own lives and take on the thoughts of the characters in the secondary world; that is, they become lost in the story. As readers stand back from the secondary world, they are able to examine both the activities within the secondary world and their own lives as illuminated by the experience of being in that world. As readers think about the secondary world, they are able to see themselves with fresh insight, or from a new perspective.

Interpretive Communities

Individual readers respond to literature, and their responses reflect their unique reading experiences. However, when readers share their responses after reading a story or poem, many readers have common responses. That is, in any group of readers there will be both individual, unique responses and common responses. The reason that readers can respond commonly to a story or poem is because they belong to an interpretive community. Interpretive communities are readers who share a common interest in reading and responding to the same story or poem (Bleich, 1978).

Members of interpretive communities usually have in common not only the experience of reading the same story or poem, but may also belong to communities that share similar values and experiences. Sharing similar experiences and values means that readers more or less automatically interpret certain events or characters in similar ways. For example, if you were to read a story about a young mother playing ball with her toddler, you would assume that the character was a good woman who loved her child very much. You would make that interpretation based on the character's actions because you have certain beliefs about motherhood that you hold in common with most other adults in our society.

The purpose of interpretive communities is to develop understandings or interpretations of literature. Readers in an interpretive community will have both common understandings of a story or poem and unique understandings. Sharing unique responses with an interpretive community expands and enriches all readers' interpretation of the story or poem. Readers develop their interpretation or understanding as they share and negotiate their individual responses with an interpretive community (Bleich, 1978).

Literary Reading and Informative Reading

Rosenblatt (1978) distinguished between two kinds of reading: efferent or informative reading and aesthetic or literary reading. She argued that readers focus their attention in various ways according to their purposes for reading. An *efferent* stance or focus of attention means that readers intend to carry information away from reading. The reader concentrates on the public, common referents of the words and symbols in the text. For example, children might use this stance when reading the directions for putting together a model ship. Their attention is focused on what they need to do, not on the experience of reading.

In contrast, the *aesthetic* stance means that readers intend to "live through" the reading experience. They concentrate on the thoughts, images, feelings, and associations evoked during reading. Readers also respond to these thoughts, images, feelings, and associations. They may respond to the language of the text and, for instance, feel carried along by the nonsensical, repetitive language of Dr. Suess. Or they may respond to symbolic meanings evoked by a text such as C. S. Lewis' Narnia tales and appreciate the meanings that are added to a story when they understand the significance of symbols. When readers read aesthetically, they do remember the stories and poems, but what they remember is their own experienced meaning and responses.

Rosenblatt suggested that any single reading experience usually calls for a balance between aesthetic and efferent reading. Readers do not just read stories and poems aesthetically and textbooks or information books efferently. Rather, in any one story, poem, or informational book readers may oscillate between taking an aesthetic stance or an efferent stance. She concluded, however, that literature should be read primarily from the aesthetic stance.

Clearly, readers need to be able to take both stances and benefit from learning to use both stances in reading stories and poems and in reading informational books. Children's literature experts agree that quality informational books should do more than provide information (Lukens, 1990). They should provide readers with a sense of wonder and stimulate curiosity as well. Such recommendations suggest that quality informational books could well be read from an aesthetic stance. On the other hand, there are times when stories and poems can be examined efferently. Probst (1988) suggested that response ought to be only one component of a literature program. He argued that students need to analyze and interpret literature as well as respond to it. Moving from students' responses to a literary work to examining sources of the responses in the text allows students to see the significance of literary components of fiction. As they analyze character, plot, or theme, they take an efferent stance.

Instructional Implications

The reader response perspective emphasizes that reading is an experience capturing readers' moment-to-moment thoughts, feelings, images, and associations, and readers simultaneously respond to these moment-to-moment experiences. Further, readers continue to respond after the reading experience is over. Teachers provide opportunities for students to articulate their first, tentative responses and experiences in order to help them construct richer, more informed responses. The reader response perspective suggests that groups of readers, interpretive communities, play particularly significant roles in helping children articulate their initial responses and construct richer, more informed responses and interpretations. Teachers make decisions about the kinds of group discussions and projects that will create supportive interpretive communities. Finally, the reader response perspective emphasizes that readers read differently for different purposes. Teachers must help students learn to recognize these different kinds of reading and support children's reading both for aesthetic and efferent purposes.

Capturing Initial Responses.   Children's initial experiences with literature are often a mixture of unarticulated feelings, puzzlements, and global evaluations of liking or disliking. They may not be sure of the meaning of what they have read. All readers need time to explore those unformed and hazy responses to literature. Corcoran (1987) claimed that teachers need to provide "meaning-space," time where children can explore stories, poems, and informational books without having to answer questions correctly or tell what a book means.

One way that teachers can provide meaning-space is by asking students to jot down their first responses after reading in *response journals*. Response journals are intended to help readers articulate what they were thinking and feeling while reading, and they should be discouraged from writing a summary of the events in a story or coming to a conclusion about the meaning of a literary work too quickly. After reading *Bunnicula* (Howe & Howe, 1979), a fifth grader wrote in her response journal:

Chapter 1: "The Arrival"
I thought the part where Toby sat on Bunnicula at the movies and then
popped out of his seat and shouted, "I sat on something!" was funny and sad.
It was funny when Toby popped out of his seat, but it was sad that
Bunnicula got squished. And I already like it even though I've only read one
chapter, and I think you would too! Oh yea, I forgot to tell about the note
around Bunnicula's neck. But none of them could read it because it was in a
different language but Harold their dog could and it said, "Take care of my
baby." Next I think Chester the cat and Harold will get jealous and run away.
Oh yea, Bunnicula is a rabbit.

Figure 4.3 presents a first grader's response to *Hey, Al* (Yorinks, 1986).

Students can also use small-group discussions as forums for exploring their initial responses to literature. Group discussions can be guided either by open-ended questions posed by the teacher or by questions generated by the students themselves.

Building an Interpretive Community. Students build an interpretive community through talk. In response-centered classrooms, students and teachers are good listeners. Students are valued for their ability to provide important insights into the interpretive process. Teachers do not try to guide students into a standard interpretation of a story or poem; rather, they allow interpretations to arise from group and individual work to which they, as the most knowledgeable literature experts, also contribute.

The kinds of questions that teachers ask can help to ensure that students' responses become the center of attention. For example, teachers can pose questions such as, "How did this poem make you feel?" or "What do you think is the most significant word in the poem?" Questions such as these will naturally lead to discussions where differences arise. Students will have different feelings about a poem and will select different words as being the most significant. Such differences lead to provocative and enriching discussions as students explain the sources of their feelings and opinions.

Another way to give students a voice is for the teacher to keep quiet. Teachers may pose one question for small groups of students to discuss and then leave the groups alone to discuss the question. (Teachers will want to be clear about what students are to produce as a result of such discussions—a list, a written answer, a role-play, for example—and rules for conducting discussions should be established beforehand.) After students have discussed the question (or prepared a role-play, etc.), the whole class can be gathered and each group shares its work.

Teachers can examine whether students actually have voices in a classroom by audiotaping literature discussions (Purves, Rogers, & Soter, 1990). Then teachers listen to the tapes and examine who talks the most, who justifies answers, whose interpretation seems to have more importance, and what kinds of connections are being made between other works of literature and to life. Teachers we work with have found this to be a very revealing exercise.

Differentiating Aesthetic and Efferent Reading. Sometimes it suits readers' purposes to read only efferently. Studying for a test, following a recipe to cook dinner, or reading a timetable to find out a train departure time are some examples of times

FIGURE 4.3   A First Grader's Response to *Hey, Al* (Yorinks, 1986)

when readers intend to read efferently. At other times, readers read only aesthetically. Reading a cookbook for pleasure or reading a chapter book for enjoyment are examples of times when readers intend to read aesthetically. More often, though, readers read a story, poem, or information book for a combination of aesthetic and efferent reasons. Reading a chapter book for enjoyment and later writing an interpretive essay about the book is one such example. Upper grade students, for example, might read David Macauley's *Cathedral: The Story of Its Construction* (1973) to appreciate his attention to detail in illustration and later use the information found in the illustrations to prepare a report on the Middle Ages.

Teachers ask different sorts of questions, depending on whether students are reading efferently or aesthetically. Questions that might stimulate efferent reading of stories, poems, or informational books include

Who were the main characters?
What happened first, second, . . . last in the story?
What was the theme of the story?
What was the most important point in the text?
How can _____ be compared to _____?
What are the steps in the process of _____?

In contrast, questions that might stimulate aesthetic reading of stories, poems, and informational books include

What did the text remind you of?
What images came to mind as you read the text?
What were your feelings as you read the text?
What do you think?

As teachers make reading assignments, devise discussion questions, and plan literature activities, they need to be aware of the differences between aesthetic and efferent reading and think about which kind of reading they want students to use for particular reading assignments. Careful consideration is needed to support students as they become better aesthetic and efferent readers.

CRITICAL PERSPECTIVE

The critical perspective is based on the assumption that studying literature involves literary criticism. Even young children are literary critics when they study literature in a systematic fashion (Sloan, 1984) as Ms. Chauvez's students did in the case study at the beginning of this chapter. These students studied the circle structure, a structure found in many stories, and they compared and contrasted stories having this structure.

Literary Structures

Studying authors and illustrators, different genres of literature such as folktales or contemporary realism, or literary elements such as character or plot is included in a systematic study of literature. These activities originated in the structuralist perspective on literature (Cullinan, 1981). Structuralists examined different genres of literature and the literature from different cultures to identify common characteristics or structures. They noticed that all stories including those from varied cultures include characters, a setting, plot, point of view, and theme. Similarly, they found that many stories from different cultures share common characteristics. For example, folktales from around the world have happy endings, one-dimensional characters, backdrop settings, and motifs (see Chapter 2 for a discussion of folktales). These commonalities across stories from different cultures are called *literary structures.*

Readers internalize knowledge of literary structures and other conventions of literature and use this knowledge, called *literary competence,* as they read and interpret literature (Culler, 1975). Readers develop literary competence as they read a variety of literature and as they learn about a variety of literary structures.

Temple (1991) described two important kinds of literary structures found in literature, and both of these structures have direct application to literature-based reading instruction. The first structure, *dramatic roles,* is based on the idea that certain kinds of characters and objects have specific purposes in stories or perform specific roles (Souriau, 1950). Six roles that characters play in a story are the lion force, sun or object, rival, moon, receiver, and judge. These six roles are explained in Figure 4.4.

All characters in a story occupy one of these six dramatic roles, and sometimes the role that a character plays changes in a story. For example, in *Rumpelstiltskin* (Zelinsky, 1986) the lion force is the miller's daughter. However, the characters and objects who fill the object, rival, and helper roles change during the story. At the beginning of the story, the king fills the rival role by forcing the miller's daughter to

FIGURE 4.4   Six Roles That Characters Play

	Role	Description
♌	The Lion Force	The character whose actions, desires, and wishes give direction to the story
☉	The Sun or Object	The character, thing, or event that the lion force character wants
♂	Mars, the Rival	The character or action that opposes the lion force character and prevents him or her from getting what is desired
☾	Moon, the Helper	The character who helps the lion force character get what he or she wants
♁	Earth, the Receiver	The character who receives the sun or object or who benefits from the lion force's actions
♎	Libra, the Judge	The character who decides whether the lion force may have the sun or object

Note: From "Seven Readings of a Folktale: Literary Theory in the Classroom" by C. Temple, 1991, *The New Advocate, 4,* p. 29. Copyright 1991 by Christopher-Gordon Publishers and C. Temple.

spin straw into gold, and Rumpelstiltskin fills the helper role by spinning the straw into gold for the miller's daughter. As the story continues, the object changes. At first, the miller's daughter wants to stay alive, but later, she wants to keep her child. Rumpelstiltskin also changes roles; at the story's end he fills the rival role by trying to take the child away from the miller's daughter who is now the queen. The role of helper is now taken by the maid who sneaks into the forest and learns Rumpelstiltskin's name.

Temple also described *literary opposites,* another literary structure common to stories across cultures (Levi-Straus, 1967). Literary opposites refers to contrasts that are found in stories: cold and hot, young and old, bad and good, strong and weak. For example, *Rumpelstiltskin* has many contrasts, especially between the miller's daughter and Rumpelstiltskin:

Miller's Daughter	*Rumpelstiltskin*
young	old
pretty	ugly
lives in a palace	lives in the woods
not talented	talented
has a child	childless

Other contrasts found in stories include what the lion character does and does not desire, what is told about a character or event and what is not told, what one character wants but another character does not. In *Rumpelstiltskin,* for instance, we are never told where Rumpelstiltskin came from or why he desired a child. We know that the miller's daughter wanted to stay alive; but we are not told what it is that she did not want.

Intertextuality

The notion that each literary work is connected to other works is central to the critical perspective. This connection between literary works is called *intertextuality* (Cairney, l990). Children notice intertextuality when they comment that Peter in *The Tale of Peter Rabbit* (Potter, 1902) reminds them of Max in *Where the Wild Things Are* (Sendak, l963). They may see the connection because Max and Peter both disobey their mother or because Max and Peter both leave home, have an adventure, meet danger, and return home safely.

Literary works are linked through textual elements such as author, style of illustration, genre, motif, theme, setting, character, and point of view. Literary works are also linked through reader elements such as the images they evoke, feelings they produce, and associations to childhood they recollect. Each of these connections provides rich sources for understanding and interpreting literature.

Instructional Implications

The critical perspective suggests that the greater children's understanding of structures found in literature, the richer their interactions with literature will be. One way children's understanding of literary structures may develop is through discussions in which teachers ask questions that focus children's attention on literary structures and their significance. Understandings of literary structures are also fostered by reading a set of several books illustrating a common literary structure.

Discussions That Focus on Structure.   Teachers can help children understand the significance of literary structures through careful questioning in literature discussion groups. A list of questions that teachers might use to explore literary structures and other questions that focus on authors and their style or on illustrators and their illustrations is presented in Figure 4.5. These questions are model questions and teachers should adapt them for stories that their students are discussing.

Teachers can also formulate questions about dramatic roles, and these questions help students to think more critically about their reading. Temple (1990) recommended that teachers help children focus on opposites in stories they read and write through these questions:

What does the character want? What does the character not want?
What is the character trying to make happen? What is the character trying not to make happen?
What do others expect the character to be like? What do others not expect the character to be like?
Think of a someone in the story who is just the opposite of the character. What do they do in the story? What do they want? (adapted from Temple, 1990, p. 39).

Contrasts can also be used to formulate questions and interpretations of literature. Questions about contrasts help children focus on the central characters and

FIGURE 4.5   *Model Questions for Critical Literature Discussions*

Questions to Explore Literary Structures

In what ways are the main characters revealed? What do they look like? do? say? think? What do other characters have to say about them? What are their relationships with other characters?
What conflicts do the main characters encounter? With nature? With others? With themselves? With society?
Do the main characters change in the story? If so, in what ways?
What do the main characters learn in the story?
In what ways is the setting important to the story? Would the story be the same in a different setting?

Questions About Authors and Their Style and Illustrators and Their Illustrations

How did the author create humor (suspense, sadness, etc.)?
How did the author appeal to your senses of sight, smell, hearing, touch, and taste?
Why did the author use objective point of view (flashbacks, the combination of fantasy and realism, etc.)?
How does the author's style compare in various books?
How do different versions of a story compare?
What style of art (artistic elements, media, etc.) did the illustrator use to create the illustrations?
How do the illustrations contribute to the story's meaning?
How do illustrations compare in various books?

their motives. Take, for example, the "Rumpelstiltskin" story. Questions that focus on contrasts between the miller's daughter and Rumpelstiltskin and the changing role of the helper and rival help readers examine the force character in more detail. Children can list the differences between the miller's daughter and Rumpelstiltskin, and they will notice that at first, the miller's daughter is helpless and dependent. In contrast, Rumpelstiltskin is clever and powerful. The miller's daughter offers Rumpelstiltskin all that she possesses (and might possess) for a short-term goal (to live at the end of the night). However, as Rumpelstiltskin changes into the rival, the miller's daughter finds a new helper, her maid. There are many important differences between Rumpelstiltskin-the-helper and maid-the-helper. Thoughtful questions can be used to help children to probe these differences. Another contrast is that Rumpelstiltskin was in control of the miller's daughter as the helper; in contrast, the miller's daughter is in control of the maid as the helper, and at the end of the story, she emerges more in control of her own life. Her goals go beyond her own survival for a day; they concern the lifelong commitment to a child.

Teachers might use the dramatic roles and the contrasts of what is and is not told in the story to examine it from other points of view. These activities help children to see each character's motivations and goals in relationship to the other characters. Most stories have characters that have conflicting motivations and goals and through dramatic roles and contrasts students can explore these differences. Students could explore the objects (or goals) of each of the other characters. For example, they might pose questions such as, what was the object desired by the king? What kind of king must he be if he was willing to kill his future wife if she didn't weave straw into gold? What was Rumpelstiltskin's desire? What did he really want with the child? We would interpret the story differently if we believed he was a lonely old man who merely wanted a child of his own than if we believed he wanted to use the child for some evil purpose.

Teachers could use the contrasts between the miller's daughter and Rumpelstiltskin to connect to other works of literature. We could compare the miller's daughter and Rumpelstiltskin to Red Riding Hood and the woodcutter. Both Red Riding Hood and the miller's daughter are naive and trusting; they are dependent. The woodcutter must save little Red Riding Hood just as Rumpelstiltskin must save the miller's daughter from death. Yet, the two stories differ. In many ways, *Rumpelstiltskin* provides a more satisfying ending for young women. The miller's daughter evolves into someone more in charge of her life while Little Red Riding Hood only promises not to talk to strangers. This comparison might lead to discussions about the role of females and males in many traditional folktales.

Literary structures offer teachers and their students many avenues for speculating on the meaning of stories. As students become familiar with the technique of finding contrasts in stories and examining dramatic roles, they will be better able to struggle with the central tensions in literature and in their own lives.

Text Sets.   A *text set* is a collection of stories, poems, and informational books on a particular topic. The topic may be a theme or issue, an author or illustrator, a style of illustration, or a literary structure. Students read the poems, stories, and informational books included in a text set, and through their reading, they intuitively acquire knowledge about literature and the topic. Figure 4.6 presents a list of stories from a text set of feminist folktales. These stories have female characters who are strong,

FIGURE 4.6   A Text Set of Feminist Folktales

de Paola, T. (1975). *Strega Nona*. New York: Prentice-Hall. (P)
Galdone, P. (1973). *The little red hen*. New York: Seabury. (P)
McCarty, T. (1981). *The skull in the snow*. New York: Delacorte. (U)
McKissack, P. (1986). *Flossie & the fox*. New York: Dial. (P–M)
Minard, R. (1975). *Womenfolk and fairy tales*. Boston: Houghton Mifflin. (U)
Munsch, R. (1980). *The paper bag princess*. Toronto, Canada: Annick Press. (P)
Phelps, E. (1981). *The maid of the north, feminist folktales from around the world*. New York: Holt.
    (M–U)
Philps, E. (1978). *Tatterhood and other tales*. Old Westburn, NY: The Feminist Press. (M–U)
Riordan, J. (1984). *The woman in the moon and other tales of forgotten heroines*. New York: Dial.
    (M–U)
Williams, J. (1973). *Petronella*. New York: Parents' Magazine Press. (M)
Williams, J. (1978). *The practical princess and other liberating fairy tales*. New York: Four Winds. (M)
Yolen, J. (1981). *Sleeping ugly*. New York: Coward-McCann. (P)

P = Primary grades (K–2); M = Middle grades (3–5); U = Upper grades (6–8)

active decision-makers who face heroic journeys into the physical and psychological unknown. These stories can be used to contrast typical folktales that have female characters who are passive, wicked, or wait to be rescued.

The steps in putting together a text set are

1. Choose the topic or identify a reason for the text set.
2. Use resources listed in Chapters 2, 3, and 8 to locate picture books, chapter books, informational books, poems, and other types of reading materials related to the topic of the text set.
3. Preview these materials to see if they are appropriate for your students. Appropriateness includes choosing books with suitable content about the topic, a range of reading levels that meets your students' needs, and the literary element or structure you wish to highlight.
4. Collect additional copies of the trade books and other materials from the public library, the school library, book clubs, and colleagues.
5. Display the text set in a special place or in a decorated box in the classroom library center.
6. Present a book talk to introduce the text set and highlight individual books in the collection.

INTERACTIVE PERSPECTIVE

The interactive perspective comes from psychological theories of how we learn, and the goal of reading according to this perspective is comprehension. This perspective explains how children become readers as well as how students understand what they read. One of the most important concepts in the interactive perspective is the notion of *schema*. Schemas are like mental file folders in which all the information related to an event, object, or person is kept. They are the key to predicting and remembering.

Schema

A schema is a mental bundle of knowledge that holds everything we know about a topic. For example, think about roaches. The first thing that might come to mind is an image of a big black bug crawling across a floor. You might think "yuck" and shudder as you recall opening a cabinet and seeing a bug scoot out of sight. You might recall when you used insecticide to kill the pests in your kitchen. The information that one teacher recalled about roaches in presented in Figure 4.7. The diagram in this figure is a representation of a schema for roaches.

This teacher's schema for roaches includes factual information (roaches are black or brown and lay eggs), unique and personal information (the time when a roach flew at him), and some misinformation (roaches have six legs, not eight!). It also illustrates an important feature of schema: they are organized. The information included in the roach schema in Figure 4.7 is organized into groups including methods for killing roaches, locations where roaches are found, and activities roaches engage in.

We have schemas for events and activities as well as schemas for objects and places. We have schemas for going to the mall (riding in the car, finding a money machine to accept our bank card, purchasing goods, carrying them back to the car), going on vacation, and visiting the dentist. We also have schemas for doing things such as solving problems (defining the problem, identifying the characteristics of the problem, generating solutions, and selecting the solution that eliminates the most characteristics of the problem). Everything we know is organized in schemas.

A second important feature of schema is that they are connected to one another. Going to the mall reminds us of going on vacation because these two schemas have the common feature of requiring money. Going to the dentist reminds us of going to the mall because both schemas have in common the feature of riding in the car.

Learning occurs when schemas grow and change. For example, children learn about bugs as they observe bugs and listen to others talk about bugs. These experiences provide information about bugs, and it becomes a part the schema which will probably be called *bug*. When children come to school they acquire additional information about bugs which is added to their bug schema. They learn the word *insects*, a new name for bugs, and may rename their bug schema *insect*. Or, they may learn information that alters their schema. Learning that a spider is not an insect might change the organization of children's schema about insects and add a new schema called *spider*. Children may realize that their insect and spider schemas can be related to another new schema called *arthropoda*.

Schema and Reading

Schemas are crucial for reading. As we read the words in a text, we call to mind schema related to those words. For example, read this text and try to imagine what is happening:

> I lay quietly on my bed. I did not rustle the sheets. I breathed slowly and silently. I was listening for a sound—a sound a friend had told me I'd never hear.

FIGURE 4.7   One Teacher's
Schema for Roaches

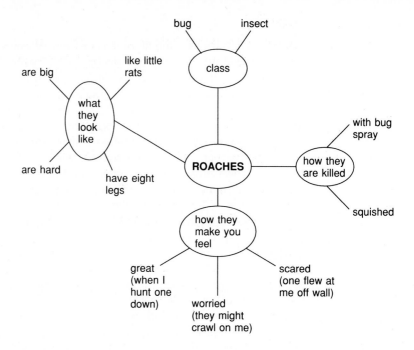

You might visualize a tired mother lying in bed with a pillow over her head. It is early evening and her husband is putting the children to bed. She is waiting for the silence that indicates her children have fallen asleep—the sound she believes she will never hear. You would have inferred a great deal of information from reading the brief text. This information is not in the text, but you borrowed information found in schemas used to understand the text.

Now read the text from *The Polar Express* (Van Allsburg, 1985) in Figure 4.8. This is an expansion of the excerpt printed in the previous paragraph. A few words have been added to the text along with the title of the story, but these additions dramatically change what readers imagine as they read the text. Most readers use their schemas related to winter and Christmas to understand the text and imagine a child who is watching out the window for Santa's sleigh. The ground outside the window is likely to be covered in snow and the child's bed is covered with many well-loved stuffed animals.

As we read, we call to mind various schemas which we think will be useful in understanding a text. We make tentative selections of schemas to use while reading and alter those choices as needed during reading. These schemas allow readers to guess or predict what will happen before reading and provide additional information not stated in the text. Readers use schemas to construct meanings as they read.

Schema and the Interactive Model of Reading

While schemas are an important part of reading, they are not the only mental processes used in reading. Reading involves the use of many mental processes, and

FIGURE 4.8 An Excerpt from *The Polar Express* (Van Allsburg, 1985)

> On Christmas eve, many years ago, I lay quietly in my bed. I did not rustle the sheets. I breathed slowly and silently. I was listening for a sound—a sound a friend had told me I'd never hear—the ringing bells of Santa's sleigh.

Note: From *The Polar Express* by Chris Van Allsburg. Copyright © 1985 by Chris Van Allsburg. Reprinted by permission of Houghton Mifflin Company. All rights reserved.

teachers must find ways to help children use all of their mental processes in reading, not merely one or two processes.

Mental Processes Used in Reading. Readers use at least six mental processes as they read:

1. Processes using schema
2. Semantic processes
3. Syntactic processes
4. Orthographic processes
5. Phonological processes
6. Processes of identifying letters

Each of these processes is important and necessary for reading and will be described in the following sections. The six processes are also summarized in Figure 4.9.

Processing schema. Readers select a schema related to the title or content of the story or other book as they begin reading. They use this schema but they may change or alternate schema as a result of their reading. One kind of schema, *story schema,* is particularly important for reading. A story schema is a mental representation of the structural components found in stories. Figure 4.10 presents a representation of a story schema. This figure shows that readers expect that stories will have a setting to introduce characters, that stories will be centered around the main character's attempts to solve a problem, and that the story will end when the problem is resolved.

Readers have schemas for many different kinds of literature. For example, experienced readers know that historical romances have a strong female character who is young, beautiful, and rebellious. This character meets an older man who is much more experienced, handsome, and virile. Similarly, experienced readers know that fables are short stories that teach a moral, and folktales have one-dimensional characters who are foolish, wicked, or good.

Readers use their story schemas and schemas for other kinds of literature to make predictions about what they will read and to remember information in different kinds of stories, poems, and informational books.

Semantic processing. A second kind of mental process used in reading is *semantic processing.* Semantics is the system of meanings associated with words. Words acquire meanings, in part, because of our experiences with the *referents* of

FIGURE 4.9   Six Mental Processes That Readers Use

---

1. Processes Using Schema
- Readers select a schema related to the title or the content of the text as they begin reading.
- Readers use story schema and schema related to literature as they read.

2. Semantic Processes
- Readers associate meanings with words based on their past experiences.
- Readers use contextual information in a sentence as an aid in determining a word's meaning.

3. Syntactic Processes
- Readers use knowledge about the order of words in sentences, word class, or part of speech to anticipate words before reading them.
- Readers use affixes and word endings to provide information about a word's meaning.

4. Orthographic Processes
- Readers use spelling patterns to recognize words quickly.
- Readers recognize how words should be pronounced.

5. Phonological Processes
- Readers recognize sounds associated with letters and letters found in frequently used spelling patterns.

6. Process of Identifying Letters
- Readers identify features of letters.
- Readers use features to identify letters.

---

words (we know what the word *chair* means because we have had numerous experiences with objects, or referents, that we call *chairs*). When we read the word *chair*, the semantic processor calls to mind our experiences with sitting in, seeing, buying, breaking, or repairing chairs.

Words also acquire meanings through their relationships with other words in sentences. For example, read the following sentences and think about the meaning of *run*.

1. Can you *run* the store?
2. Can you *run* the computer?
3. Can you *run* the mile?
4. Can you *run* in the election?
5. How long is your milk *run?*
6. How long was the copy *run?*
7. How long was the *run* on snow shovels?
8. How long was the *run* in your pantyhose?

The word *run* takes on different meanings in each sentence depending on the context established by the other words in the sentence. Because other words in a sentence provide clues to word meanings, readers often use semantic processing to guess what a word is before reading it. For example, guess the missing word in this

FIGURE 4.10   Representation of a Story Schema

Story Components	Sample Story "The Old Woman and Her Cat"
Setting, introduces characters, describes location and time	Once there was an old woman and a very curious cat who lived together on a tiny farm.
Problem, establishes goal of character	One day the cat overheard his friends the blackbirds talking on the roof of the barn. He got so curious about what they were saying that he climbed to the top of the roof. All at once he was too scared to come down.
Attempts to solve the problem	The cat began meowing for help, but the woman was hard of hearing. He decided to ask the blackbirds to fly down and tell the old woman of his predicament. The blackbirds agreed to help if he promised to have the old woman set out bread crumbs for them during the winter. The cat promised, so the blackbirds flew down and landed on the shoulder of the old woman and told her where the cat was.
Outcome of attempts to solve the problem	The old woman quickly got a ladder and climbed up to rescue her cat. The cat kept his promise, and when the winter came, he had the old woman set out bread crumbs for the blackbirds.
Resolution	And as for the cat, he never climbed to the barn roof again.

Note: From "The Videotape Answer to Independent Comprehension Activities" by L. McGee and G. Tompkins, 1981, *The Reading Teacher, 34*, p. 428. Reprinted with permission of the authors and the International Reading Association.

sentence: "The man rode to the 12th floor on the _____." Most readers recognize that the missing word is *elevator.* We use semantic processing, or context, to guess what the missing word is, but context does not always supply enough information to guess the word before reading it. For example, try to guess the missing word in this sentence: "The man was cleaning his _____." Most readers recognize that the word will be a noun but cannot guess exactly what the missing word is so they continue reading and use other mental processes to identify it.

Syntactic processing.   Readers use *syntactic processing* or their knowledge about the order of words in sentences, word classes, or parts of speech to anticipate words before they read them. For example, consider the two sentences:

1. John kissed Linda.
2. Linda kissed John.

We know that either Linda or John did the kissing because of the order in which the words appear: the first word in the sentence is the doer of the kissing action. We also anticipate that the second word in this sentence will be an action word (even though not every sentence has an action word as its second word) because action words almost always follow nouns or pronouns. The syntactic processor suggests that the word missing from the following sentence is a verb because of the order of words: "The boy _____ on his bike."

The syntactic processor also uses affixes and, in particular, word endings to provide information about meaning. The word ending *ed* in the word *jumped* indicates that an action occurred in the past, and the word ending *er* in the words *swimmer* or *colder* signals what action a person does or indicates how much.

Orthographic processing.   Another reading process is *orthographic processing,* which recognizes spelling patterns. Readers use the orthographic processor to quickly recognize words. For example, in English words the letter *t* is followed by the letter *h* (as in the word *the*) 50 times more frequently than it is followed by the next frequently occurring letter *o* (as in the word *to*) (Adams, 1990, p. 109), and this knowledge about English spelling patterns allows readers to quickly identify a word as *the* by seeing just the letter *t* before seeing the other letters in the word.

The orthographic processor also allows experienced readers to recognize how words should be read. For example, the word *preamble* is read *pre am ble* rather than *pream ble,* and the word *fathead* is read *fat head* rather than *fath ead* or *fa thead* (Adams, 1990, p. 122).

Phonological processing.   Readers use *phonological processing* to recognize sounds associated with letters, or more importantly, with the letters found in frequently used spelling patterns. While the English language is notoriously unpredictable at the letter-sound level (for example, the letter *e* is associated with the sounds found in the words *eel, elephant, sleigh, pie,* and *love* to name just a few), it is predictable at the level of spelling patterns. For example, the letter *e* always represents the same sound when it is found in words such as *bed, red, Ted, Ned, led,* and *sled.* The letters *ed* form a consistent spelling pattern associated with the sound /ed/ within the *ed word family,* and readers who see *ed* in the word *fed* automatically know how to pronounce the word even when they have never seen the word in print before.

Letter processing.   The sixth reading process is *recognizing letters.* The letter recognizer identifies *features* of letters. For example, lower case *b* has a vertical line and a closed curve features. The letter *d* has the same features, but with a different orientation. A lower case *c* also shares one feature with the lower case *b,* a curved line; however, the lower case *c* also has an open curve feature.

Experienced readers recognize letters automatically and quickly. They do not need to see all of a letter's features in order to recognize it. In contrast, young children may be confused by letters that have similar features and may need time to recognize individual letters. These youngsters are more likely to correctly identify letters when all features are available.

Interactive Model of Reading.   The *interactive model of reading* (Adams, 1990; Rumelhart, 1977; Stanovich, 1980) suggests that readers use all six processes simultaneously as they read. This model is presented schematically in Figure 4.11. This model illustrates that readers begin by both using information from the processors in the head and by looking at print. As soon as the eyes see the print, the letter recognizer begins the process of recognizing letters. However, because all of the reading processes work simultaneously and interactively, any of the other processors such as information from schema or from the orthographic processor or from the syntactic processor can interact with and influence the processing of the letter recognizer.

FIGURE 4.11   The Interactive Model of Reading

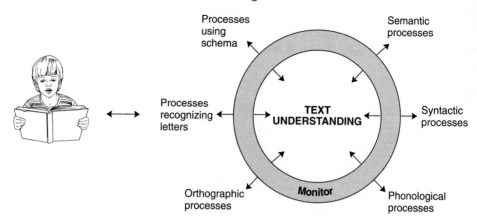

Similarly, the processing of the letter recognizer can influence or interact with the processing of any of the other processors.

To explain how this model works, suppose you are reading the sentence "Once upon a time there was a queen, and she longed for a child" and you have just fixed your attention on the printed word *child.* Before your eyes have even seen the printed word, you have already called to mind your schema for a fairy tale because the sentence begins with "Once upon a time" and it is about a queen who longs for a child, two features that are found in many fairy tales. Similarly, you have called to mind your schema about queens, and this schema provides the information that queens are beautiful, powerful, married to kings, lived long ago, wear long gowns, and are surrounded by ladies in waiting. You have also activated your schema related to longing for something, which has information about being miserable, feeling that everything else is unimportant while the longed-for-object becomes all important, and being willing to do anything to get the longed-for-object.

At the same time your semantic processor recognizes that the word you are about to read must be something that a queen—a woman—wants, and your syntactic processor is expecting a noun from the order of words in the sentence.

Simultaneously, the letter recognizer would begin recognizing the letters *c-h-i-l-d.* At the same time, the orthographic processor connects the letters *c* and *h* into the cluster *ch* and the letters *l* and *d* into the cluster *ld* because these are frequently occurring letter clusters. Further, your orthographic processor notes that the letter cluster *ch* is found at the beginning of words such as *church, chime, child,* and *chock;* at the same time your orthographic processor notes that the letter cluster *ld* is found at the end of such words as *should, would, child,* and *mild.*

All of this information arrives simultaneously, and you use some or all of it both to read the word *child* and to comprehend the sentence. In fact, expecting to read a noun and something related to what a queen wants probably speeds the identification of the letters *ch* which in turn influences the orthographic processor to suggest the highly likely word candidate *child.* The moment you are reading the word *child,* you have far more information than what the word is. You have information about the part of speech, what kinds of problems might be included in this fairy tale, and what the queen might do in the story. You have a great deal of information from which to make inferences and predictions from reading just this one sentence. Imagine how much information is available after reading an entire story!

At the moment readers read a single word, they receive information from a variety of sources, including information derived from the text and from their minds. Readers use all of this information to construct meaning, sometimes with little attention to the actual letters in words.

Monitoring.   Because all six mental processes involved in reading occur simultaneously and interactively, the interactive model of reading includes an important executive function—a decision-maker. Reading must proceed quickly, and there is not enough time for readers to consciously attend to all the information being provided by the various processors (LaBerge & Samuels, 1974). Readers must rely on some processes occurring automatically, without conscious effort or thought so that they can focus their attention on comprehension. The decision-maker monitors the six processes and determines which ones a reader will pay conscious attention to. Experienced, fluent readers attend to the comprehension of a story, poem, or informational book, and the other processes occur automatically.

Sometimes, however, readers must divert their attention to other processes of reading. They might come across words that they have never seen before or words that they do not know the meaning of. When this happens, their attention must be focused on pronouncing the word or in figuring out what the sentence might mean without knowing the word's meaning. Experienced readers monitor their efforts; they know when to reread to regain meaning or when to continue reading to find more information that will clear up confusions.

Instructional Implications

The interactive perspective emphasizes that readers focus on comprehension as they read. This focus on comprehension suggests that reading is a constructive, interactive, and strategic process, and each of these characteristics has implications for instruction.

Reading as a Constructive Process.   Reading is a constructive process because readers construct meaning by drawing on information from their schema. They use their schemas to make predictions, draw conclusions, and develop interpretations. In the case study at the beginning of this chapter, Mr. Williams capitalized on schema as a part of his lesson on caterpillars. He helped children call to mind their schema, or *prior knowledge,* about caterpillars and then helped them integrate this knowledge with what they learned from reading. He used a modification of a *KWL* (What I *k*now, What I *w*ant to know, and What I *l*earned) lesson (Ogle, 1989). This lesson asks students to call to mind what they know about a topic before reading and what they would like to learn during reading. After they read, they compare and contrast what they knew, what they thought they would learn, and what they learned. Figure 4.12 presents the steps in preparing and using a KWL chart and lesson.

Reading as an Interactive Process.   Reading is an interactive process because readers create meaning using both their prior knowledge related to the text and the

FIGURE 4.12   Steps in a KWL Lesson

1. *Teacher prepares KWL chart.* The teacher prepares a chart with these headings:

K—What We *Know*	W—What We *Want* to Know	L—What We *Learned*

2. *Students brainstorm what they know about a topic.* Students brainstorm ideas about the topic that they will read about, and the teacher or student writes them in the first column of the KWL chart.
3. *Students brainstorm a list of questions.* Students brainstorm questions that they have about the topic, and the teacher or student writes them in the second column of the KWL chart. The questions identify information that students would like to learn more about.
4. *Students read the text.* The students read the text by themselves or with a partner. Or, the teacher reads it aloud.
5. *Students list what they have learned from reading.* The students brainstorm a list of things they learned from reading. The teacher or student writes the list in the third column of the KWL chart.
6. *Students compare what they knew, questions they had, and what they learned from reading.* Students compare what they knew before reading (information in the first column of the chart) with what they learned (information in the third column of the chart). They also discuss which of their questions were answered and which questions were not answered from the information provided in the text.

Note: From "K-W-L: A Teaching Model That Develops Active Reading of Expository Text" by D. Ogle, 1986, *The Reading Teacher, 39*, p. 565. Reprinted with permission of Donna Ogle and the International Reading Association.

text that they are reading. According to this perspective, teachers provide children with strategies for using their prior knowledge and strategies for efficiently and fluently reading text. Teachers who are guided by the interactive perspective want children to have opportunities to acquire effective letter recognition and orthographic processing knowledge within the context of meaningful reading experiences. This equal emphasis on providing strategies for helping children to use reader-based processes (schema, semantics, and syntax) and text-based processes (orthographic and letter knowledge) begins with the first lesson and continues throughout a student's instructional life. Teachers guiding children's emerging reading in kindergarten and first grade recognize the importance of all reading processes through meaningful reading experiences as much as upper grade teachers do.

For example, kindergarten teachers capitalize on children's natural interest in favorite stories and poems to provide many opportunities for exploring both meaning and print during *shared readings.* Many favorite stories and poems are available in big book format. These *big books* are enlarged picture books with text and illustrations large enough for a group of children to see easily. As teachers read these stories and poems aloud to children, they pause and invite children to predict what will happen next, ask questions, and make comments. Later, teachers may read the story again and have several simple props (or just the names of the characters printed on cards with a yarn strap that can be worn around a child's neck) so that children can act out the story. These activities help children use reader-based processes and focus on meaning.

The next time teachers share the story or poem, they point to each word of the text, and invite children to read along. They invite a child to point to the words as the group rereads the stories. They also cover some of the words in the text with adhesive-backed paper and invite the children to guess the hidden words. The children practice rereading and pointing to each word in the story to figure out the hidden words. Then teachers might invite them to guess what letters the words begin and end with. Or, teachers print several words on cards and ask children to locate those words in the big book. These activities help children use text-based processes and focus on print.

While the integrity of good literature should never be sacrificed for promoting decoding skills, studying grammar, or developing vocabulary, teachers can use literature and the natural models that authors provide as a way to teach children about written language and print. Upper grade teachers, for example, may choose to explore survival as a theme. As the students read chapter books, informational books, and poetry to explore the nature of meanings found in this theme, they can also study words. Accounts of survival often include descriptions of unfamiliar plants, animals, and cultural traditions that provide a rich source of new vocabulary words and concepts. Or middle grade teachers can combine an author study of Chris Van Allsburg with learning about verbs (Tompkins, 1990). This author's vivid illustrations and active text make a natural context for learning more about using language.

Reading as a Strategic Process.   Reading is a strategic process because readers are aware when they do not understand what they are reading and have several strategies for dealing with meaning loss. Sometimes readers do not understand what they are reading, but good readers, unlike poor readers, realize when this is the case because they monitor their reading. Teachers can help students monitor reading by asking them to stop and talk about what they have read in their own words. One indication that children are not monitoring for meaning occurs when a child is reading aloud and says a word that does not make sense but continues reading without pausing. Teachers should wait until the child has finished reading the sentence and then ask, "Does that make sense?"

Mature readers use many reading strategies that enhance and enrich their understanding and appreciation of what they read. They anticipate, pause to reflect and summarize, compare events to other stories and to their own lives, and evaluate the validity of arguments. They use their knowledge of semantics, syntax, orthographics, phonology, and letters to figure out unknown words and meanings.

BALANCING THE THREE THEORETICAL PERSPECTIVES IN THE READING PROGRAM

We have described three theoretical perspectives—reader response, critical, and interactive—separately; however, these perspectives are similar in many ways. All three focus on the construction of meaning; readers actively construct meaning as they read. In addition, all three theoretical perspectives focus on reader knowledge; what readers know influences how they read and the understandings they construct.

Some teachers may feel more comfortable with one perspective than with the others; however, all three perspectives offer unique opportunities for enhancing students' reading growth. The reader response perspective could be called the *reading literature* approach. This perspective focuses on the reader rather than on literature or reading instruction. According to this perspective, teachers help readers better understand themselves and their world through their transactions with literature. This perspective is related to Louise Rosenblatt's notions about aesthetic reading. According to this perspective, teachers are concerned that readers are engaged with what they are reading; that is, they are personally interested and involved. Further, teachers recognize that readers bring many different perspectives to their reading, and they respond in various ways to a single poem, story, or informational book. These different and personal responses provide the basis for further exploration and learning about life and literature.

The critical perspective could be called the *teaching literature* approach. According to this perspective, the more students know and understand about literature—literary elements, genres, and authors—the more insightful their interpretations of literature and understandings of the information presented in literature will be. This perspective is similar to Louise Rosenblatt's efferent reading, and it suggests that teachers help students learn to appreciate and understand the structures of literature and authors' and illustrators' craft. Teachers help students use this information to deepen their interpretations of literature and extend their learning from literature.

The interactive perspective could be called the *teaching reading* approach because this perspective emphasizes the interactive nature of all the processes of reading. The focus is on teaching many kinds of reading skills and strategies—comprehension, vocabulary, and word recognition. The interactive perspective suggests that teachers will both help students better understand and interpret what they are reading and will help them develop more sophisticated reading strategies. This perspective also has much in common with Rosenblatt's efferent reading, reading to remember information. The three theoretical perspectives are summarized in Figure 4.13.

In literature-based reading, students read stories and poems for their lived-through experiences; helping students take this stance is teachers' first and most important concern no matter what students' instructional needs are. Because of this primary focus, the reader response perspective is a particularly important one. This perspective does not emphasize "getting the main idea," "analyzing a character," or "identifying metaphor." Instead, it emphasizes readers' lived-through, aesthetic experience of reading. This perspective is not to be confused with merely reacting emotionally to what is read (Rosenblatt, 1991). Rather, this perspective focuses on supporting and encouraging students to experience literature and make connections between literature and their own lives.

We believe that, with stories and poems, students should always have an opportunity to respond aesthetically to what they read. Teachers should ensure that students always have space to make their own meaning through talk, writing, art, or drama before instruction in reading strategies, vocabulary, or literary structures begins. With stories and poems, the reader response perspective plays a critical and primary role. On the other hand, we believe that when students are reading infor-

FIGURE 4.13 Summary of the Three Theoretical Perspectives

	Reader Response Perspective	**Critical Perspective**	**Interactive Perspective**
Source of theoretical perspective	Literary theories of reader response	Examinations of literature by structuralists	Theories of learning from cognitive psychology
Major focus	Reading literature	Teaching literature	Teaching reading
View of reading	Reading viewed as experience; processes readers engage in while reading	Reading viewed as acquisition of literary competence (knowledge and use of literary elements, genre, and authors and illustrators to guide reading)	Reading viewed as interaction of reader-based and text-based processes
Instructional implications	Encourage engagement, personal involvement, and personal connections to text; use these responses to build more interpretive responses	Learning about literary elements, genre, and authors and illustrators as a way to extend understandings of literature	Learn strategies for constructing and monitoring meaning

mational books to learn, the interactive perspective is appropriate. However, teachers can also approach informational books aesthetically (see Chapter 5).

Reading instruction has many purposes including teaching students to read for information, identify literary elements, appreciate an author's craft, read for enjoyment and personal insight, and use reading strategies. Each of these different purposes of instruction fits within different theoretical perspectives. For example, if teachers want students to become familiar with an author's or illustrator's craft, then the critical perspective combined with the reader response perspective best fits this purpose. If teachers want students to acquire strategies for locating, organizing, and summarizing information for reporting, then the interactive perspective best fits this purpose. If teachers want students to become lifelong readers and to find reading pleasurable, then the reader response perspective best fits this purpose. Because each of these goals is crucial and each is a part of every reading program, we recommend that teachers weave instruction from all three theoretical perspectives into their instructional programs.

Instruction based on the three theoretical perspectives can be used effectively to teach literature-based reading with students in kindergarten through eighth grade. Each of the three theoretical perspectives has implications for what readers do before reading, while reading, and after reading. An instructional framework can be used to guide students' reading from any of the three perspectives.

FROM THEORY TO INSTRUCTIONAL FRAMEWORK

Reading is a process, and readers engage in four kinds of reading activities: (a) preparing to read the story, poem, or informational book, (b) reading the text, (c) exploring the text, and (d) extending the text.

Reading Activities: Preparing, Reading, Exploring, and Extending the Text

Before they read, readers engage in certain kinds of activities that prepare them for reading. The interactive perspective suggests that readers use prior knowledge as a part of reading. That is, both before and during reading readers bring to mind information from their experiences that they anticipate will help them construct meaning as they read. The reader response perspective suggests that readers set literary or informational purposes for reading and that they take an aesthetic or efferent stance. The critical perspective indicates that readers use a special kind of prior knowledge—information about literary structures—in making predictions and setting purposes for reading.

Next readers read the text. According to the interactive perspective, readers construct meaning by drawing upon the component processes of reading in a constructive, interactive, and strategic way. From the critical perspective, a reader's knowledge of literary structures guides reading processes, and according to the reader response perspective, readers (who read for literary purposes) evoke meaning as they engage in many reading activities such as constructing images, building hypotheses, finding associations, and thinking back.

Reading does not stop here because readers continue to explore meanings they created during reading. They reread stories, poems, or informational books and negotiate meanings in discussions. The interactive perspective suggests that reading influences a reader's schemas, changing or modifying them through rearrangement or addition. Monitoring activities often lead readers to reread. All of these activities, especially a reader's own sense of meaning (continually asking, "Does this make sense?"), indicate that readers benefit from reflecting on their own reading and considering meanings again and again for different insights. These activities lead to critical reading where readers rethink what they have read from several different perspectives. The reader response perspective suggests that readers first construct tentative initial responses that are modified and enriched through discussion in an interpretive community or through other response activities.

Readers also go beyond their reading of the story, poem, or informational book through extension activities. The interactive perspective implies that readers practice new strategies and skills they have learned in other reading activities. The critical perspective emphasizes intertextuality. That is, readers connect stories, poems, or informational books they are reading with books they have previously read. The reader response perspective suggests that readers' responses to stories, poems, and informational books often are demonstrated through art, music, dancing, cooking, writing, dramatizing, or any number of other activities.

An Instructional Framework

An instructional framework is a structure for how teachers can organize instruction by making decisions about minilessons or organizing literature discussion group activities. We believe that an instructional framework should reflect the processes that readers engage in while reading and should be useful with all three theoretical perspectives. This framework includes activities that help readers to (a) prepare to read, (b) read the text, (c) explore the text, and (d) extend the text. These four types of activities are steps in the instructional framework that we will continue to use in other chapters in this book. They are summarized in Figure 4.14.

Step 1: Preparing to Read.   Preparing-to-read activities help children set purposes for reading and activate relevant literary and prior knowledge. These activities introduce the literary work. Corcoran (1987) suggested that situated context (details related to why the teacher has chosen a particular text for a particular class at a particular moment) influences children's later reading. Teachers may take this into account by helping children find paths into reading using role-plays, writing, activities that set the mood, or discussion. Preparing activities also encourage children to use strategies for thinking ahead about the kinds of ideas that they might expect to read about. In the case study at the beginning of this chapter, Mr. Williams used a modified KWL strategy to help children get prepared to read.

FIGURE 4.14   The Instructional Framework

Step 1: Preparing to Read a Story, Poem, or Informational Book

- Set purposes for reading.
- Activate prior knowledge.
- Introduce the text.
- Find paths into reading using role-plays, writing, activities that set the mood, or discussion.
- Use predicting strategies.

Step 2: Reading the Text

- Demonstrate reading strategies, such as predicting and imagining.
- Use processes such as visualizing, summarizing, restating, retrospection, rereading, empathizing, and evaluating.
- Share ideas about how to solve reading problems.

Step 3: Exploring the Text

- Reread and rethink the text.
- Articulate responses.
- Role-play, draw, construct.
- Examine the author's craft.
- Learn new vocabulary or new reading strategies.
- Consider the text from a different perspective.

Step 4: Extending the Text

- Explore connections between stories, poems, and informational books.
- Connect with listening, talking, reading, writing, and fine arts (art, music, and drama) activities.
- Think about relationships among literary works.

Step 2: Reading the Text.   Reading activities support children as they construct meaning. Teachers often demonstrate or model how they think while reading. They encourage children to use strategies such as predicting, visualizing, summarizing, restating, or rereading. Children share ideas about how they solve reading problems, such as what to do when they come to an unfamiliar word, when they are confused, or what they do to keep track of characters and complicated events in stories, poems, or informational books. Mr. Williams, in the first case study, encouraged children to predict as he read aloud.

Step 3: Exploring the Text.   Exploring activities encourage children to go back to stories, poems, or informational books and to reread and rethink about what they have read. As they reread, they examine the author's craft and learn new vocabulary or new reading strategies. These activities encourage children to consider their reading from a different perspective. They capitalize on group interaction as a means of enriching initial responses. They encourage critical thinking. The children in Mrs. Figlock's class, for example, in the case study at the beginning of this chapter explored the meaning of *The Phantom Tollbooth* through a conversation.

Step 4: Extending the Text.   Extending activities allow readers to examine the connections between several stories, poems, or informational books and between literature and other language arts, or other content areas. In the case study at the beginning of the chapter, for instance, the children in Ms. Chauvez's class extended their understanding of three stories by examining their common circle structure.

The four activities can be used to guide students as they read core literature selections in small or whole class groups or can be used in minilessons for reading workshop. Teachers plan activities that help their students develop independent strategies for preparing, reading, exploring, and extending from books of their own choice and to meet their own purposes for reading.

MAKING DECISIONS ABOUT READING INSTRUCTION

Teachers need to reflect carefully on their own beliefs and learn more about the theoretical perspectives that reading and literature theorists argue can explain reading acquisition and be used to teach reading with literature. At the beginning of this chapter, you were asked to read a list of 15 statements about teaching reading with literature and to identify five statements that reflected your beliefs. In Figure 4.15 we present our classification of those statements according to the three theoretical per-

FIGURE 4.15   Classification of the 15 Statements According to the Three Theoretical Perspectives

Reader Response Perspective
#1, #4, #5, #8, #9, #13

Critical Perspective
#3, #6, #7, #11, #12, #14

Interactive Perspective
#1, #2, #4, #8, #10, #15

FIGURE 4.16   Summary Chart for Decision Tree

<table>
<tr><td></td><td></td><td align="center">**Decision Tree**</td></tr>
<tr><td>Chapter 1</td><td>←</td><td>Using Literature in the Reading Program</td></tr>
<tr><td>Chapter 2</td><td></td><td>Choosing Literature for Children</td></tr>
<tr><td>Chapter 3</td><td></td><td>Learning About Authors and Illustrators</td></tr>
<tr><td></td><td></td><td>**Identifying Perspectives on Reading Instruction**</td></tr>
<tr><td></td><td></td><td>• **Reflect on your present beliefs about learning to read and teaching reading with literature.**</td></tr>
<tr><td>**Chapter 4**</td><td></td><td>• **Become more knowledgeable about the reader response, critical, and interactive theoretical perspectives and their implications for instruction.**</td></tr>
<tr><td></td><td></td><td>• **Consider how all three theoretical perspectives can be woven into a literature program that helps children prepare for reading, read, explore, and extend the text (story, poem, or informational book).**</td></tr>
<tr><td>Chapter 5</td><td></td><td>Teaching from a Reader Response Perspective</td></tr>
<tr><td>Chapter 6</td><td></td><td>Teaching from a Critical Perspective</td></tr>
<tr><td>Chapter 7</td><td></td><td>Teaching from an Interactive Perspective</td></tr>
<tr><td>Chapter 8</td><td></td><td>Putting It All Together</td></tr>
<tr><td>Chapter 9</td><td>↓</td><td>Assessing Students' Learning</td></tr>
</table>

spectives so that you can think about the theoretical perspective that best reflects your beliefs about reading instruction.

After you have examined your own beliefs and studied the three theoretical perspectives, you will need to consider the four activities in which readers engage: preparing for reading the story, poem or informational book; reading the text; exploring the text; and going beyond a single literary work through extension activities. Such activities help readers extend initial responses into more interpretive and critical responses and examine connections among literary works.

The important decisions that teachers make about theoretical perspectives for teaching literature-based reading include the following:

• Reflect on your present beliefs about learning to read and teaching reading with literature.
• Become more knowledgeable about the reader response, critical, and interactive theoretical perspectives and their implications for instruction.
• Consider how all three theoretical perspectives can be woven into a literature program that helps children prepare for reading, read, explore, and extend the text (story, poem, or informational book).

This information is added to the decision-making diagram, as shown in Figure 4.16.

REFERENCES

Adams, M. (1990). *Beginning to read: Thinking and learning about print.* Cambridge, MA: MIT Press.

Bleich, D. (1978). *Subjective criticism.* Baltimore: The Johns Hopkins University Press.

Cairney, M. (1990). Intertextuality: Infectious echoes from the past. *The Reading Teacher, 43,* 478–485.

Corcoran, B. (1987). Teachers creating readers. In B. Corcoran (Ed.), *Readers, texts, teachers* (pp. 41–74). Upper Montclair, NJ: Boynton/Cook.

Culler, J. (1975). *Structuralist poetics.* Ithaca, NY: Cornell University Press.

Cullinan, B. (1981). *Literature and the child.* New York: Harcourt Brace Jovanovich.

Fish, S. (1970). Literature in the reader: Affective stylistics. *New Literary History, 2,* 123–162.

Iser, W. (1978). *The act of reading.* Baltimore, MD: The Johns Hopkins University Press.

LaBerge. D., & Samuels, S. (1974). Toward a theory of automatic information processing in reading. *Cognitive Psychology, 6,* 293–323.

Langer, J. (1990). The process of understanding: Reading for literary and informative purposes. *Research in the Teaching of English, 24,* 229–260.

Levi-Strauss, C. (1967). *Structural anthropology.* Garden City, NJ: Doubleday Anchor.

Lukens, R. (1990). *A critical handbook of children's literature* (4th ed.). Glenview, IL: Scott Foresman.

McGee, L., & Tompkins, G. (1981). The videotape answer to independent comprehension activities. *The Reading Teacher, 34,* 427–433.

Moss, J. F. (1984). *Focus units in literature: A handbook for elementary teachers.* Urbana, IL: National Council of Teachers of English.

Ogle, D. (1989). The know, want to know, learn strategy. In K. Muth (Ed.), *Children's comprehension of text: Research into practice* (pp. 205–223). Newark, DE: International Reading Association.

Probst, R. (1988). *Response and analysis: Teaching literature in the junior and senior high school.* Portsmouth, NH: Boynton/Cook.

Purves, A., Rogers, T., & Soter, A. (1990). *How porcupines make love II.* New York: Longman.

Rosenblatt, L. (1978). *The reader, the text, the poem: The transactional theory of the literary work.* Carbondale, IL: Southern Illinois University Press.

Rosenblatt, L. (1991). Literature—S.O.S.! *Language Arts, 68,* 444–448.

Rumelhart, D. (1977). Toward an interactive model of reading. In S. Dornic (Ed.), *Attention and performance, VI.* Hillsdale, NJ: Erlbaum.

Sloan, G. (1984). *The child as critic* (2nd ed.). New York: Teachers College Press.

Souriau, E. (1950). *Les deux cent milles situations dramatiques.* Paris: Flammarion.

Stanovich, K. (1980). Toward an interactive-compensatory model of individual differences in the development of reading fluency. *Reading Research Quarterly, 16,* 32–71.

Temple, C. (1990). How literary theory expands our expectations for children's reading and writing. In T. Shanahan (Ed.), *Reading and writing together: New perspectives for the classroom* (pp. 23–56). Norwood, MA: Christopher-Gordon.

Temple, C. (1991). Seven readings of a folktale: Literary theory in the classroom. *The New Advocate, 4,* 25–35.

Tompkins, G. (1990). The literature connection: How one teacher puts reading and writing together. In T. Shanahan (Ed.), *Reading and writing together: New perspectives for the classroom* (pp. 201–223). Norwood, MA: Christopher-Gordon.

Tompkins, J. (Ed.). (1980). *Reader response criticism: From formalism to post-structuralism.* Baltimore: The Johns Hopkins University Press.

CHILDREN'S LITERATURE REFERENCES

Cleary, B. (1983). *Dear Mr. Henshaw.* New York: Morrow.

Drew, D. (1987). *The caterpillar diary.* South Melbourne, Australia: Thomas Nelson.

Flack, F., & Wiese, K. (1933). *The story about Ping.* New York: Viking.

Howe, D., & Howe, J. (1979). *Bunnicula: A rabbit tale of mystery.* New York: Atheneum.

Juster, N. (1961). *The phantom tollbooth*. New York: Random House.

Macaulay, D. (1973). *Cathedral: The story of its construction*. Boston: Houghton Mifflin.

Oakley, G. (1981). *Hetty and Harriet*. New York: Atheneum.

Potter, B. (1902). *The tale of Peter Rabbit*. New York: Warne.

Sendak, M. (1963). *Where the wild things are*. New York: Harper & Row.

Steig, W. (1986). *Brave Irene*. New York: Farrar, Straus & Giroux.

Van Allsburg, C. (1985). *The polar express*. Boston, MA: Houghton Mifflin.

White, E. B. (1952). *Charlotte's web*. New York: Harper and Row.

Yorinks, A. (1986). *Hey, Al*. New York: Farrar, Straus & Giroux.

Zelinsky, P. (1986). *Rumpelstiltskin*. New York: Dutton.

CHAPTER 5

TEACHING FROM A READER RESPONSE PERSPECTIVE

In this chapter you will learn to make decisions about:

- Selecting stories, poems, and informational books based on a knowledge of literature, individual preferences, and curriculum demands
- Assessing whether students need teacher-directed or independent preparing, reading, exploring, and extending activities
- Selecting an appropriate activity that meets the needs of individual learners, is consonant with the purpose of reading, and is appropriate to the selection by understanding individual learners, reading and analyzing the selection, and consulting professional resources
- Consulting school or state curriculum guides for lists of expected competencies or learning outcomes

THIS IS THE FIRST of three chapters that will explore instructional activities that develop children's reading abilities through experiences with literature. In this chapter we discuss teaching reading from a reader response perspective. In the following case studies, Mr. Sahady and Ms. Epstein teach from this perspective, believing that their students need to discover personal connections to literature as they read and respond to literature. The ways in which they interact with their students and the activities they plan illustrate each teacher's careful attention to the unique opportunities for response offered by the particular story and informational book selected for instruction.

A CASE IN POINT

Mr. Sahady's Guided Reading of Sylvester and the Magic Pebble

Mr. Sahady's third grade class is reading *Sylvester and the Magic Pebble* (Steig, 1969), a story about a donkey named Sylvester who finds a magic pebble and foolishly wishes that he were a rock. He is turned into a rock and many months pass before he becomes himself again. To introduce the story, he shows his students a small red pebble and says, "This pebble plays an important part in the story we will be reading today. Take a good look at it and guess how it might be special." One student suggests the pebble might be magic. Mr. Sahady says, "I think so too. If you hold it and make a wish, it might come true." Each student holds the pebble and makes a wish. Then Mr. Sahady reads the title and shows the cover of *Sylvester and the Magic Pebble* (Steig, 1969). He invites the children to predict how Sylvester might have found the magic pebble and to speculate what he will do with it. Rubin says, "He just found it"; Mary Ann suggests, "I think he got it as a present"; and Karen responds "Maybe his grandparents had it for a real long time and then they gave it to him." Then the children read the first few pages of the story.

Then the children role-play this part of the story as a reading step activity. Three children act out a typical day at the Duncan home making up dialogue as they improvise. The other children interview them about what they are thinking and feeling. Then the children read the next few pages, and role-play several times the scene in which Sylvester meets the lion, panics, and wishes himself into a stone. The children discuss what they were feeling as they became these characters. Then the children finish reading the story on their own and, as an exploring step activity, write in their response journals after reading.

The next day the children bring their response journals to share as they talk about *Sylvester and the Magic Pebble.* Mr. Sahady opens the conversation about the story by asking, "Who has something to say about the story or to share from a journal?" The students talk about what they liked and disliked, what the story made them think about, what puzzled them, and what other stories

Sylvester and the Magic Pebble called to mind. Rubin reads from his journal, "Sylvester reminded me of the time I went for a walk in the woods near our house and thought I was lost. I was really scared until I found the path." Mary Ann says, "I thought the picnic food was neat, but what is timothy?"

Mr. Sahady then poses two questions, "Why did the author turn Sylvester into a rock? What did Sylvester learn from his experience?" The children talk about being scared by a lion, being brave, being smart, and learning a lesson the hard way. Rubin comments, "Sylvester's parents are the ones who suffered the most even though it wasn't their fault. But everyone at the end realized how much they loved everyone else in the family."

Mr. Sahady presents to his class a list of response to literature activities, as shown in Figure 5.1. He and the children discuss the list, adding a few more activities that the children suggest. As an extending step, the children select from the list an activity to extend their understanding of *Sylvester and the Magic Pebble.* Michael and Karen read books that have magic objects. Hiram and Mary Ann write a sequel to the story. Rubin and two classmates make stick puppets of Sylvester and his mother and father. They write a puppet play of the story and dramatize it for the group. Laura makes a diorama of Sylvester as a rock.

FIGURE 5.1 Response to Literature Activities for *Sylvester and the Magic Pebble* (Steig, 1969)

Make a series of dioramas of Sylvester as a rock on the hill in autumn, winter, and spring.
Make bookmarks of the characters and distribute them to classmates.
Prepare flannel board props and retell the story.
Gather a rock collection and label the kinds of rocks in the collection.
Write a missing person poster for Sylvester.
Write a sequel for the book telling when the Duncans next use the magic pebble.
Write a newspaper article about Sylvester's disappearance.
Write a simulated diary from Sylvester's mother's or father's perspective.
Write a readers' theatre script and perform it.
Read more books by William Steig.
Read more books about magic objects, for example, *Strega Nona* (de Paola, 1975) and *The Amazing Bone* (Steig, 1976).
Locate and read poems that complement the story.
Make a plot profile.

A CASE IN POINT

Ms. Epstein's Vertebrate Animal Theme Cycle

Ms. Epstein is teaching a theme cycle on vertebrate animals. Her science curriculum specifies that her sixth grade students should be able to describe the characteristics of amphibians, lizards, fish, birds, and mammals. She has several animals in her classroom including a mouse, frog, lizard, and parrot. Near the cages is a poetree (Hopkins, 1987), a tree branch potted in a large can filled with rocks, and students have hung on the tree copies of poems about the animals that they have found in books or written themselves. A veterinarian, pet store owner, and member of the humane society have visited the classroom and been interviewed by the class.

This week Ms. Epstein and eight students are reading *Frogs, Toads, Lizards, and Salamanders* (Parker & Wright, 1991). As a preparing step for reading from this book, the students each locate and share one of the poems about frogs or lizards hanging on the poetree beside the animal cages. A list of these poems appears in Figure 5.2.

Then they read several pages of the book and write responses in their learning logs using the *content response heuristic* (Brozo, 1988). Figure 5.3 presents the response heuristic, a series of questions that are used to guide reading. Today Ms. Epstein and the students discuss pages 40 and 4l of the book, which describe the similarities and differences between amphibians and lizards. For the exploring step, they discuss these differences by reading from their learning logs and making comments. Ms. Epstein begins the discussion by saying, "Who will share the word or sentence you thought was most interesting?" Students read entries from their learning logs and respond to each other's entries. Ted says, "I like the part where toads have warty skins. But I don't get how they breathe through their skin."

FIGURE 5.2   Frog and Lizard Poems

Cambell, A. (1983). "Sally and Manda." In J. Prelutsky (Ed.), *The Random House book of poetry.* New York: Random House.

Gardner, J. (1983). "The lizard." In J. Prelutsky (Ed.), *The Random House book of poetry.* New York: Random House.

Hoban, R. "The tin frog." In M. Farber & M. Livingston (Eds.), *These small stones.* New York: Harper & Row.

Johnson, T. (1990). "Among the water lilies," "Lizard longing," and "Frog eggs." In T. Johnson, *I'm gonna tell Mama I want an iguana.* New York: Putnam.

Prelutsky, J. (1984). "The chameleon" and "The gallivanting gecko." In J. Prelutsky, *Zoo doings.* New York: Greenwillow.

Prelutsky, J. (1986). "Bullfrogs, bullfrogs on parade." In J. Prelutsky, *Ride a purple pelican.* New York: Morrow.

Roethke, T. (1983). "The lizard." In J. Prelutsky (Ed.), *The Random House book of poetry.* New York: Random House.

Wilbur, R. (1984). "What is the opposite of a prince?" in Z. Sutherland & M. Livingston (Eds.), *The Scott Foresman anthology of children's poetry.* Glenview, IL: Scott Foresman.

Yolen, J. (1986) "Song of the spring peeper." In J. Yolen, *Ring of Earth.* San Diego: Harcourt Brace Jovanovich.

FIGURE 5.3   Response Heuristic for Informational Books

---

1. What was most interesting or exciting word, phrase, sentence, or picture in the text? What idea, detail, issue, or concept did you feel most strongly about?
2. What are your feelings about this idea, detail, issue or concept? Why do you feel this way?
3. What connections can you make between your own experiences and the ideas, details, issues, and concepts in the text?
4. What places in the text made you think of something you have experienced or seen or know about? Why?

Adapted from Brozo, 1988, p. 142.

Next, the students brainstorm words and phrases that reflect what they know and feel about amphibians and lizards. Ms. Epstein urges them to select words and phrases from their learning logs, from comments made in the group discussion, and from the book they are reading. They brainstorm a list of words and phrases on the chalkboard and compose two poems as a further exploring step activity:

> *Lizards*
> *dry and cold*
> *slip away as fast as the eye can blink*
> *long legs and graceful bodies*
> *But we'll never know*
> *eggs on land*
> *sounds so grand*
> *but not caviar*

> *Amphibians*
> *ribit, ribit at the pond*
> *moist and warm*

> *no ribs*
> *just belly we guess*
> *eggs in jelly*
> *under the water*
> *how do they hatch?*

Later, for an extending step activity, the students demonstrate their knowledge of the characteristics of various vertebrate animals by writing animal stories incorporating the factual information they have been learning in their descriptions of setting and character. Students will consider three or four activities to extend their study of reptiles and amphibians and other vertebrate animals and decide to study "The Frog Prince" fairy tale by reading several versions of this brothers Grimm story including *The Frog King* (1989), *The Frog Prince* (1989), *Frog Prince* (Berenzy, 1989), and *The Frog Prince Continued* (Scieszka, 1991). They will compare these versions to a version that Ms. Epstein found in a 1945 edition of *Grimm's Fairy Tales* (Lucas, Crane, & Edwardes).

INTRODUCTION

The reader response perspective focuses on reading as a lived-through experience that involves the feelings, images, thoughts, and associations called to mind at the moment of reading. Readers respond to those feelings during and after reading. The reader response perspective also emphasizes that reading is an engaged process. Readers identify with or feel repelled by characters, and they have feelings of empathy, admiration, disgust, or any number of other emotional responses to events and images in stories and poems. Through engagement, they make personal connections to the stories and poems they read and to the content presented in informational books and magazines.

Readers' experiences and responses are at the center in this perspective. Teachers recognize that readers come to their own understanding of stories, poems, and informational books, and each student's experiences and responses will be different depending on many variables including age and developmental level, life experiences, literary experiences, and reading experiences. The teacher's role is to first help students express their responses and understandings and then provide activities that help students deepen and enrich those responses and understandings. Teachers begin by helping students express their responses. Then they help students move back into the text to clarify their understandings of the text based on personal response and then to move out of the text to expand their understandings of the world and themselves.

In the first part of this chapter we describe activities for preparing, reading, exploring, and extending that support children's reading for literary purposes, usually in stories and poems. In the second section we describe activities that support children's reading for informational purposes, usually in informational books and magazines. In the final section we discuss decisions that teachers make about teaching reading from a reader response perspective, including decisions about selecting particular activities to meet specific purposes and needs. It is important to keep in mind that some of these activities can fit within the other two theoretical perspectives, critical and interactive, as well as in the reader response perspective. In this chapter we stress how to encourage students to enjoy the lived-through experience of reading and become personally involved and engaged readers.

READING FOR LITERARY PURPOSES

When readers read for literary purposes, they enter the world of a story or poem, and it is as if readers are vicariously present in one secondary world that they construct while reading. At the same time, readers are able to step back from this secondary world to reflect on their understandings of the events and relationships of that world. They come away from their reading transformed, having gained a new understanding of themselves, their world, and their place in that world. Activities that support literary reading help students enter this secondary world; savor the language, associations, and images they construct in that world; and reflect on those experiences. The goal is to help students become engaged or personally involved with a story or poem, to be able to take on the viewpoint of the various characters or narrator, and to use personal response to develop interpretations.

Preparing Step

Activities in the preparing step are designed to develop students' engagement or personal involvement with the story or poem. Readers are personally involved when they are caught up in the plot of the story and care about the characters or when they savor the mood of a poem. Preparing activities help readers get personally involved before reading by inviting them to identify with characters or by setting the mood for a poem. Carefully selecting the order in which poems and stories are read is also an important part of the preparing step.

Encouraging Engagement and Setting Mood.   One way to encourage readers to identify with a character before reading is to ask them to imagine an event that will happen to a character or to dramatize that event. For example, having children imagine what it would be like to leave one's family behind and travel far from home to marry a stranger and raise his children helps them to feel for themselves Sarah's thoughts and emotions in *Sarah, Plain and Tall* (MacLachlan, 1985). Often a discussion or a simple improvisation will prompt children to identify with a character. In the case study at the beginning of this chapter, Mr. Sahady simply painted a stone red and invited his students to hold it, imagine that it was magic, and make a wish. This activity allowed them to step into Sylvester's footsteps and better understand this character's feelings and motivations.

Another activity that encourages readers to identify with a character is the *prereading writing assignment* (Marino et al., 1985; Noyce & Christie, 1989). In this activity children write about how they would deal with an event related to the story they are preparing to read. For example, before reading *Sylvester and the Magic Pebble,* students might write in response to this prompt:

> Imagine that you are the mother (or father) of a son who has been missing for several days. Write in your diary what you are feeling, what you have done to try to find your son, and what might happen in the future.

To prepare a prereading writing assignment, teachers pinpoint a crucial event in a story that influences characters' motivations, actions, or reactions. They describe this event and ask students to write how they would react to the event. This activity lets students weigh the consequences of actions and face the same decisions that a character must face. Doing so lets students become that character for a few moments. These assignments result in intense personal involvement with characters and their problems which, in turn, increase children's engagement as they read.

Another way teachers encourage children's engagement is to introduce the main characters to children before they read. Before reading *Bridge to Terabithia* (Paterson, 1977), teachers can introduce the members of the Aarons and Burke families by describing them or reading descriptive information about each of the family members from the story. For example, a teacher might explain, "The Aarons family lives on a small farm that can no longer support the family, so Mr. Aarons drives an old pickup truck into town to work. The family includes Momma, Dad, Brenda, Elle, Jesse, May Belle, and Joyce Ann. In contrast, the Burke family, including Leslie, her mother, and father, have recently moved to the country. To introduce the Burke family, the teacher could read portions of pages 44 and 45 in the story describing Leslie's parents. Both Mr. and Mrs. Burke are writers, but Mrs. Burke writes novels and is very famous. Mr. Burke spends more time with Leslie; he likes to work on the house, listen to music on the stereo, and read books aloud.

Finally, teachers might read the opening chapter of a book or the initial stanza in a poem as a way of engaging readers. Skillful oral readers have a way of pulling their listeners into a story or poem. After hearing a dramatic reading of a chapter opening or the beginning of a poem, children are impatient to continue reading themselves. Reading aloud can also help set the mood; the opening chapter signals whether the book is a comedy or a spooky tale. Reading an entire poem aloud sets the stage for more intense engagement as children reread it themselves.

Selecting Stories and Poems.   Readers' prior experiences with literature is an important variable in determining their responses to unfamiliar stories and poems. What readers have read before they read a particular story or poem influences their responses to it. When readers reread the same story or poem, their responses are different during the second or third reading because they are influenced and changed by their previous reading.

Carefully selecting the order in which stories or poems are read can influence the kinds of responses and interpretations that children construct. For example, reading *The Facts and Fictions of Minna Pratt* (MacLachlan, 1988) will influence the way that children subsequently interpret *Are You There, God?, It's Me, Margaret* (Blume, 1970). The first story is a richer, more complex look at what it means for a young girl to mature into womanhood, while the second story presents a more shallow, but for the time, socially acceptable picture of womanhood. Children are much more likely to be able to compare and contrast the different solutions to growing up that these two authors offer when the two stories are read in sequence.

Reading poetry before a story or reading a story before poetry is another way to prepare readers. Poems can set the mood for a story by illuminating a character trait or providing an image of a setting. Because poems are so compact, emotionally appealing, and rich in images, they stimulate personal involvement. Poetry to be read with stories should be carefully selected so that readers gain a greater understanding of both poems and stories. Stories and poems can be selected so that they have a common topic, theme, character, or event. For example, Adoff's poem "I Am Learning" (1979) about eating with chopsticks is a perfect accompaniment for *How My Parents Learned to Eat* (Friedman, 1987), and "Cynthia in the Snow" (Brooks, 1956) can set the stage for reading *The Snowy Day* (Keats, 1962). Figure 5.4 presents a list of stories and related poems that can be read together.

Reading Step

Since a reader response perspective emphasizes reading as a lived-through experience, teachers should plan few reading activities so as not interfere with children's reading. However, teachers might want to encourage personal involvement using role-playing as Mr. Sahady did in the case study at the beginning of this chapter. Role-playing encourages readers to take on the perspective of a character, experiencing the story from that character's point of view. This activity also allows children to explore the role of the narrator—what does the narrator see and know that characters do not? It also allows children to experience the story from different perspectives as they role-play various characters. Role-playing during reading is informal, and children make up dialogue as they enact the story. Teachers act as coaches, asking children what they are thinking and prompting them to include these feelings in their dialogue.

Exploring Step

Exploring activities give children ample time and space to construct their own meanings and interpretations of stories and poems. Children's initial, tentative responses to stories and poems are encouraged, accepted, and celebrated. Teachers help children build from these initial responses into more considered, informed, and interpretive responses by rereading and thinking about the story or poem that they are reading and by attending to an author's craft.

Rereading and Thinking. After students express their responses to reading, they may reread to deepen those responses in many ways. One way is by participating in grand conversations. Other activities include writing in response journals, composing simulated journals or letters, drawing, gathering materials for a story or poetry box, and dramatizing stories or poems in a tableau or readers' theatre presentation.

Response journals. *Response journals* are an excellent tool for helping children capture their initial responses to stories and poems (Corcoran, 1987). After reading a story or poem, children write in a notebook about their thoughts and feelings, rather than a summary of their reading. The purpose of response journals is for students to explore their personal reactions and understanding. Response journal entries often begin with the word *I*. Teachers and students frequently compile a list of phrases such as the following to use to prompt responses:

> I don't understand when. . . .
> This makes me think of. . . .
> This reminds me of. . . .
> This is like. . . .
> This makes me feel. . . .
> I can picture. . . .
> I like the part. . . .
> I didn't like the part. . . .
> The part I remember most is. . . .

These prompts can be written on a chart in the classroom or duplicated and stapled in the front of each student's response journal. After writing in response journals, students share their writing with their classmates. This sharing can be done in pairs, in small groups, or with the whole class.

Another way to prompt students' responses is by using a *response heuristic* (Bleich, 1978), which is a set of four prompts that stimulate students' personal reactions to reading. Students write their personal reactions to these prompts in their response journals. The prompts included in a response heuristic are

1. *Reconstruct the story or poem.* Students write in their response journals, retelling the story or poem in their own words.
2. *Find connections with the story or poem.* Students think of at least three things that the story or poem reminds them of in another story or in their own lives and write these connections to personal experiences or to literature in their response journals.
3. *Choose the most important paragraph, sentence, and word in the story or poem.* Students copy a paragraph, sentence, or word from the text and explain why that part of the text was most important to them.

FIGURE 5.4   Correlated Poems and Stories

Story	Poem
Babbitt, N. (1975). *Tuck Everlasting.* New York: Farrar, Straus & Giroux.	Hoberman, M. (1983). "Changing." In J. Prelutsky (Ed.), *The Random House Book of Poetry of Children* (p. 102). New York: Random House
Bang, M. (1985). *The Paper Crane.* New York: Greenwillow Books.	Field, G. (1985). "Home Cooking Cafe." In P. Janeczko (Comp.), *Pocket Poems.* New York: Bradbury Press.
Brett, J. (1989). *The Mitten.* New York: Putnam.	Esbensen, B. (1984). "Mittens." In B. Esbensen, *Cold Stars and Fireflies: Poems of the Four Seasons* (p. 25). New York: Crowell.
Burnett, F. (1987). *The Secret Garden.* Boston: D. R. Godine.	Field, R. (1983). "Some People." In J. Prelutsky (Comp.), *The Random House Books of Poetry for Children* (p. 56). New York: Random House.
Byars, B. (1981). *The Summer of the Swans.* New York: Puffin	Little, J. (1989). "When Someone I Love is Hurt." In J. Little, *Hey World, Here I Am!* (p. 36). New York: Harper & Row.
Cleary, B. (1983). *Dear Mr. Henshaw.* New York: Morrow.	Johnston, T. (1989). "Christmas Wish." In M. Livingston (Ed.), *Poems for Fathers* (p. 12). New York: Holiday House.
Dahl, R. (1964). *Charlie and the Chocolate Factory.* New York: Knopf.	Adoff, A. (1989). "In My Horror Fantasy Chiller." In A. Adoff, *Chocolate Dreams* (p. 22). New York: Lothrop, Lee & Shepard.
Goble, P. (1978). *The Girl Who Loved Wild Horses.* New York: Bradbury.	Whitman, W. (1989). "A Gigantic Beauty of a Stallion." In C. Sullivan (Ed.), *Imaginary Gardens: American Poetry and Art for Young People* (p. 9). New York: Henry N. Abrams.
L'Engle, M. (1962). *A Wrinkle in Time.* New York: Dell.	MacLeish, A. (1955). "Reply to Mr. Wordsworth." In H. Plotz (Ed.), *Imagination's Other Place: Poems of Science and Math* (p. 62). New York: Crowell.

4. *Choose the most important literary element in the story or poem* (for older students only). Students select the literary element (e.g., characterization, setting, symbol) that they feel most influenced them as they read.

After writing responses to the heuristic in their journals, students share their entries with their classmates in pairs or small groups. Students' comprehension and interpretations of stories and poems are enhanced by hearing several students' connections to a text and by arguing the merits of selecting different sentences or words as being the most important.

Grand conversations. Grand conversations are literary discussions in which students talk about a book or poem that everyone has read or listened to read aloud. Mr. Sahady's students had a grand conversation about *Sylvester and the Magic Pebble* in the case study at the beginning of this chapter when the students shared what they found interesting in the story.

Story	Poem
Lobel, A. (1971). *Frog and Toad Together.* New York: Scholastic.	Esbensen, B. (1986). "Frog." In B. Esbensen, *Words with Wrinkled Knees* (p. 6). New York: Crowell.
Lowry, L. (1989). *Number the Stars.* Boston: Houghton Mifflin.	Margolis, R. (1986). "How to Get Through the Memorial Service." In M. Livingston (Ed.), *Poems for Jewish Holidays* (p. 7). New York: Holiday House.
McCloskey, R. (1969). *Make Way for Ducklings.* New York: Viking.	Fyleman, R. (1965). "Regent's Park." In A. McGovern (Ed.), *Arrow Book of Poetry* (p. 47). New York: Scholastic.
McKissack, P. (1986). *Flossie & the Fox.* New York: Dial.	Schwartz, D. (1990). "I Am Cherry Alive." In N. Philip (Ed.), *Treasury of Children's Poetry* (p. 28). New York: Stewart, Tabori and Chang.
Mendez, P. (1989). *The Black Snowman.* New York: Scholastic.	Hru, D. (1990). "The Mask." In D. Slier (Ed.), *Make a Joyful Sound* (p. 46). New York: Checkerboard Press.
Paterson, K. (1980). *Jacob Have I Loved.* New York: Crowell.	Unknown, Swakiuti Indian (1983). "Prayer of a Man to Twin Children." In J. Bierhorst (Ed.), *The Sacred Path* (unpaged). New York: Morrow.
Steig, W. (1971). *Amos and Boris.* New York: Farrar, Straus & Giroux.	Fyleman, R. (1983). "Mice." In J. Prelutsky (Ed.), *The Random House Book of Poetry for Children* (p. 54). New York: Random House.
Taylor, M. (1976). *Roll of Thunder, Hear my Cry.* New York: Dial.	Walker, M. (1984). "Lineage." In C. Streich (Ed.), *Grandparents' Houses* (p. 29). New York: Greenwillow.
Waber, B. (1972). *Ira Sleeps Over.* Boston: Houghton Mifflin.	Viorst, J. (1981). "Teddy Bear Poem." In J. Viorst *If I Were in Charge of the World and Other Worries* (p. 52). New York: Aladdin Books.
White, E. (1952). *Charlotte's Web.* New York: Harper & Row.	Esbensen, B. (1986). "Spider." In B. Esbensen, *Words with Wrinkled Knees* (unpaged). New York: Crowell.

According to Mary Ann Eeds (Eeds & Wells, 1989; Peterson & Eeds, 1990), who originated the idea of grand conversations, too often teachers and children participate in "gentle inquisitions" about books in which teachers ask a series of recall level, known-answer questions. Instead, she argued, teachers need to provide a forum for children's ideas to be heard. Nancie Atwell (1987) had a similar idea. She suggested that when children talk about a book that it should be more like the way a group of adults might sit around the dinner table and discuss a book they had read or a movie they had seen. Adults do not answer recall level, known-answer questions; instead, their discussions involve a genuine give-and-take. The same kind of discussion is possible in school in a grand conversation.

In grand conversations, children tell about the parts of stories or poems that they liked and why, describe parts that puzzled them, make interpretations about why characters act as they do or what poems mean, and argue different interpretations. The difference between a grand conversation and other kinds of discussions is that children identify what they will talk about. The teacher does not ask questions which the children then discuss. The goal of a grand conversation is not for every child to accept the same, "correct" interpretation of a story or poem; rather, it is for everyone to have a chance to be heard, for ideas to be challenged, and for greater insights to emerge from the group talk.

After students have read and enjoyed a picture book or several chapters in a longer book, they meet as a class or in small groups to talk about it in a grand conversation. These conversations are brief, often lasting only 15 or 20 minutes. For these conversations it is important to use excellent literature—the kind with many layers of meaning, such as *Sarah, Plain and Tall* (MacLachlan, 1985) and *Ira Sleeps Over* (Waber, 1972).

Guidelines for group interaction during a grand conversation should be established ahead of time and posted so that everyone can see them. They might include the following rules:

> Sit in a circle so that everyone will be involved.
> Only one person talks at a time.
> Take turns.
> Stay on the topic.
> Talk at least once, but not more than three times until everyone has talked.

We believe that grand conversations have two parts. The first part provides an opportunity for children to talk about their personal responses, and the second part is sparked by a literary question that the teacher asks. These are the steps:

1. *Students share personal responses.* Students share their personal responses with the group and tell what they liked about the book. The teacher or a student leader begins the conversation by asking, "What did you think?" or "What did you like?" Students start talking immediately or they share responses they have written in their journals. Students use specific incidents from the book to support their responses or read a short excerpt from the book or show an illustration to make a point. To prepare for a grand conversation, some teachers ask students to place one or more bookmarks in their books indicating a place in the story that they want to talk about. Other teachers ask students to star one or two statements in their response journals that they would like to share. As children make comments, the teacher may want to challenge a child to think further by asking, "Why?" For example, in a grand conversation about *Sylvester and the Magic Pebble* (Steig, 1969), one child might comment that he would like to find that pebble. The teacher helps expand the response by asking, "Why?"

Teachers act as experts in children's literature during the conversation. They react to children's responses by providing the labels or terms given to literary information. As children describe how a character changes or is different at the beginning and end of the story, for instance, the teacher might introduce the term *dynamic character,* a literary term used to describe characters who grow and change in stories. As children comment that the story seemed like a dream, the teacher introduces the term *fantasy.* At one point in a grand conversation about *Sylvester and the Magic Pebble,* several of the children commented that they especially liked the pictures where the rock sat through autumn, winter, and spring. The teacher then focused on the importance of the seasons in the story, explaining that authors sometimes use seasons as *symbols.* Symbols are objects, events, or characters that have more than one meaning. Spring in the story refers to the season when flowers begin to grow, but it also means or symbolizes new life and hope. Sylvester turned back into himself, or you might say he was given new life in the spring. Winter means the season when the ground is covered with snow and most plants are dormant. It may also symbolize death or the death of hopes and dreams, and Sylvester's hopes of ever becoming himself again were the lowest in the winter.

Teachers also offer their own responses and interpretations during the conversation, including the symbols they notice in stories and poems. During a grand conversation about *Sylvester and the Magic Pebble,* for example, one sixth grade teacher talked about the pebble and what it symbolized (Smith, 1990). One interpretation, she suggested, was that the pebble is just a small stone with magical qualities. But, it might also symbolize maturity. Sylvester tried to use grown-up power, just as a mature person would, but was too foolish, too young and inexperienced to use it properly. At the end of the story, the pebble, which represented the maturity that Sylvester did not have, was put away until Sylvester was ready for it.

Another role that teachers play in grand conversations is to help children reflect on the sources of their particular responses. If children mention that a story reminds them of a particular event from their lives, teachers ask, "What is similar about the past event and the story?" Teachers ask children to identify passages from the text that call to mind recollections from their lives and to explain why the language of the text might have prompted that response. They help children return again and again to the story or poem and to their own past experiences or to connections with other literature as a way of strengthening and deepening their understanding of the text and their responses (Smith, 1990).

Teachers frequently do not participate in the personal response portion of grand conversations. Children who are familiar with the kinds of talk that are expected and the rules of the conversation should have opportunities to explore literature on their own. Students are capable of making sophisticated interpretations of literature on their own when given the opportunity.

2. *Ask literary questions.* The second part of a grand conversation is directed by one or two *literary questions* that the teacher asks (Saul, 1989). Literary questions focus on interpreting literature. Interpretation is somewhat different than comprehension. Comprehension comes first; readers must comprehend a story or poem in order to interpret it. Comprehension involves knowing the details of a story or poem—understanding what the story or poem is about or who the characters are and the events that occur. For example, when children comprehend *Sylvester and the Magic Pebble,* they know who the characters are and the events that happen in the story. Comprehension also means inferring character traits (that Sylvester is both smart for figuring out the pebble is magic and immature in panicking at the sight of a lion when he had the power of magic at his disposal).

In contrast, interpretation answers the question, "So what does this mean?" Literary discussions take readers beyond stating the sequence of events, making inferences, knowing the meaning of vocabulary, or stating an opinion. Interpretation is figuring out the significance of characters, events, dialogue, setting, rhythm, rhyme, image, or figurative language. Interpretation of *Sylvester and the Magic Pebble* involves understanding the significance of the lion appearing just as Sylvester finds a magic pebble, Sylvester's loss of identity in autumn and winter, his reawakening in spring, and the family's decision to put the magic pebble in an iron safe.

Interpretation also involves understanding theme—the statement about life and human nature that is made through the story or poem. Different readers interpret themes differently. For example, one reader might think that the theme of *Sylvester and the Magic Pebble* is that family is more powerful than all the magic in the world. Another reader may think the theme is that it is better not to become involved with things you cannot control. Still another reader may decide that the theme is that a wise person is someone with maturity rather than someone with magical qualities.

Literary questions have more than one right answer, take the reader back into the text for support, and go beyond the obvious events and stated details in the text (Saul, 1989). There are several sources for literary questions. One source is to look for basic contrasts or similarities in the story (see discussion of literary contrasts in Chapter 4). For example, *Sarah, Plain and Tall* (MacLachlan, 1985) begins and ends with the memory of a sunny day. A literary question might ask readers to explore the significance of these memories. The story takes place on the plains and Sarah is described as plain. A literary question is, "What should readers make of this?" Another source of literary questions is statements made by characters that can mean more than one thing. Caleb asks in *Sarah, Plain and Tall,* "Can my face be too clean?" What else could this question mean? When they huddle in the barn during a storm, Sarah says, "It will be all right, Jacob." What else could this mean? Another source of literary questions is to consider whether an event or detail seems particularly compelling in the story. For example, the giving of gifts in *Sarah, Plain and Tall* seems important. Readers might examine the significance of Sarah's gifts and ponder what the greatest gift in the story was.

Sometimes teachers may not include the second portion in the grand conversation. Students' responses may have earlier explored the kinds of issues that teachers had planned as the focus of their literary questions. Or, teachers may want students to be more completely in charge of the conversation.

A successful grand conversation gives students adequate time to comprehend the story or poem, question events or characters, interpret the significance of events and motivations of characters, make statements about themes, evaluate how well they liked the story or poem, and assess the effectiveness of an author or illustrator (Eeds & Wells, 1989). While the teacher can be actively involved, grand conversations are comprised primarily of student talk. Grand conversations not only help students articulate their first, tentative responses to stories, but also help them expand those responses into more considered, interpretive responses.

Moral decisions.   Another activity that encourages students to become more actively involved with characters and story events is making *moral decisions* (Johnson & Louis, 1987). To make moral decisions, students read a story to the point where a character must make an important decision. The decision must not be one for which there is clearly a correct action. Before reading the remainder of the story, students discuss the decision facing the character and the issues involved in making that decision in a small group. Then each student makes a decision and tells the group why that decision was made. For example, students might decide whether Johnny Orchard should or should not shoot his bear after reading the first portion of *The Biggest Bear* (Ward, 1952). Or students might decide whether they would drink from the spring giving eternal life after reading *Tuck Everlasting* (Babbitt, 1975). Moral decisions require students to take a stand on an issue that a character must face in a story. Students become personally involved with the character as they face making a similar decision.

Another way to engage students in considering characters' moral decisions is to have groups of students complete *discussion webs* (Alvermann, 1991). In the center of a discussion web is a statement about a decision that a character makes in a story. For example, the center of a discussion web about *Hey, Al* (Yorinks, 1986) is the statement, "Al should not have gone to the island with the bird." Students explore reasons for both agreeing and disagreeing with the statement and write justifications for agreeing with the statement on one side of the web; on the other side, they give justifications for disagreeing. Finally, the group comes to a consensus on whether they agree or disagree. The groups report their decisions to the whole class and give reasons for their decision.

Simulated journals.   Students explore a character in depth by writing a *simulated journal* from that character's viewpoint. As they write simulated journals, students pay careful attention to the events in a story, but they also make inferences about what characters think and feel. For example, students can become Anna, Caleb, Sarah, or Papa as they read *Sarah, Plain and Tall,* and after reading each chapter, they write about the events and their thoughts and feelings about the events as if they were that character. Students choose which character they will become and the events they will write about. They will select the character they most identify with and write about the events that seem most relevant to them. Figure 5.5 presents a simulated journal written by a third grader from the perspective of Sam after reading *Sam, Bangs, and Moonshine* (Ness, 1966).

Children should share their simulated journal entries with their classmates. As children share their journal entries, they learn how perspective influences memories of events and feelings. Characters in stories often have conflicting goals and emotions and sharing simulated journal entries allows children to explore those conflicting goals and emotions. It also allows children to see the story from the perspective of different characters.

Simulated letters.   Children also take on the role of a character as they write *simulated letters.* A simulated letter is written from one character to another or from a character in a story to a real or a fictitious person. Students decide why they will write letters, select the character writing the letter, and choose the topic for the letter. For example, after reading *Number the Stars* (Lowry, 1989), a story about the friendship between a Jewish girl and a Christian girl during World War II, students might assume the role of either girl and write letters to each other or to Adolph Hitler. Similarly, after reading *The Summer of the Swans* (Byars, 1970), a story about a mentally

Dear Diary,

I am a fool to fall for that baby Kangeroo trick! I thought that trick was true. Well after my bike floated away and I got a new pet gerbil I felt a little better, but I still have larengits. Bummer! I wonder if Bangs could really talk! I don't think she could.

retarded boy who goes out alone to look for wild swans and becomes lost overnight, students might take on the role of Sara, the little boy's sister who feels guilty about her brother getting lost or the role of another family member. Figure 5.6 presents two letters written by a sixth grader after reading *The Summer of the Swans.* In the first letter, she takes on the role of Sara and, in the second, the role of Sara's father.

Children should have opportunities to share their simulated letters with their classmates. As with simulated journals, these letters offer opportunities to explore character traits and motives and to examine the influence of point of view on understanding story events.

Agony column.   A variation on writing simulated letters for upper grade students is writing for an *Agony Column* (Johnson & Louis, 1987). After reading a portion of a story about a character with a problem, students adopt the perspective of a character and write a Dear Abby type letter asking for advice about a problem in the story. Other students become Abby and write replies. After reading *One-Eyed Cat* (Fox, 1984), a story about a child who feels guilty after accidentally shooting a cat, one student wrote:

> *Dear Abby:*
> *I feel just awful. My father told me never to shoot a gun, but I did it anyway. I think I shot this cat. He is in the woods and can't take care of himself. I really am responsible for the cat. I don't want him to die. What should I do?*
>
> *Troubled Conscience*

Another student replied:

> *Dear Troubled Conscience:*
> *I think you should tell your father. Most fathers will understand if you tell them you are sorry. It is important to help the cat, but more important to make up with your father.*
>
> *Abby*

Students can select which of Abby's replies that they believe is the most sensible, most likely to be used by the author, or least likely to be used by the author and explain why. This activity will prompt careful rereading to examine any clues the author gives toward solving a character's problem. After reading the story, students can compare Abby's solutions to the author's solution.

Simulated newspapers.   Children can step into the setting and times of a story by writing a *simulated newspaper* that might be published at the time of the story or poem. Students write news articles, weather forecasts, advertisements, and other articles related to the setting and events of the story they are reading. The headlines for a newspaper written for *Sylvester and the Magic Pebble* might read "Young Duncan Lost for 10 Days." Articles that children write might include interviews with Mr. and Mrs. Duncan, advertisements for Sylvester's return, and the police report of Sylvester's disappearance.

"I" poems.   Writing poetry after reading stories prompts careful rereading and interpretation. One type of poetry is an "I" poem, written from the viewpoint of a

FIGURE 5.6   A Sixth Grader's Simulated Letters for *The Summer of the Swans* (Byars, 1970)

> Dear Father,
>
> Remember me? It's Sara, your daughter. You're doing fine, aren't you? I mean, how should your own daughter know, you never talk to me. Do you know what is going on here? Charlie is missing. We woke up in the morning and he was gone. Don't you think you should support your son when he needs you the most? Please come. Put yourself in my shoes, or Charlie's, or even (yes even), Wanda's. We were deserted by our father. Just say "hi," or have a small conversation with us. Yes, it does matter. I'm just really upset, and it's not because I take after my uncle!
>
> Sincerely,
> Sara

character. "I" poems have an unrhymed form and each line begins with the word *I*. After reading *Sarah, Plain and Tall,* students might write a poem from Sarah's point of view, for example:

> *I am Sarah, plain and tall*
> *I come from the ocean, green and gray*
> *I have my memories strong*
> *I am searching, wondering*
> *I am uncertain*
> *I am Sarah, plain and tall*
> *I have found new friends*
> *I have planted flowers and hope*
> *I have seen the golden plains*

FIGURE 5.6
continued

> Dear Sara,
>
> You have to understand how I feel. I am supporting two families, and I have a job in Ohio I'd love to spend more time with you, but I just can't. Things aren't what they used to be. You kids have changed, too. Wanda is older now and is interested in boys, you are having teenaged problems, and it's hard to understand or do anything with your brother, Charlie. Anyways, your Aunt Willie spends time with you. Someday, you'll be in a position like mine. I love you, gotta go! Bye!
>
> Love,
> Dad

I am a bride
I am Sarah, plain and tall

To write "I" poems, students must make inferences about a character's thoughts and feelings and pay careful attention to descriptive details. Writing the poem allows them to become more personally involved with a character and to view the story from that character's perspective. To encourage this personal involvement, students should select the character that they wish to write about. As students share their poems about different characters in a story, they will naturally explore the story's meanings from several perspectives.

Sketch-to-stretch. An activity that encourages students to interpret what they read is the *sketch-to-stretch* activity (Harste, Short, & Burke, 1988). In this activity, students sketch a picture that represents their interpretation of a story or poem. The sketches are not drawings of events from the story; rather, they are intended to show the significance of events. These steps can be followed when using this strategy:

1. *Students read the story or poem.* The students read either the complete work or read to a selected point in a poem or story. Or the teacher reads the story or poem aloud.
2. *Students draw interpretive pictures.* Students draw a picture representing their interpretation of the story or poem. For example, a sketch-to-stretch drawing for *Bridge to Terabithia* (Paterson, 1977), a story about two lonely children who create an imaginary kingdom called Terabithia, might include a picture of Jesse and his father on two sides of a bridge. A road sign saying, "Bridge to Terabithia" might be drawn next to the bridge, and the word *Leslie* might be written across the bridge. This sketch does not depict an event in the story; it shows an interpretation of the story: that Jesse becomes closer, or bridged, to his father through Leslie's death and his involvement with her in their imaginary kingdom.
3. *Students discuss their pictures.* The students explain their pictures. They also compare and contrast their differing interpretations. Figure 5.7 presents a sketch made by a sixth grader to interpret *The Summer of the Swans* (Byars, 1970).

Students often draw different sketches to illustrate their interpretations of the same story, and teachers can discuss these differences, pointing out that one reason each picture is different is that each reader brings slightly different prior knowledge to reading. Older students can reread selected portions of the text that were particularly important in forming their sketches and write an essay about their interpretation. Figure 5.8 presents an essay written to accompany the sketched interpretation shown in Figure 5.7.

Story or poetry box.   Another activity that encourages interpretation is a *story or poetry box*. To make a story or poetry box, students gather or make materials to represent the events, images, characters, or topics of poems or stories and put them in a box. Then they prepare a list of the objects included in the box and attach it to the inside of the box lid. For example, after reading Jack Prelutsky's (1982) book of poems *The Baby Uggs Are Hatching* students might make a poetry box that contains several clay figures of Uggs for the poem "The Baby Uggs Are Hatching," a broken cup to represent "The Smasheroo," a feather to represent "The Sneezy-snoozer," a checker to represent "The Snatchits," an apple core to represent "The Creature in the Classroom," and several pebbles to represent the "Grubby Grebbles." A story box for *Sarah, Plain and Tall* might include a picture of the ocean, seashells, a map of the United States with Sarah's journey marked, a poem about storms, a poem about colors, sand, hay, a stuffed cat, and colored pencils. Students also might make a train ticket and draw a picture of Sarah to include.

Collage.   A *collage* consists of pictures, words, and other materials cut from magazines, newspapers, wallpaper books, or found in nature. Constructing a collage is a unique way for students to express their interpretations of stories and poems.

FIGURE 5.7   Sketch-to-Stretch Interpretation for *The Summer of the Swans* (Byars, 1970)

FIGURE 5.8   Interpretive Essay for *The Summer of the Swans* (Byars, 1970)

> In "The Summer of the Swans" when Sara descibes the staircase, it certainly had a lot of meaning in my mind. Through out Sara's life, she had lived in the shadows, with difficulty seeing anything right or being able to fix it. But that afternoon, it was like she had stepped out of the darkness, and into the light were she could see that she had the ability to change anything in her life she disliked, and could go as far as she wanted to go. Sara's father was at the bottom not trying to change of do anything, as if he were helpless or didn't want to make things better than they were. Then there was Charlie, who had difficult problems which were too complex for Charlie to solve, and couldn't go as far as Sara could. To Sara it was like she all of a sudden was looking through a magnifying glass and everything was much clearer to her then it ever had been, and she knew her position, in her life.

Students arrange pictures or objects to represent a theme, capture a character's feelings, or express a mood. They can also take pictures of objects, facial expressions, or dramatizations that represent the theme of a story or mood of a poem (Purves, Rogers, & Soter, 1990). For example, after reading *The Facts and Fictions of Minna Pratt* (MacLachlan, 1988), a story about a girl who learns to appreciate herself and her family, students might take pictures of an immaculate room and a room filled with interesting things that are haphazardly lying around as representations of the tensions Minna feels in her life.

Tableau. A *tableau* is a still enactment of a moment from a story or poem and is created by students who use expression, placement of body, gesture, and stance (Purves, Rogers, & Soter, 1990). Students do not act out a scene in a tableau as they do in other kinds of dramatizations. Rather, they freeze all movement just at the moment of an important event. For example, children might create a tableau for *Sylvester and the Magic Pebble* at the moment Sylvester sees the lion. Two children would participate, one as Sylvester and the other as the lion. The child posing as the lion might get down on all fours and look ferocious or perhaps confused depending on the student's interpretation. Sylvester might pose with his hand over his mouth and his eyes opened wide in fear.

Children select a scene that they consider particularly important in a story or poem for a tableau. They discuss the scene, decide how to construct the tableau, and then they practice two or three different ways to stage the tableau. When the tableau is presented to the class, the teacher rings a bell and everyone in the tableau freezes for a minute. Then the other children guess which scene is being portrayed and discuss why the tableau was effective—how the emotions of the characters were captured or the tension between two characters shown.

Selecting scenes for a tableau makes children aware of moments in stories that are particularly important for understanding and interpreting a story's meaning. Having several groups of students enact a tableau of the same moment in a story prompts discussion of the various perspectives that students bring to a story and the differences in their interpretation of that story.

Puppets. Children enjoy making and using puppets to retell a favorite story, whether the puppet show is an impromptu affair or a more elaborate and rehearsed production. Planning and staging a puppet show encourages careful reading and personal involvement with a character. These steps can be followed to prepare for and present a puppet show:

1. *Students construct puppets.* Students select which characters they wish to be and construct their puppets using information from the story about appearance. Five types of puppets that elementary and middle school students can construct using scrap materials are described in Figure 5.9 and sample puppets based on characters from children's literature are shown.

2. *Students set up a stage.* Students set up the puppet stage or create a makeshift stage using furniture in the classroom. They can hang a curtain between two desks, file cabinets, or table or make a stage from an appliance box. The stage provides a place where students can hide while they work with their puppets as well as a place where they perform the story.

3. *Students organize the presentation.* As students plan the puppet show, they will usually find it useful to organize the presentation into a beginning, middle, and end. For chapter books, children should select a chapter or a single episode to enact. They should be encouraged to ad-lib dialogue rather than memorize the text. Often students draw a picture for each part of the enactment or make notes about the sequence of events to help them keep their organization in mind.

4. *Students rehearse the puppet show.* Students rehearse the puppet show several times, using the organizational plan they developed in Step 3. During the

FIGURE 5.9   Types of Puppets

Stick Puppets

Students draw, color, and cut out a picture or construct a model out of paper or clay which they then attach to a popsicle stick, tongue depressor, ruler, or wooden dowel. In the illustration, a drawing of Mr. Willy Wonka from *Charlie and the Chocolate Factory* (Dahl, 1964) has been cut out and attached to a popsicle stick.

Paper Bag Puppets

Students decorate small paper bags with a character's face or body. (Use small paper lunch bags or bags from bakeries.) The puppet's mouth can be placed at the fold of the paper bag so that when the puppet is moved, it will look as if the character is talking. Faces can be drawn on paper, cut out, and glued on the paper bag or can be colored or painted on the bag. Also, yarn can be added for hair and scraps of paper or cloth for clothes. The crocodile paper bag puppet in the illustration represents Lyle from *The House on East 88th Street* (Waber, 1962), *Lyle, Lyle, Crocodile* (Waber, 1965), and other books in the series.

Sock Puppets

Students sew or glue scraps of fabric, buttons, yarn, and pipe cleaners on socks to make puppets. The sock can also be cut at the toe to create a mouth. The illustration shows a rabbit sock puppet from *Bunnicula: A Rabbit Tale of Mystery* (Howe & Howe, 1979).

Paper Plate Puppets

Paper plates can be used for face puppets as well as for masks. Students add junk materials to decorate the paper plates and then tape sticks or rulers to the back of the plates as handles. The mouse in the illustration represents the mouse character in *If You Give a Mouse a Cookie* (Numeroff, 1985).

Finger Puppets

Students draw, color, and cut out small figures. Then they add tabs to either side of the figure and tape the tabs together to fit around the finger. Or, they can tape a strip of paper into a ring to fit around the finger and then attach the small figure they have made. The illustration presents a finger puppet of the hen from *Rosie's Walk* (Hutchins, 1968).

first rehearsal, students focus on creating the dialogue to carry the storyline. In the second rehearsal, students practice moving their puppets and using their voices in dramatic ways. Students might want to practice a third time in front of a mirror to perfect their performance.

5. *Students present the show.* Students present the puppet show for an audience of their classmates or younger children. It often works better to have small groups in the audience because it is difficult for large groups of children to see the puppets and hear the dialogue.

Students can spend an enormous amount of time making a puppet and preparing for the show. Teachers often wonder if this is time well spent. Research shows that dramatizing stories increases students' comprehension of stories (Galda, 1982). Since puppet shows are a form of dramatization, teachers can expect that children's comprehension of stories presented in puppet shows would be increased.

Readers' theatre. Readers' theatre, another dramatization activity, presents numerous opportunities to extend comprehension of favorite stories. To present a readers' theatre, students rewrite the text of a story or informational book into a script and then read it aloud in a dramatic way. Readers use their voices to interpret the text as they read it aloud; few actions or props are involved. Students sit or stand, but they carry the whole communication of the plot, characterization, and theme through gestures, facial expressions, and voice qualities. Stories that have an action-packed plot, strong characters, and distinctive language are appropriate for readers' theatre. Figure 5.10 presents a list of stories that are appropriate for developing into readers' theatre scripts.

These steps can be followed to prepare a readers' theatre:

1. *Students learn about readers' theatre.* If students are not familiar with the format of a script or performing readers' theatre, teachers choose a story and pre-

FIGURE 5.10 Stories That Can Be Scripted for Readers' Theatre

Atwater, R., & Atwater, F. (1938). *Mr. Popper's penguins.* Boston: Little, Brown. (M)
Babbitt, N. (1975). *Tuck everlasting.* New York: Farrar, Straus & Giroux. (U)
Brittain, B. (1983). *The wish giver.* New York: Harper & Row. (M–U)
Burch, R. (1980). *Ida Early comes over the mountain.* New York: Viking. (M)
Byars, B. (1981). *The Cybil war.* New York: Viking. (M–U)
Cleary, B. (1975). *Ramona and her father.* New York: Morrow. (M)
Cohen, B. (1974). *Thank you, Jackie Robinson.* New York: Lothrop. (M–U)
Fleischman, S. (1986). *The whipping boy.* New York: Greenwillow. (M–U)
Lewis, C. S. (1950). *The lion, the witch, and the wardrobe.* New York: Macmillan. (M–U)
MacLachlan, P. (1985). *Sarah, plain and tall.* New York: Harper & Row. (M–U)
Milne, A. A. (1974). *Winnie-the-pooh.* New York: Dutton. (P–M)
Rockwell, T. (1973). *How to eat fried worms.* New York: Franklin Watts. (M–U)
Sebestyen, O. (1979). *Words by heart.* Boston: Little, Brown. (U)
Stolz, M. (1960). *A dog on Barkham Street.* New York: Harper & Row. (M)
Wallace, B. (1980). *A dog called Kitty.* New York: Holiday House. (M)

P = Primary grades (K–2); M = Middle grades (3–5); U = Upper grades (6–8).

pare a readers' theatre script based on the story. They write each character's dialogue from the story and add a narrator's part to provide background information about the setting and characters or to connect events in the story. Teachers show the script to students and explain the format of the script. Students read through the script and discuss how they might interpret each role through gesture, facial expression, or voice quality. They assume roles and perform a readers' theatre presentation.

2. *Students write a script.* Once students are familiar with the format of readers' theatre scripts, they can compose their own, based on a familiar story. They choose a story, make a list of the events and dialogue in the story, and create dialogue for the story events. They add a narrator part to provide background information and connect the events. They practice dramatizing their script making revisions as they as practice. For older students who are reading chapter books, Laughlin and Latrobe (1989) suggest that students begin by reading the entire book and thinking about its theme, characters, and plot. Next they choose a scene or scenes to script. Students make photocopies of the scene from the book and use felt-tip pens to highlight the dialogue. They adapt the scenes by adding narrators' lines to set the scene and summarize where needed. The final version of the script is typed and duplicated. Even young children can compose readers' theatre scripts. Figure 5.11 presents a readers' theatre script for *Jack and the Beanstalk* that a class of first graders composed collaboratively.

3. *Rehearsing the script.* Students practice reading the script several times. The emphasis is not on production quality; rather, it is on dramatic reading and the interpretive quality of the readers' voices and expressions. Costumes and props are unnecessary; however, adding a few props enhances interest and enjoyment, as long as they do not interfere with the dramatic quality of the reading.

4. *Staging the readers' theatre performance.* Readers' theatre can be presented on a stage or in a corner of the classroom. Students stand or sit in a row and read their lines in the script. They must stay in position through the presentation. If they are sitting, they may stand to read their lines; if they are standing, they may step forward to read.

Readers' theatre combines the effectiveness of rereading and writing to enrich students' comprehension of stories. As they prepare the readers' theatre script, students select parts of dialogue and detail which are most important to carry the storyline. As they practice rereading their script trying out different expressions or gestures, they gain fluency and word recognition skills. Being able to read fluently and select the most important parts of stories are important comprehension abilities.

Appreciating the Author's Craft.   Authors use language deliberately and carefully; their language evokes vivid images and stirs strong emotions. The reader response perspective acknowledges the importance of authors' language; according to this perspective, the language of the text serves as a blueprint to guide readers' experiences and construction of meaning. Therefore, savoring authors' language and exploring the kinds of images, emotions, associations, and thoughts that are evoked by that language is an important component of reading. Two ways to help students appreciate an author's craft are collecting notable language samples and using double-entry journals.

Notable language samples. Children become more sensitive to language and notice how an author's choice of language affects readers by collecting *notable language samples* in their response journals. Notable language samples are words, phrases, and sentences from the text which students find most interesting, moving, or fun to read. Their selections often include language that paints strong pictures, arouses intense feelings, or tickles the tongue. For example, students might collect the sentences "She filed fish-bone needles to bee-sting sharpness" and "How strange her own voice sounded! Crystal thin and harebell clear, it tinkled on the air" from *The Borrowers* (Norton, 1955, pp. 55 and 72). These sentences include unusual uses of the words *bee-sting, crystal,* and *tinkled.* Other students might copy the poem "Sunny" (Adoff, 1979) because they are fascinated with the way Arnold Adoff dropped the endings of words down a line and with the way the poem is written down the page instead of across the page. Children copy notable language samples on special pages in their response journals or add the samples to a chart that hangs on the wall in the classroom.

Double-entry journals. *Double-entry journals* is another technique that draws attention to the language of poetry and stories (Barone & Lovell, 1980; Berthoff, 1981). To construct a double-entry journal, students draw a line down the middle of a page in their response journals. On the left side of the line they copy the words from the story or poem that students find personally important, interesting, or funny. Then on the right side of the page, students write what those words called to mind. Students are not required to use double entries all the time. Instead, they are encouraged to use them when they notice certain words, phrases, or sentences as they are reading. Figure 5.12 presents a double-entry response to Judy Blume's *Superfudge* (1984), a sequel to *Tales of a Fourth Grade Nothing* (1972) about life in the Hatcher household and the tensions between brothers.

Children often select sentences that are particularly funny or that have unusual or interesting words for double entries. They should share their double entries with a partner or in small groups and describe why they selected the particular sentence or words for double entries.

A Caution About Exploring Activities. Teachers select exploring activities to meet the needs of particular students or for certain purposes. When teachers begin using the reader response perspective to guide their instruction, they feel that every response should be accepted and encouraged (Smith, 1990). Or, teachers may believe that any response activity is equally effective. They may decide, for example, to cook pasta after reading de Paola's Italian folktale *Strega Nona* (1975) about a magic pasta pot. Talking about personal experiences is a legitimate topic for a grand conversation. And, many children have enjoyed cooking pasta after reading *Strega Nona.* However, neither of these activities alone capitalizes on the power of students' responses to enrich and deepen their experiences with literature.

The reader response perspective emphasizes that supporting students' reading means helping them move beyond their initial responses into more informed, knowl-

FIGURE 5.11 Readers' Theatre Script for *Jack and the Beanstalk* (pp. 188–190)

Characters	Jack	Peddler	Giant's Wife
	Jack's Mom	Giant	Harp
	Milky White		

Setting	*Jack's House*	*Beanstalk*	*Giant's House*
	fence		cement
	garden		bushes
	trees		giant mushroom
	grass		trees
	flowers		long road
	road to town		steps
	clouds		clouds

Props	ax	food	dishes
	beanstalk	oven	milk carton
	clothing	pot	door
	window	beans	giant's table
	gold	golden egg	and chair
	hen	bed	harp
	pillow	costumes	blanket

Script

NARRATOR ONE: Once upon a time there was a poor old lady who lived in a cottage and had a son named Jack. She had a cow named Milky White and a cat named Snowy.

NARRATOR TWO: Everyday the cow gave milk, and Jack took it to market and sold it. One day the cow gave no milk.

JACK: "We need to sell the cow."

JACK'S MOM: "O.k. Take the cow to market."

COW: "Don't sell me! Don't sell me!"

JACK: "Come on. We've got to go."

NARRATOR THREE: Jack went down the road, over a bridge, and through the forest, where he met a peddler.

PEDDLER: "What a nice cow you have. Are you selling her?"

JACK: "Yes. How much money will you give me?"

PEDDLER: "I've got something better than money. Beans."

JACK: "Beans!"

PEDDLER: "They're five magic beans."

JACK: "No."

PEDDLER: "If you plant them, a beanstalk will grow to the sky."

JACK: "Then I want six."

PEDDLER: "I only have five."

JACK: "O.k."

NARRATOR FOUR: Jack went back through the forest, over the bridge, and down the road to his cottage.

JACK: "Mom, I sold the cow for five magic beans."

JACK'S MOM: "Beans! You fool! Go to your room."

NARRATOR ONE: Jack went to bed without any supper, and his mother threw the beans out the window.

FIGURE 5.11, *continued*

NARRATOR TWO:	When Jack woke up, he saw the beanstalk out the window. He left his mother and began to climb the beanstalk.
NARRATOR THREE:	When he got to the top, he found a giant house. Jack knocked on the door.
JACK:	"I'm hungry. Will you give me something to eat?"
GIANT'S WIFE:	"My husband is a giant, and he likes to eat little boys."
	THUMP! THUMP! THUMP!
	"Here he comes now. Hide behind the oven!"
GIANT (All):	"Fe Fi Fo Fum I smell the blood of an Englishman. Be he alive or be he dead, I'll grind his bones to make my bread."
GIANT'S WIFE:	"You must smell the boy from yesterday. Eat your breakfast."
	(The giant eats breakfast.)
GIANT:	"Wife, bring me my gold."
NARRATOR FOUR:	The giant began to count his gold and fell asleep. He began to snore.
(ALL):	He snored so loud, the house began to shake.
NARRATOR ONE:	Jack jumped up, grabbed the bag of gold, and ran. He climbed down the beanstalk and showed his mother the gold.
NARRATOR TWO:	One day, Jack decided to try his luck again. So he climbed the beanstalk and knocked on the door.
JACK:	"Will you give me something to eat?"
GIANT'S WIFE:	"Weren't you the little boy that came last time and stole the gold?"
JACK:	"Maybe. But I'm too hungry to talk."
GIANT'S WIFE:	"O.k. I'll give you some breakfast."
	THUMP! THUMP! THUMP!
	"Hide, quick!"
GIANT (All):	"Fe Fi Fo Fum I smell the blood of an Englishman. Be he alive or be he dead, I'll grind his bones to make my bread."
GIANT'S WIFE:	"You must smell the boy you ate from yesterday. Eat your breakfast."
	(The giant eats.)
GIANT:	"Wife, bring me my golden hen."
	(Wife brings hen.)
	"Lay, hen."
NARRATOR THREE:	The giant fell asleep. He began to snore.
(ALL):	He snored so loud, the house began to shake.
NARRATOR FOUR:	Jack jumped up, grabbed the hen, and ran. He climbed down the beanstalk and showed his mother the hen.
NARRATOR ONE:	Jack decided to try his luck again. He climbed the beanstalk and hid behind a bush.
NARRATOR TWO:	When the giant's wife left, he went in the house and hid behind a pot. The giant's wife came back.

FIGURE 5.11, *continued*

NARRATOR THREE:	Soon he heard . . .
	THUMP! THUMP! THUMP!
GIANT (All):	"Fe Fi Fo Fum
	I smell the blood of an Englishman.
	Be he alive or be he dead,
	I'll grind his bones to make my bread."
GIANT'S WIFE:	"If it's that rascal Jack, he'll be hiding in the oven."
	(They look in oven.)
GIANT'S WIFE:	"You must smell the boy from yesterday. Eat your breakfast."
	(The giant eats.)
GIANT:	"Wife, bring me my golden harp."
	(Wife brings harp.)
NARRATOR FOUR:	The giant fell asleep. He began to snore.
(ALL):	He snored so loud, the house began to shake.
NARRATOR ONE:	Jack jumped up, grabbed the harp, and ran. But the harp shouted, . . .
HARP:	"Master! Master!"
NARRATOR TWO:	The giant woke up and chased Jack. Jack climbed down the beanstalk, but the giant stopped. Then he heard the harp cry, . . .
HARP:	"Master! Master!"
NARRATOR THREE:	The giant began to climb down.
JACK:	"Mom, bring me the ax!"
	(Mom brings it, then stops—terrified.)
NARRATOR FOUR:	Jack gave the beanstalk a chop. Then another one. The giant felt the beanstalk shake. Then the giant fell to the ground, and Jack and his mother . . .
(ALL):	. . . lived happily ever after.

edgeable, and interpretive responses (Corcoran, 1987). Students who focus on their own experiences in grand conversations need help in using those experiences to better understand the story. For example, teachers can help students explain how their personal experiences are related to the story and how understanding their own experiences helps them to understand a story better.

Teachers also carefully plan exploring activities so that students have opportunities to explore a story or poem in a more interpretive fashion. For example, having students write a diary from the perspective of Big Anthony in *Strega Nona* would better help them appreciate one of the important components of the story: the irony of a big man not being able to control the magic in a cooking pot.

Teachers must acknowledge the importance of accepting and celebrating students' responses. Yet, they also need to select response activities that help students grow without imposing their own interpretations on students. Teachers balance the importance of encouraging students' responses and choices with their responsibility for fostering growth of literary appreciation and interpretation.

FIGURE 5.12   Excerpt from a Double Entry Journal Written in Response to *Superfudge* (Blume, 1980)

Page 17

I don't want to wait.

I want you to get rid of her now.

I would ask my mother if I could take her for a walk.

Page 18

You like the baby?

Oh yes she's just adorable.

You can have her for a quarter.

If Fudge asked me I would have taken her.

Extending Step

According to the reader response perspective, extending activities widen students' opportunities for response beyond the story or poem. The most important element of the extending step is choice. Students choose the kinds of extending activities that they want to engage in because each reader's responses vary. Because each reader's response to a story or poem is different, the activity that would best expand those personal responses may be different. Readers know best which direction they feel most interested in taking to extend their responses to stories and poems.

Readers may choose to read additional stories or poems that are written or illustrated by the same author or illustrator, that explore the same theme or have the same character as the core selection, or that are set in the same time period as the core selection. Students might also study a topic introduced in the core selection in greater depth. They may read a wide selection of informational books or magazines to become better informed about the Civil War after reading *Across Five Aprils* (Hunt, 1964) or read about pioneers and life on the prairie after reading *Sarah, Plain and Tall* (MacLachlan, 1985).

Possibilities for extending activities are almost endless and include sewing, cooking, constructing, drawing, painting, dancing, role-playing, writing, collecting, visiting, talking, weaving, planting, diagraming, and more. For example, students in Mr. Sahady's class in the case study at the beginning of this chapter decided to read additional books with magic objects, write a puppet play and dramatize it, construct a diorama, and write a sequel to the story. Figure 5.13 presents a list of response-to-literature activities, and children will think of others to add to the list.

READING FOR INFORMATIONAL PURPOSES

Now, we change our focus from literary texts to informational texts, and we describe instructional techniques that support children's reading for informational purposes. The reader response perspective emphasizes differences between reading for literary purposes or aesthetic reading and reading for informational purposes or efferent reading. In this section we present activities that encourage students to read informational text more aesthetically while at the same time learning information from their reading. Readers gain information from reading aesthetically as well as from reading efferently when they make personal connections to content information. When students read about history, for example, they learn a great deal by viewing history from the perspective of a participant, such as exploring the Civil War from the perspective of a soldier or a child whose brother is a soldier (Brozo & Tomlinson, 1986).

Preparing Step

Preparing activities encourage students to become personally involved with the content of informational books and magazines. Personal involvement not only encourages engagement, but also helps students remember what they have read.

Letter to the Editor. One method of encouraging personal involvement before reading informational text is to have students take a stand on an issue or declare their feelings about a topic before they read about it. Writing a *letter to the editor* is one strategy that requires readers to take a stand before reading (Tierney, Soter, O'Flahavan, & McGinley, 1989). Teachers begin by sharing example letters to the editor from local newspapers. Then they introduce an issue related to the content students will read. Students decide their position on the issue and then write a letter to the editor in which they express and justify their position on the issue. For example, students who are studying ecology might take a stand on requiring city residents to recycle. Students who are exploring the westward movement might write a letter formulating a policy about the relocation of Native Americans onto reservations. After composing their letters, students share them in small groups.

Writing a letter to the editor and taking a position on an issue causes students to be more personally involved as they read. Students read to find information that will confirm their position or cause them to reassess their stand. After reading more on the issue, students decide whether to revise their letter to the editor. They may add more persuasive information to bolster their original position or may alter their position.

Anticipation Guides.   Another preparing activity that encourages personal involvement is an *anticipation guide* (Head & Readence, 1986). The anticipation guide is a set of three to five opinion statements about the content to be read. Students agree or disagree with the statements and discuss their reasons. Follow these steps to use the anticipation guide:

1. *Identify major concepts.* Teachers read an informational book or magazine and identify the major concepts. For example, the major concepts presented in the *Cobblestone* article "The Voyage of Lief the Lucky" (Blohm, 1984) are
   a. Lief Eiriksson, not Christopher Columbus, was the first European to set foot on American soil.
   b. The story of Eiriksson is from a saga, an adventure story told by bards.
   c. Artifacts from the ruins of an ancient settlement in Newfoundland, Canada, provide evidence of the Vikings' presence in America.
2. *Create statements.* Teachers construct opinion statements related to the major concepts developed in the first step. For example, the following statements relate to the Lief Eiriksson article:
   a. Christopher Columbus discovered America.
   b. History books are the best sources of information about the past.
   c. No Europeans were in America before Columbus came in 1492.
3. *Present the statements.* The statements can be presented on an overhead projector or written on the chalkboard. Then, teachers read them aloud.
4. *Students discuss the statements briefly.* Students discuss whether they agree or disagree with each statement and give their reasons.
5. *Students read the text.* Students read the text to see what the author says about each of the anticipation statements.
6. *Students discuss the text and their responses to the guide.* Students discuss how the author would have responded to the guide and compare and contrast their opinions with those of the author. They need not agree with the author, and such a disagreement might lead to further research on the topic.

Reading these anticipation guides causes students to take a position on concepts about which they will read. Once students state what they believe and know, they read more carefully to examine whether they are correct or not. Anticipation guides can be used to stimulate lively discussions after reading. Students should be

FIGURE 5.13   Response-to-Literature Activities

Responding Through Art

1. Experiment with the illustration techniques (e.g., collage, watercolor, line drawing) used in a favorite book. Examine other books illustrated with the same technique.
2. Make a diagram or model using information from a book.
3. Create a collage to represent the theme of a book.
4. Design a book jacket for a book, laminate it, and place it on the book.
5. Decorate a coffee or potato chip can using scenes from a book. Fill the can with quotes from characters in the story. Other students can guess the identity of the characters. Or fill the can with quotes from a poem with words missing. Other students guess the missing words.
6. Construct a shoebox or other miniature scene of an episode for a favorite book (or use a larger box to construct a diorama).
7. Make illustrations for each important event in a book.
8. Make a map or relief map of a book's setting or something related to the book.
9. Construct the setting of the book in the block center or use other construction toys such as Lego's or Lincoln Logs.
10. Construct a mobile illustrating a book.
11. Make a roll-movie of a book by drawing a series of pictures on a long strip of paper. Attach ends to rollers and place in a cardboard box cut like a television set.
12. Make a comic strip to illustrate the sequence of events in a book.
13. Make a clay or soap model of a character.
14. Prepare bookmarks for a book and distribute them to classmates.
15. Prepare flannel board pictures to use in retelling the story.
16. Use or prepare illustrations of characters for pocket props to use in retelling the story.
17. Use or prepare illustrations of the events in the story for clothesline props to use in retelling the story.
18. Experiment with art techniques related to the mood of a poem.
19. Make a mural of the book.
20. Illustrate the box with scenes from a book. Place objects, poems, and illustrations that represent characters, events, or images from the book.

Responding Through Writing

21. Write a review of a favorite book for a class review file.
22. Write a letter about a book to a classmate, friend, or pen pal.
23. Dictate or write another episode or sequel for a book.
24. Create a newspaper with news stories and advertisements based on characters and episodes from a book.
25. Make a five senses cluster about the book.
26. Write a letter to a favorite character (or participate in a class collaboration letter).
27. Write a simulated letter from one book character to another.
28. Copy five "quotable quotes" from a book and list them on a poster.
29. Make a scrapbook about the book. Label all items in the scrapbook and write a short description of the most interesting ones.
30. Write a poem related to the book. Some types of poems to choose from are acrostic, concrete poem, color poem, "I wish" poem, "If I were" poem, haiku, or limerick.
31. Write a lifeline related to the book, the era, the character, or the author.
32. Write a business letter to a company or organization requesting information on a topic related to the book.

33. Keep a simulated journal from the perspective of one character from the book.
34. Write a dictionary defining specialized vocabulary in a book.
35. Write the story from another point of view (e.g., write the story of *The Little Red Hen* from the perspective of the lazy characters).
36. Make a class collaboration book. Each child dictates or writes one page.
37. Write a letter to a famous person from a character in a book.
38. Make a ladder to accomplishment listing the steps taken to achieve some goal.

Responding Through Reading

39. Read another book by the same author.
40. Read another book by the same illustrator.
41. Read another book on the same theme.
42. Read another book in the same genre.
43. Read another book about the same character.
44. Read and compare another version of the same story.
45. Listen to and compare a tape, filmstrip, film or video version of the same story.
46. Tape-record a book or excerpt from it to place in the listening center.
47. Read a poem that complements the book aloud to the class. Place a copy of the poem in the book.
48. Tape-record a book using background music and sound effects.

Responding Through Drama and Talk

49. Give a readers' theatre presentation of a book.
50. Improvise the events in a book.
51. Write a script and present a play about a book.
52. Make puppets and use them in retelling a book.
53. Dress as a character from the book and answer questions from classmates about the character.
54. Have a grand conversation with a small group or the whole class about a book.
55. Write and present a rap about the book.
56. Videotape a commercial for a book.
57. Interview someone in the community who is knowledgeable about a topic related to the book.

Responding Through Literary Analysis

58. Make a chart to compare the story with another version or with the film version of the story.
59. Make a character cluster.
60. Make a character sociogram.
61. Make a plot diagram of the book.
62. Make a plot profile of the book.

Responding Through Research

63. Research the author of the book and compile information in a chart or summary. Place the chart or summary in the book.
64. Research a topic related to the book. Present the information in a report.

Other Ways of Responding

65. Cook and eat a food described in or related to a book.
66. Collect or make objects related to the book.

FIGURE 5.14 Correlated Poems and Informational Books

Informational Book	Poem
Adler, D. (1989). *A Picture Book of Martin Luther King, Jr.* New York: Holiday House	McClester, E. (1990). "For Peace Sake." In D. Slier (Ed.), *Make a Joyful Sound* (p. 36). New York: Checkerboard Press.
Aliki. (1983). *A Medieval Feast.* New York: Crowell.	Unknown. (1988). "Sing a Song of Sixpence." In *The Real Mother Goose* (p. 62). New York: Checkerboard Press.
Alter, J. (1989). *Women of the Old West.* New York: Franklin Watts.	Benet, R. & Benet, S. (1989). "Western Wagons." In C. Sullivan (Ed.), *Imaginary Gardens: American Poetry and Art for Young People* (p. 29). New York: Henry N. Abrams.
Ballard, R. (1990). *The Lost Wreck of the Isis.* New York: Scholastic.	Brown, G. (1990). "Beachcomber." In N. Philip (Ed.), *A New Treasury of Children's Poetry* (p. 48). New York: Stewart, Tabori and Chang.
Bentley, J. (1990). *Harriet Tubman.* New York: Franklin Watts.	Greenfield, E. (1990). "Harriet Tubman." In D. Slier (Ed.), *Make a Joyful Sound* (p. 53). New York: Checkerboard Press.
Brown, T. (1986). *Hello, Amigos!* New York: Henry Holt.	Unknown. (1982). "I Like Arozzy Habichuelas." In C. Pomerantz (Comp.), *If I had a Paka: Poems in 11 Languages.* New York: Greenwillow.
Cole, J. (1989). *The Magic School Bus Inside the Human Body.* New York: Scholastic.	Hillert, M. (1990). "Puzzled." In P. Janeczko (Ed.), *The Place My Words Are Looking For* (p. 51). New York: Bradbury.
Gaes, J. (1987). *My Book for Kids with Cansur.* Aberdeen, SD: Melius and Peterson.	Silverstein, S. (1974). "Sick." In S. Silverstein, *Where the Sidewalk Ends* (p. 58). New York: Harper & Row.
Gibbons, G. (1989). *Monarch Butterfly.* New York: Holiday House.	Fleischman, P. (1988). "Chrysalis Diary." In P. Fleischman, *Joyful Noise* (p. 39). New York: Harper & Row.
Hoyt-Goldsmith, P. (1990). *Totem Pole.* New York: Holiday House.	Lopez, A. (1988). "Celebration." In T. dePaola, *Tomie dePaola's Book of Poems* (p. 11). New York: Putnam's.
Isberg, E. (1989). *Peak Performance: Sports Science and the Body in Action.* New York: Simon & Schuster.	Adoff, A. (1986). "Sports Pages." In A. Adoff, *Sports Pages* (p. 6). New York: HarperCollins.

given the opportunity to change their opinions and to explain why. They should be encouraged to refer to information from the text to support their opinions.

Poetry and Stories. Reading poetry or stories related to a topic of study is another pathway into informational texts. Poetry appeals to the senses and imagination; it sparks children's interest in topics and allows children to examine the topic in a unique way. Ms. Epstein's students in the case study at the beginning of the chapter selected and read poems about amphibians and lizards before reading an informa-

Informational Book	Poem
Jacobs, W. (1990). *Ellis Island: New Hope in a New Land.* New York: Scribners.	Martin B., Jr. (1974). *I am Freedom's Child.* Texas: DLM.
Lasky, K. (1990). *Dinosaur Dig.* New York: Morrow.	Kennedy, X.J. (1989). "Why Dinosaurs Disappeared." In X. Kennedy, *Ghastlies, Goops, and Pincushions* (p. 24). New York: Margaret K. McElderry.
Macaulay, E. (1975). *Pyramid.* Boston: Houghton Mifflin.	Unknown. (1983). "The Seven Wonders of the Ancient World." In H. Plotz (Ed.), *Eye's Delight: Poetry of Art and Architecture.* New York: Greenwillow.
Morris, A. (1990). *When Will the Fighting Stop?* New York: Atheneum.	Brooks, G. (1990). "A Little Girl's Poem." In P. Janeczko (Ed.), *The Place My Words Are Looking For* (p. 60). New York: Bradbury.
Pluckrose, H. (1989). *Look at Skin, Shell, and Scale.* New York: Franklin Watts.	Prelutsky, J. (1982). "The Baby Uggs are Hatching." In J. Prelutsky, *The Baby Uggs are Hatching* (p. 6). New York: Greenwillow.
Provensen, A. (1990). *The Buck Stops Here.* New York: Harper & Row.	Carr, R., & Benet, S. (1933). "Thomas Jefferson." In R. Carr & S. Benet, *Book of Americans.* New York: Holt, Rinehart.
Roy, R. (1987). *Whose Hat Is That?* New York: Clarion.	Margolis, R. (1984). "All My Hats." In R. Margolis *Secrets of a Small Brother.* New York: Macmillan.
Simon, S. (1988). *Volcanoes.* New York: Morrow.	Kennedy, X.J. (1989). "Backyard Volcano." In X. Kennedy, *Ghastlies, Goops and Pincushions* (p. 31). New York: Margaret K. McElderry.
Stanley, D. & Vennema, P. (1988). *Shaka, King of the Zulus.* New York: Morrow.	Oyewold, A. (1990). "Africa." In D. Slier (Ed.), *Make a Joyful Sound* (p. 40). New York: Checkerboard Press.

tional book on that topic. Figure 5.14 presents a list of poems correlated with informational books.

Stories can be used to introduce informational books as well. Many fine books of historical fiction are perfect accompaniments for social studies topics. Reading *Across Five Aprils* (Hunt, 1964), for example, can be used to open a unit on the Civil War. Topics in science are also explored in a number of stories, and reading these stories makes issues in science more relevant. *Ben's Dream* (Van Allsburg, 1990) and *Who Really Killed Cock Robin?* (George, 1971) examine issues related to ecology as does Dr. Seuss's *The Lorax* (Geisel, 1971). After reading these stories, students become more concerned with ecology than if they had merely studied the facts related to the issue.

Reading poems and stories before informational books has numerous benefits. Stories and poems offer a great deal of information about topics, build children's prior knowledge, and help students clarify their feelings about a topic of study. Poetry and stories also appeal to the emotions and help students take a personal perspective related to the science and social studies topics they are studying. Learning about history, for example, is more real and personally meaningful when students see past events through the eyes of real people who were affected by these events.

Reading Step

Reading activities encourage readers to make personal connections to the information that they are reading. For example, in the case study at the beginning of this chapter, Ms. Epstein used a content area response heuristic, presented in Figure 5.3, to guide her students' reading (Brozo, 1988). This guide prompted students' emotional responses to the information found in the book they were reading.

Another reading activity that stimulates emotional and personal involvement is the *point of view reading guide* (Wood, 1988). Point of view guides use interview questions that require students to provide information from their reading as if they were a historical personality. Figure 5.15 presents a point of view guide for *Ellis Island: New Hope in a New Land* (Jacobs, 1990).

FIGURE 5.15   Point of View Reading Guide for *Ellis Island: New Hope in a New Land* (Jacobs, 1990)

Imagine that you are an immigrant arriving in America on March 27, 1907, and answer the following questions:

1. You are a passenger on a ship in steerage. You have been on the ship for three weeks. Describe what you did and felt during those three weeks (pp. 1 & 2).
2. Tell why you have come to the United States (pp. 1, 2, & 3).
3. Describe what you see and feel on March 27, 1907, as you first glimpse the United States (pp. 1, 2, & 3).

Imagine that you are a doctor serving on Ellis Island on March 27, 1907, and answer the following questions:

4. Describe what you did and felt on March 27, 1907, on Ellis Island in your capacity as a doctor (pp. 7 & 8).
5. Describe what your friend who works at the Money Exchange did today (p. 10).
6. Describe what your friend the Inspector did today (p. 13).

Imagine that you are a 10-year-old immigrant who speaks Polish, and then answer the following questions (pp. 7–13):

7. What do you see, think, and feel as you step onto Ellis Island?
8. What happens to you in the next four hours?
9. What will you and your family do next?
10. Where will you go and how will you live?

After reading, students use point of view reading guides as a focus for discussion. They compare and contrast their responses to the guide's questions and reread to reconcile differences in factual information. Students might also role-play answering the questions and have the class interview them as if they were holding a press conference or appearing on a TV talk show.

Exploring Step

Exploring activities encourage rereading and thinking about informational books and magazines by capitalizing on students' personal responses. Students respond personally as they write in reading logs using the content response heuristic, have conversations about their reading based on the response heuristic or on a point of view reading guide, or dramatize events in history from different perspectives or interview historical figures. These activities encourage rereading and thinking about information presented in books and magazines. Students also explore authors' craft as a way of learning more about the information they are reading.

Rereading and Thinking.   Students expand their content knowledge as they participate in grand conversations; write simulated letters, journals, and newspapers; compose poetry; and paint murals or construct sculptures. Each of these activities provides many opportunities for children to reread and learn information related to the science and social studies topics they are studying.

Grand conversations.   Students hold grand conversations about informational books and magazines in the same way that they do after reading stories and poems. These conversations can be prompted by the content response heuristic or by simply asking students to discuss what they found most interesting, meaningful, or important in their reading. Grand conversations about informational texts are not disguised question-and-answer sessions in which teachers ask questions that students must answer. However, teachers should have clearly identified the major concepts they expect students to gain from reading so these concepts can be naturally explored in a grand conversation. As students discuss information relevant to each major concept, teachers invite other students to react to that information as well. They may contribute themselves, making an important point when it seems relevant to do so. However, the majority of talk in a grand conversation about informational books should consist of student talk and not teacher talk, just as in conversations about stories and poems.

Simulated journals, letters, and newspapers.   Historical events and scientific issues becomes more relevant when students examine these topics from the perspective of real people affected by the events and issues. Writing a journal or letter or pretending to interview someone and writing an article to include in a newspaper are effective techniques for helping children to walk in the footsteps of historical figures they are studying. These techniques also help students see the practical and real implications of science topics. Students might pretend to be the character Shaka and keep a journal after reading *Shaka: King of the Zulus* (Stanley & Venemma, 1988) or write a newspaper article about an event in Lincoln's life after reading *Lincoln: A Photobiography* (Freedman, 1987). Figure 5.16 presents a fifth grader's journal as she imagined being Betsy Ross.

FIGURE 5.16   Simulated Journal as Betsy Ross

May 15, 1773
Dear Diary,

This morning at 5:00 I had to wake up my husband John to get up for work, but he wouldn't wake up. I immediately called the doc. He came over as fast as he could. He asked me to leave the room so I did. An hour later he came out and told me he had passed away. I am so sad. I don't know what to do.

June 16, 1776
Dear Diary,

Today General Washington visited me about making a flag. I was so surprised. Me making a flag! I have made flags for the navy, but this is too much. But I said yes. He showed me a pattern of the flag he wanted. He also wanted six-pointed stars but I talked him into having five-pointed stars.

July 8, 1776
Dear Diary,

Today in front of Carpenter Hall the Declaration of Independence was read by Tom Jefferson. Well, I will tell you the whole story. I heard some yelling and shouting about liberty and everyone was gathering around Carpenter Hall. So I went to my next door neighbors to ask what was happening but Mistress Peters didn't know either so we both went down to Carpenter Hall. We saw firecrackers and heard a bell and the Declaration of Independence was being read aloud. When I heard this I knew a new country was born.

July 14, 1777
Dear Diary,

Today was a happy but scary day. Today the flag I made was adopted by Congress. I thought for sure that if England found out that a new flag was taking the old one's place something bad would happen. But I'm happy because I am the maker of the first American flag and I'm only 25 years old!

Found poetry.   Students create *found poems* by culling words from the informational book they are reading and arranging them as a poem. Students can add words, if necessary, to complete an idea or image. The students in Ms. Epstein's class created found poetry to consolidate their learning about amphibians and reptiles in the case study at the beginning of this chapter. A small group of third graders composed the following found poem after reading *Sarah Morton's Day: A Day in the Life of a Pilgrim Girl* (Waters, 1989):

This Is My Day

Good day.
I must get up and be about my chores.
The fire is mine to tend.
I lay the table.
I muck the garden.
I pound the spices.
I draw vinegar to polish the brass.
I practice my lessons.
I feed the fire again.

I milk the goats.
I eat dinner.
I say the verses I am learning.
My father is pleased with my learning.
I fetch the water for tomorrow.
I bid my parents good night.
I say my prayers.
Fare thee well.
God be with thee.

This writing activity prompts students to explore vocabulary and capture important concepts in a different format.

Drawing, painting, and constructing. Art is an important way that students can respond to informational books and magazines and demonstrate their understandings of concepts. Students can draw, paint, or construct sculptures to interpret events in history or scientific concepts. Then they share their art with the class explaining the significance of their work and its connection to the informational book or magazine they have been reading. For example, after reading *Trash* (Wilcox, 1988) students might construct a sculpture out of items found in a trash can that should have been recycled. Or, students might paint a mural depicting the many ways the Jews were saved during World War II after reading *Rescue: The Story of How Gentiles Saved Jews in the Holocaust* (Meltzer, 1988).

Students can also construct *dioramas* of important events from history or from the lives of others they read about in biographies. Reading *Pueblo Boy: Growing up in Two Worlds* (Keegan, 1991) might prompt students to make two dioramas, one depicting Timmy Roybal in school and one depicting him dancing in the Corn Dance.

Constructing a *life box* is another way to capture the information from a biography. Students collect objects, pictures, poems, and other items that represent important events in a famous person's life. After reading *Mary McCleod Bethune* (Greenfield, 1977), a biography of the black educator, students might collect vegetables, an old school book, a nurse's cap, and a map of the United States with the route marked from Daytona Beach, Florida, to Washington, DC, to place in a life box to represent her family's farm, her school for girls and hospital for black Americans in Daytona Beach, and her work at the National Youth Administration in Washington, DC.

Dramatizing. Students expand their understandings of content information through dramatizing. They might enact *"you were there"* moments (Norton, 1991) to emphasize important moments in history or in the life of a famous person. One "you were there" moment that students might enact after reading *Columbus* (D'Aulaire & D'Aulaire, 1955) is the moment when Christopher Columbus meets Queen Isabella. Students might also pretend to be a historical figure and answer interview questions in a press conference. They can pretend to be a person who witnessed an important event in history and tell a neighbor or friend what they witnessed. Students can conduct man-on-the-street interviews about historical events. Or they can become newscasters and report news about historical events. Students enjoy videotaping these enactments and watching themselves.

Drama is especially useful to expand the information from biographies. After reading a biography, students identify scenes from the book for improvisation; they identify characters and plan dialogue and actions. Fritz's biographies of American Revolutionary War figures, including *Where Was Patrick Henry on the 29th of May?* (1975), make excellent resources for drama. For example, students might enact Patrick Henry as he begins his law practice and does not have many clients or when he played practical jokes such as upsetting his friend's canoe (Norton, 1991). (For other biographies by Jean Fritz, see the "Children's Literature References" at the end of this chapter.)

Dramatizing an event requires careful reading of a biography to discover a historical figure's actual words and actions. Students might also enjoy researching a biography for information about props such as clothing, colloquial expressions, or weapons that can be adapted for the dramatization. Many authors of biographies, such as Diane Stanley and Jean Fritz, research these details thoroughly and their illustrations and text reflect this careful research.

Appreciating the Author's Craft.   Authors of informational books and magazines often use words that appeal to our senses about topics they write about. While these techniques often increase the enjoyment of reading informational books, readers need to recognize the effect of these techniques.

Connotative and denotative meanings.   One way authors appeal to the senses is through using connotative and denotative meanings of words. Words have both connotative and denotative meanings. *Connotative meanings* appeal to our emotions, senses, or make judgments. *Denotative meanings* are the public meanings of words. For example, *The Old Boot* (Baines, 1989) is a book about ecology that explains how several insects live together by sharing an old boot for their home. To describe the insects, Baines uses many words that have connotative appeal such as *squidgy* slug, *slimy* slug, and *creepy-crawlies*. These words conjure up vivid images for some students and call to mind unpleasant associations with bugs for others.

Authors who write historical or scientific books use words that have both connotative and denotative meanings. Readers need to be aware of authors' use of language and its effect on their understandings and feelings toward topics. Sometimes these differences are hard to detect. For example, most informational books about Christopher Columbus' accomplishments suggest that he *discovered* America, when actually he did not. Native Americans were already living in America at the time Columbus arrived and Viking explorers landed in North America hundreds of years before Columbus. The fact that we say Christopher Columbus *discovered* America implies that the Native Americans living in North America at the time of Columbus were not important and ignores the fact that the Vikings were here before Columbus. Authors write about Columbus in other ways that affect our thinking about his accomplishments. The language and images associated with Christopher Columbus and the other European explorers found in many informational books portray *hardy, enterprising, God-fearing* men who *risked their lives* for the *betterment* of all. Native peoples would use very different language and images to portray these explorers. Older students can examine informational books and magazines for authors' connotative use of language. They might compare the language used to describe important historical figures in biographies and in other informational sources.

Read-arounds. Another way to focus attention on an author's use of language is to have a read-around. A *read-around* is a rereading activity in which children select one sentence from an informational book that is the most meaningful, interesting, or memorable to them. Teachers begin the activity by asking, "Who would like to share first?" Students then take turns reading their sentences, in a random order. There is no discussion of the sentences. Sometimes read-arounds lead to quilt-making. Students write their favorite sentences on paper quilt pieces. Then the pieces are glued to a large sheet of butcher paper in a quilt design, and the quilt is hung on the wall for everyone to read.

Read-arounds support the development of fluency and attention to authors' language. Many informational books are beautifully written with metaphorical language and strong sensory appeal. Reading and writing sentences from such books on a quilt naturally highlights these qualities of an author's craft. Older students use the quilt to discuss the qualities of writing that most appeal to them.

Extending Step

Extending activities allow children to make choices about how they will extend their content learning, and they capitalize on the potential of poetry and stories to enrich content learning. Many of the activities listed in Figure 5.13 are appropriate for extending children's responses to informational books as well. In addition, children can extend their content learning by reading more from multiple sources of informational books and magazines. They also learn from interviewing experts, local community members, and other children and from examining historical artifacts and documents. They gain critical awareness as they compare and contrast the ways different authors present similar information, and these investigations allow students to evaluate the authenticity and accuracy of information they are learning. Students extend as they connect with poetry and stories, with the community and primary sources, and with the other language arts.

Connecting Through Poetry and Stories. Many stories and poems present historical or scientific information, and students can compare and contrast the information found in informational books with that found in stories or poems. Often authors alter historical information to better fit their story or poem. For example, *Across Five Aprils* (Hunt, 1964) includes a great deal of information about several battles in the Civil War, some of which is accurate and some of which Irene Hunt changed to fit her story. Students could use informational books to compare historical facts with the facts presented in Hunt's book. They might prepare a comparison chart with two columns: facts in *Across Five Aprils* and facts from informational books. Students could compare the dates of battles, the number of soldiers in the battles and the numbers killed for the North and South, and the Northern and Southern generals leading the battles.

Students can also be encouraged to collect poetry related to a topic of study. Teachers can hang a clothesline across the classroom with pictures related to the topics of study (Hopkins, 1987). Children are then challenged to find poems which the topic and pictures prompt. They can duplicate the poems and hang them on the clothesline beside the pictures. Teachers might also place several objects in a large box to prompt poetry searches or writing.

Connecting to the Community and Primary Sources.   Members of the community and other community resources are often untapped sources of learning. Community resources such as aquariums, zoos, processing plants, water stations, recycling plants, and even farms provide firsthand experiences with animals and other processes. These experiences bring information to life.

Local historical societies and some libraries provide other kinds of resources. They often have documents such as magazines, letters, journals, marriage records, or newspapers from the past. Such primary sources are invaluable in studying history. Students studying the Civil War might locate letters, diaries, or other documents from the time written by local people. Such documents present a picture of history as it was lived—an experience students miss when reading informational books or biographies. Older community members who lived through historical events and can share these memories with children are also valuable resources.

Connecting to the Other Language Arts.   One way that students can share what they are learning is through *debates*. Informal debates arise when students have differing opinions about an issue, such as off-shore oil drilling, the internment of Japanese Americans during World War II, gun control, or Christopher Columbus' reputation. Students with one opinion about the issue move to one side of the classroom, and students with a differing opinion move to the other side. If there are students with other opinions, they gather together on other sides of the classroom, and students who have not formed an opinion sit in the middle of the classroom. After hearing the arguments, students may change their minds and move to a different side of the room; if they are no longer certain which side they agree with, they take a seat in the middle.

The teacher begins the debate by asking a student on one side to state that group's opinion. After this opening statement, a student from the other side makes a statement. From then on, students on each side takes turns making and rebutting statements. Before making a rebuttal statement, students sometimes ask clarifying questions of someone who has just made a statement. The debate continues until all sides of the issue have been discussed and all opinions aired. It is not important that one side "wins" or that all students in the class agree with one opinion or another. What matters is that students have voiced their opinions and substantiated their arguments with facts and examples from their reading.

Students can also share what they are learning through writing. After reading biographies of characters, students could write *fictionalized biographies* about that person (Zarnowski, 1988). First, students learn about fictionalized biographies. They might read *Grand Papa and Ellen Aroon* (Monjo, 1976), a story about Thomas Jefferson told by his granddaughter, *Me and Willie and Pa* (Monjo, 1973), a story about Abraham Lincoln told from Tad Lincoln's perspective, or *Ben and Me* (Lawson, 1939), a story of Ben Franklin told by a mouse who lives in his hat. After students read a fictionalized biography, they then select a famous person and read biographies and informational books about him or her. They select a person to tell the story about the famous person: a son, daughter, grandchild, or pet of the famous person. Then they select events from the person's life and write about them from the perspective of the storyteller.

MAKING DECISIONS ABOUT TEACHING FROM
A READER RESPONSE PERSPECTIVE

Teachers make several decisions about teaching reading from the reader response perspective. Guided by an awareness of quality literature, sensitivity to the likes and dislikes of their students, and the expected curriculum of their school systems, they decide which stories, informational books, and poems they will select for their reading instruction.

To make decisions about planning instructional activities, teachers first carefully read and personally respond to stories, informational books, and poems that they intend to use in instruction. They may respond to humor, dialogue, mood, language play, image, or character, or to arguments and supporting details, examples, or sequence of ideas. Teachers carefully consider remembrances of life experiences or connections to other literature that is called to mind during reading. They analyze how their responses to the literature selection deepen and enrich their understanding, appreciation, and interpretation of the work. Only after teachers have responded to a literary work and reflected on their own lived-through experience are they ready to plan instruction that will best encourage children's reading and responding to a particular story, book, or poem. For example, in the case studies at the beginning of this chapter, Mr. Sahady and Ms. Epstein reflected on their own responses to *Sylvester and the Magic Pebble* and *Frogs, Toads, Lizards, and Salamanders* as a first step in making decisions about instruction. These teachers carefully selected activities that they believed would best enhance children's involvement with and response to this particular story and informational book (Chapter 8 also describes how to select activities).

Teachers also decide when students need teacher-directed preparing, reading, exploring, and extending activities and when children can engage in these activities independently. This decision must be based on an awareness of individual learners gained through careful observation. Teachers select activities that best fit students' needs and are appropriate for the particular story, poem, or informational book to be read. Figure 5.17 presents an overview of the activities included in this chapter. Teachers must be thoroughly familiar with stories, poems, and informational books. Preparing interpretive questions and selecting activities that support interpretation depend on teachers' careful and critical reading. Assessing the major concepts that students should learn from informational reading also demands critical reading. Activities that teachers select both accept children's initial responses and build from these into more interpretive responses. Teachers select activities that prompt students to become personally involved, allow students to view stories from the perspectives of several characters, and encourage students to make choices about extending their responses. Through professional reading and attending professional meets and conferences, teachers keep informed of new instructional techniques. Finally, teachers consult with local and state curriculum guides to identify mandated learning outcomes or competencies in literacy.

The decisions that teachers make about supporting children's reading from the reader response perspective are:

- Select stories, poems, and informational books based on a knowledge of literature, individual preferences, and curriculum demands.

FIGURE 5.17   Overview of Activities from a Reader Response Perspective

	Reading for Literary Purposes	Reading for Informational Purposes
Step 1: Preparing to read	Imagining or dramatizing a story event Prereading writing assignment Introducing characters Reading aloud Reading poetry as introductions to stories	Letter to the editor Anticipation guide Poetry and stories as introductions to informational books Poetrees
Step 2: Reading the text	Role-playing	Response heuristic for informational books Point of view reading guides
Step 3: Exploring the text	Response journals Response heuristic Simulated letters Simulated newspapers "I" poems Sketch-to-stretch drawings Story or poetry boxes Collages Tableau Puppets Readers' theatre Notable language samples Double-entry journals	Grand conversations Simulated journals, letters, and newspapers Found poetry Murals Sculptures Dioramas Life boxes "You were there" dramas Read-arounds Quilts
Step 4: Extending from the text	Self-selected response activities	Correlating stories with informational books Collecting poetry Interviewing and using primary sources Fictionalized biographies

- Assess whether students need teacher-directed or independent preparing, reading, exploring, and extending activities.
- Select an appropriate activity that meets the needs of individual students, is consonant with the purpose of reading, and is appropriate to the selection by understanding individual learners, reading and analyzing the selection, and consulting professional resources.
- Consult school or state curriculum guides for lists of expected competencies or learning outcomes.

This information is added to the decision-making diagram as shown in Figure 5.18.

FIGURE 5.18   Summary Chart for Decision Tree

		Decision Tree
Chapter 1		Using Literature in the Reading Program
Chapter 2		Choosing Literature for Children
Chapter 3		Learning About Authors and Illustrators
Chapter 4		Identifying Perspectives on Reading Instruction

Teaching from a Reader Response Perspective

Chapter 5

- **Select stories, poems and informational books based on a knowledge of literature, individual preferences, and curriculum demands**

- **Assess whether students need teacher-directed or independent preparing, reading, exploring, and extending activities**

- **Select an appropriate activity that meets the needs of individual learners, is consonant with purpose of reading, and is appropriate to the selection by understanding individual learners, reading and analyzing the selection, and consulting professional resources**

- **Consult school or state curriculum guides for lists of expected competencies or learning outcomes**

Chapter 6		Teaching from a Critical Perspective
Chapter 7		Teaching from an Interactive Perspective
Chapter 8		Putting It All Together
Chapter 9		Assessing Students' Learning

REFERENCES

Alvermann, D. E. (1991). The discussion web: A graphic aid for learning across the curriculum. *The Reading Teacher, 45,* 108–116.

Atwell, N. (1987). *In the middle: Writing, reading, and learning with adolescents.* Portsmouth, NH: Heinemann.

Barone, D., & Lovell, J. (1990). Michael and the show-and-tell magician: A journey through literature to self. *Language Arts, 67,* 134–143.

Berthoff, A. (1981). *The making of meaning.* Upper Montclair, NJ: Boynton/Cook.

Bleich, D. (1978). *Subjective criticism.* Baltimore, MD: Johns Hopkins University Press.

Brozo, W. (1988). Applying the reader response heuristic to expository text. *Journal of Reading, 32,* 140–145.

Brozo, W., & Tomlinson, C. (1986). Literature: The key to lively content courses. *The Reading Teacher, 40,* 288–293.

Corcoran, B. (1987). Teachers creating readers. In B. Corcoran (Ed.), *Readers, texts, teachers* (pp. 41–74). Upper Montclair, NJ: Boynton/Cook.

Eeds, M., & Wells, D. (1989). Grand conversations: An exploration of meaning construction in literature study groups. *Research in the Teaching of English, 23,* 4–29.

Galda, L. (1982). Playing about a story: Its impact on comprehension. *The Reading Teacher, 36,* 52–55.

Harste, J., Short, K., & Burke, C. (1988). *Creating classrooms for authors.* Portsmouth, NH: Heinemann.

Head, M., & Readence, J. (1986). Anticipation guides: Enhancing meaning through prediction. In E. Dishner, T. Bean, J. Readence, & D. Moore (Eds.), *Reading in the content areas: Improving classroom instruction* (2nd ed.) (pp. 229–234). Dubuque, IA: Kendall/Hunt.

Johnson, T., & Louis, D. (1987). *Literacy through literature.* Portsmouth, NH: Heinemann.

Laughlin, M., & Latrobe, K. (1989). *Readers theatre for children: Scripts and script development.* Englewood, CO: Libraries Unlimited.

Marino, J., Gould, S., & Haas, L. (1985). The effects of writing as a prereading activity on delayed recall of narrative text. *Elementary School Journal, 86,* 199–205.

Norton, D. (1991). *Through the eyes of a child: An introduction to children's literature* (3rd ed.). New York: Merrill/Macmillan.

Noyce, R., & Christie, J. (1989). *Integrating reading and writing instruction in grades K–8.* Boston: Allyn & Bacon.

Peterson, R., & Eeds, M. (1990). *Grand conversations: Literature groups in action.* Toronto, Ont: Scholastic-TAB.

Purves, A., Rogers, T., & Soter, A. (1990). *How porcupines make love II.* New York: Longman.

Saul, W. (1989). "What did Leo feed the turtle?" and other non-literary questions. *Language Arts, 66,* 295–303.

Smith, K. (1990). Entertaining a text: A reciprocal process. In K. Short & K. Pierce (Eds.), *Talking about books: Creating literate communities* (pp. 16–31). Portsmouth, NH: Heinemann.

Tierney, R., Soter, A., O'Flahavan, J., & McGinley, W. (1989). The effects of reading and writing upon thinking critically. *Reading Research Quarterly, 24,* 134–173.

Wood, K. (1988). Guiding students through informational text. *The Reading Teacher, 41,* 912–920.

Zarnowski, M. (1988). Learning about fictionalized biographies: A reading and writing approach. *The Reading Teacher, 42,* 136–142.

CHILDREN'S LITERATURE REFERENCES

Adoff, A. (1979). "I am learning." In A. Adoff, *Eats poems.* New York: Lothrop, Lee & Shepard.

Adoff, A. (1979). "Sunny." In A. Adoff, *Eats poems.* New York: Lothrop, Lee & Shepard.

Babbitt, N. (1975). *Tuck everlasting.* New York: Farrar, Straus & Giroux.

Baines, C. (1989). *The old boot.* New York: Crocodile Books.

Berenzy, A. (1989). *Frog prince.* New York: Holt, Rinehart & Winston.

Blohm, C. (1984). The voyage of Leif the Lucky. *Cobblestone,* 14–16.

Blume, J. (1970). *Are you there, God? It's me Margaret.* New York: Bradbury.

Blume J. (1972). *Tales of a fourth grade nothing.* NY: Dutton.

Blume, J. (1980). *Superfudge.* New York: Dutton.

Brooks, G. (1956). "Cynthia in the snow." In G. Brooks, *Bronzeville boys and girls.* New York: Harper & Row.

Byars, B. (1970). *The summer of the swans.* New York: Viking.

Dahl, R. (1964). *Charlie and the chocolate factory.* New York: Knopf.

D'Aulaire, I., & D'Aulaire, E. (1955). *Columbus.* New York: Doubleday.

dePaola, T. (1975). *Strega Nona.* New York: Simon & Schuster.

Fox, P. (1984). *One-eyed cat.* New York: Bradbury.

Freedman, R. (1987). *Lincoln: A photobiography.* New York: Clarion.

Friedman, I. (1987). *How my parents learned to eat.* Boston, MA: Houghton Mifflin.

Fritz, J. (1975). *Where was Patrick Henry on the 29th of May?* New York: Coward, McCann.

Geisel, T. (1971). (Dr. Seuss) *The lorax.* New York: Random House.

George, J. C. (1971). *Who really killed Cock Robin?* NY: Dutton.

Greenfield, E. (1977). *Mary McLeod Bethune.* New York: Crowell.

Grimm, J., & Grimm, W. (1989). *Frog king and other tales of the Brothers Grimm.* New York: Signet Classics.

Grimm, J., & Grimm, W. (1989). *Frog prince.* New York: North-South.

Hopkins, L. (1987). *Pass the poetry, please!* New York: Harper & Row.

Howe, D., & Howe, J. (1979). *Bunnicula: A rabbit tale of mystery.* New York: Atheneum.

Hunt, I. (1964). *Across five Aprils.* Chicago, IL: Follett.

Hutchins, P. (1968). *Rosie's walk.* New York: Macmillan.

Jacobs, W. (1990). *Ellis Island: New hope in a new land.* New York: Scribner's.

Keats, E. (1962). *The snowy day.* New York: Viking.

Keegan, M. (1991). *Pueblo boy: Growing up in two worlds.* New York: Dutton.

Lawson, R. (1939). *Ben and me.* Boston, MA: Little, Brown.

Lowry, L. (1989). *Number the stars.* Boston, MA: Houghton Mifflin.

Lucas, E., Crane, L., & Edwardes, M. (Trans.) (1945). "The frog prince." In *Grimm's fairy tales* (pp. 85–89). New York: Grosset & Dunlap.

MacLachlan, P. (1985). *Sarah, plain and tall.* New York: Harper & Row.

MacLachlan, P. (1988). *The facts and fictions of Minna Pratt.* New York: Harper & Row.

Meltzer, M. (1988). *Rescue: The story of how Gentiles saved Jews in the Holocaust.* New York: Harper & Row.

Monjo, F. (1973). *Me and Willie and Pa: The story of Abraham Lincoln and his son Tad.* New York: Simon & Schuster.

Monjo, F. (1976). *Grand Papa and Ellen Aroon.* New York: Holt, Rinehart & Winston.

Ness, E. (1966). *Sam, Bangs, & Moonshine.* New York: Holt, Rinehart & Winston.

Norton, M. (1955). *The borrowers.* New York: Harcourt Brace Jovanovich.

Numeroff, L. (1985). *If you give a mouse a cookie.* New York: Scholastic.

Parker, N., & Wright, J. (1991). *Frogs, toads, lizards, and salamanders.* New York: Greenwillow.

Paterson, K. (1977). *Bridge to Terabithia.* New York: Crowell.

Prelutsky, J. (1982). *The baby uggs are hatching.* New York: Mulberry.

Scieszka, J. (1991). *The frog prince continued.* New York: Viking.

Stanley, D., & Vennema, P. (1988). *Shaka: King of the Zulus.* New York: Morrow.

Steig, W. (1969). *Sylvester and the magic pebble.* New York: Simon & Schuster.

Steig, W. (1976). *The amazing bone.* New York: Farrar, Straus & Giroux.

Van Allsburg, C. (1990). *Ben's dream.* Boston, MA: Houghton Mifflin.

Waber, B. (1962). *The house on East 88th Street.* Boston: Houghton Mifflin.

Waber, B. (1965). *Lyle, Lyle crocodile.* Boston: Houghton Mifflin.

Waber, B. (1972). *Ira sleeps over.* Boston: Houghton Mifflin.

Ward, L. (1952). *The biggest bear.* Boston, MA: Houghton Mifflin.

Waters, K. (1989). *Sarah Morton's day: A day in the life of a Pilgrim girl.* New York: Scholastic.

Wilcox, C. (1988). *Trash!* Minneapolis: Carolrhoda.

Yorinks, A. (1986). *Hey, Al.* New York: Farrar, Straus & Giroux.

CHAPTER 6

TEACHING FROM A CRITICAL PERSPECTIVE

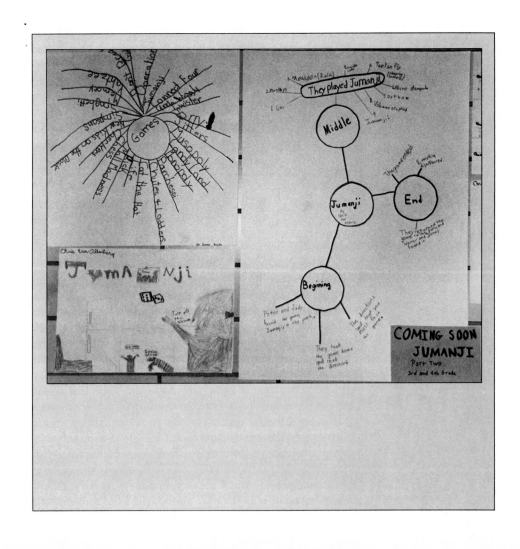

In this chapter you will learn to make decisions about:

- **Planning a literature program that includes the study of authors, illustrators, genres, and literary elements.**
- **Coordinating planning of literature programs with other teachers so that children's experiences with literature build from grade to grade and are based on previous experiences.**
- **Assessing whether students need teacher-directed or independent preparing, reading, exploring, and extending activities.**
- **Selecting an appropriate activity that meets the needs of individual learners, is consonant with the purpose of reading, and is appropriate to the selection by understanding individual learners, reading and analyzing the selection, and consulting professional resources.**
- **Consulting school or state curriculum guides for lists of expected competencies or learning outcomes.**

THIS IS THE SECOND of three chapters that explores instructional activities that extend children's reading abilities and experiences with literature. In this chapter we describe instructional activities for teaching reading from the critical perspective. We present two case studies describing Mrs. Galvin and Ms. Jacobs who teach from this perspective. These teachers are quite knowledgeable about literature and believe that their students become better readers by learning more about the characteristics, structures, and elements of literature and about authors' and illustrators' craft. They have carefully selected a story and informational book with the best qualities of literature and spent considerable time reflecting on the best activities to explore these particular selections.

A CASE IN POINT

Mrs. Galvin's Guided Reading of Sylvester and the Magic Pebble

Eight of Mrs. Galvin's third graders are sitting on the rug in the literature center of the classroom. Mrs. Galvin is reading *The Princess and the Frog* (Isadora, 1989) aloud to the group as a preparing step activity. The story is about a prince who has been turned into a frog and can only be changed back into his human form if the Princess will let him sleep in her bed for three nights. After Mrs. Galvin finishes reading, she and the students discuss the story and the characteristics of folktales found in the story. They refer to the chart listing the characteristics of folktales that they made several weeks ago at the beginning of their unit on folktales. Samantha says, "The Frog Prince has a transformation; the frog turns into a prince." Orlando adds, "It has a happy ending, you know. The prince and princess get married."

The next day the group gathers around a large table. Each of the children has a copy of *Sylvester and the Magic Pebble* (Steig, 1969). Mrs. Galvin says, "Traditional folktales, such as The Frog Prince, have no known author. These stories were told by storytellers who travelled from village to village telling stories around a campfire or after dinner. Later, two men, named Jacob and Wilhelm Grimm, listened to many of these stories as they were told aloud and wrote them down. Today, some authors write new folktales. These folktales are called modern literary tales. The story you will read today, *Sylvester and the Magic Pebble,* is a modern literary tale. This story is similar to traditional folktales but it was written by William Steig. It also has many of the same characteristics of traditional folktales that we have been studying in our unit."

The children guess which features of folktales might be included in *Sylvester and the Magic Pebble*. Paul guesses that the story will have a magic object, and Maria guesses that the story will have animals who can talk and act like humans. Idaliz thinks the story will include wishes.

Then the children read the first few pages of the story to confirm their guesses. They confirm that animals can talk and act like people in the story and that there is a magic object—the red pebble. Students make guesses about what

FIGURE 6.1   Cluster of Folktale Characteristics included in *Sylvester and the Magic Pebble* (Steig, 1969)

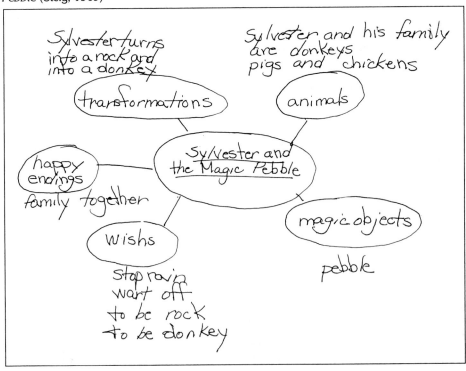

Sylvester will do with the magic pebble and then read further to the part where Sylvester is transformed into a rock. The students discuss this part of the story, and Orlando explains, "I thought that the magic would help Sylvester, but I guess it backfired." Mrs. Galvin leads them in a discussion of why the magic might have backfired. One of the students, Sheri, recalls, "I remember that in *Strega Nona* (de Paola, 1975) Big Anthony could not make the magic pasta pot stop making pasta." The students conclude that you have to be smart to control magic, and they decide that magic is not something to fool around with if you do not know

what you are doing. The students read the remainder of the story to find out how Sylvester gets out of his predicament.

The next day the students gather to discuss their reactions to the story. Mrs. Galvin encourages them to talk about what they found interesting, surprising, and confusing. Then, as an exploring step activity, Mrs. Galvin asks students to select three features of folktales from the list the group brainstormed at the beginning of their folktale unit and write them on a cluster. Then they add examples and other information about the features from *Sylvester and the Magic Pebble* to

FIGURE 6.2   Character Trait Cluster for Sylvester

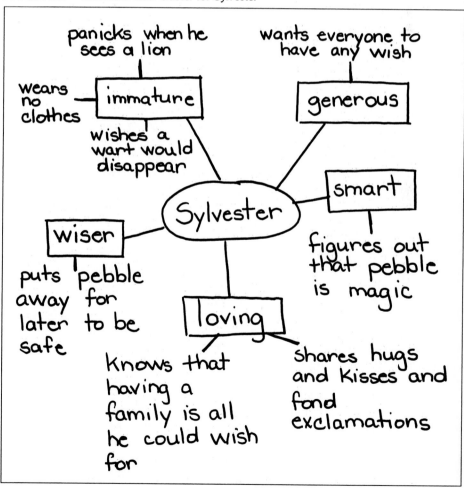

complete their cluster. Figure 6.1 presents one child's cluster.

The next day the children share their clusters describing the features of folktales included in *Sylvester and the Magic Pebble.* Then, Mrs. Galvin explains that characters in modern literary tales are more fully developed than characters in traditional folktales. Mrs. Galvin demonstrates this difference by constructing a character trait cluster about Sylvester. As the students name one of Sylvester's character traits, such as *smart,* Mrs. Galvin asks students to justify their answers, and she adds this information to the cluster as shown in Figure 6.2.

The following day Mrs. Galvin shows the children a box of "magic" objects including a red pebble, silk scarf, wand, TV remote control, and glitter (fairy dust). She says, "These objects might be magic, but only for someone who knows how to use the magic," and she invites the children to guess how each object's magic might work. They brainstorm a list of ideas about the magic objects. Then, as an extending activity, children write folktale-like stories about one of the magic objects. Some children begin rehearsing their story by writing a cluster while others quickwrite. Later Mrs. Galvin will work with the children as they revise and edit their stories before publishing them in a class book.

A CASE IN POINT

Ms. Jacobs' Vertebrate Animal Unit

Ms. Jacobs' sixth graders are studying vertebrate animals. According to the science curriculum, she is responsible for teaching reptile, amphibian, bird, fish, and mammal classes. One objective of this theme cycle is for students to compare and contrast members of these classes according to reproductive cycles, habitats, diet, and internal systems. She has several animals in her classroom including tadpoles, newts, and mice that her students will observe during the unit.

A group of eight students are researching the life cycles of frogs. As one activity they have been observing tadpoles and recording information from their observations in their learning logs. They have also been reading *Frogs, Toads, Lizards, and Salamanders* (Parker & Wright, 1991) to gain more information about frogs and lizards. Today Ms. Jacobs begins the lesson by explaining that students will be learning about an organization or structure that authors use to present information called the compare-contrast organization. As a preparing step activity, the students discuss what they know about this kind of organization, and Ms. Jacobs presents the compare-contrast organizer

shown in Figure 6.3. Ms. Jacobs prepared this organizer using the information presented on pages 40 and 41 of *Frogs, Toads, Lizards, and Salamanders.* She explains that this is a visual overview of the likenesses and differences between amphibians and lizards. She talks about the organizer, stressing both its content (features distinguishing amphibians and lizards) and how compare-contrast structures work. Students notice that amphibians and lizards are compared systematically on several features such as the type of blood, type of lungs, place where eggs are laid, and moisture of skin.

Next, students compose a paragraph about the similarities and differences between frogs and lizards using the information presented in the compare-contrast organizer. Ms. Jacobs stresses that they need to include words such as *alike, different, similarities, differences, can be compared,* and *in contrast* in their compositions.

The next day the students read their paragraphs aloud. The group gives compliments, asks clarifying questions, and discusses possible revisions. Then students read pages 40 and 41 of

FIGURE 6.3   Organizer for Pages 40 & 41 from *Frogs, Toads, Lizards, and Salamanders* (Parker & Wright, 1991)

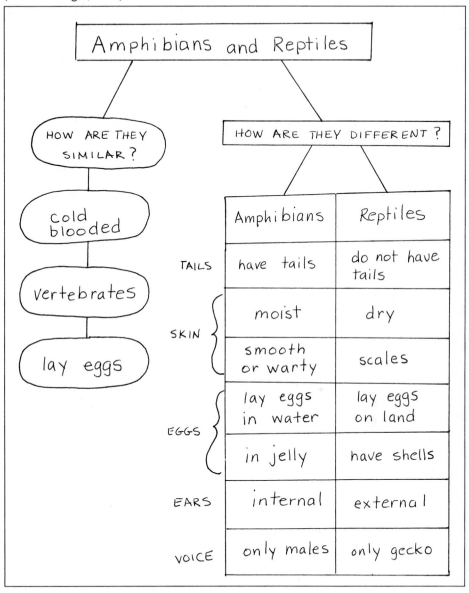

Frogs, Toads, Lizards, and Salamanders. After reading, the students discuss the content presented on these pages and the author's use of the compare-contrast structure. As an exploring activity, they compare and contrast the paragraph they composed to the author's text. They note that the author used few of the clue words that signal a compare-contrast structure. Many students decide that their compositions were easier to read because they had more clearly signaled how frogs and lizards were alike and different. The students also discuss how readers could look for a com-

FIGURE 6.4   Skeleton Compare-Contrast Organizer

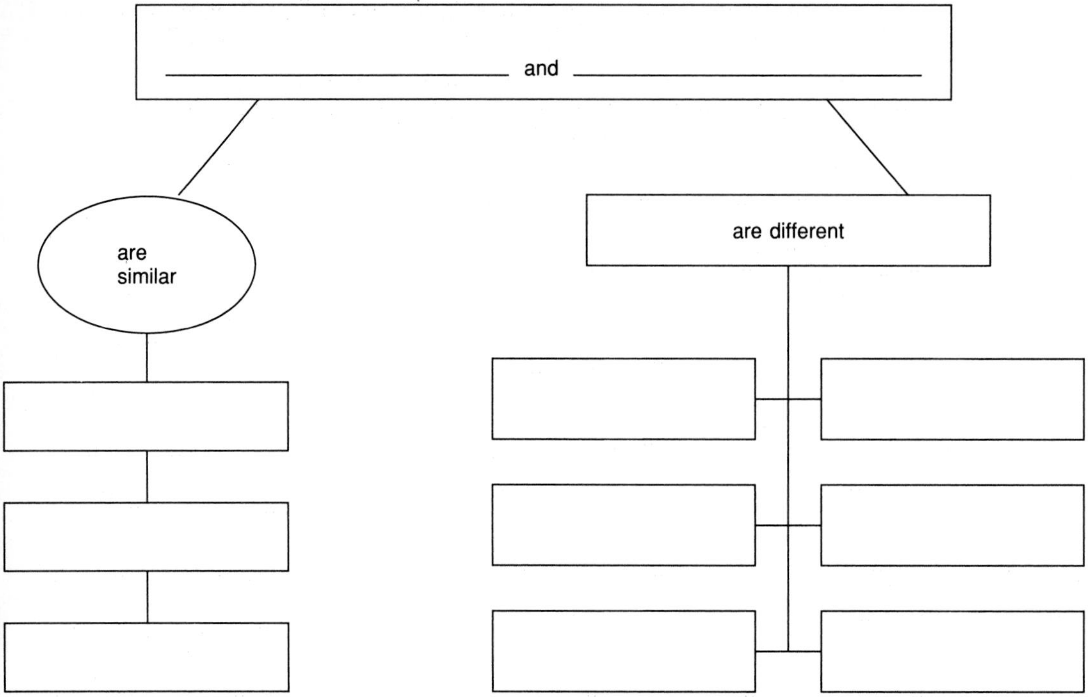

pare-contrast structure while reading. Ms. Jacobs ends the lesson by presenting and describing a skeleton organizer for a compare-contrast structure shown in Figure 6.4. She explains, "This is a skeleton organizer that you can use whenever you want to write a composition comparing and contrasting two things. You can also use this organizer to record information when you are reading a paragraph that compares and contrasts something."

The next day Ms. Jacobs introduces two new books about amphibians and reptiles: *Never Kiss an Alligator!* (Bare, 1989) and *Look at Skin, Shell, and Scale* (Pluckrose, 1989). She tells the students that these books have some portions that are written in a compare-contrast structure. She reminds them that noting these structures is an important way to learn new information. Then students divide into two groups. As an extending activity, they will read one of the two books and prepare to teach the students in the other group some new information they learned, using the compare-contrast organizer for their presentations.

As another extending activity, students later will use what they have learned about vertebrate animals to compose an alphabet book following the "A is for _____," "B is for _____," "C is for _____" formula. They will read *The Yucky Reptile Alphabet Book* (Pallota, 1986) and *The Frog Alphabet Book* (Pallota, 1986) and use these as models for their book.

INTRODUCTION

In this chapter we describe how teachers support children's reading for literary and informational purposes according to the critical perspective. The critical perspective focuses on providing children with an ever-increasing understanding of the nature of literature, literary elements and organizations, and authors and illustrators. According to this perspective, the more readers know about literature, literary elements and organizations, and authors and illustrators, the better able they will be to interpret literature and understand content information. While the critical perspective emphasizes that all literature shares common structures and that authors and illustrators use common elements, each piece of literature combines these elements in unique and creative ways. Similarly, readers draw on these elements in unique ways based on their own experiences with literature to construct personal meanings.

In the first part of the chapter we describe a variety of preparing, reading, exploring, and extending activities that support students' literary reading (usually of stories and poems), and in the second section we describe other activities that support students' informative reading (usually of informational books and magazines). While teachers need to be familiar with a wide range of possible activities, they also need to consider which activity best helps students read a particular story, book, or poem. Teachers should select activities after a careful reading of a particular selection and after determining the purposes for instruction. In the final section we discuss decisions that teachers make about teaching reading from a critical perspective. It is important to keep in mind that several of these activities can also fit the purposes of other theoretical perspectives.

READING FOR LITERARY PURPOSES

Students read for literary purposes when they read stories, poems, and sometimes other types of literature for pleasure. They also learn more about the literary elements associated with stories and poems and about authors and illustrators and their craft. In Chapters 2 and 3 we presented information about literary elements, genres and organizations, authors, and illustrators that students can learn in order to become better readers. This chapter describes instructional activities that sharpen students' understanding of those literary features.

Preparing Step

Preparing activities help students use what they know about the literary elements of stories and poems to predict what they will read about. In the case study at the beginning of this chapter, Mrs. Galvin read *The Frog Prince* aloud as a way of preparing children to read *Sylvester and the Magic Pebble,* a story with similar folktale features. Students used what they knew about the features of folktales to predict what they would read. Teachers also use preparing activities to present new information about literary elements, genres, or authors and illustrators before children read.

Many children become familiar with literary elements, characteristics of genre, and the unique qualities of an author's or illustrator's style intuitively as they listen to and read many stories and poems. Reading aloud is often an effective way to introduce an unfamiliar story or poem as well as to introduce a literary element. Mrs. Galvin read *The Frog Prince* aloud to prepare the children for reading *Sylvester and the Magic Pebble.* She selected this book because it has several of the same characteristics of folktales as *Sylvester and the Magic Pebble.* Comparing two or more stories or poems helps children to crystalize their intuitive understandings into a more conscious awareness that guides their reading and interpretation of subsequent stories and poems.

Sometimes teachers help students learn about the features of genres, literary elements, and the unique characteristics of an author or illustrator more directly. Tompkins and Hoskisson (1991) recommend an instructional strategy to teach children about literary elements, genres, or characteristics of an author's or illustrator's craft that can be used to help children prepare to read. The steps include the following:

1. *Review information about literature.* Teachers select a literary element, genre, or an author or illustrator for study and review information about the literary element, characteristics of the genre, or unique features of an author's or illustrator's style.

2. *Collect a text set.* Teachers collect stories or poems written by a particular author, illustrated by a particular illustrator, representative of a genre, or having the literary element for a text set. They preview the reading materials to further examine the characteristics of style, genre, or literary element before setting them out for students to read.

3. *Prepare focusing questions and a descriptive chart.* Teachers construct questions that will focus children's attention on characteristics of the author's or illustrator's style, the genre, or the literary element and prepare charts that list these characteristics. For example, Mrs. Galvin and her third graders constructed a chart about the characteristics of folktales.

4. *Share literature, ask focusing questions, and present chart.* The teacher reads aloud a story or poem that clearly provides examples of the literary element, genre, or style of the author or illustrator being taught. Students may read with a partner or independently. Then the teacher asks questions to focus students' attention on this element and introduces the chart as a way of summarizing the discussion. This chart can later be hung in the classroom or students can make copies of it in their literature journals.

5. *Repeat steps with another story or poem.* The teacher reads a second story or poem aloud or the children read it and discuss how it exemplifies the same characteristics of the genre, element, or author's or illustrator's style.

6. *Provide extending activities.* Teaching children to identify literary elements, characteristics of genre, or qualities of an author's or illustrator's style should be only one of many activities children use to explore literature. Children can extend their knowledge of the genre, literary element, or style through further reading, retelling, dramatizing, or writing activities.

Once children learn about a feature of literature, they should be encouraged to use this feature as they read and discuss literature. The purpose of learning about the features of literature is to enrich children's enjoyment and understanding of what they read, and children should have many opportunities to use their literary knowledge in reading for pleasure.

Reading Step

Reading activities support children as they construct meaning using their understanding of literary elements, genre, and authors and illustrators, according to the critical perspective. One method of providing this support during reading is to use a modified Directed Reading Thinking Activity (DRTA). The steps in using a DRTA are

1. *Show book cover and read title.* The teacher shows the cover of the book (or an illustration accompanying a poem) and reads the title of the story or poem.
2. *Students predict.* Students each make one or more predictions about the story or poem. Teachers encourage students to think creatively.
3. *Record predictions.* The teacher or students record the predictions on a chart or using an overhead projector. As an alternative, students can write their predictions in a literature journal. They divide the page into two columns: "What I predict" and "What happened." Students then write their predictions in the first column and record what actually happened in the second column.
4. *Students read.* Students read the story or poem (or portions of it). Or the teacher may read the selection aloud.
5. *Students discuss predictions.* Students briefly discuss their predictions and use information from the poem or story to confirm or reject their predictions.
6. *Repeat Steps 2 through 5 if appropriate.* The procedure is typically repeated two or three times depending on the length and complexity of the text.

Teachers can modify the DRTA so that children attend to literary elements as Mrs. Galvin did in the case study at the beginning of this chapter. As children predict which literary elements they expect to encounter, they make hypotheses about meaning. Then children read to confirm their hypotheses. After reading, they discuss their predictions in light of what they read in the text. Another example of using the modified DRTA is to ask children to predict what they would expect to find in a fairy tale (e.g., prince, princess, mean stepmother, witch, fairy godmother, mean sisters, transformations, enchantments, magic, magic wands or other objects, wishes) before reading the fairy tale, and students or the teacher write the predictions. After reading, students reread the list and mark those characteristics they predicted correctly. They can also add other characteristics of fairy tales they noticed while they were reading. Then they can use this list of characteristics of fairy tales to make predictions before reading modern literary tales such as *Petronella* (Williams, 1973). In this story, prediction is especially fun because the prince and princess do not behave in expected ways.

Exploring Step

Exploring activities are designed to deepen children's understanding of stories and poems through rereading and thinking about literary elements. Children grow as readers as they explore characters and their development, plot structures, and the influence of point of view and setting on meaning. Exploring activities also provide children with new strategies for examining an author's craft.

Rereading and Thinking. Children learn more about character, plot, setting, and other elements of an author's style or genre through the use of story boards, plot diagrams and profiles, character clusters, missing person reports, and literary maps. These activities call children's attention to literary elements and require careful re-reading.

Story boards. *Story boards* are the illustrations from a story mounted on cardboard. They are displayed in sequence so that readers can view the entire story's illustrations at once. Story boards draw attention to various aspects of literary elements including story structure (for example, story boards of *Sylvester and the Magic Pebble* by Steig, 1969, illustrate that the story begins and ends in the same setting), changes in perspective (e.g., story boards of *Goodnight Moon* by Brown, 1947, show how a room slowly darkens as a child gets ready for bed), and foreshadowing (e.g., story boards of *Hey, Al* by Yorinks, 1986, show how the illustrations foreshadow what will happen to Al at the island).

Teachers make story boards by glueing illustrations from a picture book version of a story or poem on sturdy cardboard. For example, to create story boards for *Sylvester and the Magic Pebble,* teachers purchase two copies of the story and cut out each illustration. Some illustrations are double spreads; that is, one illustration stretches across two pages. Each illustration is mounted on a sheet of sturdy cardboard and laminated. Teachers may also want to cut out the words of the text and glue them to the back of the story boards before laminating.

Children sequence the story boards along a wall or the ledge of a chalkboard, so that all of the illustrations are visible at once, and then they examine them, looking for new insights about the meaning of the story. Students are encouraged to retell stories from the story boards and to discuss what they learned from viewing the illustrations. For example, in *The Napping House* (Wood, 1984), a cumulative story about an afternoon nap, the perspective in the illustrations subtly shifts so that at the beginning the reader views the bedroom from eye level and at the high point views it from ceiling level. This change in perspective is more easily detected from viewing story boards than from reading the story. Story boards recreate the kind of work that artists do as they prepare illustrations (Johnson & Louis, 1990).

Where the Wild Things Are (Sendak, 1963) also lends itself to story boards. When the story boards are laid out, children notice that the illustrations at the beginning are very small and placed in the center of the page and gradually increase in size. The illustrations in the middle of the story are the largest; the high point has four connected double-spread illustrations of the wild rumpus (which should be included on a single story board). After that point in the story the illustrations diminish in size, and the illustrations at the end are as small as they were at the beginning. The increasing size of the illustrations corresponds with Max's leaving home and venturing into the land of make-believe where the wild things live. Students who retell the story from story boards are more likely to appreciate the illustrator's contribution to the story's meaning.

In addition to viewing story boards in sequence and making inferences about the contributions of the illustrations to a story's meaning, students can sequence randomly ordered story boards prior to reading. They might be asked to divide story boards into beginning, middle, and end "chapters" and invent chapter titles. Each of these activities calls for students to consider how stories are organized and the influence of that organization on interpretation.

After children become familiar with using story boards, they can examine illustrations on their own. Students can discuss how illustrations enhance a story's or poem's meaning and to evaluate the effectiveness of illustrations.

Plot structure diagrams. Plot is one of the most important elements in a story, and students gain insights into plot structures using several visual displays including clusters, diagrams, and profiles. A *beginning-middle-end (BME) cluster* highlights the basic three-part plot structure of stories. To construct a BME cluster, students write the title of the story in a center circle, draw three rays out from the circle, and label them *beginning, middle,* and *end.* The students add pictures or words about the three story parts to finish the diagram. Figure 6.5 presents two BME clusters: one for *Who's in Rabbit's House?* (Aardema, 1977) and the other for *The Little Red Hen* (Zemach, 1983). The steps in creating BME clusters are the following:

1. *Draw the cluster.* Teachers write the title of the story in a circle in the center of a chart and draw three rays from the center circle to connect to three outer circles or nodes labeled *beginning, middle,* and *end.* Students working in small groups or individually can also draw clusters on sheets of paper.

2. *Children complete the cluster.* Children identify story events that occurred at the beginning, middle, and end of the story, and the teacher or children draw or write these events on lines extending from the appropriate node. Students usually suggest three to four events for the beginning, five to seven events for the middle, and two to three events for the end. It is important that students understand that the middle is the longest part of a story and identify more events for this part of the story than for the beginning or the end.

The beginning-middle-end cluster is very useful in examining stories with repetitive events such as *The Little Red Hen* (Zemach, 1983), *The Three Little Pigs* (Galdone, 1970), and *The Great Big Enormous Turnip* (Tolstoy, 1969). These stories have words and actions that are repeated to expand the middle of the story. The BME cluster can be modified by subdividing the *middle* into repeated words and repeated events. Figure 6.5 presents a beginning-middle-end cluster for a repetitive story, *The Little Red Hen.*

Middle grade students can use more complex visuals to explore the plot. Figure 6.6 presents two diagrams that focus students' attention on the plot of a story. To complete the first diagram, students draw or write the main character, what the main character wanted, the roadblock, and the resolution in the appropriate columns. To complete the second plot diagram, students arrange the main events on the mountain-like line (Tompkins, 1990). They draw a line out from the word *problem* and write a phrase to describe the problem. In the rising section of the diagram labeled *roadblocks,* students draw lines out and describe each roadblock. Then they describe the *high point* on a line drawn out from the summit of the mountain-like diagram, and draw another line out from the *solution* section to tell how the problem was solved. This diagram visually illustrates the rising action of a story to its high point and the falling action as the story is resolved.

Still another way to explore plot is to construct a *plot profile* (Johnson & Louis, 1987). A plot profile is similar to a graph. The excitement level (high to low) of each event in the story is identified and plotted on a graph. This activity draws students'

FIGURE 6.5   Beginning-Middle-End Clusters (*Note.* From "Teaching Repetition as a Story Structure" by G. Tompkins and L. McGee, 1989. In K. Muth (Ed.), *Children's Comprehension of Text: Research into Practice* (p. 70). Newark, DE: International Reading Association. Reprinted with permission of the International Reading Association.)

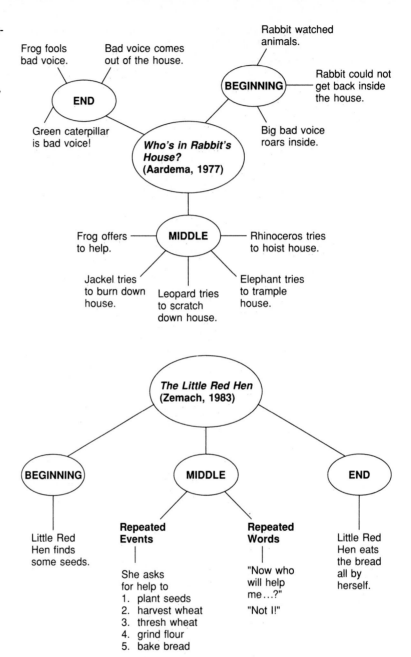

attention to the rising excitement in story events culminating in the high point or most exciting event in the story. Figure 6.7 presents a plot profile for *Hey, Al* (Yorinks, 1986). The steps in using a plot profile are the following:

   1. *Prepare a grid.* Teachers use graph paper or paper drawn with horizontal and vertical lines to create a grid. The vertical axis is labeled *excitement* with *high*

FIGURE 6.6   Plot Diagrams (*Note.* From *Response to Literature, Grades K–8* (p. 7) by J.M. Macon, D. Bewell, and M.E. Vogt, 1991. Newark, DE: International Reading Association. Reprinted with permission of the International Reading Association.)

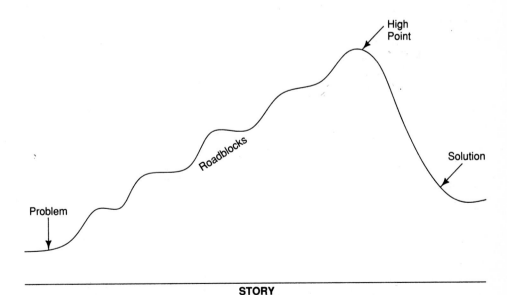

FIGURE 6.7   Plot Profile for *Hey, Al* (Yorinks, 1986)

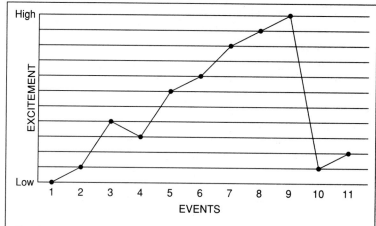

Events:
1. Al and Eddie eat, work, and watch TV together.
2. Al and Eddie argue about living in a house.
3. A bird invites Al and Eddie to be his guest.
4. Al and Eddie wait for the bird to arrive.
5. Al and Eddie arrive at the island.
6. They enjoy the island.
7. They begin turning into birds.
8. They try to fly home.
9. Eddie falls into the water.
10. Al misses Eddie.
11. Eddie comes home and they paint their room.

written at the top of the axis and *low* written at the bottom. The horizontal axis is marked with numbers to correspond with the number of events in the story. On the bottom of the sheet is a space for students to list the events in the story.

2. *Present the grid.* If students have never used a plot profile before, teachers present the grid on an overhead or a chart and explain that they will graph the events of the story and analyze how exciting each event is. First, the students brainstorm a list of the main events (usually 8 to 15 items), and the teacher writes these in order on the list.

3. *Complete the grid.* Students discuss the first event and analyze how exciting it is. Then they assign a level of excitement "score," determining where on the low to high range on the grid to place the event. Then the teacher demonstrates placing a point on the grid at the intersection of the number of the event and the level of excitement score. Students continue discussing each event and marking the excitement level. After all the events have been plotted, the teacher demonstrates drawing a line to connect the points on the plot profile.

4. *Students complete a grid.* Next, students read a story and work in small groups or with partners to complete a plot profile. They list the main events and then place points on the grid to indicate the level of excitement of each event. Then they complete the profile by drawing a line to connect the points.

Plot clusters, diagrams, and grids help students focus both on the content of stories and on their structures. Having students compose plot structure diagrams independently is one way that teachers can assess students' understanding of plot. Teachers can examine students' diagrams for accuracy, detail, and insight.

Character clusters and sociograms. Another important element in stories is character, and being able to make inferences about characters is an important part of understanding stories. Students must infer character traits and their motives in order to interpret story events. Visual displays can help students focus on characters and use evidence to support their inferences about character traits and development. In the case study at the beginning of the chapter Mrs. Galvin's students constructed a *character cluster* to examine Sylvester's character traits (see Figure 6.1). To construct a character cluster students write the character's name in the center of the cluster and draw rays for each character trait. Students can also use character clusters to study the four components of character: appearance, action, dialogue, and thoughts. Students write the character's name in the center of the cluster and then draw out four rays, one for each component of character. Then students add information about each of these four components.

The relationships among characters are often one of the most important aspects of a story. These relationships can be examined using another kind of visual display called a *character sociogram* (Johnson & Louis, 1987). To construct a character sociogram students write the names of the major characters in circles spaced around a page. They draw an arrow from one character's circle to another and write words that describe the relationship between the characters on the arrow. Figure 6.8 presents a sociogram depicting the relationships among Alex, his mother Virginia, and his step-father Jake in *Like Jake and Me* (Jukes, 1984). The following steps may be used to make a character sociogram:

1. *Present the central characters on a large chart or overhead.* Teachers write the main characters' names in circles around a chart leaving enough space between circles to draw arrows and write words describing relationships.

FIGURE 6.8   Character Sociogram for *Like Jake and Me* (Jukes, 1984)

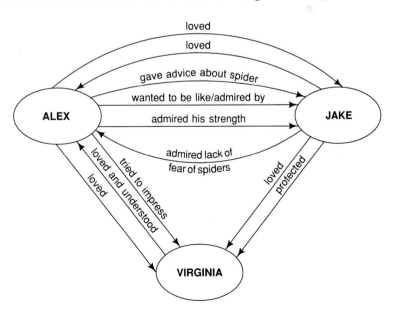

2. *Read the story aloud demonstrating how to infer relationships among characters.* If students are unfamiliar with using character sociograms, teachers demonstrate how to make an inference about a relationship by thinking aloud. For example, teachers read the first page of *Like Jake and Me,* and they explain that Alex is Jake's stepson and that Alex admires how strong Jake is. They draw an arrow from *Alex* to *Jake* and write *admires* on the arrow.

3. *Read the story and invite students to infer relationships.* When students are familiar with character sociograms, teachers read the story aloud or students read, and students describe the relationship between two characters. They draw an arrow on the sociogram between the two characters and write a word or two describing the relationship between the characters on the arrow. Students describe relationships among other characters and add arrows for those relationships to complete the sociogram.

Older students can complete sociograms independently after guided practice with teachers. They can also compare character sociograms made after reading one or two chapters of a chapter book and again at the end of the book. For example, character sociograms of *Charlotte's Web* (White, 1952) made near the beginning of the story and again at the story's end would demonstrate the changing relationships between Wilbur and Charlotte.

Missing person posters.   Another way that students can explore character is by constructing a *missing person poster* (Johnson & Louis, 1987). To construct a missing person poster students draw a picture of a character at the top of a sheet of paper and write the caption "Missing Person" or "Have You Seen This Person?" Then they write a description of the character and include details such as age, height, weight, or eye color. They include information about where the person was last seen and whom to contact with information about the person. They may want to add information about a reward. Stories with lost or missing characters such as *Miss Nelson Is Missing* (Allard, 1977), *Ping* (Flack 1933), and *The Summer of the Swans* (Byars, 1979) make good choices for this activity. Figure 6.9 presents a missing person poster for Liverwurst from *Liverwurst Is Missing* (Mayer, 1981).

Making missing person posters allows students to examine a character from the perspective of other characters. They must reread parts of the story carefully to find details about the character's appearance and to make inferences about how other characters will feel about this character's disappearance.

Literary maps.   Settings are another important component of stories, and students can examine setting by making *literary maps* (Johnson & Louis, 1987). Literary maps are drawings of the settings or portions of the settings of stories with pictures indicating where story events occurred. Figure 6.10 presents a literary map for *Flossie & the Fox* (McKissack, 1986). This map shows where Flossie hid her doll when she was called to carry eggs to the McCutchin's place and the path that she took through the woods. Each place where she stopped to talk to the fox is marked on the map. The steps in teaching literary maps are

1. *Demonstrate constructing a map.* The teacher reads aloud a simple story where the characters move around in the setting. For example, teachers could read

FIGURE 6.9   Missing Person Poster for *Liverwurst Is Missing* (Mayer, 1981)

FIGURE 6.10   Literary Map for *Flossie & the Fox* (McKissack, 1986)

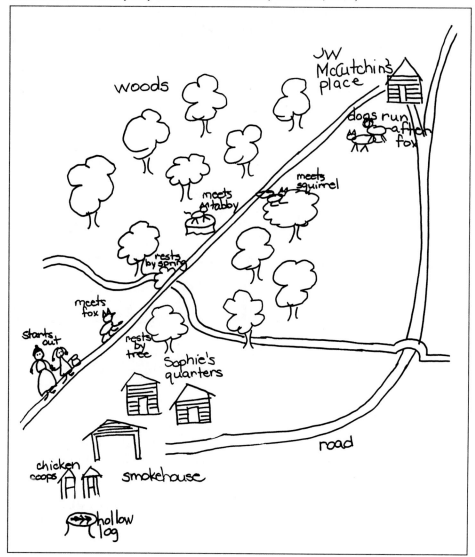

Rosie's Walk (Hutchins, 1968) and map her travels. They would draw where Rosie began her walk on a large sheet of butcher paper and then continue drawing where she went. Teachers talk aloud as they draw the map, explaining how they decided to place the objects and characters in the setting.

2. *Guide students in constructing a map.* Next, the students read a story, and the teacher guides them in making a map by discussing which parts of the setting to include on the map and where they will begin to draw the character's movements. Students make suggestions about what to include on the map, and

then one student draws the map on a chart. Students may draw literary maps in small groups, with partners, or individually.

3. *Encourage map making during independent reading.* Students should be invited to construct literary maps after reading stories in which characters take journeys or where details of houses, tunnels, or buildings or other settings are presented. Recommended stories include *The Gingerbread Boy* (Galdone, 1975), *The Ox-Cart Man* (Hall, 1979), *Little Red Riding Hood* (Hyman, 1983), *Mrs. Frisby and the Rats of NIMH* (O'Brien, 1971), *Sign of the Beaver* (Speare, 1983), and *The Hobbit* (Tolkien, 1938).

Another activity that draws attention to setting is hanging a map of the United States in the classroom on which students mark the locations of stories they have read. For example, *Make Way for Ducklings* (McCloskey, 1941) takes place in Boston, and children might mark Boston on a map with a picture of a duckling. Other books that might be marked on a United States map include *Dragonwings* (Yep, 1975), which takes place in San Francisco; *The Mixed Up Files of Mrs. Basil E. Frankweiler* (Konigsburg, 1967), which is set in New York City; and *The Wall* (Bunting, 1990), which is set in Washington, DC. Children could read *Bridge to Terabithia* (Paterson, 1977), *Sign of the Beaver* (Speare, 1983), and *A Family Apart* (Nixon, 1987) to determine their settings and add them to the settings map. Keeping a map over the school year is a graphic way of illustrating how many books children have read and the different places they traveled in their readings.

Constructing literary maps and keeping track of settings on maps require careful reading for locale and the sequence of events in a story. These activities also encourage students to visualize story events and examine the importance of setting on understanding story events.

Other literary diagrams.   Many stories have distinctive structures. For example, some stories follow a circle structure: the character begins at home, takes a journey and meets danger, and returns home safely again. Examining the structures of stories helps students see the overall organization that authors use in composing stories. *Story structure diagrams* are designed to help students recognize a variety of structures used to organize stories (Galda, 1987; Reutzel, 1985). The students in Ms. Chauvez's class in the case study at the beginning of Chapter 4 were learning about circle stories (Jett-Simpson, 1981) and used a circle structure diagram to retell events in stories with this story structure. To construct this story structure diagram students draw a circle and write words around the circle to represent the events leading from home to home again. Figure 6.11 presents a list of stories that can be diagramed with the circle structure.

Cumulative tales have a different structure. Stories with a cumulative structure involve repetitions in which each event adds a new character, sound, or activity to the story. Figure 6.12 presents a cumulative structure diagram (adapted from Indirisano & Peratore, 1987) that can be used to illustrate the structure found in *Cat Goes Fiddle-i-Fee* (Galdone, 1985). Other cumulative tales that can be explored using similar diagrams are *The Napping House* (Wood, 1984), *It Could Always Be Worse* (Zemach, 1977), *The Bun: A Tale from Russia* (Brown, 1972), and *The House that Jack Built* (Galdone, 1961; Stobbs, 1983).

FIGURE 6.11 List of Circle Stories

Alexander, L. (1978). *The first two lives of Lukas-Kasha.* New York: Dutton. (U)
Duvoisin, R. (1961). *Veronica.* New York: Knopf. (P)
Flack, M. (1932). *Angus lost.* New York: Doubleday. (P)
Flack, M. (1933). *The story about Ping.* New York: Viking. (P)
Grimm, J., & Grimm, W. (1971). *Hansel and Gretel.* New York: Delacorte Press. (P)
Hall, D. (1979). *The ox-cart man.* New York: Viking. (P)
L'Engle, M. (1962). *A wrinkle in time.* New York: Farrar, Straus & Giroux. (U)
McKinley, R. (1984). *The hero and the crown.* New York: Greenwillow. (U)
Munro, L. (1936). *The story of Ferdinand.* New York: Viking. (P)
Oakley, G. (1981). *Hetty and Harriet.* New York: Atheneum. (P–M)
Peet, B. (1965). *Chester the worldly pig.* Boston: Houghton Mifflin. (M)
Potter, B. (1903). *The tale of Peter Rabbit.* New York: Warne. (P–M)
Sendak, M. (1963). *Where the wild things are.* New York: Harper & Row. (P)
Sperry, A. (1940). *Call it courage.* New York: Macmillan. (M)
Steig, W. (1969). *Sylvester and the magic pebble.* New York: Simon & Schuster. (P–M)
Steig, W. (1976). *The amazing bone.* New York: Farrar, Straus & Giroux. (P–M)
Steig, W. (1986). *Brave Irene.* New York: Farrar, Straus & Giroux. (M)
Tolkien, J. (1938). *The hobbit.* Boston: Houghton Mifflin. (U)

P = Primary grades (K–2); M = Middle grades (3–5); U = Upper grades (6–8).

Still other stories have chained structures. In these stories, several events are tightly linked through cause and effect relationships. Figure 6.13 presents a chained structure diagram for the story *Why Mosquitoes Buzz in People's Ears* (Aardema, 1977). Indirisano and Peratore (1987) also suggest exploring *Why the Sun and Moon Live in the Sky* (Dayrell, 1968) through a chain structure diagram.

Discussion accompanies the use of all diagraming, mapping, and clustering activities. As students construct these visual displays, they use problem solving as they talk about story events in small groups or with partners. As they share their

FIGURE 6.12 Cumulative Structure for *Cat Goes Fiddle-i-fee* (Galdone, 1985)

fiddle-i-fee
chimmy-chuck, fiddle-i-fee
quack-quack, chimmy-chuck, fiddle-i-fee
swishy-swashy, quack-quack, chimmy-chuck, fiddle-i-fee
baa-baa, swishy-swashy, quack-quack, chimmy-chuck, fiddle-i-fee
griffy-gruffy, baa-baa, swishy-swashy, quack-quack, chimmy-chuck, fiddle-i-fee
moo-moo, griffy-gruffy, baa-baa, swishy-swashy, quack-quack, chimmy-chuck, fiddle-i-fee
neigh-neigh, moo-moo, griffy-gruffy, baa-baa, swishy-swashy, quack-quack, chimmy-chuck, fiddle-i-fee
bow-wow, neigh-neigh, moo-moo, griffy-gruffy, baa-baa, swishy-swashy, quack-quack, chimmy-chuck, fiddle-i-fee

FIGURE 6.13   Chain Structure for *Why Mosquitoes Buzz in People's Ears* (Aardema, 1977)

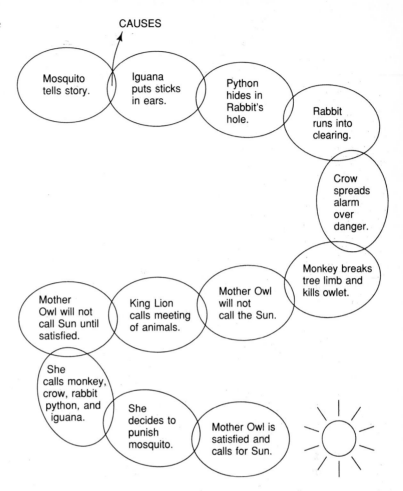

diagrams and other visual displays with classmates, the discussion that ensues provides opportunities for students to present diverse opinions and to articulate rationales, explanations, and supporting opinions about the events, character, settings, and structures of stories and their contributions to a story's meaning.

Focusing on the Author's Craft.   Children who have had many opportunities to listen to stories and poems read aloud develop an intuitive sense of author's craft. They appreciate imagery, comparisons, and the poetic elements of alliteration, repetition, rhyme, and onomatopoeia. They also expand their vocabularies related to themes that they are studying through reading, writing, and discussion activities.

Imagery.   *Imagery* is created when authors and poets appeal to the senses. Imagery is the use of words to cause readers to see, hear, taste, touch, and smell. Teachers can help students appreciate imagery by gathering stories and poems that especially appeal to one sense and sharing these with children. For example the poems "Song of the Train" (McCord, 1984), "I Speak, I Say, I Talk" (Shapiro, 1988), and "The Pickety Fence" (McCord, 1984) appeal strongly to students' sense of hearing. Teachers should read the poems aloud so that students can enjoy the sensory images. Students can discuss why they liked the poems, and such discussions will naturally lead to talk about imagery. Students can be challenged to locate poems that have strong appeals to a sense. Or, students can make five-senses clusters to explore imagery after reading a story or poem. They write the title of the story or poem in the center of the cluster and then draw five rays to circles labeled *see, smell, taste, feel,* and *hear.* Children write phrases and words from the poem or story on lines drawn from the appropriate circle.

   Comparisons.   Two types of comparisons are *similes* (when *like* or *as* is used in the comparison) and *metaphors.* Children can collect examples of effective similes and metaphors. One of children's favorite uses of figurative language is from *Owl Moon* (Yolen, 1987, unpaged): "The snow was whiter than the milk in a cereal bowl." Others come from favorite poems. In "Houses" (Fisher, 1984) the poet compares a house to a face, "The Garden Hose" (Janosco, 1984) portrays a hose as a snake, and "The Car Wash" (Livingston, 1984) likens the machines in a car wash to a large genie.

   Poetic elements.   Students also become sensitive to *alliteration* (repetition of the same initial consonant sound in successive words), *onomatopoeia* (words which, when spoken, sound like their meaning), *repetition* (repeated use of words or phrases), and *rhyme* (words that have the same ending sounds) through reading favorite stories and poems. Children do not have to study poetic elements; instead, they notice and appreciate the power of these elements by sharing favorite stories and poems aloud. Poems should usually be shared orally, rather than merely being read silently. The best poems to share are those which children love to hear again and again.

   Choral reading of favorite poems allows children to develop an intuitive sense of language features. Choral reading is a social reading activity in which individual students and small groups take turns reading aloud the lines or stanzas of a poem (or other piece of writing). Students read aloud in choral reading, but it is different from traditional round-robin reading in which individual students take turns reading aloud to the class. In choral reading, children usually read in small groups or if they read individually, they have volunteered to do so and are reading a familiar text. Choral reading requires active involvement, and students learn to appreciate the sounds, feelings, and magic of the poetry they are reading as well as how to make their own reading more dramatic. It is helpful for students to listen to commercially prepared tapes of professional readers reading poetry so that they can better understand the difference between regular reading and dramatic reading. The steps in choral reading are

   1. *Select literature to share.* Students select poems and other short pieces of writing that they enjoy for choral reading. Paul Fleischman has written two books of poetry specifically for reading aloud. They are *I Am Phoenix: Poems for Two Voices* (1985), a collection of poems about birds, and *Joyful Noise: Poems for Two Voices* (1988), a collection of poems about insects. Many other poems are appropriate for choral reading: for example, Shel Silverstein's "Boa Constrictor," "Full of the Moon" by Karla Kuskin, Laura E. Richard's "Eletelephony," and "Catch a Lit-

tle Rhyme" by Eve Merriam. Many of the poetry books mentioned in Chapter 2 can be used in choral reading interpretations.

Copies of the poem or other work for the choral reading must be made available for all children. Individual copies can be made, or the text can be written on a chart, on sentence strips to be placed in a pocket chart, or on a transparency to be shown on an overhead projector. Sometimes, the poem is available as a big book that all children can see to read together.

2. *Arrange the literature for choral reading.* Students and the teacher arrange the literature for choral reading. First, they decide how the lines and sentences of the text will be read. These are some possibilities:

- A leader reads each line, and the whole class (or a small group) repeats it.
- A leader reads the main parts of the text and the whole class (or small groups) reads the refrain or chorus together.
- Four or five solo readers are chosen to read key parts of the text, and the rest of the text is read in unison by the whole class.
- The class is divided into two groups, and the groups take turns reading the text.

The class discusses the options for arranging the reading and may experiment reading the text in several ways. After the arrangement is decided, students and the teacher mark their copies of the literature indicating who will read which portions.

Another consideration is how each line or sentence will be read. Students decide whether to read lines quickly, joyfully, staccato, or in other dramatic ways. Students consider tempo (how fast or slow to read), rhythm (which words to stress), pitch (when to raise or lower the voice), and juncture (where and how long to pause) for dramatic readings.

3. *Students rehearse the reading.* Students practice reading the literature several times to check the effectiveness of the arrangements they have chosen. Often it is necessary to make changes to make the reading more dramatic.

4. *Students present the choral reading.* For informal choral readings, students remain seated and simply read through the text for their own enjoyment. They may want to tape-record their reading so that they can listen to it. For more formal presentations, background music can be added, and students stand in groups according to the order in which they read. Students who are "leaders" or who have solo parts step forward as they read or stand apart from the rest of the class.

Having students collect examples of poetic elements from authors is one way to help students focus on this important aspect of an author's craft. Teachers might select several sentences that have examples of repeated words and sounds (for example, William Steig's uses of words and sounds in *Sylvester and the Magic Pebble*) and challenge students to find additional examples in the stories. These sentences could be collected on a poster titled "Repetition of Sounds and Words in *Sylvester and the Magic Pebble.*" Teachers could help students notice similes, metaphors, or other poetic elements in other authors' writings. Students might be encouraged to keep a special part of their response journal where they jot down examples of an author's craft that they notice while reading.

Using favorite poems and stories as models for writing is another way that children develop an intuitive appreciation for poetic elements. For example, *The Z Was Zapped* (Van Allsburg, 1987) is a good model for an ABC book. Students read this book and naturally notice the alliterative sentences Chris Van Allsburg used for each alphabet letter. Then they write their own ABC books following Van Allsburg's alliterative pattern, such as "The M made money marching to Mississippi."

Thematic word study.   Children should also have opportunities to learn the vocabulary related to a genre study. For example, as students read King Arthur stories, they learn words such as *feast, knights, companions, charger, armor, challenge, scabbard, Excalibur, Camelot, foe, lance, Guinevere,* and *courtly.* During a focus unit on myths students could be challenged to discover the meaning and origin of words related to Greek and Roman mythology such as *Achilles heel, Amazon River, ambrosia, atlas, calliope, cosmic, echo, fauna, hydra, January, narcissus, nectarine, odyssey, Olympics, phobia, scorpion, typhoon, Uranus,* and *Venus.* Students collect these words on a large chart and use them as they write or construct maps, charts, and diagrams or talk about what they have read.

Extending Step

Extending activities are particularly important, according to the critical perspective because becoming a critical reader involves more than responding to individual works of literature; it means becoming aware of systematic relationships that tie together the stories, poems, and informational books that we call literature. Therefore, extending step activities help students see the connections among several works of literature through reading and writing.

Connecting with Several Works of Literature.   Children should be immersed in reading many stories and poems that are related to one another in some way. These literary works are often part of text sets that teachers have selected to correlate with an author study or focus literature unit. Children might be reading a collection of poems by Jack Prelutsky, a set of alphabet books, folktales with noodlehead characters, or circle stories. Children need many opportunities to share the stories and poems that they are reading and to compare and contrast these works of literature. As they read many of the stories or poems included in text sets focusing on a genre or a particular author, they inductively acquire knowledge about the field of literature.

Venn diagrams.   A *Venn diagram* is one way to help students compare and contrast two or more pieces of literature. A Venn diagram consists of two overlapping circles. Characteristics that are common to two selections of literature are written in the overlapping section of the two circles, and characteristics that are unique to each selection are written in the parts of the two circles that do not overlap. Figure 6.14 shows a Venn diagram completed by a group of fourth graders after reading two of Robert Frost's poems, "The Pasture" (1982) and "Stopping by Woods on a Snowy Evening" (1982). After reading and discussing each of the poems, students talked about how the poems were alike and different. The teacher guided the discussion by having the students think about the setting, mood, people, and events in the poem as well as the narrator's role and the poetic elements Frost used. Upper grade stu-

FIGURE 6.14   Venn Diagram for Robert Frost's Poems "The Pasture" and "Stopping by Woods on a Snowy Evening"

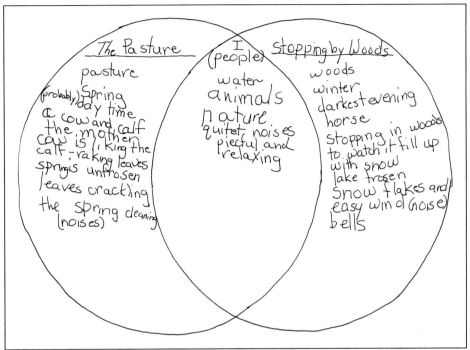

dents might use a Venn diagram to compare *Beauty: A Retelling of the Story of Beauty and the Beast* (McKinley, 1978) with *Beauty and the Beast* (de Beaumont, 1978). The first is the folktale expanded into a novel, and the second is a traditional retelling of the story. Students might compare these two versions to Mayer's beautifully illustrated picture book version of *Beauty and the Beast* (1978).

Studying different versions of the same story is an important extending activity. Students can compare and contrast various versions of *Cinderella, Jack and the Beanstalk, Sleeping Beauty,* and other traditional stories by constructing a chart to compare characters, events, repetitions, and endings. (See Chapter 3 for a list of picture book versions of familiar folktales.) For example, kindergartners used the chart shown in Figure 6.15 to compare and contrast different versions of *The Three Little Pigs.* Students can compare modern literary tales that retell folktales from particular characters' viewpoints, are sequels to the folktales, or change the setting for the stories. For example, middle grade students will appreciate the humor in *Ruby* (Emberley, 1990), a modern, urban version of *Little Red Riding Hood,* and upper grade students can analyze the mood in Anthony Browne's (1982) version of *Hansel and Gretel. The True Story of the 3 Little Pigs* (Scieszka, 1989) presents a new twist to the familiar story that all students enjoy. Even young children catch the play on the traditional story *The Emperor's New Clothes* in *The Principal's New Clothes* (Calmenson, 1989). Some modern literary tales have a decidedly feminist appeal because they allow female characters to be strong and independent. For instance,

FIGURE 6.15   Comparison Chart for Versions of *The Three Little Pigs*

	Paul Galdone (1970)	Galvin Bishop (1989)	James Marshall (1989)
What do the pigs use to build their houses?	straw sticks bricks	straw sticks bricks	straw sticks bricks
What do the pigs wear?	no clothes	shirt coat overalls	pants pants overalls
What does the wolf wear?	no clothes	jacket walkman sunglasses	T-shirt and jacket
What words does the wolf repeat?	Little pig, little pig let me in Then I'll huff and I'll puff and I'll blow your house in	Little pig, little pig let me in Then I'll huff and I'll puff and I'll blow your house in	Little pig, little pig let me in Then I'll huff and I'll puff and I'll blow your house in
What words do the pigs repeat?	No, no! Not by the hair of my chinny chin chin	No, not by the hair of my chinny chin chin	No, no, no, not by the hair of my chinny chin chin Go right ahead
Where do the wolf and the third pig go?	Mr. Smith's Merry Garden Shanklin	Mr. Smith's Merry Garden Shanklin	Farmer Jones' Merry Meadow Hog Hill
How does the story end?	boiled wolf lived happily ever after	wolf fell in pot lived happily ever after	cooked wolf gobbled him up

Jane Yolen (1981) presents a fresh perspective in her *Sleeping Ugly* (see Chapter 4 for a list of feminist folktales).

Studying different versions of folktales and other familiar stories provides opportunities for students to see the common elements among these stories as well as to appreciate the unique perspectives that authors and illustrators bring to familiar stories. As students compare and contrast versions, they gain an awareness of how an author's or illustrator's style contributes to the story's meaning. Upper grade students can examine how different people have historically viewed the messages in folktales as they examine reprinted versions of folktales written decades ago.

Comparison grids. Another way to compare two or more poems or stories is by using *comparison grids* (Johnson & Louis, 1990). A comparison grid is a chart that compares and contrasts a set of stories or poems according to the characteristics of a particular genre. The stories or poems being compared and contrasted are written across the top of a chart and the characteristics are written down the side. For example, Johnson and Louis (1990) suggested that a comparison grid of time-slip stories, fantasies in which the characters move from the present into the future or the past, should include comparisons of the main character, companions, locality #1, locality #2, portal, direction of travel, historical connection, and personal growth. Johnson and Louis devised these characteristics by reading several stories involving a time-slip such as *The Root Cellar* (Lunn, 1983) and *Tom's Midnight Garden* (Pearce, 1959). As they read these stories they noticed that the stories included a main character and a supporting character who either accompanied the main character on the time trip or who was a friendly and helpful character in the altered time setting. They noticed that there were two settings—the place where the story began and ended and the time-slip location. These stories also included a particular portal or gate where the character stepped from one time to another. Time-slip stories usually have dynamic characters who grow and change as a result of their experiences in the other location.

Upper grade students might use a comparison grid to compare the rides of Paul Revere and Jack Jouette, both Revolutionary War patriots, during a unit on the American Revolutionary War. They might compare Longfellow's famous poem of *Paul Revere's Ride* (1990) and Gail E. Haley's account of *Jack Jouette's Ride* (1973). Students could compare the poem and story by answering the questions: Who was the rider? Where did he ride? Why did he ride? Who did he warn? and Was he caught?

Teachers can make comparison grids for stories in different genre, including quests in search of adventure, quests in search of identify, hero tales, and circle stories. These stories are placed in text sets. Then as children read several stories in the text set, they compare and contrast them using a comparison grid. Grids constructed on chart-sized paper provide children with enough space to describe the characteristics of each book. Once the grid is completed, children can discuss the stories and how they illustrate the genre characteristics.

Sequels, trilogies, and series. Children make connections to other literature through sequels, trilogies, or series stories. Many favorite characters reappear in several stories. Readers meet Ramona in Cleary's *Ramona the Pest* (1968), *Ramona the Brave* (1975), *Ramona and Her Father* (1977), and *Ramona Quimby, Age 8* (1981). Another favorite character, Anastasia, appears in *Anastasia Krupnik* (Lowry, 1979), *Anastasia Again!* (Lowry, 1981), and *Anastasia at Your Service* (Lowry, 1982). Lloyd Alexander's trilogies, including *The Westmark* (1981), *The Kestrel* (1982), and *The Beggar Queen* (1984), feature the mythical land of Prydain and appeal to upper grade students as do Susan Cooper's stories about 11-year-old Will Stanton's battles between the forces of good and evil in *The Dark Is Rising* (1973), *The Grey King* (1975), and *Silver on the Tree* (1977). Children enjoy reading these series stories in order, mapping the growth of the characters and their accomplishments.

The Reading-Writing Connection to Literature.   Students expand their understanding of a story through writing, and they can expand their knowledge about a literary genre by writing stories that embody the characteristics of a genre they have studied (Tompkins, 1990). Students can also rewrite stories from different points of view and learn about the effect of perspective on other literary elements. When students write stories they use the writing process. Their experiences with literature serve as prewriting and these extensive reading activities help to make the writing successful. Students draft, revise, and edit their stories before publishing and sharing them with classmates or another appropriate audience.

Genre stories.   Writing a poem or story in a genre or that includes the literary elements being studied is a natural extension activity. Mrs. Galvin's students composed folktales in the case study at the beginning of this chapter, and students can also compose mystery stories, fables, circle stories, and formula poems after reading these genre. Students' stories or poems can be collected and published in class collaboration books. After reading several anthologies of haiku and discussing this genre, students wrote their own haiku poems. One fifth grader wrote this poem:

> *The mud feels slimy*
> *And it splashes through my toes*
> *Making them vanish*

Students use the writing process and sit in the author's chair to share their final copies with classmates. They can also publish their poems as hardbound books or in an anthology.

Pattern books.   Students also explore stories and poems through pattern writing or making innovations on an author's structure. Many stories and poems have repetitive or predictable structures, and students explore these structures by inventing their own content to fit within the structure. Young children enjoy inventing new content for *The Wheels on the Bus* (Raffi, 1987). They might compare their inventions of the story to another version written by Maryann Kovalski (*The Wheels on the Bus,* 1987). Older students might invent new episodes for Judith Viorst's tale of woe in *Alexander and the Terrible, Horrible, No Good, Very Bad Day* (Viorst, 1972) or Audrey Wood's repetitive story *The Napping House* (1984). One third grader wrote his own version of *King Bidgood's in the Bathtub* (Wood, 1985) and it begins this way:

> *Betsy Boo's in the Bathtub*
>
> *"Get out of the bathtub," said Mom.*
> *"No, no!" said Betsy Boo.*
> *"Help! Help!" cried Mom. "Betsy Boo won't get out of the bathtub!"*
> *"I'll get her out," said Dad. "Betsy, it's time to read a book."*
> *"Come in with a read, read, read. Today we read in the bathtub," shouted Betsy.*

Point of view stories.   Students can also rewrite stories from a different point of view. Teachers can introduce the idea of different perspectives or points of view using *The Pain and the Great One* (Blume, 1974), which recounts the same family events from the perspective of an older sister first and then the younger brother. *The True Story of the Three Little Pigs* (Scieszka, 1989) is another point of view spoof in which the familiar story is told from the perspective of the wolf. To compose point of view stories, students reread several versions of a familiar folktale to acquaint themselves with story events and then rewrite the familiar folktale from a character's viewpoint. *Little Red Riding Hood,* for example, might be rewritten from the perspective of the wolf, *Cinderella* from the perspective of the stepmother, or *Hansel and Gretel* from the perspective of the witch. As they rewrite the stories, students make conscious decisions about what content to change or leave out from the familiar version and what content to invent to support the character's perspective in the retelling.

READING FOR INFORMATIONAL PURPOSES

In this section we turn our attention to reading for informational purposes and describe instructional techniques that support children's reading of books and magazines for these purposes. According to the critical perspective, instructional activities focus children's attention on organizational structures that authors use to present information and help children use these structures to learn more information.

Preparing Step

One way to prepare for informational reading is to learn more about the kinds of organizational patterns or structures that authors use to present information. Authors can organize information through the expository text structures of describing, sequencing, comparing and contrasting, showing causes and effects, and presenting problems and their solutions (see Chapter 2 for a description of expository text structures). Students who learn to recognize and use these structures to guide their reading and writing understand what they read and write better than students who do not use such structures.

Teaching Informational Text Structures.   There are many ways to teach students to recognize and use informational or expository text structures. Ms. Jacobs used one method called the *structure strategy* in the case study at the beginning of this chapter. The structure strategy introduces students to information from an informational text by presenting it in an organizer (Richgels, McGee, & Slaton, 1989). Organizers are visual displays of information arranged to show a particular expository text structure. Students use the organizer to write a paragraph using the structure shown on the organizer. Then students read the passage from the informational book written in the structure used in the organizer. The steps in using this strategy are

1. *Select a passage and prepare an organizer.* Teachers select a passage from an informational book or magazine that clearly represents one of the five basic structures and that students will be reading as a part of a theme cycle. Then they prepare a graphic organizer for the passage. This organizer highlights the particular text structure that students will learn, as shown in Figure 6.3.

2. *Present the graphic organizer and teach the content.* Teachers explain through the information presented on the organizer emphasizing both the content and how the content is organized. They also point out clue words that indicate the structure.

3. *Students write a paragraph using the graphic organizer.* Students use the information presented in the organizer to write one or two paragraphs. Students

may write individually, work in small groups, or dictate the paragraph for the teacher to write on a chart or on a transparency for an overhead projector.

4. *Students read the passage and compare it to their compositions.* Students read the passage from the informational book or magazine that was selected in the first step, and teachers guide students in comparing and contrasting how information is presented in the original passage and in the paragraphs written by the students.

5. *Present skeleton organizers.* Teachers prepare skeleton organizers that illustrate the five common expository text structures: description, sequence, compare-contrast, cause-effect, and problem-solution. A skeleton organizer for the compare-contrast structure was presented in Figure 6.4 earlier in the chapter. Figure 6.16 presents skeleton organizers for description, problem-solution, sequence, and cause-effect structures. These organizers can be adapted for the unique characteristics of any passage. For example, one cause-effect passage may have one cause and four effects, whereas another might have three causes and two effects. The cause-effect skeleton organizer can be changed to reflect these differences in structure.

6. *Students read additional passages with similar structures.* Teachers select additional passages representing the structure being studied, and students use skeleton organizers to guide their reading. They are encouraged to construct their own organizers as a way of presenting information they have learned.

The structure strategy is designed to present information that will be useful for later reading. Students have opportunities to see and discuss vocabulary and concepts prior to reading. They also explore the way that the author organizes information before they are expected to detect that organization in a passage.

Becoming familiar with the five expository text structures found in informational books is important because most informational material written for young children is presented in loosely organized descriptive structures or with a combination of structures. Information that is not well organized is more difficult to remember than information presented in well-defined expository text structures. Teachers can help students read poorly organized text and text with combinations of structures. Students who are familiar with the five basic expository structures are more likely to be able to read and remember poorly organized or loosely organized text than students who are not yet familiar with well-organized texts.

Class discussion after reading is one way to build more sophisticated awareness of informational structures. Students might also rewrite information from poorly organized passages into more organized text and then use their text to reread and study content information. Students can note organizations that authors use to present information that are different from the five basic expository structures. For example, some authors present information about familiar events or objects first and then describe information about unfamiliar events or objects. Other authors describe objects from the outside to the inside or from the top to the bottom. Readers need to learn to note these organizations because they can also help readers remember information.

Graphic aids are another important organizational feature of informational books and magazines. Children can use the information presented in graphic aids

FIGURE 6.16   Skeleton Organizers for Description, Problem-Solution, Sequence, and Cause-Effect Structures

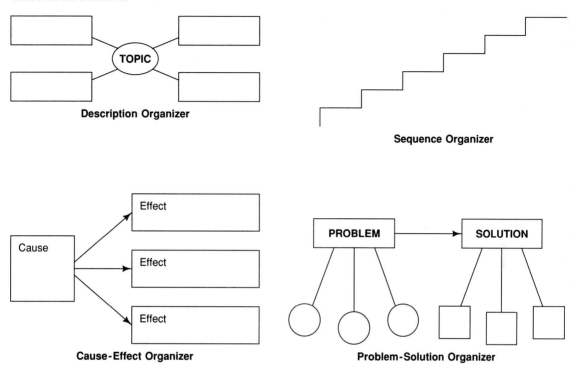

such as graphs, tables, glossaries, indexes, tables of content, and diagrams to prepare for reading. Children might examine the last page in *A Children's Zoo* (Hoban, 1985), which provides a table of zoo animals with their names, a photograph, and information about where they come from, where they live, and what they eat before reading. Two related books *Look at Skin, Shell, and Scale* and *Look at Paws and Claws* (both by Pluckrose, 1989) provide tables for organizing the information in the book. Children might use these tables to guide their reading. *The Weather Sky* (McMillan, 1991) includes weather maps, diagrams, and photographs of different weather conditions that children can examine before reading. Children should learn to preview books before they read and to read the information presented in graphic aids. They can also construct them in the reports and informational books they write.

Previewing can be used to alert students to the importance of graphic aids and to help them prepare for reading. To preview, students skim a selection, reading the table of contents, titles, and subtitles. They examine whether the selection includes an index, references, or glossary. They read any graphs, diagrams, or tables, noting the kinds of information these aids provide. As a previewing activity, students read these aids to make predictions about what they will read, to identify vocabulary to explore as they read, and to activate their prior knowledge. Students can write their predictions and lists of vocabulary words to be examined further in their learning logs.

Reading Step

As students read for informational purposes, they are reading to glean particular information. They should be encouraged to be aware of the author's organizational pattern whether they are reading independently or in guided reading. Reading activities guide students' reading of informational books and magazines by helping them attend to content and how the author presented the content.

One technique that helps students pay attention to the organization of information as they read is the *hierarchical summary procedure* (Taylor, 1982). The steps in using this procedure are

1. *Students construct a skeleton outline.* Students preview a short article from a magazine or section of an informational book to identify the number of subsections. (Teachers should select a text with at least three subsections.) Then students construct a skeleton outline that they complete as they read the selection. First, they write a capital letter (i.e., *A, B, C* and so on) for every subsection in the selection and leave five or six lines between each capital letter. As students preview the selection, they discuss the titles of the subsections and predict what they will read about.

2. *Students read and write a main idea for a subsection.* Students read the first subsection and write a one-sentence main idea statement. Then they list two, three, or four supporting ideas from the subsection.

3. *Students repeat the procedure for each subsection.* Students read each subsection and write one main idea and several supporting details.

4. *Students write a topic sentence for the entire selection.* After reading the entire passage, students consider the overall purpose and content of the selection, and they write a topic sentence to summarize the selection.

5. *Students review their hierarchical summaries and retell.* Students reread their summaries to develop an oral retelling of the selection. They give their summary to a partner and then retell the summary to the partner. Then the partner provides feedback on how much of the information from the summary the student retold.

Once students are familiar with the hierarchical summary procedure, they should discuss how to use its principles when reading and studying independently. This procedure highlights the importance of previewing a selection before reading and pausing to summarize what has been read. Students should be encouraged to use these strategies as they read on their own.

Exploring Step

During exploring activities students reread and think again about their reading to better understand information they have read. Most exploring activities help students use an author's structure to recall and organize information and explore vocabulary. Discussions following the structure strategy and the hierarchical summary procedure are useful techniques that require rereading and thinking. Students also construct timelines, lifelines, and ladders to accomplishment to explore the lives of famous people. Finally, students learn more information when they examine vocabulary with related root words.

Rereading and Thinking.   Students gain insight about how authors present information and how that presentation helps them learn through discussion, constructing visuals such as organizers and lifelines, and writing their own well-constructed passages.

   Timelines.   *Timelines* are a visual display of the sequence of events from history. To construct a timeline, students draw a horizontal line and mark the line with important dates related to a specific event or historical period. Students might construct a timeline for the building of the Greek Parthenon after reading *The Parthenon* (Woodford, 1983) or for the history of windows after reading *Let There Be Light: A Book About Windows* (Giblin, 1988).

   Lifelines are a variation of timelines. Lifelines illustrate the accomplishments of a famous person or an ordinary person who has admirable qualities. Constructing lifelines encourages careful rereading and thinking about biographies and autobiographies (Tompkins, 1990). Students use long sheets of shelf paper, construct a line with appropriate dates marked, and write the important events in the person's life. Students may also illustrate their lifelines with scenes of important moments in a person's life.

   Ladders to accomplishments are similar to lifelines. Students write the events in a person's life leading to an important accomplishment on the rungs of a ladder. Figure 6.17 presents a ladder to accomplishment constructed after reading *The Glorious Flight* (Provensen & Provensen, 1983). This book tells of Louis Bleriot's efforts to build an airplane that would fly across the English Channel.

   Constructing timelines, lifelines, and ladders to accomplishments focuses students' attention on the sequence and significance of events in history or from a person's life. Students must read critically to determine which events are important enough to include on a timeline and then reread to check the dates of these significant events.

Focusing on the Author's Craft.   Authors of informational books and materials craft their language very carefully. They use language to help students gain many concepts about content topics through their careful presentation of specialized vocabulary. Informational books present clear explanations of processes and examples of principles as they introduce students to the language and terminology related to the topic. Students' learning content material often is facilitated by carefully examining the specialized vocabulary. Teachers can use techniques such as having students keep a log of special vocabulary words that they encounter while reading, helping students use context to figure out the meanings of specialized vocabulary, and having students use new vocabulary words in quickwrites or other informal writing activities.

   Another way that students can learn more about specialized vocabulary is to learn the history of familiar word groups, such as words built from Latin and Greek roots. Many informational reading materials include words with these roots. For example, the Greek root *meter,* meaning *measure,* is found in the words *barometer, centimeter, kilometer, ceilometer, anemometer,* and *thermometer*—words fre-

FIGURE 6.17 Ladder to Accomplishment for *The Glorious Flight* (Read from bottom up.) (Provensen & Provensen, 1983)

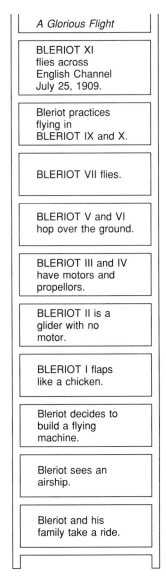

A Glorious Flight

BLERIOT XI
flies across
English Channel
July 25, 1909.

Bleriot practices
flying in
BLERIOT IX and X.

BLERIOT VII flies.

BLERIOT V and VI
hop over the ground.

BLERIOT III and IV
have motors and
propellors.

BLERIOT II is a
glider with no
motor.

BLERIOT I flaps
like a chicken.

Bleriot decides to
build a flying
machine.

Bleriot sees an
airship.

Bleriot and his
family take a ride.

quently found in informational books about weather. Therefore, knowing this root is particularly useful when the students are engaged in a theme cycle on weather. Sometimes teachers select one or two words with Latin or Greek roots for direct instruction. These words selected for direct instruction should be related to crucial concepts that the students need for the theme cycle and represent a root word which is useful in learning many words. For example, during a theme on famous scientists and their discoveries, one teacher selected the word *credible* for intensive study because many words are related to the word *credible* through the root word *cred*. The steps in teaching vocabulary with related root words are as follows (Tompkins & Hoskisson, 1991):

1. *Find out about the word.* Teachers look up the word in an unabridged dictionary, check its meaning and etymology (history), and make a list of words with the same root word. For example, the word *credible* comes from the root *cred* and means being believed or trustworthy. Other words with the root *cred* include *incredible, credulity, credulous, creed,* and *credit.*

2. *Present the word as a part of a cluster.* Teachers draw a cluster and write the root word *cred* in the center. They select a word with that root that is likely to be familiar to students, to introduce first. For example, teachers may begin the study of *cred* words with *credit card.* Teachers draw a ray from the center of the cluster and write a related word on the ray. Students tell what they know about this related word. Then teachers add other rays to the cluster for additional related words. As students discuss each word's meaning, the teacher adds the words to the cluster. Finally, students discuss how the words are related to each other and to the root word.

Students should be challenged to use words learned in direct instruction lessons in their writing and talking activities. They should be encouraged to note when words are related to one another through common root words. Teachers can help students recognize the usefulness of such knowledge for spelling as well as for reading.

Extending Step

Extending activities allow students to enjoy and learn from a wide variety of literature using their newly acquired understandings of the organizations and structures associated with informational books and magazines. Teachers can help students extend their knowledge of organization by gathering text sets that focus particularly on informational text structures. For example, students who are studying weather can extend their study of both weather and the cause-effect structure by reading *Flash, Crash, Rumble, and Roll* (Branley, 1985) and *The Weather Sky* (McMillan, 1991). Students can also extend their knowledge of content by modeling their writing on other kinds of texts with unique organizational features such as those found in alphabet books. Students can extend to stories and poems through informational book structures; some poems and stories include structures found in informational books.

Alphabet books. Alphabet books are informational books that present information in a unique structure according to the sequence of letters in the alphabet. They may also have an additional structure such as the formula "A is for _____ ," "B is for _____ ," "C is for _____ ," and so on. Students can use the structures found in alphabet books to write their own ABC books about the content information they have been studying. For example, students might want to demonstrate their understanding of weather by composing an alphabet book about weather.

Before they compose their own alphabet books, students examine alphabet books to identify the formula that authors use to present information, write the alphabet on a chart, and brainstorm key words and other information about the topic related to each letter. Students each select a letter and write one page for a class book or they can write alphabet books individually. Students use the writing process to revise and edit their pages and compile the final copies to make the class book.

Ms. Jacobs' students in the case studies at the beginning of the chapter composed an invertebrate alphabet book. The text of their alphabet book begins:

A is for animal, but not all animals have backbones.
B is for backbone, and vertebrate animals have backbones.
C is for chordata, and that's what scientists call backbones.

Expository text structures in stories.   While expository text structures are characteristically found in informational books and magazines, authors sometimes embed these structures in stories, and students can examine stories that use these structures. Students who are learning about expository text structures through reading informational books will enjoy finding the compare-contrast structure in stories such as *Two Islands* (Gantschev, 1985), *Frog and Toad Are Friends* (Lobel, 1970), *Come Away from the Water, Shirley* (Birningham, 1977), and *Sarah, Plain and Tall* (MacLachlan, 1985). Students can use a Venn diagram to compare the settings of the two islands, the characteristics of the two friends—Frog and Toad, Shirley's activities at the beach and as a pirate, and Sarah's memories of the sea in contrast to her perceptions of the prairie. Stories that have sequence structures include *The Very Hungry Caterpillar* (Carle, 1970) and *The House on Maple Street* (Pryor, 1987). Students could use the sequence organizer (shown in Figure 6.16) to explore the sequence of foods that the caterpillar eats and the sequence of events that happens on Maple Street. Cause-effect structures are found in *Why Mosquitoes Buzz in People's Ears* (Aardema, 1975), and students can examine this structure through the chained structure diagram shown in Figure 6.13. Problem-solution structures are found in *A New Coat for Anna* (Ziefert, 1986), *Huge Harold* (Peet, 1961), and *Number the Stars* (Lowry, 1989), and students can discuss how Anna's mother bartered things for Anna's new coat, how Harold solved his problem of being too big, and how Annemarie solved the problem of getting her Jewish friend Ellen Rosen to safety.

MAKING DECISIONS ABOUT TEACHING
FROM A CRITICAL PERSPECTIVE

Teachers must make several decisions about teaching reading from the critical perspective. They must decide which genres, literary characteristics, or authors and illustrators to teach and which stories, books, and poems they will select for this instruction. Most children's literature experts recommend that students in every grade be exposed to the major genres of literature and they study at least a few authors and illustrators every year.

Students should examine increasingly complex examples of the various genres from kindergarten through eighth grade. For example, in a study of folktales, kindergartners begin to learn cumulative stories such as *Henny Penny* (Galdone, 1968), *The Three Little Pigs* (Galdone, 1970), and *The Little Red Hen* (Zemach, 1983), and the repetitive features of these stories make them easier for young children to read. Middle grade students explore tall tale heroes such as Johnny Appleseed, Pecos Bill, Paul Bunyan, and Davy Crockett in conjunction with social studies themes on westward movement, and upper grade students examine Greek, Roman, and Norse myths in conjunction with social studies units on ancient civilizations.

Students should also have opportunities to develop increasingly sophisticated understandings of literary elements, expository text structures, and elements of authors' and illustrators' craft. Kindergartners might identify the main characters of stories, whereas middle grade students might examine the character traits of main characters and the relationships among characters, and upper grade students might examine how character reveals theme. However, we caution teachers that reading literature should be first and foremost an enjoyable activity. Analyzing character traits or detecting story structures should never become more important than fostering the appreciation and love of literature. Teachers must always keep in mind that students learn about literature as they enjoy it; therefore, they should plan activities that do not quell children's natural love of stories, poems, and informational books.

To make decisions about the selection of instructional activities, teachers first carefully read and respond to stories, books, and poems that they will use in instruction. They read and reread a particular story, informational book, or poem analyzing and evaluating its literary qualities (see Chapters 2 and 3). Only when teachers are thoroughly familiar with a particular literary selection and have made decisions about the qualities of the selection that merit attention are they ready to make decisions about instruction and activities that will best support children's exploration of the

FIGURE 6.18 Overview of Activities for the Critical Perspective

	Reading for Literary Purposes	**Reading for Informational Purposes**
Step 1: Preparing to read	Teach literary element, genre, author/illustrator style	Structure strategy Preview graphic aids
Step 2: Reading the text	Modified DRTA	Hierarchical summary procedure
Step 3: Exploring the text	Story boards Beginning-middle-end clusters Plot diagrams Plot profiles Character sociograms Literary maps Missing person posters Improving on author's structure Genre study of words	Organizers Lifelines Ladders to accomplishments Structure frames Intensive word study
Step 4: Extending from the text	Text sets by genre, author, element Venn diagrams Compare versions Comparison grids Sequels, series Stories from different points of view	Reports using informational structures Alphabet books Compare structures in stories and informational books

FIGURE 6.19   Summary Chart for Decision Tree

Decision Tree

Chapter 1	Using Literature in the Reading Program
Chapter 2	Choosing Literature for Children
Chapter 3	Learning About Authors and Illustrators
Chapter 4	Identifying Perspectives on Reading Instruction
Chapter 5	Teaching from a Reader Response Perspective

Teaching from a Critical Perspective

- **Plan a literature program that includes the study of authors, illustrators, genres, and literary elements.**

- **Coordinate planning of literature programs with other teachers so that children's experiences with literature build from grade to grade and are based on previous experiences.**

Chapter 6

- **Assess whether students need teacher-directed or independent preparing, reading, exploring, and extending activities.**

- **Select an appropriate activity that meets the needs of individual learners, is consonant with the purpose of reading, and is appropriate to the selection by understanding individual learners, reading and analyzing the selection, and consulting professional resources**

- **Consult school or state curriculum guides for lists of expected competencies or learning outcomes.**

Chapter 7	Teaching from an Interactive Perspective
Chapter 8	Putting It All Together
Chapter 9	Assessing Students' Learning

work. For example, in the case study at the beginning of this chapter Mrs. Galvin wanted her students to become knowledgeable about modern literary tales, and she selected *Sylvester and the Magic Pebble* to launch this instruction. She analyzed this selection and then selected clustering activities because they could be used to focus on character and motifs—critical elements in this story and in modern literary tales (Chapter 8 also addresses instructional planning).

Teachers also decide when students need teacher-directed preparing, reading, exploring, and extending activities and when students can engage in these activities independently. This decision must be based on an awareness of individual learners that comes through careful observation of students and reflective interaction with them.

Finally, teachers select activities that best fit students' needs and are appropriate for the particular story, poem, or informational book being read. Figure 6.18 presents a list of the activities introduced in this chapter. Teachers should be thoroughly familiar with the stories, poems, and informational books they plan to use in instruction. Careful attention to the literary elements and to the craft that authors and illustrators have used is essential in making a decision about any instructional activity. Each activity should be selected so that it both heightens students' enjoyment and understanding of the selection and provides opportunities for learning new information that will enrich future reading. Finally, teachers should consult with school district or state curriculum guides to become informed about the learning outcomes or literacy competencies that they are expected to teach.

The decisions that teachers must make about supporting students' reading according to the critical perspective are

- Plan a literature program that includes the study of authors, illustrators, the major genres, and literary elements.
- Coordinate planning of literature programs with other teachers so that children's experiences with literature build from grade to grade and are based on previous experiences.
- Assess whether students need teacher-directed or independent preparing, reading, exploring, or extending activities.
- Select an appropriate activity that meets the needs of individual learners, is consonant with the purposes of reading, and is appropriate for the selection by understanding individual students and by analyzing the selection.
- Consult system or state curriculum guides for lists of expected competencies or learning outcomes.

This information is added to the decision-making diagram, as shown in Figure 6.19.

REFERENCES

Galda, L. (1987). Teaching higher order reading skills with literature: Intermediate grades. In B. Cullinan (Ed.), *Children's literature in the reading program* (pp. 89–95). Newark, DE: International Reading Association.

Indirisano, R., & Paratore, J. (1987). The republic of childhood and the reading disabled. In B. Cullinan (Ed.). *Children's literature in the reading program* (pp. 139–148). Newark, DE: International Reading Association.

Jett-Simpson, M. (1981). Writing stories using model structures: The circle story. *Language Arts, 58,* 293–300.

Johnson, T., & Louis, D. (1990). *Bringing it all together: A program for literacy.* Portsmouth, NH: Heinemann.

Louis, D. & Johnson, T. (1987). *Literacy through literature.* Portsmouth, NH: Heinemann.

Macan, J. M., Bewell, D., & Vogt, M. E. (1991). *Responses to literature, grades K–8.* Newark, DE: International Reading Association.

Reutzel, D. (1985). Story maps improve comprehension. *The Reading Teacher, 38,* 400–404.

Richgels, D., McGee, L., & Slaton, E. (1989). Teaching expository text structures in reading and writing. In D. Muth (Ed.), *Children's comprehension of text: Research into practice* (pp. 167–184). Newark, DE: International Reading Association.

Taylor, B. (1982). A summarizing strategy to improve middle grade students' reading and writing skills. *The Reading Teacher, 36,* 202–205.

Tompkins, G. (1990). *Teaching writing: Balancing*

process and product. New York: Merrill/Macmillan.

Tompkins, G., & Hoskisson, K. (1991). *Language arts: Content and teaching strategies* (2nd Ed.). New York: Merrill/Macmillan.

CHILDREN'S LITERATURE REFERENCES

Aardema, V. (1975). *Why mosquitoes buzz in people's ears.* New York: Dial.

Aardema, V. (1977). *Who's in Rabbit's house?* New York: Dial.

Alexander, L. (1981). *The westmark.* New York: Dutton.

Alexander, L. (1982). *The kestrel.* New York: Dutton.

Alexander, L. (1984). *The beggar queen.* New York: Dutton.

Allard, H. (1977). *Miss Nelson is missing.* Boston: Houghton Mifflin.

Bare, C. (1989). *Never kiss an alligator!* New York: Dutton.

Birningham, J. (1977). *Come away from the water, Shirley.* New York: Harper & Row.

Bishop, G. (1989). *The three little pigs.* New York: Scholastic.

Blume, J. (1974). *The pain and the great one.* New York: Bradbury.

Branley, F. (1985). *Flash, crash, rumble, and roll* (rev. ed.). New York: Harper & Row.

Brown, M. (1947). *Goodnight moon.* New York: Harper & Row.

Brown, M. (1972). *The bun: A tale from Russia.* New York: Harcourt Brace Jovanovich.

Browne, A. (1982). *Hansel and Gretel.* New York: Watts.

Bunting, E. (1990). *The wall.* New York: Clarion.

Byars, B. (1979). *The summer of the swans.* New York: Viking.

Calmenson, S. (1989). *The principal's new clothes.* New York: Scholastic.

Cleary, B. (1968). *Ramona the pest.* New York: Morrow.

Carle, E. (1970). *The very hungry caterpillar.* New York: Viking.

Cleary, B. (1975). *Ramona the brave.* New York: Morrow.

Cleary, B. (1977). *Ramona and her father.* New York: Morrow.

Cleary, B. (1981). *Ramona Quimby, age 8.* New York: Morrow.

Cooper, S. (1973). *The dark is rising.* New York: Atheneum.

Cooper, S. (1975). *The grey king.* New York: Atheneum.

Cooper, S. (1977). *Silver on the tree.* New York: Atheneum.

Dayrell, E. (1968). *Why the sun and moon live in the sky.* Boston: Houghton Mifflin.

de Beaumont, M. (1978). *Beauty and the beast.* New York: Bradbury.

dePaola, T. (1975). *Strega Nona.* New York: Simon & Schuster.

Emberley, M. (1990). *Ruby.* Boston: Little, Brown.

Fisher, A. (1984). "Houses." In J. Cole (Sel.), *A new treasury of children's poems.* Garden City, NY: Doubleday.

Flack, M. (1933). *Ping.* New York: Viking.

Fleischman, P. (1985). *I am Phoenix: Poems for two voices.* New York: Harper & Row.

Fleischman, P. (1988). *Joyful noise: Poems for two voices.* New York: Harper & Row.

Frost, R. (1982). "The Pasture." In R. Frost, *A swinger of birches.* Owings Mill, MD: Stemmer House.

Frost, R. (1982). "Stopping by woods on a snowy evening." In R. Frost, *A swinger of birches.* Owings Mill, MD: Stemmer House.

Galdone, P. (1961). *The house that Jack built.* New York: McGraw-Hill.

Galdone, P. (1968). *Henny Penny.* New York: Seabury.

Galdone, P. (1970). *The three little pigs.* New York: Seabury.

Galdone, P. (1975). *The gingerbread boy.* New York: Seabury.

Galdone, P. (1985). *Cat goes fiddle-i-fee.* New York: Clarion.

Gantschev, I. (1985). *Two islands.* New York: Picture Book Studio.

Giblin, J. (1988). *Let there be light: A book about windows.* New York: Crowell.

Grimm, J., & Grimm, W. (1981). *Hansel and Gretel.* New York: Franklin Watts.

Haley, G. (1973). *Jack Jouett's ride.* New York: Viking.

Hall, D. (1979). *The ox-cart man.* New York: Viking.

Hoban, T. (1985). *A children's zoo.* New York: Greenwillow.

Hutchins, P. (1968). *Rosie's walk.* New York: Macmillan.

Hyman, T. (1983). *Little red riding hood.* New York: Holiday House.

Isadora, R. (1989). *The princess and the frog.* New York: Greenwillow.

Janosco, B. (1984). "The garden hose." In J. Cole (Sel.), *A new treasury of children's poems.* Garden City, NY: Doubleday.

Jukes, M. (1984). *Like Jake and me.* New York: Knopf.

Konigsburg, E. (1967). *The mixed up files of Mrs. Basil E. Frankweiler.* New York: Atheneum.

Kovalski, M. (1987). *The wheels on the bus.* Boston: Little, Brown.

Livingston, M. (1984). "The car wash." In J. Cole (Sel.), *A new treasury of children's poems.* Garden City, NY: Doubleday.

Lobel, A. (1970). *Frog and toad are friends.* New York: Harper & Row.

Longfellow, H. (1990). *Paul Revere's ride.* New York: Dutton.

Lowry, L. (1979). *Anastasia Krupnik.* Boston: Houghton Mifflin.

Lowry, L. (1981). *Anastasia again!.* Boston: Houghton Mifflin.

Lowry, L. (1982). *Anastasia at your service.* Boston: Houghton Mifflin.

Lowry, L. (1989). *Number the stars.* Boston: Houghton Mifflin.

Lunn, J. (1983). *The root cellar.* New York: Scribner's Sons.

MacLachlan, P. (1985). *Sarah, plain and tall.* New York: Harper & Row.

Marshall, J. (1989). *The three little pigs.* New York: Dial.

Mayer, E. (1978). *Beauty and the beast.* New York: Macmillan.

Mayer, M. (1981). *Liverwurst is missing.* New York: Four Winds Press.

McCloskey, R. (1941). *Make way for ducklings.* New York: Viking.

McCord, D. (1984). "The pickety fence." In J. Cole (Sel.), *A new treasury of children's poems.* Garden City, NY: Doubleday.

McCord, D. (1984). "The song of the train." In J. Cole (Sel.), *A new treasury of children's poems.* Garden City, NY: Doubleday.

McKinley, R. (1978). *Beauty: A retelling of the story of beauty and the beast.* New York: Harper & Row.

McKissack, P. (1986). *Flossie & the fox.* New York: Dial.

McMillan, B. (1991). *The weather sky.* New York: Farrar, Straus & Giroux.

Nixon, J. (1987). *A family apart.* New York: Bantam.

O'Brien, R. (1971). *Mrs. Frisby and the rats of NIHM.* New York: Scribner's.

Pallota, J. (1986). *The yucky reptile alphabet book.* Watertown, MA: Ivory Tower.

Parker, N., & Wright, J. (1990). *Frogs, toads, lizards, and salamanders.* New York: Greenwillow.

Paterson, K. (1977). *Bridge to Terabithia.* New York: Harper & Row.

Pearce, P. (1959). *Tom's midnight garden.* New York: Lippincott.

Peet, B. (1961). *Huge Harold.* Boston: Houghton Mifflin.

Pluckrose, H. (1989). *Look at paws and claws.* New York: Franklin Watts.

Pluckrose, H. (1989). *Look at skin, shell, and scale.* New York: Franklin Watts.

Provensen, A., & Provensen, M. (1983). *The glorious flight across the Channel with Louis Bleriot, July 25, 1909.* New York: Viking.

Pryor, B. (1987). *The house on Maple Street.* New York: Morrow.

Scieszka, J. (1989). *The true story of the 3 little pigs.* New York: Viking.

Sendak, M. (1963). *Where the wild things are.* New York: Harper & Row.

Shapiro, A. (1988). "I speak, I say, I talk." In T. dePaola, *Tomie dePaola's book of poems.* New York: G. P. Putnam's.

Speare, E. (1983). *Sign of the beaver.* Boston: Houghton Mifflin.

Steig, W. (1969). *Sylvester and the magic pebble.* New York: Simon & Schuster.

Steig, W. (1976). *The amazing bone.* New York: Farrar, Straus & Giroux.

Stobbs, W. (1983). *The house that Jack built.* London: Oxford University Press.

Tolkien, J. (1938). *The hobbit.* Boston: Houghton Mifflin.

Tolstoy, A. (1969). *The great big enormous turnip.* New York: Franklin Watts.

Van Allsburg, C. (1987). *The z was zapped.* Boston: Houghton Mifflin.

Viorst, J. (1972). *Alexander and the terrible,*

horrible, no good, very bad day. New York: Atheneum.

White, E. B. (1952). *Charlotte's web.* New York: Harper & Row.

Williams, J. (1973). *Petronella.* New York: Parents' Magazine Press.

Wood, A. (1984). *The napping house.* San Diego: Harcourt Brace Jovanovich.

Woodford, S. (1983). *The Parthenon.* Cambridge: Lerner.

Yep, L. (1975). *Dragonwings.* New York: Harper & Row.

Yolen, J. (1981). *Sleeping ugly.* New York: Coward-McCann.

Yolen, J. (1987). *Owl moon.* New York: Philomel.

Yorinks, A. (1986). *Hey, Al.* New York: Farrar, Straus & Giroux.

Zemack, M. (1977). *It could always be worse.* New York: Farrar, Straus & Giroux.

Zemack, M. (1983). *The little red hen.* New York: Farrar, Straus & Giroux.

Ziefert, H. (1986). *A new coat for Anna.* New York: Knopf.

CHAPTER 7

TEACHING FROM AN INTERACTIVE PERSPECTIVE

In this chapter you will learn to make decisions about:

- Considering whether students will be reading for literary or informative purposes
- Assessing whether students need teacher-directed or independent preparing, reading, exploring, and extending activities
- Selecting an appropriate activity that meets the needs of individual students, is consonant with the purposes of reading, and fits the text
- Consulting school system or state curriculum guides for lists of competencies or learning outcomes
- Keeping informed of new instructional techniques and theories by reading professional journals and books

THIS IS THE THIRD of three chapters that explore instructional activities that extend children's reading abilities through experiences with literature. In this chapter, we discuss teaching reading in a literature-based program from an interactive perspective. In the following case studies, Ms. Nee and Mr. Roberts teach reading from an interactive perspective. They provide activities during each step of the reading process to ensure that their students understand the story or informational book that they are reading and acquire more sophisticated reading strategies. In the first case study, Ms. Nee's students read for literary purposes, and in the second, Mr. Roberts' students read for informational purposes. Each of these lessons reflects careful consideration of both the purpose for instruction and the unique qualities and content of the story and informational book selected for instruction.

A CASE IN POINT

Ms. Nee's Guided Reading of *Sylvester and the Magic Pebble*

Ms. Nee gathers a group of her third graders. She asks, "What is the most important thing in the world to have? How can you get it?" Students suggest having lots of money, becoming famous, being popular, being healthy, being happy, and doing good deeds. They talk about ways they might obtain these things: by working hard, being well-behaved, listening to their parents, being talented and successful, and being smart. Then Ms. Nee explains that the character in the story they are going to read today discovers what is most important to him, and she reads the title and shows the cover of *Sylvester and the Magic Pebble* (Steig, 1969).

The children then make several predictions about what might happen in the story, and Ms. Nee records these predictions on the chalkboard: the pebble will make magic happen, a donkey named Sylvester will find a magic pebble, and a boy will find a magic pebble and turn into a donkey. Children write one or two of the predictions in their literature journals. Then children read the first part of the story and discuss whether their predictions were confirmed, rejected, or still might happen. They also compare how the story they have read so far relates to their discussion of what is most important. The children write predictions again, read several pages, and discuss these predictions. After writing several more predictions in their literature journals, the children continue reading the story independently. Later students verify their predictions by writing about the events of the story and noting how useful their predictions were.

The next day children share their journal entries and discuss the story. Ms. Nee begins the discussion by asking, "What do you think about the story?" The students tell what they liked, what was most interesting, and what questions they have about confusing parts. Then Ms. Nee shows on the overhead projector five sentences from the story, each with a word deleted (the deleted words are *perfectly, gradually, aimlessly, suddenly,* and *sadly*):

> It was flaming red, shiny, and _____ round, like a marble.
> It didn't stop _____ as rains usually do. It CEASED.
> Mr. Duncan walked _____ about while Mrs. Duncan set out the picnic food on the rock.
> "You know, Father," she said _____ , "I have the strangest feeling that our dear Sylvester is still alive and not far away."
> Mr. Duncan looked _____ at her as if to say, "How can you ask such a question?"

The children discuss the sentences and make guesses about words that would fit the deletions and tell why they would make sense. For example, the children suggest the words *very* and *nearly* to complete the first sentence. Then they reread the story, locate the words used by the author, and Ms. Nee writes them in the sentences. One student notices that all the deleted words from the story end in *ly.* Ms. Nee explains that *ly* is a suffix. She says, "Suffixes are letters added at the end of a word, and when the suffix is 'peeled off', a meaningful, real word is left." Ms. Nee demonstrates the effect of peeling off the *ly* suffix on the word *perfectly,* and she discusses the meaning of the root word *perfect* and the meaning of the word with the suffix added. Then the students peel off the *ly* suffix from the other words and discuss the meanings of the root words and the words with suffixes. Ms. Nee tells the students that it is useful to know about the *ly* suffix to figure out how to read a word or how to figure out the meaning of a word.

Then Ms. Nee passes out copies of *The Amazing Bone* (Steig, 1976), and she presents a minilesson to review the prediction and verification strategies that students used in reading *Sylvester and the Magic Pebble.* She demonstrates the strategies by thinking aloud as she reads the first few pages of *The Amazing Bone.* After reading the title, she makes three or four predictions about what might happen in the story. Then she pauses to discuss whether her predictions were verified and to elaborate on the information from the text and illustrations. After the minilesson, children read the story independently and practice the strategies.

A CASE IN POINT

Mr. Roberts' Vertebrate Animal Theme

Mr. Roberts' sixth graders are studying vertebrate animals, and he expects that they will expand their knowledge by being able to explain the characteristics of mammals, birds, reptiles, amphibians, and fish. Mr. Roberts wants his students to describe the animals' reproduction and life cycles, habitats, physical characteristics, and diet. He has live animals in the classroom including a hamster, frog, newt, salamander, and several tadpoles and fish. The science center has a collection of books about animals, magazines with information about animals, and pictures of animals. The students have learning logs in which they record their observations of the animals, summaries of books and articles they have read, and lists of theme-related words. A word wall, a large sheet of paper on which students have written over 70 words related to their study of vertebrates, hangs on one wall of the classroom.

Mr. Roberts meets with eight students at the reading table to continue reading from *Frogs, Toads, Lizards, and Salamanders* (Parker & Wright, 1991). A list of information that the students brainstormed about reptiles and amphibians before reading this book is spread out on the reading table. The list is divided into three questions: "Where do different kinds of amphibians and rep-

tiles live?" "What do different kinds of amphibians and reptiles eat?" and "What do different kinds of amphibians and reptiles do?" The students used these three questions to guide their reading of the first portion of the book, and they wrote the answers to the questions on chart paper.

Mr. Roberts explains that students will use the reciprocal teaching procedure today to read pages 40 and 41 in *Frogs, Toads, Lizards, and Salamanders*. The students are familiar with this procedure, so Mr. Roberts calls on a volunteer to begin. Al begins by making a prediction, "I see two diagrams of the insides of a frog and a lizard. I predict we'll read about the insides of a frog and a lizard." Mr. Roberts tells Al that this is a good prediction because it uses information from the illustration. He asks Al to read the first sentence on page 40 to see if that makes any difference in his prediction. After reading, Al notes that the paragraph will probably be about the differences between amphibians and reptiles. Mr. Roberts is pleased and explains, "Al's prediction is important because it will guide the kinds of information you will look for

FIGURE 7.1 Semantic Feature Analysis for *Frogs, Toads, Lizards, and Salamanders* (Parker & Wright, 1991)

	Amphibian	Reptile	Caudata	Salienta	Warm-blooded	Cold-blooded	Dry skin	Moist skin	Voiceless	Lay eggs in water	Lay eggs on land	Clawed feet
Hellbender												
California Newt												
Eastern Spadefoot Toad												
American Toad												
Bullfrog												
African Clawed Frog												
Mediterranean Gecko												
Western Skink												

Code: + = yes   − = no   ? = maybe

when you read. You should read to compare how the insides of amphibians and reptiles may be alike or different."

Then all the students read the passage independently. Next, Al asks questions about the passage, "My questions are, 'How do frogs and toads breathe?' and 'We have ribs and no tail; what do frogs have?'" Students volunteer answers. Then Al continues, "My summary is that frogs and toads breathe through their skin and have no tails. Frogs and toads are different." Mr. Roberts comments that Al's summary includes some of the important information from the passage. He tells the students that one additional detail is important; that frogs and toads are cold-blooded. The students brainstorm what they think this means and consult the glossary in the book. Another student continues the reciprocal teaching activity on page 41.

Next, Mr. Roberts presents a semantic feature analysis chart for amphibians and reptiles, as shown in Figure 7.1. The students work with partners to complete the analysis. They place a plus

(+) to indicate that the animal has the characteristic identified on the chart and a minus (−) to indicate that it does not.

The next day students share their completed semantic feature analysis charts. Then Mr. Roberts presents a text set, a collection of informational books and magazine articles, about amphibians and reptiles. Students preview the texts, and each student selects an amphibian or reptile to investigate. As a group they brainstorm questions, such as "What does this animal eat?" on the chalkboard to guide their research. They will research and write a report about their animal using at least two of the reading materials from the text set. Later, students will gather in writing groups for feedback and suggestions on how to revise their rough drafts. Mr. Roberts will present a minilesson on writing bibliographic references before students prepare a final draft with a bibliography. Students will share their reports with other students and place the reports in the science center for others to read.

INTRODUCTION

The interactive perspective to teaching reading in a literature-based program emphasizes reading as a meaningful, constructive, and strategic process. Readers simultaneously and interactively use several processes of reading, such as predicting and monitoring meaning. In this chapter we describe how teachers use the principles of an interactive perspective to plan instructional activities that will support children's reading for literary and informational purposes. It is important to keep in mind that many of the strategies we discussed in Chapters 5 and 6 are also applicable to the principles of an interactive perspective, and many of the activities we will describe in this chapter can be applied in using a critical or reader response perspective.

The focus of instruction from an interactive perspective is on helping students to better understand what they read and on supporting them as they acquire new reading strategies. In the first part of the chapter, we describe instructional activities that help students read for literary purposes. These activities encourage students' development of strategies for the preparing, reading, exploring, and extending steps in the reading process. Teachers select from among these activities and others only after they are thoroughly familiar with the specific content, ideas, themes, and topics explored in a particular story, book, or poem. In the second section, we describe instructional activities that help students read for informational purposes. In the final section, we consider the decisions that teachers make related to teaching from an interactive perspective.

READING FOR LITERARY PURPOSES

Children usually read stories and poems for literary purposes rather than to learn specific information about content, although they gain considerable knowledge about content from reading stories and poems. Reading for literary purposes includes reading for pleasure and reading to learn more about the organization of stories and poems. Teachers guide students' literary reading by helping them understand stories and poems and demonstrating the use of new reading strategies.

We describe many kinds of instructional techniques that support students' reading for literary purposes, including some that Ms. Nee used in the case study at the beginning of this chapter. It is important to keep in mind that many of the strategies we describe for literary reading can be adapted for informational reading. Similarly, many of the strategies we describe for informational reading can be adapted for literary reading.

Preparing Step

According to the interactive perspective, students activate prior knowledge, become aware of vocabulary, and set purposes for reading during the preparing step of the reading process. These activities are particularly important as readers construct meaning. In the preparing step, readers access their prior knowledge, which helps them to make inferences and draw conclusions during the reading step. They use their understandings of word meanings gained before reading to comprehend as they read. The purposes that they set before reading influence the kinds of information that they pay attention to during reading.

Activating Prior Knowledge.   Students can easily read a story or poem on a familiar topic, but it is much more difficult for them to comprehend a story or poem for which they have little or no background knowledge. Good readers are aware of how their own knowledge helps them read. They call to mind prior knowledge, or activate schema, related to the topics they will read about before reading. In the case study at the beginning of this chapter, Ms. Nee encouraged students to use their prior knowledge before reading by discussing things students believe are important to possess. This topic is crucial to understanding the story. Teachers can help students activate their prior knowledge before reading by identifying a few important topics related to a poem or story for prereading discussion. For example, students can explore their prior knowledge before reading *Roll of Thunder, Hear My Cry* (Taylor, 1976) by discussing topics such as Martin Luther King, Jr., prejudice, or small southern towns.

Students can also quickwrite or quickdraw for 5 to 10 minutes to activate their prior knowledge about a topic. For example, students might quickwrite about doing things with their parents before they read *Owl Moon* (Yolen, 1987) or about the California gold rush before they read *By the Great Horn Spoon* (Fleischman, 1963).

Quickwrites can also be used in a modification of the *Experience, Text, Relationship (ETR)* activity (Au, 1979). The purpose of ETR is to help children see the relationships between their own experiences and what they have read. The steps in using ETR are

1. *Students quickwrite.* Students quickwrite about a personal experience related to a topic or theme from a story or poem they will read. For example, before reading *Ira Sleeps Over* (Waber, 1972), children might quickwrite about sleepovers.
2. *Students share quickwrites.* Children share their quickwrites with a partner or a small group before reading the story.
3. *Students read the story or poem.* Students might read the story or poem aloud to a partner or read it independently.
4. *Students compare quickwrites with the story or poem.* After reading, children talk about how their own experiences with the topic or theme were similar to or different from the experiences described in the story or poem. For example, students compare their experiences with sleepovers to Ira's experience.

Quickwrites and ETR activities encourage students to activate prior knowledge and connect what they read with their own experiences. After introducing these activities to children, teachers can show them how to apply these principles in independent reading. For example, teachers might demonstrate pausing for a moment to think about rain before reading the poems "Rain Poem" (Coatsworth, 1988) and "Rain" (Livingston, 1988).

Introducing Vocabulary.   Even though it may seem useful to discuss the meanings of all unfamiliar words with students before reading, this practice is actually unproductive in the long run. Readers become dependent on the teacher to provide definitions of unknown words instead of learning strategies to figure out meanings of words on their own as they read. Students need to become aware that they are responsible for learning the meanings of words.

Vocabulary Prediction (Atwell & Rhodes, 1984) is an activity that encourages students to take an active part in learning words before they read. Steps in vocabulary prediction are

1. *Select vocabulary.* The teacher chooses three to eight words from a story or poem and writes them across the top of a chart or chalkboard. For example, a first grade teacher might select the words *plow, lumberjacks,* and *slopes* before reading *If the Dinosaurs Came Back* (Most, 1978), a pattern book about the ways dinosaurs could help people if they were alive today.
2. *Students brainstorm ideas related to vocabulary.* The teacher reads the first word and waits 30 seconds or so for the children to think about the word. The children dictate whatever comes to mind related to the word, and the teacher records their responses on the chalkboard. The children may also write their responses in a journal. For example, the children dictated the phrases "snow plow," "something on trucks," "something in fields," and "dig" for what they knew about the word *plow.*
3. *Students read.* The children read the story or poem with a partner or by themselves, or the teacher may also read it aloud to students.
4. *Students compare brainstormed ideas about words to ideas from the story or poem.* After reading, students find the words in the text and dis-

cuss with the teacher what the words mean. The teacher helps students compare and contrast what they knew before reading, what they learned as a result of reading, and how thinking ahead of time about words contributes to their reading effectiveness. After reading the story *If the Dinosaurs Came Back,* the students used the clues in the story to define *plow* as "digging up a field."

Students can also use this technique when reading independently. After reading a story or poem once, students select three or four words to explore during a second reading. They predict these words' meanings mentally or by thinking aloud and then reread more carefully to compare and contrast their initial ideas with their more careful analysis.

Setting Purposes for Reading.   Good readers have a purpose in mind when they read. They may read for entertainment, to compare one version of a story with another, or to find out how a character solves a problem that is similar to their own. Teachers can help students articulate the purposes for reading by discussing different purposes for reading and modeling how to read for those purposes. One way to encourage students to set purposes for reading is the *Directed Reading Thinking Activity (DRTA)* (Stauffer, 1969). DRTA arouses students' curiosity by having them predict what they will read about by using their prior knowledge and guesses about word meanings.

Reading Step

Reading activities guide readers through a story or poem. Typically teachers guide students' reading by asking questions; however, it is more effective to teach students strategies that they can use as they read independently. Two types of strategies are important: strategies that help children construct meaning and fix-up strategies that children use when they do not understand what they are reading or when they encounter an unknown word.

Meaning-Construction Strategies.   Fluent readers use strategies such as predicting, rereading, summarizing, and visualizing to construct meaning as they read. These strategies are invisible mental processes; and, therefore, it is difficult to explain them. One way of demonstrating these mental processes that readers use to construct meaning is to use *think-alouds* (Davey, 1983). In a think-aloud, teachers talk about what they think and describe what they do as they read. In the case study at the beginning of the chapter, Ms. Nee gave a short minilesson using a think-aloud about the strategies of predicting, confirming, and elaborating before students read *The Amazing Bone* independently. The steps in using a think-aloud are

1. *Prepare for think-aloud.* To prepare for a think-aloud, teachers choose one or two strategies to teach, such as prediction, visualization, or summarization. They carefully read the story or poem that the children will read marking points in the text where the strategy might be used effectively. Then, they make notes to guide their explanation during the think-aloud. Their explanation must illustrate how experienced readers think while reading and why a particular strategy was selected.

Figure 7.2 presents a list of 10 reading strategies that can be taught through think-alouds.

2. *Demonstrate a meaning-construction strategy.* Teachers explain that they will demonstrate a strategy that students can use while reading. As they read a story or poem aloud, teachers pause at the selected points to think-aloud, explaining the strategy they are using and why. Figure 7.2 also presents sample think-aloud explanations for the 10 meaning-construction strategies.

3. *Students practice the strategy.* Teachers select additional places in the story or poem where students can practice the strategy and think aloud. Students work in pairs to practice the strategy by continuing to read aloud, pausing at the marked places, and thinking aloud to their partner.

As students learn about meaning-construction strateigies, they think aloud and talk about what they do when they read. The purpose of these think-aloud activities is not to teach students how to talk about strategies that they use but to encourage them to be more aware of the different kinds of strategies that they might use when reading. Think-alouds succeed when students read strategically on their own.

Fix-up Strategies.   Sometimes readers do not understand what they are reading. Good readers realize when they lapse into misunderstanding because they monitor their reading. In contrast, poor readers are more likely to read a text word-by-word without thinking about whether what they are reading makes sense. Teachers can help students monitor the meaning by asking them to stop and talk about what they have read.

Teachers can assess whether students are monitoring when they read aloud. One indication that a child is not monitoring is when the child says a word or phrase that does not make sense and continues reading without pausing, trying to reread the word, or going back to the beginning of the sentence to start again. Teachers allow the child to finish reading the sentence and then repeat what child read and ask, "Does that make sense?" Children must expect that what they read will make sense before they see any reason to learn fix-up strategies.

Readers use fix-up strategies for two purposes: to identify unfamiliar words and to regain meaning when reading does not make sense. Good readers use several fix-up strategies to identify unknown words. They guess the meaning, use what they know about what kind of word would fit in the sentence, and attend to print clues such as initial and final letters to figure out an unknown word. Several fix-up strategies for recognizing an unfamiliar word are

1. Skip the word and continue reading to the end of the sentence.
2. Guess what word would make sense.
3. Use the beginning letters to confirm your guess.
4. Think of a familiar word that looks like the unfamiliar word.
5. Look carefully at the letters from left to right, looking for familiar letter clusters.
6. Look for a familiar root word, suffixes, and prefixes.
7. Look at the illustration.

Good readers also use several fix-up strategies to regain meaning when what they are reading does not make sense. They may stop and reread more slowly, or

FIGURE 7.2 Think-Aloud Explanations for Literary Reading and Examples from *Like Jake and Me* (Jukes, 1984)

Predicting	"I'll use what I have read and my knowledge to make a guess about what will happen next."	"I predict Alex will get hurt and Jake will save him. They will get closer."
Confirming	"I'll use what I've read so far to check whether my predictions are correct, in-correct, or not yet confirmed."	"No, Alex doesn't get hurt lighting the fire."
Visualizing	"I'll create a picture in my mind about what I'm reading."	"I see that Jake is a very large man. His arm muscles are bulging, and he is sweating as he cuts the firewood."
Elaborating	"I'll use my knowledge to make infer-ences and add information to what I read."	"I think Jake is very masculine. He probably played football and hunts. He can likely fix anything. He might like being outside all the time. He's likely very fit."
Retelling/ Paraphrasing	"I'll say to myself what I've read in my own words."	"Alex says that wolf spiders can carry their babies on their backs and do not bite if you don't bother them."
Summarizing	"I'll say to myself the important parts of what I've read so far."	"So far the story has been about Jake and his stepson, Alex. Alex wants to be like Jake but isn't."
Connecting to Literature	"I'll think of something in another book that reminds me of what I'm reading."	"I wonder if the wolf spider is like Char-lotte from *Charlotte's Web* (White, 1952). Charlotte wouldn't hurt anybody."
Connecting to Life	"I'll think of some experience or some-thing I know about that reminds me of something I'm reading."	"I remember the time that fire ants crawled on me and bit me. No wonder Jake is scared."
Connecting to Text/ Retrospecting	"I'll think of something I've read earlier in this book that makes me think about this part."	"I remember in the beginning of the book when I thought Jake could do any-thing and Alex couldn't do anything. I didn't expect Jake to be scared and Alex to be brave."
Empathizing	"I'll think about what I feel and why."	"Oh, yuck. Poor Jake. I'd hate for a spi-der to crawl in my pants. I bet he's going crazy."
Identifying	"I'll think about whether this character makes me think of myself or someone I know and why."	"I feel like Alex lots of times. When I most want to impress someone, I do something stupid. Alex wanted to im-press Jake but he fell over a pumpkin instead."
Monitoring	"I'll make sure that what I'm reading makes sense to me or I'll use a fix-up strategy."	"Wait, who is Jake talking about? Virginia or the spider?"

they may just continue to read knowing that sometimes confusions are clarified by information presented later in the text. Good readers sometimes even skip confusing sections of long stories because they know that some sections are not crucial to understanding a whole story. Teachers can prepare a chart listing these strategies and post it where children can see it during independent reading. The chart may include these fix-up strategies:

1. Stop and read more slowly.
2. Go back to the beginning of the sentence or paragraph and reread.
3. Continue to read.
4. Continue to read and then go back and reread the confusing parts more slowly.
5. Skip confusing words or sections.
6. Look at an illustration.

Teachers help students learn fix-up strategies using think-alouds and demonstrations in minilessons. These strategies are not taught just once during the year; rather, teachers who are in the habit of thinking aloud and asking students to reflect on their own thought processes often take a few moments to discuss how they and other students solve problems that naturally arise in reading lessons. Teachers encourage children to use fix-up strategies during guided and independent reading. Having children reflect on how they use these strategies reinforces their control over their own reading.

Exploring Step

During the exploring step of the reading process, teachers provide activities to deepen students' understanding of stories and poems through rereading and rethinking. Teachers also use the familiar text of a story or poem that children have read and reread to teach new reading strategies.

Rereading and Thinking Activities.   Many types of activities can encourage children to reread and think more deeply about the meaning of stories and poems. Discussing the story is probably the most frequently used exploring activity. Children learn from having to gather their own thoughts about a story or poem to participate in a discussion. They also learn from other children's comments. Good discussions bring out new ideas and clarify misunderstandings. Discussions are not guided by literal questions (questions whose answer is found directly in the text of the story or poem); rather, the best questions for guiding discussions are those that require making inferences and using higher level thinking. For example, Ms. Nee in the case study at the beginning of this chapter used an open-ended question to guide the discussion about *Sylvester and the Magic Pebble.*

Retelling and storytelling.   Retelling stories is an enjoyable and effective method for reflecting on stories and poems (Gambrell, Pfeiffer, & Wilson, 1985; Morrow, 1989). To *retell,* children tell a story or poem that they have read or listened to in their own words. The steps in the retelling strategy are

1. *Explain the retelling activity before reading.* Before reading a story, the teacher explains that the children will retell the story afterwards.
2. *Read the story.* The teacher reads the story aloud, or students read it independently.
3. *Students discuss the story.* Students identify the characters and talk about the story events.
4. *Demonstrate retelling.* The teacher demonstrates retelling the story, using props such as small objects or pictures. For example, to illustrate each event of the story teachers might prepare pictures that they hang on a clothesline as they retell the story.
5. *Invite retellings.* Teachers invite children to retell the story using the storytelling props.
6. *Prompt retellings when needed.* Teachers offer help when necessary by suggesting starting with "Once upon a time" or by using questions such as "Then what happened?" Other questions, such as "Who was the story about?" "Where did the story happen?" "What happened first, second, last?" and "How did the story end?" help children retell more complete stories (Morrow, 1989, pp. 42–43).

The retelling strategy works best with familiar stories that have predictable plots. Folktales and other stories with repetitive phrases or events or a cumulative plot are good choices. In retelling, the focus is not on remembering the exact words in the story; rather, it is on recalling important characters and events in the order in which they were presented.

Teachers can encourage children to use the retelling strategy on their own by placing storytelling props in the classroom library center. Children enjoy exploring a story again and again by retelling it to a friend or even a stuffed animal. A good way to practice this activity is with buddies. One child retells the story while the other child manipulates the storytelling props.

Older students can learn stories for *storytelling.* Storytelling differs from retelling in that students memorize some of the language of the story. Traditional stories, such as folktales, make excellent sources for storytelling. They have repetitive language and events that make them easy to remember. Students reread the story several times, identifying phrases and sentences to include in their storytelling. Repetitive dialogue and important quotations are usually selected. To aid in storytelling, students select props such as stuffed animals to represent characters or small objects to represent story objects. They practice telling the story and then tell their stories to a small group or younger children.

Rereading is another effective exploring activity (Dowhower, 1987). Young children ask for their favorite books to be read aloud again and again. As they begin to read conventionally, they continue to reread favorite stories on their own. This activity is one of the most effective ways for young children to develop fluency and to acquire many print-related skills. Older students who read the same book repeatedly also gain in fluency, word recognition, and comprehension abilities (Dowhower, 1987). This practice is especially effective with less fluent readers.

To use rereading, teachers gather two or three copies of predictable or other favorite books in the library center and encourage children to reread during independent reading times. Having multiple copies of a story or poem encourages young children to reread aloud together. For second graders and older students, the teacher and students select a short book or poem for rereading practice. Then the teacher tape-records a reading of the selection. Children listen to the tape, read along with the tape, and then reread the selection several times until they read fluently and at a rate similar to the teachers' rate of reading.

Drawing.   Drawing requires students to pay particular attention to the language in stories or poems to construct a visual representation of a character, the setting, an event, or an image. For example, after reading Madeleine L'Engle's science fiction masterpiece *A Wrinkle in Time* (1962), children can draw pictures of Mrs. Whatsit, Mrs. Who, and Mrs. Which by carefully reading the descriptions of these characters. They can draw the setting for Robert Frost's (1988) poem "Stopping by Woods on a Snowy Evening" and compare their illustrations to those of Susan Jeffers in her version of *Stopping by Woods on a Snowy Evening* (Frost, 1978). They might also construct a diorama of a setting. Such projects require careful rereading and visualizing of the details included in stories and poems.

Story charts.   Another way to explore a story in greater depth is by using a *story chart.* As shown in Figure 7.3, a story chart is a skeleton of the important parts of a story. These parts correspond to the major parts of a story schema (see Chapter 4). As children work with story charts, they strengthen their story schema. Children who have well-developed schemas for stories remember and write better stories than children who do not have such well-developed ideas about stories (Fitzgerald & Teasley, 1986).

For whole-class or small-group activities, teachers draw the chart on an overhead projector or large chart and describe each part. Then children reread a story and suggest phrases or sentences to complete the story chart, and the teacher writes

FIGURE 7.3   Story Chart

Characters	Setting
Goal	
Attempts	Outcomes
Solution	

their dictation on the chart. Or, students can work with a partner or independently to complete a story chart.

Dramatizing.   Research has shown that drama is a powerful way to think about stories and poems. Dramatization of stories improves comprehension because it encourages careful rereading and attention to sequence and detail (Christie, 1987; Galda, 1982). To dramatize a story, students can pantomime the story's actions as teachers read aloud or they can act out the story adding dialogue as they go. The steps in dramatizing a story are

1. *Students choose roles for the dramatization.* The students identify the roles needed for the dramatization and select parts. The teacher may serve as narrator or take a role in the drama. Children who do not have a role can be the audience and exchange places with the students in the drama for a second improvisation.
2. *Plan the set props.* Students and the teacher identify and collect simple props to use in the dramatization. For example, a chair becomes a tree, a child's sweater spread on the floor becomes a lake, or a desk becomes a bear's cave.
3. *Students dramatize the story.* Students begin role-playing the story, ad-libbing dialogue as needed. It is not important that the dramatization be an exact imitation of the story; rather, the goal is for students to better understand the story.
4. *Students repeat the dramatization.* Other students assume the roles and dramatize the story again.

Literature journals.   Writing about a story or poem is an effective way to have students reflect on meaning. Students who write after reading remember more than those who answer questions or participate in discussions (Marshall, 1987; McGee & Richgels, 1990). Writing after reading encourages students to recall the details of a story or poem, reflect on meanings, and reread for clarification. Many teachers have students write about stories and poems in *literature journals.* They write retellings of stories or poems, keep predictions about stories as Ms. Nee's students did in the case study, or list the main events of stories in their journals. Figure 7.4 shows an entry from a second grader's literature journal about *There's a Nightmare in My Closet* (Mayer, 1968), a story about how a boy conquers his fears about the night.

Focusing on the Text.   Children learn new strategies for reading as they focus on the text of familiar stories and poems. As children focus on the text, they extend and deepen their understandings of word meanings and acquire new sight words. They develop more sophisticated understandings about written language that they apply to decode unfamiliar words. Extending activities that help students focus on the text show them how to gain new word meanings as they read independently, apply new strategies for recognizing words, and apply knowledge about letter-sound relationships, suffixes, and prefixes in decoding.

Extending understandings of word meaning.   Extending children's understanding of words and their meanings is an important part of exploring the text. Teachers draw attention to words and their meanings as a natural part of discussion activities.

FIGURE 7.4 Entry from a Second Grader's Literature Journal from *There's a Nightmare in My Closet* (Mayer, 1968)

Theres A Nightmare In My Closet

The boy had a monster in his closet. He had a gun to shoot it. He was very, very very scrad and the monster was to. So the boy and the monster got in the bed together He lived happy ever after.

One way to make vocabulary related to the text more visible is to use a *word wall.* Teachers hang a large sheet of paper on the wall, and children collect words to write on the word wall as they read. The words written on the word wall can be used in a variety of activities.

One way to help students focus on word meaning is to make a *cluster* or *map,* a visual display of related vocabulary words or concepts. After reading *Amos and Boris* (Steig, 1971), for example, a group of second graders decided to collect words to describe Amos and Boris in clusters. As they gathered the words, they discussed what the words meant and used them to talk about the story. Figure 7.5 presents their clusters.

Another type of cluster that can be used to explore word meanings, a *definition cluster,* examines a word from several different perspectives. As shown in Figure 7.6, a definition cluster includes the word used in a sentence, the word's definition, the category in which the word fits, and one additional bit of information about the word. Figure 7.6 presents a definition cluster for the word *polar* from Van Allsburg's Christmas fantasy *The Polar Express* (1985).

Developing sight vocabulary. *Sight words* are words that children can read and know the meaning of instantly, without using word recognition strategies. Children who are mature, fluent readers have a large store of sight words, and they acquire these words as a consequence of reading, not by practicing lists of words before reading (Weaver, 1988). Because children use the multiple processes of reading simultaneously, they can read without knowing all the words before reading. Young children can read many stories, poems, songs, and chants before they have any sight words because they memorize the text. Once young children have memorized the

FIGURE 7.5   Clusters for *Amos & Boris* (Steig, 1971)

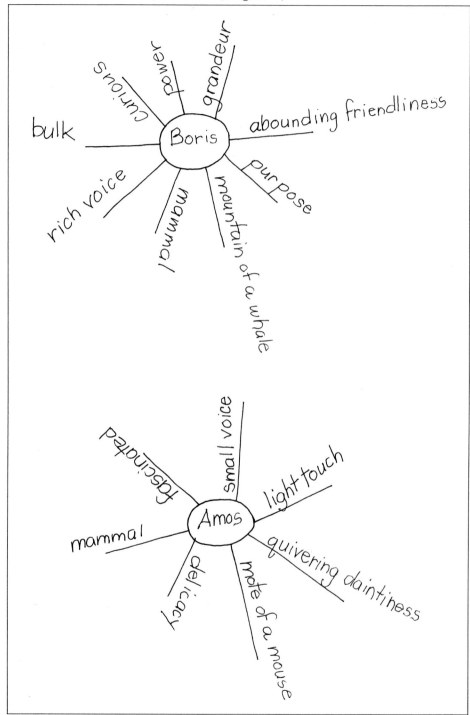

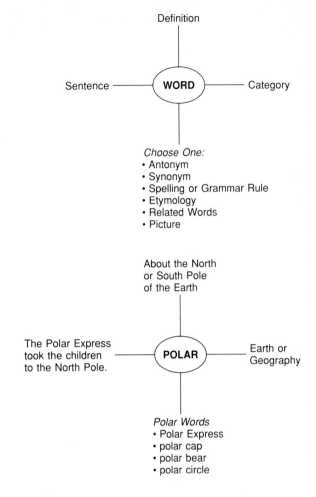

FIGURE 7.6 Definition Cluster for the Word *Polar* from *The Polar Express* (Van Allsburg, 1985)

text of a familiar song or poem, the teacher can direct their attention to words and what they look like. Many children learn their first sight words as they reread favorite stories, poems, and songs.

Rereading favorite stories, poems, and songs often takes place in shared readings of big books or charts (see Chapter 4). Children predict before reading and chant familiar refrains or repeated elements as the teacher reads. Teachers model the reading process by pointing to the print from left to right as they read and demonstrate the importance of print by asking children to recall parts of the story or poem. Then they confirm these parts by locating the information in the text (Combs, 1987). After reading, children retell, dramatize, or reread the story. They put music to the words, play musical instruments as the teacher reads, or make up a finger play to accompany the story or poem. Children extend reading through painting, modeling, building with Lego's, putting on a puppet show, writing, and listening to other familiar stories or poems (Heald-Taylor, 1987).

Rereading stories, poems, and songs is an important way that children deepen their understandings (Yaden, 1988) and begin to learn sight words (Bridge, Winograd,

& Haley, 1983). As a part of shared reading children can learn sight words through *sight word learning routine* (Johnson & Louis, 1987). The steps for this strategy are

1. *Students learn a familiar story, poem, song, or chant.* Teachers read a brief and familiar story, poem, or chant such as *The Lady with the Alligator Purse* (Westcott, 1988) by inviting children to predict what the story will be about and pausing for discussion. They reread the text again inviting children to join in the chanting. Teachers reread the text several times over the next few days using dramatization or retellings. Children are encouraged to join in until they have memorized the text.

2. *Prepare a chart or big book version.* Teachers write the story on a chart or in a big book. (Many commercial big book versions of appropriate stories, poems, and songs are currently available.) If teachers make big books, they write a line, stanza, or episode on each page of the big book as it appears in the original version. Children illustrate the big books, and then the big books are used in the following steps. Figure 7.7 presents directions for making big books with children.

3. *Students recognize familiar lines of text.* The teacher reads the chart or big book and points to each word with a pointer or yardstick while the children read along. Next the teacher invites a child to point at the words as the other children read the text. Later the teacher points to a line of text at random and invites children to read the text.

4. *Students recognize familiar words of text.* The teacher frames a word on the chart or big book using a mask and asks a student to read that word (Fisher, 1991). (A mask is a cardboard rectangle with the center cut out. Teachers need several sizes of masks to fit words of varying lengths.) The teacher demonstrates reading and pointing to each word in the line of text to identify the masked word. Then the teacher masks another word and children identify the word by rereading the line of text in which the word appears.

5. *Students identify familiar lines of text.* The teacher reads a line or sentence from the text and children locate it on the chart or in the big book. For example, the teacher asks, "Where does it say 'In came the doctor'?" and a child points to that line of text.

6. *Students identify words.* The teacher names a single word in the text and a child locates the word and masks it.

7. *Students select words to complete a modified cloze.* Teachers prepare word cards for each word in the text. They place the words cards in a pocket chart omitting several words of the text but leaving a space for each missing word card. Children read the text, identify the missing words, and place the missing word cards in the spaces. Figure 7.8 presents an example of a modified cloze pocket chart activity for *The Lady with the Alligator Purse* (Wescott, 1988).

An important caution to keep in mind is that this word learning strategy should be used only after children have memorized text and can point to each word as they read. Not all children need to use all of the steps in the strategy. This activity should be interspersed with a variety of activities that focus on meaning, such as dramatizations and retellings. Fortunately, the kinds of stories, poems, songs, and chants that

FIGURE 7.7   Directions for Making Big Books with Children

Big books are enlarged copies of favorite books, poems, or chants. There are three kinds of big books: replicas or copies of published books; new versions of published books that children have composed using the author's structure and creating new content; and original books that children have composed and illustrated. To construct a big book with children follow these directions:

1. *Gather materials.* Teachers gather several sheets of 18″ × 30″ paper, several sheets of 12″ × 18″ white construction paper, glue, two pieces of sturdy cardboard at least 18″ × 30″, and yarn, clips, or metal rings. They might gather other materials such as markers, crayons, glue, wallpaper samples, and other collage materials.
2. *Decide on the type of book to be constructed.* If children are to construct a replica or new version, they select a predictable story or poem with obvious rhythm, pattern, or rhyme. The teacher reads the book or poem several times to the children and invites them to join in the reading. If constructing an original big book, they prepare for writing by brainstorming or clustering ideas. Then students dictate a rough draft of their story, which the teacher writes on a large chart. Then the story is reread and revised.
3. *Prepare the text.* The teacher prints the text of the story, rhyme, song, or poem on white construction paper, which will be glued on the large sheets of paper. The text should be divided evenly across the pages of the book so that at least half the page is left for the illustration.
4. *Illustrate the book.* Students may use crayons, paint, markers, or other media to create illustrations for each page of the book.
5. *Add a title page with the copyright year and the names of authors and illustrators.* Students design a title page that contains the copyright year, title, author, and other important information. If the book is a replica of a favorite book, a statement such as "Retold and Illustrated by Mrs. Smith's class," might be added after the title and author. If the big book is a new version, a statement such as "Based on Bill Martin, Jr.'s *Brown Bear, Brown Bear, What Do You See?*" might be added. A dedication page can be added at the beginning of the book, and a page about the authors and a reader comment page can also be included at the back.
6. *Design covers.* A small group of students design a front and back cover. Then the teacher glues the covers to sturdy cardboard.
7. *Sequence the pages.* Students sequence the pages, and the book is put together in this order: front cover, title page, copyright page, dedication page, story, page about the authors, comment page, and back cover. Teachers use yarn, metal clips, or rings, or commercial spiraling to bind the book.

are appropriate for the word learning strategy are among children's favorites, and they ask for these favorite stories to be read again and again offering numerous opportunities for word and letter-sound learning.

Letter-sound relationships.   English is an alphabetic system in which letters represent sounds. Many children begin learning *phonics,* or letter-sound knowledge before they begin to read conventionally. They demonstrate their developing knowledge of letter-sound relationships as they write. Once children begin learning to read conventionally, they see words spelled conventionally and apply this visual information in their writing.

FIGURE 7.8   Modified Cloze Pocket Chart for *The Lady with the Alligator Purse* (Westcott, 1988)

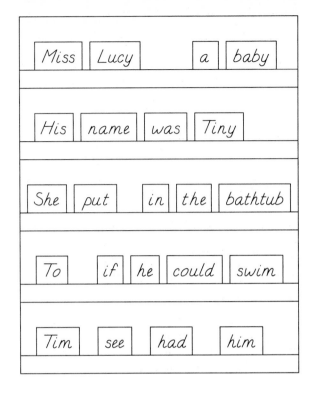

Miss	Lucy		a	baby
His	name	was	Tiny	
She	put	in	the	bathtub
To	if	he	could	swim
Tim	see	had		him

Many alphabet letter names capture the sound associated with that letter. For example, the sound associated with the letter *t, /t/,* is heard when someone says the letter name *t.* Many young children begin to learn letter-sound relationships based on the sounds found in the names of letters. But young children do not always notice the sound. Rather, they may notice that when they say a word, slowly isolating the initial or beginning sound, their mouths are in the same position as when they say the letter name. Place of articulation, the position of the mouth and lips, teeth, and tongue, is the first clue to many young spellers that letters can be related to sounds in words in predictable and knowable ways. Teaching children letter-sound relationships should capitalize on children's willingness to write and on the powerful clues of place of articulation.

Once children begin using some letter-sound relationships in writing, teachers can introduce other letters and the sounds associated with them. It is important that children learn the sound asociated with each consonant letter since these are more regular and are associated with only one sound. The letters *c, g, h, q, w,* and *x* do not have sound associations with their letter names, and many children may need help in learning these associations. In addition, the letters *c* and *g* have two sounds associated with them (soft sounds such as in the words *city* and *gem* and hard sounds such as in the words *came* and *game*). Children also need to become familiar with *consonant digraphs (ch, sh, ph, th,* and *wh).* Consonant digraphs have two letters representing a single sound unrelated to the sounds associated with either individual letter. Children also learn consonant *blends* (e.g., *br, cl, dr, fl, gl,* and *str),* combinations of two or three consonants where each letter retains its individual sound.

They also learn about the sounds associated with vowels as they begin to learn familiar *phonograms* in *word families.* Word families are sets of words that have in common a familiar spelling pattern. For example the *at* word family (e.g., *bat, cat, fat, mat, rat, sat,* and *vat)* consists of words that include the *at* spelling pattern. Figure 7.9 presents a list of phonograms or word families found in frequently occuring words.

Learning letter-sound relationships and phonograms. Letter-sound relation-ships are best taught to children through writing and then applied to reading (Freppon & Dahl, 1991). Teachers can demonstrate thinking about letters and sounds as they write on the chalkboard or take children's dictation. For example, a group of first graders might be composing collaboratively a new version of the fa-miliar song "Mary Wears a Red Dress." The children use their own names and clothes in their song. They dictate:

> *Hua wears brown pants, brown pants, brown pants.*
> *Hua wears brown pants all day long.*

FIGURE 7.9 Phonograms

back, jack, lack, pack, rack, sack, tack, shack, whack, smack
bad, Dad, had, mad, pad, sad, glad
bag, gag, hag, sag, rag, tag, stag, brag, flag
gain, rain, pain, vain, brain, plain, stain, train, strain
can, fan, man, pan, ran, tan, van, than, span
bank, rank, sank, tank, thank, blank, spank, drank
bat, cat, fat, hat, mat, rat, sat, vat, that, drat, splat
bake, make, lake, take, sake, flake, brake
bay, day, gay, hay, lay, may, pay, say, spray, play, clay
bed, fed, led, Ned, red, Ted, wed, sled
deep, keep, peep, weep, sheep, sleep, sweep
bend, lend, send, tend, mend, spend, trend
best, nest, pest, rest, test, west, vest
hide, wide, side, slide, snide, glide
bin, pin, tin, sin, thin, spin
fight, light, might, sight, right, tight, fright, bright
bill, gill, hill, Jill, kill, mill, pill, sill, till, thrill
bin, fin, in, sin, tin, win, chin, thin, spin
dip, hip, lip, rip, sip, tip, ship, chip, whip, flip, trip
ding, king, ring, sing, thing, bring, sting, fling
bold, cold, gold, hold, mold, old, sold, told
cop, hop, mop, pop, top, chop, shop, stop, flop
duck, luck, muck, suck, stuck, truck
bug, hug, mug, rug, tug, thug, smug
bunk, dunk, junk, sunk, skunk, flunk, trunk, drunk

As teachers write, they talk about letters and sounds. For example, a teacher might say, "I want to write *pants, p-ants* (saying the word slowly). I hear a /p/," and then writes the letter *p.*

Teachers also talk about letters and sounds as they respond to individual children's invented spellings. Teachers might say, "I can see this says *monster*," pointing to the *m* that a child has written. Or, looking at *no j* that a child has written, teachers can say, "I can read this. It says, 'no jumping'" (underlining the letters *n* and *o* and then the *j*). Some children need more direct help in producing invented spellings. Teachers invite these children to say their message, and they repeat the first word slowly isolating each sound. (This is called phonemically segmenting a word.) Then teachers ask, "Feel your mouth. What letter do you feel and hear?" Some children may need lots of experiences hearing a teacher segment a word's sounds and selecting a letter to represent those sounds before they are able to invent spellings independently.

Keep in mind that good readers have an intuitive sense of the regular spelling patterns of English. They may not necessarily know the terminology associated with decoding (e.g., "soft *c*", "digraph", or "silent *e*") but they do know how to use such concepts to decode words and they apply this knowledge as they read independently.

We believe that children need to learn the most regular letter-sound relationships (consonants, blends, and digraphs), the spellings associated with phonograms or familiar word families, and—through familiar word families—the sounds associated with vowel patterns. For example, the *ad* and *it* families teach the CVC pattern associated with short vowel sounds; the *ake* and *ike* families teach the CVCe (Consonant, Vowel, Consonant, silent *e*) pattern associated with long vowel sounds; and the *ail, eel,* and *owl* families, among many others, teach CVVC patterns associated with long vowel and other vowel sounds.

Applying letter-sound and phonogram knowledge.   Most children begin applying letter-sound knowledge when they use picture clues to predict the meaning of an unfamiliar word and then apply beginning letter sound knowledge. Readers who read the sentence "He was sad" as "He was scared" indicate that they are using both meaning and letter-sound relationship strategies because *scared* begins with the same letter as *sad,* and it makes sense in the sentence. Teachers can encourage strategy use by inviting children to guess what an unfamiliar word might be based on meaning and then to check their guesses using the initial letter.

Another way to apply letter-sound knowledge in reading is by using small stick-on note papers to cover words in familiar stories, songs, poems, and chants. For example, teachers might cover several words in a big book version of *The Lady with the Alligator Purse.* The children guess what the covered word is and guess the letters that spell the word. The word is uncovered and the children discuss which letters they guessed correctly.

Another strategy for recognizing unfamiliar words is to *decode by analogy* (Gaskins et al., 1987). This strategy is most appropriate for children in grades two through four who are familiar with a variety of phonograms or word families. To use the decoding by analogy strategy, children think of a word from a familiar word family that looks like an unfamiliar word. Using class charts of familiar word families, they compare the familiar "word family" word to the unfamiliar word in order to decode the unfamiliar word. The steps in the decoding by analogy procedure are

1. *Demonstrate the strategy.* The teacher demonstrates the strategy by reading a sentence that has been written on the chalkboard with a word in it that is unfamiliar to the children, such as, "I want to get a sack for the toys." The teacher says "blank" for the unknown word *sack* and finishes the sentence. Then the teacher thinks aloud: "I can use what I know about word families to figure out this word. I recognize that this word is in the *ack* family. (Teacher underlines the letters *ack* in the unfamiliar word on the board.) Now I'm thinking of a word that I know in the *ack* family—*back*. (Teacher points to the *ack* words on the word family chart hanging in the classroom and writes the word *back* on the board). I know *back*. If the letters *b-a-c-k* are *back* then the letters *s-a-c-k* must be *sack*. Now let me reread the sentence to see if *sack* makes sense."

2. *Students practice.* The teacher selects several sentences from stories or poems that the children are reading and writes them on the chalkboard. The children read the sentences saying "blank" when they encounter an unfamiliar word. Next, they identify the word family of the unfamiliar word and name one or more words from the word family that they know. Then they decode the unfamiliar word and reread the sentence to make sure the word makes sense.

3. *Students apply the strategy.* Teachers encourage students to use the strategy when they are reading independently and come across unfamiliar words. They remind children of the strategy when they are reading orally and they pause because they do not immediately recognize a word.

Learning syllables and other complex word patterns. Mature readers are unlikely to use only letter-sound relations to decode unfamiliar words; they are more likely to use word parts such as suffixes, prefixes, and familiar syllables. For example, older students can pronounce the nonsense word *monglustamer* even though they have never seen the word before. They are likely to use the familiar word parts of *mon, glu, stam,* and *er.*

It is a big step to move from using single letters or clusters to recognizing unfamiliar words to using word parts that we associate with syllables. Teaching children how to divide a word into syllables may not be the solution to helping children achieve this level of word recognition ability because rules for dividing words into syllables are complex and rely on abstract concepts and terms. Children may end up memorizing such rules, but not being able to apply them to reading.

Teachers can help children learn to recognize familiar word parts by teaching them to recognize frequently occurring prefixes and suffixes. Prefixes are word beginnings that change word meanings (*war—antiwar*) and suffixes are word endings that change tense (*walk—walked*), part of speech (*run—runner*), or number (*boy—boys*). Suffixes carry less meaning than prefixes; they mostly serve grammatical purpose (White, Sowell, & Yanagihara, 1989). Research has shown that students need to learn only the most commonly used prefixes including: *un* and *dis* (meaning not); *in, im, ir,* and *non* (meaning not); *re* (meaning again or back); *en, em, over,* and *mis* (miscellaneous meanings); and *dis, un, in,* and *im* (alternative meanings other than not) (White, Sowell, & Yanagihara, 1989, p. 305). Students need to identify the suffixes *s (es), ed, ing,* and *er* in words where adding a suffix does not require a spelling change *(talks, talked, talking)* and when adding a suffix requires a spelling change, such as when the consonant is doubled *(running, runner),* when *y* is changed to *i (happier, cried),* and when *e* is deleted *(taking).* In addition, the suffixes *ly, er, ion, able, al, y,* and *ness* should be taught.

Teaching children about prefixes and suffixes should take place in the context of meaningful text so that children understand that the purpose of the lesson is to help them learn how to better understand what they read. Teachers can take a few moments to point out words with similar prefixes or suffixes and discuss their root words, meaningful words to which prefixes and suffixes are added. For example, in the case study at the beginning of the chapter, Ms. Nee prepared an activity that focused on the suffix *ly* where the students identified the suffix and discussed the meanings of root words with and without that suffix.

Some middle and upper grade students may need more direct instruction about word parts and root words and how to use them to derive meaning from unfamiliar words. White, Sowell, and Yanagihara (1989) describe the steps for teaching students about root words and prefixes (or suffixes):

1. *Provide information about prefixes.* Teachers provide information about prefixes using a chart or overhead:
    a. A prefix is a group of letters that go in front of a word.
    b. It changes the meaning of a word.
    c. When you peel it off, a word must be left. (White, Sowell, & Yanagihara, 1989, p. 305)
2. *Provide examples and nonexamples of words with prefixes.* Teachers provide examples of words with prefixes (e.g., *unwind, rewind, unloved,* and *irresponsible*) and nonexamples (e.g., *under, read,* and *rebuke*).
3. *Select sentences illustrating prefixes.* Teachers select a prefix that appears several times in a text the students are reading. They write several sentences containing words with the prefix from the text on the chalkboard or overhead.
4. *Students locate words with prefixes, peel off prefixes, identify root words, and discuss meanings of roots words and prefixes.* Students read the sentences and locate the words with prefixes. They peel off the prefix, identify the root word, and discuss the meaning of the root word and prefix. For example, students might identify the word *irresponsible* as a word with a prefix. They note that the root word *responsible* means reliable, and *irresponsible* means not reliable because the prefix *ir* means not.

Teachers follow the same steps in teaching suffixes.

Learning to use a combination of strategies.   Children should be encouraged to use two or more strategies in combination when figuring out an unfamiliar word. Efficient word recognition requires the use of several strategies (Clay, 1979). Readers use their knowledge about context as they guess what a word will mean, their knowledge of what kinds of words fit in a particular spot in a sentence, their knowledge of letter-sound associations (especially initial sounds), their knowledge of familiar word families, and their awareness of frequent word parts together to recognize and identify the meanings of words. Children also need to learn to cross-check their solutions to word recognition problems (Clay, 1979). Cross-checking involves monitoring their solution of an unfamiliar word with two or more strategies.

Extending Step

The purpose of these extending activities is to provide opportunities for independent practice of strategies and to extend children's appreciation and understanding of literature. Students in the extending step practice using strategies they are learning in other contexts such as in reading other selections, in writing activities, or in discussion activities. Most of the extending activities used in an interactive perspective involve children in independent reading. Students must spend considerable time in independent reading if they are to improve as readers, and guided reading lessons must always be accompanied by extended periods of independent reading.

Teachers may select one or more stories or poems for independent reading as Ms. Nee did in the case study at the beginning of the chapter. She selected *The Amazing Bone* for an extending activity because this story was written by the same author as the core selection, contained similar literary elements, and was on a comparable reading level.

At other times, children self-select stories and poems for extended reading. It is particularly important that children learn to select their own books and poems for independent reading, an ability that develops over time. Children need to learn to explore a wide range of reading materials—both different topics and different difficulty levels. Students must learn to read for a variety of purposes and to select reading materials that will both fit their purposes and present challenging, but not daunting reading experiences. Teachers need to plan activities that will help children make wise choices for independent reading.

Ohlhausen and Jepsen (1992) recommended teaching students the *Goldilocks strategy* to help them select appropriate reading materials. Just as Goldilocks sampled porridge that was "too hot," "too cold," and "just right," students can learn to identify books that are, for the moment, "too hard," "too easy," or "just right." Teachers can introduce these concepts in minilessons by reading books that they find difficult, easy, and just right. Figure 7.10 presents a chart that was developed by a teacher and her students to help the students select books that are "just right" for them.

It is important that students recognize that all readers have books that are "too hard," "too easy," and "just right" and that books often change categories. Books that are "too hard" or "just right" can become "too easy" with practice and over time. Students need to spend time with all three kinds of books. "Too easy" books provide opportunities to develop fluency, use strategies automatically, and gain confidence (Ohlhausen & Jepsen, 1992). "Just right" books provide the best learning opportunities because they allow students to figure out new words from context and present challenging and engaging content. Students may spend just a little time with "too hard" books especially to see if these books might become "just right."

Another method for helping students select books for independent reading is the *five-finger method* in which students read a page of a book that they are consid-

FIGURE 7.10   How to Use the Goldilocks Strategy to Choose Books

---

"Too Easy" Books

Ask yourself these questions. If you are answering "yes," this book is probably a "Too Easy" book for you. Have fun reading it!

1. Have you read it lots of times before?
2. Do you understand the story (text) very well?
3. Do you know (can you understand) almost every word?
4. Can you read it smoothly?

"Just Right" Books

Ask yourself these questions. If you are answering "yes," this book is probably a "Just Right" book for you. Go ahead and learn from it!

1. Is this book new to you?
2. Do you understand some of the book?
3. Are there just a few words per page you don't know?
4. When you read are some places smooth and some choppy?
5. Can someone help you with this book? Who?

"Too Hard" Books

Ask yourself these questions. If you are answering "yes," this book is probably a "Too Hard" book for you. Spend a little time with it now. Give it another try later (perhaps in a couple of months).

1. Are there more than a few words on a page you don't know?
2. Are you confused about what is happening in most of the book?
3. When you read, does it sound pretty choppy?
4. Is everyone else busy and unable to help you?

Note. From "Lessons from Goldilocks: 'Somebody's Been Choosing My Books but I Can Make My Own Choices Now!'" by M. Ohlhausen and M. Jepsen, 1992, *The New Advocate, 5,* p. 36. Copyright 1992 by Christopher-Gordon Publishers and M. Ohlhausen.

ering and raise a finger each time they encounter an unknown word. If they raise all five fingers on one hand before finishing the page, then the book may be too difficult. Students should learn to use the five-finger strategy flexibly; some books may be very difficult to read, but because they are so interesting students decide to read them anyway.

READING FOR INFORMATIONAL PURPOSES

Now we turn our attention to instructional techniques that support children's reading of books and magazines for informative, rather than literary, purposes. Children read informational texts for many reasons, including to find out information about a topic or learn how to do something, to confirm or reject hypotheses or beliefs, to understand a topic better, to find answers to questions, and to study information for a test. The strategies we described in the case study about Mr. Roberts at the beginning of this chapter and those we will describe in this section are particularly suited to supporting children's reading for informational purposes.

Preparing Step

The purposes of the preparing step are to help children call to mind prior information and vocabulary that will be used during reading and to set purposes for reading. The purposes for the preparing step in informational reading are similar to those for the preparing step in literary reading.

Activating Prior Knowledge and Vocabulary.   An effective prior knowledge strategy is to have students quickwrite about topics in *learning logs* (Fulwiler, 1987), as Mr. Roberts' students did in the case study. Learning logs are a special kind of journal in which students reflect on what they know about a unit of study, what they want to learn, and what they have learned. Students take notes, list vocabulary words, make observations, describe steps and outcomes in experiments, draw diagrams and illustrations, and make conclusions (Tompkins, 1990).

Learning logs can be used for other preparing activities. Students can preview and then write *hypotheses* or predictions about what they will read in their learning logs. To preview, students skim a selection, quickly reading the title, looking at the illustrations and graphs and reading their captions, reading the subtitles, and reading the summary. Then students write hypotheses in their learning logs about what they think they will read. Teachers can demonstrate this technique through modeling and thinking aloud.

Self-questioning is another preparing activity that activates prior knowledge. Students preview a text by scanning titles, subtitles, illustrations, graphs, tables, and diagrams. After previewing, students ask themselves questions they believe will be answered from reading the text. These self-questions also guide reading. Mr. Roberts' students in the case study at the beginning of the chapter used questions they developed in a preparing activity to guide their later reading.

Setting Purposes for Reading.   Techniques such as KWL charts (see Chapter 4) and self-questioning help students set purposes for reading, but students need to learn to set their own purposes before reading. Students should always be able to answer the question "Why I am reading this?" before they begin reading. Teachers can help students think about the different kinds of purposes for reading: readers read to find out more information; to study; to confirm or disconfirm hypotheses, ideas, or beliefs; to apply knowledge to real life situations (like finding out how to construct a birdhouse or plant a tree); and to answer a question (Blanton, Woods, & Moorman, 1990). Teachers can use think-alouds to demonstrate different purposes for reading.

Reading Step

Reading activities help guide readers as they read an informational passage. These activities help readers use reading processes that meet their purposes for reading, acquire and use meaning-making strategies, and focus attention on important information to be remembered.

Reading to Satisfy Purpose.   Students vary the way they read when they are reading for different purposes. For example, when reading to answer a question, readers quickly scan the text to find information related to the question rather than reading the entire text. Readers who are reading to study for a test read slowly and stop frequently to retell what they have learned from reading. Teachers can demonstrate how students should vary their reading and use think-alouds to model these reading strategies.

Meaning-Construction Strategies.   Readers use many strategies to construct meaning, some of which are especially useful when reading for informational purposes. Readers preview, hypothesize, connect to background knowledge, revise hypotheses, question, take a position, paraphrase, and evaluate. Figure 7.11 presents a list and description of eight strategies that are useful for informational reading.

Think-alouds can be used to demonstrate these meaning-making strategies. Figure 7.11 also presents a description of the explanations that teachers can use to model thinking about the eight strategies. Teachers use the steps for think-alouds presented earlier in this chapter.

Another technique for helping students develop meaning-making strategies is *reciprocal teaching* (Palinscar & Brown, 1984). Mr. Roberts' students used this technique as they predicted, questioned, and summarized. The steps in this strategy are

1. *Select a text and become familiar with it.* Teachers select a text that may be complex or difficult to comprehend and identify text segments that will be used in the reciprocal teaching procedure. One or two paragraphs are sufficient for younger students and slightly longer sections for older students. Teachers write several predictions based on the title or first sentence and questions for each segment of the text. Then they write a summary for each segment and circle unfamilar words.

2. *Make predictions about the text.* After reading the title, teachers state the prediction prepared in the first step. They also invite students to make predictions.

3. *Read the text segment aloud.* Teachers read the text aloud or have a student read it.

4. *Ask a question about the content.* Teachers ask the question they prepared in the first step, and students answer the question.

5. *Invite students to ask questions.* Teachers ask, "Does anyone else have a question?" They encourage students to ask questions that call for higher level thinking.

6. *Summarize the text segment.* Teachers present the summary they prepared in the first step.

7. *Clarify confusing vocabulary or ideas.* Teachers lead a discussion of critical or difficult words, figurative language, or unusual and confusing ideas.

8. *Support students as they take on the teacher's role.* Students predict, ask questions, make a summary, and clarify confusing or difficult information as teachers guide them through the process. Once students are familiar with the strategy, they can use it with a partner or apply its principles to their independent reading. Teachers discuss with students the importance of pausing to predict, questioning oneself, and then summarizing their reading.

Focusing Attention on Important Information.   One way that teachers help children attend to important information is to use *reading guides* (Wood, 1988). Reading guides help students focus attention on the main ideas of a passage, make inferences

FIGURE 7.11 Think-aloud Explanations for Informational Reading and Examples from "The Nature of Time" (Cooper, 1987)

Previewing	"I'll read the title and look carefully through the book. I'll look at each illustration, map, or graph and read the subtitles."	"The title is 'The Nature of Time.' I see illustrations of a solar chronometer, a bone with pictures of the moon waxing and waning, and a picture of ancient Egyptians harvesting."
Hypothesizing	"I'll think of what I've read and what I know and guess what the book will tell me."	"The illustrations suggest that it will be about how people told time in the past. I think this article will describe different ways that people long ago used to tell time before they had watches."
Connecting to Background Information	"I'll think about what I know related to the topic."	"I know one way people tell time without a watch. They used a sundial. The shadow on the sundial moved around in a circle like the hands on a clock."
Revising Hypotheses	"I'll use what I've read so far to see whether my hypotheses were correct or need revision."	"I see from the first paragraph that this article might be about how animals tell time. No, the second paragraph tells how humans must guess seasonal times."
Questioning	"I'll make sure that what I'm reading makes sense to me or I'll ask questions about the information I don't understand."	"I do not understand. What are seasonal changes? How can people not know what season it is? We know the dates for each season."
Take a Position	"I'll say to myself what I believe about the topic."	"People should take more time to be with their families."
Evaluate	"I'll decide whether the information I've read meets my purpose, is useful, is accurate, or is important for me to know and provides the information that I expected."	"This article is hard to read. I did not find out how humans told time before they had watches as I expected to."

Additional think-aloud explanations appear in Figure 7.2.

and connections among ideas, and locate supporting arguments. They also help students study and remember the material through writing, retelling, or dramatizing. Reading guides are prepared as worksheets that indicate which page and paragraph students are to read and identify what information students should glean from this text (e.g., "list two causes of . . . ," "list three ways that . . . ," "write the major reason that . . . ," or "describe how the ideas in this paragraph are related to the event on page. . . ."). Reading guides also direct students to retell information in their own words, determine whether statements are true or false, and be ready to defend their answers, or draw illustrations and diagrams.

One kind of reading guide that is especially effective is the *interactive reading guide* (Wood, 1988). This guide directs students to complete some activities independently, some with a partner, and others with a small group. Figure 7.12 presents an interactive reading guide for *An Apple Tree Through the Year* (Schnieper, 1987). Students answer some questions independently on the reading guide and then discuss their answers with a partner or a small group and come to a consensus about the answer.

FIGURE 7.12 Interactive Reading Guide for *An Apple Tree Grows Through the Year* (Schnieper, 1987)

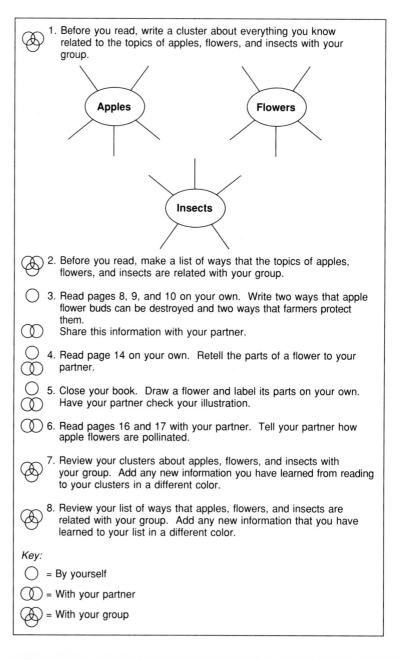

1. Before you read, write a cluster about everything you know related to the topics of apples, flowers, and insects with your group.

Apples

Flowers

Insects

2. Before you read, make a list of ways that the topics of apples, flowers, and insects are related with your group.

3. Read pages 8, 9, and 10 on your own. Write two ways that apple flower buds can be destroyed and two ways that farmers protect them.
   Share this information with your partner.

4. Read page 14 on your own. Retell the parts of a flower to your partner.

5. Close your book. Draw a flower and label its parts on your own. Have your partner check your illustration.

6. Read pages 16 and 17 with your partner. Tell your partner how apple flowers are pollinated.

7. Review your clusters about apples, flowers, and insects with your group. Add any new information you have learned from reading to your clusters in a different color.

8. Review your list of ways that apples, flowers, and insects are related with your group. Add any new information that you have learned to your list in a different color.

Key:

◯ = By yourself

◯◯ = With your partner

⊛ = With your group

Reading guides are most effective when followed by a group discussion of the material learned through the activity. The discussion should also focus on how students can use the ideas from the reading guide to direct their reading without a guide. Students can suggest activities that they practiced with the reading guide that they could do on their own.

Exploring Step

Exploring activities are particularly important when reading for informational purposes. The goal of exploring activities is to encourage critical thinking about topics. Critical thinking—reflecting on the accuracy, authenticity, and bias of information—is often more important than remembering information. Readers can reflect on the accuracy, authenticity, and bias in information when they reread text from different perspectives. For example, reading a history text to understand the sequence of events in the Civil War, for example, may not encourage critical thinking as well as rereading a text several times, first from the perspectives of slaves and then from the perspective of slave owners. Through exploring activities, students reread and rethink so they can critically examine information and learn new strategies for reading, learning, and studying.

Rereading and Thinking. Many activities lead students back into the text to reread and rethink information. Discussion of hypotheses, questions, and reading guides provide many opportunities to reread the text to support answers and clarify misunderstandings. As students talk, they examine questions and learn the kinds of information that can be used to answer them. Visualizing activities and writing provide other opportunities to examine information critically.

QAR relationships. Students need to have different strategies for answering questions about the informational text they have read. Many students try to answer questions using only information from the text, whereas other students try to answer questions using only information from their prior knowledge. It is important to point out to students that questions vary according to whether the source of answers is in the text or readers' prior knowledge. One way to help students understand these different sources of answers is to teach them the *QAR (question-answer-relationship)* technique (Raphael, 1986). Four possible relationships between questions and answers are

1. *Right There.* The answer is directly stated in the text, and the words in the question and answer are included in the same sentence in the text.
2. *Think and Search.* The answer is in the text, but the words in the question and answer are not in the same sentence.
3. *Author and Me.* The answer is not in the text, but the text provides information to use in the answer.
4. *On My Own.* The answer is not in the text; it must come from the reader's own experiences.

Steps in this QAR procedure are

1. *Prepare QAR chart.* Teachers prepare a chart with the headings *Right There, Think and Search, Author and Me,* and *On My Own* and definitions of each of the QARs. Picture clues such as of a page of print, a page of print with

words and phrases in different parts of the text highlighted, a child and an author, and a child's face with a light bulb in the forehead help illustrate the QAR concepts. First and second graders learn to distinguish only between right-there (in the text) and in-my-head (not in the text) QARs.

2. *Prepare questions.* Teachers select a short passage from an informational book that students are reading and write several questions illustrating each QAR category.

3. *Introduce the QAR technique.* Teachers introduce the chart, telling students that they will learn about four kinds of information that can help them answer questions about what they have read. Teachers read the passage aloud or have students read it. They write right-there questions on the chalkboard and invite children to find answers to these questions from the passage. After the students answer the questions, they explain to students that right-there questions have words from the text in the question and in the answer. Then teachers write several in-my-head questions and ask students to answer them. They explain that in-my-head questions have answers that are not in the text but come from the students' own experiences and knowledge. Then they present the other QARs using the same procedure.

4. *Students practice QARs.* Students read another passage, and teachers ask several questions about the passage. Working in small groups, students answer the questions and determine the type of QAR. Students develop additional questions for their classmates to answer. Students who answer these questions discuss whether they used information from the text or their experience to answer the questions. Teachers can add some questions that could be answered from either source and discuss that sometimes questions can be answered from different sources.

5. *Incorporate QARs in other activities.* Students can use the concept of QARs in self-questioning or reciprocal teaching.

This technique is not intended to help children answer questions correctly; rather, it is designed to help students learn that questions require different kinds of thinking to be answered correctly.

Clusters.   Students can explore text by making clusters to diagram main ideas and details in informational text (Tompkins & Hoskisson, 1991). One type of cluster students can construct is a *5 W's plus* how *cluster.* The topic is written in a center circle, and six rays are drawn out from the center and labeled *who, what, when, where, why* and *how.* Then students add details to explain each of the *W* words and *how.* Figure 7.13 presents a 5 *W's* plus *how* cluster constructed by second graders after reading *Cranberries* (Jaspersohn, 1991).

A second kind of cluster is a *biographical cluster* that includes information about a person's childhood, education, adulthood, and accomplishments. After reading a biography, students make a cluster by writing the person's name in the center circle, and drawing out rays for important events in the person's life. Then details are added about important events on lines drawn out from each ray.

Another cluster can be created from information related to the five senses. For example, after reading *The Hidden Life of the Meadow* (Schwartz, 1988), students could construct a *five-senses cluster* by writing the word *meadows* in the center circle, drawing out rays for each of the five senses, and adding details related to seeing, tasting, smelling, hearing, and touching.

FIGURE 7.13   5 *W*'s plus *How* Cluster for *Cranberries* (Jaspersohn, 1991)

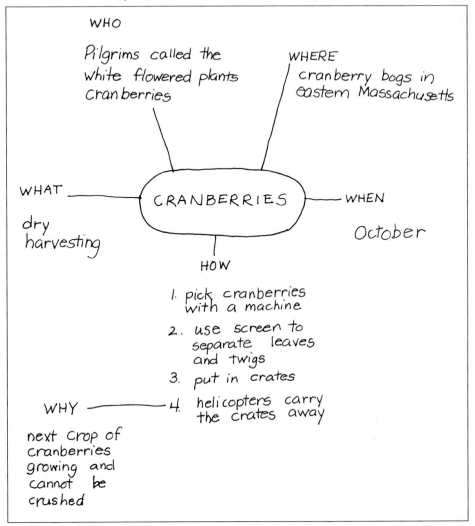

Students can identify main ideas and details to use in constructing their own clusters using the *list, group, and label activity* (Taba, 1967). First, students brainstorm a list of ideas that they remember from their reading. Each idea can be written on an index card or on a fact sheet (Hess, 1991). For example, Figure 7.14 presents a fact sheet that fourth graders wrote about thunderstorms after reading *Flash, Crash, Rumble, and Roll* (Branley, 1985). Students read the book and wrote sentences with information they learned from their reading (Figure 7.14). Next students cut up their fact sheet and arrange facts in main idea groups. Then they think of titles for their groups or categories. They glue related words of a group in a cluster or a column.

Learning logs.   Writing in learning logs engages students in rereading and rethinking about the informational text they have read. Teachers can focus entries in

FIGURE 7.14   Fact Sheet

Fact *Warm air rises inside clouds.*	Fact *Airplanes get their wings ripped off in clouds.*
Fact *Clouds grow sometimes 10 miles high.*	Fact *Lightning is a mile long.*
Fact *Water in clouds is water vapor.*	Fact *Thunder can't hurt you but lightning can.*
Fact *Clouds can have crystals.*	Fact *Go inside if it lightnings or lay down.*
Fact *Air also goes down.*	Fact *People thought lightning was God's finger.*

learning logs by asking students to write summaries of what they have read, write questions for other students to answer (Fitzgerald, 1983), or make a list of things they learned from reading. Students could also quickwrite on a topic related to the informational text or on what they remember from reading. They can also construct clusters, maps, or other diagrams in their learning logs. These entries can be used in a whole-class or small discussion of the reading or could be used as information to be included in a report or presentation. Figure 7.15 presents two learning log entries written by a third grader. The first is a quickwrite about spiders and the second is a cluster about birds.

Focusing on the Text.   Informational text can be difficult for students to read because these texts include so many technical and unfamiliar words. Students need to develop strategies to focus on the text to learn the meanings of new words as well as new meanings of familiar words. The most effective way to learn vocabulary is by reading (Nagy, 1988), and students learn many new words through reading, talking, and writing as a part of content area units. Using vocabulary for genuine reading and writing activities is more effective than looking up meanings in dictionaries or writing definitions; however, teachers can play an important role in students' vocabulary learning. They draw attention to words in the text, plan for activities to focus on particular words, and help children learn independent strategies for learning new words as they read.

The most effective vocabulary instruction helps students relate new words to their prior knowledge, be actively involved in their own learning, develop independent strategies for word learning, and develop ownership of words. Children develop ownership of words when they know words so well that they use them competently in different contexts and in reading, writing, and talking (Carr & Wixon, 1986). Teachers can begin by showing students how to apply phonics (knowledge of letter-sound relationships), structural analysis (knowledge of prefixes, suffixes, and other word parts), and context clues to word learning. A knowledge of phonics helps students identify unfamiliar sight words that they may already know the meaning of or that may be part of their speaking or listening vocabularies. Structural analysis helps students use the meanings found in prefixes, suffixes, and root words to both identify a word and know something of its meaning. Context clues involve using the surrounding words in a text to discover a word's meaning. Meanings are provided in context through definitions, synonyms, antonyms, or examples. Students are encouraged to use all these sources of information in the text, sometimes followed by reference to a dictionary or thesaurus, to determine the meanings of words.

Word walls. Teachers help students develop an awareness of words by drawing attention to vocabulary. One way is by having students construct a word wall. The teacher and students select words related to the focus unit or theme cycle from the text and add these words to the word wall. For example, a word wall for a theme cycle on weather might include the words *water vapor, crystals, electricity, funnel-shaped, tornado, cyclone, meteorologist, forecast, anemometer, rain gauge, air pressure, dew point, barometer, stratus, altostratus, cirrostratus, front,* and *pressure system.* Words are added to the word wall as students encounter them in the texts they are reading, such as when they read *Weather Forecasting* (Gibbons, 1987), view a film related to the theme cycle, or interview a meteorologist.

Definition activities. Most vocabulary activities are designed to draw attention to word definitions. Sometimes students need instruction in understanding what a definition of a word is. Good readers intuitively know the kinds of information to look for in the text in order to construct their own definitions of words. They look for examples, features or distinguishing characteristics, and more general classifications to which the word is related. For example, in constructing a definition for the word *tornado,* students would note in the text that tornadoes are powerful storms (more general classification), have moving air that spins around in a funnel shape and air that travels up to 300 miles an hour (distinguishing features), and are also called twisters, cyclones, or waterspouts (examples). Teachers can help students learn the kinds of information they should seek when learning the meanings of words using the *concept of definition procedure* (Schwartz & Raphael, 1985). The steps in using this procedure are

1. *Construct a word map and prepare examples.* Teachers construct a word map as shown in Figure 7.16, and select three or four concepts that children are familiar with such as tree, house, or swim.
2. *Introduce the concept of definition.* Teachers discuss with students that understanding the meaning of a word means knowing three kinds of information about the word: the general class (usually answers the question "what is it?"), distinguishing features (usually answers the question "what is it like?"), and examples

FIGURE 7.15 Entries from a Third Grader's Learning Logs

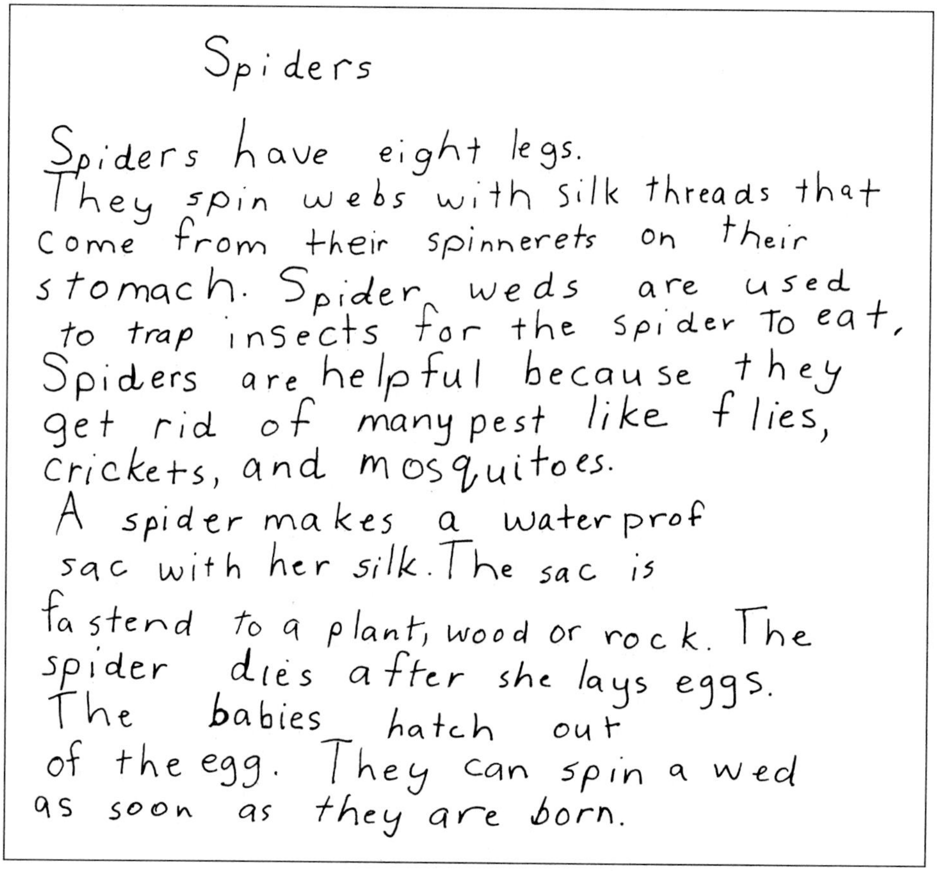

> ## Spiders
>
> Spiders have eight legs.
> They spin webs with silk threads that
> come from their spinnerets on their
> stomach. Spider weds are used
> to trap insects for the spider to eat,
> Spiders are helpful because they
> get rid of many pest like flies,
> crickets, and mosquitoes.
> A spider makes a water prof
> sac with her silk. The sac is
> fastend to a plant, wood or rock. The
> spider dies after she lays eggs.
> The babies hatch out
> of the egg. They can spin a wed
> as soon as they are born.

(usually answers the question "what are some examples?"). They show a word map and talk through the kinds of information that will be placed on the map.

3. *Work through the map with a practice word.* Teachers identify a vocabulary word and students brainstorm information to complete the map. They discuss why the information fits in a particular place on the map. Students work in small groups to complete other vocabulary words and discuss their maps with the class.

4. *Encourage students to use the concept of definitions with self-selected vocabulary.* Students construct word maps in their learning logs for unfamiliar words they have selected to learn. Or, they can create word maps for other students to complete.

Semantic feature analysis. Another way that students expand their understanding of words is by examining how one word relates to other words. The *semantic feature analysis* (Nagy, 1988) activity that Mr. Roberts used in the case study in the beginning of this chapter is designed to show students how words are related to one another. In a semantic feature analysis, students examine a group of related words

FIGURE 7.15,   *continued*

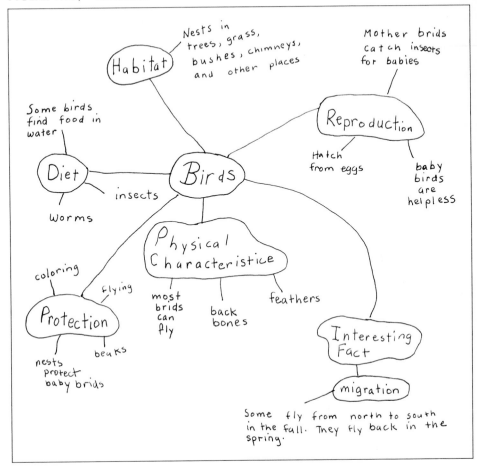

according to a list of distinguishing features or characteristics. The steps in preparing a semantic feature analysis are

1. *Select a group of related words.* Teachers select a group of 5 to 10 related words from a focus unit or theme cycle. For example, words related to land travel might include *car, bus, van, motorcycle, semi-tractor trailer, ambulance, recreational vehicle,* and *taxi.*

2. *Select the distinguishing characteristics.* Teachers make a list of several features or characteristics that can be used to compare and contrast the group of words. For example, the features of land travel words might include "two-wheeled," "four-wheeled," "more than four wheels," "carries passengers," "carries goods," "used by families," and "used to make money."

3. *Create the matrix.* Teachers make a matrix by listing the group of related words in a vertical column on the left side of a chart and the distinguishing charac-

FIGURE 7.16   Structure of a Word Map (*Note.* From "Concept of Definition: A Key to Improving Students' Vocabulary" by R. Schwartz and T. Raphael, 1985, *The Reading Teacher,* 39, p. 201. Reprinted with permission of Robert M. Schwartz and the International Reading Association.)

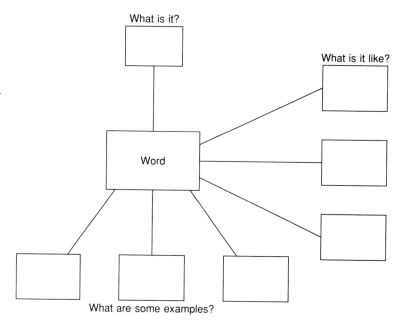

teristics in a horizontal row across the top of the chart. Then vertical and horizontal lines are drawn to construct the matrix. The matrix can be drawn on chart paper to use with the whole class or a small group, or individual copies made for each student.

4. *Present the semantic feature matrix and discuss the words.* Present the semantic feature matrix and have students discuss each word related to the features identified on the matrix. Students place a + on the matrix to indicate that the word has the feature, a − to indicate the word does not have the feature, or a ? to indicate that sometimes the feature might apply.

An adaptation of semantic feature analysis can be used with biographies. For the *biography vocabulary analysis* activity, students and teachers identify a list of words from a biography they are reading. Students decide whether or not each word relates to the famous person in the biography. For example, after reading *And Then What Happened, Paul Revere?* (Fritz, 1973) fifth graders made a list of 25 words from the biography including *porringers, anvils, sentries, congregations, lampblack,* and *forge.* Then students worked in small groups and put a + or a − by each word to signify whether or not the word related to Paul Revere. Afterwards, students discussed their choices.

Word sorts.   Another vocabulary activity is *word sorts* (Gillett & Temple, 1990) in which students look for relationships among the words. For example, as a part of a theme cycle on the California Gold Rush of 1849, a class of fourth graders sorted some of the words on their word wall into these categories:

Gold: ore, nuggets, veins, valuable, ounce, carat, precious
Prospectors: James Marshall, ruthless, panhandlers, greedy
Uses of gold: money, jewelry, red glass, gold leaf

To make a word sort, teachers or students select words from a focus or theme cycle and write them in a grid with 25 to 30 spaces. The words may be selected from a word wall, informational books, or from students' learning logs. Figure 7.17 presents a word sort grid for words from *The Magic School Bus Inside the Earth* (Cole, 1987). Teachers duplicate the word sort grid and students cut the words apart. Students sort the words and determine categories for sorting. Sometimes all the words do not fit in the categories so students can discard a few words. After sorting, students glue the words related to a category into a column or cluster.

Extending Step

Through extending activities, students integrate content area information gleaned from reading, writing, or viewing multiple texts and use reading strategies independently. Most extending activities in an interactive perspective involve students in reading text sets so that they can explore a topic of interest in greater depth. Other activities provide opportunities for students to demonstrate their new understandings about topics by writing reports.

Text sets. Teachers and students select text sets for a focus unit, theme cycle, or for topics of interest. These text sets might include informational books and other readings related to Martin Luther King, Jr., rain forests, Egypt, the American Revolution, or the water cycle. In the case study at the beginning of this chapter, Mr. Roberts prepared a text set on reptiles and amphibians, and this text set was, in turn, part of a larger text set on vertebrate animals.

Oral and written reports. Students research a topic by reading a text set and then share what they have learned by writing a report or preparing an oral report. The steps in preparing reports are

1. *Students choose a topic.* Students select a topic related to a theme cycle that puzzles them or that they are interested in learning more about. Possible topics

FIGURE 7.17   Word Sort Grid for *The Magic School Bus Inside the Earth* (Cole, 1987)

earth	marble	quartzite
minerals	slate	crust
soil	granite	igneous rock
clay	sandstone	outer core
sedimentary rock	volcano	obsidian
pumice	mantle	stalagmite
basalt	stalagtite	fossil
shale	sediment	inner core
prehistoric	metamorphic rock	lava
limestone		

related to weather include meteorologists, tornadoes, clouds, and thunderstorms. Topics should be broad enough so that they can be subdivided into several parts but narrow enough so that they are manageable. For example, weather is too broad a topic, but cumulonimbus clouds is too narrow a topic for most elementary and middle school students.

2. *Students design research questions or subtopics.* Students select questions related to a unit of study. Questions may emerge as a part of a KWL chart activity or are drafted just prior to beginning a report activity. Questions for a research report on meteorologists might include, "What do meteorologists do?" "What do meteorologists have to know?" "How are meteorologists trained?" or "Where do meteorologists work?" A report on jungle animals might include the subtopics of appearance, diet, habitat, and protection.

3. *Students gather and organize information.* Students search for answers to their questions. Kindergarten or first grade children dictate information they remember from listening to their teacher read aloud, viewing films, or interviewing guest speakers. Teachers record the information on a cluster. Older students can use a cluster or a *data chart* (McKenzie, 1979) to gather and organize information about each research question or subtopic. Figure 7.18 presents a data chart that third graders might use for a report about Native Americans. For either the cluster or data chart, students list their research questions and then record information from several sources including informational books, magazines, films, filmstrips, interviews, and encyclopedias to complete the chart. They list their sources on the

FIGURE 7.18   Data Chart on Native Americans

Source	Where did they live?	What did they live in?	What did they eat?	What did they play?

back of the chart and later write the bibliographic information about these sources on a reference page in the final copy of their reports.

4. *Students draft the report.* For written reports, students write or dictate a rough draft of their report using the information from their cluster or data chart. For oral reports they decide how to present the information they have gathered. Students prepare notecards with key words to remind them of information to present.

5. *Students revise and edit the report.* For written reports, students meet in writing groups to share their rough drafts, get feedback from classmates about how well they are communicating, and then make revisions to clarify, expand, and refine ideas. Later, they proofread their reports and correct spelling and mechanical errors. For oral reports, students might prepare visuals such as a chart, diagram, picture, or model. Students preparing an oral report on tigers, for example, might find several magazine photographs of tigers, draw pictures of the food that tigers eat, and locate where tigers live on a world map. Students rehearse their reports one or twice with a partner. The focus in this practice session is for students to speak fluently and confidently without reading or memorizing their report. They refer to their notecards as needed.

6. *Students publish their reports.* Students write a final copy with a bibliography and publish their reports or contribute their report to a class book. Students giving oral reports present their reports to the class using notecards and the visuals they have prepared.

MAKING DECISIONS ABOUT TEACHING FROM AN INTERACTIVE PERSPECTIVE

Teachers make several decisions regarding how to support students' reading from an interactive perspective. Teachers must first decide the purposes for which they want students to read. Students need opportunities to read for both literary and informational purposes and to develop more refined strategies for engaging in these kinds of reading. Teachers must carefully consider the purposes for which students read and plan activities that will encourage students to read for those purposes.

Second, teachers need to decide whether students will engage in teacher-directed or independent activities. Sometimes students need a teacher-directed preparing activity before reading independently; at other times students benefit from exploring in a self-selected activity. Not all stories, poems, or informational books that are selected as core reading selections require that teachers plan preparing, reading, exploring, and extending activities, and not all children need guidance as they move through the reading process. It is the teachers' responsibility to assess whether students need activities that guide them through reading a selected reading or whether they should engage in most of these activities on their own. In fact, the ultimate goal of instruction is for children to become independent, competent readers, and students need many opportunities to stretch their abilities on their own.

Third, after teachers have decided that they need to plan or direct a particular kind of reading activity, they select from the many options available. To make decisions about instruction and activities, teachers first carefully read and respond to the stories, informational books, and poems that they have selected for instruction. They thoughtfully read a literary work to discover themes, issues, topics, concepts, or other literary elements that are important to understand the work. For example, in the case study at the beginning of this chapter, Ms. Nee believed that the issue of discovering what is most essential for happiness contributed to an important theme in *Sylvester and the Magic Pebble*. Therefore, she planned activities that helped her students focus on this issue before and after reading (Chapter 8 also addresses selecting reading activities and making decisions about instruction). Figure 7.19 presents an overview of all the activities presented in this chapter. Teachers carefully consider which of these activities best fits the purposes of reading, the needs of the students, and the characteristics of the reading selection. Teachers make these decisions based on what skills and strategies they are accountable for teaching and on their knowledge of what their students know and need to learn.

Teachers also decide what kinds of skills and strategies they will teach. Traditionally, reading instruction has focused on teaching three broad categories of skills: comprehension (e.g., recognizing cause and effect, sequencing, identifying character traits), vocabulary (e.g., knowing the meanings of words and acquiring sight words),

FIGURE 7.19   Overview of Activities from an Interactive Perspective

	Reading for Literary Purposes	Reading for Informational Purposes
Preparing Step	Quickwrite ETR Vocabulary prediction DRTA	Learning logs Hypothesizing Self-questioning Reading for different purposes
Reading Step	Think-alouds Fix-up strategies	Think-alouds Reciprocal teaching Interactive reading guides
Exploring Step	Retelling Storytelling Rereading Drawing Story charts Literature journals Dramatizing Word walls Clusters Definition clusters Sight word learning routine Decode by analogy Prefix/suffix strategy	QARs 5 *W's* plus *how* cluster Biographical cluster Five-senses cluster List-group-label Learning logs Word walls Word maps Semantic feature analysis Word sorts
Extending Step	Extended reading Projects to extend understandings of readings	Text sets Oral and written reports

and word recognition (e.g., using context, structural analysis, and phonics). Most state and local school systems have developed lists of skills to be taught at particular grade levels, sometimes called curriculum guides, scope and sequence charts, or minimum competency lists. Some school systems require that teachers teach the skills and competencies listed in a basal reader series. In traditional instruction, these lists of skills guided and even dominated instructional programs. Teachers knew when to teach cause and effect, the *less* prefix, and words on high frequency lists by following the scope and sequence of skills or a curriculum guide.

Although teachers in these school systems may be free to use literature to teach reading, their students are still expected to pass competency tests that are correlated with a basal reading series or the state's minimum competency list. Teachers who are working in systems with these expectations need to consult the teachers' manual of the basal reader or curriculum guide to identify which skills, strategies, and competencies their students are expected to know. It is important to note that most skills listed in basal readers or curriculum guides are minimal; that is, many children already know the skills in a particular basal reader before they read it (Taylor, Frye, & Gaetz, 1990).

We want to caution teachers that most skills lists, either from basal reader series or from state or local curriculum guides, imply that reading is developed by learning a set of discrete skills, such as being able to recognize cause and effect or to know the sounds associated with consonants. Reading cannot be broken into such small, discrete skills even though good readers are able to apply these skills. Rather, this chapter has presented a broader view that readers need a repertoire of strategies which they can use to guide and improve their own reading of literature. We also caution teachers that reading literature should be first and foremost an enjoyable activity. Analyzing stories for themes or making inferences about character traits or cause and effect relationships should never become more important than fostering an appreciation and love of literature.

Teachers plan carefully so that over a year's time children have reading and other language experiences that systematically provide opportunities for growth. Making effective plans, keeping careful records of observations, and wide reading in professional journals and books all contribute to a teacher's own professional development. Perhaps nothing is more important to making decisions than a teacher's own professional knowledge about reading and language learning.

Teachers are expected to be careful observers of the learners in their classroom. Careful observation provides information about what each student can do and would benefit from learning. This information guides teachers as they select instructional activities.

The decisions that teachers make about supporting children's reading from the interactive perspective are

- Consider whether students will be reading for informative or literary purposes.
- Assess whether students need teacher-directed or independent preparing, reading, exploring, and extending activities.
- Select an appropriate activity that meets the needs of individual students, is consonant with the purposes of reading, and fits the text.

FIGURE 7.20   Summary Chart for Decision Tree

<table>
<tr><td></td><td align="center">**Decision Tree**</td></tr>
<tr><td>Chapter 1</td><td>Using Literature in the Reading Program</td></tr>
<tr><td>Chapter 2</td><td>Choosing Literature for Children</td></tr>
<tr><td>Chapter 3</td><td>Learning About Authors and Illustrators</td></tr>
<tr><td>Chapter 4</td><td>Identifying Perspectives on Reading Instruction</td></tr>
<tr><td>Chapter 5</td><td>Teaching from a Reader Response Perspective</td></tr>
<tr><td>Chapter 6</td><td>Teaching from a Critical Perspective</td></tr>
<tr><td>**Chapter 7**</td><td>

Teaching from an Interactive Perspective

- **Consider whether students will be reading for literary or informative purposes.**
- **Assess whether students need teacher-directed or independent preparing, reading, exploring, or extending activities.**
- **Select an appropriate activity that meets the needs of individual students, is consonant with the purposes of reading, and fits the text.**
- **Consult school or state curriculum guides or basal reader manuals for lists of expected competencies or learning outcomes.**
- **Keep informed of new instructional techniques and theories by reading professional journals and books.**

</td></tr>
<tr><td>Chapter 8</td><td>Putting It All Together</td></tr>
<tr><td>Chapter 9</td><td>Assessing Students' Learning</td></tr>
</table>

- Consult school system or state curriculum guides or basal reader manuals for lists of competencies or learning outcomes.
- Keep informed of new instructional techniques and theories by reading professional journals and books.

This information is added to the decision-making diagram, as shown in Figure 7.20.

REFERENCES

Atwell, M., & Rhodes, L. (1984). Strategy lessons as alternatives to skills lessons in reading. *Journal of Reading, 27,* 700–705.

Au, K. (1979). Using the experience-text-relationship method with minority children. *The Reading Teacher, 32,* 677–679.

Blanton, W., Wood, K., & Moorman, G. (1990). The role of purpose in reading instruction. *The Reading Teacher, 43,* 486–493.

Bridge, C., Winograd, P., & Haley, D. (1983). Using predictable materials vs. preprimers to teach beginning sight words. *The Reading Teacher, 36,* 884–891.

Carr, E., & Wixon, K. (1986). Guidelines for evaluating vocabulary instruction. *Journal of Reading, 29,* 588–595.

Christie, J. (1987). Play and story comprehension: A critique of recent training research. *Journal of Research and Development, 21,* 36–43.

Clay, M. (1979). *The early detection of reading difficulties.* Auckland, New Zealand: Heinemann.

Combs, M. (1987). Modeling the reading process with enlarged texts. *The Reading Teacher, 40,* 422–426.

Davey, B. (1983). Think-aloud—modeling the cognitive processes of reading comprehension. *Journal of Reading, 27,* 44–47.

Dowhower, S. (1987). Effects of repeated reading on second grade transitional readers' fluency and comprehension. *Reading Research Quarterly, 22,* 389–406.

Fisher, B. (1991). *Joyful learning: A whole language kindergarten.* Portsmouth, NH: Heinemann.

Fitzgerald, J. (1983). Helping students gain self-control. *The Reading Teacher, 37,* 249–253.

Fitzgerald, J., & Teasley, A. (1986). Effects of instruction in narrative structure on children's writing. *Journal of Educational Psychology, 78,* 424–433.

Freppon, P., & Dahl, K. (1991). Learning about phonics in a whole language classroom. *Language Arts, 68,* 190–197.

Fulwiler, T. (1987). Introduction. In T. Fulwiler (Ed.), *The journal book* (pp. 1–4). Portsmouth, NH: Heinemann.

Galda, L. (1982). Playing about a story: Its impact on comprehension. *The Reading Teacher, 36,* 52–55.

Gambrell, L., Pfeiffer, W., & Wilson, R. (1985). The effects of retelling upon reading comprehension and recall of text information. *Journal of Educational Research, 78,* 216–220.

Gaskins, I., Downer, M., Anderson, R., Cunningham, P., Gaskins, R., & Schommer, M. (1987). A metacognitive approach to phonics: Using what you know to decode what you don't know. *Remedial and Special Education, 9,* 36–41.

Gillet, J., & Temple, C. (1990). *Understanding reading problems: Assessment and instruction.* Glenview, IL: Scott Foresman.

Heald-Taylor, G. (1987). How to use predictable books for K–2 language arts instruction. *The Reading Teacher, 40,* 656–661.

Hess, M. (1991). Understanding purpose, classification, response. *Language Arts, 68,* 228–232.

Johnson, T., & Louis, D. (1987). *Literacy through literature.* Portsmouth, NH: Heinemann.

Marshall, J. (1987). The effects of writing on students' understanding of literary texts. *Research in the Teaching of English, 21,* 30–63.

McGee, L., & Richgels, D. (1990). Learning from text using reading and writing. In T. Shanahan (Ed.), *Reading and writing together: New perspectives for the classroom* (pp. 145–168). Norwood, MA: Christopher-Gordon.

McKenzie, G. (1979). Data charts: A crutch for helping pupils organize reports. *Language Arts, 56,* 784–788.

Morrow, L. (1989). Using story retelling to develop comprehension. In K. Muth (Ed.), *Children's comprehension of text: Research into practice* (pp. 37–58). Newark, DE: International Reading Association.

Nagy, W. (1988). *Teaching vocabulary to improve reading comprehension.* Urbana, IL: ERIC Clearinghouse on Reading and Communication Skills and the National Council of Teachers of English and the International Reading Association.

Ohlhausen, M. M., & Jepsen, M. (1992). Lessons from Goldilocks: "Somebody's been choosing my books but I can make my own choices now!" *The New Advocate, 5,* 31–46.

Palinscar, A., & Brown, A. (1984). Reciprocal teaching of comprehension-fostering and comprehension-monitoring activities. *Cognition and Instruction, 2,* 117–175.

Raphael, T. (1986). Teaching question-answer relationships, revised. *The Reading Teacher, 39,* 516–523.

Schwartz, R., & Raphael, T. (1985). Concept of definition: A key to improving students' vocabulary. *The Reading Teacher, 39,* 198–205.

Stauffer, R. (1969). *Directing reading maturity as a cognitive process.* New York: Harper & Row.

Taba, H. (1967). *Teacher's handbook for elementary social science.* Reading, MA: Addison-Wesley.

Taylor, B., Frye, B., & Gaetz, T. (1990). Reducing the number of reading skill activities in the elementary classroom. *Journal of Reading Behavior, 22,* 167–179.

Tompkins, G. E. (1990). *Teaching writing: Balancing process and product.* New York: Merrill/Macmillan.

Tompkins, G. E., & Hoskisson, K. (1991). *Language arts: Content and teaching strategies* (2nd Ed.). New York: Merrill/Macmillan.

Weaver, C. (1988). *Reading process and practice: From socio-psycholinguistics to whole language.* Portsmouth, NH: Heinemann.

White, T., Sowell, J., & Yanagihara, A. (1989). Teaching elementary students to use word-part clues. *The Reading Teacher, 42,* 302–308.

Wood, K. (1988). Guiding students through informational text. *The Reading Teacher, 41,* 912–920.

Yaden, D., Jr. (1988). Understanding stories through repeated read-alouds: How many does it take? *The Reading Teacher, 41,* 556–560.

CHILDREN'S LITERATURE REFERENCES

Branley, F. (1985). *Flash, crash, rumble, and roll* (rev. ed.). New York: Harper & Row.

Coatsworth, M. (1988). "Rain poem." In B. S. deRegniers, Moore, E., White, M., & Carr, J. (Sel.), *Song of popcorn.* New York: Scholastic.

Cole, J. (1987). *The magic school bus inside the earth.* New York: Scholastic.

Cooper, M. (1987). The nature of time. *Faces: The Magazine about People, 3,* 5–9.

Fleischman, S. (1963). *By the great horn spoon!* Boston: Little, Brown.

Fritz, J. (1973). *And then what happened Paul Revere?* New York: Coward-McCann.

Frost, R. (1978). *Stopping by woods on a snowy evening.* New York: Dutton.

Frost, R. (1988). "Stopping by woods on a snowy evening." In B. de Regniers (Ed.), *Sing a song of popcorn: Every child's book of poems* (p. 36). New York: Scholastic Hardcover.

Gibbons, G. (1987). *Weather forecasting.* New York: Four Winds.

Jaspersohn, W. (1991). *Cranberries.* Boston: Houghton Mifflin.

Jukes, M. (1984). *Like Jake and me.* New York: Knopf.

L'Engle, M. (1962). *A wrinkle in time.* New York: Farrar, Straus & Giroux.

Livingston, M. (1988). "Rain". In B. S. deRegniers, Moore, E., White, M., & Carr, J. (Sel.) *Sing a song of popcorn.* New York: Scholastic.

Mayer, M. (1968). *There's a nightmare in my closet.* New York: Dial.

Most, B. (1978). *If the dinosaurs came back.* San Diego, CA: Harcourt Brace Jovanovich.

Parker, M., & Wright, J. (1991). *Frogs, toads, lizards, and salamanders.* New York: Greenwillow.

Schnieper, C. (1987). *An apple tree through the year.* Minneapolis, MN: Carolrhoda Books.

Schwartz, D. (1988). *The hidden life of the meadow.* New York: Crown.

Steig, W. (1969). *Sylvester and the magic pebble.* New York: Simon & Schuster.

Steig, W. (1971). *Amos and Boris.* New York: Farrar, Straus & Giroux.

Steig, W. (1976). *The amazing bone.* New York: Farrar, Straus & Giroux.

Taylor, M. (1976). *Roll of thunder, hear my cry.* New York: Dial.

Van Allsburg, C. (1985). *Polar express.* Boston: Houghton Mifflin.

Waber, B. (1972). *Ira sleeps over.* Boston: Houghton Mifflin.

Westcott, N. (1988). *The lady with the alligator purse.* Boston: Little, Brown.

White, E. B. (1952). *Charlotte's web.* New York: Harper & Row.

Yolen, J. (1987). *Owl moon.* New York: Philomel.

CHAPTER 8
PUTTING IT ALL TOGETHER

In this chapter you will learn to make decisions about:
- Determining a focus.
- Identifying literature selections.
- Designing a program with core literature and reading workshop components.
- Considering theoretical perspectives.
- Planning reading and response activities.
- Coordinating grouping patterns with reading and response activities.
- Organizing grouping patterns with reading and response activities.
- Organizing the classroom and time.
- Managing record-keeping.
- Assessing students' learning.

IN THE FOLLOWING CASE STUDIES, we describe Mr. Kfoury's and Ms. Jones' literature-based reading programs, which reflect their decisions about "putting it all together."

A CASE IN POINT

Mr. Kfoury's Literacy Block

Mr. Kfoury, a fifth grade teacher, divides his daily schedule into five time blocks: literacy block; social studies block; science block; math block; and arts block. During the literacy block, he organizes reading and response activities into units or themes that focus on an author, genre, or theme, and these units usually last six to eight weeks. Each unit includes both a core literature component and a reading workshop component.

Mr. Kfoury begins most units by selecting a focus. For this unit, the focus is on courage, and he has decided to begin with a core literature component and then move to a reading workshop component. Since Mr. Kfoury has decided to begin

the unit with core literature, he selects a chapter book that is central to the focus to read aloud to the whole class. Mr. Kfoury selects *Number the Stars* (Lowry, 1989), a Newbery Medal story of a Christian girl's courage as she helps her Jewish friend escape from Denmark during World War II. He intends to use a reader response perspective so students will have opportunities to respond personally to the issues presented in *Number the Stars* and the other books they read in this unit. Therefore, Mr. Kfoury makes tentative plans for some response activities that he expects all students to complete. He also prepares a list of other response activities from which students may choose. Each day Mr. Kfoury plans to read aloud one or two chapters of *Number the Stars* as students follow along in individual copies of the book. They will reread portions of the book independently, write responses in response journals, discuss their reading in grand conversations, and pursue response projects they have chosen.

Mr. Kfoury also selects additional books related to the focus for students to read in small groups. He chooses these books after reading and carefully considering many books recommended by librarians, colleagues, and students. He also has "kid-tested" them in his classroom over several years of teaching. For this unit he selects *Call It Courage* (Sperry, 1968), *Julie of the Wolves* (George, 1972), *Stone Fox* (Gardiner, 1980), *The Courage of Sarah Noble* (Dalgliesh, 1982), *Trouble River* (Byars, 1969), and *The Upstairs Room* (Reiss, 1972) for small-group reading. Several days into the unit, Mr. Kfoury gives a book talk about these books; he holds each book up, tells something about the plot, reads aloud an interesting excerpt, and arouses students' interest by raising issues or posing questions. Students sign up to read one of these books, and depending on students' interests, four, five, or six small groups, called "literacy clubs," will be formed to read and respond to the books. Mr. Kfoury meets with each group two or three times a week as they read and

discuss their books. He also guides students' reading of these books and presents preparing, reading, and exploring lessons for each of the books to help students explore the book in depth. Figure 8.1 presents Mr. Kfoury's daily schedule for the core literature portion of the unit.

Mr. Kfoury uses a reading workshop approach for the second portion of his unit on courage. In this portion, students read and respond to self-selected books, conference with Mr. Kfoury about the books they are reading, attend whole-class minilessons to learn literacy strategies and skills, and share the books they are reading and responding to with classmates. Mr. Kfoury involves his students in collecting the reading materials they will read during reading workshop. They locate poems, stories, informational books, magazine articles, and newspaper stories about courage in the class library, school library, and local public library and arrange them together on a special shelf in the class library. Then students choose books and other reading materials from this collection to read independently.

Mr. Kfoury also meets with students individually in conferences during reading workshop. During the conferences he discusses the kinds of materials students have read (students keep a log of the titles of books, poems, and other materials they have read), listens to students read aloud a

FIGURE 8.1   Mr. Kfoury's Schedule for Core Literature

8:30–8:45	Arrival, Lunch Count, Attendance, Independent Reading
8:45–11:00	Literacy Block

	8:45–9:30	Read-aloud core book and response activities
	9:30–9:45	Literacy demonstrations
	9:45–10:15	Literacy club (small-group meetings, reading, and response activities)
	10:15–10:30	Recess
	10:30–11:00	Literacy club (continued)

11:00–12:00	Mathematics Block
12:00–12:45	Lunch and Recess
12:45–1:30	Science Block
1:30–2:00	Arts Block: Physical education, music, art, library
2:00–2:45	Social Studies Block
2:45	Dismissal

FIGURE 8.2   *Mr. Kfoury's Reading Workshop Schedule*

8:45–9:15	Reading Aloud to Students
9:15–9:30	Minilesson
9:30–9:35	Class Meeting
9:35–10:15	Self-Selected Reading, Response Activities and Conferences
10:15–10:30	Recess
10:30–10:45	Self-Selected Reading (continued)
10:45–11:00	Student Sharing

short passage to assess their use of strategies and their progress in interpreting stories and poems or learning information from informational books and magazines, reviews students' plans for response activities, and makes suggestions for future reading and projects. After each conference Mr. Kfoury writes brief notes about the student's progress, which he keeps in special folders. He meets with three or four students each day so that every two weeks he meets with each student in the class.

Each day Mr. Kfoury reads aloud to the students a variety of reading materials related to courage and teaches minilessons. He uses minilessons to introduce students to new reading strategies, provide a forum for students to share strategies they have found successful, model how to do particular response activities such writing a simulated diary, and share strategies and activities that students can use as they prepare, read, explore, and extend a book.

Each day reading workshop ends with several students sharing the book they have been reading and their response projects with the class. Because students work individually during reading workshop, Mr. Kfoury feels that sharing is an important social activity. Figure 8.2 presents Mr. Kfoury's schedule for the reading workshop component of the unit on courage.

A CASE IN POINT

Ms. Jones' Language Arts Block

Ms. Jones teaches first grade, and because many of her students are learning English as a second language, she places the highest priority on integrating language arts throughout the school day. She divides her day into four major time blocks: language arts, the arts and physical education, mathematics, and content (social studies and science). Figure 8.3 presents Ms. Jones' daily schedule. The five components in her language arts block are

1. *Shared Reading:* Ms. Jones and her students read big books, poems, and predictable or easy-to-read books using shared reading techniques.
2. *Response Activities:* Students respond to their reading by drawing and writing in reading logs, and they participate in response projects.
3. *Rereading:* Small groups of students reread books and poems previously introduced in shared reading with Ms. Jones.
4. *Independent Reading:* Students read self-selected books individually or with buddies and listen to books at the listening center.
5. *Conferences:* Ms. Jones meets with stu-

FIGURE 8.3   Ms. Jones' Daily Schedule

8:30–8:40	Children Arrive, Attendance, Lunch Count
8:40–11:00	Language Arts Block

	8:40–9:40	Shared reading
	9:40–9:50	Reading journals
	9:50–10:15	Rereading group, response activities, buddy reading, literacy centers
	10:15–10:35	Snack and recess
	10:35–11:00	Rereading, response activities, buddy reading, literacy centers

11:00–11:30	Arts and Physical Education Block
11:30–12:15	Lunch and Recess
12:15–1:00	Math Block
1:00–1:15	Reading Aloud to Students
1:15–2:30	Content Block (Social Studies and Science)
(2:10–2:30 Conferences)	
2:30–2:45	Sharing and Dismissal

dents in individual conferences and listens to them read aloud and talk about their reading during the afternoon content block.

Ms. Jones also incorporates language arts into other activities. She reads aloud to the whole class after lunch and incorporates reading, writing, listening, and discussion activities into the social studies and science content block in the afternoon. Content block units are *theme cycles* that focus on a content topic such as families or seasons and also include integrated listening, talking, reading, and writing activities. Often Ms. Jones incorporates theme cycles into the morning language arts block.

Ms. Jones usually takes an interactive "teaching reading" perspective in her teaching, and each of the components of the language arts and content blocks meets different instructional needs. Ms. Jones uses shared reading to introduce children to a wide variety of literature. She selects literature first for its literary qualities and appeal to young children. Her second concern is how to make the literature accessible to her emerging and beginning readers, many of whom have limited English speaking proficiency. She uses the shared reading time to model how readers respond to literature and connect literature to their

lives and to help children develop meaning-making strategies, such as predicting, visualizing, and applying fix-up strategies. In addition, she helps children focus on print and develop strategies for figuring out unknown words and their meanings.

Today the class is reading literature about winter in conjunction with a theme cycle on the four seasons, and Ms. Jones reads several literature selections during shared reading including a favorite story she has reread many times, a new selection, a poem, and a selection to focus on a strategy. First, Ms. Jones reads one of the children's favorite stories, *The Jacket I Wear in the Snow* (Neitzel, 1989) a repetitive book that describes the clothes a child puts on to play in the snow, and the children retell the story using clothesline props. This retelling activity helps children focus on sequence and allows them to repeat the words in an enjoyable and meaningful context.

Next, she reads the big book version of *The Snowy Day* (Keats, 1962) and focuses on the strategies of predicting and connecting with personal experience. While this book is too difficult for most of her children to read independently, it provides many opportunities to expand children's concepts, language, and responses. Next, she shares a chart containing Marie Louis Allen's poem "First Snow" (Prelutsky, 1983). This poem extends the images and language of winter presented in Keats' story. After reading the poem, children add words about winter to the classroom word wall.

During the next 10 or 15 minutes all the children write about their reading. Today they draw and write about what Peter liked to do in the snow in *The Snowy Day*. As the children write, Ms. Jones helps children segment words to invent spellings and invites them to read their responses to the class. During this part of the language arts block Ms. Jones focuses on informally teaching many of the phonic skills her students need.

During the next 20 minutes Ms. Jones meets with one of the three groups of seven or eight children of mixed reading abilities she has established for the current theme (the membership in the groups changes with each cycle). Ms. Jones gives each child in the group a copy of *The Wheels on the Bus* (Kovalski, 1987), a picture book version of the story in which two children shop for winter coats with their grandmother and miss the bus when they become engrossed in singing the familiar song of the same title. The children are familiar with the book from shared reading. Ms. Jones reads the book aloud, inviting the children to join in. She then asks for volunteers to read aloud a page from the story. The group rereads the story several times because of students' enthusiasm, and then Ms. Jones suggests three possible response activities for the story: using collage materials to construct a large bus for the bulletin board, writing new versions of the story in a shape book, or making stick puppets to retell the story. The group decides to make stick puppets to retell the story, and the children discuss how they will complete the tasks. They return to their seats to construct the puppets, practice for the show, and reread the story to their buddies.

The other two groups in the classroom have been reading to their buddies, completing response activities, reading self-selected books or poems, or working at the listening center, reading center, or writing center. Mrs. Morris, a part-time aide, circulates among the children helping them complete their tasks and monitoring to ensure that those who are buddy-reading record the title of the story they read and stamp the date in their reading folders.

Later, during the content block the children write poems about winter that they share with classmates while sitting in the author's chair. Some students choose to write "I like winter" poems, like this one:

> *I like winter.*
> *snowflakes*
> *cold*
> *white*
> *I like winter.*

Others write five-senses poems, following this format:

> *Snowflakes*
> *look like feathers falling*
> *sound like whispering*
> *smell like nothing*
> *feel like the refrigerator*
> *taste like vanilla ice cream*
> *I wish it would snow today!*

During the last few minutes of the afternoon content block when children are busy working on small-group or individual projects, Ms. Jones has conferences with two children each day. During the conferences Ms. Jones listens to a child read aloud part of a favorite book, and after reading she makes suggestions for other books that the child might read during the language arts block. Ms. Jones often makes a *running record* (an assessment of reading accuracy described in Chapter 9) to include in the child's *portfolio* (a collection of reading and writing samples used to document literacy growth described in Chapter 9).

INTRODUCTION

Organizing and managing a literature-based reading program is both a challenge and a joy. Teachers must make many complex decisions as they plan reading experiences for their students; however, making these decisions gives teachers an enormous sense of empowerment and satisfaction. The decisions that teachers make about selecting literature for their students to read, selecting reading and response activities, organizing the classroom, scheduling time for reading and language activities, keeping records, and assessing students' learning reflect the theoretical perspective underlying their instruction.

Mr. Kfoury and Ms. Jones made a number of decisions about their literature-based reading programs. They began by selecting literature for their students to read and identifying a focus for their reading and response activities. Mr. Kfoury focused on the theme of courage and selected books and other reading materials related to that theme, whereas Ms. Jones focused on seasons in a theme cycle that connected social studies and science to language arts. Both teachers identified one or more literature selections to share with the whole class or with small groups and collected other extended reading materials for students to read independently.

Both teachers established daily routines or schedules that allotted large blocks of time to literacy instruction and activities, and they designed their instructional program around a combination core literature and reading workshop approaches. Ms. Jones combined some components of the core literature approach and reading workshop approach in her program, and Mr. Kfoury alternated the core literature and reading workshop approaches. In addition, their students were involved in selecting literature and response activities for the whole class, small groups, partners, and individual children.

Through the literature-based reading programs that these two teachers developed, the decisions that they made about theoretical perspectives become clear. Because of his reader response stance, Mr. Kfoury provided many opportunities for his students to read and discuss literature and reach their own interpretations about literature and life. In contrast, Ms. Jones based her literature-based reading program on the interactive perspective. Her concern about teaching students how to read as well as letting them learn the joys of reading is clear from how she organized her language arts block. However, at other times during the year, for different focuses and to meet different purposes, Mr. Kfoury's and Ms. Jones' instruction reflect other perspectives.

Mr. Kfoury and Ms. Jones completed each of these steps in planning, organizing, and managing their literature-based reading programs:

1. Determine a focus.
2. Identify core and extended literature.
3. Design a program with core literature and reading workshop components.
4. Consider the instructional perspective.
5. Plan reading and response activities.
6. Coordinate grouping patterns with reading and response activities.
7. Organize the classroom and time schedules.
8. Manage record-keeping.
9. Assess students' learning.

While these steps suggest a linear order to planning a literature-based reading program, in reality, teachers can move through these steps in any order. For example,

FIGURE 8.4   Planning Cycle for
Putting It All Together

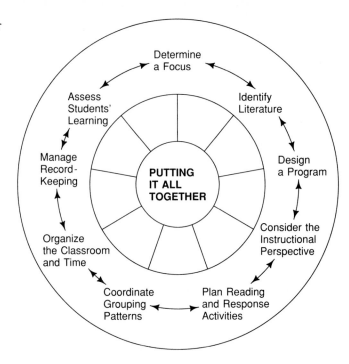

Mr. Kfoury identified his focus first and then considered components of the read-ing workshop and core literature approach before he made decisions about se-lecting literature. However, other teachers may complete the planning steps in another order. Some teachers may start their planning with the kinds of reading materials that they have available. Other teachers may start their planning with an inflexible daily schedule filled with interruptions. Figure 8.4 shows the nine steps in a planning cycle.

In this chapter we discuss how teachers put together literature-based reading programs from careful consideration of the first eight of these planning, organizing, and managing steps. We address the last step, assessing students' learning, in Chap-ter 9. While we describe the planning steps in a particular order, it is important to keep in mind that these steps can be completed in a different order.

STEP ONE: DETERMINE A FOCUS

One of the earliest steps in planning a literature-based reading program is to deter-mine the direction or focus for reading and instruction. For example, a fourth grade teacher might read *Jumanji* (Van Allsburg, 1991) aloud to the class, and the students may indicate an interest in reading and learning more about this book. The teacher would need to decide whether to focus on the book alone, to launch an author study of Van Allsburg, or to collect other stories for a unit on the fantasy genre. Sometimes teachers use topics in content subjects as a focus for reading and instruction. Second graders are often expected to study oceans and weather, most fifth graders learn about westward expansion and pioneers in America, and seventh graders examine civilization in the American and Asian cultures. These topics provide a focus for literature-based reading instruction.

Sometimes teachers plan to find a focus for reading and instruction by using just one book. At other times teachers will focus on an issue, theme, particular kind of character, literary element, or content area topic and will gather text sets to illustrate this focus. Teachers may also focus on an author, illustrator, or genre or decide to have a more open-ended focus, allowing students to choose their own reading material. Finally, teachers may focus on a broad topic that can integrate reading with content area topics. Six ways that teachers can find a focus for literature-based reading programs are

1. Focus on one book.
2. Focus on an issue, theme, or literary element.
3. Focus on a genre.
4. Focus on an author or illustrator.
5. Focus on making connections across the curriculum.
6. Choose not to have a focus.

Each of the six ways to determine a focus is described in the following sections.

Focus on One Book

Many books are so compelling that teachers decide to focus a unit around an in-depth study of that book. Teachers may read the book aloud, use shared reading so that all students—even those who are unable to read the book independently—can enjoy the literature experience, or have students read the book in guided reading lessons. Books chosen for this special attention are often award-winning or very popular books. For example, a sixth grade teacher might decide to focus a unit on Mildred Taylor's (1976) *Roll of Thunder, Hear My Cry,* the story of an African-American girl's life in the rural south.

After teachers have selected a book for a focus unit, they next decide how to use the book and what direction to take in guiding students' reading or in planning preparing, reading, exploring, and extending activities. Teachers first carefully read the book themselves often keeping a response journal as they read because their own responses provide insightful directions for instruction. Teachers should also read critically, carefully noting the author's craft in developing character and theme and analyzing the influence of setting or point of view on theme, character, or plot (Johnson & Louis, 1990). Often a single vocabulary word or event will stimulate ideas for instructional directions. For example, the word *precious* is important in interpreting *Alexander and the Wind-Up Mouse* (Lionni, 1969); the event of gift giving is crucial in *Sarah, Plain and Tall* (MacLachlan, 1985); and the contrast between the vocabulary and deeds of the mouse and whale in *Amos & Boris* (Steig, 1971) is vital for understanding theme. Sometimes an event in the story will suggest an instructional focus. One teacher responded strongly to one line of dialogue in *The Cabin Faced West* (Fritz, 1958). George Washington was dining one evening with a pioneer family living in a small cabin in western Pennsylvania. The young girl of the family was dazed through dinner thinking of all the accomplishments and the exciting life of this famous person. At the time she was bored with her life far away from friends. After dinner George Washington placed his hand on her shoulder and said, "I envy you." This teacher decided to focus her instruction around envy and what this one line of dialogue revealed about young Ann Hamilton and George Washington.

Once teachers have carefully analyzed a book, they plan preparing, reading, exploring, and extending activities that will help students develop deeper insights. Instruction should be carefully crafted so that students discover new understandings about the book through talking, listening, reading, and writing. Figure 8.5 presents a planning web with suggestions for activities that teachers may consider for a focus on a single book.

Focus on an Issue, Theme, or Literary Element

Often teachers decide to focus on theme, character, or literary element, and these units are called *focus units* (Moss, 1984). Teachers may also focus on a folktale that has several different versions. To determine the direction for instruction in focus units, teachers gather several books with a similar theme, character, literary element, or story to form a text set. For example, in the case study at the beginning of this chapter, Mr. Kfoury's class focused on courage, and they read books and other materials from a text set that dealt with that theme. Other themes that teachers may use in focus units include friendship, growing up, survival, dealing with death, and family.

Other focus units can be organized around literary elements (Norton, 1992). For example, teachers might focus on plot (e.g., books that illustrate personal conflict, conflict with society, conflict with nature, or conflict with others), character (e.g., books that demonstrate how the use of symbolism reveals character), or setting (e.g., books in which setting develops mood, provides historical background, and suggests symbolic interpretations). Other focus units can be developed around particular characters. For example, pigs play an important role in many stories for children, and reading stories about these characters can make a humorous unit (Moss, 1984). Other units can be built around favorite characters such as Ramona, Baba Yaga (a character found in Russian folktales), or monsters.

Sometimes students read all of the books included in a text set or they may read only a few books. Often the whole class reads one of the books from the text set and then small groups of students read other selected books from the set. Because all of the materials gathered for a text set have a common element—theme, character, literary element, or story—an important part of a focus unit is comparing and contrasting the various books and materials in the text set. In another important activity, students develop their own statements defining and explaining the common element in the text set. They might describe character traits and character development across several stories, the various ways that the theme of courage is illustrated in several texts, or the characteristics or definition of a literary element. Finally, students explore the common element in their own talking, writing, and dramatizing.

FIGURE 8.5   Planning Web for Focusing on One Book

• Audiotape for
  listening center
• Venn diagram
  comparison of book
  and video or film
  version
• Audiotape, videotape,
  film, filmstrip of author

• Murals
• Collages
• Sculptures
• Story boxes
• Literary maps
• Cooking
• Field trips

**Response
Projects**

**Audiovisual
Materials**

• Books by
  same author
• Books with same
  theme
• Books and poems
  on related topics

**Related
Literature**

• Notable language
  samples
• Word walls
• Vocabulary
  clusters

**Author's
Craft**

• Readers'
  theatre
• Retellings
• Puppets
• Role play

Drama

Focus on processes:
• preparing
• reading
• exploring
• extending
Focus on literary
elements:
• character
• setting
• plot
• point of view
• theme

**Strategies
and
Skills**

**FOCUS
ON A
BOOK**

**Connecting
Across the
Curriculum**

• Art
• Math
• Science
• Social
  Studies
• Music

Reading

• Read aloud
• Shared reading
• Guided reading
• Independent
  reading

**Writing
Process**

• Poetry
• Simulated
  newspapers
• Letters to the
  author
• Sequels
• Point of
  view stories

**Informal
Writing**

• Simulated journals
  and letters
• Quickwrites
• BME clusters
• Plot diagrams
  and profiles
• Response journals

**Talking
and
Listening**

• Grand conversations
• Book talks
• Sharing
• Interviews

Focus on a Genre

Another focus for literature-based reading units is to explore a genre, such as folk-tales, biographies, or poetry (Huck, Hepler, & Hickman, 1987; Norton, 1992), and Figure 8.6 presents a web with suggestions for focusing on various genre. To plan a genre focus unit, teachers and students gather into text sets several books that illustrate the genre. Students might read several of the books independently and then read one of the books together as a class.

An important goal of a genre focus unit is for students to develop their own understandings about the characteristics of the genre. They compare and contrast various books in the text set and learn about the characteristics of the genre and how

FIGURE 8.6   Planning Web for Genre Focus Units

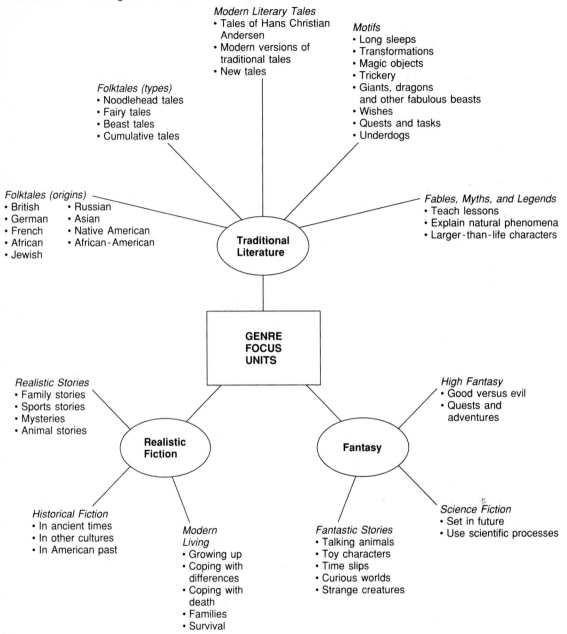

Modern Literary Tales
• Tales of Hans Christian Andersen
• Modern versions of traditional tales
• New tales

Motifs
• Long sleeps
• Transformations
• Magic objects
• Trickery
• Giants, dragons and other fabulous beasts
• Wishes
• Quests and tasks
• Underdogs

Folktales (types)
• Noodlehead tales
• Fairy tales
• Beast tales
• Cumulative tales

Folktales (origins)
• British   • Russian
• German   • Asian
• French   • Native American
• African   • African-American
• Jewish

Fables, Myths, and Legends
• Teach lessons
• Explain natural phenomena
• Larger-than-life characters

Traditional Literature

GENRE FOCUS UNITS

Realistic Stories
• Family stories
• Sports stories
• Mysteries
• Animal stories

Realistic Fiction

Fantasy

High Fantasy
• Good versus evil
• Quests and adventures

Historical Fiction
• In ancient times
• In other cultures
• In American past

Modern Living
• Growing up
• Coping with differences
• Coping with death
• Families
• Survival

Fantastic Stories
• Talking animals
• Toy characters
• Time slips
• Curious worlds
• Strange creatures

Science Fiction
• Set in future
• Use scientific processes

authors use these characteristics to structure their stories. They also apply what they learn about genres to talking, writing, drama activities, and response projects.

Focus on an Author or Illustrator

An important focus for a literature unit is to study authors and illustrators. Text sets that focus on an author or illustrator include the following components:

- a collection of books written by a particular author (or illustrated by a particular illustrator)
- biographical information about the author's or illustrator's life
- letters written by the author or illustrator to the teacher or former students
- audiotapes, videotapes, or filmstrips in which the author reads or talks about his or her work

To prepare for an author or illustrator unit, teachers carefully read and analyze their books for insights about common themes and identify the unique qualities and contributions of the author or illustrator. For example, Chris Van Allsburg's books all include some illustrations drawn from unusual perspectives, have a twist at the end, and involve the subtle interplay of reality and fantasy. Students also enjoy finding the little white dog that appears in each story. In addition, teachers prepare for the unit by reading professional articles that the author or illustrator has written discussing his or her work, professional critiques of the author's works, and biographical information about the author's or illustrator's life. Figure 3.11 in Chapter 3 provides a list of resources that teachers can use to find biographical information about authors. Appendix B lists books and audiovisual materials about famous authors and illustrators. Teachers can find critical reviews of authors' and illustrators' works in most libraries in the *Children's Book Review Index* and in *Children's Literature Review: Excerpts from Reviews, Criticism, and Commentary on Books for Children and Young People.*

An author or illustrator unit includes activities in which students discover for themselves the themes and qualities that are common in all of the author's or illustrator's work. Students also compare and contrast works and discover how the author's or illustrator's life experiences are reflected in his or her work. Students can compare their own thoughts and reflections on the works with what authors or illustrators say about their works. Students might want to write to authors or illustrators; however, it is never recommended that students be required to do so. Students might want to experiment using some of the illustrator's artistic techniques or media. Figure 3.10 in Chapter 3 provides a list of suggested activities for learning about authors and illustrators.

Focus on Making Connections Across the Curriculum

Many teachers connect literature with science or social studies topics as Ms. Jones did in the case study at the beginning of this chapter. We believe that literature-based reading programs should often be organized around integrated units called *theme cycles*. A theme cycle is a unit of study focused on a broad topic that integrates content and literature study; theme cycles involve students in reading stories, informational books, and poems about related topics. Theme cycles also allow students to make choices; the cycles evolve as teachers and students decide what projects and activities to engage in, what books and materials to read, and what questions to explore.

Selecting topics organized around a content topic may be as simple as consulting a local or state curriculum guide or textbook. In the United States, each state has identified topics in science, social studies, and health that are to be covered at every grade level. Many of these topics can become the focus of a theme cycle. However, content topics must be broadened to include themes not only from science or social studies but also from literature (Crook & Lehman, 1991; Pappas, Kiefer, & Levstik, 1990). Theme cycles in content areas are also expanded to incorporate stories and poems as well as informational books and other materials. In this way, theme cycles focus on aesthetic as well as scientific knowledge (McClure & Zitlow, 1991).

One way to begin planning a theme cycle is to identify a list of stories, poems, and informational books related to the theme. Figure 8.7 presents a planning web for a fourth grade theme cycle planned around the topic of life cycles (Crook & Lehman, 1991, p. 37). This web illustrates that students learn about the cycle of seasons studied in science and explored symbolically in literature through the circle of birth, death, and renewal. Similarly, a study of weather, for instance, focuses on information about meteorology as well as the impact of weather in stories and poems, and a theme cycle about the universe includes books about space and planets and myths about the origin and movement of the sun, moon, and stars.

Choose Not to Have a Focus

It is not always necessary to have students focus on a single book, a unit, or a theme cycle. In many literature-based reading programs, students choose books they wish to read, and within a class, students are reading a wide variety of books independently. Some students may be reading favorite authors or exploring a special interest, such as astronomy, some might be reading a book recommended by a classmate or the teacher, and others might be rereading favorite books read earlier in the year or during a previous year. Having an open-ended or no focus allows students to choose the topics they wish to pursue.

Teachers often use the first five focuses to organize their literature-based reading programs during the school year, and they usually plan these focus units with students' involvement. For example, when teachers notice that students are particularly interested in an author or illustrator, they suggest that students might want to focus on that person and his or her books. Students and the teacher plan the unit together, choosing books and planning reading and response activities. Much of the time students should have the freedom to select and read the books they are interested in, without having to read books the teacher or other students have selected.

STEP TWO: IDENTIFY LITERATURE

We believe that the single most important ingredient in a literature-based reading program is the literature that students read, and early in the planning process teach-

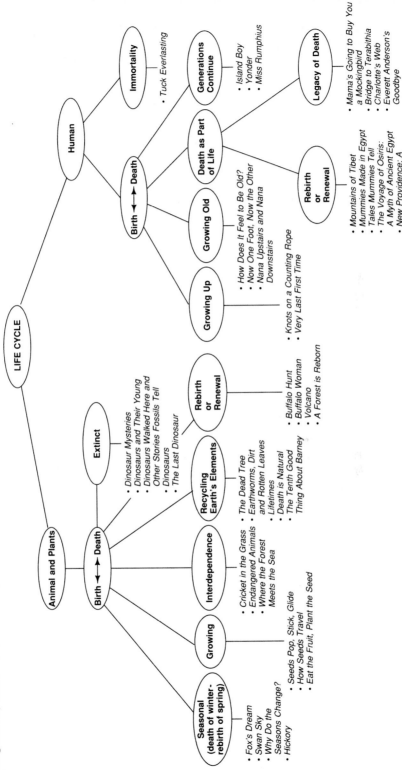

FIGURE 8.7 Planning Web for Theme Cycle on Life Cycles (*Note.* From "Themes for Two Voices: Children's Fiction and Nonfiction as 'Whole Literature'" by P. Crook and B. Lehman, 1991, *Language Arts, 68*, p. 37. Copyright 1991 by the National Council of Teachers of English. Reprinted with permission.)

ers must select literature to read aloud and to use in guided and shared reading activities and for independent reading. Teachers need to learn about children's literature and read a wide variety of children's books to be able to choose appropriate books for their classroom collections, for instructional purposes, and for focus units or theme cycles. Teachers who use either the core literature or reading workshop approach should include collections of books by particular authors and illustrators and books that represent particular genres and literary elements that students will study. Moreover, the classroom library and books selected for reading aloud, theme cycles, or units should have a cultural balance. In addition, teachers need to know their students' interests and their curricular needs in order to select books judiciously.

Choosing literature for students can feel like an overwhelming responsibility, but the guidelines we present will help teachers identify literature and plan a literature-based reading program. Students, too, will share favorite books and help to define the program by their interests and the books they check out from the school and community libraries. Once teachers have selected a focus for a literature unit or a content area theme cycle, it will suggest many other books and reading materials.

Core and Extended Literature

In a core literature approach, some of the books teachers choose will be core books and others are extended books. *Core literature selections* should be "works of compelling, intellectual, social, or moral content . . . [and] be examples of excellent language use" (California State Department of Education, 1988, p. xi). Because of their exceptional qualities, these books are selected for careful consideration in guided reading groups. They stimulate students to respond through talk, drama, writing, and further reading. Teachers have multiple copies of these books available in the classroom so that students can read them as a whole class or in a small group.

Extended literature includes the other reading materials in the classroom library that students self-select to read or read in conjunction with core books. Extended literature selections should be good literature that entertains, inspires, or informs; these selections should appeal to students and encourage their interest in reading. Usually students read extended books independently, but they might also read and discuss these books or other reading materials in small groups.

Read-Aloud Selections for Reading Workshop

Teachers also select books and other reading materials to read aloud to the class in a reading workshop approach. Some teachers choose books to focus on a theme, genre, or author (Hornsby & Sukarna, 1986). Other teachers select read-aloud books to demonstrate certain reading strategies, to illustrate an author's use of language, or simply for pleasure. Although students do not explore these books in as much detail as they do when they read core literature selections, these books are, nonetheless, an important part of the reading program. After hearing their teacher read a book aloud, many students choose to read that book independently, become interested in an author, or gain new insights into a genre or literary element based on their teacher's comments. It is important that the selections that teachers choose for reading aloud during reading workshop must also expose students to the highest quality literature.

Guides for Selecting Books

Teachers need to become knowledgeable about children's literature—about literary elements and genres, authors and illustrators, and the variety of the books available today if they are to make informed choices about which books to use in literature-based reading classrooms. In Chapter 2 we described guidelines for choosing stories, informational books, and poetry; these guidelines help teachers make better selections of children's literature.

Selecting children's books might seem easy, but it is not. Researchers who have examined the books that teachers select for classroom use have found that their choices suggest an unconscious gender or racial bias because few books that are chosen feature the experiences of female or ethnic minorities and few were written by these groups (Jipson & Paley, 1991; Shannon, 1986; Traxel, 1983). These researchers call this pattern the *selective tradition,* and they believe that books reflect and convey sociocultural values, beliefs, and attitudes to readers. It is important that teachers be aware of the ideas conveyed by their selection patterns and become more reflective about the books they choose for classroom use.

A number of resource guides are available that teachers can use in choosing children's literature, and some useful guides are listed in Figure 8.8. In some of these resource books, annotated information is provided about thousands of books; in others, lists of books related to various literary and content area themes are presented. Teachers might also consider books that have received Caldecott or Newbery Medals or books that have been selected as "Children's Choices" or "Teachers' Choices" in the annual nationwide selection process sponsored by the International Reading Association (and published annually in *The Reading Teacher*).

Finding books for readers who are just beginning to read conventionally is a difficult task, especially when teachers are trying to connect language arts with social studies and science theme cycles. Books that have repetition, rhythm, and rhyme are usually recommended for these readers, and Figure 8.9 presents a list of books for young beginning readers that include these features. In addition, teachers may find appropriate stories, poems, and informational books from publishers such as The Wright Group (19201 120th Avenue, NE, Bothell, WA 98011-9512) or Rigby (PO Box 797, Crystal Lake, IL 60014). These stories are also recommended as reading selections for students who have limited English speaking skills.

Magazines are another good source of reading materials. Today, a variety of magazines are published for children that include fiction and nonfiction articles on topics in science, social studies, and language. The stories in *Cricket,* articles on historical topics in *Cobblestone,* and the consumer issues in *Zillions,* to name only three magazines, are stimulating reading for children. Figure 8.10 lists magazines appropriate for elementary and middle school students. One way that teachers can locate articles in children's magazines related to topics of theme cycles is to use *Magazines for Young Readers* (Katz & Katz, 1991), a guide that lists articles from 30 children's magazines according to subject.

FIGURE 8.8   Guides to Use in Selecting Literature

Barron, N. (1987). *Anatomy of wonder: A critical guide to science fiction* (3rd ed.). New York: Bowker.

Barstow, B., & Riggle, J. (1989). *Beyond picture books: A guide to first readers.* New York: Bowker.

Baskin, B. H., & Harris, K. H. (1977). *Notes for a different drummer: A guide to juvenile fiction portraying the handicapped.* New York: Bowker.

Baskin, B. H., & Harris, K. H. (1984). *More notes from a different drummer: A guide to juvenile fiction portraying the disabled.* New York: Bowker.

Bernstein, J. E. (1983). *Books to help children cope with separation and loss* (2nd ed.). New York: Bowker.

Bernstein, J. E., & Rudman, M. K. (1988). *Books to help children cope with separation and loss: An annotated bibliography* (Vol. 3). New York: Bowker.

Carlin, M. G., Laughlin, J. L., & Saniga, R. D. (1990). *Hear no evil, see no evil, speak no evil: An annotated bibliography for the handicapped.* Englewood, CO: Libraries Unlimited.

Carroll, F. L., & Meacham, M. (Eds.). (1984). *Exciting, funny, scary, short, different, and sad books kids like about animals, science, sports, families, songs, and other things.* Chicago: American Library Association.

Children's books in print, 1992–93. (1992). New York: Bowker. (annual edition)

Criscoe, B. L. (1990). *Award-winning books for children and young adults.* New York: Scarecrow. (annual publication)

Fakih, K. O. (1991). *The literature of delight: A critical guide to humorous books for children.* New York: Bowker.

Freeman, J. (1990). *Books kids will sit still for: The complete read-aloud guide* (2nd ed.). New York: Bowker.

Friedberg, J. B., Mullins, J. B., & Sukiennik, A. W. (1985). *Accept me as I am: Best books of juvenile nonfiction on impairments and disabilities.* New York: Bowker.

Gillespie, J. T. (1991). *Best books for junior high readers.* New York: Bowker.

Gillespie, J. T., & Naden, C. J. (1990). *Best books for children: Preschool through grade 6* (4th ed.). New York: Bowker.

Hearne, B. (1990). *Choosing books for children* (rev. ed.). New York: Delacorte.

Hopkins, L. B. (1987). *Pass the poetry, please.* New York: HarperCollins.

Jett-Simpson, M. (Ed.). (1989). *Adventuring with books: A booklist for pre-K–grade 6.* Urbana, IL: National Council of Teachers of English.

Kennedy, D., Spangler, S. S., & Vanderwerf, M. A. (1990). *Science and technology in fact and fiction: A guide to children's books.* New York: Bowker.

Kennedy, D., Spangler, S. S., & Vanderwerf, M. A. (1990). *Science and technology in fact and fiction: A guide to young adult books.* New York: Bowker.

Deciding How Many Copies Are Needed

The number of copies of books or other reading materials that will be needed depends on how the materials will be used. For core books, teachers should consider whether the whole class will be reading a book at the same time, or if students will be reading the books in small groups. Teachers who use a core literature approach often choose four to eight books as core selections for the year and get copies for each student in the class. If core books will be used in small groups, teachers usually obtain six to eight copies of five or six different books for each unit, and students select one of these books to read. This may mean that teachers need six to eight

Kima, C. W., & Lima, J. A. (1989). *A to zoo: Subject access to children's picture books* (3rd ed.). New York: Bowker.

Kimmel, M. M., & Segel, E. (1988). *For reading out loud!* New York: Delacorte.

Kobrin, B. (1988). *Eyeopeners! How to choose and use children's books about real people, places, and things.* New York: Penguin.

Lynn, R. N. (1988). *Fantasy literature for children and young adults: An annotated bibliography* (3rd ed.). New York: Bowker.

McMullan, K. H. (1984). *How to choose good books for kids.* Reading, MA: Addison-Wesley.

Miller-Lachmann, L. (1991). *Our family, our friends, our world: An annotated guide to significant multicultural books for children and teenagers.* New York: Bowker.

Mohr, C., Nixon, D. D., & Vickers, S. (1990). *Books that heal: A whole language approach.* Englewood, CO: Libraries Unlimited.

Nilsen, A. P. (Ed.). (1991). *Your reading: A booklist for junior high and middle school students* (8th ed.). Urbana, IL: National Council of Teachers of English.

Pilla, M. L. (1987). *Resources for middle-grade reluctant readers: A guide for librarians.* Englewood, CO: Libraries Unlimited.

Pilla, M. L. (1990). *The best: High/low books for reluctant readers.* Englewood, CO: Libraries Unlimited.

Recommended readings in literature, kindergarten through grade eight (annotated). (1988 and 1990). Sacramento, CA: California State Department of Education.

Richey, V. H., & Tuten-Puckett, K. (1991). *Wordless/almost wordless picture books: A guide.* Englewood, CO: Libraries Unlimited.

Roser, N., & Frith, M. (Eds.). (1983). *Children's choices: Teaching with books children like.* Newark, DE: International Reading Association. (Annual lists of children's choices are available from the International Reading Association.)

Sinclair, P. (1992). *E for environment: An annotated bibliography of children's books with environmental themes.* New York: Bowker.

Subject guide to children's books in print, 1991–92. (1991). New York: Bowker. (annual edition)

Trelease, J. (1989). *The new read-aloud handbook.* New York: Penguin.

Tway, E. (Ed.). (1981). *Reading ladders for human relations* (6th ed.). Washington, DC: American Council on Education.

Wilson, G., & Moss, J. (1988). *Books for children to read alone: A guide for parents and librarians.* New York: Bowker.

Wilson, G., & Moss, J. (1991). *Tried and true: 500 nonfiction books children want to read.* New York: Bowker.

copies of 20 to 30 core books for small-group instruction. With so many good books available as paperbacks, collecting class and small-group sets of core literature selections is not prohibitively expensive. Often teachers who teach at the same grade level share sets of core books.

When primary grade teachers use shared reading, they use both a big book to demonstrate with and regular-sized versions of the story for children to read. Some teachers use class sets of the regular-sized versions along with the big book, whereas others have six to eight copies of the regular-sized books for small-group activities.

For extended books and books used in the reading workshop, teachers should obtain two, three, or even five copies of favorite books and poems so that more than

FIGURE 8.9   Books for Beginning Readers

Ahlberg, J., & Ahlberg, A. (1985). *Each peach pear plum.* New York: Scholastic.

Arno, E. (1985). *The gingerbread man.* New York: Scholastic.

Berenstain, S., & Berenstain, S. (1969). *Bears on wheels.* New York: Random House.

Berenstain, S., & Berenstain, S. (1971). *Bears in the night.* New York: Random House.

Brown, M. (1947). *Goodnight moon.* New York: Harper & Row.

Brown, R. (1984). *A dark, dark tale.* New York: Dial.

Cairns, S. (1987). *Oh no!* Crystal Lake, IL: Rigby.

Chase, E. (1984). *The new baby calf.* New York: Scholastic.

Cowley, J. (1987). *Mrs. Wishy-Washy.* Crystal Lake, IL: Rigby.

Eastman, P. (1960). *Are you my mother?* New York: Random House.

Eastman, P. (1961). *Go, dog. Go!* New York: Random House.

Galdone, P. (1986). *Three little kittens.* New York: Clarion.

Gelman, R. (1977). *More spaghetti, I say!* New York: Scholastic.

Hill, E. (1980). *Where's Spot?* New York: Putnam.

Melser, J., & Cowley, J. (1987). *Grandpa, Grandpa.* San Diego: The Wright Group.

Parkes, B. (1986). *Who's in the shed?* Crystal Lake, IL: Rigby.

Parkes, B., & Smith, J. (1986). *The enormous watermelon.* Crystal Lake, IL: Rigby.

Peek, M. (1981). *Roll over.* New York: Clarion.

Dr. Seuss. (1960). *Green eggs and ham.* New York: Random House.

Dr. Seuss. (1963). *Hop on pop.* New York: Random House.

Trafuri, N. (1984). *Have you seen my duckling?* New York: Greenwillow.

Westcott, N. (1981). *The lady with the alligator purse.* Boston: Little, Brown.

Ziefert, H., & Smith, M. (1989). *In a scary old house.* New York: Penguin.

Ziefert, H., & Taback, S. (1984). *Where is my dinner?* New York: Grosset & Dunlap.

---

one student can read a book at a time or so that students can read with a buddy. Having several copies of a story or poem prompts students to form informal reading groups and allows all students in a class to read a favorite book. Sometimes teachers collect extended books on particular themes, genres, or authors to use along with core or read-aloud books. Zarrillo (1989) recommended that no fewer than 40 of these related books should be available for a class of 30 students.

There can never be too many reading materials for independent reading, and teachers continue to collect books each year to add to their collections. We recommend that classroom libraries include 5 to 10 books times the number of children in the class as a minimum. Zarrillo reported that the most effective classrooms have 1,000 or more books on hand! Of course, not all of these books relate to any one focus unit, theme cycle, genre, or author study, but they provide a wide range of books and poems from which students can choose.

STEP THREE: DESIGN A PROGRAM WITH CORE LITERATURE AND READING WORKSHOP COMPONENTS

Two approaches have been developed in literature-based reading: *core literature* and *reading workshop.* A core literature approach, as the name suggests, is typically used

FIGURE 8.10   Children's Magazines

3-2-1 Contact (science and technology)
Children's Television Workshop
1 Lincoln Plaza
New York, NY 10023

Chickadee (science)
Young Naturalist Foundation
56 the Esplanada
Suite 306
Toronto, Ontario
Canada M5E 1A7

Cobblestone (history)
Box 959
Farmingdale, NY 11737

Cricket (literature)
PO Box 300
Peru, IL 61354

Ebony Jr! (social studies)
Johnson Publishing Co.
820 S. Michigan
Chicago, IL 60605

National Geographic World
Dept. 00683
17th and M St. NW
Washington, DC 20036

Odyssey (astronomy)
1027 7th St.
Milwaukee, WI 53233

Ranger Rick's Nature Magazine
8925 Leesburg Pike
Vienna, VA 22180

Scholastic Sprint (language arts)
730 Broadway
New York, NY 10003

Stone Soup (literary)
Children's Art Foundation
PO Box 83
Santa Cruz, CA 95603

Zillions (economics)
Consumers Union
256 Washington St.
Mount Vernon, NY 10553

with core literature selections when the whole class or small groups of children read a book together, usually with the guidance of a teacher. In contrast, a reading workshop approach is used when students select extended books, poems, magazines, and other reading materials from the classroom library for independent reading.

Sometimes teachers choose to use either the core literature or reading workshop methodology but more often they combine or modify the approaches according to their perspectives on teaching reading, the books they have available, their schedules, or other dimensions of their own unique teaching situations.

Core Literature Approach

The core literature approach can take either of two forms: a *whole-class core literature approach* in which everyone in the class reads or listens to a teacher read the same book and participates in response activities or a *literature unit core approach* in which small groups of children read different books related to one another by a common focus (Zarrillo, 1989). In the case study at the beginning of this chapter, Mr. Kfoury uses a combination of both forms of the core literature approach. He both reads a core book aloud to the whole class and invites students to select another core book to read with a small group of classmates.

A core literature approach involves four components: (a) reading the core selection, (b) responding to the selection, (c) teaching about reading and literature, and (d) reading independently.

Reading the Core Book.   In a whole-class core literature approach, the teacher guides students through the four stages of the reading process: preparing, reading, exploring, and extending beyond the core selection. Students read the core book at the teacher's direction, or the teacher reads aloud the core literature selection. Teachers use guided reading, shared reading, or reading aloud to students to make the core literature selection accessible to all students. When the teacher reads aloud, students follow along in their own copies of the book and later reread the book independently or with a partner. If sufficient copies of the core selection are not available, students listen to the teacher read the selection aloud, and they may have access to a tape-recorded version of the book. Students respond to the core selection by writing in response journals or completing other exploring and extending response activities.

In a literature unit core approach, students read a core book with a small group of classmates. Students meet together each day to read and discuss their reading, and the teacher usually meets with the small group to guide students through the four stages of the reading process. A literature unit core approach is virtually the same as a whole-group approach, except that students are reading in small groups, not together as a class.

Guided reading.   Teachers use guided reading as they direct small groups or the whole class through the four stages of the reading process in order to extend students' thinking about a literature selection. They instruct by demonstrating strategies and guiding students' use of strategies, and they pose challenging questions and make comments that stimulate students' engagement with literature or encourage creative and critical thinking. Mr. Kfoury used guided reading as his students read books related to the theme of courage, and Ms. Jones included guided reading in the case study at the beginning of the chapter during small-group rereading of books and poems.

An important way that teachers guide reading is by preparing special activities for students who are reading particularly challenging books or poems. When groups are formed by choice, some students in the group may be reading books that are relatively easy while other students may find the same books to be difficult. For those students who find the books difficult, teachers may provide a tape-recorded version of the book, pair these students with more adept readers for buddy reading, introduce them to the characters and describe the setting before reading, or work individually with them to construct a personal word wall.

The purpose of guided reading is to provide support for students as they develop new reading strategies, try out new ways of interpreting literature, and explore new ways of responding to books and poems. Teachers and classmates offer suggestions, demonstrations, and feedback as students extend their ways of reading and responding.

Shared reading.   Shared reading can take many forms including reading big books with students and the teacher reading aloud while students follow along in their copies of a book. Shared reading of big books usually occurs in kindergarten or primary classrooms. As teachers read from big books, they invite children to make predictions and comments or to join in reading. In the case study at the beginning of this chapter, Ms. Jones read *The Snowy Day* as a shared reading. Shared reading also occurs as teachers read aloud a core literature selection as Mr. Kfoury did when he read *Number the Stars.* Teachers may use preparing activities before reading and follow the reading with exploring or extending activities. Another form of shared reading arises when students read aloud a core literature selection such as in a readers' theatre presentation.

The purpose of shared reading is to build a community of readers through shared, common experiences with one or more selections of literature. Often teachers select literature to use in shared readings that is beyond the reading level of many of the students but provides significant opportunities for growth in understanding life and literature.

Reading aloud to students. Teachers read core literature aloud to small groups of students or the whole class as an introductory activity before students read the core book independently or when only several copies of the core book are available. Teachers model fluent reading and their own joy of reading. Reading aloud to students is similar to shared reading because it is a social experience, and teachers invite children to make predictions and other comments during reading.

Responding to the Book. After reading, students respond to the core selection as they discuss with classmates and write in response journals. Through these immediate responses, students develop and refine their interpretation of the book. Teachers plan a variety of exploring activities to help students gain new reading strategies, build from their initial responses, and learn more about literature. Students also extend their responses as they participate in other reading, writing, talk, drama, and research activities that they have chosen. For example, in the case studies at the beginning of this chapter, students in Mr. Kfoury's class selected response activities from a class-generated list of options, and Ms. Jones' students decided to make puppets to retell a story they had read. Teachers and students select extending activities that allow them to use reading strategies independently, extend responses into the arts or other language activities, or explore connections among several literature selections.

Teaching About Reading and Literature. Teachers carefully plan for instruction by considering what strategies and skills students will need to complete activities and projects. Teachers also informally observe and assess students as they read and complete activities to identify further strategies and skills that children demonstrate a need to learn. Instruction can occur during the planning, reading, and exploring activities. As teachers prepare students to read the selection, they might teach about an author or a genre, and during reading they might demonstrate using a particular word identification strategy or a prediction strategy. During the exploring activities, teachers may have students focus on the meanings of vocabulary or teach literary concepts or other language arts strategies and skills that students will apply as they extend their understanding of the core literature selection.

Mr. Kfoury, for instance, might plan to introduce students to the main characters and locate the setting on a world map as a preparing activity before he begins reading *Number the Stars.* He may demonstrate the strategy of creating images or mind pictures as he reads several portions of the story. After reading, Mr. Kfoury might examine some of the words from *Number the Stars* that he and his students added to the word wall or talk about character development.

Reading Independently.   Both the whole-class core approach and the literature unit core approach are usually supplemented with a period of self-selected independent reading. During this time students select reading materials either related to or outside of the focus unit or theme cycle, but of personal interest. The core literature approach and the self-selected independent reading component require that an adequate number of copies of core books are available and that an extensive collection of other reading materials is available for students to self-select from for independent reading.

Reading Workshop Approach

The reading workshop approach is based on the idea that students learn to read by reading and that the most important part of any reading program is sustained periods of self-selected reading. It is modeled after the writing workshop approach (Atwell, 1987). During reading workshop, students may read freely from any self-selected reading materials (Atwell, 1987), or teachers may organize a reading workshop around a particular focus or theme (Hornsby & Sukarna, 1986; Reutzel & Cooter, 1991). Six components of reading workshop are

1. reading aloud to students
2. teaching minilessons
3. reading independently
4. responding to literature
5. conferencing with students
6. sharing books and response projects

In the case study at the beginning of this chapter, Mr. Kfoury organized his reading workshop around the theme of courage and used most of these reading workshop components.

Reading Aloud to Students.   Teachers read aloud daily in reading workshop. As they read aloud, they share a wide variety of literature with students, and through the books they read, they set the stage for independent reading by introducing a theme or other focus. As teachers read aloud they demonstrate reading strategies and model how they react as readers. For example, teachers may tell students how and when they notice symbols, why they reread a sentence or paragraph slowly and carefully, how they form mental images and react to characters, how language tickles their tongues, or why certain phrases linger in the minds and beg to be reread aloud. Teachers may also simply read aloud and allow children to savor and enjoy literature for pleasure. Together, the teacher and students build the spirit of a community of readers through this component.

Teaching Minilessons.   Teachers provide instruction in reading workshop in short minilessons, no more than 15 minutes in length. At these minilessons, teachers give students information, demonstrate ways of thinking or reading, show students new activities, or guide students as they practice using new strategies or engaging in new activities. Minilessons focus on teaching (a) strategies and conventions; (b) literary elements, genre, authors and illustrators, and styles of illustration; (c) response activities; (d) record-keeping and other maintenance activities; and (e) self-evaluation.

Minilessons that focus on teaching students new strategies and conventions inform students why and how to use reading strategies (such as how to use fix-up strategies or prediction), provide information about conventions of reading (such as how to recognize a simile or metaphor), demonstrate how readers think while reading (such as how to connect personal experiences with story events), and demonstrate how to use the four stages of the reading process as they prepare to read, explore, and extend from a book or poem independently.

Minilessons can be used to teach students about literature. Teachers can focus on the common element of a genre or about other literary elements (see Chapters 2 and 6) or on authors, illustrators, and styles of illustration (see Chapter 3). Teachers plan these lessons in conjunction with a focus unit on a genre, author or illustrator, or style of illustration. Then students can apply the information the teacher has presented as they read other books, write in response to their reading, or work on response projects.

In minilessons that focus on response activities, teachers provide examples and model how to accomplish activities such as how to write different kinds of responses in response journals or how to construct a character web or story map. Minilessons can also be used to show students how to keep records and perform other related activities. Teachers can use minilessons to show students how to keep track of what they read in a reading log or buddy journal and how to plan what they intend to accomplish during a day, week, or unit. Minilessons might focus on how to select an interesting book that is appropriately challenging but not too difficult and how to share what they have been reading with the class.

Finally, minilessons focused on self-evaluation help students learn to evaluate their own work. Minilessons can include discussions of what good readers do, what a good entry in a reading response journal includes, and how to participate effectively in a grand conversation.

Reading Independently.   Students read independently each day, and this is the most important part of reading workshop. The books read during this time are self-selected, either from a text set of reading materials related to a theme, author, or genre or from any reading material available in the class or school library. Students in both Mr. Kfoury's and Ms. Jones' classes read books and poems independently as a part of their reading workshop programs.

Primary grade students begin with relatively short periods of independent reading—perhaps 10 to 15 minutes and gradually build up to 30 minutes or more. In the upper elementary grades, students often read for 45 minutes daily. Teachers who have not used reading workshop in their classrooms may find it hard to believe that students read for such lengthy periods of time, but the teachers we work with report that students enjoy this part of reading workshop the most and often beg to have more time to read books. For many students, 30 or 45 minutes just isn't enough time!

The purpose of independent reading is to increase self-motivation, develop reading fluency, and create a lifelong reading habit. Independent reading is one of the most important factors in improving students' reading; the amount of time students spend reading is significantly related to reading achievement (Anderson, Hiebert, Scott, & Wilkerson, 1985).

Responding to Literature.   Students make two types of responses to literature. First, they make exploratory responses through writing and drawing in response journals. The emphasis is on individual reflection and interpretation, not summarizing the plot of the story. Students have regular conferences with the teacher, and at these meetings, they decide together how often students will write in response journals, share response journals, and discuss the books they are reading.

In the second type of more extended response, students periodically choose one of the books they have read and respond to it more deeply through writing, art, drama, talk, or research. Students and the teacher decide together how often students will complete a self-selected extended response project for a certain number of books or poems read. Students are expected to complete one extended response activity, after reading three books, or they may complete one or two extended response activities per week.

Teachers often post a list of activities for extended response that have been planned jointly by the teacher and students in the classroom. Some teachers model each response activity in a minilesson before they expect students to complete the activity independently. These minilessons occur close to the beginning of the year so that students have an opportunity to see various ways of responding to books and poems.

At other times students and the teacher develop a list of extended response activities especially designed for a theme or focus unit and decide on a certain number of these activities which must be completed by the end of the unit.

Conferencing with Students.   Teachers have conferences with students while they are making exploratory and extended responses to literature. Students are usually encouraged to plan ahead for conferences, sign up for them, and indicate their conference plans on a record-keeping chart. Many teachers expect students to have a conference at least every two weeks and ask them to keep track of the dates of conferences on a special list. During conferences, teachers listen to students read, invite them to discuss the books and poems they are reading, teach strategies and conventions when needed, and make suggestions for future reading and response activities. Many teachers keep anecdotal records of the content of the conferences and note students' progress.

Sharing Books and Response Projects.   Each reading workshop ends with several students sharing the books they have read or their response activities with the class. This sharing is important because it confirms the value of students' reading and responding and it gives other students ideas for books they will read and types of responses they might want to try. Also, students or the teacher can discuss problems that have arisen in the workshop or announce important upcoming events such as a readers' theatre presentation or an invited guest reader.

The Special Case of Beginning Readers

Once students are reading with some fluency, typically by second or third grade, a reading workshop approach works well. However, for emergent and beginning readers, a variation on the core literature approach may be more appropriate (Holdaway, 1979; Routman, 1988). This adaptation involves shared reading of big books; participating in response activities; and repeated readings of familiar books either independently or in small groups, with partners or buddies. This approach for emergent and beginning readers has six components:

1. whole-class shared reading of big books, poems, and predictable or easy-to-read books
2. writing in reading logs or personal journals
3. small-group rereading of books and poems introduced in shared reading
4. buddy reading and individual self-selected reading
5. participating in response projects
6. reading aloud to students

Whole-class shared reading of predictable books and poems builds students' confidence in their reading abilities and a shared awareness of a large body of literature. These shared experiences are extended in several ways: through writing in reading logs or response journals, small-group rereading of shared reading selections, buddy and independent reading of the shared reading selections, and participation in response activities. Each activity provides extended opportunities to explore literature, gain print skills, and develop reading fluency. A description of this approach is found in Ms. Jones' case study at the beginning of this chapter.

Designing a Literature-Based Reading Program

As teachers design literature-based reading programs, they make choices about which components from the core literature and reading workshop methodologies they want use in their classrooms. Sometimes teachers choose one or the other of the approaches, but it is much more likely that teachers will combine or modify the methods to fit the literature they have selected and to reflect their own perspectives about reading instruction. In designing a literature-based reading program, we recommend that teachers include both core literature and reading workshop components.

While there is no one best way to plan a literature-based reading program, we believe that teachers should include in their programs the opportunities to

1. read self-selected books independently
2. read literature in small groups or with the whole class
3. respond to literature
4. share their learning with classmates
5. learn about literary elements, genres, authors and illustrators, and styles of illustration
6. learn more about reading strategies and skills

Mr. Kfoury combined both approaches by first using a core literature approach followed by a reading workshop approach in each focus unit he planned. In this way he guided students as they read and responded to selections that he felt were important to the central themes and issues in the unit, and he also allowed choice and self-direction to strengthen and deepen students' understanding of these issues and themes.

Ms. Jones modified the two approaches for her first graders. She presented core books and poems in a whole-class sharing and guided students as they reread these core books in small groups. She also extended students' reading by arranging for them to have a special friend or buddy with whom they read each day. Her students also had many opportunities to select books and poems to read independently or with classmates.

We recommend that teachers choose and adapt components because both core literature and reading workshop methodologies have strengths and weaknesses. One of the greatest strengths of the whole-class core literature approach is that a community of learners is built through shared experiences with the highest quality of literature. Also, teachers model fluent reading as they read aloud to students.

The core literature approach has disadvantages as well. Although it is certainly important to expose children to the highest quality of literature, there are no 10 or 20 or even 100 books or poems that all children should read. So, limiting students' reading to only one book every week or two does not allow them to explore the thousands and thousands of quality books and poems available today. Another disadvantage is that all students, whatever their interests or reading abilities, read and respond to one book—usually selected by the teacher and often dictated by a school or district curriculum list (Zarrillo, 1989). This core book may not interest all students or may be beyond the reading abilities of some students. Even when all students have a copy of the core selection and teachers read the selection aloud, some books are too difficult for some students later to read independently or with a partner. Without daily and sustained reading of books and poems that are interesting and appropriately challenging, students make little progress in reading ability.

A literature unit core approach eliminates some of these disadvantages when students are allowed to make choices, when books are selected on a variety of topics and reading levels, and small-group organization encourages more active talk and listening than is possible when students read together as a class.

A reading workshop approach has many strengths as well, such as providing opportunities for student choice in selecting reading materials and response activities. Students who make choices are more likely to be engaged in reading and motivated to learn. Students read at their own pace, and faster readers do not have to wait for slower readers. Students can select books and poems that are comfortable or challenging to read depending on their own preferences. Most students report that their favorite activity in literature-based reading classrooms is reading books of their own choice.

Reading workshop has several weaknesses, too. Reading workshop does not provide a time for students to read together and build a sense of community around shared experiences with books and poems. Teachers report that the lack of administrative support and funds to purchase reading materials often makes this approach difficult to manage (Zarrillo, 1989). We have also found that some teachers worry that students will not perform well on required end-of-the-year standardized or competency-based tests. However, these weaknesses can be eliminated by encouraging students to form small groups to read and respond to favorite books together, working with administrators to change budgeting practices, and becoming informed about the results of literature-based reading programs on reading achievement—research shows and teachers report that students who regularly participate in a reading workshop perform well on reading achievement tests.

STEP FOUR: CONSIDER THE INSTRUCTIONAL PERSPECTIVE

An important part of planning for literature-based reading is making decisions about beliefs and perspectives that guide instruction. In Chapter 4 we described three theoretical perspectives that underlie many teachers' literacy instruction. While students should always have an opportunity to respond personally to what they read, each of the three theoretical perspectives provides important opportunities for student learning. Teachers should reflect on their own beliefs about reading instruction when considering perspectives for instruction. And most teachers plan instruction from each of the theoretical perspectives sometime during the school year to meet instructional goals.

Consider Personal Beliefs.   Taking time to reflect on personal beliefs about how children learn to read and the role of literature in the reading program is an important way that teachers make decisions about theoretical perspectives. Many teachers feel more comfortable with an interactive perspective; they may believe that students need to learn text-based reading strategies as well as for capitalizing on reader-based knowledge. Other teachers are quite knowledgeable about children's literature, and they feel that students need to explore the world of literature and learn about great authors and illustrators. These teachers find themselves drawn to a critical perspective. Still other teachers feel it is critical for students to talk about what they read and what it means to them. These teachers find a reader response perspective most compelling. Reflecting on, identifying, and clarifying personal beliefs about reading instruction helps teachers plan more effective reading programs.

Consider Purposes for Instruction.   Another way that teachers make decisions about theoretical perspectives is by considering purposes for instruction. There are many purposes for instruction, and different purposes suggest different theoretical perspectives. In the case study at the beginning of the chapter, Mr. Kfoury carefully examined his goals for instruction and selected a reader response perspective to guide his instruction in the courage theme. He selected this perspective because he had observed his students making critical decisions based on peer pressure. He wanted his students to reflect on the kind of courage it takes to make decisions that might not be popular with others or that are morally important. Therefore, he selected the theme about courage and felt that a reader response perspective would best encourage students to personally explore this issue.

At other times Mr. Kfoury selects an interactive or critical perspective to guide instruction. His fifth graders study the American Revolution and he uses the interactive perspective during this theme cycle. He selects this perspective because he wants his students to gain information about the American Revolution. He also includes some components of the reader response perspective in this theme cycle because he feels that the study of history involves examining the historical events from the perspective of the participants. Therefore, students not only learn information about the American Revolution, but they will also explore what it was like to live during that time.

Ms. Jones used an interactive perspective to guide her instruction in the theme cycle described at the beginning of this chapter because she is concerned that her first graders learn both reader-based and text-based strategies and knowledge for fluent reading. At other times Ms. Jones selects a critical perspective such as during a focus unit on monsters. In this unit she has students explore the different kinds of monstrous creatures described in folktales and their relationship with monsters found in modern fantasies. With this purpose in mind, Ms. Jones uses a critical perspective by focusing on a study of the monster motif in traditional literature. Ms. Jones also uses a reader response perspective for a unit focused on a text set of books dealing with friendship. During this unit Ms. Jones wants students to relate their own experiences with friends to what they read.

STEP FIVE: PLAN READING AND RESPONSE ACTIVITIES

The first four steps we have discussed have laid the ground work for planning reading and response activities. Teachers begin by making preliminary plans for activities and then invite students to participate in planning and make suggestions about the books they will read and the activities in which they will participate (Crafton, 1991). Together the teacher and students plan activities for the four stages of the reading process. In these activities, students use listening, talking, reading, and writing to enjoy and appreciate literature, discover new insights and understandings, use literacy strategies and skills, and share learning with others.

Activities for the Four Stages of the Reading Process

After teachers and students fill in the planning web, teachers choose the books and activities from the web as they develop their lesson plans. Teachers should choose activities for each of the four stages of the reading process. The activities presented in Chapters 5, 6, and 7 provide many examples of ways that students prepare to read, read, explore, and extend beyond a literature selection.

To illustrate the activities that fit each of the four stages of the reading process, a fifth grade teacher might choose the following preparing to read activities for a core literature unit on *Sarah, Plain and Tall* (MacLachlan, 1985):

- locating Maine and the prairie states on a United States map
- brainstorming and clustering ideas related to the words *pioneer* and *hardship*
- reading aloud *Dakota Dugout* (Turner, 1985)

Reading activities might include

- using a Directed Reading Thinking Activity focusing on foreshadowing
- practicing think-alouds to visualize the setting and the main characters
- using fix-up strategies
- keeping a chapter-by-chapter reading journal

Exploring activities might include

- constructing a word wall and making word clusters
- making a story box, cluster, or portrait of Sarah
- constructing a story timeline and indicating foreshadowing of events
- gathering words and sentences for a Notable Language poster
- constructing a diorama of a scene from the story and explaining the importance of setting
- collecting color words from the story and using the writing process to write a color poem

Extending activities might include

- reading another book about life on the prairie and sharing it with the class
- reading another book written by Patricia MacLachlan and sharing it with the class
- writing an illustrated retelling of the story and binding it into a book for the class library
- writing a sequel for the story
- researching a prairie animal and making a poster, papier-mâché animal, or report to share with the class
- learning and singing prairie songs to the class
- making a mural of prairie life including prairie animals and plants
- viewing the film version of the story and making a Venn diagram comparing and contrasting the film and book versions
- reading an informational book about sea shells and sharing the information with the class

Other Language Arts Activities

In addition to planning for close attention to a few stories, poems, or informational books, teachers plan so that children are engaged in reading, writing, talking, and listening activities. These language activities should be genuine literacy experiences in which students use language for real life purposes. For example, in a first grade theme cycle about plants, students might be involved in the following listening activities:

- listening to the teacher share poems about plants
- listening to the teacher read informational books about plants
- listening to films, videotapes, and filmstrips about plants
- listening to a botanist or gardener talk about plants

Talk activities might include

- participating in grand conversation after reading *Jack and the Beanstalk* (Cauley, 1983)
- talking about plant experiments students are conducting
- asking a botanist or gardener questions about growing plants
- retelling or dramatizing a plant story such as *The Great Big Enormous Turnip* (Tolstoy, 1969)

Reading activities could include

- reading informational books about plants
- reading seed packets and planting guides
- reading maps showing different growing regions
- reading aloud poems about plants
- reading a classmate's hardbound book about plants
- sharing books students have written about plants

Writing activities might include

- brainstorming a list of plant-related words
- making a cluster after reading *A Tree Is Nice* (Udry, 1956)
- writing in a learning log about a plant experiment
- writing a thank you letter to a botanist or gardener who visited the class
- writing invitations to a tree-planting ceremony
- writing poems about plants (Tompkins & Hoskisson, 1991, pp. 525–526)

As teachers incorporate language arts activities into their plans for focus on a single book, focus unit, author unit, genre study, or theme cycle, they should ask themselves if they have included listening, talking, reading, and writing activities in their plans.

Literacy Strategies and Skills

An essential part of a literature-based reading program is the instruction that students receive. Most teachers are held accountable by their school system and state for teaching students certain reading and language arts strategies and skills. Teachers are expected to be familiar with these strategies and skills so they can plan appropriate assessment and instruction. Instruction of mandated skills and strategies is easily integrated into themes and focus units. For example, Ms. Jones in the case study at the beginning of this chapter is expected to teach children many skills including retelling events in sequence, using blends at the beginning of words as a tool for word recognition, and spelling words with familiar short vowel patterns such as *op*. Ms. Jones had children practice sequencing ideas as they retold *The Jacket that I Wear in the Snow* (Neitzel, 1989). Other skills can be incorporated into her repeated shared reading of *The Snowy Day* (Keats, 1962). As Ms. Jones continues to read this story, she will use modified cloze activities (see Chapter 5) to help children identify initial consonant blends in words such as *tracks, snow,* and *stick.* She will use the words *plop* and *top* in the story as a stimulus for writing other words with the *op* phonogram.

Some decisions about what strategies and skills will be taught can be made during planning. If students will write letters to an author or simulated letters from one character to another as part of a core literature unit, teachers teach conventions related to letter writing. When students are reading self-selected books, teachers plan minilessons on how to select books and how to write entries in response journals.

However, many other decisions about instruction are made as teachers observe and assess student needs. Teachers may notice that students are trying to sound out long words letter-by-letter rather than looking for familiar word parts, or they may notice that some students are trying to use dialogue in fantasies they are writing without using conventional punctuation. Teachers then plan a minilesson or other brief lessons to address these needs. Planning for instruction must be flexible enough to take into account students' instructional needs that arise as they are involved with genuine reading and writing activities.

STEP SIX: COORDINATE GROUPING PATTERNS WITH READING AND RESPONSE ACTIVITIES

Making decisions about how to group students for reading and responding to literature is an important consideration in planning literature-based reading programs. Four organization patterns for groups are whole class, small group, partners, and individuals, and each of these patterns is useful for particular types of literacy activities. Teachers must consider when to use each of these grouping patterns, the criteria used to place students into groups, and whether to use special kinds of small groups called cooperative or collaborative groups.

Grouping Patterns

Students can be grouped into whole-class, small-group, partner, or individual patterns for instruction. Whole-class groups are often teacher-led and provide opportunities for shared experiences such as viewing a film, listening to a guest speaker, or planning future directions for a theme cycle. Teachers can use whole-class groups for presenting minilessons and sharing new reading materials. Small groups may be teacher-led, jointly led by the teacher and students, or student-led. Students benefit both from being guided by a teacher and having opportunities to direct their own learning in small groups. Teachers may guide small-group reading and response daily or may only provide occasional guidance by meeting with groups once or twice a week. Students read and complete response activities on their own during the other days. Students often work with a partner for buddy-reading or work together on a response activity. Individual students work independently as they read self-selected books and complete response activities. They also meet individually with the teacher in conferences.

Experts recommend that teachers use all four grouping patterns in literature-based reading programs (Hiebert & Colt, 1989). Mr. Kfoury used the whole-class group to provide instruction related to reading *Number the Stars* and guided reading in small groups. He also provided ample time for independent learning during reading workshop. Ms. Jones used all four grouping schemes in her reading and language program. Students shared big books as a whole class, reread books in small groups with the guidance of a teacher, read books with a partner, and read independently.

Criteria for Grouping Students

An important decision regarding grouping is how to group students. Most teachers are familiar with *homogeneous groups,* grouping students together who have similar reading abilities. This practice has long been recommended because it was believed to better meet the needs of students. With grouping by ability, teachers can select reading materials that are appropriately challenging without being too difficult and plan instruction on specific strategies when they have groups of students on similar reading levels and with similar strategy needs.

However, the practice of grouping students by ability has recently received much criticism. Research has shown that students in low ability groups receive different kinds of instruction than students in high ability groups, stay in low groups throughout their school lives, and are at much greater risk for failing and dropping out of school. Students in low ability groups usually receive instruction focused on decoding and word recognition, while students in high ability groups usually receive instruction focused on comprehension (Allington, 1983; Hiebert, 1983). These findings have been misinterpreted by some schools as a need to use more whole-group instruction and do away with small groups entirely (Anderson, Hiebert, Scott, & Wilkinson, 1985).

Because this grouping pattern offers some advantages that other patterns do not, we do not feel that the use of small groups should be abandoned. Small groups allow teachers to personalize instruction, offer opportunities for shy children to participate more comfortably, and provide more practice for each individual child. Teachers can use ability groupings sparingly and with caution to meet short-term needs. A few students who demonstrate a need for a particular strategy or skill can be grouped for a lesson or to read a particular book or poem where the strategy can be applied.

Our recommendation is that teachers use *heterogeneous groups,* grouping students by criteria other than ability. Children can be grouped by interest or choice. For example, students who show an interest in Lloyd Alexander's books can be grouped together to read several of his books. Or children can be grouped when they choose a particular book or poem to read. Mr. Kfoury's students were grouped according to the book they selected to read. Groups formed by choice or by interest allow students to work with a variety of different children. Low ability children benefit from working with high ability children, and all children gain a greater respect for the strengths of their classmates. Grouping by interest and choice means that teachers will be especially mindful of children who have taken on a challenging reading task and provide them with the individual support and guidance they need. Teachers may also need to help students make choices that allow them to read materials that are not always too difficult.

Some teachers keep children in the same heterogeneous group for an entire year, whereas other teachers change groups for each theme cycle or core literature book. Teachers may want to experiment with group membership to see if some children work better with particular children than other children. Sometimes, teachers experiment with small groups of children until they have identified several groups of children who seem to work well together. Then these groups of children form a stable reading group (Keegan & Shrake, 1991).

Cooperative and Collaborative Groups

Cooperative groups are groups of students who teach each other content information, guide each other in learning to use a new strategy, collaborate to complete a joint project, or share insights and interpretations of a story, poem, or informational book (Slavin, 1983). Members of cooperative groups are responsible for learning, sharing their learning with others, and making sure each member of the group performs as well as possible. Cooperative groups provide an alternative to teacher-directed instruction and teacher-led guided reading groups; students themselves provide instruction and guidance for their classmates.

One form of cooperative group learning is called a *jigsaw* (Slavin, 1986). Students first become an expert on a strategy or on information about a topic and then teach the strategy or information to other students in a small group. To organize a jigsaw activity, teachers prepare reading materials that will present information that students will read, learn, and teach to other students. Teachers may prepare a reading guide (see Chapters 5 and 7) for the material to facilitate students' learning. Or teachers may plan lessons to demonstrate a new strategy that students will later demonstrate to other students. A small group of students, who will become experts, reads the material or participates in a demonstration lesson. The expert students work together as a group to recall the text material or practice the strategy until each of them knows the information or can perform the strategy. Then each expert returns to a different small group and teaches the students in that group the information or strategy. All students in the small group either are quizzed on the information by writing what they learned or answering questions or must perform the strategy while reading. Each student receives a score for his or her performance, and all of the scores for the students in a group are added together. Each student is then given the total score of the group. This practice encourages all members of the group to help each other learn the information or strategy so that the group will receive a higher score.

Collaborative groups are groups in which students work together as they learn. One kind of collaborative group is called a *conversational discussion group* that can be used as an alternative to a teacher-guided group discussion or grand conversation (O'Flahavan, 1988). Teachers introduce students to guidelines for a group discussion and then provide one interpretive question that will guide students' discussion. Examples of rules that can be used to guide a collaborative group discussion are

- Talk one at a time.
- Let other people talk.
- Give reasons for statements: "I liked it because. . . ." "I thought it was funny because. . . ." "I thought the man was mean because. . . ."
- Use ideas from the book or poem to back up what you say.
- Use your own experiences to back up what you say.
- Listen to what others say and comment on their statements.
- Stick to the topic.

These rules should be posted in the classroom where everyone can see them and refer to them during the group discussion. Interpretive questions should focus on broad issues related to themes or controversies. For example, interpretive questions for *Charlotte's Web* (White, 1952) might include "What invitations of friendship were offered in the book? What was the most important of these invitations?" or "Why was it important that Charlotte was a spider?" Questions should be written so that students are clear about the topic of their discussion.

Small groups of students can also work collaboratively to read a common book or poem or on response activities. Students make decisions about how many chapters of a book they will read before they meet to discuss it and can plan activities that will demonstrate their learning. They can work together to write and perform a readers' theatre, make a mural, or write a retelling of a favorite story. Teachers help students set realistic goals and evaluate their own performance.

STEP SEVEN: ORGANIZE THE CLASSROOM AND TIME

Teachers carefully consider the physical layout of their classrooms to facilitate the activities and group work planned for themes and focus units, and they arrange a schedule that enables students to have sufficient time to engage in reading and response activities.

The Physical Layout

A literature-based reading program dictates some features of the classroom arrangement. First and foremost, classrooms need a large class library stocked with at least several hundred books and other reading materials. The library must be both accessible to students and comfortable enough for them to stay and read if they choose to do so (see Chapter 1). Within the classroom library, a special area is designated where books and other reading materials related to the focus book, author unit, literature theme, or content area theme cycle are accessible to students. This location might be a special table, bookcase, or rolling cart where the materials are housed. Other features of the classroom layout include

1. a well-stocked art center where students have access to paper, markers, paint, glue, scissors, and other supplies for making books and completing other response projects
2. a listening center where students can listen to shared reading and to tapes of authors and illustrators describing their craft
3. a large area for puppet shows, readers' theater presentations, and other whole-class sharing activities
4. space for keeping projects-in-progress and displaying finished response projects
5. desks and chairs arranged in groups to facilitate whole-group and small-group gatherings

Many teachers use *centers,* locations in a classroom designed for specific activities such as reading or writing or drama, to organize their classroom. Some teachers, especially kindergarten and primary grade teachers, have as many as six to eight centers throughout the classroom (see the Kindergarten Action Plan for a description of kindergarten centers). Other teachers prefer to set up centers around the edge of their classrooms leaving space for groups of desks. These desks are used for whole-group and small-group work, and the centers provide additional spaces for individual or small-group activities. Figure 8.11 presents a third grade classroom with some centers and desks arranged in groups. Classroom spaces should be both flexible and

FIGURE 8.11   A Classroom Arranged in Centers

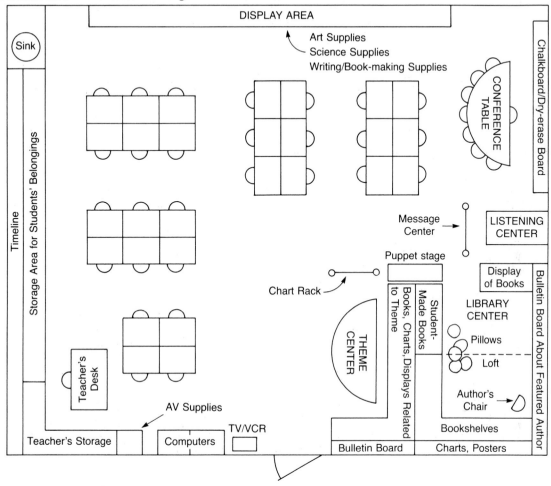

jointly planned with students. Students who feel they have a voice in classroom arrangement and organization are more likely to take responsibility for keeping track of supplies, use equipment and materials carefully and wisely, and take pride in class displays.

Schedules

Literature-based reading programs require large blocks of time, lasting at least two hours, in which students read, listen, talk, and write. The reading time is integrated with language arts into one large block, and often it is integrated with one or more of the content areas. Language arts instruction, including instruction in reading, is not limited to the morning; often language instruction is integrated into afternoon content instruction. The traditional subjects—spelling, handwriting, grammar, and writing—are integrated with reading.

Establishing a predictable schedule is as important in a literature-based reading program as in any program, even though the integrated approach often necessitates overlapping activities. Students, especially younger children, operate best when they follow a familiar routine. Schedules should include daily time for teachers to read aloud and for students to read independently and share with their peers. Both Mr. Kfoury and Ms. Jones planned their schedules so that their students could participate in shared reading, guided reading, and independent reading. They allowed ample time for activities and for sharing.

STEP EIGHT: MANAGE RECORD-KEEPING

Teachers are held accountable not only for providing instruction but also for tracking students' progress and assessing their learning. Teachers must plan ways to document what each student does and learns. We have already described many forms of record-keeping such as keeping a list of titles that students have read, dates that students have had conferences, and activities students have completed. Teachers also keep anecdotal records of conferences they have with students and make notes as they observe students involved in reading and responding activities. Two other ways to keep records are state-of-the-class reports and assignment sheets.

State-of-the-Class Reports

In the reading workshop approach, teachers and students keep track of what they intend to do each day through *state-of-the-class reports* (Atwell, 1987; Reutzel & Cooter, 1991). Teachers and students meet for a state-of-the-class report before beginning to read independently or work on response activities. Students report to the class what they plan to accomplish during the work period and record their intentions on a class chart. Figure 8.12 presents a portion of a state-of-the-class record-keeping chart. This chart shows the number of pages that students intend to read, or whether they will write in their response journals, read with a partner, complete a response activity, or conference with the teacher.

The state-of-the-class record-keeping chart informs the teacher and individual students about what should be accomplished during a reading workshop. One way that students can be evaluated is whether they frequently accomplish what they intend and how well they learn to set and stick to realistic expectations. Students become more responsible as they complete the chart for themselves each day and as they evaluate their own progress in achieving their goals.

Assignment Sheets

Another form of record-keeping is an assignment sheet (Tompkins, 1990). A copy of an assignment sheet for a core literature unit on *Sarah, Plain and Tall* (MacLachlan, 1985) is presented in Figure 8.13. This assignment sheet is developed with students and distributed at the beginning of the focus unit. Students keep track of their work during the unit and sometimes negotiate to change the assignment sheet as the unit evolves. They may staple the assignment sheet inside a folder in which they will keep

FIGURE 8.12 State-of-the-Class Report Chart

Student	Monday	Tuesday	Wednesday	Thursday	Friday
Gregory	10CB,RJ*	10SB,RA-map			
Kristen	RA-web,15SB	20CB,RJ			
Juan	RA-web,15SB	C,RJ,RA-word wall			
Carlos	10CB,RJ*	10CB,RA-map			
Margaret	RA-web,10SB	10CB,RJ			
Anne-Marie	10CB,RJ*	10CB,RA-sew			
Montgomery	30SB,C	20CB,RJ,RA-note language			

CB = core book, SB = self-selected book, RJ = response journal, RA = response activity, C = conference with teacher, * = read pages with buddy

337

FIGURE 8.13   Assignment Checklist for *Sarah, Plain and Tall* (MacLachlan, 1985)

	Student	Teacher
Name: _____		
1. Keep a response journal and write five entries.	_____	_____
2. Make a map with prairie states, Maine, and Sarah's trip marked.	_____	_____
3. Help make a portrait of one character (or make a cluster or story box).	_____	_____
4. Make a poster of words and sentences from the story.	_____	_____
5. Help draw or paint a prairie mural showing animals and plants of the region.	_____	_____
6. Write a color poem.	_____	_____
7. Do a project of your choice.	_____	_____
8. Share your project with the class.	_____	_____

their work for the focus unit. Students identify which projects they will complete and check these off as they are finished.

Teachers may use the assignment sheet for assessment purposes. They may check off that they have reviewed the assignment or may record quality points for the assignment. Students can also evaluate their assignments and include their evaluation in the folder of completed work. Chapter 9 will describe additional assessment procedures and methods.

MAKING DECISIONS ABOUT PUTTING IT ALL TOGETHER

Teachers make many decisions as they put together a literature-based reading program. We described eight steps that teachers use in planning, managing, and organizing a literature-based reading program including choosing literature and identifying a focus. Teachers organize their teaching around core literature selections, focus units, or theme cycles and use core literature and reading workshop components. They consider theoretical perspective and plan reading and response activities. Finally, they make decisions about record-keeping and assessment.

The decisions that teachers make in putting together a literature-based reading program are to

- Determine a focus.
- Identify literature.
- Design the program with core literature and reading workshop components.
- Consider theoretical perspectives in light of personal beliefs and purposes for instruction.
- Plan reading and response activities.
- Coordinate grouping patterns with reading and response activities.
- Organize the classroom and time.
- Manage record-keeping.
- Assess students' learning.

This information is added to the decision-making diagram as shown in Figure 8.14.

FIGURE 8.14   Summary Chart for Decision Tree

	Decision Tree
Chapter 1	Using Literature in the Reading Program
Chapter 2	Choosing Literature for Children
Chapter 3	Learning About Authors and Illustrators
Chapter 4	Identifying Perspectives on Reading Instruction
Chapter 5	Teaching from a Reader Response Perspective
Chapter 6	Teaching from a Critical Perspective
Chapter 7	Teaching from an Interactive Perspective
Chapter 8	**Putting It All Together** • **Determine a focus.** • **Identify literature.** • **Design the program with core literature and reading workshop components.** • **Consider theoretical perspective in light of personal beliefs and purposes for instruction.** • **Plan reading and response activities.** • **Coordinate grouping patterns with reading and response activities.** • **Organize the classroom and time.** • **Manage record-keeping.** • **Assess students' learning.**
Chapter 9	Assessing Students' Learning

REFERENCES

Allington, R. (1983). The reading instruction provided readers of differing ability. *Elementary School Journal, 83,* 255–265.

Anderson, R., Hiebert, E., Scott, J., & Wilkinson, I. (1985). *Becoming a nation of readers: The report of the commission on classroom.* Washington, DC: The National Institute of Education.

Atwell, N. (1987). *In the middle.* Portsmouth, NH: Heinemann.

Children's book review index. (Vols. 1–13). Detroit: Gale Research Co.

Children's literature review: Excerpts from re-views, criticism, and commentary on books for children and young people. Detroit, MI: Gale Research Company.

Crafton, L. (1991). *Whole language: Getting started . . . Moving forward.* New York: Richard C. Owens.

Crook, P., & Lehman, B. (1991). Themes for two voices: Children's fiction and nonfiction as "whole literature." *Language Arts, 68,* 34–41.

Hiebert, E. (1983). An examination of ability grouping for reading instruction. *Reading Research Quarterly, 18,* 231–255.

Hiebert, E., & Colt, J. (1989). Patterns of literature-based reading instruction. *The Reading Teacher, 43,* 14–20.

Holdaway, D. (1979). *The foundations of literacy.* Portsmouth, NH: Heinemann.

Hornsby, D., & Sukarna, C., with J. Parry (1986). *Read on: A conference approach to reading.* Portsmouth, NH: Heinemann.

Huck, C., Hepler, S., & Hickman, J. (1987). *Children's literature in the elementary school.* New York: Holt, Rinehart & Winston.

Jipson, J., & Paley, N. (1991). The selective tradition in teachers' choice of children's literature: Does it exist in the elementary classroom? *English Education, 23,* 148–159.

Johnson, T., & Louis, D. (1990). *Bringing it all together.* Portsmouth, NH: Heinemann.

Katz, B., & Katz, L. (1991). *Magazines for young people.* (2nd ed.). New Providence, NJ: R.R. Bowker.

Keegan, S., & Shrake, K. (1991). Literature study groups: An alternative to ability grouping. *The Reading Teacher, 44,* 542–547.

McClure, A., & Zitlow, C. (1991). Not just the facts: Aesthetic response in elementary content area studies. *Language Arts, 68,* 27–33.

Moss, J. F. (1984). *Focus units in literature: A handbook for elementary teachers.* Urbana, IL: National Council of Teachers of English.

Norton, D. (1992). *The impact of literature reading.* New York: Merrill/Macmillan.

O'Flahavan, J. (1988, December). *Conversational discussion groups: A study of second graders leading their own discussions.* Paper presented at the National Reading Conference, Tucson, Arizona.

Pappas, C., Kiefer, B., & Levstik, L. (1990). *An integrated language perspective in the elementary school.* New York: Longman.

Recommended readings in literature: Kindergarten through grade eight. (1988). Sacramento: California State Department of Education.

Reutzel, D., & Cooter, Jr., R. (1991). Organizing for effective instruction: The reading workshop. *The Reading Teacher, 44,* 548–554.

Routman, R. (1988). *Transitions from literature to literacy.* Portsmouth, NH: Heinemann.

Shannon, P. (1986). Hidden within the pages: A study of social perspective in young children's favorite books. *The Reading Teacher, 39,* 656–661.

Slavin, R. (1983). *Cooperative learning.* New York: Longman.

Slavin, R. E. (1986). *Using student team learning* (3rd ed.). Baltimore, MD: Johns Hopkins University, Center for Research on Elementary and Middle Schools.

Tompkins, G. (1990). The literature connection: How one teacher puts reading and writing together. In T. Shannahan (Ed.), *Reading and writing together: New perspectives for the reading* (pp. 201–223). Norwood, MA: Christopher-Gordon.

Tompkins, G., & Hoskisson, K. (1991). *Language arts: Content and teaching strategies* (2nd ed.). New York: Merrill/Macmillan.

Traxel, J. (1983). The American Revolution in children's fiction. *Research in the Teaching of English, 17,* 61–83.

Zarrillo, J. (1989). Teachers' interpretations of literature-based reading. *The Reading Teacher, 43,* 22–28.

CHILDREN'S LITERATURE REFERENCES

Byars, B. (1969). *Trouble river.* New York: Viking.

Cauley, L. (1983). *Jack and the beanstalk.* New York: Putnam.

Dagliesh, A. (1982). *The courage of Sarah Noble.* New York: Scribner.

Fritz, J. (1958). *The cabin faced west.* New York: Coward-McCann.

Gardiner, J. (1980). *Stone fox.* New York: Harper & Row. Greenwillow.

Keats, E. (1962). *The snowy day.* New York: Puffin.

Kovalski, M. (1987). *The wheels on the bus.* Boston: Little, Brown.

Lionni, L. (1969). *Alexander and the wind-up mouse.* New York: Pantheon.

Lowry, L. (1989). *Number the stars.* Boston: Houghton Mifflin.

MacLachlan, P. (1985). *Sarah, plain and tall.* New York: Harper & Row.

Neitzel, S. (1989). *The jacket I wear in the snow.* New York: Greenwillow.

Reiss, J. (1972). *The upstairs room.* New York: Harper & Row.

Sperry, A. (1968). *Call it courage.* New York: Collier.

Steig, W. (1969). *Sylvester and the magic pebble.* New York: Farrar, Straus & Giroux.

Steig, W. (1971). *Amos & Boris.* New York: Farrar, Straus & Giroux.

Taylor, M. (1976). *Roll of thunder, hear my cry.* New York: Dial.

Tolstoy, A. (1969). *The great big enormous turnip.* New York: Watts.

Turner, A. (1985). *Dakota dugout.* New York: Aladdin.

Udry, J. M. (1956). *A tree is nice.* New York: Harper.

White, E. (1952). *Charlotte's web.* New York: Harper & Row.

CHAPTER 9

ASSESSING STUDENTS' LEARNING

In this chapter you will learn to make decisions about:

- **Identifying who will use assessment information and how it will be used**
- **Identifying instructional goals**
- **Documenting learning**
- **Analyzing learning**
- **Evaluating learning**

I N THIS CHAPTER we focus on how teachers assess students' learning in literature-based reading programs. In the following case study, Mrs. Reeves and her third graders use portfolios to assess their reading growth.

A CASE IN POINT

Mrs. Reeves' Students Use Portfolios

At the beginning of the school year Mrs. Reeves explains to her class of third graders, "Each of you will keep records about what you read and collect samples of the work that you do. You will keep your records and work samples for the entire school year in a large folder we'll call a 'portfolio.' The papers in your portfolio will show me and your parents how much you have learned this year."

Then Mrs. Reeves shows the students Jameel's portfolio, a student who was in her classroom last year. The students examine the contents of Jameel's portfolio; they read the list of books that he read, his response journal entries, and some of the stories and reports he wrote, clusters he constructed, and pictures he drew. They are impressed by the amount of reading Jameel accomplished in one year. Mrs. Reeves assures everyone, "You will read just as much or even more than Jameel did last year and you will have lots of fun selecting books that you want to read this year."

Mrs. Reeves passes out large sheets of tag board and shows students how to fold the sheets—like an envelope—to make their own portfolios. Students staple the edges of their envelopes together, write their names on the portfolios, and decorate them. Students place their portfolios in a special box in the classroom.

The next day, Mrs. Reeves asks students to think for a few moments about what they would like to do and learn in reading this year. Several students volunteer ideas about what they would like to accomplish. Carey answers, "I want to read lots of big, thick books without any pictures," and Sarah comments, "I want to read every one of Chris Van Allsburg's books all by myself." Then the students break into small groups and share their goals among themselves. Afterwards, students write a list of three or more goals and put their lists in their portfolios. Mrs. Reeves reminds students that they can review this list and the other materials they will put in their portfolios whenever they wish.

During the next two weeks Mrs. Reeves meets with students in individual conferences and listens to them read excerpts from three books aloud (about five to ten pages). As students read, she takes a running record using a special marking system that captures what students say as they read. The purpose of running records is to get a quick indication of students' reading levels and the strategies they use as they read. (See the discussion of running records later in this chapter.) Mrs. Reeves knows this is only a rough estimate that is influenced by the student's interest in the topic of the book or familiarity with the text. Even so, the running record provides a quick assessment of each student's reading level at the beginning of the school year and an initial guide for instructional planning.

Students select the books they will read aloud from Mrs. Reeves' classroom library and these books range from easy-to-read to very difficult for most third graders. Most students select books from a collection of predictable books, favorite folktales, and easy-to-read stories such as *Teeny Tiny* (Bennett, 1985), *Mouse Soup* (Lobel, 1977), and *The Good-bye Book* (Viorst, 1988) that they read aloud with buddies or in small groups during the first few days of school. Other students are independently reading *The Mouse and the Motorcycle* (Cleary, 1965), *On My Honor* (Bauer, 1986), and other chapter books.

Mrs. Reeves analyzes each student's running record and puts the running record and her analysis of reading level and strategy use in each student's portfolio. Running records provide information about whether students are reading a passage that is easy or difficult and about students' use of strategies such as monitoring meaning and attending to print cues. One way that she uses this information is to guide her selection of books for the upcoming theme cycles. Mrs. Reeves wants to be sure she has a range of books that will meet everyone's needs and interests. She also uses the information to plan minilessons on reading strategies.

During the next few weeks of school Mrs. Reeves teaches her students to carefully document what they are reading and how they are responding to literature. For each focus unit or theme cycle, students keep a folder with checklists, reading logs, and other materials. For instance, students keep a list of books they read independently and in a literature study group, notes about conferences they have with Mrs. Reeves, and response activities they complete.

At the end of each focus unit or theme cycle, Mrs. Reeves asks students to review the contents of their folders and to self-evaluate their work. Students meet with Mrs. Reeves individually or in small groups to talk about their progress and how well they met the goals they had set for themselves. They select entries from their reading journals, response activities, and checklists to place in their portfolios. These samples represent what students consider to be their best work or show their growth as readers and writers. Mrs. Reeves also takes photos of students' projects to place in their portfolios. As a part of these self-evaluation lessons, students discuss why they selected certain samples, and they set goals for the next unit or cycle based on the criteria of good reading and response developed in their discussions. Students also make notes to attach to their samples to explain why each piece has been selected for inclusion in the portfolio.

Twice during the school year, Mrs. Reeves gathers small groups of students to evaluate their learning as reflected in the portfolio samples. Students each read through their portfolios to find ways they believe they have grown. She asks them to find things they can do in their latest work samples that they could not do in their earlier samples. After they examine their portfolios, students meet with Mrs. Reeves in small groups to share their observations. At one small group meeting, Carey observes, "I found a lot of words that I could not spell in September and October that I can spell now, and I think I am writing a lot more now," and Sarah explains, "I can't believe that I wrote that cluster with only five details. My clusters now have 11 or 12 details. I also never used to talk about another book in my response logs—I only talked about the book I was reading. Now I can think of at least one other book and compare it to what I'm reading."

Mrs. Reeves also collects additional information to assess students' literacy development and places some of this information in the students' portfolios, including

- anecdotal notes as she observes students' activities and behaviors during reading workshop
- notes about conferences
- checklists about students' contributions in grand conversations
- several more running records collected periodically during the year

Mrs. Reeves believes that assessment is part of the learning process, and she wants her students to be involved in the entire process, so she places most assessment records that she makes in students' portfolios. Making her records accessible to students has changed some of the ways that Mrs. Reeves writes anecdotal notes, records conference meetings, and marks checklists. She ex-

plains, "I find that I focus more on my students' strengths, and I compare how they are working and behaving now to their previous levels. The biggest difference is that I keep my students' goals in mind as well as my own."

Some of Mrs. Reeves' assessment activities are part of her school's assessment plan. Together with her colleagues, Mrs. Reeves has been working for three years to develop a school-wide portfolio assessment plan. All teachers have agreed to keep running records of their students' oral reading three times a year, checklists of grand conversations four times a year, samples from response journals six times a year, and samples of process writing four times a year. One of the process writing samples must be a report project in which students gather information after reading several sources. In this way, some of the information included in the portfolio is used in school-wide assessments of the language arts program while the majority of information is used for classroom-based decisions.

INTRODUCTION

Assessment is an important consideration for all teachers, but it is particularly important for teachers who are implementing literature-based reading programs. Many of the theories and practices on which literature-based reading programs are based conflict with traditional methods of assessment (Valencia & Pearson, 1987). Traditional methods of literacy assessment are based on practices such as identifying a list of skills and assessing whether students have mastered those skills. Usually students' knowledge of these skills is examined in isolation—word recognition skills of single words in isolation or knowledge of the meanings of isolated vocabulary words—using tests with multiple choice formats and questions that have only one right answer. These tests examine students' ability to read short, contrived passages, not genuine reading materials.

Traditional methods of assessment do not adequately serve the needs of students who develop strategies for solving their own reading difficulties, stress multiple and personal interpretations of text, and focus on whole stories, poems, or informational books in literature-based reading programs. Other assessment techniques such as those Mrs. Reeves used in the case study are needed to assess students' literacy learning. In this chapter we discuss the issues related to assessment in literature-based reading programs and describe how teachers can document, analyze, and evaluate their students' literacy development.

PLANNING TO ASSESS STUDENTS' LITERACY LEARNING

Assessment is changing to reflect both teachers' beliefs about how children learn to read and write and the instruction in literature-based reading classrooms. Tests and other traditional forms of assessment are being replaced with more authentic assessment techniques such as analysis of student work samples and running records. As teachers make plans for assessment they must keep in mind three considerations: they must be aware of purposes of assessment, the people who will use the assessment information, and the characteristics of effective assessment.

Goals for Assessment

One of the first questions teachers ask as they think about assessment ought to be, "What do I assess?" To answer this question, teachers must be clear about what they want students to learn because goals for instruction should guide assessment. For that reason, we have placed the chapters about instruction before this chapter on assessment.

Teachers begin their planning for assessment by clarifying instructional goals, and these goals emerge from teachers' beliefs about literacy learning and the theoretical perspectives underlying their instruction (Winograd, Paris, & Bridge, 1991). As they begin planning, teachers should carefully reflect on their beliefs about literacy learning and the implications of their theoretical perspective for assessment. These beliefs suggest goals for instruction. Once instructional goals are identified, teachers begin to make decisions about how these goals will be assessed in ways that match teachers' beliefs and theoretical perspectives. No other step in assessment is as important as clarifying goals for instruction.

Classroom-Based Assessment

An important question in planning assessment is, "Who will use the information from assessment?" Students, parents, teachers, specialists, counselors, administrators, policy makers, and the public are all potential users of assessment information. Students use assessment information to evaluate their strengths, measure their learning, and help them set goals for future learning. Parents use assessment information to monitor their children's progress. Teachers use assessment information to judge the effectiveness of their instruction, to evaluate learners, and to plan instruction. Reading teachers, special educators, school psychologists, and other specialists use assessment information to make judgments about placing students in special learning programs. Counselors use assessment information to guide students' decisions about programs of study, and administrators evaluate teachers and programs using this information. Outside groups, such as policy makers and the public, use assessment information to gauge the effectiveness of school systems in educating future citizens.

Because each of these groups has different needs, the kinds of assessments that will provide them the information that they need differ. We are concerned in this chapter with classroom-based assessments, assessments that inform students, parents, and teachers. We will make suggestions on how classroom assessments may also meet the needs of administrators and local policy makers. For example, in the case study at the beginning of this chapter Mrs. Reeves used portfolios as the primary method of classroom-based assessment, and her school uses some information from portfolios in school-based assessment.

The purposes of classroom-based literacy assessment are to (a) inform students what and how well they are learning, (b) inform parents what and how well their children are learning, (c) inform teachers about students' developmental and instructional needs, and (d) inform principals and other district policy makers how well students are progressing.

Portfolio Assessment

Portfolio assessment is an alternative method of documenting and evaluating students' learning that can be used to meet classroom-based assessment needs. Portfolio assessment consists of the systematic collection and analysis of data to help teachers assess students' achievement, improvement, learning processes, and effort (Tierney, Carter, & Desai, 1991). It is more than a collection of students' samples and teachers' notes or checklists. Portfolio assessment is a process; the process in which students and teachers select data to use in assessment, and then analyze data, evaluate data, and share the data.

Mrs. Reeves used portfolio assessment in the case study at the beginning of this chapter. She and her students collected specific kinds of data—work samples, running records, lists, and checklists—that were selected and then placed in a folder. Mrs. Reeves and her students analyzed the data included in the portfolio—students made self-evaluations, and Mrs. Reeves analyzed student samples, running records, and anecdotal notes. Finally, the data were shared with students, parents, and the school principal.

Portfolios can be used to inform parents and others of students' progress. Teachers and students collect evidence that is used to compare students' current achievement with their past accomplishments (Flood & Lapp, 1989). Teachers share the information from portfolios with parents so that they can see a breadth of information about their child rather than a single grade or test score. For example, a first grade teacher might record at several times over the year the number of words that students can read aloud in one minute and the number of words students can write in their journals within 10 minutes (Pils, 1991). These numbers can be plotted on a graph, placed in a portfolio, and shared with parents at the end of each grading period.

Characteristics of Effective Assessment

Teachers regularly collect all sorts of assessment information about students, but not all information is effective. To be effective, assessment must provide useful information to students, parents, teachers, and administrators. Characteristics of effective assessment are that it is (a) grounded in theory, (b) authentic, (c) continuous and inseparable from instruction, (d) multi-dimensional, (e) collaborative, (f) concerned with both process and product, and (g) evolving (Harp, 1991; Tierney, Carter, & Desai, 1991). As teachers plan for assessment, they need to consider these seven characteristics of effective assessment and find ways to make their own assessment plans more useful.

Assessment Is Grounded in Theory.   Literature-based reading programs are based on reader response, critical, and interactive theories of reading. These theories portray readers as strategic, constructive learners who use a sophisticated knowledge of literature as they engage in reading for a variety of purposes including both aesthetic and efferent purposes. Therefore, assessment should examine students' lived through experiences as they read and respond to a wide variety of stories and poems through talk, writing, and other activities. Assessment should capture students' ability to interpret literature and learn information as well as their ability to share responses, interpretations, and information with others through talk, writing, and other reporting techniques. Assessment should also reflect students' growing sophistication in selecting materials to read for pleasure and for learning.

Winograd, Paris, and Bridge (1991) identified three characteristics of good readers that are consistent with the reader response, critical, and interactive perspectives: Good readers are skilled, motivated, and independent. Skilled readers focus on meaning; they read fluently and accurately so that they can comprehend and interpret what they read. Skilled readers are motivated to stick with difficult tasks and spend considerable time reading and responding to books and poems of their choice. Motivated readers are open to ideas about interpretation of books and poems; they are able to communicate their own impressions and ideas about books and poems but are willing to listen to their classmates' comments. In addition, motivated readers have favorite authors and illustrators and respond enthusiastically and knowledgeably to their works. Independent readers transfer the strategies and knowledge they learned in one situation to new contexts and new activities, and they plan their reading activities based on their purposes for reading because they have strategies for monitoring their reading based on those purposes. These three characteristics of readers—skilled, motivated, and independent—suggest goals for instruction and help to define the shape of assessment.

In addition to capturing the goals of instruction, assessment reflects the kinds of experiences children engage in. Assessment should document the diversity of literacy activities that are a part of the literature-based reading program. If students participate in grand conversations, write reports, keep learning logs, write in response journals, construct character webs, write to authors and illustrators, publish simulated newspapers, and compose stories and poems in response to literature, then these activities ought to be a part of the assessment process.

Figure 9.1 presents an *assessment planning guide* that identifies the goals for instruction and activities that are planned to meet these goals. The assessment planning guide presented in Figure 9.1 illustrates some of the goals that a third grade teacher identified for her students and her ideas about how she might collect information about each of the instructional goals based on the kinds of activities that she

FIGURE 9.1   Assessment Planning Guide

Instructional Goals	Activities to Meet Goals	Assessment
Fluently reads increasingly difficult books	Daily independent reading, core literature, small group guided reading	Running record of texts on various levels
Selects books for enjoyment and sustains engagement in books	Daily independent reading	Lists of books read & self-evaluation. Anecdotal notes during reading
Interprets books and poems using personal experiences and support from text	Guided reading/Grand conversations	Response checklist
Reads for information and learn from reading	Theme cycles, reports, and quickwrites	Vocabulary clusters KWL charts, reports, quickwrites

planned for her reading program. The teacher completed the guide early in the school year and used it to make decisions about what kinds of assessment activities she needed to complete, such as keeping anecdotal records and checklists (which are explained later in this chapter). As the year progressed, she modified and changed her plan to reflect input from students and her new insights into instructional needs.

Assessment Is Authentic.   Literacy learning takes place as students engage in reading and response activities for authentic purposes. That is, students learn to read as they read to discover how to take care of a pet frog in the classroom, laugh at the antics of the animals in *Bunnicula: A Rabbit Tale of Mystery* (Howe & Howe, 1979), or find out how pioneers lived as they crossed thousands of miles of prairie. Assessments help teachers evaluate how well students are learning from these authentic experiences with reading, and it must take place as students are engaged in authentic reading and language activities.

Teachers observe students as they read with a partner, write letters to authors, or participate in grand conversations. They write anecdotal notes of their observations, collect samples of letters students have written, or tape-record students' reading or discussion in grand conversations for later analysis. One reason effective assessment is authentic is that teachers observe students as they are engaged in genuine literacy activities rather than simply collecting finished products.

Teachers also observe students to determine directions for future instruction. Teachers note particular students who need more support in using a certain strategy independently or students who need to learn a new reading strategy or written language convention. Teachers use these observations to make decisions about instruction in the upcoming days or weeks. Effective assessments are authentic because they influence the on-going instruction in the classroom.

Assessment Is Continuous and Inseparable from Instruction.   Teachers plan so they collect assessment information continuously throughout the school year. Many teachers identify particular assessments that they make monthly, at the beginning of each semester, at the end of each grading period, or according to some other schedule. In the case study at the beginning of this chapter, Mrs. Reeves planned to collect oral readings and running records as students read favorite and other books three times during the year—in September, January, and June. She also planned to observe each student in a grand conversation and collect drafts and final copies of writing projects to document each student's use of the writing process four times a year (once during each grading period). These continuous and planned assessments help the teacher determine students' progress and what changes need to be made in instructional plans.

Other assessments are not planned, but nonetheless are collected continuously throughout the school year. Teachers are continuously involved in observing students, and most teachers keep anecdotal notes of their observations over the school year. Anecdotal notes can provide the best evidence of student growth because teachers who are careful to capture spontaneous classroom events and dialogue can often trace when students' understanding of new strategies and understandings emerges.

Teachers also help students select various reading and writing samples to include in their portfolios. Mrs. Reeves guided her students as they collected samples for their portfolios after each theme cycle. These samples provide a continuous record of students' reading and response activities and accomplishments.

Planning continuous assessment activities is a natural and inseparable part of instruction. Mrs. Reeves planned self-evaluation conferences where her students identified criteria for effective reading and response activities. As students discuss these criteria they are learning more about themselves as readers and writers as they evaluate their own learning. Such assessments have a strong instructional component as well as an evaluation component.

Assessment Is Multi-dimensional.   Effective assessment is multi-dimensional because teachers use information from a variety of sources including anecdotal records, running records, checklists, and students' samples. These samples include response journal entries, process writing compositions, and readers' theatre scripts. Teachers observe students as they interact in whole-group, small-group, and individual learning situations, and they observe students' choices, interests, and attitudes as well as their academic work. Samples of work-in-progress as well as finished products can be examined. As teachers plan for assessment, they should take care that the assessment reflects the diversity of students' experiences and interactions.

Assessment Is Collaborative. Students in traditional classrooms are rarely part of the assessment process, yet helping students become independent and lifelong readers implies that they will be able to set and assess the attainment of their goals and achievements. When students play a role in setting criteria by which their reading and response activities will be assessed, assessment can empower rather than police them.

Self-evaluation is one of the underlying principles of portfolio evaluation (Tierney, Carter, & Desai, 1991). In the case study at the beginning of this chapter, Mrs. Reeves helped her students evaluate their learning as a part of the assessment plans she used in her classroom. Students collaborate with the teacher both to select the materials and samples that will be placed in their portfolios and to evaluate those materials and samples.

Assessment Is Concerned with Process and Product. Many goals of literature-based reading programs relate to processes, the mental activities and strategies that students use while reading and responding to literature. Often these processes are reflected in products that students say or write as they respond to literature. For example, one process we want students to be able to demonstrate is the use of imagery, the process of forming a mental picture of a setting or character. Two products that reflect students' use of imagery are quickwrites that might provide descriptive detail about an imagined setting or quickdraws that may include details about a character's appearance and activities. As teachers analyze students' quickwrites, they make inferences about students' use of the imagery strategy—a process—and about their writing fluency and insight—a product.

Teachers want to assess how well students have learned to use the processes of writing (e.g., preparing to write by brainstorming ideas on a cluster or a quickwrite) as well as to assess their written products (e.g., the variety of sentence structures or support for an argument). Assessing both processes and products involved in reading and writing is a part of every assessment plan.

Assessment Is Evolving. Classroom-based assessment requires that teachers develop and fine-tune many observation, recording, and analysis skills. Teachers have found that the ability to collect assessment information and develop assessment instruments, such as observation checklists, requires some practice (Paradis, Chatton, Boswell, Smith, & Yovich, 1991; Pils, 1991). The development of useful checklists and other procedures for collecting assessment information is a slow process and depends on teachers' careful reflection on their goals. Many teachers find that at first they tend to collect data in a flurry right before a grading period ends. With practice, they begin to collect data more systematically throughout the school year. Developing the professional skills used in classroom-based, portfolio assessment is a continuously evolving process.

DOCUMENTING STUDENTS' LITERACY LEARNING

Once teachers have identified goals for instruction, then the second step in assessment is to identify procedures for collecting samples and other information that will document students' growth related to the instructional goals. Many kinds of information can be used to document students' literacy learning including anecdotal notes, checklists, student samples and records, and running records.

Anecdotal Notes

Anecdotal notes are informal notes that teachers write about what they observe in their classroom. Anecdotal notes should describe an event or process rather than evaluate (Rhodes & Nathenson-Mejia, 1992). To take anecdotal notes, teachers observe individual students as they read in a variety of situations. What teachers observe depends on the situation, the student, and the purposes for observation. Teachers may observe what students are reading and writing, students' comments about reading and writing, aspects of text students attend to, students' use of information from instruction in their reading, misconceptions students have, the way students solve problems in reading, or students' use of reading to learn (Rhodes & Nathenson-Mejia, 1992; Siu-Runyan, 1991).

For example, one teacher we work with was observing one of her students, Harrison, participate in a book talk group at the group meeting. Harrison described the most exciting parts of *Redwall* (Jacques, 1987), a book in the class library, and spontaneously read aloud a sentence from the book to the group. The teacher noted this event because she knows that Harrison struggles with reading and never seems to enjoy it. This incident clearly shows that Harrison has found a book he likes and is willing to share with others. The teacher also noticed that Dominique, another reluctant reader in her classroom, read independently for 35 minutes on a particular day. The teacher knows this indicates real growth for Dominique because at the beginning of the year she had been reading only 4 to 5 minutes before beginning to get restless.

Many teachers have found that keeping a pad of sticky-backed notepaper close at hand during students' independent reading time is an effective way to record observations (Reardon, 1991). Teachers write one observation per page, date it, and then stick the paper on a clipboard or the cover of a notebook (Figure 9.2). At the end of the day, they transfer the note pages from the clipboard into a special observation notebook with pages labeled for each child.

Sometimes teachers make observations of specific activities or behaviors. For example, teachers might want to observe all students for indications of engagement or personal involvement with a book or to monitor students' use of fix-up strategies. In these focused observations, teachers keep a checklist of students' names, and they check off each name or write brief notes as they observe students. Sticky-backed notepaper also works well for recording focused observations when teachers want to capture students' behaviors as they occur rather than observing each student and marking "yes" or "no."

FIGURE 9.2   Anecdotal Notes About a Third Grader

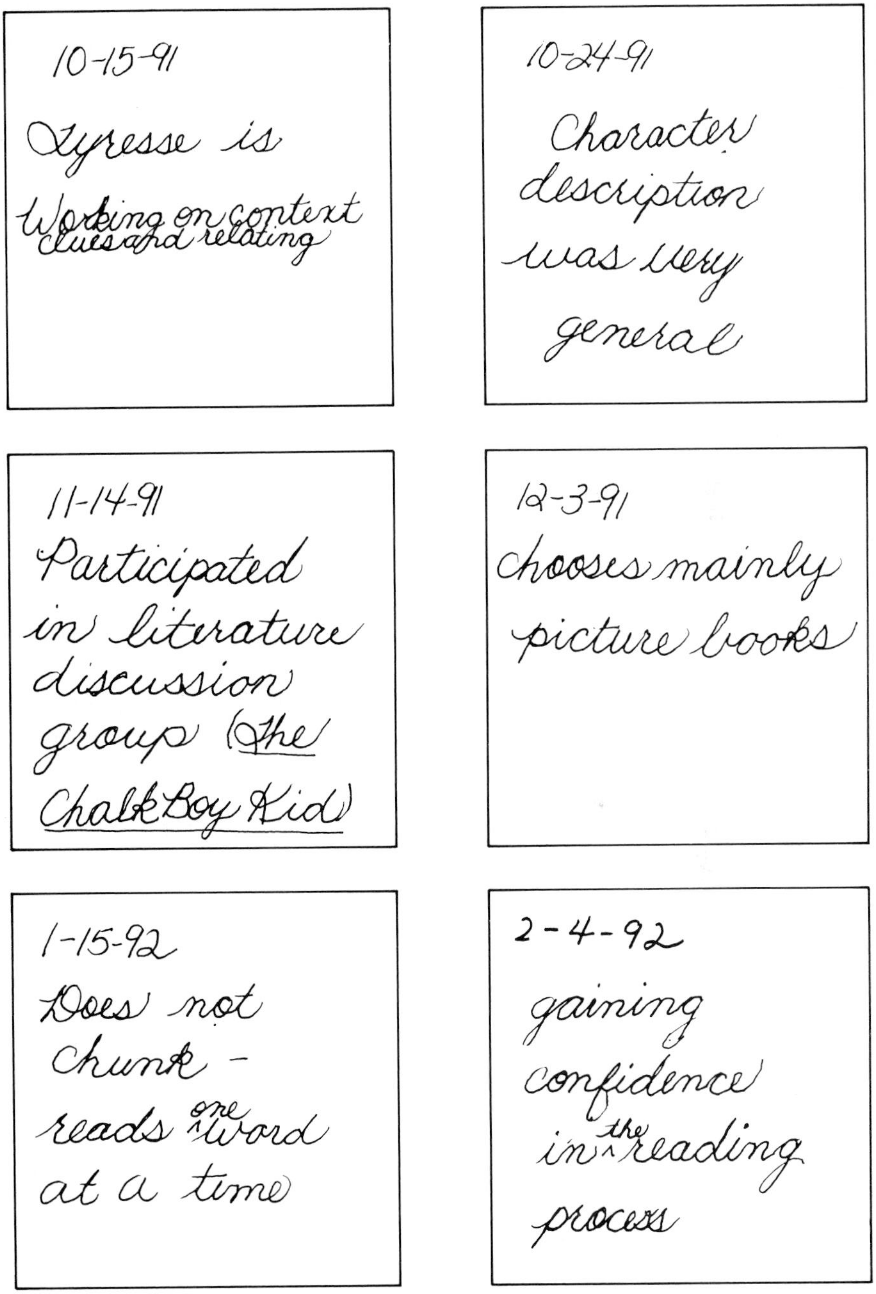

10-15-91

Tyresse is Working on context clues and relating

10-24-91

Character description was very general

11-14-91

Participated in literature discussion group (The Chalk Boy Kid)

12-3-91

chooses mainly picture books

1-15-92

Does not chunk – reads one word at a time

2-4-92

gaining confidence in the reading process

Focused observation can also be used to check to see how students are using their time during reading workshop. If students use status-of-the-class record charts (see Chapter 8), teachers might observe whether students actually work on the projects that they recorded on the chart, how quickly they finish everything they recorded, or whether they finish the projects they list each day. Observations such as these help teachers determine whether students are being realistic and self-guided in their use of independent reading and response time.

Another kind of anecdotal notes that teachers can keep are more general observations of classroom activities or groups of students. Teachers keep an observational notebook in which they write at least one entry daily. For example, some excerpts from one teacher's observational notebook included:

8/29   Most students are having difficulty sustaining reading beyond 10 minutes. Many students spend nearly 5 minutes looking through several books before selecting one that they look through or read quickly. They spend more time finding a second book.

9/12   Some students are selecting chapter books now, but many students are still taking too long to locate books. Many students still select inappropriately.

Writing anecdotal notes during many response activities involving talk is an important form of documentation. For example, teachers can take anecdotal notes as children role-play or perform puppet plays, readers' theatre, or other drama activities. Teachers can also use anecdotal notes to capture students' participation in interviews or "You were there" enactments. These talk activities are an important way that students demonstrate their engagement and interpretation of literature, and because they do not usually include a written product, they are often not included in assessments.

Teachers will want to keep anecdotal records of students' individual conferences. They keep records of books students decide to share in the conferences, comments students make about their reading or responses to the books, and observations of students' reading strategies.

Anecdotal records can also provide information about the day-to-day activities of individual students and the class as a whole. They document teachers' careful observations of what they see and their fleeting reflections on how things are going. Most teachers see things during the day which surprise them or confirm that students are learning and using information from instruction. Keeping anecdotal notes allows teachers to capture these fleeting moments before they are forgotten in the busy world of the classroom.

Checklists

Checklists are prepared lists of behaviors or activities that are used to guide observation. Some checklists are designed to help teachers document how effectively students are using reading, writing, and talking processes. For example, Figure 9.3 presents one kind of checklist that can be used to document students' use of writing processes. The teacher or individual students can use this checklist to assess their use of the writing process for one particular writing project, or they can make entries

FIGURE 9.3   Writing Process Checklist

Name: _____ Date: _____

Title: _____

Prewriting

1. Student considers purpose, audience, and form for the writing.   _____
2. Student gathers and organizes ideas before writing.   _____

Drafting

3. Student writes one or more rough drafts.   _____
4. Student labels paper as a "draft" and double-spaces text.   _____
5. Student places a greater emphasis on content than on mechanics.   _____

Revising

6. Student meets in a writing group and shares his or her writing.   _____
7. Student makes changes to reflect suggestions made by classmates and the   _____
   teacher.

Editing

8. Student proofreads his or her writing to identify mechanical errors.   _____
9. Student meets with teacher to identify and correct errors.   _____
10. Student makes a final copy.   _____

Sharing

11. Student shares writing with an appropriate audience.   _____

for each writing project and then examine their growth in using the writing process over the school year.

Other checklists help students keep track of activities and projects that they complete during focus units and theme cycles. For example, in Chapter 8 we presented an assignment list that students could use to document activities and projects related to *Sarah, Plain and Tall* (MacLachlan, 1985).

Teachers might also develop a checklist to document students' participation in individual conferences. For example, Figure 9.4 presents a checklist that a fourth grade teacher uses to document the reading workshop and other independent reading conferences. This checklist includes information about the genre of literature that students are reading, their choices for selecting certain literature, and their discussion of books or poems they have read. Teachers would, of course, supplement this checklist with anecdotal notes and other comments.

Checklists can also be developed in collaboration with students for them to use as they evaluate their own learning. For example, Figure 9.5 presents a checklist that a group of fourth grade students developed to use as they participate in response groups. Students use this checklist to evaluate their reading of a core literature selection, preparation for their "book conversation," and participation in the conversation.

Teachers and students work collaboratively to develop many self-evaluation checklists. For example, students can use self-evaluation checklists as they write folktales, give oral reports, or write inquiry letters.

FIGURE 9.4   Conference Checklist

Student's Name: _____ Date: _____

Title: _____

Genre: Story _____   Poem _____   Informational Book _____

Reason Title was Selected: _____
_____

Response Activity: yes _____   no _____

What will be read next: _____

Discussion included:	Simple	Some Elaboration	Elaborated
Recall			
Global evaluations			
Inferences characters/events			
Evaluations characters/events			
Reference to personal experience			
Reference to other literature			
Reference to theme			
Reference to structure			
References to author's craft			
References to language of text			

Difficulties student reported: _____
_____
_____

Strategies student used: _____
_____
_____
_____

Comments:

Some checklists can be devised to document children's changing reading behaviors as they develop in reading ability. These checklists are especially appropriate in documenting young children's learning as they move from emergent to conventional beginning reading (Heald-Taylor, 1987). Figure 9.6 presents an emerging reading checklist that can be used with kindergarten and first grade children. To use the checklist, teachers observe children as they read with buddies, independently, or in an individual conference and then record their reading behaviors. Teachers observe children several times during the year so that they can illustrate how children's reading behaviors change over time as they move toward more conventional reading.

Checklists are an effective assessment tool; they provide a focus for teachers' observations of students and for students' reflection about their own learning and behavior. When they are used carefully and thoughtfully, checklists can provide useful

FIGURE 9.5   Response Group Self-Evaluation Checklist

Name: _____

3 = I always do this.   2 = I sometimes do this.   1 = I didn't do this.

_____ 1. I read the number of assigned pages.
_____ 2. I think as I write in my response journal.
_____ 3. I am prepared for the book conversation because I
- have read the book or poem
- bring my response journal
- mark pages in the book or places in the poem I want to talk about

_____ 4. I listen in the book conversation.
_____ 5. I take turns in the book conversation.
_____ 6. I tell about how I thought about events in my life during the conversation.
_____ 7. I tell about how I thought about other literature during the conversation.
_____ 8. I support my statements.

My goals for the next response group are:

---

and valuable information; however, they must be used cautiously. A good checklist pinpoints the exact behaviors that indicate reading and response processes. Teachers should tailor checklists to meet specific needs, and students should collaborate with teachers to develop checklists—especially those used for students' self-evaluations. We also recommend that teachers use anecdotal notes to supplement checklists in order to provide a context for the assessment and to elaborate on students' behaviors, use of strategies, or response activities.

Students' Work Samples and Records

Student work samples include examples of all the activities, projects, and events that occur in a classroom as part of a literature-based reading program. They include students' response activities, entries from their response journals and learning logs, and compositions. Other samples consist of audiotapes of book discussions, videotapes of readers' theatre or dramatic presentations, photographs of art projects, or other response activities. These samples provide a great deal of information about the kinds of activities students engage in, the processes students use as they complete these activities, and their achievements. Some possible samples of students' work that teachers collect are

- literature response activities, such as

webs	word sorts
charts	notable language posters
diagrams	written DRTA's

FIGURE 9.6   Emergent Reading Checklist

Child's Name: _____ Date: _____

Rereading

- Rereading not matched to pictures or text   _____
- Rereading related to pictures but not text   _____
- Rereading closely matched to text but not related to pages of text   _____
- Rereading closely matched to text and related to pages of text   _____
- Rereading exact match to text   _____

Directionality

- Sweeps finger from left to right across page (not tracking words or lines) while retelling   _____
- Moves finger from left to right across page (tracking each line) while retelling   _____
- Moves finger from left to right across page (tracking each word) while retelling   _____

Voice to Print Match

- Points to words and assigns segment of oral speech (matches words in text to oral syllables)   _____
- Points to each word in text while saying a word (matches text with oral rereading exactly)   _____
- Points to words in text while rereading (tracks print) and can find specific words in text by tracking   _____
- Identifies words in text   _____
- Identifies words out of text   _____

Cue Systems

- Uses memory to cue reading   _____
- Uses pictures and meaning to cue reading   _____
- Uses letter-sound relationships (phonics) to cue reading   _____
- Integrates memory, tracking, known words, and phonics to cue reading   _____

Independent Reading

- Familiar predictable books   _____
- Unfamiliar predictable books   _____
- Familiar books (not predictable)   _____
- Unfamiliar books   _____

simulated letters,   poems
   journals, newspapers   quilts
comparison grids   Venn diagrams
clusters   literary maps
stories   reports
readers' theatre scripts   letters to authors and others
drawings, paintings   constructions
story boxes   sociograms
timelines   retellings

- entries from learning logs and response journals
- rough drafts and published compositions
- audiotapes of students' oral reading, read-arounds, grand conversations and retellings
- videotapes of oral reports, puppet shows, and theatrical productions

Many of students' response activities and projects are done in groups, and these group projects may be difficult if not impossible to place in a portfolio. For instance, students may work together to create a mural, quilt, or model. Teachers can take several photos of these projects and place one print in each student's portfolio.

Teachers cannot keep all of the response activities, response journals, learning logs, or drafts and published compositions that students produce during a school year. Students will want to share many of these products with their parents, and parents will expect that students will bring home many projects that reflect their classroom activities. In the case study at the beginning of this chapter, Mrs. Reeves has her students keep most of their response activities for a focus unit or theme cycle in a special folder. At the end of the unit or cycle, she and her students select work samples to put in their portfolios and the other activities are sent home.

Students can also keep important records that document their literacy learning. They might keep records of books and poems that they have read, response activities they have completed, and times they have conferenced with the teacher. In the case study, Mrs. Reeves' students keep lists of goals they set for their reading and lists of books and poems they found easy and difficult to read. As her students chose particular work samples to include in their portfolios, they wrote explanations for their choices. These explanations also become an important source of information that teachers can use to document language arts development.

Running Records

Running records are records that teachers make of students' oral reading and are intended to capture all reading behaviors including substitutions, omissions, insertions, reversals, repetitions, and self corrections (Clay, 1985). An analysis of running records illustrates the kinds of reading strategies and cues that students use as they read. That is, oral reading provides a window into students' reading processes that teachers can use to make decisions about instruction. For example, some students rely almost exclusively on graphophonic cues or phonics as they read and pay relatively little attention to meaning. Other students overrely on context, and their oral reading shows little concern for attention to print. Knowing this information provides teachers with important directions for instruction.

Teachers do not need special forms or materials to collect a running record; however, they do need to become familiar with the system of marking miscues or errors. Many teachers practice recording several students' reading before they feel comfortable that they are capturing all of a student's reading behaviors. Figure 9.7 presents a text, a key to the marking system used to generate this record, and a running record of a student's reading of the text. Teachers write the running record on a lined sheet of paper so that each line of their record will correspond to each line of the text that students read.

FIGURE 9.7 Running Record

TEXT:

The Three Billy Goats

Once upon a time there were three billy goats who lived in a meadow by a river. One billy goat was very large, one billy goat was middle-sized, and one billy goat was very small. The three billy goats ate all the grass in their meadow and decided to cross the river to a new meadow where the grass was thick and green. To cross the river the three billy goats had to go over a bridge. And under the bridge there lived a very ugly and very mean troll. The troll had eyes as big as saucers and a nose as long as a sausage. He liked to eat billy goats most of all.

EXAMPLES:

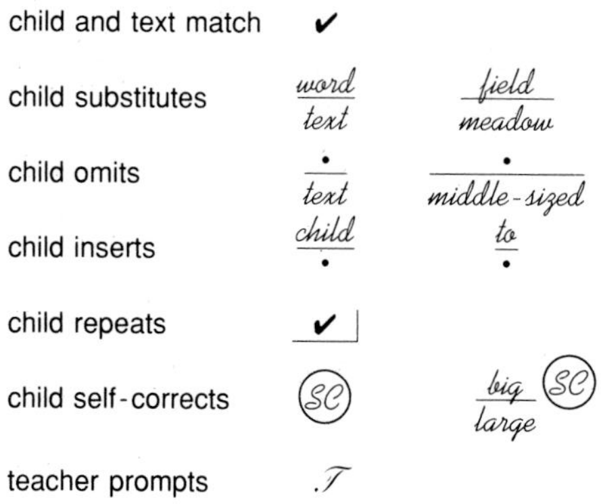

child and text match   ✔

child substitutes   *word / text*   *field / meadow*

child omits   *·̄ / text*   *·̄ / middle-sized*

child inserts   *child / ·*   *to / ·*

child repeats   ✔ |

child self-corrects   (SC)   *big / large* (SC)

teacher prompts   .T

RUNNING RECORD:

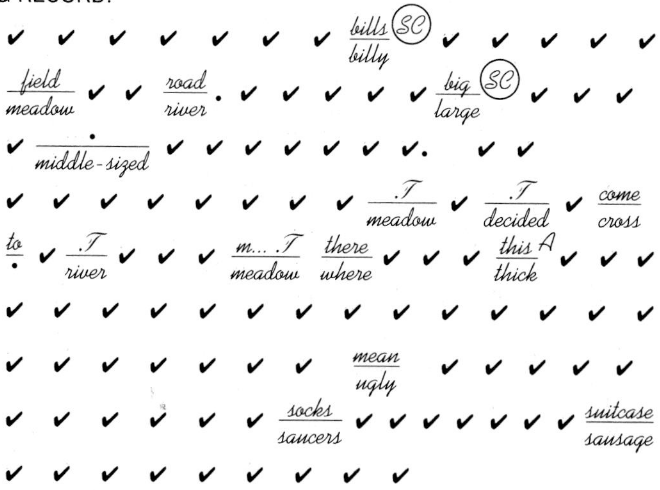

Running records are made on reading material that students have previously read in guided reading or independently. Running records are usually taken on three texts: one used in guided reading, one that is a little easier than the guided reading text, and one that is a little more difficult than the guided reading text. Reading easy, instructional, and difficult texts allows teachers to appreciate students' strengths and weaknesses. Texts should be at least 100 words in length unless students are reading from shorter dictated stories or literature with few words. If students are reading short books, then they should read three complete texts, and teachers do not need to count out 100 words.

Running records can be used with all levels of readers. They can be used with young children who are not yet reading conventionally but who enjoy reading memorized predictable stories or stories they dictated. They are also useful in kindergarten and first grade and help document the print strategies that young children are learning through shared reading experiences.

ANALYZING STUDENTS' LITERACY LEARNING

The third step in assessment is analyzing students' learning. It is not enough that teachers make anecdotal notes, mark checklists, collect students' work samples, and take running records of students' oral reading. Teachers must analyze the assessment materials they have compiled to find indications of students' current knowledge, development, and instructional needs.

Analyzing Anecdotal Notes

Analysis of anecdotal notes consists of explaining the significance of a behavior or event that was observed. To analyze anecdotal records, teachers must separate what they see in observations from their explanations and evaluations. Suppose a teacher observed two boys, Jake and Darek, reading together in the library center of a first grade classroom. They select *Green Eggs and Ham* (Seuss, 1960), and Jake begins reading. Darek stops Jake and says, "That's not *would*; it's *could*. See the *c*." The teacher might make an anecdotal note of this incident as shown in Figure 9.8, and the note is a description of just what was seen.

The analysis of this incident depends on what the teacher knows about these students' previous behaviors. The teacher might know, for example, that Darek, who made the comment about the word *could* beginning with the letter *c*, has not previously demonstrated using phonics to cue his own reading. Instead, he has relied only on his memory and has never monitored the print to see if what he says matches the print. Knowing this, a teacher can analyze this incident—it documents that Darek is beginning to use memory and attention to print, namely initial letters in words, to monitor and cue reading. This analysis is also presented in Figure 9.8. This figure presents a form with space for the observations and for teachers' comments or analysis (Baskwill & Whitman, 1988).

Sometimes single incidents or events recorded in anecdotal notes do not warrant analysis, but over time, teachers may begin to see patterns of behaviors. For

FIGURE 9.8   Anecdotal Note and Analysis Form

| Name _____ |
Date	Note	Analysis
10/14	Jake and Darek in the library center. Jake reading *Green Eggs and Ham.* Darek says thats not would. It's could. See the C.	Darek is using letters to cue readings of memorized story for the first time.

example, anecdotal notes may show that Jake always reads with a stronger reader and lets these readers correct words for him as he did when Darek corrected his reading of the word *would*. Over time the teacher may notice that Jake never reads alone or with a weaker reader and never self-corrects his own reading. To discover patterns in students' behaviors, teachers might read over their observation notebooks monthly or even weekly (Baskwill & Whitman, 1988).

Rereading anecdotal notes allows teachers to reflect carefully on the needs and growth of each student and the class as a whole. For example, after reading over her anecdotal notes about her students' writing (see Figure 9.2), one teacher decided that the students could benefit from several minilessons on selecting books. She introduced the Goldilocks strategy (see Chapter 7) and the five-finger method of selecting books. She also gave many book talks on easy-to-read chapter books that were appropriate for many of the readers in her class.

9/20   Gave book talks on several Patricia Reilly Giff books. Several children selected these books and immediately began reading. Nearly everyone found a book within 2 minutes today. Many children now use the five-finger method effectively.

This note documents that students were beginning to use information from her minilessons to select books for independent reading.

Analyzing Checklists

Information provided on checklists can also be analyzed for patterns of behavior and indications of development or instructional needs. One way that teachers can analyze checklists is by examining how children's behaviors and attitudes change over time. That is, checklists that are completed several times during a year can be used to demonstrate patterns in students' learning. Teachers can examine checklists on students' emergent reading behavior, individual conferences, or use of writing processes collected over time for changes indicating growth or needed instruction. Examining self-evaluation checklists that students complete several times during the year can also provide information about students' growth as independent learners.

FIGURE 9.9   Categories of Responses to Literature

Response	Examples from *Rosie's Walk* (Hutchins, 1968)
Recall of text events	"The hen was walking past and the fox was walking."
Global evaluations	"This story is awesome." "I like the whole thing." "It was funny."
Inferences about character or events	"She [Rosie] didn't see the rake hit him." "He [fox] wanted to catch her [Rosie], but it didn't work."
Evaluation of character or events	"He [fox] was really stupid." "It's not really funny to get a bee sting."
Reference to personal experience	"Once I got stung by bees and it wasn't funny."
Reference to other literature	"Once I saw a cartoon like 'Tom and Jerry' and the cat always gets his nose right off." "This is like the Roadrunner."
Inferences based on personal experience or other literature	"Rosie is leading the fox around and the fox is always getting hurt, like the roadrunner is always getting hurt so Rosie is setting a trap for the fox."
Personal reactions	"I would like it if I fell in the haystack." "He said, 'Alright what's this hay keeping me up? OOOOPs OWWWWW."
Thematic statements	"If you're mean, that's what you get for being bad."
Comments about structure	"In the end of the story Rosie went back to where she started."
Comments about craft	"Those were short sentences."
Comments about language or illustrations	"Her [Rosie's] eyes were pointing straight ahead so she didn't see the fox."

Sometimes completing a checklist requires analysis. For example, an important checklist might be developed to analyze students' participation in grand conversations or other kinds of book discussions. However, to use a grand conversation checklist, teachers must be able to analyze the kinds of responses that students share in grand conversations. Students make global evaluations of stories, recall events, make inferences and evaluations of characters and events, make thematic statements, recall personal experiences related to the text, recall characters and events from other related literature, and comment on the author's craft and language (Five, 1988; Galda, 1983). Figure 9.9 presents a list of the categories of responses that students might make during grand conversations or other book discussions and sample statements taken from a first grade grand conversation about *Rosie's Walk* (Hutchins, 1968).

Figure 9.10 shows a grand conversation checklist that helps teachers analyze the product—what the students say about the book or poem they are discussing, and the process—the processes students use as they participate in the group interaction during the discussion. This checklist reflects the kinds of responses that students

FIGURE 9.10 Grand Conversation Checklist

Student's Name: _____

Name of the Book or Poem: _____

Other members of the Group:

PRODUCT: What the Student Said   **Comments:**

Recalled story events and characters

Made global evaluations of story

Made thematic statements

Evaluated a character

Inferred a character's feelings, thought, motivations, traits

Inferred about events

Referred to other literature

Referred to personal experience

Shared personal reactions

Made thematic statements

Commented about structure of text

Commented about author or illustrator

Commented on the author's craft

Commented on the illustrations

Commented on language of text

PROCESS: How the Student Participated   **Comments:**

Asked questions

Made hypotheses

Used examples to support statements

Gave positive feedback to others

Acknowledged comments of others

Called for clarification, support

Challenged thinking of others

Spoke one at a time

make in a grand conversation (and in their response journals) that were presented in Figure 9.9 and lists the processes, such as making hypotheses and talking one at a time, that students use as they talk about literature.

In the case study at the beginning of this chapter, Mrs. Reeves used such a checklist to document and analyze her students' interpretations of and responses to literature in grand conversations. She tape-recorded grand conversations four times a year and completed a grand conversation checklist for each of her students. She found it necessary to tape-record the conversations because she became too absorbed in the children's talk during the conversations and was distracted as she tried to complete the checklists. She found that her records of the conversations are much more detailed if she listens to a tape recording as soon as possible after the conversation and completes a checklist for each student using the taped conversation.

Figure 9.11 presents a transcription of first grade grand conversation about *Hey, Al* (Yorinks, 1986), and Figure 9.12 presents a grand conversation checklist for Annie, one of the first graders who participated in the *Hey, Al* conversation. This checklist shows that Annie recalled story events, responded to symbols, made inferences about characters, referred to the illustrations to support her inferences, asked questions, and made evaluative comments.

Analyzing Students' Work Samples and Records

Entries from response journals, compositions such as stories, poems, or informational texts that students write in response to reading, and other response activities such as plot diagrams, character clusters, and word webs provide teachers with a great deal of information about students' literacy development, their strengths, and instructional needs. As they analyze these samples, teachers describe what students know about reading and writing as reflected in their current work samples and search through the samples looking for patterns of change. In addition, teachers can help students analyze their own work as a part of self-evaluation of their learning. Teachers can gain valuable insights into students' growing awareness of reading processes, literature, and responses to literature by looking at students' self-evaluations.

Analyzing Response Journals.   Students' entries in response journals provide indications of the processes they are using to read and respond to literature and their current understandings and interpretations of what they read (Barone, 1990; Dekker, 1991). Teachers can use the categories of responses presented in Figure 9.9 for analyzing the entries in students' response journals. Teachers examine entries in students' response journals for recall of story events and characters, global evaluations, thematic statements, evaluations of a character, inferences about a character's feelings, thoughts, motivations, or traits, references to personal experience or other literature, or comments about the author, illustrator, or the author's craft, illustrations, or language of the text.

For younger students who respond to a whole book or poem with one entry, teachers gather several response journal entries completed around the same time for analysis. For older students who respond after reading every chapter or two in a chapter book, teachers collect all the responses to the book for analysis. To analyze a collection of students' response journal entries, teachers begin by reading entries and making notes about the kinds of responses that students are making.

Figure 9.13 presents three entries from a first grader's response journal. These entries were made after her teacher read *Rosie's Walk* (Hutchins, 1968), *Hey, Al* (Yorinks, 1986), and *The Pain and the Great One* (Blume, 1974). The first entry shows that Shanna responds to books by recalling text events. The second entry shows that she not only recalls text events, but also reacts personally—she invented dialogue for Al ("I'm going. So long.") even though she does not use the conventions of commas and quotation marks. The third entry demonstrates that Shanna evaluates characters based on character traits and she infers based on criteria she uses to make judgments in her own life—she believes that boys are a pain because they are

FIGURE 9.11   First Graders' Grand Conversation about *Hey, Al* (Yorinks, 1986)

TEACHER (T): What did you think of the story?

CHRIS: I like the part when he turns into a bird. The dog and Eddy.

RYAN: Hey! Eddy's the dog. I like the part when he's laying down in the water, and the birds bring him food and stuff and he's wearing the old hat that he used to have and I like the dog too.

ANNIE: I liked the part when they were going back to their own house and Eddy fell into the ocean.

T: Why did you like that part?

ANNIE: Because it was gonna be okay.

T: Did you know that for sure?

JOHN: No, no.

CHRIS: Yea! because if they were on earth they wouldn't be birds

ANNIE: I like the part when they got home and they painted everything yellow so everything would be okay. Al's dog came back so Al wouldn't be afraid that he didn't have a dog anymore.

ALICE: I liked the part when he was a janitor but then he said, there's no-like when he was gonna go up there, and he was gonna change his mind, but he didn't.

RYAN: I like the part when the bird comes to say, "He Al," and he jumps when he's shaving his face and the bird came and say, "Al, A" and he jumped and said, "Who's that?" and the razor came out of his hand.

JOHN: Yea, it was funny.

ALICE: I liked those birds with all those big, big legs.

JOHN: I liked the part when he was waiting in the bathroom because the bird came to get him. He just grabbed him and they just went out.

ANNIE: I like the part when they were going up there and Al lost his luggage. Hey! Look at that! Look at at that hand! (Annie points to part of illustration where one of the birds has a hand that looks human).

T: Oh, where?

ANNIE: He's turning back.

T: Look what Annie's found.

stupid. We assume that Shanna is evaluating the character of The Pain in the story; however, she could be reacting even more personally. That is, she may be making a personal statement about boys in general. These three entries show that Shanna responds personally to literature by assuming the roles of characters and by inferring and judging characters (or people, in general). She also comprehends literature as shown by her accurate recall of an exciting event from a story.

Figure 9.14 presents a fourth grader's response to *The Garden of Abdul Gasazi* (Van Allsburg, 1979). This entry shows that Lori makes inferences about story events: "I do think that he did turn Fritz into a duck. But the spell only lasted a short time and Fritz ran home with the hat." She also makes very insightful inferences about characters: "I think that the magician was really Miss Hester." She connects this story to another one she has read and makes explicit the reason for the connection: "I think this story is a lot like *The Lion the Witch and the Wardrobe.* Because

JOHN: He was a person.

ANNIE: All of them were persons.

RYAN: They were all persons?

ANNIE: People! All of these were people! Look at his hands.

JOHN: I know that's what I said.

CHRIS: If they all stay there, they'll all be birds.

ANNIE: Oh, look, how can he be changed back?

ALICE: I could tell he was an old man because look at his skin.

ANNIE: I think all the animals were humans before they came out there because one of these animals was the real one and they turn real people into

JOHN: animals.

RYAN: Yeah, birds and they have to go back but they don't know how to get back because some of them don't have wings.

ERIC: I like the bird there with the hand in the cage with the funny mouth.

JOHN: I liked the part when he fell in that place up in the air.

ANNIE: in the water.

JOHN: No when he fell in the place in the sky. When the bird was dropping him down into the place.

T: Well, What do you think Al found out at the island?

ANNIE: I think he would be better as a janitor instead of up there.

RYAN: If he stayed up there, he would really be a bird and we don't know if he could change back again and his whole body would be a bird.

JOHN: He loves his house.

T: How do you know?

JOHN: Because he was happy to be back and the dog came back and they painted it.

ANNIE: They painted it yellow like the place. He was happy at the end.

CHRIS: Yea, and he got a new shirt like it wasn't the shirt from, like he was a janitor again, but he's got a nicer shirt and he looks happy.

ALICE: Eddy is smiling. Yea. The story has a happy ending.

the Lion was the Professor in the Lion the Witch and the wardrobe." Later she shared with the class that Hester was like the magician just as Aslan and the professor had the same voice in *The Lion the Witch and the Wardrobe.* She noted that Hester looked like the Magician and that other stories had characters in both real worlds and fantasy worlds such as in *The Wizard of Oz.* Clearly Lori's entry shows a sophisticated level of response for a fourth grader. She supported her inferences and referred to other literature to more deeply understand the story she was reading.

Figure 9.15 presents an entry from a sixth grader's response journal. Vicki wrote this response after reading *Faithful Elephants* (Tsuchiya, 1988), a true story of the elephants in the Tokyo zoo who refused to die despite their caregivers' attempts to euthanize them during World War II, and the entry shows that she responds to theme: ". . . book about war and elephants and what happens to animals when a war begins . . . Everybody has to STOP and think about war. . . . And enough people unit-

FIGURE 9.12 Analysis of Annie's Participation in a Grand Conversation

Student's Name: _Annie_

Name of the Book or Poem: _Hey, Al_

Other members of the Group: _Chris, Ryan, John, Alice_

Product: What the student said   **Comments:**

✔ Recalled story events and characters

  Made global evaluations of story

✔ Made thematic statements —————————— _better as a janitor_

  Evaluated a character

✔ Inferred a characters' feelings, ———————— _Al's not afraid_
    thoughts, motivations, traits   _anymore_

✔ Inferred about events —————————— _it was gonna be okay_
                                            when they got back

  Made reference to other literature

  Made reference to personal experience

  Shared personal reactions

  Made thematic statements

  Commented about structure of text

  Commented about author or illustrator

✔ Commented about the author's craft — _could be noting symbol_
                                          of yellow color/happy

✔ Commented about the illustrations ———— _notice foreshadowing_
  Commented about language of text   _of hand in picture_

Process: How the student participated   **Comments:**

✔ Asked questions ———————————— _thought all birds_

✔ Made hypotheses ———————————— _were people before_

  Gave positive feedback to others

  Acknowledged comments of others

  Called for clarification, support

  Challenged thinking of others

  Spoke one at a time

ing can help stop WARS." She also describes her lived-through experience of reading the book: "This book inspired me and made me cry. It made me think about the wars in the Past, Present, and Future." She makes judgments about the genre of the book: "This Boo Hoo Book." She even evaluates its quality ("is great"). Vicki's response entry also demonstrates her awareness of audience. She addresses comments directly to the reader: "So think about what I said and come up with some ideas about

FIGURE 9.13 Three Entries from Shanna's Response Journal

FIGURE 9.14   Entry from Lori's Response Journal

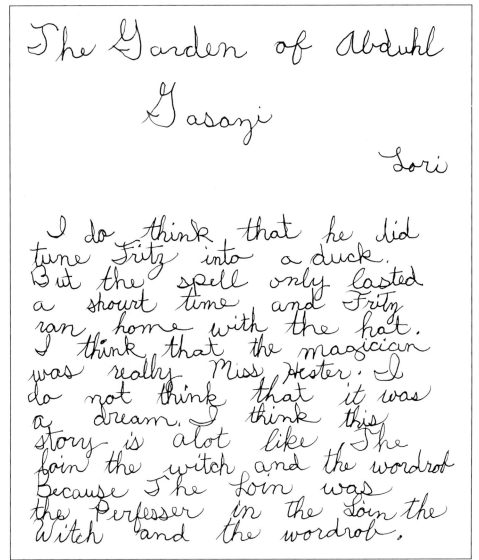

ways to begin to stop the wars." She is writing persuasively, with the intent both to convince her reader to read the book and to think about stopping war—a purpose that reflects the author's purpose in writing the book.

Teachers can analyze students' response journal entries several times over the year and examine how their responses grow and develop over time. Some teachers have found that entries in response journals become more reflective as teachers model different kinds of responses during minilessons (Dekker, 1991). Teachers can analyze students' responses before and after such minilessons to evaluate the effectiveness of their instruction.

FIGURE 9.15   Entry from Vicki's Response Journal

Faithful Elephants Retold By, Yukio Tsuchiya

Good books don't come around much, but when they do you know right away. This Boo Hoo Book is great and to check it out visit the School Library. Faithful Elephants, Retold by Yukio Tsuchiya, is an inspiring book about war and elephants and what happens to animals when a war begins. This book inspired me and made me cry, It made me think about the wars in the Past, Present, and Future. Everybody has to STOP and think about war. It's not pretty. And enough people uniting can help stop WARS. So think about what I said and come up with some ideas about ways to begin to stop the wars.

John The Ele-Phants Tomb

RIP

eNE
s A
t c
 E

FIGURE 9.16   Kristen's Composition: The Sore OLD Homs. (Transcription: *The Scary Old House,* "Come in the house," said Ghostie. "I don't like you. You are not nice.")

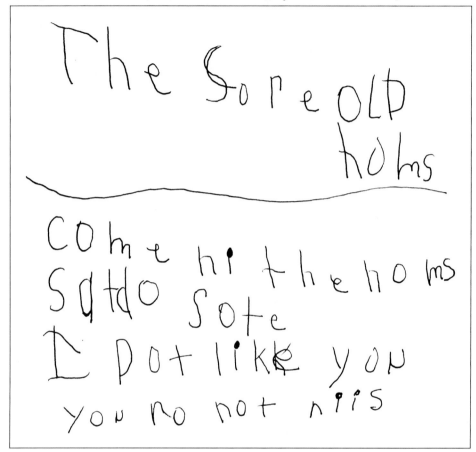

Analyzing Compositions.   Compositions that students write in response to books and poems they have read can also reveal a great deal about students' understandings about literature. Compositions reveal whether students notice organizational structures such as the structures found in circle stories or cumulative tales. Compositions also reveal students' awareness of the author's craft such as use of repetition, figurative language, symbols, or images. Finally, compositions reveal students' awareness of the written language system and how it works.

Figure 9.16 presents a first grader's composition. Kristen wrote this composition and illustrated it at the writing center during response activity time. Earlier in the week she had read *In a Scary Old House* (Ziefert & Smith, 1989) several times both at school and at home. This story has repetitive language and predictable language structures. The teacher observed that Kristen knew many of the words from the story and tracked print as she read. She also observed that Kristen relied on her memory of the story and the illustrations to read some of the story. After completing her composition, Kristen asked to share her composition and illustration with the class; she explained many of the parts of her illustration. As she pointed to various objects in her illustration, she said, "These are the scary old bats, and these are the scary old birds. This is a crooked shutter, and this is a crooked shutter, and this is a crooked shutter."

Later Kristen's teacher analyzed Kristen's composition, illustration, and shared talk. The teacher noted that while the text of Kristen's composition did not reflect the repetitive patterns found in the text of *In a Scary Old House,* Kristen's talk about her illustration revealed that she was sensitive to its repetitive language. Her composition shows that she notices titles—Kristen capitalized three of the four words in her title and separated it from the rest of the story with a line. The composition also reveals that Kristen notices the form of dialogue although she does not yet use conventions such as commas or quotation marks to indicate dialogue. The teacher noted that not only is Kristen demonstrating sensitivity to author's craft and literary structures, but she is also sensitive to print and how written language works. Her composition demonstrates that she knows

- print is written from left to right in lines
- some capital letters and most lower case letters (with some reversals such as the letter *u*)
- some conventional spellings (*the, old, come, I, like, you,* and *not*)
- some spellings that are influenced by attention to visual appearance in print rather than to sounds (*ni* for *in, satd* for *said,* and *dot* for *don't.* Her use of *homs* for *house* reflects an awareness of the spelling of *home.*)
- some spellings that indicate attention to most sounds within a word (*Sore* for *scary, o sote* for *ghostie, niis* for *nice,* and *homs* for *house*—notice the relation of *homs* to the spelling for *home,* a similar meaning word, with the ending *s* related to the ending sound in *house*)
- a spelling that indicates awareness that all words must have a vowel (*ro* for *are*)
- a spelling that indicates awareness that long vowel sounds must be spelled differently than just a single letter (*niis* for *nice*)

When teachers analyze students' compositions, the focus is on determining what students' compositions, illustrations, and talk reveal about what they know about literature and written language. Teachers notice what students know and identify a few instructional needs. Kristen's teacher, for example, noted that she might benefit from being encouraged to write stories using repetitive patterns, and she might be shown a strategy of checking her spellings during the editing process to see if they both sound and look right. She might also be asked to apply this strategy to her reading—using two kinds of cue systems, visual and sounding out, when she comes to an unknown word.

Analyzing Other Responses. Character clusters, plot diagrams, literary maps, Venn diagrams, comparison grids, notable language samples, and other response to literature activities provide a great deal of information about students' literacy learning if teachers know how to analyze them. For example, teachers might analyze students'

FIGURE 9.17 Two Clusters for *A Chair for My Mother* (Williams, 1982)

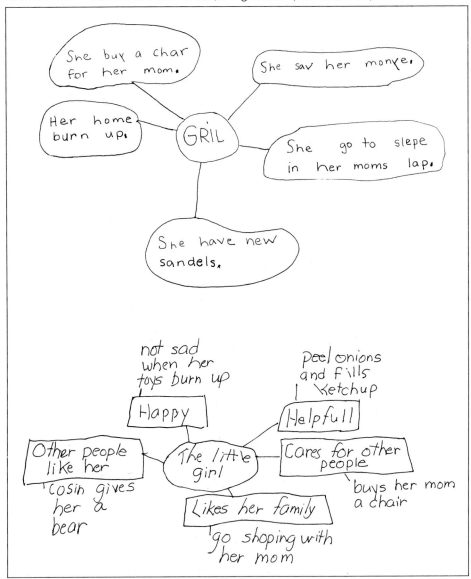

character clusters for accuracy, insightfulness, and detail (Norton, 1992). Students must be familiar with the strategy of clustering and construct clusters independently before these responses can be used effectively in assessment. Figure 9.17 presents two students' clusters about the little girl in *A Chair for My Mother* (Williams, 1982). In this realistic fiction picture book, the little girl helps her family save money to re-place the furniture and other belongings they lost when their apartment was destroyed by fire. The first cluster shows that the student was accurately recalling character descriptions, but made few inferences and did not support inferences with details from the text. The second cluster shows that the student was not only accurate, but also made insightful inferences that are backed by references to the text.

Analyzing plot diagrams is another way teachers can assess students' understanding of and responses to literature. After students have constructed several plot diagrams with the teachers' guidance and collaboratively in groups, they can individually develop a diagram that teachers can use in assessment. Teachers can examine the diagrams for sequence of events, understanding of plot and other elements of story structure, and insight into the characters' motivations. Other response activities such as Venn diagrams, comparison grids, and story charts can be analyzed in a similar manner.

Word clusters are also effective tools for gathering information about students' vocabulary knowledge and growth. Teachers might construct a cluster with several words from a story or an informational book that the students will soon read. Students would write meanings, synonyms, or related ideas on the cluster before reading and then add newly learned information to the cluster with a different color pen after reading. Teachers can analyze the changes in the clusters that students made after reading to see how students grow in their awareness of word meanings.

Helping Students Analyze Their Work

An important way that students grow as independent and lifelong learners is by learning how to evaluate their own learning. Teachers can learn about students' growing ability to reflect on themselves as learners by analyzing their self-evaluations. One component of self-evaluation is learning how to select work samples that demonstrate one's own best work, effort, and growth. Helping students set standards for selecting work to include in portfolios is an important part of self-assessment. Another component of self-selection is being able to describe why certain works were selected and what they reveal. Teachers can analyze both the work samples that students choose and their reasons for their selections.

Analyzing Students' Selection of Work Samples.   Students have a number of decisions to make as they select work to be placed in portfolios or to be used in teachers' evaluations. They must decide whether to include everything they have completed or to select particular samples and whether to include only finished work or to include work-in-progress and drafts (Tierney, Carter, & Desai, 1991). Teachers must help students reflect on their choices and develop criteria for selection. Some criteria to use in selecting work samples are

- stories, poems, or informational texts that are favorites
- reports that they think are interesting
- works that show a new development (called *pivotal pieces*)
- works that show understanding of literary structures or the author's craft
- letters or messages

- favorite journal entries
- papers that represent best work
- papers that represent a difficult activity (adapted from Tierney, Carter, & Desai, 1991, pp. 112–113)

Teachers analyze whether students are reflective and use multiple criteria or are less reflective and use only a few criteria for selecting their samples; whether their work samples represent a wide range of genre and activities or reflect a preference for a few, routine genre or activities; and whether their work samples include pivotal pieces (Tierney, Carter, & Desai, 1991). They might notice whether students' assessments of their best work or hardest activities fit with their own assessments.

Analyzing Students' Self-Evaluations of Work Samples.   Evaluation is a natural part of the selection process, and students must evaluate their work samples to make decisions about which samples to select. However, most teachers want students to more consciously reflect on their work, and so they have students write comments and evaluations to accompany each work sample selected for a portfolio or to be used in a teacher's evaluation. Students can write their comments on notecards or sticky-backed notes and attach them to the work sample (Tierney, Carter, & Desai, 1991). At the end of a theme, unit, grading period, or the school year, students can write a short overview and analysis of the whole group of samples they have selected.

To help students evaluate their own work, teachers may present a series of questions for students to discuss in small groups such as

- Why was this sample selected?
- What is good about this sample?
- What do you like about this sample?
- What is important to you about this sample?
- How is this sample the same or different from your other work?
- What does this sample show about your strengths?
- What does this sample show that you have learned? (adapted from Tierney, Carter, & Desai, 1991, p. 115)

As students talk together to explain their choices of individual work samples, they get feedback from their classmates. They also make explicit the criteria they used in their selection process. Teachers can analyze students' self-evaluations for whether they represent global comments or focus on a variety of specific criteria.

Teachers should also guide students in an evaluation of their work samples over time. In the case study at the beginning of this chapter, Mrs. Reeves helped her students evaluate the contents of their portfolios in January and June so they could see for themselves how they are developing as readers and writers. She used small-group lessons to help students find ways in which they had grown and identify strategies and conventions they had learned.

Teachers should also analyze students' self-evaluative comments over time. Students' self-evaluations can be analyzed to see whether they include a greater number of comments and comments that focus on more aspects of their work, expected conventions, that compare works, and reveal a greater awareness of overall strengths (Tierney, Carter, & Desai, 1991). In general, teachers can expect students' self-evaluations to become more sophisticated as they learn to use specific and insightful assessment criteria.

Analyzing Running Records

An analysis of a running record can indicate a student's reading level, the strategies and cues students use to read, and their ability to monitor their reading. To analyze a running record teachers first determine the reader's accuracy percentage, or the percentage of words read correctly. To calculate the accuracy percentage, teachers count the number of errors a student made in reading a passage. All substitutions, omissions, insertions, repetitions, and reversals are errors except for those that students self-correct; self-corrected miscues are not counted as errors. Next, teachers subtract the number of errors students made while reading a passage from the total number of words in that passage and divide this number by the total number of words in the passage. The next step is to use the accuracy percentage to determine the difficulty level of the passage. According to Clay (1985, p. 17) the accuracy rates for easy, instructional, and difficult passages are

Easy text	95–100%
Instructional text	90–94%
Difficult text	less than 90%

Teachers must have some knowledge of the level of reading material that students read from in order to plan to have a variety of reading materials available to meet every student's needs. Mrs. Reeves in the case study at the beginning of this chapter had her students read from a collection of stories and informational books on different reading levels. After analyzing her students' running records, she had a rough idea of the levels of texts that were easy, instructional, and difficult for each of her students. She did not use that information to group her students for instruction; rather, she used the information to guide her selection of reading materials in the classroom. She wanted to make sure that each student could select from texts that were at both easy and instructional levels. Information about the kinds and levels of texts that are easy, instructional, and difficult for each student in a class helps teachers plan for the kinds of reading materials that they will need to meet the needs of their students.

The third step in analyzing a running record is to analyze students' oral reading behavior with a *miscue analysis* (Goodman & Burke, 1972). A miscue analysis provides information about the semantic, syntactic, and graphophonic cueing systems (see Chapter 5) that students use while reading. Clay (1985) recommended that teachers examine every error made by students and ask, "What made the student say that?" (p. 21). Students might be relying on meaning (semantics), the structure of sentences (syntax), or print (graphophonics). If the miscue, or error, was made by paying too much attention to semantics, it would not change the meaning of the

FIGURE 9.18   Miscue Analysis Chart

Child/Text	Does not change meaning	Does not change syntax	Looks like word beginning	mid-dle	end	Self-corrects	Comments
bills/billy		✔	✔	✔		✔	
field/meadow	✔	✔					
road/river		✔	✔				*makes sense*
big/large	✔	✔				✔	
T/meadow							
T/decided							
this/thick			✔	✔		*A*	
mean/ugly							
socks/saucers		✔	✔				*makes sense*
suitcase/sausage		✔	✔				*makes sense*
Totals	*2/10*	*6/10*	*5/10*	*2/10*	*0/10*	*2/10*	

sentence; if the error was made by paying too much attention to syntax, it would not change the structure of the sentence; or if the error was made by paying too much attention to graphophonics, it may look like or have sound patterns similar to the word in the text. Errors may be caused by relying on more than one cue system such as attending to both meaning and print. Teachers can usually figure out the cause of the difficulty by thinking about the child's error and the correct word.

Students' self-corrections provide an important source of information about how students monitor their reading, and examining self-corrections is an important part of miscue analysis. All readers make self-corrections, but good readers are more likely to make corrections when the meaning is disturbed. An analysis of readers' self-corrections indicates if readers are monitoring print as they read word-by-word or if they are monitoring the meaning of what they read.

Some teachers construct a miscue analysis chart for each student's running record. Figure 9.18 presents a miscue analysis chart for Max's running record that appeared in Figure 9.7. This chart shows that Max relies heavily on syntax because a few of his miscues changed the structure of the sentence. Even though many miscues changed the meaning of the sentences, they still made sense. Max also relied on graphophonics—particularly initial consonants, and self-corrected two errors (20%). One of the self-corrections occurred when the miscue did not make sense (*bills* for *billy*), and Max appealed to the teacher "That doesn't make sense") when another miscue did not make sense (*this* for *thick*). He frequently used more than one cueing system (both syntax and graphophonics in 4 of the 10 miscues).

Analyzing running records provides teachers with information for instruction. For example, Max can read nearly all of the high frequency words (e.g., *there, three, were,* and *to*) but had difficulty with content words (*meadow, river, ugly*) and multisyllabic words (*saucers, sausage, middle-sized*). He uses graphophonics in conjunction with syntax, but relies primarily on beginning consonants. Max would benefit from rereading stories and examining unknown words more thoroughly—at least checking the endings of words. He also needs more difficult reading material with more content and multisyllabic words.

Analyzing students' running records and miscue analyses collected at various times over a year provides an important source of information about reading development. Teachers should expect that students will make greater strides in monitoring their meaning (as indicated by the number and kinds of self-corrections) and read a greater variety of texts and more difficult texts as the year progresses.

EVALUATING STUDENTS' LITERACY LEARNING

Evaluating students' work and grading for the purpose of reporting to parents and administrators are difficult responsibilities for all teachers but especially for teachers using literature-based reading programs. Traditional practices such as teaching reading in ability groups and teaching skills, providing practice, and then testing how well students learned the skills made evaluating and assigning grades relatively simple. In contrast, literature-based reading programs help students think critically and creatively and to evaluate their own learning as they move toward conventional and expected standards of reading and language use (Linek, 1991). Evaluating students' movement toward conventional and expected standards and assigning grades in literature-based reading programs is considerably more difficult. Nonetheless, all teachers have the professional responsibility of reporting students' progress to parents and administrators. Some teachers may be able to report this progress through parent conferences and reports; however, most teachers are expected to report grades for students' achievement periodically throughout the year.

Standards of Evaluation

The first step in evaluating learning is to determine the standards by which students will be evaluated. There are four methods of setting standards for evaluating progress toward conventional and expected levels of language arts competence: (a) compare each student's growth to past achievement, (b) compare each student's achievements to established criteria of performance, (c) compare each student's achievements to the achievements of the other students in a class and (d) compare each student's achievements to the achievement of a large sample of students such as is done with norm-referenced testing (Linek, 1991). We recommend that teachers use the first two methods for setting standards and evaluating students' learning.

In the first case, in which a student's present performance is compared to that student's past performance, the teacher and student set individual goals for achievement and activities together and then evaluate how well these goals are met (Atwell, 1987). Each student's goals for achievement may differ, but evaluation is based on how well each student approaches his or her own goals. Some teachers who use this method of evaluation help students develop contracts that specify the requirements for grades.

In the second case, students' performance is compared to an established criteria. Teachers carefully set criteria for class performance and then examine how well each student has achieved those criteria. Criteria are established as teachers carefully consider their goals for instruction, the needs of students, and expected levels of performance for their specific group of students. Many teachers share these criteria with students as a part of instruction, help students select samples of their best work as reflected by the criteria, and guide students as they evaluate how well they have achieved the criteria.

We do not recommend that teachers set standards by comparing students in a class to one another or use the results of norm-referenced tests. With these practices students who do well in a class or on a test receive high grades, and students who do poorly receive low grades. This practice does not allow students who are performing below the class average but who have made great strides in achievement and self-motivation to receive high grades, whereas it ensures that students whose achievement is high but who are not motivated and engaged learners receive high grades.

The best method for setting standards for evaluation is probably a combination of comparing students to themselves and comparing students to established criteria. Teachers must be able to justify that their students are moving toward expected levels of conventions (which could be illustrated through using criteria) and reward individual learners who show initiative, effort, and achievement toward personal goals (which could be achieved by evaluating students on individual growth).

Grading

Nothing seems harder than reducing hours, days, and weeks of classroom activities and instruction into a few grades. Reporting students' learning through parent conferences or reports provides far more information about what the students are learning and doing than a single letter grade or indication that students *always, sometimes,* or *never,* for example, read for pleasure. We recommend that teachers always supplement report cards with letters or reports to parents and samples of students' work even when they are not mandated by the school. This practice is especially important when the philosophy behind a report card differs from the philosophy of a teacher's reading program. Many report cards have changed little in format or content from report cards used in traditional programs. These report cards may ask teachers to evaluate behaviors that have little relevance to the behaviors expected in their literature-based reading programs.

While most teachers cannot ignore report cards or change their formats, they can supplement them with narrative comments and samples of students' work. Teachers can also become more involved in their local districts and volunteer to serve on committees reviewing report cards and setting policies for student evaluation.

The assessment practices that we recommend in this chapter might seem enormously time consuming. They do take some time and require planning and thoughtful reflection. However, most of the assessments we discuss can supplant rather than supplement the practice of grading papers. The time that teachers would

FIGURE 9.19   Summary Chart for Decision Tree

		Decision Tree
Chapter 1		Using Literature in the Reading Program
Chapter 2		Choosing Literature for Children
Chapter 3		Learning About Authors and Illustrators
Chapter 4		Identifying Perspectives on Reading Instruction
Chapter 5		Teaching from a Reader Response Perspective
Chapter 6		Teaching from a Critical Perspective
Chapter 7		Teaching from an Interactive Perspective
Chapter 8		Putting It All Together
		Assessing Students' Learning
		• **Identify who will use assessment information and how it will be used**
Chapter 9		• **Identify instructional goals**
		• **Document learning**
		• **Analyze learning**
		• **Evaluate learning**

normally use to grade papers can be used to analyze and evaluate running records, student samples, and anecdotal records. The benefit of these efforts is a greater understanding of each student's learning and enhanced communication with parents and administrators about the benefits and outcomes of a literature-based reading program.

MAKING DECISIONS ABOUT ASSESSING STUDENTS' LEARNING

Teachers make many decisions related to assessment. Because literature-based reading programs are not based on traditional beliefs and practices, teachers cannot rely on commercially available tests. Instead, they must be knowledgeable about the characteristics of effective assessment and be clear about who will use information from assessment. Teachers must make the following decisions:

- Identify who will use assessment information and how it will be used
- Identify instructional goals
- Document learning
- Analyze learning
- Evaluate learning

This information is added to the decision-making diagram as shown in Figure 9.19.

REFERENCES

Atwell, N. (1987). *In the middle: Writing, reading, and learning with adolescents.* Portsmouth, NH: Heinemann.

Barone, D. (1990). The written responses of young children: Beyond comprehension to story understanding. *The New Advocate, 3,* 49–56.

Baskwill, J., & Whitman, P. (1988). *Evaluation: Whole language, whole child.* New York: Scholastic.

Clay, M. (1985). *The early detection of reading difficulties* (3rd ed.). Portsmouth, NH: Heinemann.

Dekker, M. (1991). Books, reading, and response: A teacher-researcher tells a story. *The New Advocate, 4,* 37–46.

Five, C. (1986). Fifth graders respond to a changed reading program. *Harvard Educational Review, 56,* 395–405.

Flood, J., & Lapp, D. (1989). Reporting reading progress: A comparison portfolio for parents. *The Reading Teacher, 42,* 508–514.

Galda, L. (1983). Research in response to literature. *Journal of Research and Development in Education, 16,* 1–7.

Goodman, Y, & Burke, C. (1972). *The reading miscue inventory.* New York: Macmillan.

Harp, B. (1991). Principles of assessment and evaluation in whole language classrooms. In B. Harp (Ed.), *Assessment and evaluation in whole language programs* (pp. 35–50). Norwood, MA: Christopher-Gordon.

Heald-Taylor, G. (l987). Predictable literature selections and activities for language arts instruction. *The Reading Teacher, 41,* 6–12.

Linek, W. (1991). Grading and evaluation techniques for whole language teachers. *Language Arts, 68,* 125–132.

Norton, D. (1992). *The impact of literature-based reading.* New York: Merrill/Macmillan.

Paradis, E. E., Chatton, B., Boswell, A., Smith, M., & Yovich, S. (1991). Accountability: Assessing comprehension during literature discussion. *The Reading Teacher, 45,* 8–17.

Pils, L. J. (1991). Soon anofe you taut me: Evaluation in a first grade whole language classroom. *The Reading Teacher, 45,* 46–50.

Reardon, S. (1991). A collage of assessment and evaluation from primary classrooms. In B. Harp (Ed.), *Assessment and evaluation in whole language programs* (pp. 87–108). Norwood, MA: Christopher-Gordon.

Rhodes, L. K., & Natheson-Mejia, S. (1992). Anecdotal records: A powerful tool for ongoing literacy assessment. *The Reading Teacher, 45,* 502–509.

Siu-Runyan, Y. (1991). Holistic assessment in intermediate classes: Techniques for informing our teaching. In B. Harp (Ed.), *Assessment and evaluation in whole language programs* (pp. 109–136). Norwood, MA: Christopher-Gordon.

Tierney, R., Carter, M., & Desai, L. (1991). *Portfolio assessment in the reading-writing classroom.* Norwood, MA: Christopher-Gordon.

Valencia, S., & Pearson, P. (1987). Reading assessment: Time for a change. *The Reading Teacher, 40,* 726–732.

Winograd, P., Paris, S., & Bridge, C. (1991). Improving the assessment of literacy. *The Reading Teacher, 45,* pp. 108–116.

CHILDREN'S LITERATURE REFERENCES

Bauer, M. D. (1986). *On my honor.* Boston: Houghton Mifflin.

Bennett, J. (1985). *Teeny tiny.* New York: Putnam.

Blume, J. (1974). *The pain and the great one.* New York: Dell.

Cleary, B. (1965). *The mouse and the motorcycle.* New York: Morrow.

Howe, D., & Howe, J. (1979). *Bunnicula: A rabbit tale of mystery.* New York: Atheneum.

Hutchins, P. (1968). *Rosie's walk.* New York: Scholastic.

Jacques, B. (1987). *Redwall.* New York: Putnam.

Lobel, A. (1977). *Mouse soup.* New York: Harper & Row.

MacLachlan, P. (1985). *Sarah, plain and tall.* New York: Harper & Row.

Numeroff, L. J. (1985). *If you give a mouse a cookie.* New York: Harper & Row.

Seuss, Dr. (1960). *Green eggs and ham.* New York: Random House.

Tsuchiya, Y. (1988). *Faithful elephants.* Boston: Houghton Mifflin.

Van Allsburg, C. (1979). *The garden of Abdul Gasazi.* Boston: Houghton Mifflin.

Viorst, J. (1988). *The good-bye book.* New York: Macmillan.

Williams, V. (1982). *A chair for my mother.* New York: Scholastic.

Yorinks, A. (1986). *Hey, Al.* New York: Farrar, Straus & Giroux.

Ziefert, H., & Smith, M. (1989). *In a scary old house.* New York: Puffin.

PART II
Action Plans

READING AND COMPARING "GINGERBREAD MAN" STORIES

MRS. ALVAREZ USES A COMBINATION of whole-class and center-based activities in her half-day kindergarten classroom. "I'm lucky," she says. "With a student teacher this semester and several parent volunteers who help out in the classroom once each week, I can do so many more things with my children than if I were the only adult in the classroom." Mrs. Alvarez uses weekly units that integrate language arts, math, science, and social studies, and this action plan describes Mrs. Alvarez's week-long focus on "The Gingerbread Man" story.

To begin the unit, Mrs. Alvarez collects many versions of "The Gingerbread Man" story and related running-away stories, including these:

- *The Gingerbread Man* (Galdone, 1985), a traditional retelling of the folktale in which the cookie runs away from an old man and woman, a cow, a horse, threshers, mowers, and then he is tricked and eaten by a fox.
- *The Bun: A Tale from Russia* (Brown, 1972), a Russian version in which an old man and woman make a bun and it rolls away from them, and then past a hare, a wolf, and a bear before being eaten by a fox.
- *The Pancake Boy* (Cauley, 1988), a Norwegian folktale in which a pancake rolls away from a family with seven children, past Manny Panny, Henny Penny, Cocky Locky, Ducky Lucky, Goosey Poosey, Gander Pander, and Piggy Wiggy, until it is tricked and eaten by Piggy Wiggy.
- *The Pancake* (Lobel, 1978), an easy-to-read version that is very similar to Cauley's *The Pancake Boy.*
- *Journey Cake, Ho!* (Sawyer, 1953), an Appalachian version about a boy who must leave home with only a journey cake to eat because his family is so poor. The journey cake rolls down the path, attracts a cow, a duck, two sheep, a pig, some hens, and a donkey, and leads them back to the boy's home.
- *You Can't Catch Me!* (Oppenheim, 1986), an adaptation of "The Gingerbread Man" story in which a pesky fly taunts a cow, a goat, a horse, a fox, a bear, a pig, and a sheep until it is caught and eaten by a turtle.

Mrs. Alvarez has two or three copies of each of these books, and she will read aloud each version during the focus unit. Copies will be available for children to look at and retell in the reading center. In addition, she has a big book of Ed Arno's traditional version of *The Gingerbread Man* (1985) and 10 copies of the matching small books.

Next, Mrs. Alvarez constructs a planning web to identify possible activities for her focus unit, and this web is presented in Figure 1. This web capitalizes on the centers that she has in her classroom and identifies special reading and writing activities for the whole class. Mrs. Alvarez selects activities from this web to include in each of her centers and as part of shared reading and writing activities.

Mrs. Alvarez uses a combination of reader response, critical, and interactive perspectives to guide her instruction. She plans grand conversations after reading each version of "The Gingerbread Man" stories (reader response), and explains, "I believe in allowing my children an opportunity to talk about each story we read,

FIGURE 1   Mrs. Alvarez's Planning Web

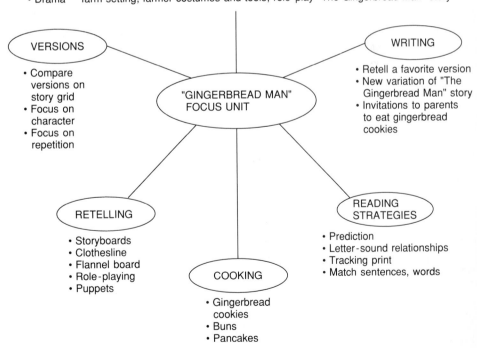

CENTERS

- Art — collage to decorate gingerbread boys; literary maps
- Writing — gingerbread boy shape paper; journals
- Math — button patterns on gingerbread boys; graph favorite versions
- Listening — tapes of two versions
- Reading — several copies of each version; storyboards; flannel board; clothesline
- Sand — cookie recipe on chart; measuring tools
- Drama — farm setting; farmer costumes and tools; role-play "The Gingerbread Man" story

VERSIONS
- Compare versions on story grid
- Focus on character
- Focus on repetition

WRITING
- Retell a favorite version
- New variation of "The Gingerbread Man" story
- Invitations to parents to eat gingerbread cookies

"GINGERBREAD MAN" FOCUS UNIT

RETELLING
- Storyboards
- Clothesline
- Flannel board
- Role-playing
- Puppets

COOKING
- Gingerbread cookies
- Buns
- Pancakes

READING STRATEGIES
- Prediction
- Letter-sound relationships
- Tracking print
- Match sentences, words

and I learn a lot about them and about their interpretations of the story as they talk." Mrs. Alvarez teaches from a critical stance when she uses a comparison grid to contrast different versions of "The Gingerbread Man" story. She explains, "Some people may think that kindergartners are too young to learn about literature, but they're not. They can compare and contrast "The Gingerbread Man" stories and they are really proud of themselves when they finish the story grid chart." She draws children's attention to print and focuses on letter-sound relationships as they read big books and write the comparison grid; these activities are typical of the interactive perspective. "Of course, I also am teaching my children how to read and write, and the best way I've found to focus on skills and strategies is during authentic reading and writing activities," Mrs. Alvarez says.

Mrs. Alvarez's classroom has a large carpeted area used for shared reading and other whole-class activities. This area includes a big book easel, an easel with large chart paper, a choice board that the children use to select centers, charts of favorite songs, poems, and chants, and pointers, markers, and several big and small books. Next to this area is a large bulletin board that Mrs. Alvarez uses for the story grid comparing the versions of "The Gingerbread Man" story. The remainder of the room is arranged into seven centers: reading, listening, writing, art, drama, math, and sand and water table. Each center contains a special activity for the "The Gingerbread Man" focus unit as well as a variety of materials that remain the same throughout the year. The materials included in each center are described in Figure 2.

MRS. ALVAREZ'S DAILY SCHEDULE

Mrs. Alvarez's half-day kindergarten is three hours long, and her daily schedule is

9:00–9:15	Opening and Calendar
9:15–10:00	Reading and Writing Time
10:00–11:00	Center Time
11:00–11:15	Clean-Up and Sharing Time
11:15–11:30	Outside Recess
11:30–11:50	Story Time
11:50–12:00	Closing

COMPONENTS OF THE KINDERGARTEN LANGUAGE ARTS PROGRAM

The components of Mrs. Alvarez's daily schedule that involve language arts are reading and writing time, center time, sharing time, and story time.

Reading and Writing Time

At the beginning of reading and writing time, Mrs. Alvarez and the children read and sing a favorite song from a chart or reread a familiar poem aloud. After singing or

FIGURE 2   Materials in the Kindergarten Centers (pp. 389–390)

The Reading Center

The reading center consists of a large class library with over 200 books, some as big books and others as small books. Many of the books have repetitive language. Props for storytelling, including a flannel board, a story clothesline, story boards, puppets, and other objects are available in the reading center. For this focus unit, a special crate has been set out that contains several copies of each version of the "Gingerbread Man" story. In addition, there are small copies of Arno's *The Gingerbread Man* and retelling props to accompany them. Mrs. Alvarez has made a story clothesline for Galdone's version, flannel board props for Oppenheim's *You Can't Catch Me!,* and story boards for Cauley's *The Pancake Boy,* and these materials are available in the center for children to use.

The Listening Center

The listening center is set up on a small table next to the reading center and holds a tape recorder and several sets of headphones. A special tub next to the table holds dozens of plastic bags, each with an audiotape and one or more copies of a book. Mrs. Alvarez has prepared audiotapes for two of the "Gingerbread Man" versions, one for Ed Arno's version and one for Marcia Brown's *The Bun: A Tale from Russia.*

The Writing Center

The writing center is a large table next to shelves loaded with a supply of writing materials including markers, pencils, plastic letters, crayons, writing paper, construction paper, note paper, envelopes, file folders, index cards, stamps and stamp pads, and a date stamp. Children's journals are kept in a plastic crate next to the shelves. This crate contains hanging folders for each child, and children place their journals and other writing samples in their folders. Children write in their journals daily, drawing pictures and writing using invented spelling. For this unit, special gingerbread-shaped paper is available in the writing center.

The Art Center

The art center is located on a table near the sink in the classroom. Next to the table is a double easel where children may paint. Mrs. Alvarez has tempera paints, crayons, markers, clay, chalk, tissue paper, collage materials, wallpaper samples, scissors, and glue available for art projects in this center. For this unit, children are using collage materials to decorate gingerbread men that they cut from construction paper.

The Drama Center

The drama center takes many forms in Mrs. Alvarez's classroom. At the beginning of the year it was a housekeeping center with a table and chairs, stove, refrigerator, and sink. At other times this center becomes a hospital, office, hair salon, bank, or restaurant. In addition, the center contains a collection of dress-up clothes and props that children use to enact favorite stories. The center includes a puppet theater and a collection of puppets. The drama center has been arranged as a farm for several weeks, and during this unit, students have special props to use including a stuffed doll of the Gingerbread Man, aprons, straw hats, and farm tools—a rake and hoe—to role-play the "Gingerbread Man" story.

The Math Center

The math center includes a large table and several math manipulatives such as peg boards, Cuisenaire rods, Unifix cubes, pattern blocks, dice, geoboards, beads, buttons, and an assortment of dried beans. The math center also contains a set of large unit blocks that children use in building on a nearby carpet. For this unit, Mrs. Alvarez made several task cards of little gingerbread men each with

FIGURE 2   *continued*

a different pattern of buttons. Other blank gingerbread men shapes are available for students to use with the button collection to match the patterns on the task cards.

The Sand and Water Table

The sand and water table is a special table in which Mrs. Alvarez places sand, water, rice, macaroni, and other materials. There are several measuring instruments housed nearby including measuring spoons and cups, pitchers, different-sized containers, and scoops. For this unit, Mrs. Alvarez posts a recipe for making gingerbread boy cookies and sets out the necessary measuring tools. The children pretend to make cookies by reading the recipe chart and measuring the ingredients with sand.

reading, children invent new versions of the songs or poems by substituting new words for the words in the songs or poems. Mrs. Alvarez writes the words they dictate on sticky-backed notes and places them over the words on the chart as children sing or read the new version (Fisher, 1991). As she writes, Mrs. Alvarez talks briefly about letters, sounds, and words.

For this focus unit, Mrs. Alvarez uses a chart with "Old MacDonald Had a Farm" that children are familiar with from a recent theme about the farm. This week, they will sing the familiar song and then make up new versions by adding characters from "The Gingerbread Man" stories. As Mrs. Alvarez writes the words for the new versions, she asks children to predict the letters that the new words begin with and compares short and long words like *gingerbread* and *man.*

The second activity is reading (or rereading) aloud a big book. On Monday, Mrs. Alvarez introduces the big book version of *The Gingerbread Man* and continues rereading it throughout the week. The first time she reads the book for pleasure, she invites children to predict and comment. On Tuesday, she rereads the book letting children take turns pointing to the words as she reads the story several times. On Thursday, the children reread the book and match sentence strips to sentences in the story, and on Friday, they reread together and match word cards to words in the story.

Mrs. Alvarez includes role-playing and storytelling in this focus unit. On Monday, the children dramatize Arno's version of *The Gingerbread Man* and on Tuesday, Wednesday, and Thursday Mrs. Alvarez tells other "The Gingerbread Man" stories using the story props she has made. The children join in the retelling by helping to manipulate the props and adding the refrains.

An important part of this focus unit is the comparison grid that Mrs. Alvarez uses to contrast the five versions of "The Gingerbread Man" story that she reads aloud. She begins the comparison grid after reading the first version of the folktale and then children add information after reading each version. Mrs. Alvarez focuses on characters and repetition, and she encourages the children to name the characters in each version and then tell something that is repeated. Mrs. Alvarez draws children's attention to words, letter names, and letter sounds by encouraging students to predict what she writes. Each day she selects several children to draw pictures of the story characters to illustrate the newly added information on the comparison grid during center time. Figure 3 shows the completed grid.

FIGURE 3   A Comparison Grid for "Gingerbread Man" Stories

Version	Who ran away?	What happened?	Other Characters	How did the story end?
The Pancake Boy		He rolled away so he wouldn't be eaten.	Goody Poody, Goodman Poody, 7 children, Manny Panny Henny Penny, Cocky Locky, Ducky Lucky, Goosey Loosey, Gander Pander, and Piggy Wiggy	Piggy Wiggy ate the pancake.
The Gingerbread Boy		He ran away.	Old woman, old man, cow, horse, threshers, mowers, and a fox	The fox ate the cookie.
You Can't Catch Me!		The fly bothered the animals.	A cow, a goat, a horse, a fox, a bear, a pig, a sheep, and a turtle	The turtle ate the pesky fly.
Journey Cake, Ho!		It rolled off down the path.	Old woman, old man, Johnny, a cow, a duck, two sheep, a pig, some hens, and a donkey	The old woman, the old man, and Johnny ate the journey cake.
The Bun: A Tale from Russia		It rolled away.	Old woman, old man, a hare, a wolf, a bear, and a fox	The fox ate the bun.

On Monday, Mrs. Alvarez introduces the special thematic activities in each center. She explains the center activities and talks with children about what they might do with the activities. After using each story retelling prop, Mrs. Alvarez places it in the reading center and encourages children to sequence and retell the story using the props.

On Thursday, Mrs. Alvarez uses some of the reading and writing time to make gingerbread boy cookies. Together as a class, they read the recipe chart that has been posted at the sand and water center, measure and mix the ingredients, and cut out the cookies. Later, the children decorate and eat the cookies with the volunteer parent-helper.

Center Time

Each day children spend some time at the reading, math, and writing centers. These three centers are the "must-do" centers and the other four are "your-choice" centers. At the reading center, they reread familiar books using the big book and pointer or reading with a partner, retell stories using story props, or read other books from the classroom library. At the writing center, they write about a topic of their own choice in their journals each day. At the math center, they complete a math activity daily, and Mrs. Alvarez or her student teacher often visit this center to teach informal lessons. They are also free to select from among the other centers in the classroom each day.

The children use their class choice board to indicate which centers they visit each day. Mrs. Alvarez modeled her choice board after the one described by Bobbi Fisher (1991). The children's names are posted on a pegboard with a peg under each name. Color-coded circles hang above the names on the board. The circles are coded for each of the centers in the classroom (red for reading, yellow for listening, and so on). Mrs. Alvarez expects the children to go to the choice board after they visit a center and hang one of the color-coded circles under their names to indicate they have completed the center. At the end of the day, Mrs. Alvarez checks that each child has visited the three "must do" centers and notes which of the "your-choice" centers each child has been to as indicated by the circles hanging on the pegboard.

Mrs. Alvarez's student teacher, Ms. Medrano, works at the writing center during this focus unit. Each day she works with a small group of four or five children to make a collaborative book retelling "The Gingerbread Man" story. The children dictate the story, and Ms. Medrano writes it on several large pieces of writing paper. Then children illustrate the pages, and Ms. Medrano encourages them to include the gingerbread man in their pictures and to label him with the letters *GB*. One page of the group's retelling is presented in Figure 4. Afterwards, they sequence the pages, make a title page and a page for comments to go at the back of the book, and decorate a cover. Then they bind their book and make plans to share it with the class during the sharing time later in the morning.

Mrs. Alvarez is in the math center on Monday and Tuesday. She observes children's patterning and encourages them to begin patterns with repetitions of three. While she is there, she initiates several informal sorting and categorizing activities to supplement the other activities. On Wednesday and Friday, Mrs. Alvarez is in the reading center to observe children as they reread books and retell stories using the story props. Mrs. Jones, the mother of a child in the classroom, comes every Thursday and helps bake the gingerbread boy cookies and works with small groups of children, assisting as they decorate and eat their cookies. Mrs. Best, an aide from the instructional services center (ISC), comes into the classroom on Friday morning for one hour to work with a small group of students on a computer that she rolls in from the ISC.

Sharing Time

During sharing time, several children share what they did during center time, and other children share special objects they have brought from home. Children often share what they wrote at the writing center, and Mrs. Alvarez has a special author's chair for children to sit in as they share their writings. The children who wrote and illustrated their version of "The Gingerbread Man" story at the writing center with Ms. Medrano also share their book with the class. After someone shares, children ask questions and give compliments.

Story Time

Mrs. Alvarez introduces children to a wide variety of books by reading aloud daily. She always mentions the title and author, asks children to predict what will happen

FIGURE 4   A Page from a Dictated "Gingerbread Man" Book

The [Gingerbread Man] said,
"I'm a quarter gone."
"I'm almost gone."
"I'm three-quarters gone."

Then he didn't say anything at all because he was all gone.

GB→

Bye, Bye, [Gingerbread Man]!

in the book, and encourages them to make comments about the books. Sometimes she draws children's attention to specific concepts or vocabulary, but often she reads simply for pleasure. The books that Mrs. Alvarez reads during story time are often reread during reading and writing time. On most days after listening to Mrs. Alvarez read a story, the class participates in a grand conversation. They scoot back on the rug to make a circle. Mrs. Alvarez begins by asking, "Who wants to share first?" and

FIGURE 5   One-Week Lesson Plan for the "Gingerbread Man" Focus Unit

	MONDAY	TUESDAY	WEDNESDAY	THURSDAY	FRIDAY
9:00 – 9:15	Opening and Calendar • Counting with calendar • Days of the week				
9:15 – 10:00 *Reading and Writing Time*	"Old MacDonald Had a Farm" Big Book — *The Gingerbread Man* • Role-play • Introduce centers	"Old MacDonald" Variation Retell *The Pancake Boy* with story boards • Start story grid • Reread GB big book	Choice Songs Retell *The Gingerbread Boy* using story clothes-line • Add to story grid • Sentence match in the big book	Choice Songs Retell *You Can't Catch Me!* on flannel board • Add to story grid • Mix and bake GB cookies	"Old MacDonald" Variation Read *The Bun: A Tale from Russia* • Add to story grid • Match words in the big book
10:00 – 11:00 *Center Time*	SPECIAL ACTIVITIES FOR FOCUS UNIT Reading Center — Story clothesline, story boards, flannel board props Listening Center — Tape of two GB stories Writing Center — GB shape paper		Art Center — GB collage Sand Center — GB recipe and measure tools Math Center — GB task cards for button patterns Drama Center — Farm and GB costumes		
	• Student Teacher — Writing Center — Collaborative retellings of GB into books				
	Teacher — Math Center	Teacher — Math Center	Teacher — Reading Center • Anecdotal notes	Mrs. Jones — Decorate cookies and eat them	Mrs. Best — Computer Teacher — Reading Center
11:00 – 11:15	Sharing Time — Children sit in circle and share books and projects				
11:15 – 11:30	Outside Recess				
11:30 – 11:50 *Story Time*	*The Pancake Boy*	*The Gingerbread Boy*	*You Can't Catch Me!*	*Journey Cake, Ho!*	*The Bun: A Tale from Russia*
	Grand conversation each day after reading aloud				
11:50 – 12:00	Closing				

the children take turns commenting on the book. She listens carefully to their comments because she is interested in learning what makes books so appealing to her students. Mrs. Alvarez explains, "At the beginning of the year, my children are so eager to talk, I don't think they listen to each other. But, you know, they grow and before long they do listen to each other and build on each other's comments." During this focus unit, Mrs. Alvarez reads a different version of "The Gingerbread Man" story each day.

MRS. ALVAREZ'S ONE-WEEK LESSON PLAN

Mrs. Alvarez's week-long lesson plan for a "Gingerbread Man" focus unit is presented in Figure 5. This lesson plan includes each of the components of her daily schedule. Mrs. Alvarez plans specific activities for Reading and Writing Time and Story Time as well as on-going activities, and she keeps the center activities the same throughout the week-long focus unit.

MRS. ALVAREZ'S RECORD-KEEPING AND ASSESSMENT PROCEDURES

Mrs. Alvarez uses a variety of record-keeping and assessment procedures. She uses the choice board to keep track of which centers children visit each day, and she notes whether or not children have been to the three "must-do" centers and which of the "your-choice" centers children prefer. Either Mrs. Alvarez or her student teacher transfers this information to a chart to keep a permanent record of the children's participation in center activities.

Mrs. Alvarez makes anecdotal records as she observes children working in centers and during other language arts activities. When she visits the reading center on Wednesday and Friday, she assesses individual children's retelling strategies and print-matching skills using an emerging reading checklist as well as anecdotal notes. Mrs. Alvarez uses the emerging reading checklists developed by the kindergarten and first grade teachers in her district (see Figure 9.6 in Chapter 9). As she observes various reading behaviors and engages children in retelling familiar stories, she writes anecdotal notes on the checklist as she completes it. Mrs. Alvarez also observes children's language competencies as they talk about books in grand conversations, participate in dramatic activities and in the housekeeping center, and share during sharing time. She makes brief notes about her observations.

Mrs. Alvarez places the checklists, anecdotal notes, and children's writing samples in their language arts portfolios.

REFERENCES

Fisher, B. (1991). *Joyful learning: A whole language kindergarten.* Portsmouth, NH: Heinemann.

CHILDREN'S LITERATURE REFERENCES

Arno, E. (1985). *The gingerbread man.* New York: Scholastic.

Brown, M. (1972). *The bun: A tale from Russia.* New York: Harcourt Brace Jovanovich.

Cauley, L. B. (1988). *The pancake boy.* New York: Putnam.

Galdone, P. (1975). *The gingerbread boy.* New York: Seabury.

Lobel, A. (1978). *The pancake.* New York: Greenwillow.

Oppenheim, J. (1986). *You can't catch me!* Boston: Houghton Mifflin.

Sawyer, R. (1953). *Journey cake, ho!* New York: Viking.

GRADE 1 ACTION PLAN

CELEBRATING MARTIN LUTHER KING, JR.'S, BIRTHDAY

MRS. EDISON IS A FIRST grade teacher at Western Hills Elementary School. Each year her first graders celebrate Martin Luther King, Jr.'s birthday in January, and her students read, write, and talk about this great civil rights leader. Mrs. Edison is an African American and many of her students are too. She describes herself as a "multi-cultural teacher" and explains, "I want my students to know about Dr. King because most television coverage of African Americans is negative. Seldom do we make noteworthy headlines, and my students need inspirational role models to help them develop their self-esteem."

Mrs. Edison bases the week-long unit on David A. Adler's *A Picture Book of Martin Luther King, Jr.* (1989). This core book presents an overview of the civil rights leader, his childhood, adult life, and contributions. At the end of the book is a lifeline of Dr. King's life. On each page, there are several sentences of text, and Robert Casilla's sensitive, watercolor illustrations extend the text. Several of the children in the classroom can read the book themselves, and Mrs. Edison has 15 copies of the book available for children to read and reread individually or with buddies. She also uses language experience to take children's dictation about Dr. King and his contributions and a chart with the song "We Shall Overcome" that Dr. King and other civil rights workers sang.

Mrs. Edison uses a combination of all three perspectives as her students read this core book, but of the three, she probably places the greatest emphasis on reader response. "I use this core book about Dr. King because he is a human success story; he has made a significant contribution to our society," Mrs. Edison explains. "I'm proud of what he did and I want my students to be proud, too." Later in the school year, Mrs. Edison plans for her students to learn about Ronald McNair, an African American astronaut, and people from other cultures who have made significant contributions to our society.

The week-long celebration culminates on Friday afternoon at the weekly school assembly when the class presents the book about Dr. King that they have written and illustrated. Before the book is bound, Mrs. Edison makes a transparency of each page. At the assembly, the students read their book to the school by placing each page on the overhead projector and reading the text aloud.

MRS. EDISON'S DAILY SCHEDULE

Mrs. Edison has two language arts periods each day. The students spend 1½ hours in the morning engaged in reading and writing activities and 1 hour in the afternoon. The schedule is

9:15–9:30	Students Read Self-Selected Books
9:30–10:00	Read the Core Book
10:00–10:30	Respond to the Core Book
10:30–10:45	Minilesson on Language Arts Skills and Strategies
10:45–11:40	Math
11:40–12:45	Lunch and Recess
12:45–1:05	Read Aloud to Students
1:05–1:30	Write in Personal Journals and Share Their Writing in Author's Chair
1:30–1:45	Reread the Core Book or Related Texts

COMPONENTS OF MRS. EDISON'S CORE LITERATURE UNIT

The components of the core literature unit are reading self-selected books, reading the core book, responding to the core book, minilessons, reading aloud, journal writing, and rereading. Mrs. Edison plans independent reading, journal writing, and rereading activities to be sure that her first graders are actively involved in language arts activities.

Independent Reading Time

Mrs. Edison has a large class library with hundreds of books under the windows on one wall of her classroom. She has special baskets for books related to core books as well as baskets for books related to science and social studies theme cycles. She also has special sections for books she has read aloud in class, books students have already read, easy-to-read books, books made by the class, and books with tapes for the listening center. Each day students begin with 15 minutes of independent reading time.

Many teachers fear that first graders aren't interested or able to read independently for 15 minutes, but these students do. At the beginning of the school year, Mrs. Edison introduced several strategies for independent reading. She suggested that students "read" the book by focusing on the illustrations and inventing the text. She also recommended that students reread familiar books or read with a buddy. They are also welcome to listen to a book at the listening center during this time. Class books are also popular during independent reading. Some students sit at their desks and others spread out on the carpet squares in the library area.

At the end of the independent reading period, several students briefly share the books they have been reading with the class, and students who have finished a book add it to the list of books they have read that they keep in their reading notebooks. By January of their first grade year, most children have read 100 books!

During the week that students were learning about Dr. King, several students read other books about Dr. King or other biographies, but because there are so few biographies for first graders, most students selected and read books unrelated to the core book. After students return their books to the class library and join Mrs. Edison in the reading circle for the core literature book, the child who is librarian for the week remains in the library area for several minutes to tidy it.

Reading the Core Book

Mrs. Edison plans most core literature units for a week, and during the week she introduces the book to the whole class and reads it aloud. Then students reread the book several times during the week and participate in talk and writing response activities. She has class sets of some books and for other books she has only quarter- or half-class sets. To get enough books for the students, she often trades books with other first grade teachers at Western Hills School and in the school district.

Sometimes the core literature book that Mrs. Edison wants to use is too difficult for many of her students to read independently. When this is the case, as in *A Picture Book of Martin Luther King, Jr.,* she uses language experience activities, a book that the students write, and supplemental reading materials, such as a poem or song, to provide students with additional reading experiences.

During the first reading of the book, she tape-records her reading and places the audiotape in the listening center for students to listen to and read during the week—during independent reading time and at other times during the school day. She plans other activities using story boards of the biography that she has made from two copies of the book that were cut apart, backed with poster board and laminated.

Mrs. Edison hangs a sheet of butcher paper for a word wall each time she begins a new core literature book. After reading, she and the students write words related to the book on the word wall and they refer to these words for all response activities during the week. They will continue to add words to the list during the week as the book is reread and as other books related to the core book are shared. The list of words that Mrs. Edison and her students compiled for their unit on Martin Luther King, Jr. is presented in Figure 1.

Responding to the Core Book

Students respond to the core book in a variety of ways. Their first exploratory responses are through grand conversations and reading logs. Sometimes students write first in their reading logs and share their writings to begin the grand conversation, and at other times students first share their ideas orally and then write in their reading logs. Both sequences are effective. The order is usually determined by how long the students have been sitting and whether Mrs. Edison feels they need to get up and move around before the grand conversation.

FIGURE 1   Word Wall for *A Picture Book of Martin Luther King, Jr.* (Adler, 1989)

Martin Luther King, Jr.	boycott
great leader	equal rights
powerful speaker	civil rights
protests	sit-ins
marches	marches for freedom
unfair-fair	March on Washington
Atlanta, Georgia	Washington, DC
Alfred Daniel (A. D.)	Nobel Peace Prize
Willie Christine	riots
pastor	violence
minister	Memphis, Tennessee
Reverend King	assassinated
preach	James Earl Ray
slaves	hate
love each other	prejudice
Coretta Scott King	"I'm free at last."
Montgomery, Alabama	third Monday in January
Rosa Parks	federal holiday
White Only	

For their more extended responses, Mrs. Edison's first graders often dramatize the story or write a retelling of it. Sometimes the whole class works on a single response as they do in their class book about Dr. King. At other times students choose five response activities and Mrs. Edison sets up centers for students to work at.

As a part of this unit, students write their own class book about Dr. King. Mrs. Edison plans this response activity so that the students will think more deeply about Dr. King's contributions to create a book about Dr. King that the students can read. To begin, students retell the events in Dr. King's life using story boards. Using the story boards as prompts, students make a lifeline of Dr. King on a long roll of paper. (Mrs. Edison has drawn the line and marked off the years of Dr. King's life in advance.) Then students identify significant events in Dr. King's life and add them to the lifeline. Students work in pairs, and each pair chooses an event to write about, making an illustration and a rough draft of a sentence to describe the illustration. Next, Mrs. Edison and her students revise and edit their sentences and then copy them on the page with their illustrations. Finally they compile the pages to make a class book. As the culminating activity for the unit, students will share their class book at the school assembly on Friday afternoon. A page from the class's book is shown in Figure 2.

Minilessons on Language Arts Skills and Strategies

Mrs. Edison spends 15 minutes each day teaching a minilesson. These lessons focus on various reading or language arts skills, including reading skills and strategies, handwriting, vocabulary, and phonics. She often ties the lessons to the core book and as students read about Dr. King, Mrs. Edison teaches minilessons on writing abbreviations, sequencing events in the biography, handwriting, words from the word

FIGURE 2   A Page from the Class Book About Dr. King

Martin Luther King, Jr. won the Nobel Peace Prize. He receive d a Medal and $54,600.00.

wall, and words that rhyme with *king.* These lessons are for the whole class and students participate orally, use manipulative materials like story boards or word cards, and often write on the chalkboard. They rarely use worksheets.

Reading Aloud to Students

Mrs. Edison reads aloud to students several times a day, and during the 20-minute period from 12:45 to 1:05, she usually reads a book related to the core book. Mrs. Edison would like to read other biographies about African Americans, but very few are appropriate for first graders. Instead, this week will be a "your-choice week," and she will read and reread favorite books that the students request. After reading, students spend five minutes or so discussing the book in a grand conversation.

Writing in Personal Journals

Students spend 25 minutes writing entries in personal journals and sharing their entries in the author's chair. Students are free to write on self-selected topics, but Mrs. Edison has found that students who complain "I don't know what to write about" often choose to write about the book she just read. Students use invented spelling as they write. Mrs. Edison circulates around the classroom, encouraging students to invent their own spellings. She also uses this time for informal phonics lessons as students ask how to spell words or which letters they should use to spell specific sounds. At the same time, she keeps track of what her students who spell words with only one or two letters are writing so that she can help them to reread their writing.

As students finish writing, they show their writing to Mrs. Edison and then move to the author's chair. After four children are sitting in the reading circle, the sharing begins, and students take turns sharing while Mrs. Edison continues to work with students who are still writing. Not everyone will share each day, but those students who don't share one day will begin sharing the following day and will write afterwards.

Rereading Activities

Mrs. Edison knows her first graders need many opportunities to read and she plans a 15-minute "rereading" time each afternoon. Sometimes students echo-read the core book that Mrs. Edison read aloud in the morning, sometimes they buddy-read the book, and sometimes at the end of the week students participate in a read-around in which they reread aloud their favorite sentences from the book. At other times, students dictate sentence strips and language experience stories and reread them during this rereading time. They also reread poems, songs, and other supplemental reading materials. In the unit on Dr. King, students reread dictated sentence strips and use choral reading to reread the song "We Shall Overcome."

MRS. EDISON'S WEEK-LONG LESSON PLAN

Mrs. Edison's lesson plan for her week-long unit on Dr. King using David A. Adler's *A Picture Book of Martin Luther King, Jr.* is presented in Figure 3. The lesson plan includes both the morning and afternoon reading and language arts activities. Most of the activities are planned to help students read and respond to the book. Mrs. Edison also plans language experience activities and a song chart to provide additional reading opportunities for her students.

MRS. EDISON'S RECORD-KEEPING AND ASSESSMENT PROCEDURES

Mrs. Edison uses a weekly checklist of language arts activities in her classroom. Each week she makes a list of the activities for the week and makes copies of it for each child. She keeps the copies herself and makes notes about each child during the week. By Thursday she concentrates on those children she has not already observed or those who need more thorough observation and conferencing. Then she puts these checklists in the language arts folders she keeps for each child. A copy of the checklist Mrs. Edison uses for the unit on Dr. King is presented in Figure 4.

Mrs. Edison also collects work from the students at the end of each unit. For a week-long unit on Dr. King, she collects these materials:

- reading log
- list of abbreviations
- sentence strip (cut apart and in envelope)
- quickwrite/cluster on vocabulary word

FIGURE 3 A Week-Long Lesson Plan for a Focus Unit on Martin Luther King, Jr.

	MONDAY	TUESDAY	WEDNESDAY	THURSDAY	FRIDAY
9:15 – 9:30 *Independent Reading*	Students read self-selected books from the class library				
9:30 – 10:00 *Reading the Core Book*	• Introduce concept of biography • True story • Person's life • Introduce M.L.K., Jr. Read aloud *A Picture of Martin Luther King, Jr.*	• Reread book • Add to word wall • Make lifeline on chart paper • Mark locations on U.S. map	• Introduce song "We Shall Overcome" • Pass out copies for choral reading to four groups	• Sequence story boards • Reread lifeline • Students choose events for class book	• Finish class book • Do title page and covers • Collate • Bind book
10:00 – 10:30 *Responding to the Core Book*	• Begin word wall • Grand conversation • Write in reading logs • Share entries	• Students choose word from wall and write a quickwrite or cluster in log • Share	• Retell book using story boards • Begin talking about class book	• Work in pairs to draw pictures and rough draft sentences. • In small groups, students reread book at listening center	• Rehearse reading the collaborative book and choral reading for the assembly
10:30 – 10:45 *Minilesson*	*Abbreviations* • Dr., Rev., Mr., Mrs., Ms., Jr., capital letters, and periods	*Sequence* • Sequence story boards • Compare to lifeline	*Handwriting* • Practice word wall words and sentences from book	*Vocabulary* • Review word wall • Make word posters and share	*Phonics* • Review -*ing* rhyme • King ⟶ *ing* • Write words in reading log
12:45 – 1:05 *Reading Aloud*	"Your-Choice" Week • Students choose books they want me to read aloud • Grand conversations after reading				
1:05 – 1:30 *Journal Writing*	Students write personal journal entries and share them in the author's chair				
1:30 – 1:45 *Rereading*	• Dictate sentences about Dr. King on sentence strips • Read aloud	• Reread sentence strips • Share • Cut apart & rebuild	• Reread choral reading and sentence strips	• Read around rough draft of class book • Revise	• Share book and perform choral reading at the assembly

FIGURE 4   Mrs. Edison's Assessment Checklist

Core Book: *A Picture Book of Martin Luther King, Jr.* (Adler, 1989)

Name: _____ Week of January 16

Independent Reading

_____

Grand Conversations

_____

Minilessons

a. Abbreviations (*Dr., Jr., Mr., Ms., Rev.*)
b. Sequence
c. Handwriting
d. Vocabulary
e. Phonics (*-ing*)

_____

Informal Writing

a. Reading logs
b. Personal journals

_____

Reading and Rereading

a. Core book
b. Dictated sentences
c. Choral reading "We Shall Overcome"

_____

Activities

a. Class book
b. Performing at assembly

_____

- word poster
- rough draft of page for the Dr. King book

These pieces of writing document that the children in Mrs. Edison's class are reading, writing, and learning about written language. As she reviews these materials, Mrs. Edison looks for evidence that her students are becoming more proficient readers and writers and she makes notes on the papers to highlight their strengths.

CHILDREN'S LITERATURE REFERENCES

Adler, D. A. (1989). *A picture book of Martin Luther King, Jr.* New York: Holiday House.

GRADE 2 ACTION PLAN

READING AND WRITING ABOUT DINOSAURS

MRS. WASHINGTON USES theme cycles in her second grade classroom at Fox Ridge School, and now her students are studying about dinosaurs. "My students are wild about dinosaurs," Mrs. Washington explains. "At the beginning of the school year when we first talked about which social studies and science themes they were interested in, everyone wanted to learn more about dinosaurs." As she was getting ready to begin this theme cycle, Mrs. Washington shared some of her plans with her students and they suggested other things they would like to do. One of their ideas was to divide into groups and make large papier-mâché dinosaurs. While she wasn't sure she could handle it, Mrs. Washington got some help from the art teacher at the junior high school and a stegosaurus, a pteranadon, a tyrannosaurus rex, and a diplodocus are taking shape at one end of the classroom. Students also wanted to meet a real paleontologist, and Mrs. Washington has arranged for a scientist from the local university to come and talk to her class.

Mrs. Washington's students are involved in activities related to dinosaurs almost all day long. She has divided the school day into three large blocks: language arts, math, and social studies/science, but she works to integrate the theme cycle into all three blocks because she believes children learn better that way. Many of the activities related to dinosaurs go on during the afternoon social studies and science block; in this action plan, we will focus on the theme-related activities during the language arts block.

Mrs. Washington teaches from the reader response and interactive perspectives. She explains: "At the beginning of the year, I think I focus on teaching children how to read, but as soon as they develop some fluency, I try to back off and let them read. I know the best way for them to learn to read is by reading books they're interested in." Mrs. Washington usually asks students to read most stories, informational books and poems two times. They read first to have fun, and they reread if they need to remember something. "I know reading's not that simple, but I wanted to separate Louise Rosenblatt's concepts of aesthetic and efferent reading for my 7- and 8-year-olds," she explains.

LANGUAGE ARTS BLOCK SCHEDULE

Mrs. Washington's language arts block is two hours long, from 9:00 to 11:00, and she has divided the block into four components:

9:00–9:15	Minilesson
9:15–9:30	Personal Journals
9:30–10:00	Independent Reading
10:00–11:00	Theme Cycle Connection

COMPONENTS OF MRS. WASHINGTON'S LANGUAGE ARTS BLOCK

Mrs. Washington plans four components in her language arts block. The first three—teaching a minilesson on language arts skills and strategies, writing in personal journals, and reading independently—remain the same all year. The fourth component is the theme cycle connection, and during this one-hour period, Mrs. Washington involves her students in a variety of language arts activities related to the theme cycle.

Teaching Minilessons

Each morning Mrs. Washington begins the language arts block with a 15-minute minilesson during which she focuses on a language arts skill or strategy. Because her students are reading informational books about dinosaurs and writing about dinosaurs in the theme cycle, she is teaching these related skills and strategies during the minilessons:

- how to pronounce names of dinosaurs
- differences between stories, informational books, and poems
- how to read charts and figures in informational books
- how to use a table of contents
- how to use a glossary
- how to identify main ideas and details
- how to take notes in a cluster format
- when to use capital letters in writing about dinosaurs

Mrs. Washington begins by explaining the skill or strategy and then gives examples using the books students are reading or the writing they are doing. Then she asks her students to apply what she has taught in their reading and writing. She doesn't use worksheets because she says, "I think children learn better through real reading and writing, not by doing busy-work!"

Writing in Personal Journals

After the minilesson, Mrs. Washington passes out students' journals and they spend the next 15 minutes writing and drawing in their journals. Students are free to choose their own topics for writing, and some students write about their family and friends, about a television program they watched last night, or their sports teams, but many students write about the theme cycle. Mrs. Washington encourages the children to "tell me more" and to invent their own spellings for words that are not on the theme cycle word wall. At the end of 15 minutes, she collects the journals. She checks each student's journal at least once a week and writes a brief note back to the child. As she reviews their journal entries, Mrs. Washington notes the children's increasing use of conventional spelling and other mechanical skills.

Reading Independently

Mrs. Washington's students read independently for 20 minutes and then use the last 10 minutes of the period to share the books they are reading with classmates. Her students choose books from the class library, the school library, and the local public library to read, and many students read books related to the theme cycle. Mrs. Washington has a large collection of easy-to-read books and predictable books so some books are appropriate for each child in the class. Sometimes Mrs. Washington reads with a small group of less fluent readers to give them more access to books they could not read independently, and she also has a listening center set up in the classroom. At the listening center, small groups of students follow along in individual copies books as they listen to stories and other books.

Students keep a reading list in their language arts folders and after they read each book, they write the date and the title of the book on this reading list. They also evaluate the book by marking a face with a smile, a straight line, or frown mouth. Most of the students also write the number of pages in each book on their reading lists. Mrs. Washington doesn't ask them to do this; students do it on their own because they are so proud of their reading and are impressed by how many pages they are reading. A copy of the reading list that Mrs. Washington uses is presented in Figure 1. (Toward the end of the school year, Mrs. Washington encourages students to also write the author's name beside the title on the reading list.)

When she is not working with a group of children, Mrs. Washington walks around the classroom and observes children who are reading, gives assistance when needed, notes which books children have chosen, and stops to chat briefly with children about their books.

During the last 10 minutes of independent reading time, students get into a circle, and Mrs. Washington invites students to share their books informally. She tries to have every child share each week so that children will have the experience of talking about their books and so that classmates will learn about the books in the classroom library.

Connecting with the Theme Cycle

During this one-hour component of the language arts block, Mrs. Washington plans reading, writing, and other language arts activities in connection with the social studies and science theme cycle. For the three-week theme cycle on dinosaurs, Mrs. Washington plans reading and writing opportunities for her students.

FIGURE 1   A Second Grade Reading List

Books I Have Read

Name: _____

Date: Title and Author: Good or Bad?

_____

_____

_____

_____

_____

_____

_____

_____

Week One: Reading Informational Books About Dinosaurs.   During the first week, students divide into four groups to read *If the Dinosaurs Came Back* (Most, 1978), *Dinosaurs* (Gibbons, 1987), *Dinosaur Time* (Parish, 1974) or *Dinosaurs Are Different* (Aliki, 1985). Mrs. Washington begins the week by giving a book talk on the books and inviting students to sign up to read one of the four books. As soon as they choose their books, the students get together to preview the book they chose and begin to read. They continue reading on Tuesday in their small groups. As they read in small heterogeneous groups, Mrs. Washington circulates among the groups, helping to identify unfamiliar words, but most of the time someone in each group knows the words and students are able to read without frustration. After reading, students quickwrite about the book and then share their quickwrites as they discuss the book.

On Wednesday, students reread their books with a partner. Their purpose in rereading is to collect facts to use in making a cluster about dinosaurs. Students spend Wednesday and Thursday rereading and making a cluster on a large sheet of poster board. Mrs. Washington asks students to write the title of the book in the middle of the sheet of poster board, draw a circle around it, draw out four, five, or six rays, write main ideas, and then add details to each main idea. Students often make clusters in Mrs. Washington's class and they understand what they are to do. When Mrs. Washington first introduced clusters, she read a book aloud and together as a class they developed a cluster; now she is pleased to note that the children are working confidently in small groups. One group's cluster of facts from Gail Gibbons' *Dinosaurs* (1987) is presented in Figure 2.

On Friday, each group shares its cluster with the class, and Mrs. Washington points out that each group has "found" many facts and written them on the clusters. She explains that next week students will be writing their own "All About Dinosaurs" books and they may want to use some of these facts in their reports. A few minutes remain in the period after the four groups have shared, so Mrs. Washington invites students to reread favorite sentences from their books in a class read-around. Even though the children are reading sentences from four different books, they are all sharing information about dinosaurs, and the read-around effectively summarizes the information children have gleaned about dinosaurs.

FIGURE 2 A Facts Cluster on *Dinosaurs* (Gibbons, 1987)

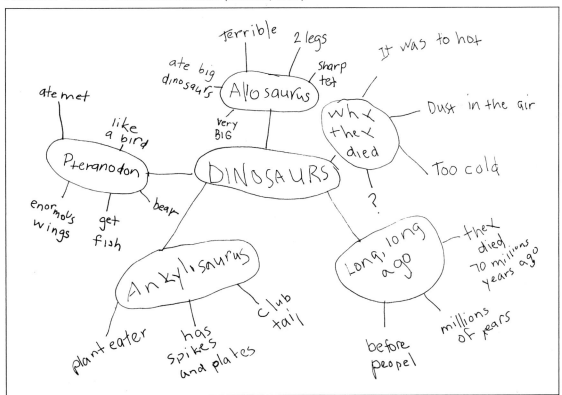

Week Two: Writing Dinosaur Books.   Students write "All About Dinosaurs" books using the writing process during the second week. On Monday, they brainstorm facts about dinosaurs together as a class. Next they decide how to construct their books: a cover, title page, four or five pages of information, and an author page. Then students collect paper for their books and then begin drawing illustrations and drafting facts. On Tuesday they continue writing and drawing. Then they meet with Mrs. Washington and several classmates in writing groups to share their rough drafts and get feedback about how to make their writing clearer and more complete. Students make at least two changes and then edit their reports to correct spelling and other mechanical errors. Then they make the final copy of their books by writing their corrected compositions on the pages with their illustrations. Students add a title page and an author page with information about themselves and a small photo. (Mrs. Washington duplicated copies of their school pictures and students glue one of these copies onto their author pages.) Then students bind their books together and begin sharing them with classmates. The few students who do not finish their books this week will finish next week, and they will also continue sharing their books during the third week.

Week Three: Reading Poems About Dinosaurs.   During the third week, Mrs. Washington shares Jack Prelutsky's book of dinosaur poems, *Tyrannosaurus Was a Beast* (1988), and students read and respond to five of the poems during the week. Mrs. Washington's procedure for sharing a poem is to copy it on a chart and use shared reading to introduce it. Then the students read the poem a second time together in unison and a third time in small groups as a choral reading.

Then they talk about any confusing parts, and she asks about "10-dollar words." Earlier in the year, Mrs. Washington explained that poets use lots of 10-dollar or expensive words. These words that might be hard to pronounce or might sound strange but they are good words to know. She has duplicated rectangles of papers decorated to look like 10-dollar bills but with a picture of a dinosaur instead of a president in the middle. She writes the words that students find difficult on these 10-dollar bills and hangs them on a clothesline across one corner of the room. Students volunteer to illustrate or write an explanation of the word and attach it to the 10-dollar bill. These words from Prelutsky's poems were honored as 10-dollar words: *slaughtered, perpetual, immense, vacuous, inedible, miniscule, cudgel,* and *ravenous.* While these words may seem well beyond the ability of most second graders, within the context of Prelutsky's poems and Mrs. Washington's 10-dollar words concept, her students grasped their meaning and enjoyed using them. They impressed their parents with them, too.

Next, Mrs. Washington passed out copies of the dinosaur poem for the day and students read the poem with partners. Then students clapped out the rhythm of the poem, dramatized the poem, and wrote a quickwrite about the poem, telling what they liked or how the poem made them feel. David wrote this brief response after reading "Diplodocus":

> *Plodding, plodding Diplodocus.*
> *Plodding, plodding David.*
> *When I have too much*

FIGURE 3   A Three-Week Lesson Plan on Dinosaurs

	MONDAY	TUESDAY	WEDNESDAY	THURSDAY	FRIDAY
WEEK 1	• Book talk to introduce *If the Dinosaurs Came Back, Dinosaurs, Dinosaur Time,* and *Dinosaur Are Different* • Choose books • Get into groups • Preview books	• Read books in small groups • Remind students to read for enjoyment • Quickwrite • Discuss book • Add words to Dinosaur Word Wall	• Read books with partners • Purpose is to gather facts for cluster • Make one cluster in each group (cluster diagram with "Title")	• Finish clusters • If time, bring class together and share clusters	• Share clusters • Point out facts that students might use in dinosaur books they will write next week • Have a read-around if time
WEEK 2	• Brainstorm facts and topics for "All About Dinosaurs" books • Discuss book covers, title page, 4 – 5 pages, and author page • Begin drawing and drafting	• Continue drafting • As students get ready, begin writing groups to share writing and give feedback • Remind students to make two changes	• Continue writing groups and revising • Begin editing to correct spelling and other errors	• Continue revising and editing	• Continue editing • Make final copies • Bind books • Begin sharing finished books
WEEK 3	• Share *Tyrannosaurus Was a Beast* • Read "Tyrannosaurus" • Identify $10 words • Other activities • Share students' dinosaur books	• Read "Anklyosaurus" • Identify $10 words • Quickwrite • Other activities	• Read "Diplodocus"	• Read "Brachiosaurus"	• Read "Allosaurus"

> *to carry home from school*
> *I go plodding, plodding, plodding.*

Not only did David connect the poem to his own life, but he also used repetition much like Jack Prelutsky did in his poem.

Students also spend 20 minutes each day sharing their "All About Dinosaurs" books with the class. After children read and show their illustrations, the class clapped and offered compliments.

MRS. WASHINGTON'S THREE-WEEK LESSON PLAN ON DINOSAURS

The lesson plan presented in Figure 3 shows the activities Mrs. Washington has planned to connect language arts with the theme cycle on dinosaurs for three weeks. During the first week, students read informational books on dinosaurs, in the second week they write their own informational books that Mrs. Washington calls "All About Dinosaurs" books, and in the third week they read dinosaur poems.

MRS. WASHINGTON'S RECORD-KEEPING AND ASSESSMENT PROCEDURES

Mrs. Washington reads her children's personal journal entries and analyzes them for signs of writing growth, and she keeps track of their independent reading by reviewing

FIGURE 4   Checklist for Language Arts Activities Related to the Dinosaur Theme Cycle

Name: _____

Week 1: Read a dinosaur book.

_____ Read the book.
_____ Quickwrite about the book.
_____ Talk about the book.
_____ Help make a cluster.
_____ Be a good group member.

Week 2: Write a dinosaur book.

_____ Draw pictures.
_____ Write a rough draft.
_____ Meet in a writing group.
_____ Make two changes.
_____ Edit.
_____ Make a final copy.
_____ Add a title page.
_____ Add an author page.

Week 3: Read dinosaur poems.

_____ Read five poems.
_____ Quickwrite about the poems.
_____ Illustrate a $10 word.

the lists of books they have read. For the one-hour of activities related to the dinosaur theme cycle, Mrs. Washington has her students mark a checklist of activities over the three-week theme cycle. At the end of the cycle, Mrs. Washington reviews the checklists and students' other written work. A copy of Mrs. Washington's checklist for the dinosaur theme cycle is presented in Figure 4.

CHILDREN'S LITERATURE REFERENCES

Aliki. (1985). *Dinosaurs are different.* New York: Harper & Row.

Gibbons, G. (1987). *Dinosaurs.* New York: Holiday House.

Most, B. (1978). *If the dinosaurs came back.* San Diego: Harcourt Brace Jovanovich.

Parish, P. (1974). *Dinosaur time.* New York: Harper & Row.

Prelutsky, J. (1988). *Tyrannosaurus was a beast.* New York: Greenwillow.

GRADE 3 ACTION PLAN

MRS. MOREHOUSE'S CLASS LEARNS "WE ARE ALL PILGRIMS"

MRS. MOREHOUSE TEACHES third grade at Shaffer School, and many of the children in her class have recently emigrated to America from Poland, Portugal, Japan, Mexico, Cambodia, the Philippines, and Puerto Rico. Other students trace their roots more distantly to Italy, England, and Ireland. One of her core literature selections is *How Many Days to America? A Thanksgiving Story* (Bunting, 1988), a story of modern-day refugees who embark on a dangerous boat trip to America to escape political persecution in their country. Mrs. Morehouse explains, "My students really relate to this story because they, too, have escaped to America. *How Many Days to America?* is a special book even for those who have been here a long time like I have."

Mrs. Morehouse uses core literature selections as the basis for her literacy block, and she usually connects the core books with a social studies or science theme cycle. During the two-week theme cycle on pilgrims, students will read about the pilgrims of 1620 and modern-day pilgrims. Mrs. Morehouse has a half of a class set (16 copies) of the core book. She also reads aloud *Molly's Pilgrim* (Cohen, 1983), the story of Molly's Jewish mother who helps her make a Pilgrim doll for a Thanksgiving display at school and dresses the doll as she dressed before leaving Russia to seek religious freedom in America. Mrs. Morehouse's students ask their parents to help them make a doll showing their own heritage. Students also interview their parents to learn about their family's roots, and they share what they learn with the class.

"The reason we study pilgrims," Mrs. Morehouse explains, "is because I want my students to learn that we are all pilgrims." Mrs. Morehouse's perspective is mostly reader response. She encourages her students to read for aesthetic purposes and to connect what they are reading to their own lives.

MRS. MOREHOUSE'S LITERACY BLOCK SCHEDULE

Mrs. Morehouse teaches reading and writing for two hours each morning, and the daily schedule is:

9:00–9:30	Independent Reading
9:30–10:00	Core Literature Book

10:00–10:30	Response Activities
10:30–11:00	Read Aloud to Students

THE COMPONENTS OF MRS. MOREHOUSE'S LITERACY BLOCK

Mrs. Morehouse plans four half-hour activities in her literacy block: independent reading, core literature books, response activities, and reading aloud to students.

Independent Reading

Mrs. Morehouse's students begin the literacy block with independent reading for 20 minutes and then spend the last 10 minutes sharing books they have read with the class. Students read books from the class library, and some of Mrs. Morehouse's students usually reread books that they have read as core books with the class previously. Sometimes several students read the same book together as a group. Mrs. Morehouse sets out a special display of books related to the focus or theme being studied. She does a book talk to highlight these books, and often students will ask for a particular book as soon as she finishes introducing it.

Mrs. Morehouse has a special display of books related to pilgrims in an old sea chest. She has three or four copies of most of her books. The books related to her unit are listed in Figure 1. She presents a book talk on the first Monday and students quickly select Pilgrim-related books to read.

FIGURE 1   Books About Pilgrims in the Class Library

Bulla, C. R. (1954). *Squanto: Friend of the pilgrims.* New York: Crowell.
Bunting, E. (1988). *How many days to America? A Thanksgiving story.* New York: Clarion.
Coerr, E. (1986). *Lady with a torch.* New York: Harper & Row.
Coerr, E. (1988). *Chang's paper pony.* New York: Harper & Row.
Cohen, B. (1983). *Molly's pilgrim.* New York: Lothrop.
Dalgliesh, A. (1954). *The Thanksgiving story.* New York: Aladdin Books.
Fleming, A. (1988). *The King of Prussia and a peanut butter sandwich.* New York: Scribner.
Friedman, I. R. (1984). *How my parents learned to eat.* Boston: Houghton Mifflin.
Harvey, B. (1987). *Immigrant girl: Becky of Eldridge Street.* New York: Clarion.
Haskins, J. (1986). *The Statue of Liberty: America's proud lady.* Minneapolis: Lerner.
Hayward, L. (1990). *The first Thanksgiving.* New York: Random House.
Khalsa, D. K. (1986). *Tales of a gambling grandma.* New York: Clarkson N. Potter/Putnam.
Kroll, S. (1988). *Oh, what a Thanksgiving!* New York: Scholastic.
Levinson, R. (1985). *Watch the stars come out.* New York: Dutton.
McGovern, A. (1969). *. . . If you sailed on the Mayflower in 1620.* New York: Scholastic.
Polacco, P. (1988). *The keeping quilt.* New York: Simon & Schuster.
Sandin, J. (1981). *The long way to a new land.* New York: Harper & Row.
San Souci, R. (1991). *N. C. Wyeth's pilgrims.* San Francisco: Chronicle Books.
Surat, M. M. (1983). *Angel child, dragon child.* Milwaukee: Raintree.
Tran-Khanh-Tuyet. (1987). *The little weaver of Thai-Yen village.* San Francisco: Children's Book Press.
Waters, K. (1989). *Sarah Morton's day: A day in the life of a pilgrim girl.* New York: Scholastic.

As students read for 20 minutes, Mrs. Morehouse walks around the room briefly to make sure students are on task. Then, because she knows that what you do sends a more powerful message to children than what you say, she sits down and reads a book on pilgrims herself.

Students spend the last 10 minutes of the independent reading period sharing books they have read with classmates. Mrs. Morehouse expects that each student will share a book every two or three weeks.

Core Literature

Mrs. Morehouse uses two approaches for reading core literature books. One is the whole-class approach in which all of the students in the class read a core literature book together, and the second approach is study groups in which students read a core book in small groups. Usually each heterogeneous group is reading a different book related to the same theme.

Whole-Class Approach.   In this approach, the whole class reads the same book. In each theme cycle or focus unit, Mrs. Morehouse selects a core book, and she has enough copies of the book for each student or for every two students. Typically, she reads the book aloud as students follow along in their own copies. If it is a picture book, students reread it with buddies and retell it with story boards. They also quick-write about the book and participate in grand conversations.

In the theme cycle on Pilgrims, Mrs. Morehouse's students read *How Many Days to America?* together as a class during the first of the two weeks. After reading, they reread the book with partners, explore their understanding in a quickwrite, and talk about the book in a grand conversation.

Study Groups Approach.   In the second approach, Mrs. Morehouse has sets of several different books related to the theme. She introduces each book through a book talk, and students sign up for the book they want to read. Students spend the second of two weeks reading and responding to the book in small groups that Mrs. Morehouse calls "lit groups." At the end of the week, each group shares its book with the entire class. The four books that Mrs. Morehouse has chosen about pilgrims are

1. *The Long Way to a New Land* (Sandin, 1981), an easy-to-read book about Carl Erik and his family who leave Sweden in 1868 for a new chance in America.
2. *Sarah Morton's Day: A Day in the Life of a Pilgrim Girl* (Waters, 1989), a realistic account of a pilgrim's daily activities on November 12, 1627. It is illustrated with photos taken at Plimouth Plantation.
3. *. . . If You Sailed on the Mayflower in 1620* (McGovern, 1969), a collection of 48 questions and answers about the Pilgrims' famous voyage.
4. *Chang's Paper Pony* (Coerr, 1988), an easy-to-read chapter book about Chinese immigrants, Chang and his grandfather, who prepare food at a California mining camp during the Gold Rush.

Response Activities

After students read the core literature selection, they pursue response activities and projects. Sometimes students work in small groups or individually to complete self-selected activities. At other times, the whole class is involved in the same activity. In the theme cycle on pilgrims, students are involved in response activities related to the pilgrim books they read.

After reading *How Many Days to America?* students pretend that it was their family who escaped to America and write simulated letters to Uncle to tell him about the journey. Students use the writing process to draft, revise, and edit their letters. This is David's letter to Uncle:

> *Dear Uncle,*
>
>   *My journey to America was awful. This is how it went. The soldier came to our house. We had to leave by boat. By then when we were on the boat our motor died. We had to use clothes for sails. We didn't have any food or water. Then it was just like our motor died again. The sails stopped. It was going a little bit. Then it stopped again. A whale went by our boat. My mom told the whale to push us but my mom can't communicate with a whale. Then we got robbed by robbers. Then we found land. My dad jumped out with some others. My mom said, "Don't." The soldiers gave us fruit and then we were off. We clapped for joy when we saw AMERICA! The people in America clapped when they saw us. We had THANKSGIVING dinner here and my sister said, "Can we stay?" and my dad said, "Yes, we can stay."*

Mrs. Morehouse has a large Hmong story quilt hanging in the classroom, and students decide to make their own story quilts to tell about the family's trip to America. Students use construction paper and pens rather than fabric in their small quilts. Even so, the students' quilts tell a story. One student's story quilt is shown in Figure 2.

After reading *Molly's Pilgrim,* students make dolls with their parents like Molly and her mother made. Students also research their own "pilgrim" stories and interview their parents about how they came to America. Mrs. Morehouse also shows students the film version of *Molly's Pilgrim* and as a class they make a Venn diagram to compare the book and film.

In their literature study groups, students respond to the books they are reading through quickwrites and grand conversations. They also plan a way to briefly share the book with the class. Students might make a mural or a chart, perform a skit, do an interpretive reading, or write a poem to share.

Reading Aloud to Students

During the last 30 minutes of the literacy block, Mrs. Morehouse reads aloud to her students. She usually reads a book related to the theme cycle, and as she reads the book she tape-records it and places it in the listening center so that students can

FIGURE 2   A Student's Story Quilt for *How Many Days to America?* (Bunting, 1988)

reread the book later. During the two-week theme cycle on pilgrims, Mrs. Morehouse reads both fiction and nonfiction books about pilgrims.

MRS. MOREHOUSE'S TWO-WEEK LESSON PLAN

Mrs. Morehouse's lesson plan for the literacy block during the two-week theme cycle on pilgrims is presented in Figure 3. The four components—independent reading, core literature, response activities, and reading aloud—are included for each week. Mrs. Morehouse uses a KWL Chart to introduce the theme cycle and during the unit students continue to add to the chart, listing additional questions to the "Want to Know" section and information to the "What We Learned" section. On the last day of the theme cycle, students finish the KWL chart and reflect on what they have learned during the theme cycle.

FIGURE 3 Two-Week Lesson Plan for Theme Cycle on Pilgrims

	MONDAY	TUESDAY	WEDNESDAY	THURSDAY	FRIDAY
9:00 – 9:30 *Independent Reading*	• Introduce theme • Start word wall • KWL chart on pilgrims	• Students read self-selected books • 9:20 — Students share	→		↑ ↑
9:30 – 10:00 *Core Literature*	• Read aloud *The Thanksgiving Story* and *How Many Days to America*	• Buddy-read *How Many Days to America?* • Quickwrite	• Retell *HMDTA* with story boards • Discuss illustrations	• Introduce Hmong story quilts • Make quilts about *HMDTA*	• Finish quilts • Read-around
10:00 – 10:30 *Response Activities*	• Grand conversation about pilgrims	• Plan project to research own roots • Questions • Sharing	• Write simulated letters to Uncle	• Share and revise letters	• Edit letters • Final copies
10:30 – 11:00 *Read Aloud*	• Book talk to introduce sea chest of pilgrim books	• Read *Molly's Pilgrim* • Quickwrite • Grand conversation	• Trace pilgrims' journey to America • Students share own stories →	• Venn diagram HMDTA Molly — me	• Share diagrams • Write class letter to parents about making dolls ↑

FIGURE 3 *Continued*

	MONDAY	TUESDAY	WEDNESDAY	THURSDAY	FRIDAY
9:00 – 9:30 *Independent Reading*	• Students read self-selected books • 9:20 — Share	→			→
9:30 – 10:00 *Core Literature*	• Book talk on four books • Divide into lit groups	• Lit groups 1. *Sarah Morton's Day* 2. *The Long Way to a New Land* 3. *If You Sailed on the Mayflower* 4. *Chang's Paper Pony*	→		• Read • Quickwrite • Discuss • Project to share w/ class
10:00 – 10:30 *Response Activities*	• Design pilgrim display • Begin sharing dolls	• Continue with display • Continue sharing dolls	→	• View film of *Molly's Pilgrim* →	• Share projects • Finish KWL chart
10:30 – 11:00 *Read Aloud*	• Read *The Keeping Quilt* • Quickwrite • Discuss	• Read *The Statue of Liberty* • Quickwrite • Discuss	• Read *The King of Prussia and a Peanut Butter Sandwich* • Quickwrite • Discuss	• Quickwrite • Make Venn diagram to compare book and film	• Evaluation quickwrite

FIGURE 4   Assessment Checklist for Theme Cycle on Pilgrims

Name: _____   Date: _____

1. Independent Reading
   • One book on pilgrims   _____
   • Any other book   _____
2. Reading Log
   • KWL chart   _____
   • *How Many Days to America?* QW   _____
   • *Molly's Pilgrim* QW   _____
   • Venn diagram   _____
   • Compare book and movie   _____
   • Self-evaluation QW   _____
3. Lit Group
   • Read a book   _____
   • Write in log   _____
   • Talk about the book   _____
   • Share with class   _____
4. Response Projects
   • Letter to Uncle   _____
   • Story quilt   _____
   • Interview parents   _____
   • Doll   _____

QW = quickwrite

MRS. MOREHOUSE'S RECORD-KEEPING AND ASSESSMENT PROCEDURES

Mrs. Morehouse uses checklists to keep track of the reading and response activities her students are involved in. At the beginning of the theme cycle, she passes out the checklist, and students mark items when they complete them. This checklist is divided into four categories: (a) independent reading, (b) reading log, (c) lit group, and (d) response projects. A copy of Mrs. Morehouse's checklist is presented in Figure 4. (This checklist contains only the literacy activities; students have a second checklist with the social studies, science, and other across the curriculum activities.)

Mrs. Morehouse's students keep the checklists and other reading and writing materials in theme cycle folders. They also keep their reading logs (20 pages stapled together) and the book they are reading independently in the folder. "This system works well for me," Mrs. Morehouse says, "because my students have all their reading and writing materials organized and together in one place." Her students rarely lose quickwrites or other papers because they are in the reading log.

In addition to the checklists, Mrs. Morehouse has each student write an evaluation of the theme cycle. In their quickwrites, Mrs. Morehouse asks students to reflect on what they have learned, what they enjoyed, and how they have worked. In a notebook she also keeps anecdotal information about her observations of students as they read and respond to literature.

CHILDREN'S LITERATURE REFERENCES

Bunting, E. (1988). *How many days to America? A Thanksgiving story.* New York: Clarion.

Coerr, E. (1988). *Chang's paper pony.* New York: Harper & Row.

Cohen, B. (1983). *Molly's pilgrim.* New York: Lothrop.

McGovern, A. (1969). *. . . If you sailed on the Mayflower in 1620.* New York: Scholastic.

Sandin, J. (1981). *The long way to a new land.* New York: Harper & Row.

Waters, K. (1989). *Sarah Morton's day: A day in the life of a pilgrim girl.* New York: Scholastic.

GRADE 4 ACTION PLAN

FOCUS UNIT ON THE SIGN OF THE BEAVER

CAROL OCHS, A FOURTH GRADE TEACHER at Jackson Elementary School, alternates reading workshop with core literature units that focus on one book or a collection of short stories. In this action plan, we describe how Mrs. Ochs teaches a four-week core literature unit on one of her favorite chapter books, Elizabeth George Speare's award-winning *The Sign of the Beaver* (1983), a wilderness survival story set in 1768. In the story, 12-year-old Matt spends the summer in the family's new cabin in the Maine wilderness while his father returns to Massachusetts to bring the rest of the family north to their new home. While his father is away, Matt tries bravely to survive on his own and is befriended by an Indian chief and his grandson, Attean. Matt expects his family to arrive in August, but when Matt's family doesn't arrive by fall, the Indians invite him to join the Beaver tribe and move north with them. Matt decides to continue waiting for his family and at long last they finally arrive—but not until after the first snows of winter. Mrs. Ochs says, "I like this story so much because Matt is making the same kinds of difficult decisions about what is important in his life that my 10- and 11-year-olds are making about their own lives."

Mrs. Ochs begins planning the core literature unit by selecting the book and reading it two or three times if she can make time to do so. She thinks about her goals for the unit, the activities she would like to include, and related materials to use in teaching the unit. Then she brainstorms activities on a cluster, as shown in Figure 1. She includes more activities and materials than she will be able to use in the four-week unit on the cluster; however, she likes using the cluster to plan a unit because it provides options from which she can choose.

Another decision that Mrs. Ochs makes is about the perspective from which she will teach this unit. She decides to use primarily a critical perspective, but she will select activities from the other perspectives that highlight and focus on character development in her literature study, as shown in the cluster. Some of the literature study activities that she considers using include writing simulated literature journals (which she calls diaries) from Matt or Attean's viewpoints, sorting vocabulary words according to character, drawing portraits of characters, dramatizing scenes from the story according to the characters' viewpoints, developing character maps, writing poems about the characters, making a list of opposites at the beginning and again

FIGURE 1   Cluster for a Unit on *The Sign of the Beaver* (Speare, 1983)

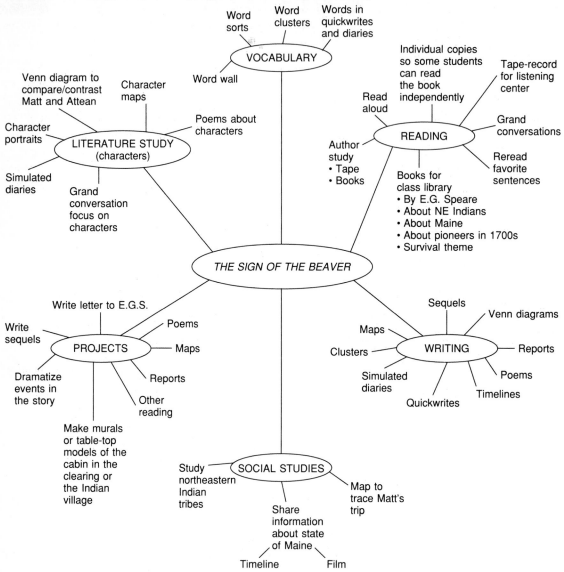

at the end of the story, making a Venn diagram to compare and contrast the characters, and writing a sequel from one viewpoint or another.

    After considering her possibilities, Mrs. Ochs develops lesson plans for the four
weeks she has allotted to the unit. She plans to read *The Sign of the Beaver* aloud
while students follow in their own copies of the book. She will have a word wall to list
vocabulary words from each chapter, and she'll use the vocabulary in various activities. Students will write simulated diary entries from Matt or Attean's viewpoint and
participate in grand conversations after reading each chapter. They do this because

Mrs. Ochs believes that students should have the opportunity to express their understanding about the book before she teaches character development. She'll also plan literature study activities on character development and allow time for projects at the end of the unit.

MRS. OCHS' DAILY SCHEDULE

Mrs. Ochs fits core literature activities into a two-and-one-half hour language arts block time frame. This is the schedule:

8:45–9:05	Students Read Self-Selected Books Related to the Focus Unit or Theme
9:05–9:15	Students Share Simulated Diary Entries
9:15–9:45	Teacher Reads *The Sign of the Beaver* Aloud, Chapter by Chapter, as Students Follow in Their Books
9:45–10:00	Students Participate in a Grand Conversation
10:00–10:15	Students Write Simulated Diary Entries
10:15–10:30	Break
10:30–11:10	Students Participate in Activities (Vocabulary, Literature Study, Projects)
11:10–11:15	Students Reread Favorite Sentences

COMPONENTS OF THE FOCUS UNIT

The components of the focus unit are independent reading, reading the core book, grand conversations, simulated diaries, vocabulary activities, literature study, projects, and rereading. The literature study is a particularly important component because it is designed to help students acquire a more critical awareness of character. Mrs. Ochs uses activities from the other two perspectives to complement the critical perspective in her teaching.

Independent Reading

Mrs. Ochs has put together a text set of picture books, chapter books, and informational books about the New England colonies, Maine, American Indians, stories with a theme of courage, and other books written by Elizabeth George Speare. These books are related to *The Sign of the Beaver,* and they are set out on a special shelf in the library center. At the beginning of the unit, students select a book from this shelf or another book related to the core book to read independently during this period. Toward the end of the unit, students will share their books during this period.

Shared Reading with Students

Mrs. Ochs has a class set of *The Sign of the Beaver,* and she reads the book aloud, chapter by chapter, while students follow in their individual copies. Mrs. Ochs explains why she reads the book aloud, "The reading level of the book is too difficult for some of my students. By reading the book aloud, I make it accessible to everyone. I encourage those students who can read the book independently to move into a quiet corner of the classroom to read silently at their own pace." Mrs. Ochs also tape-records her reading of each chapter and places the cassette tapes in the listening center so that students can "reread" the chapter or so that children who are absent can catch up.

Grand Conversations

After Mrs. Ochs finishes reading the one or two chapters for that day, the students move their chairs into a large circle for the grand conversation. During this 15-minute discussion, students first share their comments, opinions, and questions about the story. Mrs. Ochs asks that each student make at least one comment and no one may offer more than three comments until everyone has participated. Then she asks one or two questions to direct the discussion during the last few minutes to focus students' attention on the character development in the story.

Writing in Simulated Diaries

After reading each chapter, students take 15 minutes to write simulated diary entries, written either from Matt or Attean's viewpoints. Here is one child's simulated diary entry, written from Matt's point of view:

> Dear Diary,
>
> Yesterday Attean left. He brought me some presents though. His grandmother gave me some molasses and a pair of snowshoes. They looked great. Attean gave me his dog. I thought I ought to give him something, so I went inside and got my watch. "Here," I said to Attean and gave him the watch. I showed him how to wind it. Then we said goodbye, and he left.
>
> Today nothing much has happened yet. I might go hunting. The dog that Attean gave to me is a good companion. He may be scruffy, but he is a nice dog. I hope Pa gets home soon because the lake has started to freeze and food will be scarce. I set some snares and a deadfall. Tomorrow I plan to go fishing.

To begin each morning's reading activities, students share the simulated diary entries they wrote the previous day. First they share in small groups and then one student is selected from each group to share with the class. Mrs. Ochs starts with this activity because she has found it to be a good way to review the chapter read the previous day and get students ready for today's reading.

Activity Time

In the activity time, Mrs. Ochs includes three types of activities. At the beginning of the unit, the focus is on vocabulary, then on literature study activities, and during the last week of the unit, students work on projects to extend their reading.

Vocabulary Activities.   Mrs. Ochs hangs a large sheet of butcher paper on a wall of the classroom for a word wall. As she reads each chapter, Mrs. Ochs and her students write new and unusual words on the word wall. She tries to use different colored marking pens for each chapter to keep track of the words. For chapter one, they added these words and phrases: *reckoned, ashamed, spruce trees, haul, notch, snugly, splints, silence coiled around Matt, high time, Penobscot River, Quincy, Massachusetts, loft, puncheon table, daubed, chink in the log wall, battered, compass, you aim to leave it, aye, yourn, mite, powder horn, matchlock, ruefully,* and *johnnycake.*

Later they will use some of these words for vocabulary activities, such as word clusters, word sorts, and labels for murals and models. Students are also encouraged to use these new words in their simulated diary entries and the grand conversations. Mrs. Ochs also takes words from the word wall and weaves them into her conversation. Before long her students are listening intently, waiting to catch her use one of the word wall words.

Literature Study Activities

Mrs. Ochs and her students explore characters through a variety of activities. She begins the character study when she asks students to keep a simulated diary as though they were Matt or Attean. Other activities include a word sort in which students sort words from the word wall according to specific characters in the book, and making a list of opposites related to characters at the beginning of the book and again at the end. Students will draw portraits of the characters and work in groups to make a character cluster. As a final activity, students will make a Venn diagram to compare and contrast Matt and Attean, and one student's Venn diagram is presented in Figure 2.

Projects

Mrs. Ochs and the students use the activity time during the last week of the unit to work on projects. Most of the students will decide to write sequels to the story, but a few choose other activities, such as researching Northeastern Indian tribes, preparing and presenting a dramatization of the story, or writing a letter to Elizabeth George Speare.

Class Read-Around

Mrs. Ochs spends the last five minutes having students reread favorite sentences from the chapter read earlier that morning. She explains, "Rereading is a great way to settle students down and end our language arts block." As students finish the activities, they return to their seats and skim through the chapter looking for a sentence special enough to share. (Some students use a pencil to mark a favorite sentence during the first reading so that they are ready to reread.) As soon as most of the class is ready, students begin taking turns rereading favorite sentences aloud. There is no set order for the rereading; rather, one student begins reading and after that student ends, there is a brief pause, and then another student reads. It is not necessary

FIGURE 2   A Fourth Grader's Venn Diagram to Compare Matt and Attean

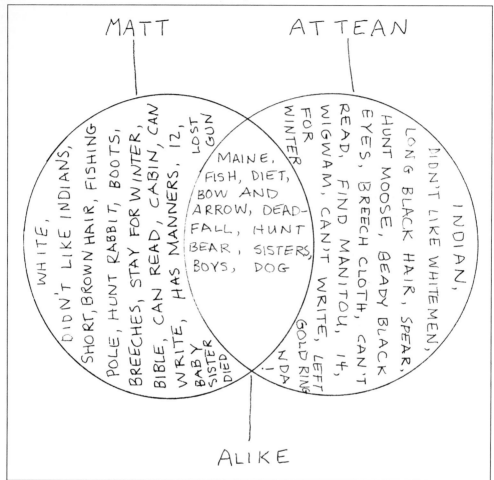

to call on students; they simply take turns and whenever there is a pause someone begins. Not every student shares every day but Mrs. Ochs asks that everyone share at least once every week. These sentences are not read in any particular order, but as students read back and forth through the chapter, they effectively review it.

MRS. OCHS' LESSON PLAN FOR ONE WEEK

A one-week lesson plan for Mrs. Ochs' focus unit on *The Sign of the Beaver* is presented in Figure 3. This lesson plan is for the third week of the four-week unit. Each of the components for Mrs. Ochs' language arts block is listed, and then particular activities for this week are detailed. The students begin the language arts block each day with independent reading of self-selected books related to the core literature

FIGURE 3 A One-Week Lesson Plan from a Focus Unit on *The Sign of the Beaver* (Speare, 1983)

	MONDAY	TUESDAY	WEDNESDAY	THURSDAY	FRIDAY
8:45 – 9:05	Independent reading of self-selected books from text set				
9:05 – 9:15	Students shared the simulated journal entries they wrote yesterday. Share in small groups. Then one student from each group shares w/ class.				
9:15 – 9:45 *Reading Core Book*	Chs. 17 – 18 *The Sign of the Beaver* 1. Read aloud while students follow in their books 2. Add words to word wall 3. Have students reread silently, if time allows * DON'T FORGET TO TAPE-RECORD EACH CHAPTER!!!	Chs. 19 – 20	Chs. 21 – 22	Chs. 23 – 24	Ch. 25
9:45 – 10:00	Grand conversations —————————————————————————————————→				
10:00 – 10:15	Students write in simulated journals —————————————————→				
10:15 – 10:30	BREAK				
10:30 – 11:00 *Activities* This week literature study on characters	• Talk about characters • Main and supporting characters • Four ways authors reveal characters: appearance, action, dialogue, and monologue • Quickwrite about favorite character	• Share quickwrites • Choose five words from word wall about favorite character • Divide into groups according to favorite character • Plan and rehearse skits	• Rehearse skits • Perform • In small groups, make character cluster • Prepare word sort	• Have students sort words according to character • Share word sorts and character clusters	• Venn diagram to compare Matt and Attean • Begin essay to compare/contrast characters • Review form for essay
11:00 – 11:15 *Read-Around*	Students reread favorite sentences from chapters read that day				

selection. Then in small groups they share the simulated journal entries they wrote the previous day, and one student from each group shares with the class. Then Mrs. Ochs reads aloud one or two chapters from *The Sign of the Beaver* while the students follow along in their books. On Friday of week three the class finishes reading the story. (During week four they will be involved in response activities.) After reading, students participate in a grand conversation and write in their simulated journals.

After the break, students participate in activities that focus on characters during this week. On Monday, Mrs. Ochs introduces characters and shares information about how authors reveal characters. (See Chapter 2 for more information about characters.) During the week, students write about their favorite character, dramatize a scene from the story featuring a favorite character, make character clusters, do a word sort according to characters, and make a Venn diagram to compare and contrast two main characters. Students end the language arts block each day by rereading favorite sentences from the chapters read that day.

MRS. OCHS' RECORD-KEEPING AND ASSESSMENT PROCEDURES

Mrs. Ochs develops a checklist with all the assignments students are to complete and gives copies of it to students when they begin the unit. A copy of her assessment checklist for *The Sign of the Beaver* is presented in Figure 4. Students keep the checklist inside their reading folders and mark off each assignment as they complete it in the column of boxes marked "Student's Check."

FIGURE 4   Assessment Checklist for *The Sign of the Beaver* Unit

Name: _____   Date: _____

Student's Check	Teacher's Check	
_____	_____	1. Read *The Sign of the Beaver*.
_____	_____	2. Make a map of Matt's journey in 1768. (10)
_____	_____	3. Keep a simulated diary for Matt or Attean. (20)
_____	_____	4. Do a word sort by characters. (5)
_____	_____	5. Listen to Elizabeth George Speare's taped interview and do a quickwrite about her. (5)
_____	_____	6. Draw a portrait of one of the characters. (5)
_____	_____	7. Make a character map of one of the characters. (5)
_____	_____	8. Make a Venn diagram to compare/contrast Matt or Attean to yourself. (10)
_____	_____	9. Contribute to a model or mural of the Indian village or the clearing. (15)
_____	_____	10. Write a sequel to *The Sign of the Beaver* or do another project. (20)
_____	_____	11. Write a self-assessment about your work, behavior, and effort in this unit. (5)

At the end of the unit, students turn in all written assignments in their reading folder with the assessment checklist on top. Students have already marked the check-list and written the self-assessment so they have a good idea of how well they have done in this unit. Mrs. Ochs has found that students assume more responsibility for their own work and her grading is simplified. Teachers can grade each item using their own grading scale or they can assign points to each item (as shown in Figure 4). Then teachers award the points in the column marked "Teacher's Check" and total the points for a unit grade. Mrs. Ochs tries to have the total number of points equal 100 to simplify grading.

CHILDREN'S LITERATURE REFERENCES

Speare, E. G. (1983). *The sign of the beaver.*
    Boston: Houghton Mifflin.

TUESDAY IS POETRY WORKSHOP DAY

AT WILSON ELEMENTARY SCHOOL, fifth grade teacher Ms. Cochran is known as the poetry lady. Because she enjoys poetry and wants her students to overcome their fear of it, Ms. Cochran's students spend the first two weeks of the school year immersed in reading and writing poetry. She says, "Most poems are short visual images or word plays, and after our two-week initiation, my students find themselves as bewitched by poetry as I am." Ms. Cochran's students continue their focus on reading and writing poetry every Tuesday morning. Tuesday is the "short" day at Wilson Elementary School, when students leave one hour early so that teachers can have meetings. To further complicate matters, Ms. Cochran has several schedule changes that day including a trip to the school library for students to check out books and to a first grade classroom for buddy-reading. Because of the weekly disruptions, Ms. Cochran and her students have decided to make Tuesday special—Poetry Workshop Day.

Ms. Cochran's classroom library is housed in plastic crates that ring the wall of the classroom. Each crate has a label—folktales, life cycle books, California books, Roald Dahl books, biographies, and so on. On one side of the room, seven crates are filled with books of poetry. Posters of favorite poems decorate the wall above the book crates. A six-foot tall (dead) tree stands near the poetry books. This is the class poetree (Hopkins, 1987), and students hang copies of favorite poems and small response projects on the tree's branches. Ms. Cochran also has a notebook with pictures and biographical information about Shel Silverstein, Jack Prelutsky, Bryd Baylor, Eve Merriam, and other poets.

Ms. Cochran introduces her students to poetry during the first two weeks of the school year. On the first day of school, she begins by reading aloud the first chapter of *Anastasia Krupnik* (Lowry, 1979) and talking about poetry. The students make a list of rules about poetry and hang it in their classroom (Tompkins & Hoskisson, 1991). Each day her students read poems and share them with the class. She shares strategies for writing poems and introduces students to several simple formulas so that they will feel instant success as they write poems. Several days later she brings in a piece of fruit for each child and invites them to "bite in and enjoy the taste." Then she shares Eve Merriam's "How to Eat A Poem" (Dunning, Lueders, & Smith, 1966) in which the poet compares reading a poem to eating a piece of fruit, and they continue discussing poetry. Students talk about many concerns: how to choose poems, what to do when they don't understand a poem, why poems are arranged on the page as they are, how to choose words and images for poems they are writing, and so on.

THE TUESDAY POETRY WORKSHOP SCHEDULE

After the two-week focus unit on poetry, Judy plans for poetry workshop every Tuesday morning. The morning schedule is broken into two sections by the weekly library visit; the first half of the workshop focuses on reading poetry and the second half on writing poetry. Ms. Cochran's schedule is

8:30–9:00	Students Read Poems Independently
9:00–9:30	Students Share Poems They Have Read with Buddies or in Small Groups
9:30–9:45	Teacher Leads a Minilesson Called "A Closer Look" on Reading Poetry
9:45–10:15	Weekly Trip to Library to Check Out Books
10:15–10:30	Teacher Leads a Second Minilesson Called "The Poet's Craft" on Writing Poetry
10:30–11:00	Students Write Poems or Responses to Poems They Have Read
11:00–11:15	Students Share Their Writing with Classmates
11:15–11:30	Students Complete "Poetry Workshop Evaluations"

COMPONENTS OF THE TUESDAY POETRY WORKSHOP

The Tuesday Poetry Workshop includes students reading poetry, teacher-directed minilessons, students writing poetry, two sharing sessions, and an evaluation component.

Reading Poems Independently

Ms. Cochran's students choose books of poetry from the classroom collection to read or they read library books or books of poetry that they bring from home or have checked out from the public library. Independent reading of poems lasts for 30 minutes, and as they read, students often stick small tabs on pages to mark favorite poems to share with classmates later. Some students have favorite poets and always want to read a particular poet. Jack Prelutsky is the students' favorite; he visited the school two years ago and hasn't been forgotten. Ms. Cochran expects that her students will read at least five poems during the independent reading period and select at least two poems to share with classmates.

The mood in the classroom is different when students are reading poetry, compared to when they are reading stories and informational books. Students are mumbling as they read the poems to themselves, moving their bodies to the rhythm of the poems, and giggling in response to a humorous poem. Students also turn to classmates for help in pronouncing or understanding an unfamiliar word or phrase.

During independent reading time, Ms. Cochran circulates around the classroom, conferencing briefly with students about their reading. She uses a set of pink index cards to take notes about each student. She says, "I use pink cards for Poetry Workshop because *P* is for pink and for poetry. It's a great mnemonic device!" She takes notes about which poems and poets students are reading, their comments about their choices and interests, their developing concepts of poetry and their increasing use of poetic terminology.

Sharing Poems with Classmates

For the second 30 minutes of the Tuesday Poetry Workshop, students share favorite poems they have read with partners or in small groups. (About once every six or eight weeks, students get into a big circle and share interesting poems with the whole class to develop a strong sense of a shared community of readers.) Ms. Cochran believes in the power of sharing. She says, "Sharing is one of the most important activities in our Tuesday Poetry Workshop. Most poems aren't meant to be read silently. When students read to each other the poems they have read come to life and my students become poets."

Teaching "A Closer Look" Minilesson

Ms. Cochran takes 15 minutes to teach "A Closer Look" minilesson that focuses on reading poetry. She explains, "My students complained that some poems were hard to understand so they gave me the idea for 'A Closer Look.' In this minilesson, we share poems and talk about them." Students nominate "confusing" poems or "poems too good to miss" or poems that illustrate something they've talked about in a previous minilesson for Ms. Cochran to use in the minilesson. They suggest these poems anytime during the week, and especially while they are reading and sharing poems on Tuesday morning. Then Ms. Cochran chooses several poems and while students are sharing, she quickly duplicates copies of the poems for each student and makes transparencies to use on the overhead projector.

During the minilesson, Ms. Cochran distributes copies of one of the poems, reads it aloud once or twice, and the student who nominated it talks about the poem, offering comments and questions. Other students share their opinions and insights and usually the student's confusion is resolved. When necessary Ms. Cochran clarifies a point. The class repeats the procedure for each poem and spends about five minutes on each one.

During the school year, Ms. Cochran plans to focus on the following topics through the "A Closer Look" minilessons: rhyme, repetition, alliteration, onomatopoeia, imagery, comparisons, symbols, and wordplay. For each of these concepts, she shares poems that illustrate the concept, introduces the concept and term, and invites students to find other poems that illustrate the poetic device or technique. She also uses this minilesson to share information about poets and to introduce new books of poetry that she will place in the class library.

Teaching "The Poet's Craft" Minilesson

Ms. Cochran leads a second 15-minute minilesson that focuses on writing poetry called "The Poet's Craft." She introduces poetic forms and formulas that students can use in writing poetry such as lies poems, color poems, "If I were" poems, apology poems (Koch, 1970, 1973) as well as haikus, acrostics, limericks, and free verse. She also talks about how to arrange poems on a page, how to unwrite and take out unnecessary words, and how to use capital letters and punctuation marks in poems.

For each minilesson, Ms. Cochran shares some poems that illustrate the strategy she wants to teach, explains the strategy, and then her class writes or revises a poem together to practice the strategy. Her students keep poetry notebooks, and Ms. Cochran asks them to take notes about the strategy she has taught at the end of the minilesson.

When students move into the next component of poetry workshop, writing poems, Ms. Cochran encourages them to experiment with the strategy she has taught in the minilesson, and many do, but they don't have to.

Writing Poems or Responses to Poems

Students spend 30 minutes writing poems or responses to poems they read earlier in the morning. Many students will continue to write, using the ideas Ms. Cochran shared in the "The Poet's Craft" minilesson, but others will look back through their poetry notebooks for ideas shared earlier in the year or will write poems related to their interests. Sometimes, too, students will return to a poem they read during independent reading time or a poem Ms. Cochran shared in the "A Closer Look" minilesson and write about these poems.

During this writing time, students share rough drafts of poems with classmates and informally get feedback about how well they are communicating. Sometimes Ms. Cochran sits in on these brief writing group meetings, and other times she is busy working with other students. Because most of the poems that students write are short, students can share their poems and get feedback quickly.

Ms. Cochran circulates around the room during this independent writing time, observing students as they work and briefly conferencing with them. She makes additional notes on her pink poetry cards, noting what students are writing, poetic devices and other techniques they are experimenting with, and poetic terminology they are using. She also notes their interest in writing poetry, the connections they make to poems they have read, and whether they go beyond rhyme to use other poetic devices.

Sharing Writing with Classmates

Students move their chairs into a large circle and spend 15 minutes sharing poems they have written and other responses to poems they have read. Students take turns sharing and after each student reads, classmates take turns offering several compliments, asking questions, or making suggestions. The sharing time is brief and only about a quarter of the class shares each week. Ms. Cochran expects that all students will share a poem or response to a poem at least once a month.

Completing "Poetry Workshop Evaluation" Sheets

Students spend the last 10 to 15 minutes of the Tuesday Poetry Workshop summarizing and evaluating their work during the workshop. Students write their evaluations on a form Ms. Cochran has developed which is shown in Figure 1. Ms. Cochran collects and reads these evaluation sheets and writes notes back to the students on the sheets. Then students file the sheets in the back of their poetry notebooks.

MS. COCHRAN'S LESSON PLAN FOR A TUESDAY POETRY WORKSHOP

A lesson plan for one Tuesday Poetry Workshop is presented in Figure 2. Students are reading, writing, and sharing poetry on this change-of-pace day. Ms. Cochran teaches two minilessons, one on reading poetry and one on writing poetry.

In the "A Closer Look" minilesson, Ms. Cochran shares Walter de la Mare's "Someone" (de Regniers, 1988), a two-stanza poem about sounds heard at night. Allison nominated the poem and she comments, "I liked reading this poem, but I don't think I understand it. Was it a ghost? Who is the 'someone'?" As the class talks about the poem, they talk about how many of them have heard sounds at night and that they were scared. Someone asks what *nought,* one of the words in the poem, means, and after five minutes of discussion, students decide this is a good poem to remember when they feel frightened at night and that the "someone" in the poem might be a ghost or, perhaps, just your imagination.

The second poem is Jack Prelutsky's "Louder than a Clap of Thunder!" (1984). Marty selected it and he reads it aloud with great relish. Then he explains that he chose this one because Ms. Cochran talked about comparisons last Tuesday, and he found this poem in which Prelutsky compares the noise a father makes snoring to a variety of other things. Students point out their favorite comparisons in the poem and then arrange the poem for choral reading.

The last poem Ms. Cochran shares in the minilesson is Laura Richards' "Eletelephony" (Prelutsky, 1983), a nonsense verse about an elephant that is tangled

FIGURE 1   Tuesday Poetry Workshop Evaluation Sheet

	Summary	Evaluation
Reading Poetry		
Writing Poetry		
Sharing		

FIGURE 2   Tuesday Poetry Workshop Lesson Plan

	TUESDAY
8:30 – 9:00 *Reading*	Students choose and read poems independently
9:00 – 9:30 *Sharing*	Students share poems they have read with classmates in small groups
9:30 – 9:45 *Minilesson* "A Closer Look"	1. Choose and share a "confusing" poem 2. Choose and share a favorite poem 3. Read "Eletelephony" and introduce invented words
9:45 – 10:15 *Library*	Students go to the library to check out books
10:15 – 10:30 *Minilesson* "The Poet's Craft"	1. Share odes 2. List characteristics 3. Write class poem "Ode to Raisins" ∗ Bring raisins
10:30 – 11:00 *Writing*	Students write odes, other poems, or responses to poetry
11:00 – 11:15 *Sharing*	Students share their writing with the class
11:15 – 11:30 *Evaluation*	Students complete "Poetry Workshop Evaluation" sheets

up with a telephone. She chose this poem because it's one of her favorites and she wants to talk about invented words. After reading the poem, the students identify the invented words and try to make up some other combinations of *elephant* and *telephone*. Ms. Cochran hangs a chart labeled "Invented Words" and writes *eletelephony* on it. One child remembers that *Bunnicula* (Howe & Howe, 1979), the title of a favorite fantasy book, is an invented word (*bunny* and *dracula*) and other children mention *brunch* (*breakfast* and *lunch*) and *smog* (*smoke* and *fog*). These students add their words on the chart, and then Ms. Cochran invites students to look for invented words in the poems they read and to pick out some to share next week.

    In the second minilesson on "The Poet's Craft," Ms. Cochran introduces odes, poems in which the author addresses a plant, animal, or other object. She has made transparencies of four odes from *The Random House Book of Poetry for Children*

(Prelutsky, 1983): Hilda Conkling's "Dandelion," Amy Lowell's "Sea Shell," Walter Brooks' "Ode to Spring," and Jack Prelutsky's "City, Oh, City!" She presents each ode on the overhead projector and reads it aloud. Together she and the students identify some of the unique characteristics of odes, and Ms. Cochran writes them on a chart that she hangs on the classroom wall.

Then Ms. Cochran passes out some raisins to each student and suggests that together as a class, they might like to write an ode to these raisins. Her students live in an agricultural area of California where raisins are grown so this idea meets with great enthusiasm. Within a minute or two, students are talking to the raisins in their hands, rehearsing lines for the class poem. Ms. Cochran takes their dictation and writes a rough draft of their poem. Students offer suggestions for revisions, and within minutes, they have written this poem:

> *Ode to a California Raisin*
> *Raisin, oh, raisin,*
> *You're nothing but a sun-dried grape.*
> *Do you remember the sunny summer days*
> *when you hung with your brothers and sisters*
> *growing plump on a grape vine?*
> *Raisin, oh, raisin,*
> *You used to be a Thompson seedless grape*
> *but in early autumn workers cut you down*
> *and laid you low in the dirt to dry out.*
> *Have you looked in the mirror lately?*
> *Raisin, oh, raisin,*
> *Now you're wrinkled, brown, and sticky*
> *turned into a nutritious, tasty snack*
> *full of ten minerals and flavor, too.*
> *Do you mind if we eat you?*
> *"Of course not," said the raisin.*

As the minilesson ends and students move into independent writing time, many begin to write odes to their pets, their jackets, and other personal objects.

MS. COCHRAN'S RECORD-KEEPING AND ASSESSMENT PROCEDURES

Ms. Cochran expects her students to read poems, write poems, and share their reading and writing experiences with classmates. She does not give grades for the poetry workshop, but she asks her students to summarize and evaluate their work each week. "Getting past the grades barrier has been hard," Ms. Cochran admits. "But I think I've succeeded—at least on Tuesdays." She uses the evaluation sheet presented in Figure 1. It took her several weeks to demonstrate to students how to summarize and evaluate their work, but now she is pleased with the work they are doing and their ability to reflect on their reading and writing experiences.

REFERENCES

Hopkins, L. B. (1987). *Pass the poetry, please!* New York: Harper Trophy.

Koch, K. (1970). *Wishes, lies, and dreams: Teaching children to write poetry.* New York: Vintage Books.

Koch, K. (1973). *Rose, where did you get that red? Teaching great poetry to children.* New York: Vintage Books.

Tompkins, G. E., & Hoskisson, K. (1991). *Language arts: Content and teaching strategies.* New York: Merrill/Macmillan.

CHILDREN'S LITERATURE REFERENCES

de Regniers, B. S. (selector). (1988). *Sing a song of popcorn: Every child's book of poems.* New York: Scholastic.

Dunning, S., Lueders. E., & Smith, H. (1966). *Reflections on a gift of watermelon pickle and other modern verse.* Glenview, IL: Scott, Foresman.

Howe, D., & Howe, J. (1979). *Bunnicula: A rabbit-tale of mystery.* New York: Atheneum.

Lowry, L. (1979). *Anastasia Krupnik.* Boston: Houghton Mifflin.

Prelutsky, J. (1984). *The new kid on the block.* New York: Greenwillow.

Prelutsky, J. (selector). (1983). *The Random House book of poetry for children.* New York: Random House.

"READERS AT WORK" IN MR. DIAZ'S CLASSROOM

MR. DIAZ HAS A SIGN hanging on the outside of his classroom door at Deer Creek Elementary School saying "Readers at Work," and his sixth graders are really readers. For six weeks of every quarter, Mr. Diaz's students participate in a reading workshop cycle, and each student in the classroom is reading a different book. (During the other three weeks, they read core literature books in small groups or as a class.) Mr. Diaz says, "The hardest thing for me to accept was that children learn to read by reading. It's just that simple, but I kept thinking that there must be more to it than that." He has read many of the books that his students are reading, and his students often read and pass favorite books from classmate to classmate so usually there are several people in the classroom who are familiar with just about any book a student might be reading. After several months of reading workshop, Mr. Diaz remembers that it finally dawned on him that it is not really important whether or not he has read the book that a student is reading. What really matters, he concluded, was that the student is reading and enjoying it.

During the six-week reading workshop cycles, students read two, three, or more self-selected books. They talk about the books they have read with classmates and with Mr. Diaz in conferences, share the books with their classmates in sharing sessions, and extend their reading through response projects.

Mr. Diaz's classroom library is stocked with hundreds books that he has collected. Most of the books are paperbacks that he has ordered from book clubs over the past four or five years, many with free points earned from his students' personal book club purchases. Others are gift books that students have presented to the class library on their birthdays, and others are on loan from the school library and the local public library. Students also bring some of their own books to share with classmates. Students take turns serving as the class librarian and keeping the library area orderly.

MR. DIAZ'S DAILY SCHEDULE FOR READING WORKSHOP

Mr. Diaz's class spends two-and-a-half hours each morning in reading workshop. The schedule is

8:45–9:15	Teacher Reads Aloud to Students
9:15–9:30	Teacher Gives a Minilesson
9:30–10:15	Students Read Self-Selected Books
10:15–10:30	Break
10:30–11:00	Students Participate in Response Activities
11:00–11:15	Students Share Books They Are Reading or Response Projects with the Class

THE READING WORKSHOP COMPONENTS

The components in Mr. Diaz's reading workshop approach are reading aloud to students, minilessons, reading of self-selected books, response activities, and sharing.

Reading Aloud to Students

Mr. Diaz spends the first 30 minutes of each reading workshop session reading aloud a chapter book to the whole class. He reads one or two chapters each day and then for the remainder of the time, students discuss the chapter(s) in a grand conversation.

Minilessons

Mr. Diaz holds a 10 to 15 minute minilesson for the whole class. He chooses topics for these brief lessons on skills from district and state curriculum guides as well as on topics he wants to teach. For example, he might focus on how a particular author uses dialogue to develop character, a reading strategy such as visualization, or talk about the author's craft by sharing a poem and talking about alliteration. He often uses excerpts from the book he is reading aloud as examples for the minilesson. It is important to note that Mr. Diaz integrates reading with the other language arts and he teaches reading, writing, and language skills and strategies in these minilessons.

Students Read Self-Selected Books

Mr. Diaz says, "Reading time is sacred. I never sacrifice a minute of it. The best thing I can do is to give time for my students to read during class; therefore, I save 45 minutes every day." During the first 10 minutes of this 45-minute period, Mr. Diaz reads a book, magazine, or newspaper that he brings to class. Then during the remainder of the period, he circulates while his students continue to read, and the students do read for the entire period.

Mr. Diaz has organized students' desks into five groups and students choose where they sit. He visits with each student in one group each day so that he can meet with every student in the class every week. Mr. Diaz squats down beside students and asks, "What are you reading?" in a hushed voice. Students tell him the name of the book, the author, and explain a little about the book and why they like it. Sometimes they softly read a brief excerpt aloud to prove a point or share a favorite episode.

Mr. Diaz carries a clipboard with checklists for each student with him as he visits with students and makes notes about each student's reading.

At first, Mr. Diaz's students had trouble selecting books to read. He taught students the five-finger strategy for choosing a book at the appropriate reading level. (Students open a book to the middle and read the page, raising a finger for each unfamiliar word. If students raise all five fingers, the book may be too difficult and students should consider choosing something else.) He also helped them become more aware of the books available to choose from through book talks he gave about books in the class library. Sometimes he'd suggest that students read another book in the same genre or another book written by a favorite author. At other times he suggested that a student might like to read a book he had already read aloud to the class. He found this problem resolved itself once students started reading and sharing their books with classmates.

Mr. Diaz says that he believes in this approach and that it can meet every student's reading needs, even Seth who was reading at a second grade level at the beginning of the school year. The first book he read was *Chicken Little* (Kellogg, 1985); by April he was reading *Tales of a Fourth Grade Nothing* (Blume, 1972).

Response Activities

During this response activity time, students write in buddy journals about the book they are currently reading, they meet in small groups with the teacher to talk about the books they are reading, and they work on response projects about the self-selected book they have read.

Buddy Journals.   After reading, students write in buddy journals (spiral notebooks) twice a week and they share their journals with another student or the teacher. They must write to the teacher once every two weeks. Two buddy journal entries are shown in Figure 1. The first is Lisa's letter to Mr. Diaz about *Stone Fox* (Gardiner, 1980), and the second is a classmate's letter to Lisa about *The Borrowers Afloat* (Norton, 1959). In these journal entries, students use the friendly letter form and underline the titles of books. At the beginning of the school year, Mr. Diaz modeled how to write these friendly letters in a minilesson, and he continues to model the form and content in the letters he writes back to students. After writing, students put their journals on another student's desk or the teacher's desk. Then students and the teacher write responses and return the journals.

Small-Group Conferences.   While most of the students are writing in their buddy journals, Mr. Diaz meets with small groups of five or six students to talk about their reading. Students sign up on a list on the chalkboard when they finish reading and are ready to meet in a conference. Students have each read a different book so Mr. Diaz asks questions that are generic enough to be appropriate for almost any book. Each student introduces his or her book to the group, and then the group talks about story events, characters, theme, genre, or authors. The session ends with each student reading a favorite excerpt to the group. The purpose of these small-group conferences is for students to have an opportunity to share what they are reading

FIGURE 1   Two Buddy Journal Entries

1-10

Dear Mr. Diaz,

    <u>Stone Fox</u> is one of the saddest books I've ever read. It was really sad when he carried him across the finish line. It was also one of the best books I've ever read. I liked the way she would use similies and keep you in suspence. I can't wait to see the movie,

           Your friend,
           Lisa

3/19
Dear Lisa,
    I am reading <u>The Borrowers Afloat</u>. I know the name sounds dumb, but you'd like it, - promise.
    It's about Arriety, Pod, & Homily. They think Humons are just for borrowing from. Read it!

           D.D.

and their personal responses, to talk about the literary elements in stories, and to make connections among books.

Response Projects.   Mr. Diaz and his students have developed a list of response projects that hangs on the classroom wall. After every three or four books, students choose one book on which to do a response activity. They choose an activity from the list, or they can think of a different activity. For example:

- Elizabeth is making a table-top diorama of the kitchen and living room from *Bunnicula: A Rabbit-tale of Mystery* (Howe & Howe, 1979).
- Aaron is constructing a gameboard after reading *Jumanji* (Van Allsburg, 1981).
- Carl is researching chocolate after reading *Charlie and the Chocolate Factory* (Dahl, 1964). He'll share what he learns in an oral report.
- Mary Catherine and three friends are writing a skit adapted form *Huge Harold* (Peet, 1961) that they will perform for the class.

Sharing.   Students sit in a circle for 15 minutes or so to share books they are reading or have finished reading and response projects they have completed with their classmates. All students come to sharing except one or two who might be at a critical moment in their reading or are finishing a response project. To begin the session, Mr. Diaz asks, "Who's ready to share?" Students take turns sharing their books and response projects. As they share, Mr. Diaz makes notes on students' checklists about their sharing.

MR. DIAZ'S LESSON PLAN FOR READING WORKSHOP

A one-week lesson plan for Mr. Diaz's reading workshop is presented in Figure 2. This lesson plan is for the second week of the six weeks that Mr. Diaz's class will spend in reading workshop. Each of the components for Mr. Diaz's reading workshop is listed, and then particular activities for this week are detailed. Mr. Diaz is reading aloud Roald Dahl's *James and the Giant Peach* (1961), a chapter each day, and in Monday's minilesson he provides background information about the author. On Tuesday, Wednesday, and Thursday, he focuses on metaphors and similies, using *James and the Giant Peach* as well as the books students are reading independently for examples. On Friday, he turns his attention to punctuation and begins a review of commas that will continue into the following week. During the reading period, students read their self-selected books and he monitors their reading, visiting briefly with students in one group each day.

After the break, students write in buddy journals and discuss the books they have read in a conference with Mr. Diaz and several classmates. On Thursday, Mr. Diaz changes pace and spends the activities period talking to the whole class about response projects. Students choose a response activity and begin working independently or in small groups on their projects on Thursday or Friday. During the last 15 minutes of the reading workshop, Mr. Diaz and his students meet to share their reading (and later in the cycle they share their projects) with the class.

FIGURE 2   A One-Week Lesson Plan from a Reading Workshop Cycle

	MONDAY	TUESDAY	WEDNESDAY	THURSDAY	FRIDAY
8:45–9:15 *Read Aloud*	Ch. 5	Ch. 6	Ch. 7	Ch. 8	Ch. 9
	James and the Giant Peach After reading, grand conversation in small groups each day to discuss the story				
9:15–9:30 *Minilesson*	(Continued from last week) • Share author information about Roald Dahl from author file and *Boy*	• Introduce comparison (similies and metaphors) • Use examples marked in *J&GP*	(Continued) • Ask students to locate and share samples from books they are reading	• Make chart to hang in classroom with samples	• Review commas • In series • Day and year • City and state • Quotes • Compound sentences
9:30–10:15 *Reading*	• Students read independently in self-selected books • Teacher briefly visits with students in one group each day to monitor their reading * Remember to make notes on Reading Workshop Checklist				
	Group 3	Group 4	Group 5	Group 1	Group 2
10:15–10:30	BREAK				
10:30–11:00 *Response Activities*	• Students write in buddy journals • Conferences with small groups (5–6 students) to discuss books they are reading			• Talk about response projects • Add new activities to chart	• Students choose response projects and begin work
11:00–11:15 *Sharing*	Students sit in a large circle to share books they have read and their response projects				

445

FIGURE 3   Weekly Reading Workshop Checklist

Name: _____ Week: _____

Minilessons

Reading Self-Selected Books

Buddy Journals

Conferences

Response Projects

Sharing

FIGURE 4   A Weekly Contract for Reading Workshop

Weekly Reading Workshop Record

Name: _____ Week: _____
Book: _____
Project: _____

	Mon	Tues	Wed	Thurs	Fri
Minilesson					
Reading					
Buddy Journal					
Conference					
Response Project					
Sharing					

0 = not done   1 = done   A = absent

MR. DIAZ'S RECORD-KEEPING AND ASSESSMENT PROCEDURES

Mr. Diaz keeps records on each student and students keep their own records. Mr. Diaz says, "I've tried all kinds of record-keeping techniques, and checklists work best for me." He uses a checklist with the reading workshop components listed on it, as shown in Figure 3. He makes a copy of the checklist for each student and keeps them on a clipboard. Mr. Diaz carries his clipboard around during reading workshop and makes notes as he meets with students and observes them. After each reading workshop cycle, Mr. Diaz places the completed checklists in reading-writing portfolios that he keeps for each student.

Each student has a reading folder, the kind with two inside pockets. During the reading workshop cycle, students keep all records in this folder. One record is a list of the books the student has read. On a second sheet, students keep a record of the types of response activities they have done. Other records include notes from the minilessons and weekly contracts. A weekly contract is shown in Figure 4 and students keep track of their daily activities on this checklist. Students also keep their buddy journals in this folder.

CHILDREN'S LITERATURE REFERENCES

Blume, J. (1972). *Tales of a fourth grade nothing.* New York: Dutton.

Dahl, R. (1961). *James and the giant peach.* New York: Knopf.

Dahl, R. (1964). *Charlie and the chocolate factory.* New York: Knopf.

Gardiner, J. R. (1980). *Stone fox.* New York: Harper & Row.

Howe, D., & Howe, J. (1979). *Bunnicula: A rabbit-tale of mystery.* New York: Atheneum.

Kellogg, S. (1985). *Chicken little.* New York: Mulberry.

Norton, M. (1959). *The borrowers afloat.* New York: Harcourt Brace Jovanovich.

Peet, B. (1961). *Huge Harold.* Boston: Houghton Mifflin.

Van Allsburg, C. (1979). *Jumanji.* Boston: Houghton Mifflin.

PARTICIPATING IN LITERATURE DISCUSSION GROUPS

MS. DANIEL TEACHES seventh and eighth grade reading classes at South Rock Creek School. Her students change classes every 50 minutes so the time she spends with each group of students is very limited. After several years of trying to parcel out bits of time to teach reading skills, Ms. Daniel turned to the reading workshop approach. "I modeled my program on Nancie Atwell's *In the Middle* (1988) and I trusted my students," she explains. "I think that's the most important thing I did. I needed to know they could read on their own, and they needed to know they didn't need me to be able to interpret a book."

Ms. Daniel alternates reading books with students together as a class and having students read and discuss books in small groups. She calls these two approaches "teacher-led" and "student-led." When she reads books with students (teacher-led), Ms. Daniel takes a more active role in asking questions and focusing students' attention on characters or another structural element, the author's craft, or stylistic devices, such as alliteration or symbolism. In contrast, when students are working in small groups (student-led), Ms. Daniel wants them to be in charge of their own learning, and she refrains from directing the course of their discussions. Her perspective for reading instruction is reader response.

In this action plan, we describe Ms. Daniel's four-week student-led reading workshop plan for *Tuck Everlasting* (Babbitt, 1975). In this fantasy set in the 1880s, young Winnie Foster travels with the Tuck family who have drunk water from a magic spring many years before and realize that the water they drank has given them everlasting life. Winnie must decide whether she will drink the water, and the Tucks must stop a sinister stranger who wants to find the magic water and sell it. Wheels and circles in the story symbolize the cycle of life and how the cycle is broken when someone drinks the magic water.

"This is what I call 'real life reading,' " Ms. Daniel says. "My students think deeply about the question of immortality. They're glad that Winnie didn't drink the water, but at the same time, the question for most students is not whether they'd want to drink the water and live forever, but when to take the drink. Some students would wait until they were 16 so that they could drive a car, and others say that they'd wait until they were 21 so they could drink, drive, and do everything they're looking forward to doing."

MS. DANIEL'S DAILY SCHEDULE

Ms. Daniel meets with each class for 50 minutes each day, and during student-led reading workshop, students read independently, respond to their reading in reading logs, and participate in discussion groups. Ms. Daniel gives her students a great deal of responsibility. She specifies the number of days the class will spend on each book, and students in each discussion group organize themselves and set their own schedule for reading, writing, and discussing the book.

COMPONENTS OF MS. DANIEL'S READING WORKSHOP PROGRAM

The three components in Ms. Daniel's student-led reading workshop for *Tuck Everlasting* are reading the book, responding in a reading log, and participating in a discussion group.

Reading the Book

Ms. Daniel and her students jointly select most books that they read. She selects several favorably reviewed books, reads them, and gives a book talk to introduce the books. Then her students decide which one they want to read. Sometimes the class decides to read the same book, and sometimes students divide into groups to read different books. Other books that Ms. Daniel's students have read in teacher-led or student-led formats this year include Judy Blume's *Iggie's House* (1970), S. E. Hinton's *The Outsiders* (1967), and Paula Danziger's *The Cat Ate My Gymsuit* (1974).

As they read, students sit with friends and then get together in groups of seven or eight to talk about their reading. "I put them in discussion groups according to reading speed," Ms. Daniel explains, "because I want them to discuss their reading as soon as possible." This technique works well because each group includes a range of reading abilities. All reading is done at school because Ms. Daniel acknowledges that she has no control over what they do outside of school hours.

Responding in a Reading Log

After students finish reading and before they meet in discussion groups, they write about their reading in reading logs. Ms. Daniel doesn't give any prompts; students are encouraged to write their reflections, predictions, questions, confusions, personal connections, and anything else they want to write. In some books, students write after every chapter, but for *Tuck Everlasting,* they write after reading each two, three, or four chapters because this book has 25 chapters, and each chapter averages 5 pages.

Students put notebook paper into folders for their reading logs, and they divide each page into two columns. The first column is headed "Reading Notes" and the second column "Discussion Notes." After reading, students write in the first column. After the discussion group meeting, they reflect on what they have learned, list opinions they have changed, and write other notes in the second column. A page from one student's reading log is presented in Figure 1.

FIGURE 1   A Page from a Student's Reading Log

Reading Notes	Discussing Notes
Why does Winnie have to stay with them for a couple of days?	so they can explain about the water
pg.45 What did Winnie mean when she said she had discovered the wings she wished she had?	Because she finally ran away
pg.46 What did Tuck mean when he said they brung a real honest-to-goodness natural child?	They drink the water and Winnie didn't
pg.48 Why did Tuck have a sad look on his face?	
Why was Tuck so happy that Winnie found out about them?	Because they had never told anyone about it

Participating in a Discussion Group

The group decides how to divide the reading of the book, how often to meet, and what they do during their discussion group meetings. No one is assigned to be the group leader; instead, students work together collaboratively. They try to keep all group members productive, and even prompt each other, saying, "Jason, you haven't said anything in three days" or "Suzanne, what questions did you have about these three chapters?"

In their discussions, students talk about personal associations they have made with the book, make comments and ask questions about details in the book, offer predictions, share interpretations, and make comments to maintain the conversation. Students often build on each other's ideas. Sometimes they read what they have written, and at other times, their talk is more spontaneous. Ms. Daniel's students often find that vocabulary in the story is a problem. They have several strategies available when they want to know the meaning of a word. They can ask each other, guess from the context, ask the teacher, or look it up in the dictionary. If students think the word is important, they record it in their reading logs.

The discussion continues until all ideas have been shared and all questions and interpretations have been discussed. Then students decide how much to read before the next discussion group meeting and when the group will meet again. Then students disband to write in their reading logs, read the next two or three chapters, and write in their reading logs before meeting together again.

MS. DANIEL'S FOUR-WEEK LESSON PLAN

Ms. Daniel's four-week lesson plan for *Tuck Everlasting* is presented in Figure 2. On most days, students are participating in reading workshop and involved in reading the book independently, writing in reading logs, and meeting in discussion groups. During the final week, students spend two days watching the film version of *Tuck Everlasting* and comparing it to the book.

MS. DANIEL'S RECORD-KEEPING AND ASSESSMENT PROCEDURES

Students keep track of their reading workshop activities in their reading logs, and at the end of the book they write letters to Ms. Daniel reflecting on their work, how well they met their own goals, and what they will work on in the next reading workshop. The grades are for participation and effort. Ms. Daniel says, "I try very hard to get out of the competitive mode. I create a safe learning environment and I expect my students to do their best."

Ms. Daniel observes her students as they read, write, and participate in discussion groups, and she writes anecdotal notes about students' behavior, their enthusiasm, and the interpretations and personal connections they share. The following are excerpts from her anecdotal notes:

FIGURE 2 Ms. Daniel's Four-Week Lesson Plan for *Tuck Everlasting* (Babbitt, 1975)

	MONDAY	TUESDAY	WEDNESDAY	THURSDAY	FRIDAY
WEEK 1	• Begin reading *Tuck Everlasting* • Divide class into four lit discussion groups according to reading speed	READING WORKSHOP 1. Independent reading 2. Reading logs 3. Discussion groups	→		
WEEK 2	READING WORKSHOP 1. Independent reading 2. Reading logs 3. Discussion groups		→		
WEEK 3	READING WORKSHOP 1. Independent reading 2. Reading logs 3. Discussion groups		→		
WEEK 4	READING WORKSHOP 1. Independent reading 2. Reading logs 3. Discussion groups	Show film of *Tuck Everlasting* →		→	Final discussion group meeting to talk about the film and wrap things up

- Was Winnie kidnapped? Aaron answers, "Yeah, she was when you get right down to it." He asks, "Does Winnie have any brothers or sisters?" "She doesn't? She just lives with her mom, grandma, and her dad?"

- Ellen asked me what Queen Anne's Lace was. I told her what I thought it was, asked if she had looked it up—no—then I asked why she didn't look things up in the dictionary. I'm trying to encourage her.

- Pat asks for her discussion group's predictions about what the man in the yellow suit will do.

- Good discussion today. David asks, "Do you think _____?" several times.

- Darlene and Laura not reading again today. I asked Laura to PLEASE read. She and Darlene came to my desk. Laura showed me where it talked of "Black Magic." "Is this what this book is about?" "No." "It's strange, and I told my mother about this part." "No, this book is not about Black Magic." "Are you sure?" "Yes, I'm sure." "Well, it is strange." Now I know why they haven't been reading! Focused on one statement that they have been taught to avoid. They felt that they were compromising under coercion. Passive resistance.

- Erica is absent. I expect the group to be different today. Probably more people will participate. Sky asks what "willy-nilly" means. Jason looked it up and read it. Daniel read it! Then they looked up "helter skelter." This seems like a waste of time. If I were in the group I would tell them the answer and go on to the story. But is that like the teacher who gets through the entire book regardless of what the kids have learned? They are probably learning more doing it their way.

- Jason knew about "flapjacks." He's had them in restaurants—in his experience. His group didn't trust him; he looked it up, confirmed his answer, and laughed!

- Cathy is filling Erica in on what she missed yesterday. Erica gasped when Cathy told her about hitting the man in the yellow suit in the skull.

- Josh predicts what the man in the yellow suit is going to do. Talking about Tuck shooting himself. They need clarification.

- Daniel told Jeremy to shut up. Laura told Jeremy to shut up. I hate how rude they are to him, but he continues to ask his questions.

- Billy joins the discussion. He was absent so I told him to just read and try to catch up. I walked over to him because he was staring into space. His book was open to Chapter 11. I asked him if he had read that far. He said he had. I asked, "How?" He answered, "I've been reading ahead when I am here." I told him to join the discussion group.

She uses these notes to reflect on students' participation in the groups, group dynamics, and students' interpretation of the book.

REFERENCES

Atwell, N. (1988). *In the middle.* Portsmouth, NH:
　Heinemann.

CHILDREN'S LITERATURE REFERENCES

Babbitt, N. (1975). *Tuck everlasting.* New York:
　Farrar, Straus & Giroux.
Blume, J. (1970). *Iggie's house.* New York: Dell.

Danziger, P. (1974). *The cat ate my gymsuit.* New
　York: Delacorte.
Hinton, S. E. (1967). *The outsiders.* New York: Dell.

AWARD-WINNING BOOKS FOR CHILDREN

CALDECOTT MEDAL BOOKS

The Caldecott Medal is named in honor of Randolph Caldecott (1846–1886), a British illustrator of children's books. The award is presented each year to "the artist of the most distinguished American picture book for children" published during the preceding year by the American Library Association. The award was first given in 1938 and is awarded annually. The winning book receives the Caldecott Medal and one or more runners-up are also recognized as "Honor" books.

1992 *Tuesday,* David Wiesner (Clarion). **Honor book:** *Tar beach,* Faith Ringgold (Crown).

1991 *Black and white,* David Macaulay (Houghton Mifflin). **Honor books:** *Puss in boots,* Charles Perrault, illustrated by Fred Marcellino (Farrar, Straus & Giroux); *"More, more, more" said the baby,* Vera B. Williams (Morrow).

1990 *Lon Po Po, A Red Riding Hood story from China,* Ed Young (Philomel). **Honor books:** *Bill Peet: An autobiography,* William Peet (Houghton Mifflin); *Color zoo,* Louis Ehlert (Lippincott); *Herschel and the Hanukkah goblins,* Eric A. Kimmel, illustrated by Trina Schart Hyman (Holiday House); *The talking eggs,* Robert D. San Souci, illustrated by Jerry Pickney (Dial).

1989 *Song and dance man,* Jane Ackerman, illustrated by Stephen Gammell (Knopf). **Honor books:** *Goldilocks,* James Marshall (Dial); *The boy of the three-year nap,* Diane Snyder, illustrated by Allen Say (Houghton Mifflin); *Mirandy and Brother Wind,* Patricia McKissack, illustrated

by Jerry Pickney (Knopf); *Free fall,* David Wiesner (Lothrop).

1988 *Owl moon,* Jane Yolen, illustrated by John Schoenherr (Philomel). **Honor book:** *Mufaro's beautiful daughters: An African tale,* John Steptoe (Morrow).

1987 *Hey, Al,* Arthur Yorinks, illustrated by Richard Egielski (Farrah, Straus & Giroux). **Honor books:** *Alphabatics,* Suse MacDonald (Bradbury); *Rumplestiltskin,* Paul O. Zelinsky (E. P. Dutton); *The village of round and square houses,* Ann Grifalconi (Little, Brown).

1986 *The polar express,* Chris Van Allsburg (Houghton Mifflin). **Honor books:** *King Bidgood's in the bathtub,* Audrey Wood (Harcourt Brace Jovanovich); *The relatives came,* Cynthia Rylant (Bradbury).

1985 *Saint George and the dragon,* Margaret Hodges, illustrated by Trina Schart Hyman (Little, Brown). **Honor books:** *Hansel and Gretel,* Rika Lesser, illustrated by Paul O. Zelinsky (Dodd, Mead); *Have you seen my duckling?* Nancy Tafuri (Greenwillow); *The story of jumping mouse,* John Steptoe (Lothrop, Lee & Shepard).

1984 *The glorious flight: Across the channel with Louis Bleriot,* Alice and Martin Provensen (Viking). **Honor books:** *Little red riding hood,* Trina Schart Hyman (Holiday); *Ten, nine, eight,* Molly Bang (Greenwillow).

1983 *Shadow,* Blaise Cendrars, translated and illustrated by Marcia Brown (Scribner). **Honor books:** *A chair for my mother,* Vera B. Williams

(Greenwillow); *When I was young in the mountains,* Cynthia Rylant, illustrated by Diane Goode (E. P. Dutton).

1982 *Jumanji,* Chris Van Allsburg (Houghton Mifflin). **Honor books:** *On Market Street,* Arnold Lobel, illustrated by Anita Lobel (Greenwillow); *Outside over there,* Maurice Sendak (Harper & Row); *A visit to William Blake's inn: Poems for innocent and experienced travelers,* Nancy Willard, illustrated by Alice and Martin Provensen (Harcourt Brace Jovanovich); *Where the buffaloes begin,* Olaf Baker, illustrated by Stephen Gammell (Warne).

1981 *Fables,* Arnold Lobel (Harper & Row). **Honor Books:** *The Bremen-Town musicians,* Ilse Plume (Doubleday); *The grey lady and the strawberry snatcher,* Molly Bang (Four Winds); *Mice twice,* Joseph Low (Atheneum); *Truck,* Donald Crews (Greenwillow).

1980 *Ox-cart man,* Donald Hall, illustrated by Barbara Cooney (Viking); **Honor books:** *Ben's trumpet,* Rachel Isadora (Greenwillow); *The garden of Abdul Gasazi,* Chris Van Allsburg (Houghton Mifflin); *The treasure,* Uri Shulevitz (Farrar, Straus & Giroux).

1979 *The girl who loved wild horses,* Paul Goble (Bradbury). **Honor books:** *Freight train,* Donald Crews (Greenwillow); *The way to start a day,* Byrd Baylor, illustrated by Peter Parnall (Scribner).

1978 *Noah's ark: The story of the flood,* Peter Spier (Doubleday). **Honor books:** *Castle,* David Macaulay (Houghton Mifflin); *It could always be worse,* Margot Zemach (Farrar, Straus & Giroux).

1977 *Ashanti to Zulu,* Margaret Musgrove, illustrated by Leo and Diane Dillon (Dial). **Honor books:** *The amazing bone,* William Steig (Farrah, Straus & Giroux); *The contest,* Nonny Hogrogian (Greenwillow); *Fish for supper,* M. B. Goffstein (Dial); *The Golem: A Jewish legend,* Beverly Brodsky McDermott (J. B. Lippincott); *Hawk, I'm your brother,* Byrd Baylor, illustrated by Peter Parnall (Scribner).

1976 *Why mosquitoes buzz in people's ears,* Verna Aardema, illustrated by Leo and Diane Dillon (Dial). **Honor books:** *The desert is theirs,* Byrd Baylor (Scribner), illustrated by Peter Parnall; *Strega Nona,* Tomie dePaola (Prentice-Hall).

1975 *Arrow to the sun,* Gerald McDermott (Viking). **Honor book:** *Jambo means hello: A Swahili alphabet book,* Muriel Feelings, illustrated by Tom Feelings (Dial).

1974 *Duffy and the devil,* Harve and Margot Zemach (Farrar, Straus & Giroux). **Honor books:** *Cathedral: The story of its construction,* David Macaulay (Houghton Mifflin); *The three jovial huntsmen,* Susan Jeffers (Bradbury).

1973 *The funny little woman,* Arlen Mosel, illustrated by Blair Lent (E. P. Dutton). **Honor books:** *Hosie's Alphabet,* Hosea, Tobias, and Lisa Baskin, illustrated by Leonard Baskin (Viking); *Snow-White and the seven dwarfs,* translated by Randall Jarrell from the Brothers Grimm, illustrated by Nancy Ekholm Burkert (Farrar, Straus & Giroux); *When clay sings,* Byrd Baylor, illustrated by Tom Bahti (Scribner).

1972 *One fine day,* Nonny A. Hogrogian (Macmillan). **Honor books:** *Hildilid's night,* Cheli Duran Ryan, illustrated by Arnold Lobel (Macmillan); *If all the seas were one sea,* Janina Domanska, (Macmillan); *Moja means one: Swahili counting book,* Muriel Feelings, illustrated by Tom Feelings (Dial).

1971 *A story, a story,* Gail E. Haley (Atheneum). **Honor books:** *The angry moon,* William Sleator, illustrated by Blair Lent (Atlantic-Little); *Frog and Toad are friends,* Arnold Lobel (Harper & Row); *In the night kitchen,* Maurice Sendak (Harper & Row).

1970 *Sylvester and the magic pebble,* William Steig (Windmill/Simon & Schuster). **Honor books:** *Alexander and the wind-up mouse,* Leo Lionni (Pantheon); *Goggles!* Ezra Jack Keats (Macmillan); *The judge: An untrue tale,* Harve Zemach, illustrated by Margot Zemach (Farrar, Straus & Giroux). *Pop Corn and Ma Goodness,* Edna Mitchell Preston, illustrated by Robert Andrew Parker (Viking); *Thy friend, Obadiah,* Brinton Turkle (Viking).

1969 *The fool of the world and the flying ship,* Arthur Ransome, illustrated by Uri Shulevitz (Farrar, Straus & Giroux). **Honor book:** *Why the sun and the moon live in the sky: An African folktale,* Elphinstone Dayrell, illustrated by Blair Lent (Houghton Mifflin).

1968 *Drummer Hoff,* Barbara Emberley, illustrated by Ed Emberley (Prentice-Hall). **Honor books:** *Frederick,* Leo Lionni (Pantheon); *Seashore story,* Taro Yashima (Viking); *The emperor and the kite,* Jane Yolen, illustrated by Ed Young (Harcourt Brace Jovanovich).

1967 *Sam, Bangs & Moonshine,* Evaline Ness (Holt, Rinehart & Winston). **Honor book:** *One wide river to cross,* Barbara Emberley, illustrated by Ed Emberley (Prentice-Hall).

1966 *Always room for one more,* Sorche Nic Leodhas, illustrated by Nonny Hogrogian (Holt). **Honor books:** *Hide and seek fog,* Alvin Tresselt, illustrated by Roger Duvoisin (Lothrop); *Just me,* Marie Hall Ets (Viking); *Tom tit tot,* Evaline Ness (Scribner).

1965 *May I bring a friend?,* Beatrice Schenk de Regniers, illustrated by Beni Montresor (Atheneum). **Honor books:** *Rain makes applesauce,* Julian Scheer, illustrated by Marvin Bileck (Holiday House); *The wave,* Margaret Hodges, illustrated by Blair Lent (Houghton Mifflin); *A pocketful of cricket,* Rebecca Caudill, illustrated by Evaline Ness (Holt).

1964 *Where the wild things are,* Maurice Sendak (Harper & Row). **Honor books:** *Swimmy,* Leo Lionni (Pantheon); *All in the morning early,* Sorche Nic Leodhas, illustrated by Evaline Ness (Holt); *Mother Goose and nursery rhymes,* illustrated by Philip Reed (Atheneum).

1963 *The snowy day,* Ezra Jack Keats (Viking). **Honor books:** *The sun is a golden earring,* Natalia M. Belting, illustrated by Bernarda Bryson (Holt); *Mr. Rabbit and the lovely present,* Charlotte Zolotow, illustrated by Maurice Sendak (Harper & Row).

1962 *Once a mouse . . . ,* Marcia Brown (Scribner). **Honor books:** *The fox went out on a chilly night: An old song,* Peter Spier (Doubleday); *Little bear's visit,* Else Holmelund Minarik, illustrated by Maurice Sendak (Harper & Row); *The day we saw the sun come up,* Alice E. Goudey, illustrated by Adrienne Adams (Scribner).

1961 *Baboushka and the three kings,* Ruth Robbins, illustrated by Nicolas Sidjakov (Parnassus). **Honor book:** *Inch by inch,* Leo Lionni (Obolensky).

1960 *Nine days to Christmas,* Marie Hall Ets & Aurora Labastida, illustrated by Marie Hall Ets (Viking). **Honor books:** *Houses from the sea,* Alice E. Goudey, illustrated by Adrienne Adams (Scribner); *The moon jumpers,* Janice May Udry, illustrated by Maurice Sendak (Harper & Row).

1959 *Chanticleer and the fox,* Barbara Cooney (Crowell). **Honor books:** *The house that Jack built: A picture book in two languages,* Antonio Frasconi (Harcourt Brace Jovanovich); *What do you say, dear?,* Sesyle Joslin, illustrated by Maruice Sendak (Scott); *Umbrella,* Taro Yashima (Viking).

1958 *Time of wonder,* Robert McCloskey (Viking). **Honor books:** *Fly high, fly low,* Don Freeman (Viking); *Anatole and the cat,* Eve Titus, illustrated by Paul Galdone (McGraw-Hill).

1957 *A tree is nice,* Janice May Udry, illustrated by Marc Simont (Harper & Row). **Honor books:** *Mr. Penny's race horse,* Marie Hall Ets (Viking); *1 is one,* Tasha Tudor (Walck); *Anatole,* Eve Titus, illustrated by Paul Galdone (McGraw-Hill); *Gillespie and the guards,* Benjamin Elkin, illustrated by James Daugherty (Viking); *Lion,* William Pene du Bois (Viking).

1956 *Frog went a-courtin',* John Langstaff, illustrated by Feodor Rojankowsky (Harcourt Brace Jovanovich). **Honor books:** *Play with me,* Marie Hall Ets (Viking); *Crow boy,* Taro Yashima (Viking).

1955 *Cinderella, or the little glass slipper,* Charles Perrault, translated and illustrated by Marcia Brown (Scribner). **Honor books:** *Book of nursery and Mother Goose rhymes,* illustrated by Marguerite de Angeli (Doubleday); *Wheel on the chimney,* Margaret Wise Brown, illustrated by Tibor Gergely (Lippincott); *The Thanksgiving story,* Alice Dalgliesh, illustrated by Helen Sewell (Scribner).

1954 *Madeline's rescue,* Ludwig Bemelmans (Viking). **Honor books:** *Journey cake, ho!,* Ruth Sawyer, illustrated by Robert McCloskey (Viking); *When will the world be mine?,* Miriam Schlein, illustrated by Jean Charlot (Scott); *The steadfast tin solider,* Hans Christian Andersen, illustrated by Marcia Brown (Scribner); *A very special house,* Ruth Krauss, illustrated by Maurice Sendak (Harper & Row); *Green eyes,* A. Birnbaum (Capitol).

1953 *The biggest bear,* Lynd Ward (Houghton Mifflin). **Honor books:** *Puss in boots,* Charles Perrault, translated and illustrated by Marcia Brown (Scribner); *One morning in Maine,* Robert McCloskey (Viking); *Ape in a cape: An alphabet of odd animals,* Fritz Eichenberg (Harcourt Brace Jovanovich); *The storm book,* Charlotte Zolotow, illustrated by Margaret Bloy Graham (Harper & Row); *Five little monkeys,* Juliet Kepes (Houghton Mifflin).

1952 *Finders keepers,* William Lipkind, illustrated by Nicholas Mordvinoff (Harcourt Brace Jovanovich). **Honor books:** *Mr. T. W. Anthony Wood: The story of a cat and a dog and mouse,* Marie Hall Ets (Viking); *Skipper John's cook,* Marcia Brown (Scribner); *All falling down,* Gene Zion, illustrated by Margaret Bloy Graham (Harper & Row); *Bear party,* William Pene du Bois (Viking); *Feather mountain,* Elizabeth Olds (Houghton Mifflin).

1951   *The egg tree,* Katherine Milhous (Scribner). **Honor books:** *Dick Whittington and his cat,* Marcia Brown (Scribner); *The two reds,* William Lipkind, illustrated by Nicholas Mordvinoff (Harcourt Brace Jovanovich); *If I ran the zoo,* Dr. Seuss (Random House); *The most wonderful doll in the world,* Phyllis McGinley, illustrated by Helen Stone (Lippincott); *T-bone, the baby sitter,* Clare Newberry (Harper & Row).

1950   *Song of the swallows,* Leo Politi (Scribner). **Honor books:** *America's Ethan Allen,* Stewart Holbrook, illustrated by Lynd Ward (Houghton Mifflin); *The wild birthday cake,* Lavinia Davis, illustrated by Hildegard Woodward (Doubleday); *The happy day,* Ruth Krauss, illustrated by Marc Simont (Harper & Row); *Bartholomew and the oobleck,* Dr. Seuss (Random House); *Henry fisherman,* Marcia Brown (Scribner).

1949   *The big snow,* Berta & Elmer Hader (Macmillan). **Honor books:** *Blueberries for Sal,* Robert McCloskey (Viking); *All around the town,* Phyllis McGinley, illustrated by Helen Stone (Lippincott); *Juanita,* Leo Politi (Scribner); *Fish in the air,* Kurt Wiese (Viking).

1948   *White snow, bright snow,* Alvin Tresselt, illustrated by Roger Duvoisin (Lothrop). **Honor books:** *Stone soup: An old tale,* Marcia Brown (Scribner); *McElligot's pool,* Dr. Seuss (Random House); *Bambino the clown,* George Schreiber (Viking); *Roger and the fox,* Lavinia Davis, illustrated by Hildegard Woodward (Doubleday); *Song of Robin Hood,* Anne Malcolmson, illustrated by Virginia Lee Burton (Houghton Mifflin).

1947   *The little island,* Golden MacDonald, illustrated by Leonard Weisgard (Doubleday). **Honor books:** *Rain drop splash,* Alvin Tresselt, illustrated by Leonard Weisgard (Lothrop); *Boats on the river,* Marjorie Flack, illustrated by Jay Hyde Barnum (Viking); *Timothy turtle,* Al Graham, illustrated by Tony Plazzo (Viking); *Pedro, the angel of Olvera Street,* Leo Politi (Scribner); *Sing in praise: A collection of the best loved hymns,* Opal Wheeler, illustrated by Marjorie Torrey (Dutton).

1946   *The rooster crows . . . ,* illustrated by Maud & Miska Petersham (Macmillan). **Honor books:** *Little lost lamb,* Golden MacDonald, illustrated by Leonard Weisgard (Doubleday); *Sing Mother Goose,* Opal Wheeler, illustrated by Marjorie Torrey (Dutton); *My mother is the most beautiful woman in the world,* Becky Reyher, illustrated by Ruth Gannett (Lothrop); *You can write Chinese,* Kurt Wiese (Viking).

1945   *Prayer for a child,* Rachel Field, illustrated by Elizabeth Orton Jones (Macmillan). **Honor books:** *Mother Goose: seventy-seven verses with pictures,* illustrated by Tasha Tudor (Walck); *In the forest,* Marie Hall Ets (Viking); *Yonie Wondernose,* Marguerite de Angeli (Doubleday); *The Christmas Anna angel,* Ruth Sawyer, illustrated by Kate Seredy (Viking).

1944   *Many moons,* James Thurber, illustrated by Louis Slobodkin (Harcourt Brace Jovanovich). **Honor books:** *Small rain: Verses from the Bible,* selected by Jessie Orton Jones, illustrated by Elizabeth Orton Jones (Viking); *Pierre pigeon,* Lee Kingman, illustrated by Arnold E. Bare (Houghton Mifflin); *The mighty hunter,* Berta & Elmer Hader (Macmillan); *A child's good night book,* Margaret Wise Brown, illustrated by Jean Charlot (Brown); *Good luck horse,* Chih-Yi Chan, illustrated by Plato Chan (Whittlesey).

1943   *The little house,* Virginia Lee Burton (Houghton Mifflin). **Honor books:** *Dash and dart,* Mary & Conrad Buff (Viking); *Marshmallow,* Clare Newberry (Harper & Row).

1942   *Make way for ducklings,* Robert McCloskey (Viking). **Honor books:** *An American ABC,* Maud & Miska Petersham (Macmillan); *In my mother's house,* Ann Nolan Clark, illustrated by Velino Herrera (Viking); *Paddle-to-the-sea,* Holling C. Holling (Houghton Mifflin); *Nothing at all,* Wanda Gag (Coward-McCann).

1941   *They were strong and good,* Robert Lawson (Viking). **Honor book:** *April's kittens,* Clare Newberry (Harper & Row).

1940   *Abraham Lincoln,* Ingri & Edgar Parin d'Aulaire (Doubleday). **Honor books:** *Cock-a-doodle do: The story of a little red rooster,* Berta & Elmer Hader (Macmillan); *Madeline,* Ludwig Bemelmans (Simon & Schuster); *The ageless story,* Lauren Ford (Dodd).

1939 *Mei Li,* Thomas Handforth (Doubleday). **Honor books:** *The forest pool,* Laura Adams Armer (Longmans); *Wee Gillis,* Munro Leaf, illustrated by Robert Lawson (Viking); *Snow White and the seven dwarfs,* Wanda Gag (Coward); *Barkis,* Clare Newberry (Harper & Row); *Andy and the lion: A tale of kindness remembered or the power of gratitude,* James Daugherty (Viking).

1938 *Animals of the Bible,* Helen Dean Fish, illustrated by Dorothy P. Lathrop (Stokes). **Honor books:** *Seven Simeon: A Russian tale,* Boris Artzybasheff (Viking); *Four and twenty blackbirds: Nursery rhymes of yesterday recalled for children of today,* Helen Dean Fish, illustrated by Robert Lawson (Stokes).

NEWBERY MEDAL BOOKS

The Newbery Medal is named in honor of John Newbery (1713–1767), a British publisher and bookseller in the 1700s. Newbery is known as the "father of children's literature" since he was the first to propose publishing books specifically for children. The award is presented each year by the American Library Association to "the author of the most distinguished contribution to American literature for children" published during the preceding year. The award was first given in 1922 and is awarded annually. The winning book receives the Newbery Medal and one or more runners-up are also recognized as "Honor" books.

1992 *Shiloh,* Phyllis Reynolds Naylor (Atheneum). **Honor books:** *Nothing but the truth,* Avi (Orchard); *The Wright brothers: How they invented the airplane,* Russell Freedman (Holiday).

1991 *Maniac Magee,* Jerry Spinelli (Little, Brown). **Honor book:** *The true confessions of Charlotte Doyle,* Avi (Orchard).

1990 *Number the stars,* Lois Lowry (Houghton Mifflin). **Honor books:** *Afternoon of the elves,* Janet Taylor Lisel (Orchard); *Shabanu, daughter of the wind,* Susan Fisher Staples (Knopf); *The winter room,* Gary Paulsen (Orchard).

1989 *Joyful noise: Poems for two voices,* Paul Fleishman (Harper & Row). **Honor books:** *In the beginning,* Virginia Hamilton (Harcourt Brace Jovanovich); *Scorpions,* Walter Dean Myers (Harper & Row).

1988 *Lincoln: A photobiography,* Russell Freedman (Clarion). **Honor books:** *After the rain,* Norma Fox Mazer (Morrow); *Hatchet,* Gary Paulsen (Bradbury).

1987 *The whipping boy,* Sid Fleischman (Greenwillow). **Honor books:** *A fine white dust,* Cynthia Rylant (Bradbury); *On my honor,* Marion Dane Bauer (Clarion); *Volcano: The eruption and healing of Mount St. Helen's,* Patricia Lauber (Bradbury).

1986 *Sarah, plain and tall,* Patricia MacLachlan (Harper & Row). **Honor books:** *Commodore Perry in the land of the Shogun,* Rhoda Blumberg (Lothrop, Lee & Shepard); *Dog song,* Gary Paulsen (Bradbury).

1985 *The hero and the crown,* Robin McKinley (Greenwillow). **Honor books:** *Like Jake and me,* Mavis Jukes (Alfred A. Knopf); *The moves make the man,* Bruce Brooks (Harper & Row); *One-eyed cat,* Paula Fox (Bradbury).

1984 *Dear Mr. Henshaw,* Beverly Clearly (Morrow). **Honor books:** *The sign of the beaver,* Elizabeth George Speare (Houghton Mifflin); *A solitary blue,* Cynthia Voigt (Atheneum); *Sugaring time,* Kathryn Lasky (Macmillan); *The wish giver,* Bill Brittain (Harper & Row).

1983 *Dicey's song,* Cynthia Voigt, (Atheneum). **Honor books:** *The blue sword,* Robin McKinley (Greenwillow); *Doctor DeSoto,* William Steig (Farrar, Straus & Giroux); *Graven images,* Paul Fleischman (Harper & Row); *Homesick: My own story,* Jean Fritz (Putnam); *Sweet Whispers, Brother Rush,* Virginia Hamilton (Philomel).

1982 *A visit to William Blake's inn: Poems for innocent and experienced travelers,* Nancy Willard (Harcourt Brace Jovanovich). **Honor books:** *Ramona Quimby, age 8,* Beverly Clearly (Morrow); *Upon the head of the goat: A childhood in Hungary, 1939–1944,* Aranka Siegal (Farrar, Straus & Giroux).

1981 *Jacob have I loved,* Katherine Paterson (Crowell). **Honor books:** *The fledgling,* Jane Langton (Harper & Row); *A ring of endless light,* Madeleine L'Engle (Farrar, Straus & Giroux).

1980 *A gathering of days: A New England girl's journal, 1830–1832,* Joan W. Blos (Scribner). **Honor book:** *The road from home: The story of an Armenian girl,* David Kerdian (Greenwillow).

1979 *The westing game,* Ellen Raskin (Dutton). **Honor book:** *The great Gilly Hopkins,* Katherine Paterson (Crowell).

1978 *Bridge to Terabithia,* Katherine Paterson (Crowell). **Honor books:** *Anpao: An American Indian odyssey,* Jamake Highwater (Lippincott); *Ramona and her father,* Beverly Clearly (Morrow).

1977 *Roll of thunder, hear my cry,* Mildred Taylor (Dial). **Honor books:** *Abel's Island,* William Steig (Farrar, Straus & Giroux); *A string in the harp,* Nancy Bond (Atheneum).

1976 *The grey king,* Susan Cooper (Atheneum). **Honor books:** *Dragonwings,* Laurence Yep (Harper & Row); *The hundred penny box,* Sharon Bell Mathis (Viking).

1975 *M. C. Higgins, the great,* Virginia Hamilton (Macmillan). **Honor books:** *Figgs and phantoms,* Ellen Raskin (E. P. Dutton); *My brother Sam is dead,* James Lincoln Collier and Christopher Collier (Four Winds); *The perilous gard,* Elizabeth Marie Pope (Houghton Mifflin); *Philip Hall likes me, I reckon maybe,* Bette Green (Dial).

1974 *The slave dancer,* Paula Fox (Bradbury). **Honor book:** *The dark is rising,* Susan Cooper (Atheneum).

1973 *Julie of the wolves,* Jean C. George (Harper & Row). **Honor books:** *Frog and Toad together,* Arnold Lobel (Harper & Row); *The upstairs room,* Johanna Reiss (Crowell); *The witches of worm,* Zilpha Keatley Snyder (Atheneum).

1972 *Mrs. Frisby and the rats of Nimh,* Robert C. O'Brien (Atheneum). **Honor books:** *Annie and the old one,* Miska Miles (Atlantic-Little); *The headless cupid,* Zilpha Keatley Snyder (Atheneum); *Incident at Hawk's Hill,* Allan W. Eckert (Little, Brown); *The planet of Junior Brown,* Virginia Hamilton (Macmillan); *The tombs of Atuan,* Ursula K. LeGuin (Atheneum).

1971 *The summer of the swans,* Betsy Byars (Viking). **Honor books:** *Enchantress from the stars,* Sylvia Louise Engdahl (Atheneum); *Kneeknock rise,* Natalie Babbitt (Farrar, Straus & Giroux); *Sing down the moon,* Scott O'Dell (Houghton Mifflin).

1970 *Sounder,* William Armstrong (Harper & Row). **Honor books:** *Journey outside,* Mary Q. Steele (Viking); *Our Eddie,* Sulamith Ish-Kishor (Pantheon); *The many ways of seeing: An introduction to the pleasures of art,* Janet Gaylord Moore (Harcourt Brace Jovanovich).

1969 *The high king,* Lloyd Alexander (Holt, Rinehart & Winston). **Honor books:** *To be a slave,* Julius Lester (Dial); *When Shlemiel went to Warsaw and other stories,* Isaac Bashevis Singer (Farrar, Straus & Giroux).

1968 *From the mixed-up files of Mrs. Basil E. Frankweiler,* E. L. Konigsburg (Atheneum). **Honor books:** *The black pearl,* Scott O'Dell (Houghton Mifflin); *The Egypt game,* Zilpha Keatley Snyder (Atheneum); *The fearsome inn,* Isaac Bashevis Singer (Scribner); *Jennifer, Hecate, Macbeth, William McKinley, and Me, Elizabeth,* E. L. Konigsburg (Atheneum).

1967 *Up a road slowly,* Irene Hunt (Follett). **Honor books:** *The jazz man,* Mary Hays Weik (Atheneum); *The King's Fifth,* Scott O'Dell (Houghton Mifflin); *Zlateh the goat and other stories,* Isaac Bashevis Singer (Harper & Row).

1966, *I, Juan de Pareja,* Elizabeth Borton de Trevino (Farrar, Straus & Giroux). **Honor books:** *The animal family,* Randall Jarrell (Pantheon); *The black cauldron,* Lloyd Alexander (Holt, Rinehart & Winston); *The noonday friends,* Mary Stolz (Harper & Row).

1965 *Shadow of a bull,* Maia Wojciechowska (Atheneum). **Honor book:** *Across five Aprils,* Irene Hunt (Follett).

1964 *It's like this, cat,* Emily Neville (Harper & Row). **Honor books:** *The loner,* Ester Wier (McKay); *Rascal,* Sterling North (E. P. Dutton).

1963 *A wrinkle in time,* Madeleine L'Engle (Farrar, Straus & Giroux). **Honor books:** *Thistle and thyme: Tales and legends from Scotland,* Sorche Nic Leodhas (Holt); *Men of Athens,* Olivia Coolidge (Houghton Mifflin).

1962 *The bronze bow,* Elizabeth George Speare (Houghton Mifflin). **Honor books:** *Frontier living,* Edwin Tunis (World); *The golden goblet,*

Eloise McCraw (Coward); *Belling the tiger,* Mary Stolz (Harper & Row).

1961 *Island of the blue dolphins,* Scott O'Dell (Houghton Mifflin). **Honor books:** *America moves forward,* Gerald W. Johnson (Morrow); *Old Ramon,* Jack Schaefer (Houghton Mifflin); *The cricket in Times Square,* George Selden (Farrah, Straus & Giroux).

1960 *Onion John,* Joseph Krumgold (Crowell). **Honor books:** *My side of the mountain,* Jean Craighead George (Dutton); *America is born,* Gerald W. Johnson (Morrow); *The gammage cup,* Carol Kendall (Harcourt Brace Jovanovich).

1959 *The witch of blackbird pond,* Elizabeth George Speare (Houghton Mifflin). **Honor books:** *The family under the bridge,* Natalie Savage Carlson (Harper & Row); *Along came a dog,* Meindert DeJong (Harper & Row); *Chucaro: Wild pony of the Pampa,* Francis Kalnay (Harcourt Brace Jovanovich); *The perilous road,* William O. Steele (Harcourt Brace Jovanovich).

1958 *Rifles for Watie,* Harold Keith (Crowell). **Honor books:** *The horsecatcher,* Marie Sandoz (Westminister); *Gone-away lake,* Elizabeth Enright (Harcourt Brace Jovanovich); *The great wheel,* Robert Lawson (Viking); *Tom Paine, freedom's apostle,* Leo Gurko (Crowell).

1957 *Miracles on Maple Hill,* Virginia Sorensen (Harcourt Brace Jovanovich). **Honor books:** *Old Yeller,* Fred Gipson (Harper & Row); *The house of sixty fathers,* Meindert DeJong (Harper & Row); *Mr. Justice Holmes,* Clara Ingram Judson (Follett); *The corn grows ripe,* Dorothy Rhoads (Viking); *Black fox of Lorne,* Marguerite de Angeli (Doubleday).

1956 *Carry on, Mr. Bowditch,* Jean Lee Latham (Houghton Mifflin). **Honor books:** *The secret river,* Marjorie Kinnan Rawlings (Scribner); *The golden name day,* Jennie Linquist (Harper & Row); *Men, microscopes, and living things,* Katherine Shippen (Viking).

1955 *The wheel on the school,* Meindert De-Jong (Harper & Row). **Honor books:** *The courage of Sarah Noble,* Alice Dalgliesh (Scribner); *Banner in the sky,* James Ullman (Lippincott).

1954 *... and now Miguel,* Joseph Krumgold (Crowell). **Honor books:** *All alone,* Claire Huchet Bishop (Viking); *Shadrach,* Meindert DeJong (Harper & Row); *Hurry home, Candy,* Meindert

DeJong (Harper & Row); *Theodore Roosevelt, fighting patriot,* Clara Ingram Hudson (Follett); *Magic maize,* Mary & Conrad Buff (Houghton Mifflin).

1953 *Secret of the Andes,* Ann Nolan Clark (Viking). **Honor books:** *Charlotte's web,* E. B. White (Harper & Row); *Moccasin trail,* Eloise McGraw (Coward-McCann); *Red sails to Capri,* Ann Weil (Viking); *The bears on Hemlock Mountain,* Alice Dalgliesh (Scribner), *Birthdays of freedom, vol. 1,* Genevieve Foster (Scribner).

1952 *Ginger Pye,* Eleanor Estes (Harcourt Brace Jovanovich). **Honor books:** *Americans before Columbus,* Elizabeth Baity (Viking); *Minn of the Mississippi,* Holling C. Holling (Houghton Mifflin); *The defender,* Nicholas Kalashnikoff (Scribner); *The light at Tern Rock,* Julia Sauer (Viking); *The apple and the arrow,* Mary & Conrad Buff (Houghton Mifflin).

1951 *Amos Fortune, free man,* Elizabeth Yates (Aladdin). **Honor books:** *Better known as Johnny Appleseed,* Mabel Leigh Hunt (Lippincott); *Gandhi, fighter without a sword,* Jeanette Eaton (Morrow); *Abraham Lincoln, friend of the people,* Clara Ingram Judson (Follett); *The story of Appleby Capple,* Anne Parish (Harper & Row).

1950 *The door in the wall,* Marguerite de Angeli (Doubleday). **Honor books:** *Tree of freedom,* Rebecca Caudill (Viking); *The blue cat of castle town,* Catherine Coblentz (Longmans); *Kildee house,* Rutherford Montgomery (Doubleday); *George Washington,* Genevieve Foster (Scribner); *Song of the pines: A story of Norwegian lumbering in Wisconsin,* Walter & Marion Havighurst (Winston).

1949 *King of the wind,* Marguerite Henry (Rand McNally). **Honor books:** *Seabird,* Holling C. Holling (Houghton Mifflin); *Daughter of the mountains,* Louise Rankin (Viking); *My father's dragon,* Ruth S. Gannett (Random House); *Story of the negro,* Arna Bontempts (Knopf).

1948 *The twenty-one balloons,* William Pene du Bois (Viking). **Honor books:** *Pancakes-Paris,* Claire Huchet Bishop (Viking); *Le Lun, lad of courage,* Carolyn Treffinger (Abingdon Press); *The quaint and curious quest of Johnny Longfoot, the shoe-king's son,* Catherine Besterman (Bobbs); *The cow-tail switch, and other West African stories,* Harold Courlander (Holt); *Misty* *of Chincoteaque,* Marguerite Henry (Rand McNally).

1947 *Miss Hickory,* Carolyn Sherwin Bailey (Viking). **Honor books:** *Wonderful year,* Nancy Barnes (Messner); *Big tree,* Mary & Conrad Buff (Viking); *The heavenly tenants,* William Maxwell (Harper & Row); *The avion my uncle flew,* Cyrus Fisher (Appleton); *The hidden treasure of Glaston,* Eleanore Jewett (Viking).

1946 *Strawberry girl,* Lois Lenski (Lippincott). **Honor books:** *Justin Morgan had a horse,* Marguerite Henry (Rand McNally); *The moved-outers,* Florence Crannell Means (Houghton Mifflin); *Bhimsa, the dancing bear,* Christine Weston (Scribner); *New found world,* Katherine Shippen (Viking).

1945 *Rabbit hill,* Robert Lawson (Viking). **Honor books:** *The hundred dresses,* Eleanor Estes (Harcourt Brace Jovanovich); *The silver pencil,* Alice Dalgliesh (Scribner); *Abraham Lincoln's world,* Genevieve Foster (Scribner); *Lone journey: The life of Roger Williams,* Jeannette Eaton (Harcourt Brace Jovanovich).

1944 *Johnny Tremain,* Esther Forbes (Houghton Mifflin). **Honor books:** *The happy golden years,* Laura Ingalls Wilder (Harper & Row); *Fog magic,* Julia Sauer (Viking); *Rufus M.,* Eleanor Estes (Harcourt Brace Jovanovich); *Mountain born,* Elizabeth Yates (Coward).

1943 *Adam of the road,* Elizabeth Janet Gray (Viking). **Honor books:** *The middle Moffat,* Eleanor Estes (Harcourt Brace Jovanovich); *Have you seen Tom Thumb?,* Mabel Leigh Hunt (Lippincott).

1942 *The matchlock gun,* Walter D. Edmonds (Dodd). **Honor books:** *Little town on the prairie,* Laura Ingalls Wilder (Harper & Row); *George Washington's world,* Genevieve Foster (Scribner); *Indian captive: The story of Mary Jemison,* Lois Lenski (Lippincott); *Down Ryton water,* Eva Roe Gaggin (Viking).

1941 *Call it courage,* Armstrong Sperry (Macmillan). **Honor books:** *Blue willow,* Doris Gates (Viking); *Young Mac of Fort Vancouver,* Mary Jane Carr (Crowell); *The long winter,* Laura Ingalls Wilder (Harper & Row); *Nansen,* Anna Gertrude Hall (Viking).

1940 *Daniel Boone,* James Daugherty (Viking). **Honor books:** *The singing tree,* Kate Seredy (Viking); *Runner of the mountain tops: The life of Louis Agassiz,* Mabel Robinson (Random House); *By the shores of Silver Lake,* Laura Ingalls Wilder (Harper & Row); *Boy with a pack,* Stephen W. Meader (Harcourt Brace Jovanovich).

1939 *Thimble summer,* Elizabeth Enright (Rinehart). **Honor books:** *Nino,* Valenti Angelo (Viking); *Mr. Popper's penguins,* Richard & Florence Atwater (Little); *"Hello the boat!"* Phyllis Crawford (Holt); *Leader by destiny: George Washington, man and patriot,* Jeannette Eaton (Harcourt Brace Jovanovich); *Penn,* Elizabeth Janet Gray (Viking).

1938 *The white stag,* Kate Seredy (Viking). **Honor books:** *Pecos Bill,* James Cloyd Bowman (Little); *Bright island,* Mabel Robinson (Random House); *On the banks of Plum Creek,* Laura Ingalls Wilder (Harper & Row).

1937 *Roller skates,* Ruth Sawyer (Viking). **Honor books:** *Phoebe Fairchild: Her book,* Lois Lenski (Stokes); *Whistler's van,* Idwal Jones (Viking); *Golden basket,* Ludwig Bemelmans (Viking); *Winterbound,* Margery Bianco (Viking); *Audubon,* Constance Rourke (Harcourt Brace Jovanovich); *The codfish market,* Agnes Hewes (Doubleday).

1936 *Caddie Woodlawn,* Carol Ryrie Brink (Macmillan). **Honor books:** *Honk, the moose,* Phil Strong (Dodd); *The good master,* Kate Seredy (Viking); *Young Walter Scott,* Elizabeth Janet Gray (Viking); *All sail set: A romance of the flying cloud,* Armstrong Sperry (Winston).

1935 *Dobry,* Monica Shannon (Viking). **Honor books:** *Pageant of Chinese history,* Elizabeth Seeger (Longmans); *Davy Crockett,* Constance Rourke (Harcourt Brace Jovanovich); *Day on skates: The story of a Dutch picnic,* Hilda Van Stockum (Harper & Row).

1934 *Invincible Louisa: The story of the author of "Little Women,"* Cornelia Meigs (Little). **Honor books:** *The forgotten daughter,* Caroline Snedeker (Doubleday); *Swords of steel,* Elsie Singmaster (Houghton Mifflin); *ABC bunny,* Wanda Gag (Coward); *Winged girl of Knossos,* Erik Berry (Appleton); *New land,* Sara Schmidt (McBride); *Big tree of Bunlahy: Stories of my own countryside,* Padraic Colum (Macmillan); *Glory of the seas,* Agnes Hewes (Knopf); *Apprentice of Florence,* Ann Kyle (Houghton Mifflin).

1933 *Young Fu of the upper Yangtze,* Elizabeth Foreman Lewis (Winston). **Honor books:** *Swift rivers,* Cornelia Meigs (Little); *The railroad to freedom: A story of the Civil War,* Hildegarde Swift (Harcourt Brace Jovanovich); *Children of the soil: A story of Scandinavia,* Nora Burglon (Doubleday).

1932 *Waterless mountain,* Laura Adams Armer (Longmans). **Honor books:** *The fairy circus,* Dorothy P. Lathrop (Macmillan); *Calico bush,* Rachel Field (Macmillan); *Boy of the South Seas,* Eunice Tietjens (Coward); *Out of the flame,* Eloise Lownsbery (Longmans); *Jane's island,* Marjorie Allee (Houghton Mifflin); *Truce of the wolf and other tales of old Italy,* Mary Gould Davis (Harcourt Brace Jovanovich).

1931 *The cat who went to heaven,* Elizabeth Coatsworth (Macmillan). **Honor books:** *Floating island,* Anne Parrish (Harper & Row); *The dark star of Itza: The story of a pagan princess,* Alida Malkus (Harcourt Brace Jovanovich); *Queer person,* Ralph Hubbard (Doubleday); *Mountains are free,* Julia Davis Adams (Dutton); *Spice and the devil's cave,* Agnes Hewes (Knopf); *Meggy Macintosh,* Elizabeth Janet Gray (Doubleday); *Garram the hunter: A boy of the hill tribes,* Herbert Best (Doubleday); *Ood-Le-Uk the wanderer,* Alice Lide & Margaret Johansen (Little).

1930 *Hitty, her first hundred years,* Rachel Field (Macmillan). **Honor books:** *Daughter of the Seine: The life of Madame Roland,* Jeanette Eaton (Harper & Row); *Pran of Albania,* Elizabeth Miller (Doubleday); *Jumping-off place,* Marian Hurd McNeely (Longmans); *Tangle-coated horse and other tales of New England,* Julia Davis Adams (Dutton); *Little blacknose,* Hildegarde Swift (Harcourt Brace Jovanovich).

1929 *The trumpeter of Krakow,* Eric P. Kelly (Macmillan). **Honor books:** *Pigtail of Ah Lee Ben Loo,* John Bennett (Longmans); *Millions of cats,* Wanda Gag (Coward); *The boy who was,* Grace Hallock (Dutton); *Clearing weather,* Cornelia Meigs (Little); *Runaway papoose,* Grace Moon (Doubleday); *Tod of the fens,* Elinor Whitney (Macmillan).

1928 *Gayneck, the story of a pigeon,* Dhan Gopal Mukerji (Dutton). **Honor books:** *The wonder Smith and his son: A tale from the golden childhood of the world,* Ella Young (Longmans); *Downright Dencey,* Caroline Snedeker (Doubleday).

1927 *Smoky, the cowhorse,* Will James (Scribner). **Honor books:** None.

1926 *Shen of the sea,* Arthur Bowie Chrisman (Dutton). **Honor book:** *Voyagers: Being legends and romances of Atlantic discovery,* Padraic Colum (Macmillan).

1925 *Tales from silver lands,* Charles Finger (Doubleday). **Honor books:** *Nicholas: A Manhattan Christmas story,* Anne Carroll Moore (Putnam); *Dream coach,* Anne Parrish (Macmillan).

1924 *The dark frigate,* Charles Hawes (Atlantic/Little). **Honor books:** None.

1923 *The voyages of Doctor Dolittle,* Hugh Lofting (Lippincott). **Honor books:** None

1922 *The story of mankind,* Hendrik Willem van Loon (Liveright). **Honor books:** *The great quest,* Charles Hawes (Little); *Cedric the forester,* Bernard Marshall (Appleton); *The old tobacco shop: A true account of what befell a little boy in search of adventure,* William Bowen (Macmillan); *The golden fleece and the heroes who lived before Achilles,* Padraic Colum (Macmillan); *Windy hill,* Cornelia Meigs (Macmillan).

CORETTA SCOTT KING AWARD

The Coretta Scott King Award is presented annually by the American Library Association to an African American author and an African American illustrator for distinguished inspirational and educational contributions to literature. Many of the books that receive this recognition are appropriate for children in kindergarten through eighth grade. The award commemorates the life and work of Martin Luther King, Jr., and honors his widow, Coretta Scott King, for her continuing work for peace and world brotherhood. The award was first given in 1970.

1992 **Author Award:** *Now is your time: The African American struggle for freedom,* Walter Dean Myers (HarperCollins). **Honor book:** *Night on Neighborhood Street,* Eloise Greenfield, illustrated by Jan Spivey Gilchrist (Dial). **Illustrator Award:** *Tar beach,* Faith Ringgold (Orchard). **Honor books:** *All night, all day: A child's first book of African American spirituals,* Ashley Bryan (Atheneum); *Night on Neighborhood Street,* Eloise Greenfield, illustrated by Jan Spivey Gilchrist (Dial).

1991 **Author Award:** *The road to Memphis,* Mildred T. Taylor (Dial). **Honor books:** *Black dance in America,* James Haskins (Crowell); *When I am old with you,* Angela Johnson (Orchard). **Illustrator Award:** *Aida,* Leontyne Prince, illustrated by Leo and Diane Dillon (Harcourt Brace Jovanovich).

1990 **Author Award:** *A long hard journey: The story of the Pullman porter,* Patricia & Frederick McKissack (Walker). **Honor books:** *Nathaniel talking,* Eloise Greenfield (Black Butterfly); *The bells of Christmas,* Virginia Hamilton (Harcourt Brace Jovanovich); *Martin Luther King, Jr. and the freedom movement,* Lillie Patterson (Facts on File). **Illustrator Award:** *Nathaniel talking,* Eloise Greenfield, illustrated by Jan Spivey Gilchrist (Black Butterfly). **Honor book:** *The talking eggs,* Robert D. San Souci, illustrated by Jerry Pinkney (Dial).

1989 **Author Award:** *Fallen angels,* Walter Dean Myers (Scholastic). **Honor books:** *A thief in the village and other stories,* James Berry (Orchard); *Anthony Burns: The defeat and triumph of a fugitive slave,* Virginia Hamilton (Knopf). **Illustrator Award:** *Mirandy and brother wind,* Patricia C. McKissack, illustrated by Jerry Pinkney (Knopf). **Honor books:** *Under the Sunday tree,* Eloise Greenfield, illustrated by Amos Ferguson (Harper & Row); *Storm in the night,* Mary Stolz, illustrated by Pat Cummings (Harper & Row).

1988 **Author Award:** *The friendship,* Mildred D. Taylor (Dial). **Honor books:** *An enchanted hair tale,* Alexis de Veaux (Harper & Row); *The tales of Uncle Remus: The adventures of Brer Rabbit,* Julius Lester (Dial). **Illustrator Award:** *Mufaro's beautiful daughters,* John Steptoe (Lothrop). **Honor books:** *What a morning! The Christmas story in Black spirituals,* John Langstaff, illustrated by Ashley Bryan (Macmillan); *The invisible hunters: A legend from the Miskito Indians of Nicaragua,* Harriet Rohmer et al., illustrated by Joe Sam (Children's Book Press).

1987 **Author Award:** *Justin and the best biscuits in the world,* Mildred Pitts Walter (Lothrop). **Honor books:** *Lion and the ostrich chicks and other African folktales,* Ashley Bryan (Atheneum); *Which way freedom?* Joyce Hansen (Walker). **Illustrator Award:** *Half a moon and one whole star,* Crescent Dragonwagon, illustrated by Jerry Pinkney (Macmillan). **Honor books:** *Lion and the ostrich chicks and other African folk tales,* Ashley Bryan (Atheneum); *C.L.O.U.D.S.,* Pat Cummings (Lothrop).

1986 **Author Award:** *The people could fly: American Black folktales,* Virginia Hamilton (Knopf). **Honor books:** *Junius over far,* Virginia Hamilton (Harper & Row); *Trouble's child,* Mildred Pitts Walter (Lothrop). **Illustrator Award:** *The patchwork quilt,* Valerie Flournoy, illustrated by Jerry Pinkney (Dial). **Honor book:** *The people could fly: American Black folktales,* Virginia Hamilton, illustrated by Leo & Diane Dillon (Knopf).

1985 **Author Award:** *Motown and Didi,* Walter Dean Myers (Viking). **Honor books:** *Circle of Gold,* Candy Dawson Boyd (Scholastic); *A little love,* Virginia Hamilton (Philomel).

1984 **Author Award:** *Everett Anderson's goodbye,* Lucille Clifton (Holt). **Honor books:** *The magical adventures of Pretty Pearl,* Virginia Hamilton (Harper & Row); *Lena Horne,* James Haskins (Coward-McCann); *Bright Shadow,* Joyce Carol Thomas (Avon); *Because we are,* Mildred Pitts Walter (Lothrop). **Illustrator Award:** *My mama needs me,* Mildred Pitts Walter, illustrated by Pat Cummings (Lothrop).

1983 **Author Award:** *Sweet whispers, Brother Rush,* Virginia Hamilton (Philomel). **Honor book:** *This strange new feeling,* Julius Lester (Dial). **Illustrator Award:** *Black child,* Peter Magubane (Knopf). **Honor books:** *All the colors of the race,* Arnold Adoff, illustrated by John Steptoe (Lothrop); *I'm going to sing: Black American spirituals,* Ashley Bryan (Atheneum).

1982 **Author Award:** *Let the circle be unbroken,* Mildred D. Taylor (Dial). **Honor books:** *Rainbow Jordan,* Alice Childress (Coward-McCann); *Lou in the limelight,* Kristin Hunter (Scribner); *Mary: An autobiography,* Mary E. Mebane (Viking). **Illustrator Award:** *Mother crocodile: An Uncle Amadou tale from Senegal,* Rosa Guy (trans.), illustrated by John Steptoe (Delacorte). **Honor**

book: *Daydreamers,* Eloise Greenfield, illustrated by Tom Feelings (Dial).

1981 Author Award: *This life,* Sidney Poitier (Knopf). **Honor book:** *Don't explain: A song of Billie Holiday,* Alexis de Veaux (Harper & Row). **Illustrator Award:** *Beat the story drum pumpum,* Ashley Bryan (Atheneum). **Honor books:** *Grandma's joy,* Eloise Greenfield, illustrated by Carole Byard (Philomel); *Count on your fingers African style,* Claudia Zaslavsky, illustrated by Jerry Pinkney (Crowell).

1980 Author Award: *The young landlords,* Walter Dean Myers (Viking). **Honor books:** *Movin' up,* Berry Gordy (Harper & Row); *Childtimes: A three-generation memoir,* Eloise Greenfield & Lessie Jones Little (Harper & Row); *Andrew Young: Young man with a mission,* James Haskins (Lothrop); *James Van Der Zee: The picture takin' man,* James Haskins (Dodd); *Let the lion eat straw,* Ellease Southerland (Scribner). **Illustrator Award:** *Cornrows,* Camille Yarbrough, illustrated by Carole Byard (Coward-McCann).

1979 Author Award: *Escape to freedom: A play about young Frederick Douglass,* Ossie Davis (Viking). **Honor books:** *Skates of Uncle Richard,* Carol Fenner (Random House); *Justice and her brothers,* Virginia Hamilton (Greenwillow); *Benjamin Banneker,* Lillie Patterson (Abingdon Press); *I have a sister, my sister is deaf,* Jeanne W. Peterson (Harper & Row). **Illustrator Award:** *Something on my mind,* Nikki Grimes, illustrated by Tom Feelings (Dial).

1978 Author Award: *Africa dream,* Eloise Greenfield (Crowell). **Honor books:** *The days when the animals talked: Black folktales and how they came to be,* William J. Faulkner (Follett); *Marvin and Tige,* Frankcina Glass (St. Martin's Press), *Mary McCleod Bethune,* Eloise Greenfield (Crowell); *Barbara Jordan,* James Haskins (Dial); *Coretta Scott King,* Lillie Patterson (Garrard); *Portia: The life of Portia Washington Pittman, the daughter of Booker T. Washington,* Ruth Ann Steward (Doubleday).

1977 Author Award: *The story of Stevie Wonder,* James Haskins (Lothrop). **Honor books:** *Everett Anderson's friend,* Lucille Clifton (Holt); *Roll of thunder, hear my cry,* Mildred D. Taylor (Dial); *Quiz book on Black America,* Clarence N. Blake & Donald F. Martin (Houghton Mifflin).

1976 Author Award: *Duey's tale,* Pearl Bailey (Harcourt Brace Jovanovich). **Honor books:** *Julius K. Nyerere: Teacher of Africa,* Shirley Graham (Messner); *Paul Robeson,* Eloise Greenfield (Crowell); *Fast Sam, cool Clyde and stuff,* Walter Dean Myers (Viking); *Song of the trees,* Mildred Taylor (Dial).

1975 Author Award: *The legend of Africania,* Dorothy Robinson (Johnson Publishing).

1974 Author Award: *Ray Charles,* Sharon Bell Mathis (Crowell). **Honor books:** *A hero ain't nothin' but a sandwich,* Alice Childress (Coward-McCann); *Don't you remember?* Lucille Clifton (Dutton); *Ms. Africa: Profiles of modern African women,* Louise Crane (Lippincott); *Guest in the promised land,* Kristin Hunter (Scribner); *Mukasa,* John Nagenda (Macmillan). **Illustrator Award:** *Ray Charles,* Sharon Bell Mathis, illustrated by George Ford (Crowell).

1973 Author Award: *I never had it made: The autobiography of Jackie Robinson,* Alfred Duckett (Putnam).

1972 Author Award: *17 black artists,* Elton C. Fax (Dodd).

1971 Author Award: *Black troubadour: Langston Hughes,* Charlemae Rollins (Rand McNally). **Honor books:** *I know why the caged bird sings,* Maya Angelou (Random House); *Unbought and unbossed,* Shirley Chisholm (Houghton Mifflin); *I am a Black woman,* Mari Evans (Morrow); *Every man heart lay down,* Lorenz Graham (Crowell); *The voice of the children,* June Jordan & Terri Bush (Holt); *Black means,* Gloom Grossman (Hill & Wang); *Ebony book of Black achievement,* Margaret W. Peters (Johnson Publishing); *Mary Jo's grandmother,* Janice May Udry (Whitman).

1970 Author Award: *Dr. Martin Luther King, Jr., man of peace,* Lillie Patterson (Garrard).

APPENDIX B

RESOURCES ABOUT AUTHORS AND ILLUSTRATORS

BOOKS ABOUT AUTHORS AND ILLUSTRATORS

ANDERSEN, HANS CHRISTIAN Greene, C. (1991). *Hans Christian Andersen: Prince of storytellers.* Chicago: Childrens Press. (P–M)*

BLEGVAD, ERIK Blegvad, E. (1979). *Self-portrait: Erik Blegvad.* Reading, MA: Addison-Wesley. (P–M–U)

BOSTON, LUCY Boston, L. M. (1979). *Perverse and foolish: A memoir of childhood and youth.* New York: Atheneum. (U)

BULLA, CLYDE Bulla, C. R. (1985). *A grain of wheat: A writer begins.* Boston: David R. Godine. (M)

BURNETT, FRANCES HODGSON Carpenter, A. S., & Shirley, J. (1990). *Frances Hodgson Burnett: Beyond the secret garden.* Minneapolis: Lerner Books. (U)

CARSON, RACHEL Wadsworth, G. (1991). *Rachel Carson: Voice for the earth.* Minneapolis: Lerner Books. (U)

CLEARY, BEVERLY Cleary, B. (1988). *A girl from Yamhill: A memoir.* New York: Morrow. (M–U)

COWLEY, JOY Cowley, J. (1988). *Seventy kilometres from ice cream: A letter from Joy Cowley.* Katonah, NY: Richard C. Owens. (P)

DAHL, ROALD Dahl, R. (1984). *Boy: Tales of childhood.* New York: Farrar, Straus & Giroux. (M–U)

DE PAOLA, TOMIE de Paola, T. (1989). *The art lesson.* New York: Putnam. (P)

DILLON, LEO and DIANE Preiss, B. (1981). *The art of Leo and Diane Dillon.* New York: Ballantine. (M–U)

DUNCAN, LOIS Duncan, L. (1982). *Chapters: My growth as a writer.* Boston: Little, Brown. (U)

FRITZ, JEAN Fritz, J. (1982). *Homesick: My own story.* New York: Putnam. (M–U)

GOODALL, JOHN Goodall, J. S. (1981). *Before the war, 1908–1939. An autobiography in pictures.* New York: Atheneum. (M–U)

HENRY, MARGUERITE Henry, M. (1980). *The illustrated Marguerite Henry.* Chicago: Rand McNally. (M–U)

HUGHES, LANGSTON Walker, A. (1974). *Langston Hughes, American poet.* New York: Crowell. (M–U)

HYMAN, TRINA SCHART Hyman, T. S. (1981). *Self-portrait: Trina Schart Hyman.* Reading, MA: Addison-Wesley. (P–M–U)

LEWIS, C. S. Lewis, C. S. (1985). *Letters to children.* New York: Macmillan. (M–U)

MELTZER, MILTON Meltzer, M. (1988). *Starting from home: A writer's beginnings.* NY: Viking. (U)

NAYLOR, PHYLLIS Naylor, P. R. (1978). *How I came to be a writer.* New York: Atheneum. (U)

PEET, BILL Peet, B. (1989). *Bill Peet: An autobiography.* Boston: Houghton Mifflin. (M–U)

---

*P = Primary grades (K–2); M = Middle grades (3–5); U = Upper grades (6–8)

POTTER, BEATRIX   Aldis, D. (1969). *Nothing is impossible: The story of Beatrix Potter.* New York: Atheneum. (M); Collins, D. R. (1989). *The country artist: A story about Beatrix Potter.* Minneapolis: Carolrhoda. (M)

RYLANT, CYNTHIA   Rylant, C. (1992). *Best wishes.* Katonah, NY: Richard C. Owen. (P–M)

SINGER, ISAAC BASHEVIS   Singer, I. B. (1969). *A day of pleasure: Stories of a boy growing up in Warsaw.* New York: Farrar, Straus & Giroux. (U)

YOLEN, JANE   Yolen, J. (1992). *A letter from Phoenix Farm.* Katonah, NY: Richard C. Owens. (P–M–U)

WILDER, LAURA INGALLS   Blair, G. (1981). *Laura Ingalls Wilder.* New York: Putnam. (P–M); Greene, C. (1990). *Laura Ingalls Wilder: Author of the little house books.* Chicago: Childrens Press. (P–M)

ZEMACH, MARGOT   Zemach, M. (1978). *Self-portrait: Margot Zemach.* Reading, MA: Addison-Wesley. (P–M–U)

INDIVIDUAL ARTICLES PROFILING AUTHORS AND ILLUSTRATORS

ADOFF, ARNOLD   White, M. L. (1988). Profile: Arnold Adoff. *Language Arts, 65,* 584–591.

ALEXANDER, LLOYD   Greenlaw, M. J. (1984). Profile: Lloyd Alexander. *Language Arts, 61,* 406–413; Tunnell, M. O. (1989). An interview with Lloyd Alexander. *The New Advocate, 2,* 83–96.

ANNO, MITSUMASA   Aoki, H. (1983). A conversation with Mitsumasa Anno. *Horn Book Magazine, 59,* 132–145; Swinger, A. K. (1987). Profile: Mitsumasa Anno's journey. *Language Arts, 64,* 762–766.

BAYLOR, BYRD   Bosma, B. (1987). Profile: Byrd Baylor. *Language Arts, 64,* 315–318.

BEHN, HARRY   Roop, P. (1985). Profile: Harry Behn. *Language Arts, 62,* 92–94.

BRETT, JAN   Raymond, A. (April 1992). Jan Brett: Making it look easy. *Teaching PreK–8, 22,* 38–40.

BROWN, MARCIA   Brown, M. (1983). Caldecott Medal Acceptance. *Horn Book Magazine, 59,* 414–422.

BROWN, MARGARET WISE   Hurd, C. (1983). Remembering Margaret Wise Brown. *Horn Book Magazine, 59,* 553–560.

BROWNE, ANTHONY   Marantz, S., & Marantz, K. (1985). An interview with Anthony Browne. *Horn Book Magazine, 61,* 696–704.

BRYAN, ASHLEY   Marantz, S., & Marantz, K. (1988). Interview with Ashley Bryan. *Horn Book Magazine, 64,* 173–179; Swinger, A. K. (1984). Profile: Ashley Bryan. *Language Arts, 61,* 305–311.

BUNTING, EVE   Raymond, A. (October, 1986). Eve Bunting: From Ireland with love. *Teaching PreK–8, 17,* 38–40.

BYARS, BETSY   Robertson, I. (1980). Profile: Betsy Byars—writer for today's child. *Language Arts, 57,* 328–334.

CARLE, ERIC   Yolen, J. (1988). In the artist's studio: Eric Carle. *The New Advocate, 1,* 148–154

CIARDI, JOHN   Odland, N. (1982). Profile: John Ciardi. *Language Arts, 59,* 872–876.

CLEARY, BEVERLY   Cleary, B. (1984). Newbery Medal acceptance. *Horn Book Magazine, 50,* 429–438; Reuter, D. (1984). Beverly Cleary. *Horn Book Magazine, 50,* 439–443.

CLIFTON, LUCILLE   Sims, R. (1982). Profile: Lucille Clifton. *Language Arts, 59,* 160–167.

COLLIER, JAMES and CHRISTOPHER   Raymond, A. (January, 1988). Meet James and Christopher Collier. *Teaching PreK–8, 18,* 35–38.

CONRAD, PAM   Raymond, A. (November/December, 1990). Pam Conrad: She said to herself, 'Now what?' *Teaching PreK–8, 21,* 38–40.

DEGAN, BRUCE   Elliot, I. (October, 1991). Bruce Degan: Doing what he likes best. *Teaching PreK–8, 21,* 44–47.

DEJONG, MEINDERT   Hearne, B. (1984). Meindert DeJong. *Horn Book Magazine, 60,* 566–568.

DR. SEUSS   Roth, R. (1989). On beyond zebra with Dr. Seuss. *The New Advocate, 2,* 213–226.

EGIELSKI, RICHARD   Egielski, R. (1987). Caldecott Medal acceptance. *Horn Book Magazine, 63,*

433–435; Yorinks, A. (1987). Richard Egielski. *Horn Book Magazine, 63,* 436–438.

ENRIGHT, ELIZABETH Cameron, E. (1984). A second look: Gone-away Lake. *Horn Book Magazine, 60,* 622–626.

FEELINGS, TOM Feelings, T. (1985). The artist at work: Technique and the artist's vision. *Horn Book Magazine, 61,* 685–695.

FLEISCHMAN, SID Fleischman, P. (1987). Sid Fleischman. *Horn Book Magazine, 63,* 429–432; Fleischman, S. (1987). Newbery Medal Acceptance. *Horn Book Magazine, 63,* 423–428; Johnson, E. R. (1982). Profile: Sid Fleischman. *Language Arts, 59,* 754–759.

FOX, MEM Manning, M., & Manning, G. (March, 1990). Mem Fox: Mem's the word in down under? *Teaching PreK–8, 20,* 29–31.

FREEDMAN, RUSSELL Dempsey, F. J. (1988). Russell Freedman. *Horn Book Magazine, 64,* 452–456; Freedman, R. (1988). Newbery Medal acceptance. *Horn Book Magazine, 64,* 444–451.

FRITZ, JEAN Ammon, R. (1983). Profile: Jean Fritz. *Language Arts, 60,* 365–369; Fritz, J. (1985). Turning history inside out. *Horn Book Magazine, 61,* 29–34; Heins, E. L. (1986). Presentation of the Laura Ingalls Wilder Medal. *Horn Book Magazine, 62,* 430–431.

GERSTEIN, MORDICAI Yolen, J. (1990). In the artist's studio: Mordicai Gerstein. *The New Advocate, 3,* 25–28.

GIFF, PATRICIA REILLY Raymond, A. (April 1987). Patricia Reilly Giff: A writer who believes in reading. *Teaching PreK–8, 17,* 34–37.

GILSON, JAMIE Johnson, R. (1983). Profile: Jamie Gilson. *Language Arts, 60,* 661–667.

GOBLE, PAUL Stott, J. C. (1984). Profile: Paul Goble. *Language Arts, 61,* 867–873.

GOFFSTEIN, M. B. Marantz, S., & Martantz, K. (1986). M. B. Goffstein: An interview. *Horn Book Magazine, 62,* 688–694; Shannon, G. (1983). Goffstein and friends. *Horn Book Magazine, 59,* 88–95.

GREENFIELD, ELOISE Kiah, R. B. (1980). Profile: Eloise Greenfield. *Language Arts, 57,* 653–659.

HALEY, GAIL E. Haley, G. E. (1990). Of mermaids, myths, and meaning: A sea tale. *The New Advocate, 3,* 1–12.

HAMILTON, VIRGINIA Hamilton, V. (1986). Coretta Scott King Award acceptance. *Horn Book Magazine, 62,* 683–687.

HENKES, KEVIN Elliot, I. (January, 1989). Meet Kevin Henkes: Young man on a roll. *Teaching PreK–8, 19,* 43–45.

HOOVER, H. M. Porter, E. J. (1982). Profile: H. M. Hoover. *Language Arts, 59,* 609–613.

HOWE, JAMES Raymond, A. (February, 1987). James Howe: Corn, ham and punster cheese. *Teaching PreK–8, 17,* 32–34.

HYMAN, TRINA SCHART Hyman, K. (1985). Trina Schart Hyman. *Horn Book Magazine, 61,* 422–425; Hyman, T. S. (1985). Caldecott Medal acceptance. *Horn Book Magazine, 61,* 410–421; Saul, W. (1988). Once-upon-a-time artist in the land of now: An interview with Trina Schart Hyman. *The New Advocate, 1,* 8–17; White, D. E. (1983). Profile: Trina Schart Hyman. *Language Arts, 60,* 782–792.

JONAS, ANN Marantz, S., & Marantz, K. (1987). Interview with Ann Jonas. *Horn Book Magazine, 63,* 308–313; Raymond, A. (December, 1987). Ann Jonas: Reflections 1987. *Teaching PreK–8, 18,* 44–46.

KEATS, EZRA JACK Lanes, S. G. (1984). Ezra Jack Keats: In memoriam. *Horn Book Magazine, 60,* 551–558; Pope, M., & Pope, L. (1990). Ezra Jack Keats: A childhood revisited. *The New Advocate, 3,* 13–24.

KONIGSBURG, E. L. Jones, L. T. (1986). Profile: Elaine Konigsburg. *Language Arts, 63,* 177–184.

LASKY, KATHRYN Lasky, K. (1990). The fiction of history: Or, what did Miss Kitty really do? *The New Advocate, 3,* 157–166.

L'ENGLE, MADELEINE Raymond, A. (May, 1991). Madeleine L'Engle: Getting the last laugh. *Teaching PreK–8, 21,* 34–36; Samuels, L. A. (1981). Profile: Madeleine L'Engle. *Language Arts, 58,* 704–712.

LESTER, JULIUS Lester, J. (1988). The storyteller's voice: Reflections on the rewriting of Uncle Remus. *The New Advocate, 1,* 137–142.

LIVINGSTON, MYRA COHN Porter, E. J. (1980). Profile: Myra Cohn Livingston. *Language Arts, 57,* 901–905.

LOBEL, ANITA Raymond, A. (November/December, 1989). Anita Lobel: Up from the crossroad. *Teaching PreK–8, 20,* 52–55.

LOBEL, ARNOLD Lobel, A. (1981). Caldecott Medal acceptance. *Horn Book Magazine, 57,* 400–404; Lobel, A. (1981). Arnold at home. *Horn*

Book Magazine, 57, 405–410; White, D. E. (1988). Profile: Arnold Lobel. *Language Arts, 65*, 489–494.

LOWRY, LOIS Lowry, L. (1988). *Rabble Starkey. Horn Book Magazine, 64*, 29–31; Lowry, L. (1990). *Number the stars:* Lois Lowry's journey to the Newbery Award. *The Reading Teacher, 44*, 98–101; Raymond, A. (October, 1987). 'Anastasia,' and then some. *Teaching PreK–8, 18*, 44–46.

MACAULAY, DAVID Ammon, R. (1982). Profile: David Macaulay. *Language Arts, 59*, 374–378.

MACLACHLAN, PATRICIA Babbitt, N. (1986). Patricia MacLachlan: The biography. *Horn Book Magazine, 62*, 414–416; Courtney, A. (1985). Profile: Patricia MacLachlan. *Language Arts, 62*, 783–787; MacLachlan, P. (1986). Newbery Medal acceptance. *Horn Book Magazine, 62*, 407–413; MacLachlan, R. (1986). A hypothetical dilemma. *Horn Book Magazine, 62*, 416–419; Raymond, A. (May, 1989). Patricia MacLachlan: An advocate of 'Bare boning.' *Teaching PreK–8, 19*, 46–48.

MARTIN, BILL, JR. Larrick, N. (1982). Profile: Bill Martin, Jr. *Language Arts, 59*, 490–494.

MAYER, MARIANNA Raymond, A. (January, 1991). Marianna Mayer: Myths, legends, and folklore. *Teaching PreK–8, 21*, 42–44.

MCDERMOTT, GERALD McDermott, G. (1988). Sky father, earth mother: An artist interprets myth. *The New Advocate, 1*, 1–7; White, D. E. (1982). Profile: Gerald McDermott. *Language Arts, 59*, 273–279.

MCKINLEY, ROBIN McKinley, R. (1985). Newbery Medal acceptance. *Horn Book Magazine, 61*, 395–405; Windling, T. (1985). Robin McKinley. *Horn Book Magazine, 61*, 406–409.

MCKISSACK, PATRICIA Bishop, R. S. (1992). A conversation with Patricia McKissack. *Language Arts, 69*, 69–74.

MERRIAM, EVE Cox, S. T. (1989). A word or two with Eve Merriam: Talking about poetry. *The New Advocate, 2*, 139–150; Sloan, G. (1981). Profile: Eve Merriam. *Language Arts, 58*, 957–964.

MIKOLAYCAK, CHARLES White, D. E. (1981). Profile: Charles Mikolaycak, *Language Arts, 58*, 850–857.

MOHR, NICHOLASA Zarnowski, M. (1991). An interview with author Nicholasa Mohr. *The Reading Teacher, 45*, 100–107.

MONTRESOR, BENI Raymond, A. (April 1990). Beni Montresor: Carmen, Cannes and Caldecott. *Teaching PreK–8, 20*, 31–33.

MOORE, LILIAN Glazer, J. I. (1985). Profile: Lilian Moore. *Language Arts, 62*, 647–652.

MOSER, BARRY Moser, B. (1987). Artist at work: Illustrating the classics. *Horn Book Magazine, 63*, 703–709; Moser, B. (1991). Family photographs, gathered fragments. *The New Advocate, 4*, 1–10.

MUNSCH, ROBERT Jenkinson, D. (1989). Profile: Robert Munsch. *Language Arts, 66*, 665–675.

MYERS, WALTER DEAN Bishop, R. S. (1990). Profile: Walter Dean Myers. *Language Arts, 67*, 862–866.

O'DELL, SCOTT Roop, P. (1984). Profile: Scott O'Dell. *Language Arts, 61*, 750–752.

PARKER, NANCY WINSLOW Raymond, A. (May, 1990). Nancy Winslow Parker: 'I knew it would happen.' *Teaching PreK–8, 20*, 34–36.

PATERSON, KATHERINE Jones, L. T. (1981). Profile: Katherine Paterson. *Language Arts, 58*, 189–196; Namovic, G. I. (1981). Katherine Paterson. *Horn Book Magazine, 57*, 394–399; Paterson, K. (1981). Newbery Medal acceptance. *Horn Book Magazine, 57*, 385–393.

PRELUTSKY, JACK Raymond, A. (November/December 1986). Jack Prelutsky . . . Man of many talents. *Teaching PreK–8, 17*, 38–42; Vardell, S. (1991). An interview with Jack Prelutsky. *The New Advocate, 4*, 101–112.

PROVENSEN, ALICE and MARTIN Provensen, A., & Provensen, M. (1984). Caldecott Medal acceptance. *Horn Book Magazine, 50*, 444–448; Willard, N. (1984). Alice and Martin Provensen. *Horn Book Magazine, 50*, 449–452.

RASKIN, ELLEN Bach, A. (1985). Ellen Raskin: Some clues about her life. *Horn Book Magazine, 61*, 62–67.

RICE, EVE Raymond, A. (April, 1989). Meet Eve Rice: Author/artist/doctor (doctor?). *Teaching PreK–8, 19*, 40–42.

RYLANT, CYNTHIA Silvey, A. (1987). An interview with Cynthia Rylant. *Horn Book Magazine, 63*, 695–702.

SCHOENHERR, JOHN Gauch, P. L. (1988). John Schoenherr. *Horn Book Magazine, 64*, 460–463; Schoenherr, J. (1988). Caldecott Medal acceptance. *Horn Book Magazine, 64*, 457–459.

SCHWARTZ, ALVIN   Vardell, S. M. (1987). Profile: Alvin Schwartz. *Language Arts, 64,* 426–432.

SENDAK, MAURICE   Sendak, M. (1983). Laura Ingalls Wilder Award Acceptance. *Horn Book Magazine, 59,* 474–477.

SEWALL, MARCIA   Sewall, M. (1988). *The pilgrims of Plimoth. Horn Book Magazine, 64,* 32–34.

SHULEVITZ, URI   Raymond, A. (January 1992). Uri Shulevitz: For children of all ages. *Teaching PreK–8, 21,* 38–40.

SPINELLI, JERRY   Spinelli, J. (1991). Capturing Maniac Magee. *The Reading Teacher, 45,* 174–177.

STEIG, BILL   Raymond, A. (August/September 1991). Jeanne and Bill Steig: It adds up to magic. *Teaching PreK–8, 21,* 52–54.

STEPTOE, JOHN   Bradley, D. H. (1991). John Steptoe: Retrospective of an imagemaker. *The New Advocate, 4,* 11–24.

TAFURI, NANCY   Raymond, A. (January 1987). Nancy Tafuri . . . Nature, picturebooks, and joy. *Teaching PreK–8, 17,* 34–36.

TAYLOR, MILDRED D.   Dussel, S. L. (1981). Profile: Mildred D. Taylor. *Language Arts, 58,* 599–604.

TAYLOR, THEODORE   Bagnall, N. (1980). Profile: Theodore Taylor: His models of self-reliance. *Language Arts, 57,* 86–91.

UCHIDA, YOSHIKO   Chang, C. E. S. (1984). Profile: Yoshiko Uchida. *Language Arts, 61,* 189–194.

VAN ALLSBURG, CHRIS   Keifer, B. (1987). Profile: Chris Van Allsburg in three dimensions. *Language Arts, 64,* 664–671; Macaulay, D. (1986). Chris Van Allsburg. *Horn Book Magazine, 62,* 424–426; McKee, B. (1986). Van Allsburg: From a different perspective. *Horn Book Magazine, 62,* 566–571; Van Allsburg, C. (1982). Caldecott Medal acceptance. *Horn Book Magazine, 58,* 380–383; Van Allsburg, C. (1986). Caldecott Medal acceptance. *Horn Book Magazine, 62,* 420–424.

VOIGT, CYNTHIA   Kauffman, D. (1985). Profile: Cynthia Voigt. *Language Arts, 62,* 876–880; Voigt, C. (1983). Newbery Medal Acceptance. *Horn Book Magazine, 59,* 401–409.

WHITE, E. B.   Hopkins, L. B. (1986). Profile *in memoriam:* E. B. White. *Language Arts, 63,* 491–494; Newmeyer, P. F. (1985). The creation of E. B. White's *The Trumpet of the Swans:* The manuscripts. *Horn Book Magazine, 61,* 17–28; Newmeyer, P. F. (1987). E. B. White: Aspects of style. *Horn Book Magazine, 63,* 586–591.

WILLARD, NANCY   Lucas, B. (1982). Nancy Willard. *Horn Book Magazine, 58,* 374–379; Willard, N. (1982). Newbery Medal Acceptance. *Horn Book Magazine, 58,* 369–373.

WILLIAMS, VERA B.   Raymond, A. (October, 1988). Vera B. Williams: Postcards and peace vigils. *Teaching PreK–8, 19,* 40–42.

WORTH, VALERIE   Hopkins, L. B. (1991). Profile: Valerie Worth. *Language Arts, 68,* 499–501.

YOLEN, JANE   White, D. E. (1983). Profile: Jane Yolen. *Language Arts, 60,* 652–660; Yolen, J. (1989). On silent wings: The making of *Owl moon. The New Advocate, 2,* 199–212; Yolen, J. (1991). The route to story. *The New Advocate, 4,* 143–149.

YORINKS, ARTHUR   Raymond, A. (November/December 1991). Arthur Yorinks: Talent in abundance. *Teaching PreK–8, 21,* 51–53.

ZALBEN, JANE BRESKIN   Yolen, J. (1990). In the artist's studio: Jane Breskin Zalben. *The New Advocate, 3,* 175–178.

AUDIOVISUAL MATERIALS PROFILING AUTHORS AND ILLUSTRATORS

ALEXANDER, LLOYD   "Meet the Newbery author: Lloyd Alexander," American School Publishers (sound filmstrip). (U)

ANDERSEN, HANS CHRISTIAN   "Meet the author: Hans Christian Andersen," American School Publishers (sound filmstrip or video). (M)

ARMSTRONG, WILLIAM H.   "Meet the Newbery author: William H. Armstrong," American School Publishers (sound filmstrip). (M–U)

BABBITT, NATALIE   "Meet the Newbery author: Natalie Babbitt," American School Publishers (sound filmstrip). (U)

BERENSTAIN, STAN and JAN "Meet Stan and Jan Berenstain," American School Publishers (sound filmstrip). (P)

BLUME, JUDY "First choice: Authors and books—Judy Blume," Pied Piper (sound filmstrip). (M–U)

BROWN, MARC "Meet Marc Brown," American School Publishers (video). (P–M)

BULLA, CLYDE "First choice: Authors and books—Clyde Bulla," Pied Piper (sound filmstrip). (M)

BYARS, BETSY "Meet the Newbery author: Betsy Byars," American School Publishers (sound filmstrip). (M–U)

CLEARY, BEVERLY "First choice: Authors and books—Beverly Cleary," Pied Piper (sound filmstrip). (M); "Meet the Newbery author: Beverly Cleary," American School Publishers (sound filmstrip). (M)

COLLIER, JAMES LINCOLN and CHRISTOPHER "Meet the Newbery authors: James Lincoln Collier and Christopher Collier," American School Publishers (sound filmstrip). (U)

COOPER, SUSAN "Meet the Newbery author: Susan Cooper," American School Publishers (sound filmstrip). (U)

DAHL, ROALD "The author's eye: Roald Dahl," American School Publishers (kit with video). (M–U)

DR. SEUSS "Who's Dr. Seuss?: Meet Ted Geisel," American School Publishers (sound filmstrip). (P–M)

FLEISCHMAN, SID "First choice: Authors and books—Sid Fleischman," Pied Piper (sound filmstrip). (M–U)

FRITZ, JEAN "Homesick: My own story," American School Publishers (sound filmstrip). (M–U)

GEORGE, JEAN CRAIGHEAD "Meet the Newbery author: Jean Craighead George," American School Publishers (sound filmstrip). (U)

GIOVANNI, NIKKI "First choice: Poets and poetry—Nikki Giovanni," Pied Piper (sound filmstrip). (M–U)

GREENE, BETTE "Meet the Newbery author: Bette Greene," American School Publishers (sound filmstrip). (M–U)

HALEY, GAIL E "Tracing a legend: The story of the green man by Gail E. Haley," Weston Woods (sound filmstrip). (M); "Creating Jack and the bean tree: Tradition and technique," Weston Woods (sound filmstrip). (M)

HAMILTON, VIRGINIA "First choice: Authors and books—Virginia Hamilton," Pied Piper (sound filmstrip). (U); "Meet the Newbery author: Virginia Hamilton," American School Publishers (sound filmstrip). (U)

HENRY, MARGUERITE "First choice: Authors and books—Marguerite Henry," Pied Piper (sound filmstrip). (M–U); "Meet the Newbery author: Marguerite Henry," American School Publishers (sound filmstrip). (M)

HIGHWATER, JAMAKE "Meet the Newbery author: Jamake Highwater," American School Publishers (sound filmstrip). (M–U)

KEATS, EZRA JACK "Ezra Jack Keats," Weston Woods (Film). (P)

KELLOGG, STEVEN "How a picture book is made," Weston Woods (video). (P–M)

KONIGSBURG, E. L. "First choice: Authors and books—E. L. Konigsburg," Pied Piper (sound filmstrip). (M–U)

KUSKIN, KARLA "First choice: Poets and poetry—Karla Kuskin," Pied Piper (sound filmstrip). (M–U); "Poetry explained by Karla Kuskin," Weston Woods (sound filmstrip). (M–U)

L'ENGLE, MADELEINE "Meet the Newbery author: Madeleine L'Engle," American School Publishers (sound filmstrip). (U)

LIVINGSTON, MYRA COHN "First choice: Poets and poetry—Myra Cohn Livingston," Pied Piper (sound filmstrip). (M–U)

LOBEL, ARNOLD "Meet the Newbery author: Arnold Lobel," American School Publishers (sound filmstrip). (P–M)

MACAULAY, DAVID "David Macaulay in his studio," Houghton Mifflin (video). (M–U)

MCCLOSKEY, ROBERT "Robert McCloskey," Weston Woods (film). (P–M)

MCCORD, DAVID "First choice: Poets and poetry—David McCord," Pied Piper (sound filmstrip). (M–U)

MCDERMOTT, GERALD "Evolution of a graphic concept: The stonecutter," Weston Woods (sound filmstrip). (P–M)

MERRIAM, EVE "First choice: Poets and poetry—Eve Merriam," Pied Piper (sound filmstrip). (M–U)

MILNE, A. A. "Meet the author: A. A. Milne (and Pooh)," American School Publishers (sound filmstrip or video). (P)

O'DELL, SCOTT "Meet the Newbery author: Scott O'Dell," American School Publishers (sound filmstrip). (U); "A visit with Scott O'Dell," Houghton Mifflin (video). (U)

PATERSON, KATHERINE   "The author's eye: Katherine Paterson," American School Publishers (kit with video). (M–U); "Meet the Newbery author: Katherine Paterson," American School Publishers (sound filmstrip). (M–U)

PEET, BILL   "Bill Peet in his studio," Houghton Mifflin (video) (M)

PINKNEY, JERRY   "Meet the Caldecott illustrator: Jerry Pinkney," American School Publishers (video). (P–M)

POTTER, BEATRIX   "Beatrix Potter had a pet named Peter," American School Publishers (sound filmstrip or video). (P)

RYLANT, CYNTHIA   "Meet the Newbery author: Cynthia Rylant," American School Publishers (sound filmstrip or video). (M–U); "Meet the picture book author: Cynthia Rylant," American School Publishers (video). (P–M)

SENDAK, MAURICE   "Sendak," Weston Woods (film). (P–M)

SINGER, ISAAC BASHEVIS   "Meet the Newbery author: Isaac Bashevis Singer," American School Publishers (sound filmstrip). (U)

SOBOL, DONALD J.   "The case of the Model-A Ford and the man in the snorkel under the hood: Donald J. Sobol," American School Publishers (sound filmstrip). (M)

WHITE, E. B.   "Meet the Newbery author: E. B. White," American School Publishers (sound filmstrip). (M–U)

WILDER, LAURA INGALLS   "Meet the Newbery author: Laura Ingalls Wilder," American School Publishers (sound filmstrip). (M–U)

WILLARD, NANCY   "Meet the Newbery author: Nancy Willard," American School Publishers (sound filmstrip). (M–U)

YEP, LAURENCE   "Meet the Newbery author: Laurence Yep," American School Publishers (sound filmstrip). (U)

ZOLOTOW, CHARLOTTE   "Charlotte Zolotow: The grower," American School Publishers (sound filmstrip). (P–M)

ADDRESSES FOR AUDIOVISUAL MANUFACTURERS

American School Publishers
P.O. Box 408
Hightstown, NJ 08520

Houghton Mifflin
2 Park Street
Boston, MA 02108

Pied Piper
P.O. Box 320
Verdugo City, CA 91046

Weston Woods
Weston, CT 06883

TITLE AND AUTHOR INDEX

SUBJECT INDEX

ABOUT THE AUTHOR

Gail E. Tompkins is a Professor of Literacy and Early Education at California State University–Fresno. She teaches courses in literature-based reading and integrated language arts to preservice and in-service teachers and conducts staff development workshops for teachers in California and across the United States. She regularly visits elementary classrooms to observe teachers as they implement the core literature and reading workshop approaches and to demonstrate literature-based reading techniques. Dr. Tompkins has published widely in professional journals, including *Language Arts* and *The Reading Teacher,* and has written two other books published by Merrill/Macmillan. She is coauthor of *Language Arts: Content and Teaching Strategies* (Second Edition) and author of *Teaching Writing: Balancing Process and Product.*

Lea M. McGee is an Associate Professor of Curriculum and Instruction at Boston College, where she teaches graduate and undergraduate courses in children's literature, language arts, and reading. She has made several inservice presentations and has worked collaboratively with teachers in developing literature-based reading programs. She has published numerous articles about literacy development in a variety of journals, including *The Reading Teacher, Language Arts,* and *Childhood Education.* Her research, which focuses on young children's concepts about print, expository text structures, and children's responses to literature, appears in journals such as *Reading Research Quarterly* and *Journal of Reading Behavior.* She is previous Associate Editor of the *Journal of Reading Behavior* and is coauthor of the text *Literacy's Beginnings: Supporting Young Children's Reading and Writing.*

ISBN 0-67-521303-7

90000>

9 780675 213035